MyWritingLab™ has helped students like you from all over the country.

MyWritingLab™ can help you become a better writer and help you get a better grade.

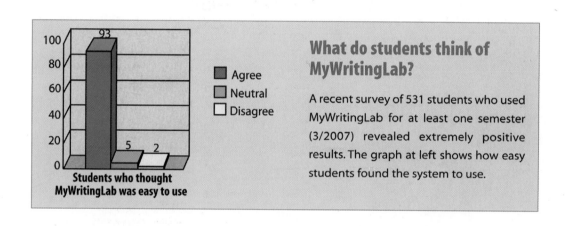

What do students think of MyWritingLab?

A recent survey of 531 students who used MyWritingLab for at least one semester (3/2007) revealed extremely positive results. The graph at left shows how easy students found the system to use.

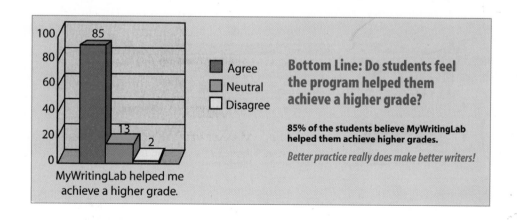

Bottom Line: Do students feel the program helped them achieve a higher grade?

85% of the students believe MyWritingLab helped them achieve higher grades.

Better practice really does make better writers!

Registering for MyWritingLab™...

It is easy to get started! Simply follow these steps to get into your MyWritingLab course.

1) **Find Your Access Code** (it is either packaged with your textbook, or you purchased it separately). You will need this access code and your course ID to join your MyWritingLab course. Your instructor has your course ID number, so make sure you have that before logging in.

2) **Click on "Students"** under "First-Time Users." Here you will be prompted to enter your access code, enter your e-mail address, and choose your own Login Name and Password. After you register, you can **click on "Returning Users"** to use your new login name and password every time you go back into your course in MyWritingLab.

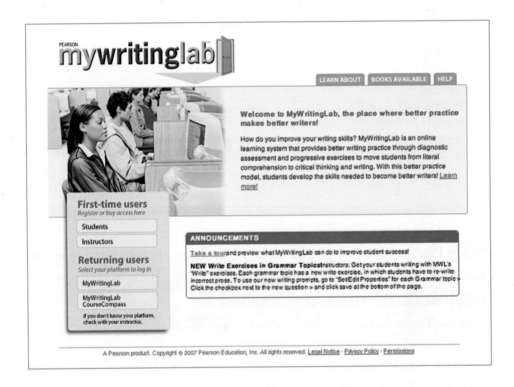

After logging in, you will see all the ways MyWritingLab can help you become a better writer.

The Homepage . . .

Here is your MyWritingLab HomePage.
You get a bird's eye view of where you are in your course every time you log in.

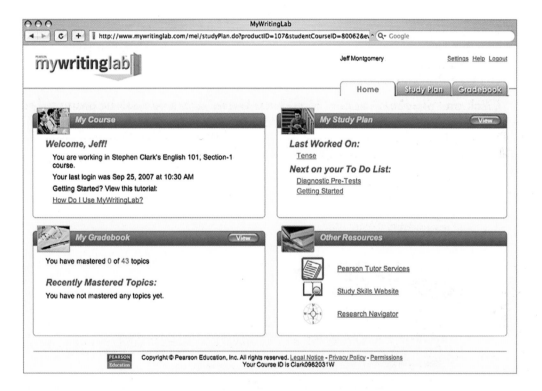

Your **Course** box shows your class details.

Your **Study Plan** box shows what you last completed and what is next on your **To Do** list.

Your **Gradebook** box shows you a snapshot of how you are doing in the class.

Your **Other Resources** box supplies you with amazing tools such as:

- **Pearson Tutor Services**—click here to see how you can get help on your papers by qualified tutors . . . before handing them in!

- **Research Navigator**—click here to see how this resembles your library with access to online journals for research paper assignments.

- **Study Skills**—extra help that includes tips and quizzes on how to improve your study skills

Now, let's start practicing to become better writers. Click on the Study Plan tab. This is where you will do all your course work.

The Study Plan . . .

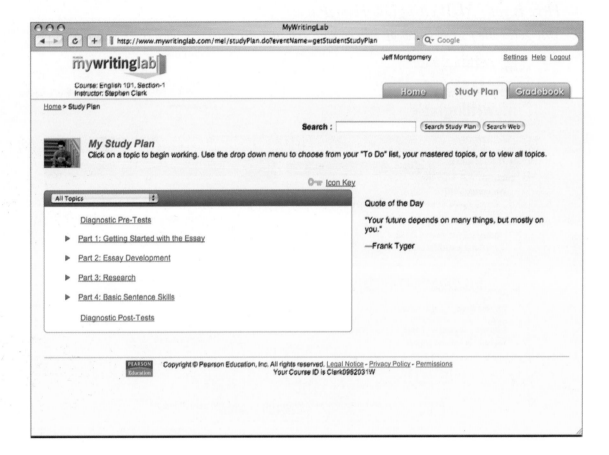

MyWritingLab provides you with a simple Study Plan of the writing skills that you need to master. You start from the top of the list and work your way down. You can start with the Diagnostic Pre-Tests.

The Diagnostic Pre-Tests . . .

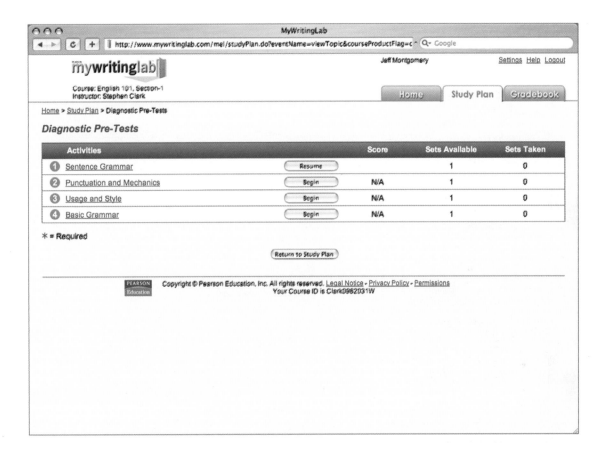

MyWritingLab's Diagnostic Pre-Tests are divided into four parts and cover all the major grammar, punctuation, and usage topics. After you complete these diagnostic tests, MyWritingLab will generate a personalized Study Plan for you, showing all the topics you have mastered and listing all the topics yet unmastered.

The Diagnostic Pre-Tests . . .

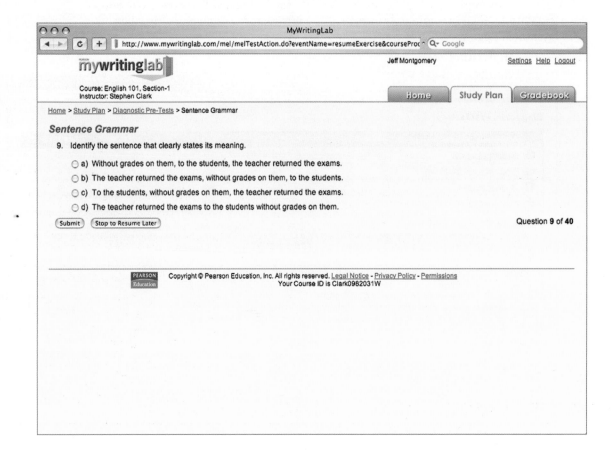

The Diagnostic Pre-Tests contain five exercises on each of the grammar, punctuation, and usage topics. You can achieve mastery of the topic in the Diagnostic Pre-Test by getting four of five or five of five correct within each topic.

After completing the Diagnostic Pre-Test, you can return to your Study Plan and enter any of the topics you have yet to master.

Watch, Recall, Apply, Write . . .

Here is an example of a MyWritinglab Activity set that you will see once you enter into a topic. Take the time to briefly read the introductory paragraph, and then watch the engaging video clip by clicking on "Watch: Tense."

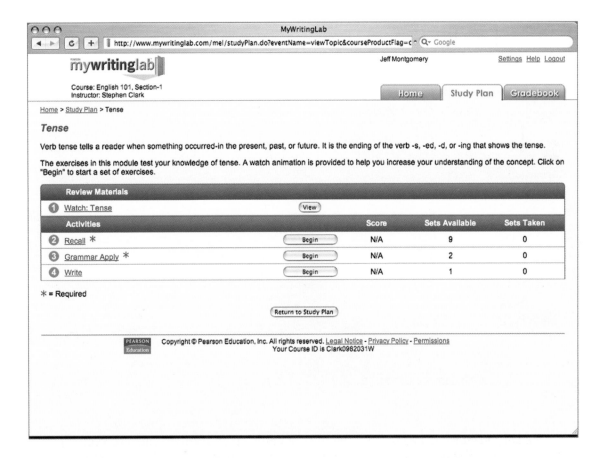

The video clip provides you with a helpful review.
Now you are ready to start the exercises. There are three types:

- Recall—activities that help you *recall* the rules of grammar

- Apply—activities that help you *apply* these rules to brief paragraphs or essays

- Write—activities that ask you to demonstrate these rules of grammar in your own writing

Watch, Recall, Apply, Write . . .

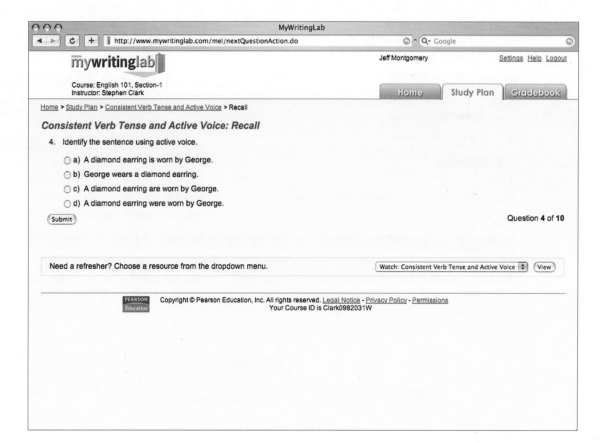

Recall questions help you recall the rules of grammar and writing when you complete multiple-choice questions, usually with four possible answers. You get feedback after answering each question, so you can learn as you go!

There are many sets available for lots of practice. As soon as you are finished with a set of activities, you will receive a score sheet with helpful feedback, including the correct answers. This score sheet will be kept in your own gradebook, so you can always go back and review.

www.mywritinglab.com

Watch, Recall, Apply, Write . . .

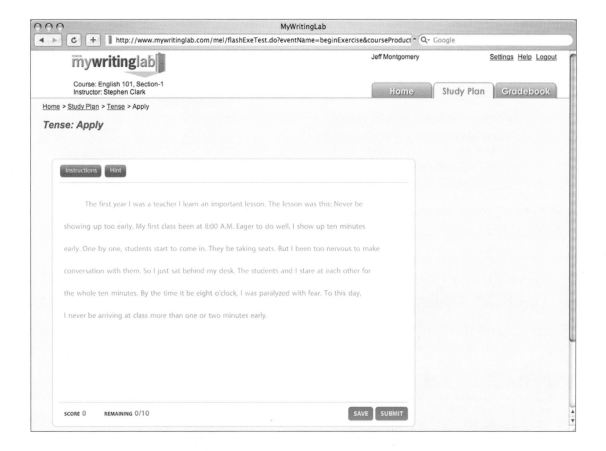

Apply exercises help you *apply* writing and grammar rules to brief paragraphs or essays. Sometimes these are multiple-choice questions, and other times you will be asked to identify and correct mistakes in existing paragraphs and essays.

Your instructor may also assign **Write exercises**, which allow you to demonstrate writing and grammar rules in your own writing.

Helping Students Succeed . . .

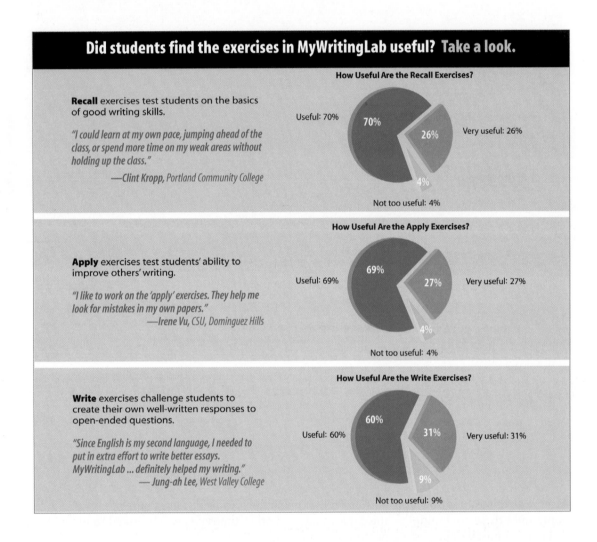

How Useful Are the Recall Exercises?

Recall exercises test students on the basics of good writing skills.

"I could learn at my own pace, jumping ahead of the class, or spend more time on my weak areas without holding up the class."

　　　　　—*Clint Kropp, Portland Community College*

Useful: 70% 70% 26% Very useful: 26% 4%

Not too useful: 4%

How Useful Are the Apply Exercises?

Apply exercises test students' ability to improve others' writing.

"I like to work on the 'apply' exercises. They help me look for mistakes in my own papers."
　　　　　—*Irene Vu, CSU, Dominguez Hills*

Useful: 69% 69% 27% Very useful: 27% 4%

Not too useful: 4%

How Useful Are the Write Exercises?

Write exercises challenge students to create their own well-written responses to open-ended questions.

"Since English is my second language, I needed to put in extra effort to write better essays. MyWritingLab ... definitely helped my writing."
　　　　　— *Jung-ah Lee, West Valley College*

Useful: 60% 60% 31% Very useful: 31% 9%

Not too useful: 9%

Students just like you are finding MyWritingLab's Recall, Apply, and Write exercises useful in their learning.

The Gradebook . . .

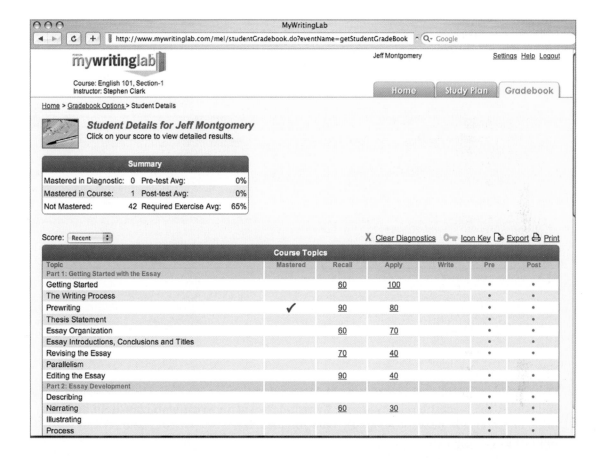

Let's look at how your own on-line gradebook will help you track your progress.

Click on the "Gradebook" tab and then the "Student Detail" report.

Here you are able to see how you are doing in each area. If you feel you need to go back and review, simply click on any score and your score sheet will appear.

You also have a Diagnostic Detail report so you can go back and review your diagnostic Pre-Test and see how much MyWritingLab has helped you improve!

Here to Help You ...

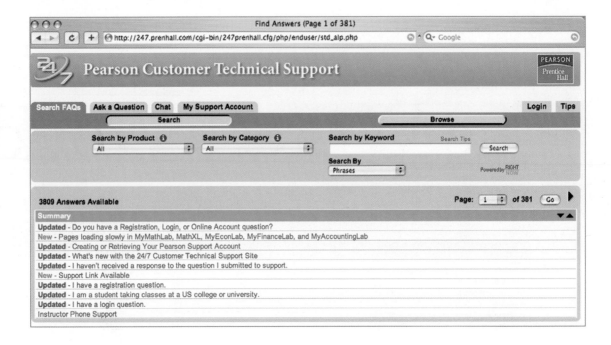

Our goal is to provide answers to your MyWritingLab questions as quickly as possible and deliver the highest level of support. By visiting **www.mywritinglab.com/help.html**, many questions can be resolved in just a few minutes. Here you will find help on the following:

- System Requirements

- How to Register for MyWritingLab

- How to Use MyWritingLab

For student support, we also invite you to contact Pearson Customer Technical Support (shown above). In addition, you can reach our Support Representatives online at **http://247.pearsoned.com**. Here you can do the following:

- Search Frequently Asked Questions about MyWritingLab

- E-mail a Question to Our Support Team

- Chat with a Support Representative

www.mywritinglab.com

LYNNE GAETZ

Lionel Groulx College

SUNEETI PHADKE

St. Jerome College

The Writer's World

Paragraphs and Essays

SECOND EDITION

PEARSON

Prentice
Hall

Upper Saddle River, New Jersey 07458

Library of Congress Cataloging-in-Publication Data

Gaetz, Lynne

    The writer's world : paragraphs and essays / Lynne Gaetz, Suneeti Phadke.—2nd ed.
      p. cm.
    Includes index.
    ISBN-13: 978-0-13-615218-7 (student ed.)
    ISBN-10: 0-13-615218-X (student ed.)
1. English language—Paragraphs—Problems, exercises, etc. 2. English language—
Rhetoric—Problems, exercises, etc.   3. Report writing—Problems, exercises, etc.
4. English language—Grammar—Problems, exercises, etc. I. Phadke, Suneeti
II. Title.
    PE1439.G254 2008
    808'.042—dc22

                                        2007050175

Editorial Director: Leah Jewell
Editor in Chief: Craig Campanella
Editorial Assistant: Deborah Doyle
Director of Marketing: Megan Galvin-Fak
Marketing Manager: Thomas DeMarco
Marketing Assistant: Sara Fry
Text Permissions Specialist: Jane Scelta
Development Editor in Chief: Rochelle Diogenes
Development Editor: Leslie Taggart
Permissions Assistant: Peggy Davis
Senior Operations Supervisor: Sherry Lewis
Director, Image Resource Center: Melinda Patelli
Manager, Image Rights and Permissions: Zina Arabia
Manager, Visual Research: Beth Brenzel

Image Permissions Coordinator: Ang'John Ferreri
Image Researcher: Sheila Norman
Interior Designer: Laura Gardner
Cover Designer: Anne DeMarinis
Cover art: Young man: Hans Neleman/Taxi/Getty Images; young
    woman: ColorBlind Images/Juperimages/Blend Images; other: Getty
Full-Service Project Management: Karen Berry, Pine Tree
    Composition, Inc.
Copyeditor: Laura Patchkofsky
Composition: Pine Tree Composition, Inc.
Printer/Binder: Quebecor World
Cover Printer: Phoenix Color Corporation
Text Font: 11/13 Janson

For permission to use copyrighted material, grateful acknowledgment is made to the copyright holders on pages 621–622, which are considered an extension of this copyright page.

Pearson Education Ltd.
Pearson Education Singapore, Pte. Ltd
Pearson Education, Canada, Ltd
Pearson Education–Japan
Pearson Education Australia Pty, Limited

Pearson Education North Asia Ltd
Pearson Educación de Mexico, S.A. de C.V.
Pearson Education Malaysia, Pte. Ltd
Pearson Education, Upper Saddle River, NJ

10 9 8 7 6 5 4
ISBN-13: 978-0-13-615218-7
ISBN-10:   0-13-615218-X

Contents

PART I — The Writing Process   2

CHAPTER 1 Exploring   3

CHAPTER 2 Developing   19

CHAPTER 3 Revising and Editing   41

PART II — Paragraph Patterns   58

CHAPTER 4 Illustration   59

Complex Sentences   290

 Sentence Variety   303

SECTION 2   Common Sentence Errors ▪ *Section Theme* PSYCHOLOGY

 **Fragments
and Run-Ons**   317

 **Faulty Parallel
Structure**   331

SECTION 3   Problems with Verbs ▪ *Section Theme* ESPIONAGE

 **Present and
Past Tenses**   340

 Other Verb Forms   367

Past Participles   355

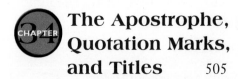
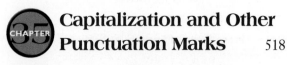
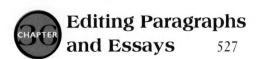

Appendices

Welcome to the Second Edition of *The Writer's World: Paragraphs and Essays*

Thank you for making the first edition of *The Writer's World* a resounding success. We are delighted that the book has been able to help so many students across the country. This second edition, too, can help your students produce writing that is technically correct and richly detailed whether your classes are filled with students who have varying skill levels, whether students are native or nonnative speakers of English, or whether they learn better through the use of visuals. When we started the first edition, we set out to develop practical and pedagogically sound approaches to these challenges, and we are pleased to hear that the book is helping students succeed in their writing courses.

In this second edition, we have refined the approach to give students more opportunities to collaborate, more information to help them boost their vocabularies, and more hints about grammar in the writing chapters. We have also extended the very popular visual program through Part V. We will discuss these new features, but first, for those new to the book, we will provide some background to give a more complete picture.

A Research-Based Approach

We began with the idea that this project should be a collaboration with other developmental writing teachers. So we met with more than forty-five instructors from around the country, asking for their opinions and insights regarding (1) the challenges posed by the course, (2) the needs of today's ever-changing student population, and (3) the ideas and features we were proposing in order to provide them and you with a more effective teaching and learning tool. Prentice Hall also commissioned dozens of detailed manuscript reviews from instructors, asking them to analyze and evaluate each draft of the manuscript. These reviewers identified numerous ways in which we could refine and enhance our key

features. Their invaluable feedback was incorporated throughout *The Writer's World*. The text you are seeing is truly the product of a successful partnership between the authors, publisher, and well over one hundred developmental writing instructors.

How We Organized *The Writer's World*

The Writer's World is separated into five parts for ease of use and convenience.

Part I: The Writing Process teaches students (1) how to formulate ideas (Exploring); (2) how to expand, organize, and present those ideas in a piece of writing (Developing); and (3) how to polish writing so that they convey their message as clearly as possible (Revising and Editing). The result is that writing a paragraph or an essay becomes far less daunting because students have specific steps to follow.

Part II: Paragraph Patterns gives students a solid overview of the patterns of development. Using the same easy-to-understand process (Exploring, Developing, and Revising and Editing), each chapter in this section explains how to convey ideas using one or more writing patterns. As they work through the practices and write their own paragraphs and essays, students begin to see how using a writing pattern can help them fulfill their purpose for writing.

Part III: The Essay covers the parts of the essay and explains how students can apply the nine patterns of development to essay writing. This section also discusses the role research plays in writing and explains some ways that students can incorporate research in their essays.

Part IV: The Editing Handbook is a thematic grammar handbook. In each chapter, the examples correspond to a theme, such as work, fads, and cultural icons. As students work through the chapters, they hone their grammar and editing skills while gaining knowledge about a variety of topics. In addition to helping build interest in the grammar practices, the thematic material provides a spark that ignites new ideas that students can apply to their writing.

Part V: Reading Strategies and Selections offers tips, readings, and follow-up questions. Students learn how to write by observing and dissecting what they read. The readings relate to the themes found in Part IV: The Editing Handbook, thereby providing more fodder for generating writing ideas.

How *The Writer's World* Meets Students' Diverse Needs

We created *The Writer's World* to meet your students' diverse needs. To accomplish this, we asked both the instructors in our focus groups and the reviewers at every stage not only to critique our ideas but to offer their suggestions and recommendations for features that would enhance the learning process of their students. The result has been the integration of many elements that are not found in other textbooks, including our visual program, coverage of nonnative speaker material, and strategies for addressing the varying skill levels students bring to the course.

The Visual Program

A stimulating, full-color book with more than 70 photos, *The Writer's World* recognizes that today's world is a visual one, and it encourages students to become better communicators by responding to images. Chapter-opening visuals in Parts I, II, and III help students to think about the chapter's key concept in a new way. For example, in the Chapter 9 opener, a photograph of a candy store sets the stage for classification. Chocolates are grouped by type, which helps students understand the premise of classification. In Part IV, chapter-opening photos help illustrate the theme of the examples and exercises. These visual aids can also serve as sources for writing prompts.

Each **At Work** box in Part II features an image from the workplace, along with content on how that particular pattern of development is utilized on the job.

The visuals in Part V provide students with another set of opportunities to write in response to images, with Photo Writing activities and Film

Writing activities that encourage them to respond using particular paragraph and essay patterns.

Throughout *The Writer's World*, words and images work together to encourage students to explore, develop, and revise their writing.

Seamless Coverage for Nonnative Speakers

Instructors in our focus groups noted the growing number of nonnative/ESL speakers enrolling in developmental writing courses. Although some of these students have special needs relating to the writing process, many of you still have a large portion of native speakers in your courses whose more traditional needs must also be satisfied. In order to meet the challenge of this rapidly changing dynamic, we have carefully implemented and integrated content throughout to assist these students. *The Writer's World* does not have separate ESL boxes, ESL chapters, or tacked-on ESL appendices. Instead, information that traditionally poses a challenge to nonnative speakers is woven seamlessly throughout the book. In our extensive experience teaching writing to both native and nonnative speakers of English, we have learned that both groups learn best when they are not distracted by ESL labels. With the seamless approach, nonnative speakers do not feel self-conscious and segregated, and native speakers do not tune out detailed explanations that may also benefit them. Many of these traditional problem areas receive more coverage than you would find in other textbooks, arming the instructor with the material to effectively meet the needs of nonnative speakers. Moreover, the Annotated Instructor's Edition provides over seventy-five ESL Teaching Tips designed specifically to help instructors better meet the needs of their nonnative speaking students.

Issue-Focused Thematic Grammar

In surveys, many of you indicated that one of the primary challenges in teaching your course is finding materials that are engaging to students in a contemporary context. This is especially true in grammar instruction. **Students come to the course with varying skill levels**, and many students are simply not interested in grammar. To address this challenge, we have introduced **issue-focused thematic grammar** into *The Writer's World*.

Each chapter centers on a theme that is carried out in examples and activities. These themes include topics related to culture, psychology, espionage, college life, inventions and discoveries, health care, the legal world, and the workplace. The thematic approach enables students to broaden their awareness of subjects important to American life, such as understanding advertising and consumerism and thinking about health care issues and alternative medicine. The thematic approach makes reading about grammar more engaging. And the more engaging grammar is, the more likely students will retain key concepts—raising their skill level in these important building blocks of writing.

We also think that it is important to teach grammar in the context of the writing process. Students should not think that grammar is an isolated exercise. Therefore, **each grammar chapter includes a warm up writing activity**. Students write and edit their paragraphs, paying particular attention to the grammar point covered in the chapter. The end of each grammar section also contains paragraph and essay writing topics that are related to the theme of the section and that follow different writing patterns. Suggestions are given for readings in these chapters in Part V that relate to the grammar themes.

What Tools Can Help Students Get the Most from *The Writer's World*?

Overwhelmingly, focus group participants and reviewers asked that both a larger number and a greater diversity of exercises and activities be incorporated into *The Writer's World*. In response, we have developed and tested the following learning aids in *The Writer's World*. We are confident they will help your students become better writers.

Hints In each chapter, **Hint** boxes highlight important writing and grammar points. Hints are useful for all students, but many will be particularly helpful for nonnative speakers. For example, in Chapter 12, one Hint encourages students to state an argument directly and a second Hint points out the need to avoid circular reasoning. In Chapter 21, a Hint discusses checking for consistent voice in compound sentences. Hints include brief discussions and examples so that students will see both concept and application.

The Writer's Desk Parts I, II, and III include **The Writer's Desk** exercises that help students get used to practicing all stages and steps of the writing process. As the chapter progresses, students warm up with a prewriting activity, and then use specific methods for developing, organizing (using paragraph and essay plans), drafting, and finally, revising and editing to create a final draft.

Paragraph Patterns at Work To help students appreciate the relevance of their writing tasks, Chapters 4–12 highlight an authentic writing sample from work contexts. Titled **Illustration at Work, Narration at Work,** and so on, this feature offers a glimpse of how people use writing patterns in different workplace settings.

Reflect On It Each **Reflect On It** is a chapter review exercise. Questions prompt students to recall and review what they have learned in the chapter.

The Writer's Room The Writer's Room contains writing activities that correspond to general, college, and workplace topics. Some prompts are brief to allow students to freely form ideas while others are expanded to give students more direction.

There is something for every student writer in this end-of-chapter feature. Students who respond well to visual cues will appreciate the photo writing exercises in **The Writer's Room** in Part II: Paragraph Patterns. Students who learn best by hearing through collaboration will appreciate the discussion and group work prompts in **The Writers' Circle** section of selected **The Writer's Rooms.** In Part III: The Essay, students can respond to thought-provoking quotations. To help students see how grammar is not isolated from the writing process, there are also **The Writer's Room** activities at the end of sections 1 to 8 in Part IV: The Editing Handbook.

New to the Second Edition
Visualizing the Writing Process

To give students an early example of a writer's complete process, Chapter 1 now includes a section in which student writer Wade Vong explores, develops, and revises and edits a paragraph about cities. This graphic example gives students an overview of the process and examples of each stage. Revising and editing stages are shown separately to help students distinguish the two tasks.

The Writers' Exchange

The Writers' Exchange now opens each Part II chapter to give students an activity they can work on together that will help them understand a writing pattern. These collaborative activities also help students build confidence about their knowledge before having to apply it in writing. Writers' Exchanges are particularly helpful for students who like to listen to acquire knowledge.

Vocabulary Boost

Throughout Part II of *The Writer's World*, new Vocabulary Boost boxes give students tips to improve their use of language and to revise and edit their word choices. For example, a Vocabulary Boost in Chapter 4 asks students to replace repeated words with synonyms, and the one in Chapter 5 gives specific directions for how to vary sentence openings. These lessons give students concrete strategies and specific advice for improving their diction.

Expanded Research Coverage

Chapter 15, Enhancing Your Writing with Research, has new coverage on gathering information using library and Internet sources, as well as expanded coverage of evaluating sources. The discussions of paraphrasing and summarizing have been expanded, and the Works Cited information has been revised. A new sample student paper on Goya is annotated with comments about MLA style and formatting.

Thematic Organization in Part Five

A new thematic organization in Part V groups readings into four broad categories: Culture and Psychology, Espionage and Great Discoveries, College Life and Health Care, and The Legal World and the Workplace. Each theme ends with Photo Writing and Film Writing prompts. Five new readings update the selections with multicultural perspectives and high-interest topics.

Readings Listed by Rhetorical Mode

The Part V readings are grouped by theme in the table of contents and on the Part V opener (page 540) by theme and dominant writing pattern. A new table of contents has been added directly after the regular table of contents in the front of the book so that you can see which readings are organized in whole or in part by the various rhetorical modes.

Acknowledgments

Many people have helped us produce *The Writer's World*. First and foremost, we would like to thank our students for inspiring us and providing us with invaluable feedback. Their words and insights pervade this book.

We also benefited greatly from the insightful comments and suggestions from over two hundred instructors across the nation, all of whom are listed in the opening pages of the Annotated Instructor's Edition. Our colleagues' feedback was invaluable and helped shape *The Writer's World* series content, focus, and organization.

We are indebted to the team of dedicated professionals at Prentice Hall who have helped make this project a reality. They have boosted our spirits and have believed in us every step of the way. Special thanks to Leslie Taggart for her careful job in polishing this book and to Craig Campanella for trusting our instincts and enthusiastically propelling us forward. We owe a deep debt of gratitude to Yolanda de Rooy, whose encouraging words helped ignite this project. Karen Berry's attention to detail in the production process kept us motivated and on task and made *The Writer's World* a much better resource for both instructors and students. We would also like to thank Laura Gardner for her brilliant design, which helped keep the visual learner in all of us engaged.

Finally, we would like to dedicate this book to our husbands and children who supported us and who patiently put up with our long hours on the computer. Manu, Octavio, and Natalia continually encouraged us. We especially appreciate the help and sacrifices of Diego, Becky, Kiran and Meghana.

Lynne Gaetz and Suneeti Phadke

A Note to Students

Your knowledge, ideas, and opinions are important. The ability to clearly communicate those ideas is invaluable in your personal, academic, and professional life. When your writing is error-free, readers will focus on your message, and you will be able to persuade, inform, entertain, or inspire them. *The Writer's World* includes strategies that will help you improve your written communication. Quite simply, when you become a better writer, you become a better communicator. It is our greatest wish for *The Writer's World* to make you excited about writing, communicating, and learning.

Enjoy!

Lynne Gaetz & Suneeti Phadke
thewritersworld@prenhall.com

Call for Student Writing!

Do you want to be published in *The Writer's World*? Send your paragraphs and essays to us along with your complete contact information. If your work is selected to appear in the next edition of *The Writer's World*, you will receive an honorarium, credit for your work, and a copy of the book!

Lynne Gaetz and Suneeti Phadke
thewritersworld@prenhall.com

Lynne Gaetz and family in Mexico.

Suneeti Phadke and family in Turkey.

PART I

The Writing Process

An Overview

The writing process is a series of steps that most writers follow to get from thinking about a topic to preparing the final draft. Generally, you should follow the process step by step; however, sometimes you may find that your steps overlap. For example, you might do some editing before you revise, or you might think about your main idea while you are prewriting. The important thing is to make sure that you have done all of the steps before preparing your final draft.

Before you begin the chapters that follow, review the steps in the writing process.

Exploring

Step 1: Think about your topic.

Step 2: Think about your audience.

Step 3: Think about your purpose.

Step 4: Try exploring strategies.

Developing

Step 1: Narrow your topic.

Step 2: Express your main idea.

Step 3: Develop your supporting ideas.

Step 4: Make a plan or an outline.

Step 5: Write your first draft.

Revising and Editing

Step 1: Revise for unity.

Step 2: Revise for adequate support.

Step 3: Revise for coherence.

Step 4: Revise for style.

Step 5: Edit for technical errors.

> ❝ *Writing is an exploration. You start from nothing and learn as you go.* ❞
>
> —E. L. DOCTOROW
> *American author (b. 1931)*

CONTENTS

Before creating a final image, a pastel artist takes the time to consider what to create. Similarly, before developing a draft, a writer needs to explore the topic.

The Paragraph and the Essay

Most of the writing that we do—e-mail messages, work reports, college papers—is made up of paragraphs and essays. A **paragraph** is a series of sentences that are about one central idea. Paragraphs can stand alone, or they can be part of a longer work such as an essay, a letter, or a report. An **essay** is a series of paragraphs that are about one central idea. Both the paragraph and the essay are divided into three parts.

Characteristics of a Paragraph

- The **topic sentence** introduces the subject of the paragraph and shows the writer's attitude toward the subject.

- The **body** of the paragraph contains details that support the topic sentence.

- The paragraph ends with a **concluding sentence.**

Characteristics of an Essay

- The **introduction** engages the reader's interest and contains the **thesis statement.**

- The **body** paragraphs each support the main idea of the essay.

- The **conclusion** reemphasizes the thesis and restates the main points of the essay. It brings the essay to a satisfactory close.

Look at the relationship between paragraphs and essays. Both examples are about real-life heroes. However, in the essay, each supporting idea is expanded into paragraph form.

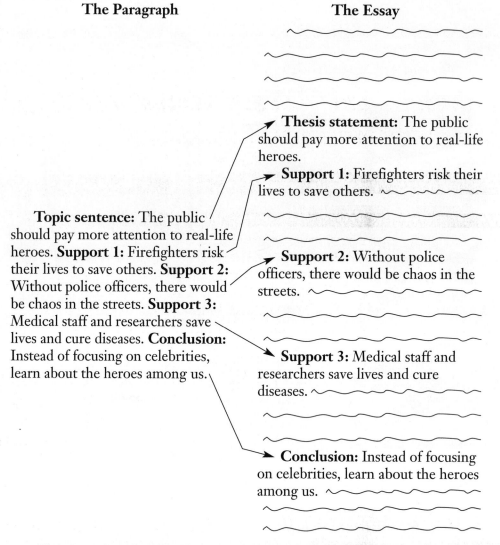

The Paragraph

The Essay

Topic sentence: The public should pay more attention to real-life heroes. **Support 1:** Firefighters risk their lives to save others. **Support 2:** Without police officers, there would be chaos in the streets. **Support 3:** Medical staff and researchers save lives and cure diseases. **Conclusion:** Instead of focusing on celebrities, learn about the heroes among us.

Thesis statement: The public should pay more attention to real-life heroes.

Support 1: Firefighters risk their lives to save others.

Support 2: Without police officers, there would be chaos in the streets.

Support 3: Medical staff and researchers save lives and cure diseases.

Conclusion: Instead of focusing on celebrities, learn about the heroes among us.

All writing begins with ideas. In the next section of this chapter, you will practice ways to explore ideas.

Visualizing the Writing Process

Wade Vong, a college student, was asked to write a paragraph about cities. Follow the writing process that Wade used to write his paragraph.

Exploring

Wade's topic was "cities." First, Wade narrowed the topic by listing ideas related to cities. Then he chose the narrowed topic, "Las Vegas, my hometown." His audience was his college instructor, and his purpose for writing was to entertain. In the exploring stage, there are several prewriting techniques that can help a writer develop a topic. Wade used a prewriting technique called brainstorming. He listed some ideas and did not worry about his grammar, spelling, or punctuation.

- lots of tourists
- beautiful parks and canyons

- superhot summers, too hot
- roads lined with palm trees
- lots of beige and pink buildings with clay-tiled roofs
- variety of great entertainment
- close to the Grand Canyon
- fast-paced glitzy tourist strip
- sea of neon lights in the casino area

Developing

In the developing stage, Wade wrote a sentence that expressed the idea that he would develop in his paragraph. Then he created a plan and organized his ideas logically. Below is the first complete draft of his paragraph.

You may notice that Wade's paragraph has errors. He will correct these when he gets to the revising and editing stage of the process.

> Las Vegas is a vibrant city of extremes. Peaceful suburbs integrate the desert landscape. Neighborhoods have pink and beige buildings with clay-tiled roofs, many yards contain various species of cactus. White roads are lined with palm trees. There are beautifull parks and canyons. Other parts of the city are extremely fast-paced and glitzy. On the Las Vegas Strip, neon lights illuminate the night sky. Crowds of tourists gaze at massive replicas of the pyramids, the Statue of liberty, and the Eiffel Tower. The strip is also vibrant because of the great entertainment available, including gambling for every taste and budget. The city attract world-class entertainment. Such as Celine Dion. The Cirque du Soleil has permanent shows. Even small clubs have magicians and hypnotists. If you would like to visit a truly unique city, go to Las Vegas.

Revising and Editing

In the revising stage, Wade removed some sentences that did not relate to his topic, and he added more sentences to make his paragraph more complete. He also added words to help link his ideas. Look at his revisions for unity, support, coherence, and style.

> Las Vegas is a vibrant city of extremes. ~~Peaceful~~ ^{First, peaceful} suburbs
> ^{stunning} ~~Some neighborhoods~~
> integrate the desert landscape. ~~Neighborhoods~~ have pink and
>
> beige buildings with clay-tiled roofs, many yards contain various
> ^{lead to}
> species of cactus. White roads ~~are~~ lined with palm trees. ~~There are~~
> ^{In contrast, other}
> beautiful parks and canyons. ~~Other~~ parts of the city are extremely
> ^{for instance,}
> fast-paced and glitzy. On the Las Vegas Strip, neon lights
> ^{jostling}
> illuminate the night sky. Crowds of tourists gaze at massive replicas
>
> of the pyramids, the Statue of liberty, and the Eiffel Tower. The strip

is also vibrant because of the great entertainment available,

In addition, the

including gambling for every taste and budget. ~~The~~ city attract

world-class entertainment. Such as Céline Dion. The Cirque du Soleil

, and even

has permanent shows. ~~Even~~ small clubs have magicians and

hypnotists. If you would like to visit a truly unique city, go to Las Vegas.

In the editing stage, Wade corrected errors in grammar, spelling, punctuation, capitalization, and mechanics.

Las Vegas is a vibrant city of extremes. First, peaceful suburbs

integrate the stunning desert landscape. Some neighborhoods have

and

pink and beige buildings with clay-tiled roofs, many yards contain

cacti

various species of ~~cactus~~. White roads lined with palm trees lead to

beautiful

~~beautifull~~ parks and canyons. In contrast, other parts of the city are

extremely fast-paced and glitzy. On the Las Vegas Strip, for

instance, neon lights illuminate the night sky. Crowds of jostling

tourists gaze at massive replicas of the pyramids, the Statue of

Liberty

~~liberty~~, and the Eiffel Tower. The strip is also vibrant because of the

great entertainment available, including gambling for every taste

attracts

and budget. In addition, the city attract world-class entertainment~~.~~

such

~~Such~~ as Céline Dion. The Cirque du Soleil has permanent shows,

and even small clubs have magicians and hypnotists. If you would

like to visit a truly unique city, go to Las Vegas.

When he finished editing, Wade typed a final draft of his paragraph.

Las Vegas is a vibrant city of extremes. First, peaceful suburbs integrate the stunning desert landscape. Some neighborhoods have pink and beige buildings with clay-tiled roofs, and many yards contain various species of cacti. White roads lined with palm trees lead to beautiful parks and canyons. In contrast, other parts of the city are extremely fast-paced and glitzy. On the Las Vegas Strip, for instance, neon lights illuminate the night sky. Crowds of jostling tourists gaze at massive replicas of the pyramids, the Statue of

Liberty, and the Eiffel Tower. The strip is also vibrant because of the great entertainment available, including gambling for every taste and budget. In addition, the city attracts world-class entertainment such as Céline Dion. The Cirque du Soleil has permanent shows, and even small clubs have magicians and hypnotists. If you would like to visit a truly unique city, go to Las Vegas.

Before handing in his assignment, Wade read it through one last time to check for typos.

What Is Exploring?

Have you ever been given a writing subject and then stared at the blank page, thinking, "I don't know what to write?" Well, it is not necessary to write a good paragraph or essay immediately. There are certain things that you can do to help you focus on your topic.

Understand Your Assignment

As soon as you are given an assignment, make sure that you understand what your task is. Answer the following questions about the assignment:

- How many words or pages should I write?
- What is the due date for the assignment?
- Are there any special qualities my writing should include?

After you have considered your assignment, follow the four steps in the exploring stage of the writing process.

EXPLORING

STEP 1	➤	**Think about your topic.** Determine what you will write about.
STEP 2	➤	**Think about your audience.** Consider your intended readers and what interests them.
STEP 3	➤	**Think about your purpose.** Ask yourself why you want to write.
STEP 4	➤	**Try exploring strategies.** Experiment with different ways to generate ideas.

ESSAY LINK

When you plan an essay, you should follow the four exploring steps.

Topic

Your **topic** is what you are writing about. When an instructor gives you a topic for your writing, you can give it a personal focus. For example, if the instructor asks you to write about "travel," you can take many approaches to the topic. You might write about the dangers of travel, describe a trip that you have taken, or explain the lessons that travel has taught you. When you are given a topic, find an angle that interests you and make it your own.

When you think about the topic, ask yourself the following questions.

- What about the topic interests me?
- Do I have special knowledge about the topic?
- Does anything about the topic arouse my emotions?

Audience

Your **audience** is your intended reader. In your personal, academic, and professional life, you will often write for a specific audience; therefore, you can keep your readers interested by adapting your tone and vocabulary to suit them. **Tone** is your general attitude or feeling toward a topic. You might write in a tone that is humorous, sarcastic, serious, friendly, or casual. For example, in an e-mail to your friend, you might use a very casual tone, with abbreviations such as *ttyl*, which means *talk to you later*. In an e-mail to your employer, you would use a more formal, business-like tone.

When you consider your audience, ask yourself the following questions.

- Who will read my assignment—an instructor, other students, or people outside the college?
- Do my readers have a lot of knowledge about my topic?
- Will my readers expect me to write in proper, grammatically correct English?

In academic writing, your audience is generally your instructor or other students, unless your instructor specifically asks you to write for another audience such as the general public, your employer, or a family member.

 **Instructor as the Audience**

When you write for your instructor, use standard English. In other words, try to use correct grammar, sentence structure, and vocabulary. Also, do not leave out information because you assume that your instructor is an expert in the field. Generally, when your instructor reads your work, he or she will expect you to reveal what you have learned or what you have understood about the topic.

PRACTICE I

E-mail messages A and B are about career goals. As you read the messages, consider the differences in both the tone and the vocabulary the writer uses. Then answer the questions that follow. Circle the letter of the correct answer.

1. Who is the audience for E-mail A?
   a. A friend   b. A family member
   c. A potential employer   d. An instructor

2. Who is the audience for E-mail B?
   a. A friend   b. A family member
   c. A potential employer   d. An instructor

3. In a word or two, describe the tone in each e-mail.
   E-mail A: _____   E-mail B: _____

4. **Language clues** are words or phrases that help you determine the audience. What language clues helped you determine the audience of e-mails A and B? The first clue in each e-mail message has been identified for you.

   E-mail A: _____   E-mail B: _____

   hey marco, sup?   *Dear Mr. Elliot:*

   _____   _____

   _____   _____

   _____   _____

E-mail A

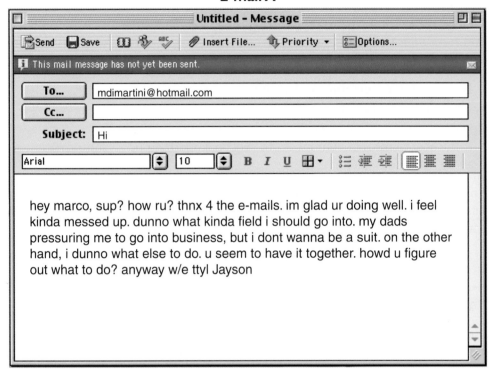

To... mdimartini@hotmail.com

Cc...

Subject: Hi

hey marco, sup? how ru? thnx 4 the e-mails. im glad ur doing well. i feel kinda messed up. dunno what kinda field i should go into. my dads pressuring me to go into business, but i dont wanna be a suit. on the other hand, i dunno what else to do. u seem to have it together. howd u figure out what to do? anyway w/e ttyl Jayson

E-mail B

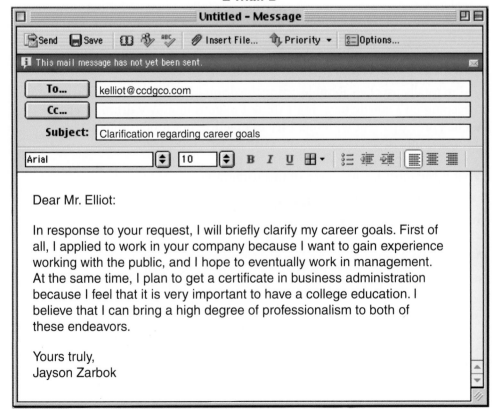

To... kelliot@ccdgco.com

Cc...

Subject: Clarification regarding career goals

Dear Mr. Elliot:

In response to your request, I will briefly clarify my career goals. First of all, I applied to work in your company because I want to gain experience working with the public, and I hope to eventually work in management. At the same time, I plan to get a certificate in business administration because I feel that it is very important to have a college education. I believe that I can bring a high degree of professionalism to both of these endeavors.

Yours truly,
Jayson Zarbok

Purpose

Your **purpose** is your reason for writing. Keeping your purpose in mind will help you focus your writing.

When you consider your purpose, ask yourself the following questions.

- Is my goal to **entertain?** Do I want to tell a story?
- Is my goal to **persuade?** Do I want to convince the reader that my point of view is the correct one?
- Is my goal to **inform?** Do I want to explain something or give information about a topic?

Sometimes you may have more than one purpose. For example, a narrative paragraph or essay about a personal experience can also inform the reader about something interesting. It is possible to write for a combination of reasons.

 **General and Specific Purpose**

Your **general purpose** is to entertain, to inform, or to persuade. Your **specific purpose** is your more precise reason for writing. For example, imagine that you have to write a piece about music. Your general purpose may be to inform while your specific purpose may be to explain how to become a better musician.

PRACTICE 2

Selections 1 to 3 are about music; however, each has a different purpose, has been written for a different audience, and has been taken from a different source. To complete this practice, read each selection carefully. Then underline any language clues (words or phrases) that help you identify its source, audience, and purpose. Finally, answer the questions that follow each selection.

EXAMPLE:

Slang ➤   I'm totally <u>psyched</u> about learning the drums. It's taken me a while to get used to keeping up a steady beat, but I think I'm getting it. My drum teacher is <u>cool</u>,
Slang, informal tone ➤ and he's <u>pretty patient</u> with me. I try to practice, but it bugs the neighbors when I hit the cymbals.

What is the most likely source of this paragraph?

   a. Web site article   b. textbook   ⓒ personal letter

What is its purpose? _To inform_

Who is the audience? _Friend or family member_

1.   Lomax also found a relationship between polyphony, where two or more melodies are sung simultaneously, and a high degree of female participation in food-getting. In societies in which women's work is responsible for at least half of the food, songs are likely to contain more than one simultaneous melody, with the higher tunes usually sung by women.

What is the most likely source of this paragraph?

   a. novel   b. textbook   c. personal letter

What is its purpose? _____

Who is the audience? _____

_____

2.   When dealing with club managers, it is *imperative* that you act professionally. Get all the details of a gig in advance. Doing so will eliminate any confusion or miscommunication that could result in a botched deal. It will also instantly set you apart from the legions of flaky musicians that managers must endure on a daily basis. That's a good thing.

What is the most likely source of this paragraph?

a. Web site article   b. novel   c. personal letter

What is its purpose? _____

Who is the audience? _____

_____

3.   But there was no reason why everyone should not dance. Madame Ratignolle could not, so it was she who gaily consented to play for the others. She played very well, keeping excellent waltz time and infusing an expression into the strains which was indeed inspiring. She was keeping up her music on account of the children, she said, because she and her husband both considered it a means of brightening the home and making it attractive.

What is the most likely source of this paragraph?

a. novel   b. textbook   c. personal letter

What is its purpose? _____

Who is the audience? _____

_____

PRACTICE 3

View the following cartoon. What is the topic? Who is the audience? What is the purpose? Does the cartoon achieve its purpose?

"Oh no, not homework again."

Exploring Strategies

After you determine your topic, audience, and purpose, try some **exploring strategies**—also known as **prewriting strategies**—to help get your ideas flowing. The four most common strategies are freewriting, brainstorming, questioning, and clustering. It is not necessary to do all of the strategies explained in this chapter. Find the strategy that works best for you.

You can do both general and focused prewriting. If you have writer's block, and do not know what to write, use **general prewriting** to come up with possible topics. Then, after you have chosen a topic, use **focused prewriting** to find an angle of the topic that is interesting and which could be developed in your paragraph.

 **When to Use Exploring Strategies**

You can use exploring strategies at any stage of the writing process.

- To find a topic
- To narrow a broad topic
- To generate ideas about your topic
- To generate supporting details

Freewriting

Freewriting is writing for a limited period of time without stopping. The point is to record the first thoughts that come to mind. If you have no ideas, you can indicate that fact in a sentence such as "I don't know what to write." As you write, do not be concerned with your grammar or spelling. If you use a computer, let your ideas flow and do not worry about typing mistakes.

TECHNOLOGY LINK

On a computer, try typing without looking at the screen or with the screen turned off. Don't worry about mistakes.

Sandra's Freewriting

College student Sandra Ahumada did freewriting about work. During her freewriting, she wrote everything that came to mind.

> Work. I've only worked in a restaurant. A lotta reasons to work in a restaurant. Schedules are good for college students. Can work nights or weekends. Serving people so different from studying. You can relax your brain, go on automatic pilot. But you have to remember people's orders so it can be hard. And some customer are rude, rude, RUDE. What else . . . It is hard to juggle a job and college work. But it forces me to organize my time. What types of jobs pay a good salary? Day-care work? In some jobs, you get tips in addition to the salary. Should people always tip servers? Don't know. The tips can be very good. Like for hairdressers. Taxi drivers.

Sandra's Focused Freewriting

After Sandra did her general freewriting, she underlined ideas that she thought could be expanded into a complete paragraph. Then she looked at her underlined ideas to decide which one to write about. Her purpose was to persuade, so she chose a topic that she could defend. She did focused freewriting about tipping.

> I think people should always tip in restaurants. Why. Well, the waitresses need the cash. I dont earn a lot, so the tips are really important. I gotta lot a bills, and can't pay everything with minimum wage. What else? Diners should just consider the tip as a part of the cost of eating out. If they don't wanna tip, they should cook at home. Also, lots of other

service people get tips and nobody cares. And bad service. It could be the cook's fault. Some customers blame me when the restaurant is really crowded and I'm run off my feet. They should be more understanding. We need those tips. Sure do.

The Writer's Desk Freewriting

Choose one of the following topics and do some freewriting. Remember to write without stopping.

The family   Travel   Sports

Brainstorming

Brainstorming is like freewriting except that you create a list of ideas, and you can take the time to stop and think when you create your list. As you think about the topic, write down words or phrases that come to mind. Do not be concerned about grammar or spelling; the point is to generate ideas.

Chul's Brainstorming

College student Chul Yee brainstormed about cities. He made a list of general ideas.

- living in a city vs. living in a town
- my favorite cities
- the bad side of city life
- reasons people move to large cities
- Los Angeles full of pollution
- reasons to get out of cities

Chul's Focused Brainstorming

After he had brainstormed some general ideas, Chul chose one idea and did some focused brainstorming about the reasons people move out of cities.

- cities are too crowded and impersonal
- smaller towns everybody knows each other
- cities are too dangerous (car jacking last week in this neighborhood)
- cost of living in the city is higher, rents are higher
- want to know neighbors and feel like a part of a community
- desire the slower pace of life in the country

The Writer's Desk Brainstorming

Choose one of the following topics and brainstorm. Write down a list of ideas.

Ceremonies   Gossip   Good or bad manners

Questioning

Another way to generate ideas about a topic is to ask yourself a series of questions and write responses to them. The questions can help you define and narrow your topic. One common way to do this is to ask yourself *who, what, when, where, why,* and *how* questions. As with other exploring strategies, questioning can be general or focused.

Clayton's Questioning

College student Clayton Rukavina used a question-and-answer format to generate ideas about binge drinking.

What is binge drinking?	having too much alcohol in a short time
Who binge-drinks?	students who are away from home for the first time, or insecure students
Why do students drink too much?	peer pressure, want to be more relaxed, don't think about consequences
When do students drink too much?	spring break, weekends, to celebrate legal age
How dangerous is binge drinking?	may get alcohol poisoning, may choke, and may drink and drive
Where does it happen?	dorm rooms, house parties, fraternities
Why is it an important topic?	can die from binge drinking or drunk driver can kill somebody else

The Writer's Desk   Questioning

Choose one of the following topics and write questions and answers. Try to ask *who, what, when, where, why,* and *how* questions.

Beliefs   Patriotism   Health

Clustering

Clustering is like drawing a word map; ideas are arranged in a visual image. To begin, write your topic in the middle of the page and draw a box or a circle around it. That idea will lead to another, so write the second idea, and draw a line connecting it to your topic. Keep writing, circling, and connecting ideas until you have groups or "clusters" of them on your page. You can cluster to get ideas about a general or a specific topic.

Mahan's Clustering

College student Mahan Zahir used clustering to explore ideas about crime. He identified some main topics.

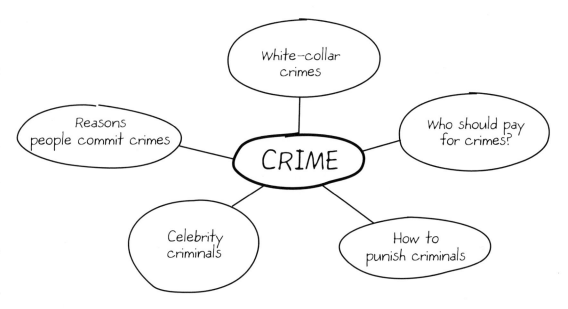

Mahan's Focused Clustering

Mahan decided to write about the reasons that people commit crimes. He added clusters to that topic.

The Writer's Desk Clustering

Choose one of the following topics and make a cluster on a separate sheet of paper. Begin by writing the key word in the middle of the space. Then connect related ideas.

Jobs   College   Relationships

Hint   **More About Exploring**

When you explore a topic using any of the listed strategies, keep in mind that a lot of the ideas you generate may not be useful. Later, when you develop your ideas, be prepared to cut irrelevant information.

Journal and Portfolio Writing

Keeping a Journal

You may write for work or school, but you can also practice writing for pleasure. One way to practice your writing is to keep a journal. A **journal** is a book, a computer file, or a blog (Web log) where you record your thoughts, opinions, ideas, and impressions. Journal writing gives you a chance to practice your writing without worrying about your readers and what they might think about it. It also gives you a source of material when you want to write about a topic of your choice. According to the author Anaïs Nin, "Keeping a diary is a way of making everyday life seem as exciting as fiction."

In your journal, you can write about any topic that appeals to you. Here are some topics for journal writing.

- Anything related to your personal life, such as your feelings about your career goals, personal problems and solutions, opinions about your college courses, reflections about past and future decisions, or feelings about your job
- Your reactions to controversies in the world, in your country, in your state, in your city, or in your college
- Facts that interest you
- Your reflections on the opinions and philosophies of others, including your friends or people that you read about in your courses

Keeping a Portfolio

A **writing portfolio** is a binder or an electronic file folder where you keep samples of all of your writing. The purpose of keeping a portfolio is to have a record of your writing progress. In your portfolio, keep all drafts of your writing assignments. When you work on new assignments, review your previous work in your portfolio. Identify your main problems, and try not to repeat the same errors.

REFLECT ON IT

Think about what you learned in this chapter. If you do not know an answer, review that topic.

1. Before you write, you should think about your topic, audience, and purpose. Explain what each one is.

    a. topic: _____

    b. audience: _____

    c. purpose: _____

2. Briefly define each of the following exploring styles.

    a. freewriting: _____

    b. brainstorming: _____

    c. questioning: _____

    d. clustering: _____

 The Writer's Room   **Topics to Explore**

Writing Activity I

Choose one of the following topics, or choose your own topic. Then generate ideas about the topic. You may want to try the suggested exploring strategy.

General Topics

1. Try freewriting about a strong childhood memory.

2. Try brainstorming and list any thoughts that come to mind about anger.

3. Try clustering. First, write "Rules" in the middle of the page. Then write clusters of ideas that connect to the general topic.

4. Ask and answer some questions about cosmetic surgery.

College and Work-Related Topics

5. Try freewriting about a comfortable place. Include any emotions or other details that come to mind.

6. Try brainstorming about study habits. List any ideas that come to mind.

7. To get ideas, ask and answer questions about recent celebrity scandals.

8. Try clustering. First, write "cell phones" in the middle of the page. Then write clusters of ideas that relate to the general topic.

Writing Activity 2

Look carefully at the poster. First, determine the topic, audience, and purpose. Whom is the poster trying to convince? What is the purpose? Is the purpose fulfilled? Then try exploring the topic. Use questioning as your exploring strategy. Ask and answer *who, what, when, where, why,* and *how* questions.

EXPLORING CHECKLIST

As you explore your topics, ask yourself the following questions.

☐ What is my topic? (Consider what you will write about.)

☐ Who is my audience? (Think about your intended reader.)

☐ What is my purpose? (Determine your reason for writing.)

☐ How can I explore? (You might try freewriting, brainstorming, questioning, or clustering.)

Developing
CHAPTER 2

> *You can only learn to be a better writer by actually writing.*
>
> —Doris Lessing
> *British author (b. 1919)*

After finding an idea, an artist begins to define shapes and layer on colors. Like an artist, a writer shapes ideas to create a solid paragraph or essay.

What Is Developing?

In Chapter 1, you learned how to use exploring strategies to formulate ideas. In this chapter, you will focus on the second stage of the writing process: **developing**. There are five key steps in the developing stage.

ESSAY LINK

When you develop an essay, you follow similar steps. For details about essay writing, see Chapter 13.

DEVELOPING

STEP 1 ⟶ **Narrow your topic.** Focus on some aspect of the topic that interests you.

STEP 2 ⟶ **Express your main idea.** Write a topic sentence (for a paragraph) or a thesis statement (for an essay) that expresses the main idea of the piece of writing.

STEP 3 ⟶ **Develop your supporting ideas.** Find facts, examples, or anecdotes that best support your main idea.

STEP 4 ⟶ **Make a plan.** Organize your main and supporting ideas, and place your ideas in a plan or an outline.

STEP 5 ⟶ **Write your first draft.** Communicate your ideas in a single written piece.

Reviewing Paragraph Structure

Before you practice developing your paragraphs, review the paragraph structure. A **paragraph** is a series of related sentences that develop one central idea. Because a paragraph can stand alone or be part of a longer piece of writing, it is the essential writing model. You can apply your paragraph writing skills to longer essays, letters, and reports.

A stand-alone paragraph generally has the following characteristics.

- A **topic sentence** states the topic and introduces the idea the writer will develop.
- **Body sentences** support the topic sentence.
- A **concluding sentence** ends the paragraph.

Catherine's Paragraph

College student Catherine Niatum wrote the following paragraph. Read her paragraph and notice how it is structured.

The topic sentence expresses the idea that Catherine develops in the paragraph.

Catherine supports the paragraph with examples.

The concluding sentence brings the paragraph to a satisfying close.

> **The commercialization of traditional holidays helps our economy.** First, toy stores and other gift shops benefit when people buy presents for loved ones. Toy Village, for instance, posted record profits during December's gift-giving season. Second, it helps the clothing industry because people spend money on new outfits. Marie Senko, a fashion store owner, says, "During the winter holiday season, we do almost the entire year's business." Moreover, specialty stores see their sales increase when customers buy lights, candles, and other decorations for their homes. Grocery stores and restaurants also profit because people prepare feasts, and companies have staff parties in restaurants and hotels. A Houston accounting firm, for example, celebrates every New Year's Eve in a local restaurant. Finally, the travel industry has a financial windfall during celebrations because people cross the nation to visit their loved ones. According to American Airlines employee Annie Sung, seat sales increase by 70 percent during Thanksgiving. The next time someone complains about the commercialization of holidays, remind the person that holiday spending is very beneficial for our economy.

Hint   **Paragraph Form**

When you write a paragraph, make sure that it has the following form.

- Always indent the first word of a paragraph. Move it about one inch, or five spaces, from the left-hand margin.
- Try to leave a margin of an inch to an inch and a half on each side of your paragraph.

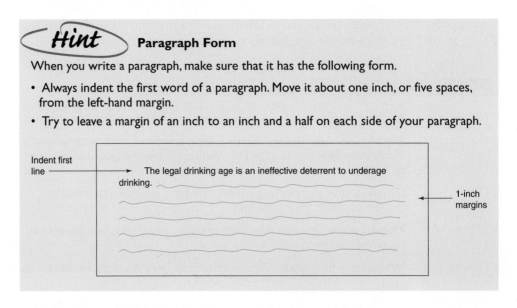

Indent first line → The legal drinking age is an ineffective deterrent to underage drinking.

1-inch margins

Narrow the Topic

A paragraph has one main idea. If your topic is too broad, you might find it difficult to write only one paragraph about it. When you **narrow** your topic, you make it more specific.

To narrow your topic, you can use exploring strategies such as freewriting, brainstorming, and questioning. These strategies are explained in more detail in Chapter 1, "Exploring."

Review the following examples of general and narrowed topics.

General Topic	**Narrowed Topic**
The job interview	How to dress for a job interview
College	My misconceptions about college life
Rituals	The high school prom

ESSAY LINK

An essay contains several paragraphs and can have a broader topic than a paragraph.

> *Hint* **Narrowing the Topic**
>
> One way to narrow your topic is to break it down into smaller categories.

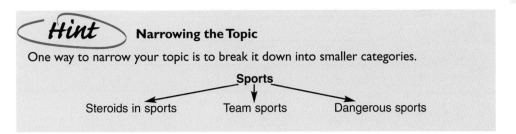

Sandra's Example of Narrowing a Topic

College student Sandra Ahumada practiced narrowing a topic by thinking of ideas about work.

- types of work: paid work, housework, homework
- jobs I have done in the service industry: server, cashier
- reasons to work in a restaurant
- how to find a job
- bad jobs that I have had
- finding the right career
- dangerous jobs such as firefighter, police officer
- are online job sites useful?

The Writer's Desk **Narrow the Topic**

Topics 1 to 5 are very broad. Practice narrowing topics by writing three ideas for each one.

EXAMPLE:

Crime: *white-collar crime*

           why people steal

           types of punishment

1. The family: _____

_____

_____

2. Gossip: _____

_____

_____

3. Travel: _____

_____

_____

4. Sports: _____

_____

_____

5. Jobs: _____

_____

_____

ESSAY LINK

Just as a topic sentence expresses the main point of a paragraph, the thesis statement expresses the main point of an essay. Both have a controlling idea.

The Topic Sentence

After you have narrowed the topic of your paragraph, your next step will be to write a topic sentence. The **topic sentence** has specific characteristics.

- It introduces the topic of the paragraph.
- It states the paragraph's controlling idea.
- It is the most general sentence in the paragraph.
- It is followed by other sentences that provide supporting facts and examples.

The **controlling idea** makes a point about the topic and expresses the writer's opinion, attitude, or feeling. You can express different controlling ideas about the same topic. For example, the following topic sentences are about youth offenders, but each sentence makes a different point about the topic.

        narrowed topic   controlling idea

Youth offenders should not receive special treatment from the correctional system.

                          controlling idea   narrowed topic

Rehabilitation and education are the best ways for the state to handle **youth offenders.**

PRACTICE I

Read each topic sentence. Underline the topic once and the controlling idea twice.

EXAMPLE:

Learning to play the guitar requires practice, patience, and perseverance.

1. Music education is essential in public schools.

2. My furnished room has everything a student could need.

3. You can learn to make decisions and think critically with a liberal arts education.

4. Several interesting events happened during the Stanford Prison Experiment.

5. The new youth center has a very impressive design.

6. There should not be a lower legal drinking age in our state.

7. We encountered many problems on our journey to Honduras.

8. Rory was known for his rumpled, unfashionable clothing.

9. IQ tests are not always accurate and valid.

10. The Beatles went through many musical phases.

Identifying the Topic Sentence

Before you write topic sentences, practice finding them in paragraphs by other writers. To find the topic sentence of a paragraph, follow these steps.

- Read the paragraph carefully.
- Look for a sentence that sums up the paragraph's subject. Professional writers may place the topic sentence anywhere in the paragraph.
- After you have chosen a sentence, see if the other sentences in the paragraph provide evidence that supports that sentence.

If you find one sentence that sums up what the paragraph is about and is supported by other sentences in the paragraph, then you have identified the topic sentence.

PRACTICE 2

Underline or highlight the topic sentences in paragraphs A, B, and C. Remember that the topic sentence is not always the first sentence in the paragraph.

EXAMPLE:

> Researchers say they have found the remains of a rodent the size of a buffalo in South America. Fossils suggest a 1,545-pound rodent that was a plant eater lived 6 million to 8 million years ago in what was then a lush, swampy forest. Marcelo R. Sanchez-Villagra of the University of Tubingen in Germany described the creature as "a weird guinea pig . . . with a long tail for balancing on its hind legs." The fossils were found in a desert area some 250 miles west of Caracas, Venezuela.
>
> —Lee Krystek, "Strange Science," *Unnatural Museum.com*

A. The idea of controlling music in society has been around for a long time. About 2,400 years ago, the Greek philosopher Plato said that the types of music people listened to should be controlled by the state. During the Middle Ages and the Renaissance, it was the Church that specified how music should be composed and performed. And in later centuries, secular rulers held a virtual monopoly over the music that was allowed in their realm. Often, composers had to submit a work to a committee before it was allowed to be published or performed.

—Jeremy Yudkin, *Understanding Music*

B. Cosmetic surgery is not like fooling around with a bottle of hair dye or getting a set of fake fingernails. The procedures are invasive, the recovery sometimes painful, and mistakes, while not common, can be difficult or impossible to correct. Breast implants may rupture, noses sink inward, and smiles turn unnaturally tight. People who merely wanted fat vacuumed from their thighs have died, while balding men have found themselves sporting new hair in symmetrical rows like tree farms. Stephen Katz, a sociologist at Trent University in Ontario, Canada, says, "To have plastic surgery, you have to think of your body as an object. It's a kind of social madness."

—Patricia Chisholm, "The Body Builders," *MacLean's*

C. Imagine a society without laws. People would not know what to expect from one another (an area controlled by the law of contracts), nor would they be able to plan for the future with any degree of certainty (administrative law); they wouldn't feel safe knowing that the more powerful or better armed could take what they wanted from the less powerful (criminal law); and they might not be able to exercise basic rights which would otherwise be available to them as citizens of a free nation (constitutional law).

—Frank Schmalleger, *Criminal Justice Today*

TECHNOLOGY LINK

If you write your paragraph on a computer, make your topic sentence bold (ctrl B). Then you and your instructor can easily identify it.

Writing an Effective Topic Sentence

When you develop your topic sentence, avoid some common errors by asking yourself these three questions.

1. **Is my topic sentence a complete sentence that has a controlling idea?**
   You might state the topic in one word or phrase, but your topic sentence should always reveal a complete thought and have a controlling idea. It should not announce the topic.

Incomplete:	Working in a restaurant.
	(This is a topic but *not* a topic sentence. It does not contain both a subject and a verb, and it does not express a complete thought.)
Announcement:	I will write about part-time jobs.
	(This announces the topic but says nothing relevant about it. Do not use expressions such as *My topic is . . .* or *I will write about. . . .*)
Topic sentence:	Part-time jobs help college students build self-esteem.

2. **Does my topic sentence make a valid and supportable point?**
   Your topic sentence should express a valid point that you can support with your evidence. It should not be a vaguely worded statement, and it should not be a highly questionable generalization.

Vague:	Beauty is becoming more important in our culture.
	(Beauty is more important than what?)
Invalid point:	Beauty is more important than it was in the past.
	(Is this really true? Cultures throughout history have been concerned with notions of beauty.)
Topic sentence:	Fashion magazines do not provide people with enough varied examples of beauty.

3. **Can I support my topic sentence in a single paragraph?**
   Your topic sentence should express an idea that you can support in a paragraph. It should not be too broad or too narrow.

Too broad:	Love is important.
	(It would be difficult to write a paragraph about this topic. There are too many things to say.)
Too narrow:	My girlfriend was born on March 2nd.
	(What more is there to say?)
Topic sentence:	During my first relationship, I learned a lot about being honest.

ESSAY LINK

If you find that your topic is too broad for a paragraph, you might want to save it so you can try using it for an essay.

> (*Hint*) **Write a Clear Topic Sentence**
>
> Your topic sentence should not express an obvious or well-known fact. When you clearly indicate your point of view, your topic sentence will capture your readers' attention and make them want to continue reading.
>
> | | |
> |---|---|
> | **Obvious:** | Money is important in our world. |
> | | (Everybody knows this.) |
> | **Better:** | There are several effective ways to save money. |

PRACTICE 3

Choose the word from the list that best describes the problem with each topic sentence. Correct the problem by revising each sentence.

Announces	Incomplete	Narrow
Broad	Invalid	Vague

EXAMPLE: This paragraph is about television advertisements.

Problem: *Announces*

Revised statement: *Television advertisements should be banned during children's programming.*

1. How to pack a suitcase.

   Problem: _____

   Revised statement: _____

2. I will write about negative political campaigns.

   Problem: _____

   Revised statement: _____

3. Today's journalists never tell both sides of the story.

   Problem: _____

   Revised statement: _____

4. History teaches us lessons.

Problem: _____

Revised statement: _____

5. Deciding to go to college.

Problem: _____

Revised statement: _____

6. The subject of this paragraph is annoying coworkers.

Problem: _____

Revised statement: _____

7. Everybody wants to be famous.

Problem: _____

Revised statement: _____

8. The coffee shop walls are painted green.

Problem: _____

Revised statement: _____

PRACTICE 4

The following paragraphs do not contain topic sentences. Read the paragraphs carefully and write appropriate topic sentences for each.

1. _____

_____

_____

First, computer technology allows people to work from their own homes, curtailing the need to have face-to-face interaction with other people. Business people can do conference calls, receive and send business documents, and access a lot of information without ever having to go to the office. Next, ATMs and on-line banking make it convenient for people to take out money or pay bills without having to communicate with bank personnel. Before Internet banking, people used to go to the bank regularly to pay bills or take out money. Most bank tellers knew their clients by name and took the time to chat with them. Nowadays, many people simply interact with a machine. Furthermore, consumers can do their shopping on-line. They never have to go to a store, further reducing their contact with other people. Indeed, modern technology has led to a way of life where people interact with each other less than before.

2. _____

_____

_____

Indeed, eye contact is a crucial ingredient to communicate thoughts and feelings. Many people have made a first social invitation with a future partner through eye contact. On the other hand, people discourage social interaction by avoiding eye contact. Next, hand gestures also communicate many messages. Through hand gestures, people greet, insult, or laugh at each other. For example, students show their knowledge by raising a hand to give a response, hitchhikers ask for a lift by using their thumb, and antiwar protesters convey their philosophy of peace with two fingers in the form of a V. Those who are extremely angry gesture with a fist. Most importantly, facial gestures are a fundamental element for nonverbal communication. People reveal their emotions through smiling, frowning, and rolling their eyes. If people really want to know what someone else is thinking or feeling, they should look closely at the person's body language.

The Writer's Desk Write Topic Sentences

Narrow each of the topics in this exercise. Then, write a topic sentence that contains a controlling idea. You could look at the Writer's Desk: Narrow the Topic on pages 21–22 for ideas.

EXAMPLE: Crime

　　Narrowed topic:　　*Why people steal*

　　Topic sentence:　　*People steal for several reasons.*

　　_____

1. The family

　　Narrowed topic:　_____

　　Topic sentence:　_____

　　_____

2. Gossip

　　Narrowed topic:　_____

　　Topic sentence:　_____

　　_____

3. Travel

　　Narrowed topic:　_____

　　Topic sentence:　_____

　　_____

4. Sports

　　Narrowed topic:　_____

　　Topic sentence:　_____

　　_____

5. Jobs

　　Narrowed topic:　_____

　　Topic sentence:　_____

　　_____

ESSAY LINK

When writing an essay, place the thesis statement in the introduction. Then each supporting idea becomes a distinct paragraph with its own topic sentence.

The Supporting Ideas

Once you have written a clear topic sentence, you can focus on the **supporting details**—the facts and examples that provide the reader with interesting information about the subject matter. There are three steps you can take to determine your paragraph's supporting details.

- Generate supporting ideas.
- Choose the best ideas.
- Organize your ideas.

Generating Supporting Ideas

You can try an exploring strategy such as brainstorming or freewriting to generate ideas.

Mahan's Supporting Ideas

College student Mahan Zahir narrowed his topic and wrote his topic sentence. Then he listed ideas that could support his topic sentence.

People steal for several reasons.
- need money for food
- want luxury items
- for thrills
- addiction
- for drugs
- minimum wage not enough to buy groceries
- alcohol-related crimes
- unemployment
- want to consume
- lack a moral code
- think they deserve something for nothing
- lack of parental attention
- too lazy
- adrenaline rush

The Writer's Desk List Supporting Ideas

Choose two of your topic sentences from the Writer's Desk on page 27. For each topic sentence, develop a list of supporting ideas.

Choosing the Best Ideas

An effective paragraph has **unity** when all of its sentences directly relate to and support the topic sentence. Create a unified paragraph by selecting three or four ideas that are most compelling and that clearly support your topic sentence. You may notice that several items in your list are similar; therefore, you can group them together. If some ideas do not support the topic sentence, remove them.

Mahan's Best Supporting Ideas

Mahan grouped together related ideas and crossed out some ideas that did not relate to his topic sentence.

People steal for many reasons.
- need money for food
- want luxury items
- for thrills
- addiction
- for drugs
- minimum wage not enough to buy groceries
- alcohol related crimes
- unemployment
- want to consume
- ~~lack of moral code~~
- think they deserve something for nothing
- ~~lack of parental attention~~
- ~~too lazy~~
- adrenaline rush

 **Hint**   **Identifying the Best Ideas**

There are many ways that you can highlight your best ideas. You can circle the best supporting points and then use arrows to link them with secondary ideas. You can also use highlighter pens or asterisks (*) to identify the best supporting points.

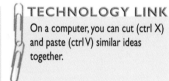
TECHNOLOGY LINK
On a computer, you can cut (ctrl X) and paste (ctrl V) similar ideas together.

PRACTICE 5

College student Sandra Ahumada brainstormed ideas about tipping. Her purpose was to persuade, so she created a topic sentence that expressed her opinion about the issue.

Underline three ideas from her list that you think are most compelling and that most clearly illustrate the point she is making in her topic sentence. Then group together any related ideas under each of the main subheadings. If any ideas do not relate to her topic sentence, remove them.

TOPIC SENTENCE: <u>Customers should always tip restaurant servers.</u>
- part of the cost of going to a restaurant
- shows appreciation for the server's work

– servers need tips to have an adequate standard of living

– their salaries below the standard minimum wage

– some customers are rude

– servers often don't get benefits such as health care

– you tip hairdressers and taxi drivers

– mistakes aren't always the server's fault

– slow service could be the cook's fault

– sometimes there are not enough servers

– some people in the service industry get good money (cooks, I think)

The Writer's Desk   Choose the Best Ideas

Choose *one* of the two lists of supporting ideas that you prepared for the previous Writer's Desk on page 28. Identify some compelling ideas that clearly illustrate the point you are trying to make. If any ideas are related, you can group them together. Cross out any ideas that are not useful.

ESSAY LINK

In an essay, you can use time, space, or emphatic order to organize your ideas.

Organizing Your Ideas

To make your ideas easy for your readers to follow, organize your ideas in a logical manner. You can use one of three common organizational methods: (1) time order, (2) emphatic order, or (3) space order.

Transitional expressions help guide the reader from one idea to another. A complete list of transitional expressions appears on page 47 in Chapter 3.

Time Order

When you organize a paragraph using **time order (chronological order),** you arrange the details according to the sequence in which they have occurred. When you narrate a story, explain how to do something, or describe a historical event, you generally use time order.

first   then   after that

Here are some transitional expressions you can use in time-order paragraphs.

after that	first	later	next
eventually	in the beginning	meanwhile	suddenly
finally	immediately	months after	then

The next paragraph is structured using time order.

> One day, some gentlemen called on my mother, and I felt the shutting of the front door and other sounds that indicated their arrival. Immediately, I ran upstairs before anyone could stop me to put on my idea of formal clothing. Standing before the mirror, as I had seen others do, I anointed my head with oil and covered my face thickly with powder. Then I pinned a veil over my head so that it covered my face and fell in folds down to my shoulders. Finally, I tied an enormous bustle round my small waist, so that it dangled behind, almost meeting the hem of my skirt. Thus attired, I went down to help entertain the company.
>
> —Helen Keller, *The Story of My Life*

Emphatic Order

When you organize the supporting details of a paragraph using **emphatic order**, you arrange them in a logical sequence. For example, you can arrange details from least to most important, from least appealing to most appealing, and so on.

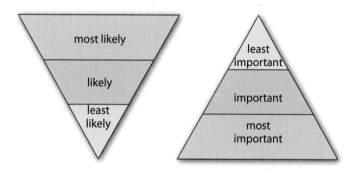

Here are some transitional expressions you can use in emphatic-order paragraphs.

above all	especially	moreover	principally
clearly	in particular	most importantly	the least important
first	last	of course	the most important

The following paragraph uses emphatic order. The writer presents the conditions from bad ones to worst ones.

> The conditions experienced by the eager young volunteers of the Union and Confederate armies included massive, terrifying, and bloody battles, apparently unending, with no sign of victory in sight. First, soldiers suffered from the uncertainty of supply, which left troops, especially in the South, without uniforms, tents, and sometimes even food. They also endured long marches over muddy, rutted roads while carrying packs weighing fifty or sixty pounds. Most importantly, disease was rampant in their dirty, verminous, and unsanitary camps, and hospitals were so dreadful that more men left them dead than alive.
>
> — Adapted from John Mack Faragher et al., *Out of Many: A History of the American People*

 **Using Emphatic Order**

When you organize details using emphatic order, use your own values and opinions to determine what is most or least important, upsetting, remarkable, and so on. Another writer might organize the same ideas in a different way.

Space Order

When you organize ideas using **space order,** you help the reader visualize what you are describing in a specific space. For example, you can describe something or someone from top to bottom or bottom to top, from left to right or right to left, or from far to near or near to far.

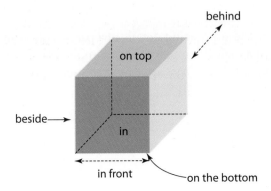

Here are some transitional expressions you can use in space-order paragraphs.

above	beneath	nearby	on top
behind	closer in	on the bottom	toward
below	farther out	on the left	under

In the next paragraph, the writer describes a location beginning at the beach and ending up at the front of the house.

> Their house was even more elaborate than I expected. It was a cheerful red-and-white Georgian Colonial mansion overlooking the bay. The lawn started at the beach and ran toward the front door for a quarter of a mile, jumping over sundials and brick walks and burning gardens—finally, when it reached the house, drifting up the side in bright vines as though from the momentum of its run. The front was broken by a line of French windows.
>
> —F. Scott Fitzgerald, *The Great Gatsby*

PRACTICE 6

Read each paragraph and underline the topic sentence. Then decide what order the writer used: time, space, or emphatic.

A. During the night of the great storm, we were filled with terror. That night, I lay awake and anxiously listened to the thunder as it continued to get closer and louder. Then I couldn't hear the thunder any more as it was replaced by another sound. I had never heard that sound before but I knew what it had to be. A split second later, I yelled "Tornado!" My wife jumped about two feet. We couldn't even get out of bed. Suddenly, everything was moving, and all we could do was hold on to each other. The roar, the sound of splintering wood, and the screeching sound of tearing sheet metal seemed to last forever. In fact, it lasted about fifteen seconds. Finally, silence returned like someone flipping a switch.

—Louis M. Tursi, "The Night Crawler"

Order: _____

B. Many factors contribute to racist attitudes. First, there are often higher levels of racist incidents in societies that have historically had very little contact with different ethnic groups. According to writer and political analyst Gwynne Dyer, such isolated societies may feel threatened when there is an influx of immigrants. Moreover, racist attitudes become more prevalent when various ethnic communities do not intermingle. If different cultural communities do not work and study together, stereotypes about other groups become entrenched. Most importantly, high levels of poverty contribute to racist reactions; immigrants become easy and available scapegoats when there is competition for limited jobs.

—Eliot Mandel, student

Order: _____

C. The tiny interior of the shop was in fact uncomfortably full, but there was almost nothing in it of the slightest value. The floor space was very restricted because all round the walls were stacked innumerable dusty picture-frames. In the window, there were trays of nuts and bolts, worn-out chisels, penknives with broken blades, tarnished watches that did not even pretend to be in going order, and other miscellaneous rubbish. Only on a small table in the corner was there a litter of odds and ends—lacquered snuffboxes, agate brooches, and the like—which looked as though they might include something interesting. As Winston wandered towards the table, his eye was caught by a round, smooth thing that gleamed softly in the lamplight, and he picked it up.

—George Orwell, *1984*

Order: _____

PRACTICE 7

Read the following topic sentences. Decide what type of order you can use to develop the paragraph details. Choose space, time, or emphatic order. (There may be more than one correct organizational method.)

EXAMPLE:

Learning to play the guitar requires practice, patience,
and perseverance.   *Emphatic*

1. Music education is essential in public schools.   _____

2. My furnished room has everything a student could need.   _____

3. You can learn to make decisions and think critically with
   a liberal arts education.   _____

4. Several interesting events happened during the Stanford Prison Experiment.   _____

5. The new youth center has a very impressive design.   _____

6. There should not be a lower legal drinking age in our state.   _____

7. We encountered many problems on our journey to Honduras.   _____

8. Rory was known for his rumpled, unfashionable clothing.   _____

9. IQ tests are not always accurate and valid.   _____

10. The Beatles went through many musical phases.   _____

The Paragraph Plan

A **plan,** or **outline,** of a paragraph is a map showing the paragraph's main and supporting ideas. To make a plan, write your topic sentence, and then list supporting points and details. Remember to use emphatic, time, or space order to organize the supporting points. In a more formal outline, you can use letters and numbers to indicate primary and secondary ideas.

Mahan's Paragraph Plan

Mahan completed his paragraph plan. He narrowed his topic, wrote a topic sentence, and thought of several supporting details. Here is his paragraph plan.

ESSAY LINK

Make a plan when you write an essay. In essay plans, each supporting idea becomes a separate paragraph.

TOPIC SENTENCE: People steal for many reasons.
  Support 1:   Poverty is a primary motivation for people to steal.
    Details: —some people are unemployed,
        —others working at low-paying jobs
        —need money for food, rent, clothing
  Support 2:   Some criminals are greedy.
    Details: —want to live a life of luxury
        —crave to conspicuously consume
        —wish for a larger yacht or faster jet
  Support 3:   Some people steal due to drug or alcohol addictions
    Details: —addicts steal to buy drugs
        —alcohol ruins good judgment
  Support 4:   Some people steal for the kicks.
    Details: —experience the thrill
        —receive an adrenaline rush when stealing

Hint — Adding Specific Details

When you prepare your paragraph plan, ask yourself if the details clearly support your topic sentence. If not, then you could add details to make your points stronger. For example, when Mahan first brainstormed a list of supporting details (page 28) he did not think of specific details to support his point about greed. In his paragraph plan, however, he added a couple of more details (larger yacht, faster jet) to make that point stronger and more complete.

The Writer's Desk Write a Paragraph Plan

Look at the topic sentence and the organized list of supporting ideas that you created for the previous Writer's Desk exercises. Now, in the space provided, make a paragraph plan. Remember to include details for each supporting idea.

Topic
sentence: _____

_____

Support 1: _____

Details: _____

_____

Support 2: _____

Details: _____

_____

Support 3: _____

Details: _____

_____

Writing the Concluding Sentence

A stand-alone paragraph may have a **concluding sentence** that brings it to a satisfactory close. There are several ways to write a concluding sentence.

- Restate the topic sentence in a new, refreshing way.
- Make an interesting final observation.
- End with a prediction, suggestion, or quotation.

ESSAY LINK

Essays end with a concluding paragraph. For more information, see pages 195–197.

Hint Problems with Concluding Sentences

When you write your concluding sentence, do not introduce a contradictory idea or change the focus of the paragraph. For example, in Mahan's paragraph about crime, he should not end with a statement that questions or contradicts his main point.

Weak: But nobody really understands why people break the law.

(This concluding sentence undermines the main point, which is that people steal for many reasons.)

Better: Knowing why people steal may help social services and law makers deal with criminals more effectively.

(This prediction brings the paragraph to a satisfactory close.)

PRACTICE 8

The topic sentences in paragraphs A and B are underlined. For each paragraph, circle the letter of the most effective concluding sentence, and then explain why the other choice is not as effective.

EXAMPLE:

Picasso painted many different types of people that he saw in the Paris neighborhood of Montmartre. He painted musicians, prostitutes, street vendors, circus performers, and fellow artists, as well as his many lovers. During his blue period, he was drawn to emaciated figures; impoverished mothers and hungry children populated his art.

a. Picasso painted many different types of people.

(b.) The human body was ultimately the most important and repeated image in his paintings and sculptures.

Why is the other choice not as effective?

Sentence "a" just repeats the topic sentence.

A. Our state should insist that day-care centers provide more flexible hours for families. Today, in many families, both parents work outside the home. These parents do not necessarily work from nine to five. For example, nurses and factory employees work in shifts. For such parents, flexible day care is very important. Also, many parents who are in the service and retail industry work on weekends. For these parents, it is important to have adequate child-care facilities during their work hours.

a. The current opening hours of most day-care centers do not meet the needs of a great number of families.

b. However, maybe day-care owners do not want to open on nights and weekends.

Why is the other choice not as effective?

_____

B. College students should find part-time jobs that require them to exercise different muscles. If a business student spends hours sitting in front of a computer screen, then he should try to find a job that requires physical activity. If an engineering student has to do advanced calculus, then maybe her part-time job should allow her to rest her brain. Students who do a lot of solitary study could try to find jobs that allow them to interact socially.

a. Some college students should not take part-time jobs because they need to concentrate on their studies.

b. Humans need to do a variety of activities to be mentally and physically strong, so college students should keep that in mind when they look for work.

Why is the other choice not as effective?

_____

PRACTICE 9

Read the next paragraph. Then answer the questions that follow.

Leonardo Da Vinci exemplified the characteristics of the Renaissance archetype. Da Vinci is most famous for being a master painter. His paintings *The Mona Lisa* and *The Last Supper* are two of the most admired in the world. Da Vinci was also an inventor, having been credited for an early model of a helicopter. He also made designs for a tank, a calculator, the double hull for ships, and a hang glider. Furthermore, Leonardo Da Vinci was a scientist. He studied anatomy by dissecting corpses, which helped him to draw human figures more precisely. He was also interested in animal and plant studies. His scientific writings are found in four journals kept in famous museums such as the Louvre and The British National Museum.

1. What is the topic of this paragraph?

    _____

2. Underline the topic sentence.

3. List the supporting details.

    _____

    _____

    _____

4. Write two possible concluding sentences for his paragraph.

    a. _____

        _____

    b. _____

        _____

The First Draft

After making a paragraph plan, you are ready to write your first draft, which is a very important step in the writing process. Your first draft includes your topic sentence, some supporting details, and a concluding sentence.

As you write your first draft, you might find it difficult sometimes to say what you mean. If you are having trouble, underline that section or put a check mark beside it so that you can come back to revise it later. If possible, put your first draft aside for a few hours before rereading it. Then, when you revise your paragraph, you will read it with a fresh perspective. The next chapter contains information about revising a paragraph.

Mahan's First Draft

Here is Mahan Zahir's first draft. You may notice that his paragraph has errors. He will correct these when he gets to the revising and editing stage of the process.

People steal for many reasons. Poverty is a primary motivation for people to steal. Because some people are unemployed and others may be underemployed. They may not have enough money for food, clothing rent. Stealing money or food may be very tempting. As a means of survival. Some criminals do fraud because they are greedy. In fact, some extremely wealthy people steal simply because they want to acquire a larger yacht or a faster jet. Another important reason that people engage in stealing is due to addiction to drugs or alcohol. Addicts steal to buy drugs and overuse of alcohol may lead to poor judgement. Finally, people also steal for kicks. Criminals get an adrenaline rush when they outwit the cops.

The Writer's Desk   Write Your First Draft

In the previous Writer's Desk on page 35, you made a paragraph plan. Now use the plan's information to type or write your first draft paragraph.

REFLECT ON IT

Think about what you have learned in this chapter. If you do not know an answer, review that topic.

1. What is a topic sentence? _____

   _____

2. What is time order? _____

   _____

3. What is emphatic order? _____

   _____

4. What is space order? _____

   _____

Are the following sentences true or false? Circle the best answer.

5. A paragraph has more than one main idea.   True   False

6. A paragraph's details support its topic sentence.   True   False

The Writer's Room Topics to Develop

Writing Activity 1

In the Writer's Room in Chapter 1, "Exploring," you used various strategies to find ideas about the following topics. Select one of the topics and write a paragraph. Remember to follow the writing process.

General Topics

1. a childhood memory
2. anger
3. rules
4. cosmetic surgery

College and Work-Related Topics

5. a comfortable place
6. study or work habits
7. college life
8. cell phones

Writing Activity 2

Choose a topic that you feel passionate about and write a paragraph. Your topic could be an activity (painting, basketball) or an interest (music, politics). Your topic sentence should make a point about the topic.

DEVELOPING CHECKLIST

As you develop your paragraph, ask yourself the following questions.

☐ Have I narrowed my topic?

☐ Does my topic sentence make a valid and supportable point about the topic?

☐ Is my topic sentence interesting?

☐ Does my paragraph focus on one main idea?

☐ Do the details support the topic sentence?

☐ Do the supporting details follow a logical order?

☐ Does my paragraph end in a satisfactory way?

How Do I Get a Better Grade?

mywritinglab

Visit www.mywritinglab.com for audio-visual lectures and additional practice sets about developing. *Get a better grade with MyWritingLab!*

Revising and Editing

CHAPTER 3

> *Life is trying things to see if they work.*
>
> —RAY BRADBURY
> *American author (b. 1920)*

The revising and editing stage of the writing process is similar to adding the finishing touches to an artwork. Small improvements can make the work more solid and complete.

What Is Revising and Editing?

After you have written the first draft of your paragraph, the next step in the writing process is to revise and edit your work. When you **revise,** you modify your writing to make it stronger and more convincing. You do this by reading your first draft critically, looking for faulty logic, poor organization, or poor sentence style. Then you reorganize and rewrite it, making any necessary changes. When you **edit,** you proofread your final draft for errors in grammar, spelling, punctuation, and mechanics.

There are five key steps to follow during the revising and editing stage.

REVISING AND EDITING

| STEP I | ➤ | **Revise for unity.** Ensure that all parts of your work relate to the main idea. |

| STEP 2 | ➤ | **Revise for adequate support.** Determine that your details effectively support the main idea. |

STEP 3 ———► **Revise for coherence.** Verify that your ideas flow smoothly and logically.

STEP 4 ———► **Revise for style.** Ensure that your sentences are varied and interesting.

STEP 5 ———► **Edit for technical errors.** Proofread your work and correct errors in grammar, spelling, mechanics, and punctuation.

ESSAY LINK

When revising and editing your essay, check that the body paragraphs support the thesis statement. Also, ensure that each body paragraph has unity.

Revise for Unity

Every idea in a paragraph should move in the same direction just as this bridge goes straight ahead. There should be no forks in the road.

Unity means that all of the sentences in a paragraph support the topic sentence. If a paragraph lacks unity, then some sentences drift from the main idea that a writer has expressed in the topic sentence. To check for unity, ensure that every sentence in the body of the paragraph relates to one main idea.

Paragraph Without Unity

In the next paragraph, the writer drifted away from her main idea. Some sentences do not relate to the topic sentence. If the highlighted sentences are removed, then the paragraph has unity.

The writer took a detour here. ➤

> **During World War II, the status of women changed profoundly.** The military industry needed "manpower" to fight the war, but it also needed womanpower. From 1940 to 1944, about 17 million women joined the work force. They filled jobs in defense industries, steel mills, shipyards, and aircraft factories. By the end of the war, women had proved that they could be invaluable workers. Today, many women work in these industries, and it isn't considered unusual. In fact, according to Brigid O'Farrell, women represent over 17 percent of all blue-collar workers in the United States. Now women earn the same salary as men in most jobs. When men returned home in 1945, most women left the factories; however, women developed confidence and earning power, and North America's workplace changed forever.

PRACTICE I

Paragraphs A and B contain problems with unity. In each paragraph, underline the topic sentence and cross out any sentences that do not support the controlling idea.

A. Car-based cell phones should be banned. One study published by the *New England Journal of Medicine* found that the risk of a collision quadruples if drivers use a cellular phone. The findings indicate that the major problem with cell phones is that they affect the driver's concentration. Jeffrey Blain repairs roads, and he says that sometimes drivers using their phones go through barriers and into road repair sites because they are so distracted. I also hate it when people use their cell phones in movie theaters. At a recent movie, I heard the beeps of various cell phones at least five times during the film. The problem is especially bad in cars, though. Our government should outlaw cell phones in motor vehicles.

B. Orville and Wilbur Wright had an unlikely dream, but they turned it into reality. When the brothers first tried to make a plane fly, they were unsuccessful. In fact, in 1901, a frustrated Wilbur Wright said that humans wouldn't fly for a thousand years. However, just two years later, on December 17, 1903, Wilbur and Orville Wright flew a plane for 105 feet. The brothers were overjoyed; their hard work and planning had finally paid off. Since that time, air travel has changed a lot. Many different types of planes exist today. Jets fly across our skies and can go from London to New York in a few hours. Eventually the Wright brothers produced nineteen types of aircraft. By sticking with an idea and persevering, the Wright brothers made their dream a reality.

Revise for Adequate Support

ESSAY LINK

When revising your essay, ensure that you have adequately supported the thesis statement. Also ensure that each body paragraph has sufficient supporting details.

A bridge is built using several well-placed support columns. Like a bridge, a paragraph requires adequate support to help it stand on its own.

A paragraph has **adequate support** when there are enough details and examples to make it strong, convincing, and interesting. The following paragraph attempts to persuade, but it does not have any specific details that make a strong point.

Paragraph Without Adequate Support

In European films, the star can be wrinkled or overweight. **Unfortunately, American filmmakers have not figured out that people like to see reflections of themselves on screen.** To get a job, American movie actors must be in perfect shape and have perfect bodies. It is often hard to believe that the beautiful actor is really the waiter or car mechanic that is pictured on screen. The problem is especially acute when the star is older. You can be sure that he or she has had a lot of surgery to look as young as possible. Ordinary audience members have trouble identifying with surgically enhanced actors. Perhaps one day American producers will use regular-looking people in their films.

PRACTICE 2

When the preceding paragraph about film stars is expanded with specific details and examples, the paragraph becomes more convincing. Try adding details on the lines provided. You can do this alone or with a partner.

In European films, the star can be wrinkled or overweight. Unfortunately, American filmmakers have not figured out that people like to see reflections of themselves on screen. To get a job, American movie actors must be in perfect shape and have perfect bodies. For example, _____ and _____ are incredibly good-looking. It is often hard to believe that the beautiful actor is really the waiter or car mechanic that is pictured on screen. In the movie titled _____, the actor _____ looks too perfect to be a _____. The problem is especially acute when the star is older. You can be sure that he or she has had a lot of surgery to look as young as possible. For instance, _____ looks much younger than the actor's real age. Ordinary audience members have trouble identifying with surgically enhanced actors. Perhaps one day American producers will use regular-looking people in their films.

Avoiding Circular Reasoning

Circular reasoning means that a paragraph restates its main point in various ways but does not provide supporting details. The main idea goes in circles and never progresses. Avoid using circular reasoning by providing a clear, concise topic sentence and by supporting the topic sentence with facts, examples, statistics, or anecdotes.

CELIA'S PARAGRAPH

Celia Raines, a student, wrote the following paragraph about a popular proverb. In the paragraph, she repeats her main point over and over and does not provide any evidence to support her topic sentence.

Circular   Those who make the most noise usually get what they want. People sometimes shout and make a fuss and then others listen to them. Those who are quiet get ignored and their opinions do not get heard. It is important for people to speak up and express their needs. This attitude is expressed in the proverb, "The squeaky wheel gets the grease."

In the second version of this paragraph, Celia added a specific example (an anecdote) that helped illustrate her main point.

Revised Paragraph   Those who make the most noise usually get what they want. Those who are quiet get ignored, and their opinions do not get heard. For example, two years ago, the local government started a passenger train service that helped local commuters get into the city. Many citizens loved commuting by train, but those who live near the train tracks complained about the noise. They made petitions, wrote to newspapers, and lobbied the local government to cancel the train service. Those people were so loud and persistent that they got their wish, and the train service was canceled. The silent majority disagreed with that lobby group, but as the proverb says, "The squeaky wheel gets the grease."

Circular reasoning in a paragraph is like a Ferris wheel. The main idea of the paragraph does not seem to progress.

PRACTICE 3

Paragraphs A and B use circular reasoning. There is no specific evidence to support the topic sentence. List supporting examples for each paragraph. With numbers, indicate where you would place the supporting examples.

EXAMPLE:

American teenagers go through several rites of passage. These rites of passage help the teenager navigate the transition from childhood to
(1)
adulthood. Some rites of passage are shared with the community.
(2)
These rites are an important part of every youth's life.

Examples: *(1) The first date and the first kiss are important.*

The first job is also a special step.

(2) During the high school prom, the community

members gathered together.

A. Police officers have an important function in our society. They provide many useful and necessary services in the community. If there were no police officers, there would be anarchy in the streets. Law-enforcement officers deserve our respect and appreciation.

Examples: _____

_____

_____

_____

_____

_____

B. When you move out of your family home and live on your own, you should plan your budget carefully. There are many things that you will have to pay for, and a lot of items will be expensive. You will need to pay for services. Even small household items add up. It is expensive to live on your own.

Examples: _____

_____

_____

_____

_____

_____

ESSAY LINK

To create coherence in an essay, you can place transitional expressions at the beginning of each body paragraph.

Revise for Coherence

When you drive along a highway and you suddenly hit a pothole, it is an uncomfortable experience. Readers experience similar discomfort if they encounter potholes in a piece of writing. Make your writing as smooth as possible by ensuring that it has **coherence:** the sentences should flow smoothly and logically.

Transitional Expressions

Transitional expressions are linking words or phrases, and they ensure that ideas are connected smoothly. Here are some common transitional expressions.

Just as bolts link pieces of a bridge, transitional expressions can link ideas in a paragraph.

Function	Transitional Word or Expression	
Addition	again	in addition
	also	in fact
	besides	last
	finally	moreover
	first (second, third)	next
	for one thing	then
	furthermore	
Concession of a point	certainly	of course
	even so	no doubt
	indeed	to be sure
Comparison and contrast	as well	likewise
	equally	nevertheless
	even so	on the contrary
	however	on the other hand
	in contrast	similarly
	instead	
Effect or result	accordingly	otherwise
	as a result	then
	consequently	therefore
	hence	thus
Example	for example	in particular
	for instance	namely
	in other words	specifically
		to illustrate
Emphasis	above all	least of all
	clearly	most important
	first	most of all
	especially	of course
	in fact	particularly
	in particular	principally
	indeed	
Reason or purpose	for this purpose	the most important reason
	for this reason	
Space	above	near
	behind	nearby
	below	on one side/on the other side
	beneath	on the bottom
	beside	on the left/right
	beyond	on top
	closer in	outside
	farther out	to the north/east/south/west
	inside	under
Summary or conclusion	in conclusion	therefore
	in other words	thus
	in short	to conclude
	generally	to summarize
	on the whole	ultimately
Time	after that	later
	at that time	meanwhile
	at the moment	months after
	currently	now
	earlier	one day
	eventually	presently
	first (second, etc.)	so far
	gradually	subsequently
	immediately	suddenly
	in the beginning	then
	in the future	these days
	in the past	

GRAMMAR LINK

For more practice using transitions in sentences, see Chapter 17, "Compound Sentences," and Chapter 18, "Complex Sentences."

 **Use Transitional Expressions with Complete Sentences**

When you add a transitional expression to a sentence, ensure that your sentence is complete. Your sentence must have a subject and a verb, and it must express a complete thought.

Incomplete: For example, the rules posted on the wall.

Complete: For example, the rules <u>were</u> posted on the wall.

PRACTICE 4

The next paragraph contains eight transitional expressions that appear at the beginning of sentences. Underline each expression, and then, in the chart, indicate its purpose. The first one has been done for you.

> For those who love eating out, a new type of dining experience is rearing its ugly head. <u>Indeed</u>, service with a sneer is popping up in Canada and the United States. For instance, in the New York City teahouse Tea and Sympathy, customers must follow a rigid list of rules. Those who plan to wait for friends are sharply told to leave. Moreover, patrons who manage to get a table are kicked out as soon as they finish their tea. Similarly, in Vancouver, the Elbow Room Café posts rules on the wall, including one that asks customers to get their own coffee and water. Also, the owner and staff members ridicule customers who order decaf tea or butter-free toast. Even so, clients keep coming back, comparing the experience to going to a show. The bad service trend has always been there. However, people in previous decades would have left such eateries without leaving a tip. These days, customers line up to be abused.

Transitional Expression   **Function**

1. *Indeed*   *Emphasis*

2. _____   _____

3. _____   _____

4. _____   _____

5. _____   _____

6. _____   _____

7. _____   _____

8. _____   _____

PRACTICE 5

Add appropriate transitional expressions to the following paragraph. Choose from the following list, and use each transitional word once. There may be more than one correct answer for each blank.

consequently   furthermore   on the other hand
for example   first   therefore

Workplace gossip has both positive and negative effects. _____, when two colleagues share secrets about others, it helps build trust and creates intimacy. _____, in large organizations, gossip helps form small social groups that provide workplace support systems. _____, overly negative gossip can undermine employee moral. An employee who hears malicious gossip may suspect that he or she is also the subject of office chatter. _____, Latisha Bishop, an employee at CR Industries, says that she felt devastated when she realized that her coworkers were spreading information about her private life. _____, she seriously considered leaving her job. _____, when office workers gossip, they should try to do so without malice.

Revise for Style

When you revise for sentence **style,** you ensure that your paragraph has concise and appropriate language and sentence variety. You can ask yourself the following questions.

- Have I used a **variety of sentence patterns?** (To practice using sentence variety, see Chapter 19.)
- Have I used **exact language?** (To learn about slang, wordiness, and overused expressions, see Chapter 31.)
- Are my sentences **parallel in structure?** (To practice revising for parallel structure, see Chapter 21.)

ESSAY LINK

You should revise your essays for style, ensuring that sentences are varied and parallel. Also, ensure that your language is exact.

MAHAN'S REVISION

On pages 37–38 in Chapter 2, you read the first draft of student Mahan Zahir's paragraph about crime. Look at his revisions for unity, support, coherence, and style.

First, poverty

People steal for many reasons. ~~Poverty~~ is a primary motivation for people to steal. Because some people are unemployed and others may be underemployed. They may not have enough money for food, clothing

◄ Transition

Transition ➤

Better word ➤

rent. Stealing money or food may be very tempting. As a means of
Next, some   perpetrate
survival. ~~Some~~ criminals ~~do~~ fraud because they are greedy. In fact, some

extremly wealthy people steal simply because they want to acquire a

Add specific examples ➤

larger yacht or a faster jet. *For example, the directors of Enron and*

WorldCom were found guilty of stealing from shareholders, none of

Add indirect quotation ➤

these directors lacked personal wealth. According to Lisa Bloom, a

reporter for court tv, the rich steal for the same reason as the poor:

they love getting something for nothing. Another important reason that

people engage in stealing is due to addiction to drugs or alcohol. Addicts

steal to buy drugs and overuse of alcohol may lead to poor judgment.

Add statistic ➤

According to the Bureau of Justice Statistics, 68 percent of jailed

inmates reported that their substance abuse problems contributed

to there decisions to commit crimes. In addition, people steal for

kicks. *Martin Jeffs, a twenty three year old mugger who spoke to*

BBC News, say that excitement is a major motivation for many street

Add quotation ➤

criminals: "It gives a lot of people a buzz to know that they have got

the power to overpower someone and take his possessions."

Better word ➤

police
Criminals get an adrenaline rush when they outwit the ~~cops~~. *Knowing*

Add concluding sentence ➤

the different reasons that people steal may help social workers and

lawmakers deal with criminals more effectively.

Hint   **Adding Strong Support**

When you revise, look at the strength of your supporting details. Ask yourself the
following questions.

• Are my supporting details interesting, and do they grab the reader's attention? Should
I use more vivid words?

• Is my concluding sentence appealing? Could I end the paragraph in a more interesting
way?

PRACTICE 6

In Chapters 1 and 2, you saw examples of Sandra Ahumada's prewriting and planning. Now look at the first draft of Sandra's paragraph, and revise it for unity, support, and coherence. Also, ask yourself what you could do to enhance her writing style.

> Customers should always tip restaurant servers. Servers need tips to live. Their salary is very low. They depend on tips to pay for food, housing, and other necessities. They do not get benefits such as health care. If you do not like the service, remember that mistakes are not always the server's fault. Poor service could be the cook's fault. Sometimes there are not enough servers. I work as a server in a restaurant, I know how hard it is when customers leave bad tips. Always tip your restaurant server.

Edit for Errors

When you **edit,** you reread your writing and make sure that it is free of errors. You focus on the language, and you look for mistakes in grammar, punctuation, mechanics, and spelling.

There is an editing guide at the back of this book. It contains some common error codes that your teacher may use. It also provides you with a list of things to check for when you proofread your text.

GRAMMAR LINK
For more editing practice, see Chapter 36.

TECHNOLOGY LINK
Word processors have spelling and grammar checkers. Do not always choose the first suggestion for a correction. Make sure that suggestions are valid before you accept them.

Editing Tips

The following tips will help you proofread your work more effectively.

- Put your writing aside for a day or two before you do the editing. Sometimes, when you have been working closely with a text, you might not see the errors.
- Begin your proofreading at any stage of the writing process. For example, if you are not sure of the spelling of a word while writing the first draft, you could either highlight the word for later verification or immediately look up the word in the dictionary.
- Keep a list of your common errors in a separate grammar log. When you finish a writing assignment, consult your error list, and make sure that you have not repeated any of those errors. After each assignment has been corrected, you can add new errors to your list. For more information about grammar and spelling logs, see Appendix 7.

MAHAN'S EDITED PARAGRAPH

Mahan Zahir edited his paragraph about crime. He corrected errors in spelling, capitalization, punctuation, and grammar.

People steal for many reasons. First, poverty is a primary

motivation for people to steal. Because some people are unemployed

, they

and others may be underemployed. ~~They~~ may not have enough

, and

money for food, clothing ^ rent. Stealing money or food may be very

as

tempting. ~~As~~ a means of survival. Next, some criminals perpetrate fraud

extremely

because they are greedy. In fact, some ~~extremly~~ wealthy people steal

simply because they want to acquire a larger yacht or a faster jet. For

example, the directors of Enron and WorldCom were found guilty of

. N

stealing from shareholders, ~~none~~ of these directors lacked personal

Court TV

wealth. According to Lisa Bloom, a reporter for ~~court tv~~, the rich steal

for the same reason as the poor: they love getting something for nothing.

Another important reason that people engage in stealing is due to

addiction to drugs or alcohol. Addicts steal to buy drugs and overuse of

alcohol may lead to poor judgment. According to the Bureau of Justice

Statistics, 68 percent of jailed inmates reported that their substance

their

abuse problems contributed to ~~there~~ decisions to commit crimes.

twenty-three-year-

In addition, people steal for kicks. Martin Jeffs, a ~~twenty three year~~

says

old mugger who spoke to *BBC News*, ~~say~~ that excitement is a major

motivation for many street criminals: "It gives a lot of people a buzz to

know that they have got the power to overpower someone and

take his possessions." Criminals get an adrenaline rush when they outwit the police. Knowing the different reasons that people steal

may help social workers and lawmakers deal with criminals more

effectively.

The Writer's Desk **Revise and Edit**

Choose a paragraph you wrote for Chapter 2, or choose one that you have written for another assignment. Carefully revise and edit the paragraph. You can refer to the Revising and Editing Checklist at the end of this chapter.

Peer Feedback

After you write a paragraph or essay, it is useful to get peer feedback. Ask another person such as a friend, family member, or fellow student to read your work and give you comments and suggestions on its strengths and weaknesses.

 **Offer Constructive Criticism**

When you peer-edit someone else's writing, try to make your comments useful. Phrase your comments in a positive way. Look at these examples.

Instead of saying . . .	**You could say . . .**
Your sentences are boring.	Maybe you could combine some sentences.
Your supporting ideas are weak.	You could add more details here.

You can use the following peer feedback form to evaluate written work.

Peer Feedback Form

Written by: _____   Feedback by: _____

Date: _____

1. What is the main point of the written work?

   _____

2. What details effectively support the topic sentence?

   _____

   _____

3. What, if anything, is unclear or unnecessary?

   _____

   _____

4. Give some suggestions about how the work could be improved.

   _____

   _____

5. What is an interesting or unique feature of this written work?

   _____

   _____

Write the Final Draft

When you have finished making revisions on the first draft of your paragraph, write the final draft. Include all of the changes that you have made during the revision and editing phases. Before you hand in your final draft, proofread it one last time to ensure that you have caught any errors.

The Writer's Desk Write Your Final Draft

You have developed, revised, and edited your paragraph. Now write the final draft. Before you offer it to readers, proofread it one last time to ensure that you have found all of your errors.

 **Spelling, Grammar, and Vocabulary Logs**

- **Keep a spelling and grammar log.** You probably repeat, over and over, the same types of grammar and spelling errors. You will find it very useful to record your repeated grammar mistakes in a spelling and grammar log. You can refer to your list of spelling and grammar mistakes when you revise and edit your writing.

- **Keep a vocabulary log.** Expanding your vocabulary will be of enormous benefit to you as a writer. In a vocabulary log, you can make a list of unfamiliar words and their definitions.

See Appendix 7 for more information about spelling, grammar, and vocabulary logs.

REFLECT ON IT

Think about what you have learned in this chapter. If you do not know an answer, review that topic.

1. What are four things that you should look for when revising?

   _____   _____

   _____   _____

2. Circle the best answer(s). A paragraph is unified if

   a. there are no irrelevant supporting details.

   b. there are many facts and statistics.

   c. all details support the topic sentence.

3. Circle the best answer: Transitional words are _____ that help ideas flow in a logical manner.

   a. links   b. sentences   c. verbs

4. The Editing Handbook in Part IV includes information about grammar, spelling, and punctuation errors. In what chapter would you find information about the following topics? Look in the table of contents to find the chapter number.

   a. capitalization   _____

   b. subject–verb agreement   _____

   c. faulty parallel structure   _____

   d. commas   _____

   e. commonly confused words   _____

The Writer's Room **Paragraph Topics**

Writing Activity 1

Choose a paragraph that you have written for your job or for another course. Revise and edit that paragraph, and then write a final draft.

Writing Activity 2

Choose any of the following topics, or choose your own topic. Then write a paragraph. Remember to follow the writing process.

General Topics

1. interesting things about yourself
2. how to write a paragraph
3. heroes in the media
4. the meaning of the quotation at the beginning of this chapter
5. bad service

College and Work-Related Topics

6. something you learned in a college course or on campus
7. an unusual work experience
8. reasons to turn down a job
9. telemarketing
10. an interesting job

✔ REVISING AND EDITING CHECKLIST

When you revise and edit, ask yourself the following questions. (For a more detailed editing checklist, refer to the inside back cover of this book.)

Unity

☐ Is my paragraph unified under a single topic?

☐ Does each sentence relate to the topic sentence?

Support

☐ Does my paragraph have an adequate number of supporting details?

Coherence

☐ Is my paragraph logically organized?

☐ Do I use transitional words or expressions to help the paragraph flow smoothly?

Style

- Do I use a variety of sentence styles?

- Is my vocabulary concise?

- Are my sentences parallel in structure?

Editing

- Do my sentences contain correct grammar, spelling, punctuation, and mechanics?

How Do I Get a Better Grade?

Visit www.mywritinglab.com for audio-visual lectures and additional practice sets about revising and editing. **_Get a better grade with MyWritingLab!_**

Paragraph Patterns

What Is a Paragraph Pattern?

A pattern or mode is a method used to express one of the three purposes: to inform, to persuade, or to entertain. Once you know your purpose, you will be able to choose which writing pattern or patterns can help you to express it.

Patterns can overlap, and it is possible to use more than one pattern in a single piece of writing. For example, imagine you are writing a paragraph about bullying, and your purpose is to inform the reader. You might use *definition* as your predominant pattern, but in the supporting details, you might use *comparison and contrast* to compare a bully and a victim. You might also use *narration* to highlight an incident in which a bully harassed a victim.

Before you work through the next chapters, review the paragraph patterns.

Illustration
To illustrate or prove a point using specific examples

Narration
To narrate or tell a story about a sequence of events that happened

Process
To inform the reader about how to do something, how something works, or how something happened

Description
To describe using vivid details and images that appeal to the reader's senses

Definition
To define or explain what a term or concept means by providing relevant examples

Classification
To classify or sort a topic to help readers understand different qualities about that topic

Comparison and contrast
To present information about similarities (compare) or differences (contrast)

Cause and effect
To explain why an event happened (the cause) or what the consequences of the event were (the effects)

Argument*
To argue or to take a position on an issue and offer reasons for your position

*Argument is included as one of the nine patterns, but it is also a purpose in writing.

Illustration

CHAPTER 4

> *A wisely chosen illustration is essential to fasten the truth upon the ordinary mind.*
>
> —HOWARD CROSBY
> *American preacher and educator (1826—1891)*

CONTENTS

Exploring
- What Is Illustration?
- The Illustration Paragraph
- Explore Topics

Developing
- The Topic Sentence
- The Supporting Ideas
- The Paragraph Plan
- The First Draft

Revising and Editing
- Revise and Edit an Illustration Paragraph

Vendors offer many examples of a product to interest consumers and to make a sale. In illustration writing, you give examples to support your point.

Writers' Exchange

Work with a team of two or three other students. You have three minutes to list as many words as you can that are examples of the following parts of speech.

Noun   Verb   Adjective   Adverb

What Is Illustration?

When you write using **illustration**, you include specific examples to clarify your main point. You illustrate or give examples anytime you want to explain, analyze, narrate, or give an opinion about something. As a writer, you can use many different types of examples to help your reader acquire a deeper and clearer understanding of your subject. You can include personal experience or factual information, such as a statistic.

You give examples every day. When telling a friend why you had a good day or a bad day, you might use examples to make your story more interesting. At college, you might give an oral presentation using examples that will help your audience better understand your point. At work, you might give examples to show clients where or how they might market their products.

Illustration at Work

Patti Guzman is a registered nurse at a large hospital. She was invited to speak to nursing students in a local university. In the following excerpt from her speech, she gives examples to explain why a nurse must be in good physical health.

Physically, the job of a nurse is demanding. On a daily basis, we must lift patients and move them. When patients are bedridden for prolonged periods, we must change their positions on their beds. When new patients arrive, we transfer them from stretchers to beds or from beds to wheelchairs. If patients fall, we must be able to help them stand up. If patients have difficulty walking, we must assist them. Patients who have suffered paralysis or stroke need to be lifted and supported when they are bathed and dressed. Keep in mind that some patients may be quite heavy, so the job requires a good level of physical strength.

ESSAY LINK

You can develop illustration essays with a series of examples or extended examples.

The Illustration Paragraph

There are two ways to write an illustration paragraph.

- **Use a series of examples** to illustrate your main point. For example, if you are writing a paragraph about an innovative teacher that you had, you might list things that the teacher did such as wear a costume, let students teach parts of the course, and use music to make a point.

- **Use an extended example** to illustrate your main point. The example can be an anecdote or a description of an event. For example, if you are writing about a stressful vacation, you might describe what happened when you lost your wallet.

PRACTICE I

Read the next paragraph and answer the questions.

> Across the country, lawmakers are coming up with inventive ways to punish criminals. Some judges in New Orleans, for example, treat offenders like unruly children. In 2003, one of the judges ordered a shoplifter in Baton Rouge to stand in front of a Dillard's store holding a sign that says "I will not shoplift anymore," and another judge ordered an offender to write "I will not steal other people's property" 2,500 times. In Florida, a hardworking judge orders drunk drivers to put bumper stickers on their cars that read, "How's my driving? The judge wants to know." The stickers feature a toll-free number. A Kentucky judge sometimes instructs **deadbeat dads** to choose between jail or a **vasectomy.** The best creative sentencing is done by a judge from Santa Fe, New Mexico. Judge Frances Gallegos, arguing that traditional anger management courses are ineffective, sentences violent offenders to tai chi, meditation, and Japanese flower-arranging classes.
>
> —Rebecca Bloom, student

deadbeat dad:
a father who avoids paying for his child's upkeep

vasectomy:
medical procedure to sterilize a male

1. Underline the topic sentence of this paragraph. (The topic sentence expresses the main idea of the paragraph.)

2. What type of illustration paragraph is this? Circle the best answer.
   a. Series of examples   b. Extended example

3. List the examples that the writer gives to illustrate her point.

   _____

   _____

   _____

   _____

PRACTICE 2

Read the next paragraph and answer the questions.

> If there is a single trait that most distinguishes entrepreneurs, it is this: they have an uncanny ability to anticipate and supply what large numbers of people want. For example, here's how Akio Morita, the legendary founder of Sony, got his idea for the Sony Walkman. He would go to the beach with his children, and the kids and their friends would listen to high-volume ghetto blasters from morning to evening. Morita asked himself, "Why should I have to listen to this **ghastly** music?" And he wondered, "Why should they have to carry those **cumbersome** machines?" Morita told his engineers to figure out a way to build a small radio and cassette player that would sound like a high-quality car stereo and yet could be attached to a person's head. They obliged, and the Sony Walkman stormed the market.
>
> —Dinesh D'Souza, "Billionaires," *Business 2.0*

ghastly:
terrible

cumbersome:
large and heavy

1. Underline the topic sentence.

2. What does the writer use to present his supporting details? Circle the best answer.
   a. a series of examples   b. an extended example

3. What example(s) does the writer give to illustrate his point? _____

_____

4. What are the main events in the narrative? List them.

_____

_____

_____

_____

_____

_____

Explore Topics

In the Warm Up, you will try an exploring strategy to generate ideas about different topics.

The Writer's Desk Warm Up

Think about the following questions and write the first ideas that come to your mind. Try to think of two to three ideas for each topic.

EXAMPLE:
What are some effective ways to market a product?

use colorful packaging

create a funny advertisement

give free samples

1. What are some habits or behaviors that really annoy you?

_____

_____

2. What are some traits of an effective leader?

_____

_____

_____

3. What are some qualities that you look for in a mate?

_____

_____

_____

DEVELOPING

The Topic Sentence

The topic sentence of the illustration paragraph is a general statement that expresses both your topic and your controlling idea. To determine your controlling idea, think about what point you want to make.

topic   controlling idea
Part-time jobs teach students valuable skills.

controlling idea   topic
Our father became anxious **when my sister started dating.**

> **ESSAY LINK**
>
> In an illustration essay, the thesis statement expresses the controlling idea.

The Writer's Desk   Write Topic Sentences

Write a topic sentence for each of the following topics. You can look for ideas in the previous Writer's Desk. Remember to narrow your topic. Each topic sentence should contain a general statement that expresses both your topic and your controlling idea.

EXAMPLE:

Topic: Effective marketing strategies

Topic sentence: *Advertisers have many clever ways to interest consumers.*

_____

1. Topic: Things that are annoying

   Topic sentence: _____

   _____

2. Topic: Traits of an effective leader

   Topic sentence: _____

   _____

3. Topic: Qualities in a mate

   Topic sentence: _____

   _____

The Supporting Ideas

After you have developed an effective topic sentence, generate supporting ideas. In an illustration paragraph, you can give a series of examples or an extended example.

When you use a series of examples, you can arrange your examples in emphatic order. Emphatic order means that you can place your examples from the most to the least important or from the least to the most important. If you use an extended example, you can arrange your ideas using time order.

The Writer's Desk Generate Supporting Ideas

Generate some supporting examples under each topic. Make sure your examples support the topic sentences that you wrote for the previous Writer's Desk.

EXAMPLE:
Effective marketing strategies

-use a catchy, memorable jingle

-offer free samples

-have a contest or sweepstakes

-do product placement in TV shows

1. Things that annoy you

2. Traits of an effective leader

3. Qualities you look for in a mate

ESSAY LINK

In an illustration essay, place the thesis statement in the introduction. Then, structure the essay so that each supporting idea becomes a distinct paragraph with its own topic sentence.

The Paragraph Plan

A paragraph plan helps you organize your topic sentence and supporting details before writing a first draft. When you write a paragraph plan, ensure that your examples are valid and relate to the topic sentence. Also include details that will help clarify your supporting examples. Organize your ideas in a logical order.

TOPIC SENTENCE: Advertisers have many clever ways to interest consumers.

Support 1: Relate the product to an interesting character.

Details: —The Pillsbury Dough Boy is cute.

—Ronald McDonald appeals to children.

Support 2: Give free samples to consumers.

Details: —Shampoo samples and granola bars come with junk mail.

—Perfume samples are passed out on street corners.

Support 3: Put the product in popular movie or television programs.

Details: —*American Idol* judges drink particular brands.

—Car companies have their products in reality shows.

Support 4:   Offer rebates to consumers.

   Details: —Products have special discounts.

—Consumers must mail in a form to get the rebate.

The Writer's Desk **Write a Paragraph Plan**

Choose one of the topic sentences that you wrote for the previous Writer's Desk. Write a paragraph plan using some of the supporting ideas that you have generated. Include details for each supporting idea.

Topic sentence: _____

_____

Support 1: _____

   Details: _____

_____

Support 2: _____

   Details: _____

_____

Support 3: _____

   Details: _____

_____

Support 4: _____

   Details: _____

_____

The First Draft

After you outline your ideas in a plan, you are ready to write the first draft. Remember to write complete sentences. You might include transitional words or expressions to help your ideas flow smoothly.

Transitional Words and Expressions

Transitional expressions can help you introduce an example or show an additional example. The next transitional words are useful in illustration paragraphs.

To Introduce an Example		To Show an Additional Example	
for example	namely	also	in addition
for instance	specifically	first (second, etc.)	in another case
in other words	to illustrate	furthermore	moreover

 **Writing Complete Sentences**

A fragment is an incomplete sentence. When you give an example, ensure that your sentence is complete. Avoid fragment errors.

Fragment: For example, too many parties.

Correction: For example, some students go to too many parties.

See Chapter 20 for more information about fragments.

The Writer's Desk Write the First Draft

In the previous Writer's Desk, you developed a paragraph plan. Now write the first draft of your illustration paragraph. Before you write, carefully review your paragraph plan and make any necessary changes.

REVISING AND EDITING

Revise and Edit an Illustration Paragraph

When you finish writing an illustration paragraph, review your work and revise it to make the example(s) as clear as possible to your readers. Check to make sure that the order of ideas is logical, and remove any irrelevant details. Before you work on your own paragraph, practice revising and editing a student paragraph.

PRACTICE 3

Read the next student paragraph and answer the questions.

> Advertisers have many clever ways to get the consumer's attention. First, to make the product memorable, they can link it with an interesting character. When people see the character, they instantly remember the product. For example, any child will recognize Ronald McDonald, the Energizer Bunny, or the Green Giant. Also, the Pillsbury Dough Boy. Furthermore, free samples help consumers become familiar with the item. Sometimes, when people are walking downtown, somebody gives you a snack or a perfume sample. Who can resist getting something for nothing? Another smart advertising method is to place products in popular television shows and movies. On *American Idol*, for instance, the judges promote certain soft drinks. In reality shows such as *Survivor*, the contestants win particular car models, and millions of people hear about the car's features. The best marketing strategy is somewhat devious, though. Many companies, especially in the high-tech field, offer mail-in rebates. Consumers are lured by the possibility of a large discount. For instance, I bought anti-virus software for my computer because there was a $40 rebate, but the method of getting the

rebate was time-consuming. I had to photocopy my receipt, fill out a form, and mail it. Apparently, large numbers of consumers simply forget to mail the rebate form in, so they never actually receive the discount. Every year, advertisers come up with better and more innovative marketing ideas.

Revising

1. Underline the topic sentence.

2. List the main supporting points.

   _____

   _____

   _____

   _____

3. What order does the author use?
   a. time order
   b. space order
   c. emphatic order

Editing

4. Underline a pronoun error. Write your correction in the space below.

   Correction: _____

5. This paragraph contains a fragment, which is an incomplete sentence. Underline the fragment. Then correct it in the space below.

   Correction: _____

> **GRAMMAR LINK**
>
> See the following chapters for more information about these grammar topics:
> Pronouns, Chapter 28
> Fragments, Chapter 20

---

vo•cab•u•lar•y BOOST

Avoid Repetition
Read through the first draft of your paragraph and identify some words that you frequently repeat. Replace those words with synonyms.

The Writer's Desk Revise and Edit Your Paragraph

Revise and edit the paragraph that you wrote for the previous Writer's Desk. Ensure that your paragraph has unity, adequate support, and coherence. Also, correct any errors in grammar, spelling, punctuation, and mechanics.

REFLECT ON IT

Think about what you have learned in this chapter. If you do not know an answer, review that topic.

1. In an illustration paragraph, you _____

2. There are two ways to write illustration paragraphs. Explain each of them.

    a. Using a series of examples: _____

    b. Using an extended example: _____

3. List three transitional expressions that indicate an additional idea.

    _____

 The Writer's Room   **Topics for Illustration Paragraphs**

Writing Activity I

Choose any of the following topics, or choose your own topic. Then write an illustration paragraph.

General Topics

1. ridiculous fads or fashions
2. good or bad habits
3. great things in life that are free
4. activities that relieve stress
5. possible future inventions
6. impolite behavior

College and Work-Related Topics

7. reasons to finish college
8. qualities that can help you succeed
9. claustrophobic work environments
10. qualities of a good instructor
11. tools or equipment needed for your job
12. reasons to take time off before starting college

WRITING LINK

More Illustration Writing Topics

Chapter 21, Writer's Room topic 1 (page 339)

Chapter 24, Writer's Room topic 1 (page 376)

Chapter 28, Writer's Room topic 1 (page 434)

READING LINK

More Illustration Readings

"The Old-Time Pueblo World" by Leslie Marmon Silko (page 546)

"The Case for Affirmative Action" by Dave Malcolm (page 579)

"When the Legal Thing Isn't the Right Thing" by Deborah Mead (page 594)

Writing Activity 2

The image depicts a man who feels like he is walking on a tightrope, and the image expresses anxiety. What things make you feel worried? Write an illustration paragraph about things that make you feel worried or stressed.

✔ ILLUSTRATION PARAGRAPH CHECKLIST

After you write your illustration paragraph, review the checklist on the inside front cover. Also ask yourself the following questions.

- Does my topic sentence make a point that can be supported with examples?

- Does my paragraph contain sufficient examples that clearly support the topic sentence?

- Do I use transitions to smoothly connect my examples?

- Have I arranged my examples in a logical order?

How Do I Get a Better Grade?

Visit www.mywritinglab.com for audio-visual lectures and additional practice sets about illustration writing. **Get a better grade with MyWritingLab!**

5 Narration

 It's all storytelling, you know. That's what journalism is all about.

—TOM BROKAW
American broadcast journalist (b. 1940)

CONTENTS

When investigating a crime scene, a detective must try to find answers to the questions who, what, when, where, why, and how. You answer the same questions when you write a narrative paragraph.

Writers' Exchange

Work with a team of at least three students, and choose a popular fairy tale. Then you will retell the fairy tale, but you will update it and make it more contemporary. First, one of you begins and says one sentence. Then, switching speakers, each person adds one sentence to the tale.

EXAMPLE: Yesterday, a young woman living in Queens decided to visit her grandmother.

EXPLORING

What Is Narration?

When you **narrate,** you tell a story about what happened. You generally explain events in the order in which they occurred, and you include information about when they happened and who was involved in the incidents.

You use narration every day. You may write about the week's events in your personal journal, or you might send a postcard to a friend detailing what you did during your vacation. At college, you may explain what happened during a historical event or what happened in a novel that you have read. At work, you might use narration to explain an incident involving a customer or co-worker.

Narration is not only useful on its own; it also enhances other types of writing. For example, Jason must write an argument essay about youth crime. His essay will be more compelling if he includes a personal anecdote about the time a gang of youths attacked him in a subway station. In other words, narration can provide supporting evidence for other paragraph or essay patterns.

Narration at Work
Joseph Roth, a boiler and pressure vessel inspector, used narrative writing in a memo he wrote to his supervisor.

As you know, I recently inspected the boiler and pressure vessels in the refinery on Highway 11. I had a few problems that I would like to mention. When I first arrived, the manager of the unit was uncooperative and initially tried to stop me from examining the boiler! After much discussion, I was finally permitted into the boiler room where I noticed several defects in the operation and condition of the equipment. Immediately, I saw that the low-water fuel cut-off chamber was filled with sludge and could not possibly function properly. Then I realized that the boiler heating surfaces were covered with scale. Finally, I found stress cracks in the tube ends and in tube seats. This is a sure sign of caustic imbrittlement, making the boiler unsafe to operate and in danger of exploding. I have asked that the boiler be taken out of service immediately. We must follow up to make sure that measures are being taken to replace the boiler.

The Narrative Paragraph

There are two main types of narrative paragraphs.

1. **Use first-person narration (autobiography).**

    In first-person narration, you describe a personal experience from your point of view. You are directly involved in the story. You use the words *I* (first-person singular) or *we* (first-person plural). For example: "When I was a child, I thought

ESSAY LINK

In a narrative essay, you can use first- or third-person narration.

that the world began and ended with me. I didn't know, or care, how other children felt. Thus, when schoolmates ridiculed a shy boy, I gleefully joined in."

2. **Use third-person narration.**

   In third-person narration, you do not refer to your own experiences. Instead, you describe what happened to somebody else. The story is told in the third person using *he, she, it,* or *they*. You might tell a story about your mother's childhood, or you might explain what happened during the last election. In this type of narration, you are simply an observer or storyteller; you are not a participant in the action. For example: "The students gathered to protest against the war. One student threw a chair through the window of the student center. Suddenly, people started pushing and shoving."

 **Choose an Interesting Topic**

When you write a narrative paragraph, try to choose a topic that will interest the reader. For example, the reader might not be interested if you write about the act of eating your lunch. However, if you write about a time when your best friend argued with a waiter during a meal, you could create an entertaining narrative paragraph.

   Think about a topic that you personally find very interesting, and then share it with your readers. Try to bring your experiences to life so that your readers can share it with you.

Explore Topics

In the Warm Up, you will try an exploring strategy to generate ideas about different topics.

The Writer's Desk **Warm Up**

Think about the following questions, and write down the first ideas that come to your mind. Try to think of two or three ideas for each topic.

EXAMPLE: What interesting stories have family members told you about their lives?

My dad's story about his arrival in this country—funny story about his first job. Uncle Pancho likes to talk about when he bought some land. The day my sister won a piano competition (she's annoying). What else? When my mom met my dad.

1. What are some serious decisions that you have made? Think about decisions related to school, personal relationships, work, and so on.

   _____

   _____

   _____

2. What are some memorable parties or celebrations that you have attended?

_____

_____

_____

3. Think about interesting true events that have happened to family members or friends. Are some stories particularly funny, sad, or inspiring? List some ideas.

_____

_____

_____

PRACTICE 1

The author of the next paragraph was born in 1876 and was raised on the Pine Ridge Reservation in South Dakota. In 1888, at the age of twelve, she was sent to a Quaker missionary school. Read the paragraph and answer the questions.

> There were eight in our party of bronzed children who were going East with the missionaries. We had anticipated much pleasure from a ride on the train, but the **throngs** of staring palefaces disturbed and troubled us. Fair women, with tottering babies on each arm, stopped their haste and **scrutinized** the children of absent mothers. Large men, with heavy bundles in their hands, halted nearby and **riveted** their glassy blue eyes upon us. I sank deep into the corner of my seat, for I resented being watched. Directly in front of me, children who were no larger than I hung themselves upon the backs of their seats with their bold white faces toward me. Sometimes they took their forefingers out of their mouths and pointed at my moccasined feet. Their mothers, instead of **reproving** such rude curiosity, looked closely at me and attracted their children's further notice to my blanket. This embarrassed me and kept me constantly on the verge of tears.
>
> —Adapted from Sitkala Sa, *Impressions of an Indian Childhood*

throngs:
crowds or groups

scrutinized:
examined in detail

riveted:
concentrated; focused intently

reproving:
criticizing severely

1. Underline the topic sentence of this paragraph. (Remember, the topic sentence is not always the first sentence.)

2. What type of narration is this? Circle the best answer.
   a. First person   b. Third person

3. Who or what is the paragraph about? _____

_____

4. In a few words, explain what happened in this paragraph. _____

_____

5. When did it happen? _____

6. Where did it happen? _____

7. By combining your answers to questions 3 through 6, write a one-sentence summary of the paragraph. Someone who has never read the paragraph should have a clear idea of the paragraph's content after reading your sentence.

_____

_____

_____

PRACTICE 2

Read the next paragraph and answer the questions.

> During the 1960s, there were profound social upheavals. The period began with optimism and excitement, as the young and charismatic John F. Kennedy was elected president of the United States. Idealistic civil rights workers, both black and white, sought to increase registration of black voters in the South and end housing discrimination in the North. The Reverend Dr. Martin Luther King attracted nationwide attention as he fought with **unprecedented** success (and immense dignity) to end segregation and racism in America without the use of violence. Soon, however, the idealism and optimism were shattered. President Kennedy was assassinated in 1963. The passage of the Civil Rights Act in 1965 was regarded by many new militant black groups as "too little, too late." Riots broke out in many cities in the summers of 1965–68. In 1968, both Martin Luther King and Robert Kennedy, the president's brother, were gunned down. But the most divisive force in American society in the 1960s was the Vietnam War.
>
> —Jeremy Yudkin, *Understanding Music*

unprecedented:
something that never happened before; without precedent

1. Who or what is the paragraph about? _____

2. Underline the topic sentence of this paragraph.

3. What type of narration is this? Circle the best answer.
   a. First person   b. Third person

4. How does the writer support the topic sentence? List the smaller events that make up this narrative.

_____

_____

_____

_____

_____

_____

_____

5. Do the supporting facts provide adequate support for the topic sentence?

_____

DEVELOPING

The Topic Sentence

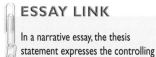

ESSAY LINK

In a narrative essay, the thesis statement expresses the controlling idea.

When you write a narrative paragraph, it is important to express a main point. If you simply describe a list of activities, it is boring for the reader. To make your paragraph interesting, make sure that your topic sentence has a controlling idea.

topic   controlling idea

When somebody broke into my house, <u>I felt totally invaded.</u>

controlling idea   topic

<u>Jay learned to be responsible</u> **during his first job.**

Make a Point

In a narrative paragraph, the topic sentence should make a point. To help you find the controlling idea, you can ask yourself the following questions.

- What did I learn?
- How did I change?
- How did it make me feel?
- What is important about it?

EXAMPLE:

Topic:	Moving out of the family home
Possible controlling idea:	Becoming more independent

topic   controlling idea

When I moved out of the family home, <u>I became more independent.</u>

PRACTICE 3

Practice writing topic sentences. Complete the following sentences by adding a controlling idea.

1. When I moved out of the family home, I felt _____

   _____

2. In my first job, I learned _____

   _____

3. When I heard the news about _____, I realized _____

   _____

The Writer's Desk **Write Topic Sentences**

Write a topic sentence for each of the following topics. You can look for ideas in the Writer's Desk Warm Up on pages 72–73. Each topic sentence should mention the topic and express a controlling idea.

EXAMPLE:

Topic: A family story

Topic sentence: *When my father found his first job in America, there was a humorous misunderstanding.*

1. Topic: A serious decision

   Topic sentence: _____

   _____

2. Topic: A celebration or party

   Topic sentence: _____

   _____

3. Topic: A story about someone

   Topic sentence: _____

   _____

The Supporting Ideas

A narrative paragraph should contain specific details so that the reader understands what happened. To come up with the details, ask yourself a series of questions. Your paragraph should provide answers to these questions.

- Who is the paragraph about?
- What happened?
- When did it happen?
- Where did it happen?
- Why did it happen?
- How did it happen?

When you recount a story to a friend, you may go back and add details, saying, "I forgot to mention something." When you write a narrative paragraph, however, your sequence of events should be clearly chronological so that your reader can follow your story.

The Writer's Desk **Develop Supporting Ideas**

Generate supporting ideas for each topic. List what happened.

EXAMPLE: A family story

dad saw an ad _____

"busboy" job _____

bowling alley _____

dad didn't understand ad _____

man gave him a dishcloth _____

1. A serious decision

_____

_____

_____

_____

_____

2. A celebration or party

_____

_____

_____

_____

_____

3. A story about someone

_____

_____

_____

_____

_____

The Paragraph Plan

Before you write a narrative paragraph, it is a good idea to make a paragraph plan. Write down main events in the order in which they occurred. To make your narration more complete, include details about each event.

ESSAY LINK

In a narrative essay, you place the thesis statement in the introduction. Each main event is developed in a supporting paragraph.

TOPIC SENTENCE: When my father found his first job in America, there was a humorous misunderstanding.

Support 1: In a newspaper, he found an ad for a busboy.
    Details: —job was in a bowling alley
    —dad didn't speak English

Support 2: He went to the bowling alley.
    Details: —applied for the job, and got it
    —was excited

Support 3: On his first day, his boss asked him to put on an apron and told him to pick up some dishes in the bowling alley's restaurant.
    Details: —father was disappointed and asked, "Where's the bus?"
    —thought that a "busboy" would work on a bus

The Writer's Desk **Write a Paragraph Plan**

Choose one of the topic sentences that you wrote for the previous Writer's Desk. Write a paragraph plan using some of the supporting ideas that you have generated. Include details for each supporting idea.

Topic sentence: _____

_____

Support 1: _____

   Details: _____

_____

_____

Support 2: _____

   Details: _____

_____

_____

Support 3: _____

   Details: _____

_____

_____

The First Draft

After you outline your ideas in a plan, you are ready to write the first draft. Remember to write complete sentences. You might include transitional words or expressions to help your ideas flow smoothly.

Transitional Words and Expressions

Transitions can help you show a sequence of events. The following transitional words are useful in narrative paragraphs.

To Show a Sequence of Events			
afterward	finally	in the end	meanwhile
after that	first	last	next
eventually	in the beginning	later	then

 **Using Quotations**

When you insert a direct quotation into your writing, capitalize the first word of the quotation, and put the final punctuation inside the closing quotation marks.

- Place a comma after an introductory phrase.

   Vladimir screamed, "The kitchen's on fire."

- Place a colon after an introductory sentence.

   Vladimir watched me coldly: "We have nothing to discuss."

See Chapter 34 for more information about using quotations.

The Writer's Desk **Write the First Draft**

In the previous Writer's Desk, you developed a paragraph plan. Now write the first draft of your narrative paragraph. Before you write, carefully review your paragraph plan and make any necessary changes.

REVISING AND EDITING

Revise and Edit a Narrative Paragraph

When you finish writing a narrative paragraph, carefully review your work and revise it to make the events as clear as possible to your readers. Check that you have organized events chronologically, and remove any irrelevant details. Before you revise and edit your own paragraph, practice revising and editing a student paragraph.

PRACTICE 4

Read the next student paragraph and answer the questions.

When my father found his first job in America, there was a humorous misunderstanding. My father, originally from Mexico City, had just moved to Dallas, Texas, and he did not speak English. One day, he sees an ad for a busboy job. He wanted the job, so he called the number in the ad. Later that day, he went for an interview in a bowling alley. The restaurant manager spoke with my father and offered him the job. That night, my father went home feeling very excited. The next day, when he arrived for work, the manager gave him an apron and asked him to pick up some dishes in the bowling alley restaurant. My father, feeling confused and dissapointed, asked, "Where is the bus?" He thought that a busboy would work on a bus collecting tickets. The owner laught and explained what a busboy's job is. When my father told the family this story, everybody thought it was funny, but they were also proud of his perseverance because today he has a university degree and a good job.

Revising

1. Write down the two parts of the topic sentence.

               topic   +   controlling idea

      _____

2. What type of order do the specific details follow? Circle the best answer.
   a. Space
   b. Time
   c. Emphatic
   d. No order

3. What are some transitional expressions that the author used?

      _____

4. What type of narration is this?
   a. First person
   b. Third person

Editing

GRAMMAR LINK

See the following chapters for more information about these grammar topics:
   Tense consistency, Chapter 31
   Spelling, Chapter 32

5. This paragraph contains a tense inconsistency. The tense shifts for no apparent reason. Identify the incorrect sentence. Then write the correct sentence in the space below.

    Correction: _____

    _____

6. This paragraph contains two misspelled words. Identify and correct them.

Misspelled words	Corrections
_____	_____
_____	_____

---

vo•cab•u•lar•y BOOST

Using Varied Language

1. Underline the opening word of every sentence in your first draft. Check to see if some are repeated.
2. Replace repeated opening words with adverbs, such as *usually, generally,* or *fortunately,* or a prepositional phrase such as *On the side* or *Under the circumstances.* You can also begin the sentences with a modifier such as *Leaving the door open.* In other words, avoid beginning too many sentences with a noun or transitional word.

Repeated First Words

   We opened the door of the abandoned house. We looked nervously at the rotting floorboards. We thought the floor might collapse. We decided to enter. We walked carefully across the kitchen floor to the bedroom, one by one.

Variety

   My cousins and I opened the door of the abandoned house. Nervously, we looked at the rotting floorboards. Thinking the floor might collapse, we decided to enter. One by one, we walked across the kitchen floor to the bedroom.

The Writer's Desk Revise and Edit Your Paragraph

Revise and edit the paragraph that you wrote for the previous Writer's Desk. Ensure that your paragraph has unity, adequate support, and coherence. Also correct any errors in grammar, spelling, punctuation, and mechanics.

REFLECT ON IT

Think about what you have learned in this chapter. If you do not know an answer, review that topic.

1. In narrative writing, you _____

2. What are the differences between the two following types of narration?

    First person: _____

    _____

    Third person: _____

    _____

3. What are some questions that you should you ask yourself when you write a narrative paragraph?

    _____

4. What organizational method is commonly used in narrative paragraphs? Circle the best answer.

    a. space order   b. time order   c. emphatic order

The Writer's Room

Topics for Narrative Paragraphs

Writing Activity 1

Choose any of the following topics, or choose your own topic. Then write a narrative paragraph.

General Topics

1. an interesting decade
2. a risky adventure
3. a move to a new place
4. an unforgettable holiday
5. a disturbing news event
6. an unexpected gift

College and Work-Related Topics

7. an embarrassing incident at college or work
8. an inspiring teacher or instructor
9. a positive or negative job interview
10. a difficult co-worker
11. your best experience at work
12. a proud moment at work or college

WRITING LINK

More Narrative Writing Topics
Chapter 28, Writer's Room topic 2 (page 434)
Chapter 30, Writer's Room topics 1 and 2 (page 461)

READING LINK

More Narrative Readings
"Why I Worked with La Migra" by Veronica Ortega (page 591)
"A Faith in Others Versus Security" by Barbara Card Atkinson (page 596)

Writing Activity 2

Have you ever lived through an earthquake, a tornado, a flood, a large storm, an extended power outage, or any other event caused by nature? What happened? What did you do? Write a narrative paragraph about a big storm or a natural event that you have lived through.

✔ NARRATIVE PARAGRAPH CHECKLIST

As you write your narrative paragraph, review the checklist on the inside front cover. Also ask yourself the following questions.

- ☐ Does my topic sentence clearly express the topic of the narration?

- ☐ Does my topic sentence contain a controlling idea that is meaningful and interesting?

- ☐ Does my paragraph answer most of the following questions: *who, what, when, where, why, how?*

- ☐ Do I use transitional expressions that help clarify the order of events?

- ☐ Do I include details to make my narration more interesting?

How Do I Get a Better Grade?

Visit www.mywritinglab.com for audio-visual lectures and additional practice sets about narration writing.
Get a better grade with MyWritingLab!

Description

"The beginning of human knowledge is through the senses, and the writer begins where human perception begins."

—FLANNERY O'CONNOR
American author (1925–1964)

CONTENTS

Pablo Picasso, "Mandolin and Guitar" 1924, oil and sand on canvas, The Solomon R. Guggenheim Museum, NYC/The Granger Collection.

The artist uses a variety of colors and brushstrokes to make an impression on the viewer. In descriptive writing, you use words to create a visual image.

Writers' Exchange

Work with two or three students. First, think about a famous person. Then describe that person, but do not name him or her. Speak nonstop about that person for about twenty seconds. Your teammates must guess the person that you are describing. Then switch speakers.

What Is Description?

Description creates vivid images in the reader's mind by portraying people, places, or moments in detail.

You use description every day. At home, you might describe a new friend to your family, or you might describe an object that you bought. At college, you might describe the structure of a cell or the results of a lab experiment. At work, you may describe a new product to a client, or you could describe the qualities of potential clients to your boss.

Description at Work

In this excerpt from an Alba Tours travel brochure, the writer describes the amenities offered at a vacation resort.

With its lavish open-air lobby complete with curving staircase, the gleaming marble columns, and the rich mahogany furniture, Sandals Dunn's River captures the romance of an Italian-style Mediterranean paradise. The centerpiece of this spectacular resort is one of Jamaica's largest swimming pools with its own cascading waterfall and swim-up bar. You can try out the facilities at the open-air fitness center, play some tennis, or shoot a round of golf at the Sandals Golf and Country Club where greens fees and transfers are included. After that, why not take a complimentary tour of the world-famous Dunn's River Falls or just relax in the Oriental hot and cold plunge pools followed by a soothing sauna?

ESSAY LINK

In descriptive essays, you should also create a dominant impression, express your attitude toward the subject, and include concrete details.

The Descriptive Paragraph

When you write a descriptive paragraph, focus on three main points.

1. **Create a dominant impression.**
   The dominant impression is the overall atmosphere that you wish to convey. It can be a strong feeling, mood, or image. For example, if you are describing a business meeting, you can emphasize the tension in the room.

2. **Express your attitude toward the subject.**
   Do you feel positive, negative, or neutral toward the subject? For example, if you feel positive about your best friend, then the details of your paragraph should convey the good feelings you have toward him or her. If you describe a place that you do not like, then your details should express how uncomfortable

that place makes you feel. You might make a neutral description of a science lab experiment.

3. **Include concrete details.**

Details will enable a reader to visualize the person, place, or situation that is being described. You can use active verbs and adjectives so that the reader imagines the scene more clearly. You can also use **imagery,** which is description using the five senses. Review the following examples of imagery.

Sight	At five-foot-nine, and a hundred and seventy-four pounds, I was muscularly inferior to the guys on the same athletic level and quite conscious of the fact.
	—H. D., "Dying to Be Bigger"
Sound	They hooked wrist-thick hanks of laghmien noodles and shoveled them into their mouths, slurping, sucking, inhaling, and chomping off portions. . . .
	—Jeffrey Tayler, "A Cacophony of Noodles"
Smell	For several days the wind blew, full of dust scents and the dryness of sagebrush, carrying eastward our own autumn smell of falling maple leaves, green walnuts, and the warm lemon odor of quince and yellow apples.
	—Josephine Johnson, "September Harvest"
Touch	My heart started racing, perspiration dripped down my face causing my glasses to slide, and I had a hard time breathing.
	—Bebe Moore Campbell, "Dancing with Fear"
Taste	I asked for fresh lemonade, and got it—delicious, and cold, and tangy with real fruit.
	—Mary Stewart, *My Brother Michael*

PRACTICE I

Read the next paragraph and answer the questions.

Whenever my wife and I travel by air, I try to get a window seat so that I can help the pilots fly the planes and also keep a close watch on our progress to make sure we don't get lost. It always surprises and disappoints me to find that they don't really need my help. The very thought that I am soaring far above the lives of ordinary people keeps me watching out the tiny window in case, some lucky day, I might get a glimpse, or at least a feeling, of real flight. One winter, on our flight home from a trip to Mexico, feeling a bit let down and vaguely sad, I sat in a window seat on the left side as we flew over the Florida Keys. It was nearing sunset when, flying up the Mississippi Valley at forty thousand feet, the plane's captain turned on the seat belt sign and announced that we were approaching a storm front. That got my attention! I at once went back to looking out the window at scattered clouds below and a big thunderhead far in the distance, black against the setting sun. A few moments later, the plane seemed to stand on its right wing, and suddenly I was looking up ten thousand feet at a brilliant, silvery cloud top, silhouetted against the blue-black sky. All too soon, the plane levelled out, and I was looking into the middle of a dark cloud, lighted occasionally by the reflection of a flash of lightning within it. Again the plane banked, this time to the left, and I gazed in awe straight down to where, in the middle of the deep, purple shadows of the cloud bottoms, was one tiny sunlit scrap of the earth. Some ten minutes later, after several more turns with vistas that made me gasp in wonder, we passed from glorious beauty into boring level flight over featureless clouds far below. Becoming aware of my surroundings, I found myself gripping my wife's hand while she leaned on my shoulder, and I realized that she too had been gazing out at the glorious views.

—Gene Swain, "Flight"

1. What is the attitude of the writer toward the subject of the paragraph? Circle the best answer.

   a. positive   b. negative   c. neutral

2. Write at least two examples to support your answer to question 1.

   _____

   _____

   _____

   _____

3. What is the dominant impression the author creates about his experience of flying through a thunderstorm?

   a. boredom   b. fear   c. wonder   d. surprise   e. sorrow

4. Write at least two examples from the text that show the dominant impression.

   _____

   _____

5. What senses does the writer use to describe the scene?

   a. touch   b. sight   c. smell   d. sound   e. taste

6. Give examples of imagery to support your answer to question 5.

   _____

   _____

Explore Topics

In the Warm Up, you will try an exploring strategy to generate ideas about different topics.

The Writer's Desk **Warm Up**

Think about the following questions, and write down the first ideas that come to your mind. Try to think of two or three ideas for each topic.

EXAMPLE: What are some useless products or other items that you own?

The plastic apple cutter (makes six perfect pieces). Never use it. Useless toy called a Furby. As a kid, I used it a couple of times. The juicer. It sits and collects dust.

1. What were some very emotional moments in your life? (Think about two or three moments when you felt extreme joy, sadness, excitement, anxiety, or other strong emotions.)

   _____

   _____

   _____

2. Describe your food quirks. What are your unusual tastes or eating habits? Which foods do you really love or hate?

   _____

   _____

   _____

3. What are some very busy places?

   _____

   _____

   _____

DEVELOPING

When you write a descriptive paragraph, choose a subject that lends itself to description. In other words, find a subject to describe that appeals to the senses. For example, you can describe the sounds, sights, and smells in a bakery.

ESSAY LINK

In a descriptive essay, the thesis statement expresses the controlling idea.

The Topic Sentence

In the topic sentence of a descriptive paragraph, you should convey a dominant impression about the subject. The dominant impression is the overall impression or feeling that the topic inspires.

topic   controlling idea
The abandoned buildings in our neighborhood are an eyesore.

topic   controlling idea
Lady Patricia was a perfect example of beauty that is but skin deep.

—Nancy Mitford, *Love in a Cold Climate*

 **How to Create a Dominant Impression**

To create a dominant impression, ask yourself how or why the topic is important.

Poor: The parade was noisy.

(Why should readers care about this statement?)

         topic   controlling idea

Better: **The parade participants** loudly celebrated the arrival of the New Year.

The Writer's Desk Write Topic Sentences

Write a topic sentence for each of the following topics. You can look for ideas in the previous Writer's Desk. Remember to narrow each topic. Each topic sentence should state what you are describing and contain a controlling idea.

EXAMPLE:

 Topic: A useless product

 Topic sentence: *When I was nine years old, I was desperate to own a Furby.*

 _____

1. Topic: An emotional moment

 Topic sentence: _____

 _____

2. Topic: Food quirks (unusual food habits or foods you love or hate)

 Topic sentence: _____

 _____

3. Topic: A busy place

 Topic sentence: _____

 _____

The Supporting Ideas

After you have developed an effective topic sentence, generate supporting details. The details can be placed in space, time, or emphatic order.

Show, Don't Tell

Your audience will find it more interesting to read your written work if you *show* a quality of a place or an action of a person rather than just state it. For example, if you want to describe a person whom you remember, write about the person's memorable actions.

Example of Telling: I remember my fifth-grade teacher fondly because she was very nice.

Example of Showing: My fifth grade teacher, at the time she taught me, was already beloved of two generations. What I chiefly remember is how she brought her own life's interests into our classroom. Back in the days when "opening exercises" included five or ten minutes of hymn singing, this teacher—a barbershop singer—graced those minutes by teaching us the hymns in four-part harmony. She had founded her own chapter of barbershoppers, quitting her original group in protest when it barred a black singer from joining. This story, too, she shared with us.

—Robyn Sarah, excerpt taken from "Notes that Resonate a Lifetime"

PRACTICE 2

Choose one of the following sentences, and write a short description that shows—not tells—the quality of the person, place, thing, or event.

1. The food smelled delicious.

2. It was a hot day.

3. The child's room was messy.

List Sensory Details

To create a dominant impression, think about your topic, and make a list of your feelings and impressions. These details can include imagery (images that appeal to sight, sound, hearing, taste, and smell).

ESSAY LINK

When you plan a descriptive essay, it is useful to list sensory details.

TOPIC: An abandoned building

Details: —damp floors
—boarded-up windows
—broken glass
—graffiti on the walls
—musty
—gray bricks
—chipping paint

---

vo•cab•u•lar•y BOOST

Using Vivid Language

When you write a descriptive paragraph, try to use **vivid language**. Use specific action verbs and adjectives to create a clear picture of what you are describing.

vulgar.
The lawyer was ~~not nice.~~

(Use a more vivid, specific adjective.)

barked
The boss ~~shouted~~ at the employee.

(Use a more vivid, specific verb or image.)

Think about other words or expressions that more effectively describe these words:

Hungry: _____

Not friendly: _____

Cry: _____

Speak: _____

The Writer's Desk   List Sensory Details

Think about images, impressions, and feelings that the following topics inspire in you. Refer to your topic sentences on page 88, and make a list under each topic.

EXAMPLE: A useless product:

Furby looks like a strange bird

black and white fur

round owl-like eyes

pointy beak that opens

a hard plastic body under the fur

speaks in a low, gurgling voice

not cuddly

1. An emotional moment: _____

   _____

   _____

   _____

   _____

   _____

2. Food quirks: _____

   _____

   _____

   _____

   _____

   _____

   _____

3. A busy place: _____

   _____

   _____

   _____

   _____

   _____

   _____

The Paragraph Plan

A descriptive paragraph should contain specific details so that the reader can clearly imagine what is being described. When you make a paragraph plan, remember to include concrete details. Also think about the organizational method that you will use.

TOPIC SENTENCE:	When I was nine years old, I was desperate to own a Furby.
Support 1:	The toy looks like a small owl.
Details:	—large round eyes —small yellow beak
Support 2:	It learns to speak and repeat words.
Details:	—has a low, gurgling voice —does not say many things
Support 3:	The hard plastic body is not cuddly.
Details:	—cannot bring it to bed —sits on a counter
Support 4:	The toy becomes boring quickly.
Details:	—after it says a few words, the novelty wears off —cannot really be played with because it is fragile

ESSAY LINK

In a descriptive essay, place the thesis statement in the introduction. Then, develop each supporting idea in a body paragraph.

The Writer's Desk Write a Paragraph Plan

Choose one of the topic sentences that you wrote for the Writer's Desk on page 88, and write a detailed paragraph plan. You can include some of the sensory details that you have generated in the previous Writer's Desk.

Topic sentence: _____

_____

Support 1: _____

Details: _____

_____

Support 2: _____

Details: _____

_____

Support 3: _____

Details: _____

_____

The First Draft

After you outline your ideas in a plan, you are ready to write the first draft. Remember to write complete sentences. You might include transitional words or expressions to help your ideas flow smoothly.

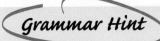 **Using Modifiers**

When you revise your descriptive essay, check that your modifiers are placed near the item that they are modifying.

Incorrect: The young man drank the coffee slowly wearing a blue suit.

Correct: The young man wearing a blue suit drank the coffee slowly.

See Chapter 30 for more information about misplaced modifiers.

Transitional Words and Expressions

You can use space order to describe a person, place, or thing. The following transitions are useful in descriptive paragraphs.

To Show Place or Position

above	beyond	in the distance	outside
behind	closer in	nearby	over there
below	farther out	on the left/right	under
beside	in front	on top	underneath

The Writer's Desk **Write the First Draft**

In the previous Writer's Desk, you developed a paragraph plan. Now write the first draft of your descriptive paragraph. Before you write, carefully review your paragraph plan and make any necessary changes.

REVISING AND EDITING

Revise and Edit a Descriptive Paragraph

When you finish writing a descriptive paragraph, carefully review your work and revise it to make the description as clear as possible to your readers. Check that you have organized your steps logically, and remove any irrelevant details.

PRACTICE 3

Read the following student paragraph and answer the questions.

When I was nine years old, I was desperate to own a Furby. In 1998, an onslaught of television commercials announced the product, and a Furby craze developed. I begged my mother for the furry little toy. Even though it was expensive and hard to find. I whined so much that my mother bought me one for my birthday. When I opened the package, I was initialy thrilled. It looked like a small owl, with large round eyes and a yellow pointy beak. Black and white fur covered its hard plastic body. Unfortunately, I could not cuddle it and bring it to bed because it was too fragile. The toy was suppose to speak, but the instructions were complicated. I became disappointed because it only repeated a few words in a low gurgling voice, and the toy quickly became boring. After two weeks, I dropped my Furby, and it stopped speaking, so I never played with it again. I have other toys that I stopped using soon after I bought them. Now the Furby is in a box somewhere in my closet, and I feel ridiculous for having wanted such a useless product.

Revising

1. Underline the topic sentence.

2. What is the dominant impression in this paragraph? Circle the best answer.
   a. anger   b. disappointment   c. joy   d. tension

3. Highlight three vivid verbs in the paragraph.

4. Revise the paragraph for unity. Cross out a sentence that does not belong.

Editing

5. A fragment lacks a subject or verb and is an incomplete sentence. Identify and correct one fragment in the paragraph.

6. This paragraph contains a misspelled word. Circle it and correct it.

7. This paragraph contains a past participle error. Circle and correct it.

> ## GRAMMAR LINK
>
> See the following chapters for more information about these topics:
> Fragments, Chapter 20
> Spelling, Chapter 32
> Past Participles, Chapter 23

The Writer's Desk Revise and Edit Your Paragraph

Revise and edit the paragraph that you wrote for the previous Writer's Desk. Ensure that your paragraph has unity, adequate support, and coherence. Also correct any errors in grammar, spelling, punctuation, and mechanics.

REFLECT ON IT

Think about what you have learned in this chapter. If you do not know an answer, review that topic.

1. What are the main features of a descriptive paragraph? _____

_____

_____

2. Define imagery. _____

3. Look at the familiar words below. Write down at least two more descriptive ways to say each word. Try to find words that are more specific.

a. cute _____   b. angry _____

c. sad _____   d. mean _____

The Writer's Room Topics for Descriptive Paragraphs

Writing Activity 1

Choose any of the following topics, or choose your own topic. Then write a descriptive paragraph.

General Topics

1. a coffee shop
2. an interesting house or building
3. a useless product or item
4. an evening out
5. a scene from nature
6. a silly fashion trend

College and Work-Related Topics

7. a quiet area on campus
8. an unusual student or co-worker
9. a loud place
10. an uncomfortable uniform
11. a place with a good or bad odor
12. an embarrassing moment at work

WRITING LINK

More Descriptive Writing Topics

Chapter 26, Writer's Room topic 1 (page 397)

Chapter 30, Writer's Room topic 2 (page 461)

Chapter 35, Writer's Room topic 4 (page 526)

Writing Activity 2

Visit a public place and take notes about the sights, sounds, and smells. Then, write a paragraph describing that place. Include vivid details.

✓ DESCRIPTIVE PARAGRAPH CHECKLIST

As you write your description paragraph, review the checklist on the inside front cover. Also ask yourself the following questions.

- Does my topic sentence clearly show what I will describe?

- Does my topic sentence have a controlling idea that makes a point about the topic?

- Does my paragraph make a dominant impression?

- Does my paragraph contain supporting details that appeal to the reader's senses?

- Do I use vivid language?

READING LINK

More Descriptive Readings
"Bound Feet" by Jung Chang (page 548)
"Aunt Tee" by Maya Angelou (page 586)

How Do I Get a Better Grade?

Visit www.mywritinglab.com for audio-visual lectures and additional practice sets about description writing.
Get a better grade with MyWritingLab!

Process

> *It is easier to know how to do something than it is to do it.*
> —CHINESE PROVERB

CONTENTS

A sushi chef follows a process to create a tasty meal. In process writing, you describe how to do something.

Writers' Exchange

Choose one of the following topics, and have a group or class discussion. Describe the steps you would take to do that process.

1. How to go grocery shopping
2. How to be a bad date
3. How to bathe your dog or cat
4. How to annoy your parents or children

What Is a Process?

A **process** is a series of steps done in chronological order. In process writing, you explain how to do something, how an incident took place, or how something works.

You explain processes every day. At home, you may explain to a family member how to use an electronic appliance. You may need to give written instructions to a baby-sitter or caregiver. At college, you may explain how to perform a scientific experiment or how a new product was invented. At work, you may explain how to operate a machine or how to do a particular job.

Process at Work

In this memo to fellow employees, Mawlid Abdul Aziz, a network administration assistant, uses process writing to explain how to install antivirus software on a computer.

Due to a new security threat circulating on the Internet, the IT department strongly recommends that you update your antivirus software. To do so, double-click on the antivirus icon at the bottom right on your computer screen (system tray). The correct icon should appear at the far left of the row of icons. Then, a window will appear that is called the virus scan console. In this window, there are several items, one of which is labeled "Automatic Update." By double-clicking on that button, another window will appear that contains the button "Run Now." Click on it, and after a minute or two, there will be a message box saying "completed." Please do not hesitate to contact the IT department if you encounter any difficulty with this procedure.

The Process Paragraph

There are two main types of process paragraphs.

- **Complete a process.** This type of paragraph contains directions on how to complete a particular task. For example, a writer might explain how to paint a picture, how to repair a leaky faucet, or how to get a job. The reader should be able to follow the directions and complete the task.

- **Understand a process.** This type of paragraph explains how something works or how something happens. In other words, the goal is to help the reader understand a process rather than do a process. For example, a writer might explain how the heart pumps blood to other organs in the body or how a country elects its political leaders.

ESSAY LINK

Process essays also focus on completing or understanding a process.

PRACTICE 1

A framed painting hanging on a wall creates its own imaginary world. Understanding and responding to a painting does not have to be difficult. First, get up close. When you approach a picture, step into its universe. Put your nose up close and observe the picture as a physical object. Drink in its visual and physical properties. Next, take a step back and look at the picture as a whole. Look at the arrangement or composition of the picture's elements: background or foreground, implied movement, and dramatic action. Is there a story? Who are the human figures? Are there symbols? What feelings or ideas does it stimulate in you? Then, think and apply what you know. Study the picture in historical context. This knowledge can help identify the style or movement to which a picture belongs. It can tell you the work's patron or something significant about the artist's life and how this work fits into that story. Finally, respond with your own thoughts and feelings. Look at what it shows you and listen to what it says and record that experience for yourself in a journal or notebook. This personal reflection fixes the impression and helps you recall this picture as something you've become acquainted with.

—Philip E. Bishop, *A Beginner's Guide to the Humanities*

1. a. What is the topic of this paragraph? _____

   _____

   b. What is the controlling idea in the topic sentence? _____

   _____

2. List the main steps the author suggests to help to understand a painting.

   _____

   _____

   _____

   _____

PRACTICE 2

Scrabble, one of the world's most popular board games, has an interesting history. Read the next paragraph and answer the questions.

Alfred Mosher Butts, a quiet architect from Poughkeepsie, New

York, was unemployed when he invented the world's most popular word

game. Lexico was played without a board, and players earned points

based on the lengths of words that they could build. By carefully

analyzing the *New York Times*, Butts discovered that *S* is the most

frequently used letter, so he reduced the number of *S*'s in the game, and he gave additional points to letters such as *J*, *Q*, and *Z*. Unable to interest game companies, Butts produced the games himself and sold them to friends. Then in 1938, inspired by crossword puzzles, Butts combined the letters with a playing board and renamed his game Criss-Cross, but game manufacturers continued to reject his idea. Things finally changed for Butts in 1948, when a small entrepreneur, James Brunot, picked up Butts's game and renamed it Scrabble. By 1953, the demand for Scrabble was so great that a large manufacturer licensed and mass-produced the game. According to Mattel Incorporated, Scrabble is now the world's best-selling board game, with over 100 million copies sold in 29 different languages.

—Iannick Di Sanza, student

1. Underline the topic sentence of this paragraph.
2. What type of process paragraph is this? Circle the best answer.
    a. complete a process   b. understand a process
3. Look at the paragraph and number the steps that Alfred Butts took to complete his board game.

PRACTICE 3

For each of the following topics, write *C* if it explains how to complete a process, or write *U* if it explains how to understand a process (how something works or how something happens).

1. How to train a pet dog   _____
2. The stages in a child's development   _____
3. How a child learns to read   _____
4. How to avoid being mugged   _____
5. Five ways to keep your motorcycle in top condition _____
6. The chemical process of a firefly's light   _____

Explore Topics

In the Warm Up, you will try an exploring strategy to generate ideas about different topics.

The Writer's Desk Warm Up

Think about the following questions, and write down the first ideas that come to your mind. Try to think of two or three ideas for each topic.

EXAMPLE: Imagine that you have a new opportunity and want to leave your current job. What are some things that you should do before you quit your job?

-give supervisor a lot of notice (needs time to hire someone else)

-ask for a reference letter (I might need it later)

-have a going-away party, and thank co-workers and supervisor

1. What are some steps you can take to enjoy life?

2. What are some things you should do to succeed in college?

3. Think about a particular holiday or celebration that you enjoy. What are some things you do to prepare for that holiday?

DEVELOPING

ESSAY LINK

In a process essay, the thesis statement expresses the controlling idea.

When you write a process paragraph, choose a process that you can easily cover in a single paragraph. For example, you might be able to explain how to send an e-mail message in a single paragraph; however, you would need much more than a paragraph to explain how to use a particular computer software program.

The Topic Sentence

In a process paragraph, the topic sentence states what process you will be explaining and what readers will be able to do or understand after they have read the paragraph.

topic   controlling idea

To calm your child during a tantrum, <u>follow the next steps.</u>

controlling idea   topic

<u>With inexpensive materials,</u> **you can redecorate a room in your house.**

Make a Point

Your topic sentence should not simply announce the topic. It should make a point about the topic.

Announces: This is how you do speed dating.

                          controlling idea   topic

Correct: It is surprisingly easy and efficient **to meet someone using speed dating.**

The Writer's Desk   Write Topic Sentences

Write a topic sentence for each of the following topics. You can look for ideas in the previous Writer's Desk. Remember to narrow each topic. Each topic sentence should state the process and should contain a controlling idea.

EXAMPLE:

Topic: How to leave a job

Topic sentence: *If you want to leave your job on a positive note, there are a few things that you should consider.*

1. Topic: How to enjoy life

   Topic sentence: _____

   _____

2. Topic: How to succeed in college

   Topic sentence: _____

   _____

3. Topic: How to prepare for a holiday or celebration

   Topic sentence: _____

   _____

The Supporting Ideas

A process paragraph contains a series of steps. When you develop supporting ideas for a process paragraph, think about the main steps that are necessary to complete the process. Most process paragraphs use time order.

Give Steps, Not Examples

When you explain how to complete a process, describe each step. Do not simply list examples of the process.

ESSAY LINK

In an essay, each body paragraph could describe a process. For example, in an essay about how to get rich, one body paragraph could be about buying lottery tickets and another could be about inventing a product.

Topic: How to Get Rich

List of Examples
- write a best seller
- win the lottery
- invent a product
- inherit money

Steps in the Process
- do market research
- find a specific need
- invent a product to fulfill that need
- heavily promote the product

The Writer's Desk **List the Main Steps**

Think about three or four essential steps in each process. Make a list under each topic.

EXAMPLE: How to leave a job

explain your reason for going

give enough notice

ask for a reference letter

find out about benefits

1. How to enjoy life

_____

_____

_____

_____

2. How to succeed in college

_____

_____

_____

_____

3. How to prepare for a holiday or a celebration

_____

_____

_____

_____

ESSAY LINK

In a process essay, place the thesis statement in the introduction. Then use each body paragraph to explain a step in the process.

The Paragraph Plan

A paragraph plan helps you organize your topic sentence and supporting details before writing a first draft. Decide which steps and which details your reader will really need to complete the process or understand it. Write down the steps in chronological order.

TOPIC SENTENCE: If you want to leave your job on a positive note, there are a few things that you should consider.

Step 1: Give positive reasons for leaving.
Details: —do not complain about the company
—say you need a new challenge
Step 2: Give employers enough notice.
Details: —the company might need time to hire a replacement
Step 3: Ask for a reference letter.
Details: —may need it in the future
Step 4: Find out about employment benefits.
Details: —might get unused vacation pay

 **Include Necessary Tools or Supplies**

When you are writing a plan for a process paragraph, remember to include any special tools or supplies a reader will need to complete the process. For example, if you want to explain how to pack for a move, you should mention that you need boxes, felt-tip markers, newsprint, twine, scissors, and tape.

The Writer's Desk Write a Paragraph Plan

Choose one of the topic sentences that you wrote for the Writer's Desk on page 101, and then list the main steps to complete the process. Also add details and examples that will help to explain each step.

Topic sentence: _____

_____

Supporting points:

Step 1: _____

Details: _____

_____

Step 2: _____

Details: _____

_____

Step 3: _____

Details: _____

_____

Step 4: _____

Details: _____

_____

Step 5: _____

Details: _____

_____

The First Draft

After you outline your ideas in a plan, you are ready to write the first draft. Remember to write complete sentences. You might include transitional words or expressions to help your ideas flow smoothly.

 **Using Commands**

In process writing, address the reader directly. For example, instead of writing "You should travel in a group," you could simply write "Travel in a group."

Transitional Words and Expressions

Most process paragraphs explain a process using time (or chronological) order. The following transitions are useful in process paragraphs.

To Begin a Process	To Continue a Process		To End a Process
(at) first	after that	later	eventually
initially	afterward	meanwhile	finally
the first step	also	second	in the end
	furthermore	then	ultimately
	in addition	third	

The Writer's Desk **Write the First Draft**

In the previous Writer's Desk, you developed a paragraph plan. Now write the first draft of your process paragraph. Before you write, carefully review your paragraph plan and make any necessary changes.

REVISING AND EDITING

Revise and Edit a Process Paragraph

When you finish writing a process paragraph, carefully review your work and revise it to make the process as clear as possible to your readers. Check to make sure that you have organized your steps chronologically and remove any irrelevant details.

PRACTICE 4

Read the following student paragraph and answer the questions.

If you want to leave your job on a positive note, there are a few things that you should consider. First, give a positive reason for leaving. Instead of complaining about something in the company, you could say that you need a change and want a different challenge. Give as much notice as possible, this will leave a favorable impression. It will also give your boss time to find a replacement. If you think you deserve it, ask for a reference letter. Even if you already have a new job, the reference letter could be useful at a future date. Find out if you are entitled to benefits. You may be eligible for back pay or vacation pay. Business consultant Cho Matsu says "The impression you make when you leave a job could have an impact on your future career".

Revising

1. Underline the topic sentence.

2. The author uses *first* to introduce the first step. Subsequent steps would be more clearly recognizable if the writer had used more transitions. Indicate, with a number, where more transitional expressions could be added, and write possible examples on the lines provided.

   _____

   _____

   _____

3. How does the writer conclude the paragraph?
   a. With a prediction   b. With a suggestion   c. With a quotation

Editing

4. This paragraph contains a type of run-on sentence called a comma splice. Two complete sentences are incorrectly connected with a comma. Identify and correct the comma splice.

5. This paragraph contains two punctuation errors in the direct quotation. Correct the mistakes directly on the paragraph.

> **GRAMMAR LINK**
>
> See the following chapters for more information about these grammar topics:
> Run-Ons, Chapter 20
> Quotations, Chapter 34

vo•cab•u•lar•y BOOST

Look at the first draft of your process essay. Underline the verb that you use in each step of the process. Then, when possible, come up with a more evocative or interesting verb. Use your thesaurus for this activity.

The Writer's Desk **Revise and Edit Your Paragraph**

Revise and edit the paragraph that you wrote for the previous Writer's Desk. Ensure that your paragraph has unity, adequate support, and coherence. Also correct any errors in grammar, spelling, punctuation, and mechanics.

REFLECT ON IT

Think about what you have learned in this unit. If you do not know an answer, review that topic.

I. What are the two types of process paragraphs? Briefly explain each type.

a. _____

_____

_____

b. _____

_____

_____

2. What organizational method is generally used in process writing? Circle the best answer.

a. space order   b. time order   c. emphatic order

3. Why are transitional words important in process writing?

_____

_____

_____

WRITING LINK

More Process Writing Topics

Chapter 19, Writer's Room topic 3
(page 316)
Chapter 26, Writer's Room topic 2
(page 397)
Chapter 32, Writer's Room topic 4
(page 490)

READING LINK

More Process Reading

"How Spies Are Caught"
(page 562)
"Control Your Temper" by
Elizabeth Passarella (page 583)

The Writer's Room

Topics for Process Paragraphs

Writing Activity I

Choose any of the following topics, or choose your own topic. Then write a process paragraph.

General Topics

1. how to make your home safe
2. how to decorate a room with very little money
3. how to find a good roommate
4. how to break up with a mate
5. how to train a pet
6. how to build or fix something

College and Work-Related Topics

7. how to choose a college
8. how to stay motivated at college
9. how to prepare for a job interview
10. how to get along with your co-workers
11. how to organize your desk or tools
12. how something was discovered

Writing Activity 2

Pop artist Andy Warhol once said that everyone would be famous for fifteen minutes. Think of some processes related to fame. Some ideas might be how to become famous, how to stay famous, how to lose fame, how to survive fame, or how to meet a celebrity. Then, write a process paragraph.

✔ PROCESS PARAGRAPH CHECKLIST

As you write your process paragraph, review the checklist on the inside front cover. Also ask yourself the following questions.

- Does my topic sentence make a point about the process?

- Do I include all of the steps in the process?

- Do I clearly explain each step so my reader can accomplish the process or understand it?

- Do I mention all of the supplies that my reader needs to complete the process?

- Do I use transitions to connect all of the steps in the process?

How Do I Get a Better Grade?

Visit www.mywritinglab.com for audio-visual lectures and additional practice sets about process writing.
Get a better grade with MyWritingLab!

CHAPTER 8

Definition

"A successful marriage requires falling in love many times, always with the same person."

—MIGNON MCLAUGHLIN
American journalist (1913–1983)

For many people, the definition of happiness is listening to great music. In definition writing, you define what a term means.

Writers' Exchange

Work with a partner or a team of students. Try to define the following terms. Think of some examples that can help define each term.

netiquette   chick flick   poseur

What Is Definition?

When you **define,** you explain the meaning of a word. Some terms have concrete meanings, and you can define them in a few words. For example, a pebble is "a small stone." Other words, such as *culture, happiness,* or *evil,* are more abstract and require longer definitions. In fact, it is possible to write a paragraph, an essay, or even an entire book on such concepts.

The simplest way to define a term is to look it up in a dictionary. However, many words have nuances that are not necessarily discussed in dictionaries. For example, suppose that your boss calls your work "unsatisfactory." You might need clarification of that term. Do you have poor work habits? Do you miss deadlines? Is your attitude problematic? What does your boss mean by "unsatisfactory?"

The ability to define difficult concepts is always useful. At home, a friend or loved one may ask you to define *commitment.* If you mention that a movie was *great,* you may need to clarify what you mean by that word. In a political science class, you might define *socialism, capitalism,* or *communism.* At work, you might define your company's *winning strategy.*

Definition at Work
In the following memo to a parent, reading specialist Amanda Wong defines a common reading disorder.

As we have discussed, your daughter exhibits signs of a reading disorder commonly referred to as dyslexia. Dyslexia is not the result of damage to the brain or nervous system. It is, more accurately, a problem that is often found in visual learners. Such learners associate pictures with words. For example, your daughter would associate the word *tiger* with the animal, but she has no image to associate with words such as *a* or *the.* Therefore, she may become confused when she reads such words. A feeling of disorientation when reading the letters in words can further compound the problem. She may not perceive individual letters in sequence but might interpret them in a variety of orders and directions. Thus, a dyslexic child may see the word *dog* as *god* or *bog.* In our next meeting, I will give you some strategies to help your daughter with her reading.

The Definition Paragraph

When you write a definition paragraph, try to explain what a term means to you. For example, if someone asks you to define *bravery,* you might tell stories to illustrate the meaning of the word. You may also give examples of acts of bravery. You might even explain what bravery is not.

When you write a definition paragraph, remember the following two points.

- **Choose a term that you know something about.** You need to understand a term in order to say something relevant and interesting about it.
- **Give a clear definition.** In your first sentence, write a definition that is understandable to your reader, and support your definition with examples. Do not simply give a dictionary definition because your readers are capable of looking up the word themselves. Instead, describe what the word means to you.

 **Consider Your Audience**

When you write a definition paragraph, consider your audience. You may have to adjust your tone and vocabulary, depending on who reads the paragraph. For example, if you write a definition paragraph about computer viruses for your English class, you will have to use easily understandable terms. If you write the same paragraph for your computer class, you can use more technical terms.

PRACTICE I

Read the paragraph, and then answer the questions.

Atmospherics is the use of color, lighting, scents, furnishings, sounds, and other design elements to create a desired setting. Marketers manipulate these elements to create a certain feeling about the retail environment. Kinney's Colorado Stores, which sell high-end outdoor clothing, for example, are designed to make the shoppers feel they're out in nature. The stores pipe in New Age background music, interrupted occasionally by the sound of a thunderstorm or a babbling brook. Motion sensors in the ceiling activate displays as a shopper approaches, so a person who walks near an arrangement of beach shoes may hear the sound of waves crashing. The owners of these stores believe that getting people in the mood makes them more likely to buy what they see. To make its stores more appealing to customers, Taco Bell sought to use décor to change its image from cheap fast food to a kind of "Starbucks with a Spanish accent." To attract a wider range of customers, Taco Bell used more wood, natural fibers, and new colors.

—Solomon, Marshall, and Stuart. *Marketing*

1. Underline the topic sentence.

2. What is the writer defining? _____

3. Who is the likely audience for this paragraph? _____

4. What two examples does the author give to develop the definition?

   _____

   _____

5. Think of another example to add to this paragraph.

   _____

   _____

Explore Topics

In the Warm Up, you will try an exploring strategy to generate ideas about different topics.

The Writer's Desk **Warm Up**

Think about the following questions, and write down the first ideas that come to your mind. Try to think of two or three ideas for each topic.

EXAMPLE: What is slang? Think of some examples of slang.

—*words people use for effect*

—*cool, dude, bro*

—*different cultural groups have their own slang terms*

1. What is a white lie? Give some examples of white lies.

_____

_____

_____

2. What is talent? Give examples of talent.

_____

_____

_____

3. What are some characteristics of a workaholic?

_____

_____

_____

DEVELOPING

The Topic Sentence

A clear topic sentence for a definition paragraph introduces the term and provides a definition. There are three basic ways to define a term.

- By synonym
- By category
- By negation

ESSAY LINK

In a definition essay, the thesis statement expresses the controlling idea. In the thesis, you can define the term by synonym, category, or negation.

Definition by Synonym

The easiest way to define a term is to supply a synonym (a word that has a similar meaning). This type of definition is useful if the original term is difficult to understand and the synonym is a more familiar word.

	term	+	synonym
A Mickey Mouse course			is an easy course to complete.
I am a procrastinator,			which means I tend to put things off.

Definition by Category

A more effective way to define a term is to give a definition by category (or class). When you define by category, you determine the larger group to which the term belongs. Then you determine what unique characteristics set the term apart from others in that category.

term	+	category	+	detail
Netiquette is		proper behavior		regarding communication on the Internet.
Luddites are		people		who are skeptical about new technology.

Definition by Negation

When you define by negation, you explain what a term does not mean. You can then include a sentence explaining what it does mean. Definition by negation is especially useful when your readers have preconceived ideas about something. Your definition explains that it is not what the reader thought.

term	+	what it is not	+	what it is
Alcoholism		is not an invented disease;		it is a serious physical dependency.
Hackers		are not playful computer geeks;		they are criminals.

Grammar Hint   **Using Semicolons**

When you write a definition by negation, you can join the two separate and independent sentences with a semicolon.

Independent clause	;	independent clause

Feminists are not man haters; they are people who want fairness and equality for women.

PRACTICE 2

A. Write a one-sentence definition by synonym for each of the following terms. Your definition should include the term and a synonym. If necessary, you can look up the terms in the dictionary; however, define each one using your own words.

EXAMPLE:

To capitulate _means to give up or surrender._

1. To procrastinate _____

2. A celebrity _____

3. Malaria _____

B. Write a one-sentence definition by category for the following terms. Make sure that your definition includes the term, a category, and details.

EXAMPLE:

A cockroach *is an insect that lives in the cracks and crevices of buildings.*

_____

4. A knockoff _____

_____

5. Paparazzi _____

_____

6. A deadbeat parent _____

_____

C. Write a one-sentence definition by negation for the following terms. Explain what each term is not, followed by what each term is.

EXAMPLE:

A placebo *is not a real drug; it is a sugar pill.* _____

_____

7. A television addict _____

_____

8. Good parents _____

_____

9. A dog _____

_____

Use the Right Word

When you write a definition paragraph, it is important to use the precise words to define the term. Moreover, when you define a term by category, make sure that the category for your term is correct. For example, look at the following imprecise definitions of insomnia.

Insomnia is the (inability) to sleep well.
(Insomnia is not an ability or an inability.)

Insomnia is (when) you cannot sleep well.
(*When* refers to a time, but insomnia is not a time.)

Insomnia is the (nights) when you do not get enough sleep.
(Insomnia is not days or nights.)

Insomnia is (where) it is hard to fall asleep.
(*Where* refers to a place, but insomnia is not a place.)

Now look at a better definition of insomnia.

Insomnia is a **sleeping disorder** characterized by the inability to sleep well.

> ## Hint   Make a Point
>
> Defining terms by synonym, category, and negation are guidelines for the writing of topic sentences. Keep in mind that your paragraph will be more interesting if you express an attitude or point of view in your topic sentence.
>
> **No point:**   Anorexia is an eating disorder.
>
> **Point:**   Anorexia is a tragic eating disorder that is difficult to cure.

PRACTICE 3

Revise each sentence using precise language.

EXAMPLE:

Tuning out is when you ignore something.

Tuning out is the action of ignoring something.

1. A scapegoat is when a person gets blamed for something.

   _____

   _____

2. Claustrophobia is the inability to be in a small place.

   _____

   _____

3. A bully is the abuse of power over others.

   _____

   _____

4. Adolescence is where you are between childhood and adulthood.

   _____

   _____

5. Ego surfing is when you surf the Internet to find references to yourself.

   _____

   _____

The Writer's Desk **Write Topic Sentences**

Write a topic sentence in which you define each of the following topics. You can look for ideas in the Warm Up on page 111. Remember to use precise language in your definition.

EXAMPLE:

Topic: Slang

Topic sentence: _Slang is informal language that changes rapidly and_ _exists in various forms among different cultural groups._

1. Topic: A white lie

   Topic sentence: _____

   _____

2. Topic: Talent

   Topic sentence: _____

   _____

3. Topic: A workaholic

   Topic sentence: _____

   _____

The Supporting Ideas

After you have developed an effective topic sentence, generate supporting ideas. In a definition paragraph, you can give examples that clarify your definition.

Think about how you will organize your examples. Most definition paragraphs use emphatic order, which means that examples are placed from the most to the least important or from the least to the most important.

PRACTICE 4

The following topic sentences are from definition paragraphs. First, underline the term that will be defined. Then write a possible supporting idea. You can write an example or anecdote.

1. Tiny cute dogs have become fashion accessories for many stars.

   _____

   _____

2. Posttraumatic stress disorder is a psychological ailment that afflicts survivors of horrible events.

_____

_____

3. Some people consider themselves fashionistas.

_____

_____

The Writer's Desk Develop Supporting Ideas

Choose one of your topic sentences from the Writer's Desk on page 115. List three or four examples that best illustrate the definition.

EXAMPLE: *Slang is informal language that changes rapidly and exists in various forms among different cultural groups.*

—words change in different eras

—rappers, punks, goths have own terms

—used like a code between friends

—words show inventive creative thinking

Topic sentence: _____

_____

Supports: _____

_____

_____

_____

ESSAY LINK

In a definition essay, the thesis statement is in the introduction. Each supporting idea is in a distinct body paragraph with its own topic sentence.

The Paragraph Plan

A good definition paragraph includes a complete definition of the term and provides adequate examples to support the central definition. When creating a definition paragraph plan, make sure that your examples provide varied evidence and do not just repeat the definition. Also add details that will help clarify your supporting examples.

TOPIC SENTENCE: Slang is informal language that changes rapidly and exists in various forms among different cultural groups.

Support 1:   Slang is a type of code used between friends.

Details: —Punks might call each other emo or poseurs.
—People outside the group might not understand slang.
—Words often help define relationships among group members.

Support 2:   Slang words often show very inventive and creative thinking.

   Details: —Computer users have come up with a wide variety of net slang terms.
   —Some terms are very illustrative and visual.

Support 3:   Many slang words come and go quickly.

   Details: —In the 1920s, people used words that have gone out of fashion.
   —In the 1950s, people used words such as hipster or swell.
   —Slang words from the early 2000s, such as homie, are already becoming obsolete.

The Writer's Desk Write a Paragraph Plan

Create a detailed paragraph plan using one of the topic sentences that you wrote for the Writer's Desk on page 115. Arrange the supporting details in a logical order.

Topic sentence: _____

_____

Support 1: _____

   Details: _____

_____

_____

Support 2: _____

   Details: _____

_____

_____

Support 3: _____

   Details: _____

_____

_____

The First Draft

After you outline your ideas in a plan, you are ready to write the first draft. Remember to write complete sentences. You might include transitional words or expressions to help your ideas flow smoothly.

Transitional Words and Expressions

Transitional expressions can show different levels of importance. The following transitions are useful in definition paragraphs.

To Show the Level of Importance	
clearly	next
first	one quality . . . another quality
most of all	second
most important	undoubtedly

The Writer's Desk **Write the First Draft**

In the previous Writer's Desk, you developed a paragraph plan. Now write the first draft of your definition paragraph. Before you write, carefully review your paragraph plan and make any necessary changes.

REVISING AND EDITING

Revise and Edit a Definition Paragraph

When you finish writing a definition paragraph, carefully review your work and revise it to make the definition as clear as possible to your readers. Check that you have organized your steps logically, and remove any irrelevant details.

PRACTICE 5

Read the following student paragraph and answer the questions.

Slang is informal language that changes rapidly and exists in various forms among different cultural groups. It is a type of code used between friends. Punks call each other *emo* or *poseurs*. Such words denote a persons status in the group. Often, those outside the group might not understand slang. My grandmother, for example, doesn't know what a homeboy is. Soldiers, athletes, music subcultures, and even wealthy industrialists come up with their own particular jargon. The rich might put down social climbers as wannabes. They might call a spouse a trophy wife or husband. Slang words often show very inventive and creative thinking. Computer users have come up with a wide variety of net slang terms such as blog, flamer, troll, cyberspook, or flamebait. Some terms are very illustrative. Jerk sounds like a fast movement. Whipped is similar to the sound a whip makes. Most slang words come and go quick, and they change over time. In the 1920s, men would call a women's legs "gams" and money "clams." In the 1950s, people used words such as hipster, swell, hepcat, or squaresville, and those word are outdated. Even slang words from the early 2000s, such as homie and hoser, are already becoming obsolete.

Revising

1. Underline the topic sentence.

2. What type of definition does the topic sentence contain? Circle the best answer.
   a. Definition by synonym   b. Definition by category
   c. Definition by negation

3. This paragraph lacks sentence variety. Revise the paragraph to give it more sentence variety by combining sentences or changing the first word of some sentences. (For more information about combining sentences and sentence variety, see Chapters 17–19.)

4. The paragraph lacks transitions to show the order of ideas. Add some transitional words or expressions.

5. The paragraph needs a concluding sentence. Add a concluding sentence in the lines provided.

_____

_____

Editing

6. There is one apostrophe error. Circle and correct the error.

7. There is an error in adverb form. Circle and correct the error.

GRAMMAR LINK

See the following chapters for more information about these grammar topics:
   Apostrophes, Chapter 34
   Adjectives and Adverbs,
      Chapter 28

vo•cab•u•lar•y BOOST

Using Your Thesaurus

Work with a partner and brainstorm synonyms or expressions that can replace each word listed below. If you have trouble coming up with ideas, use your thesaurus.

1. optimist   _____

2. depressed   _____

3. lazy   _____

4. reckless   _____

When you finish coming up with synonyms, reread your definition paragraph. Circle three words that you have repeated several times. Using your thesaurus, find possible replacements for those words.

The Writer's Desk Revise and Edit Your Paragraph

Revise and edit the paragraph that you wrote for the previous Writer's Desk.

Ensure that your paragraph has unity, adequate support, and coherence. Also correct any errors in grammar, spelling, punctuation, and mechanics.

REFLECT ON IT

Think about what you have learned in this chapter. If you do not know an answer, review that topic.

1. In definition writing, you _____

   _____

2. Explain each of the following types of definitions. Then give an example of each definition. Use your own ideas.

   a. Explain definition by synonym. _____

   _____

   Give an example of a definition by synonym. _____

   _____

   b. Explain definition by category. _____

   _____

   Give an example of a definition by category. _____

   _____

   c. Explain definition by negation. _____

   _____

   Give an example of a definition by negation. _____

   _____

The Writer's Room **Topics for Definition Paragraphs**

Writing Activity 1

Choose any of the following topics, or choose your own topic. Then write a definition paragraph.

General Topics

1. a miracle
2. sex appeal
3. a spoiled child
4. fashion police
5. bling bling
6. mind games

College and Work-Related Topics

7. integrity
8. a slacker
9. a headhunter
10. an opportunist
11. the glass ceiling
12. an apprentice

WRITING LINK

More Definition Writing Topics
Chapter 19, Writer's Room topic 1 (page 316)
Chapter 24, Writer's Room topic 4 (page 376)
Chapter 35, Writer's Room topic 1 (page 526)

Writing Activity 2

Write a paragraph in which you define censorship. What sorts of things get censored? Think of some interesting examples that support your definition.

READING LINK
More Definition Readings
"I'm a Banana and Proud of It" by Wayson Choy (page 551)
"Dancing with Fear" by Bebe Moore Campbell (page 556)

✔ DEFINITION PARAGRAPH CHECKLIST

As you write your definition paragraph, review the checklist on the inside front cover. Also ask yourself the following questions.

☐ Does my topic sentence contain a definition by synonym, negation, or category?

☐ Do all of my supporting sentences relate to the topic sentence?

☐ Do I use concise language in my definition?

☐ Do I include enough examples to help define the term?

How Do I Get a Better Grade?

Visit www.mywritinglab.com for audio-visual lectures and additional practice sets about definition writing.
Get a better grade with MyWritingLab!

Classification

> *Inanimate objects are classified scientifically into three major categories: those that don't work, those that break down, and those that get lost.*
>
> —RUSSELL BAKER
> *American Journalist (b. 1925)*

In a candy store, chocolates are classified according to the amount of cacao in the chocolate and the kinds of fillings inside the chocolates. In classification writing, you divide a topic into categories to explain it.

Writers' Exchange

Work with a partner or a group. Divide the next words into three or four different categories. What are the categories? Why did you choose those categories?

mechanic	fertilizer	kitchen
garden	cook	programmer
microwave	landscaper	wrench
office	computer	garage

What Is Classification?

When you classify, you sort a subject into more understandable categories. Each of the categories must be part of a larger group, yet they must also be distinct. For example, you might write a paragraph about the most common types of pets and sort the subject into cats, dogs, and birds.

Classification occurs in many situations. At home, you could classify the responsibilities of each person in the family, or you could classify your bills. In a biology course, you might write a paper about the different types of cells, or in a commerce course, you may write about the categories in a financial statement. On the job, you might advertise the different types of products or services that your company sells.

Classification at Work

Robert Luzynski, an allergy specialist, wrote the following information in a brochure for his patients.

If you exhibit allergic symptoms to animals, there are three types of treatment that you can follow. The most effective is to avoid contact with known allergens. Thus, avoid bringing pets into the home. If you have a pet, consider using an air cleaner, vacuum two to three times a week, and ensure that the animal is groomed frequently to remove loose fur and dander. The second type of treatment consists of medications. Antihistamines help alleviate the symptoms of allergic reactions, but they do not cure allergies. It is important to read the labels carefully as some antihistamines cause drowsiness. A final method, desensitization, is an extended treatment involving allergy shots. You would be exposed to gradually increasing amounts of specific allergens. The treatment lasts for an extended period of time, and the goal is to reduce your sensitivity to the allergens.

ESSAY LINK

Classification essays also require a classification principle and distinct categories.

The Classification Paragraph

To find a topic for a classification paragraph, think of something that can be sorted into different groups. Also determine a reason for classifying the items. When you are planning your ideas for a classification paragraph, remember these two points.

1. **Use a common classification principle.** A **classification principle** is the overall method that you use to sort the subject into categories. To find the classification principle, think about one common characteristic that unites the different categories. For example, if your subject is "the telephone," your classification principle might be any of the following:

- types of annoying phone calls
- reasons that people buy cell phones
- types of long-distance services
- types of customer reactions to telephone salespeople

2. **Sort the subject into distinct categories.** A classification paragraph should have two or more categories.

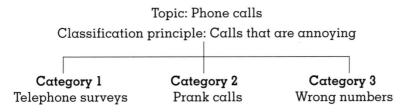

Topic: Phone calls

Classification principle: Calls that are annoying

| **Category 1** | **Category 2** | **Category 3** |
| Telephone surveys | Prank calls | Wrong numbers |

PRACTICE 1

Read the next paragraph and answer the questions.

> Hackers come in three stripes, according to Drew Williams, a computer security specialist for Maryland-based Axent Technologies. There are the "newbies," or inexperienced hackers, who generally stumble upon a Web site offering free hacking software. They try to break into targets through their Web sites as an after-school hobby. "White hat" hackers are more talented—and serious—but they use their talents to expose weak security. According to Williams, "They hack for a cause." White hat infiltrators might squirm into the computer innards of a bank or government ministry and steal a few nuggets of data, but the white hat hacker will then expose his deed to his victim and offer security suggestions—often for a fee. Then there are the "black hat" hackers whose **depredations** include sabotage of government Web sites; the Pentagon and Department of Justice are among favorite targets. They plunder bank deposits, shut down public services such as telephones and electricity, and steal trade secrets, Williams said.
>
> —Kim Krane, "Computer Crime Tops $100 Million," *APBnews.com*

depredations:
acts of destruction

1. Underline the topic sentence of this paragraph.

2. State the three categories that the author discusses and list some details about each category.

   a. _____

      Details: _____

   b. _____

      Details: _____

   c. _____

      Details: _____

3. Who is the audience for this paragraph?

   _____

4. What is the purpose of this paragraph? Circle the best answer.

   a. to persuade   b. to inform   c. to entertain

vo·cab·u·lar·y BOOST

Classifying Parts of Words

A prefix is added to the beginning of a word, and it changes the word's meaning. A suffix is added to the end of a word, and it also changes the word's meaning. Review the list of ten common prefixes and suffixes. Then come up with at least two more words using the listed prefix or suffix.

Prefixes	Example	
anti = against	antiwar	_____
un = not	unable	_____
re = again	redo	_____
bi = two	bilingual	_____
mis = wrong	misspell	_____

Suffixes	Example	
er = doer	teacher	_____
ment = condition	agreement	_____
ly = characteristic of	honestly	_____
ous = full of	courageous	_____
ful = filled with	respectful	_____

Explore Topics

In the Warm Up, you will try an exploring strategy to generate ideas about different topics.

The Writer's Desk Warm Up

Think about the following questions, and write down the first ideas that come to your mind. Try to think of two or three ideas for each topic.

EXAMPLE: What are some different types of diets?

Some people don't eat at all. Starvation diets?

Fad diets. Some diet books become bestsellers.

Protein shakes. Aren't there diet pills?

1. List some clothing that you own. You might think about old clothing, comfortable clothing, beautiful clothing, and so on.

_____

_____

_____

2. What are some different types of consumers? To get ideas, you might think about some people you know and the way that they shop.

_____

_____

_____

3. List some skills or abilities people need for different jobs. As you brainstorm ideas, consider manual labor as well as academic or office jobs.

_____

_____

_____

Making a Classification Chart

A **classification chart** is a visual representation of the main topic and its categories. Making a classification chart can help you identify the categories more clearly so that you will be able to write more exact topic sentences.

When you classify items, remember to use a single method of classification and a common classification principle to sort the items. For example, if you are classifying movies, you might classify them according to their ratings: General Audience, Parental Guidance, and Restricted. You could also classify movies according to their country of origin: British, American, and French, for example. Remember that one classification principle must unite the group.

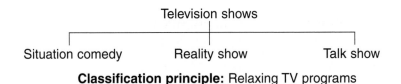

Television shows

| Situation comedy | Reality show | Talk show |

Classification principle: Relaxing TV programs

 **Categories Should Not Overlap**

When sorting a topic into categories, make sure that the categories do not overlap. For example, you would not classify drivers into careful drivers, aggressive drivers, and bad drivers because aggressive drivers could also be bad drivers. Each category should be distinct.

PRACTICE 2

In the following classification charts, a subject has been broken down into distinct categories. The items in the group should have the same classification principle. Cross out one item in each group that does not belong. Then write down the classification principle that unites the group.

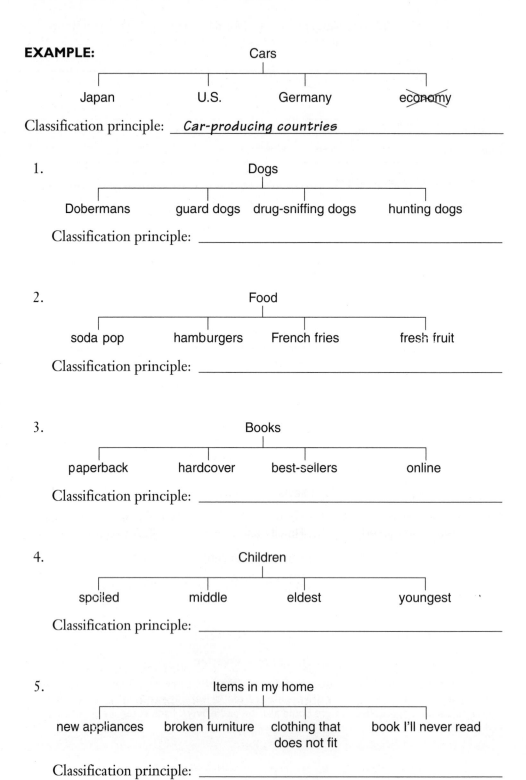

EXAMPLE:

Cars

| Japan | U.S. | Germany | ~~economy~~ |

Classification principle: *Car-producing countries*

1.

Dogs

| Dobermans | guard dogs | drug-sniffing dogs | hunting dogs |

Classification principle: _____

2.

Food

| soda pop | hamburgers | French fries | fresh fruit |

Classification principle: _____

3.

Books

| paperback | hardcover | best-sellers | online |

Classification principle: _____

4.

Children

| spoiled | middle | eldest | youngest |

Classification principle: _____

5.

Items in my home

| new appliances | broken furniture | clothing that does not fit | book I'll never read |

Classification principle: _____

The Writer's Desk **Find Distinct Categories**

Break down the following topics into three distinct categories. Remember to find categories that do not overlap. You can look for ideas in the Warm Up on pages 126–127.

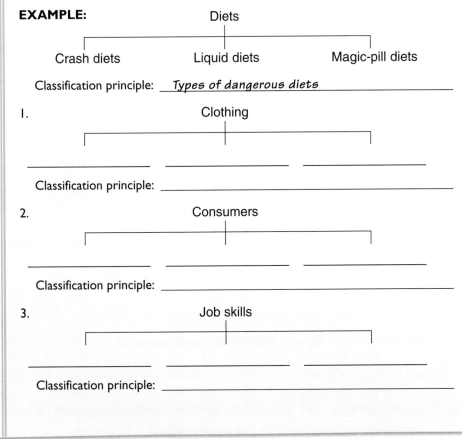

EXAMPLE: Diets

Crash diets   Liquid diets   Magic-pill diets

Classification principle: *Types of dangerous diets*

1.   Clothing

Classification principle: _____

2.   Consumers

Classification principle: _____

3.   Job skills

Classification principle: _____

DEVELOPING

The Topic Sentence

The topic sentence in a classification paragraph clearly indicates what you will classify. It also includes the controlling idea, which is the classification principle that you use.

> Several types of students can completely disrupt a classroom.

Topic: Students

Classification principle: Disruptive types

You can also mention the types of categories in your topic sentence.

> The most annoying telephone calls are surveys, prank calls, and wrong numbers.

Topic: Telephone calls

Classification principle: Types of annoying calls

ESSAY LINK

In a classification essay, the thesis statement expresses the controlling idea or classification principle.

Make a Point

To make interesting classification paragraphs, try to express an attitude, opinion, or feeling about the topic. For example, you can write a paragraph about types of diets, but it is more interesting if you make a point about the types of diets.

Poor: Types of diets

Better: Types of **dangerous** diets
Types of **effective** diets

Grammar Hint

Use parallel structure when words or phrases are joined in a series.

drug allergies

The three categories of allergies are animal allergies, food allergies, and ~~people who are allergic to medicine~~.

See Chapter 21 for more information about parallel structure.

The Writer's Desk **Write Topic Sentences**

Look again at what you wrote in the Warm Up on pages 126–127. Also look at the classification charts that you made for each topic. Now write clear topic sentences. Remember that your topic sentence can include the different categories you will be discussing.

EXAMPLE: Topic: Diets

Topic sentence: *Dieters sometimes use dangerous methods to lose weight, such as the high-fat diet, the liquid diet, and the magic-pill diet.*

1. Topic: Clothing

   Topic sentence: _____

   _____

2. Topic: Consumers

   Topic sentence: _____

   _____

3. Topic: Job skills

   Topic sentence: _____

   _____

The Supporting Ideas

After you have developed an effective topic sentence, generate supporting ideas. In a classification paragraph, you can list details about each of your categories.

The Paragraph Plan

You can make a standard paragraph plan. You can also create a pie chart to help you visualize the different categories.

Finally, an effective way to visualize your categories and supporting ideas is to make a detailed classification chart. Break down the main topic into several categories, and then give details about each category.

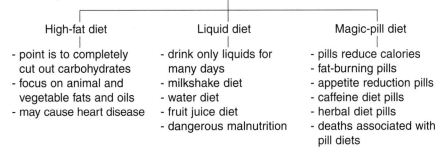

Dieters sometimes use dangerous methods to lose weight, such as the high-fat diet, the liquid diet, and the magic pill diet.

High-fat diet	Liquid diet	Magic-pill diet
- point is to completely cut out carbohydrates - focus on animal and vegetable fats and oils - may cause heart disease	- drink only liquids for many days - milkshake diet - water diet - fruit juice diet - dangerous malnutrition	- pills reduce calories - fat-burning pills - appetite reduction pills - caffeine diet pills - herbal diet pills - deaths associated with pill diets

The Writer's Desk **Make a Detailed Classification Chart**

Choose one of the topic sentences that you wrote for the previous Writer's Desk, and make a detailed classification chart. Arrange the supporting details in a logical order. You can refer to the information you generated in the Warm Up.

Topic sentence: _____

_____

ESSAY LINK

You can make a detailed classification chart when you develop your classification essay. Each supporting idea would become a distinct paragraph.

   **Use the Chart as a Plan**

Your classification chart can also serve as your paragraph plan. Like a paragraph plan, your chart contains your topic sentence, your categories, and details about each category.

The First Draft

After you outline your ideas in a classification chart or plan, you are ready to write the first draft. Remember to write complete sentences. You might include transitional words or expressions to help your ideas flow smoothly.

Transitional Words and Expressions

Some classification paragraphs use transitional words and expressions to show which category is most important and to signal a movement from one category to the next. The following transitions are very useful in classification writing.

To Show Importance	To Show Types of Categories
above all	one kind . . . another kind
clearly	the first/second type
the most important	the first/second kind
most of all	the last category
particularly	

The Writer's Desk   **Write the First Draft**

Write the first draft of your classification paragraph. Before you write, carefully review your detailed classification chart and make any necessary changes.

REVISING AND EDITING

Revise and Edit a Classification Paragraph

When you finish writing a classification paragraph, carefully review your work and revise it to make sure that the categories do not overlap. Check to make sure that you have organized your paragraph logically, and remove any irrelevant details.

PRACTICE 3

Read the following student paragraph and answer the questions.

Dieters sometimes use dangerous methods to lose weight, such as the high-fat diet, the liquid diet, the fad diet, and the magic pill diet. With high-fat diets, the point is to cut out carbohydrates. The dieter can eat as much animal protein and fat as he or she likes. However, this diet can cause high cholesterol. Another dangerous weight-loss method is the liquid diet. People have liquid meals, but if they continue this diet for a long time, they can become malnourished. One more common type of diet is the fad diet. Somebody promotes a new, improved weight-loss method, and people blindly follow this latest diet fad. For example, in the Atkins diet, dieters limit their intake of carbohydrates, or in the liquid protein diet, you just drink a protein beverage. The last type of diet, the magic pill diet. People rely on pills such as caffeine or appetite-reduction medication to lose weight. The fen-phen diet was very popular for a while, but the pills sometimes had fatal side effects.

Revising

1. What is the classification principle in this paragraph? _____

2. What are the four categories? _____
   _____

3. Which category is not valid? _____
   Explain why. _____
   _____

4. This paragraph does not have a concluding sentence. Write a concluding sentence in the space. The concluding sentence can restate the main idea of the paragraph.
   _____
   _____

Editing

5. A fragment lacks a subject or verb and is an incomplete sentence. Identify and correct one fragment.

GRAMMAR LINK

See the following chapters for more information about these grammar topics:

Fragments, Chapter 20
Pronouns, Chapter 28

6. One sentence contains a pronoun shift. The noun and the subsequent pronoun are not consistent. Identify and correct the pronoun shift.

The Writer's Desk Revise and Edit Your Paragraph

Revise and edit the paragraph that you wrote for the previous Writer's Desk. Ensure that your paragraph has unity, adequate support, and coherence. Also correct any errors in grammar, spelling, punctuation, and mechanics.

REFLECT ON IT

Think about what you have learned in this chapter. If you do not know an answer, review that topic.

1. What is classification? _____

_____

2. What is the classification principle? _____

_____

3. Give examples of various classification principles that you can use to classify the following items.

   EXAMPLE: Cars   _Types of owners, degrees of fuel efficiency, price_

   a. Animals _____

   b. Sports _____

4. Now choose one classification principle for each item in question 3. Write down three possible categories for that item.

   EXAMPLE: Cars

   Classification principle: _Types of owners_ _____

   Categories: _SUV owners, sports car owners, and tiny eco car owners_ _____

   a. Animals

   Classification principle: _____

   Categories: _____

   b. Sports

   Classification principle: _____

   Categories: _____

5. Why is it useful to make a classification chart? _____

_____

The Writer's Room

Topics for Classification Paragraphs

Writing Activity 1

Choose any of the following topics, or choose your own topic. Then write a classification paragraph.

General Topics

Types of . . .

1. parents
2. problems in a relationship
3. friends
4. people who read
5. games
6. greetings

College and Work-Related Topics

Types of . . .

7. campus fashions
8. housing
9. roommates
10. bosses
11. cheating
12. co-workers

WRITING LINK

More Classification Writing Topics

Chapter 21, Writer's Room topic 3 (page 339)

Chapter 24, Writer's Room topic 2 (page 376)

Chapter 35, Writer's Room topic 3 (page 526)

Writing Activity 2

Examine this photo, and think about some classification topics. For example, you might discuss types of risky behavior, dangerous jobs, entertainment involving animals, or culturally specific entertainment. Then write a classification paragraph based on the photo or your related topic.

READING LINK

More Classification Readings

"Fads" by David A. Locher (page 554)

"Dealing with People" by Greg McGrew (page 588)

CLASSIFICATION PARAGRAPH CHECKLIST

As you write your classification paragraph, review the checklist on the inside front cover. Also ask yourself the following questions.

- Does my topic sentence explain the categories that will be discussed?

- Do I use a common classification principle to unite the various items?

- Do I offer sufficient details to explain each category?

- Do I arrange the categories in a logical manner?

- Does all of the supporting information relate to the categories that are being discussed?

- Do I include categories that do not overlap?

How Do I Get a Better Grade?

Visit www.mywritinglab.com for audio-visual lectures and additional practice sets about classification writing. *Get a better grade with MyWritingLab!*

Comparison and Contrast

> *Life is often compared to a marathon, but I think it is more like a sprint; there are long stretches of hard work punctuated by brief moments in which we are given the opportunity to perform at our best.*
>
> —MICHAEL JOHNSON
> *American sprinter (b. 1967)*

Shoppers compare prices in order to make an informed decision. In this chapter, you will practice comparing and contrasting.

Writers' Exchange

Work with a partner. Each of you should discuss your food preferences. Then make a short list showing which food preferences you share and which ones you do not share.

What Is Comparison and Contrast?

When you want to decide between options, you compare and contrast. You **compare** to find similarities and **contrast** to find differences. The exercise of comparing and contrasting can help you make judgments about things. It can also help you better understand familiar things.

You often compare and contrast. At home, when you watch TV, you might compare and contrast different programs. At college, you might compare and contrast different psychological or political theories. On the job, you might need to compare and contrast computer operating systems, shipping services, or sales figures.

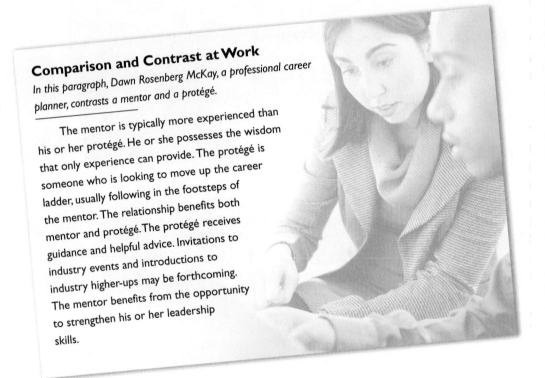

Comparison and Contrast at Work

In this paragraph, Dawn Rosenberg McKay, a professional career planner, contrasts a mentor and a protégé.

The mentor is typically more experienced than his or her protégé. He or she possesses the wisdom that only experience can provide. The protégé is someone who is looking to move up the career ladder, usually following in the footsteps of the mentor. The relationship benefits both mentor and protégé. The protégé receives guidance and helpful advice. Invitations to industry events and introductions to industry higher-ups may be forthcoming. The mentor benefits from the opportunity to strengthen his or her leadership skills.

The Comparison and Contrast Paragraph

In a comparison and contrast paragraph, you can compare and contrast two different subjects, or you can compare and contrast different aspects of a single subject. For example, you might contrast married life and single life, or you might write only about marriage but contrast the expectations people have before they get married versus what realistically happens after marriage.

When you write a comparison or contrast paragraph, remember to think about your specific purpose.

- **Your purpose could be to make judgments about two things.** For example, you might compare and contrast two restaurants in order to convince your readers that one is preferable.

- **Your purpose could be to describe or understand two familiar things.** For example, you might compare two stories to help your readers understand their thematic similarities.

Comparison and Contrast Patterns

Comparison and contrast texts follow two common patterns. One pattern is to present the details point by point. Another is to present one topic and then the other topic.

When you are thinking about ideas for writing a comparison and contrast paragraph, you can choose one of two methods to organize your supporting ideas: point by point or topic by topic.

Point by Point

Present one point about Topic A and then one point about Topic B. Keep following this pattern until you have a few points for each topic. You go back and forth from one side to the other like tennis players hitting a ball back and forth across a net.

Topic by Topic

Present all points related to Topic A in the first few sentences, and then present all points related to Topic B in the last few sentences. So, you present one side and then the other side, just as lawyers might in the closing arguments of a court case.

Kyle's Example

Kyle is trying to decide whether he should take a job in another city or stay at his current job in his hometown. His goal is to decide whether he should move or stay where he is. Kyle could organize his information using a point-by-point or topic-by-topic method.

POINT BY POINT		TOPIC BY TOPIC	
Job A	Low salary	Job A	Low salary
Job B	Good salary		Parents nearby
Job A	Parents nearby		Like my colleagues
Job B	Parents far away		
Job A	Like my colleagues	Job B	Better salary
Job B	Don't know colleagues		Parents far away
			Don't know colleagues

> **ESSAY LINK**
>
> To write a comparison and contrast essay, organize *each paragraph* in point-by-point or topic-by-topic form.

PRACTICE I

Read the next two paragraphs and answer the questions.

A. Fashion is fashion and teen fashion is meant to shock. According to my son, the girls in his school like to wear decorative thongs and let them peek out from over the tops of their low-slung jeans "for all the boys to see in English class." Their T-shirts are tiny, about the size of face cloths. Covering up the back is optional. Oddly, it is my son who finds this style of dressing shocking (among other things). It is not a flattering fashion, for sure, but I dare not complain. In high school, I wore a micro miniskirt, and I am sure the boys could see my panties as I climbed the stairs in front of them. I seldom wore a bra (which bothered a friend's father so much, I was not allowed into her house). So, when my son brings home his first near-naked girlfriend, I will not act shocked; I will merely crack a conspiratorial smile.

—Dorothy Nixon, "Teen Fashion"

1. Underline the topic sentence.

2. What aspects of fashion does the author compare? _____

   _____

3. What pattern of comparison does the author follow? Circle the correct answer.

   a. Point by point   b. Topic by topic

4. What does this paragraph focus on? Circle the correct answer.

   a. Similarities   b. Differences

B. Women's sports lag behind men's in media attention, prize money, and salaries. Some recent comparisons tell the story. The Women's Sport Foundation, a charitable educational organization established in 1974 by Billie Jean King, reports that over 90 percent of all print column inches and hours of televised sports still goes to men's sports. It has only been since 1991 that women's sports received more coverage than horse and dog racing. On the money front, the average prize earnings of the top ten professional male athletes were at least double that of their female counterparts in tennis, bowling, golf, skiing and beach volleyball. There is a huge difference in salaries as well. In professional basketball, the average salary of male players during the 1995–1996 season was 140 times higher than the average salary of female players in the now-**defunct** American Basketball League during its 1996–1997 season. Well, I think you get the picture, and it is not pretty. Now, if we could turn back Father Time and compare the women's games of today to the same developmental period in men's sports, a comparison might seem more legitimate.

—Ellen Zavian, "Men's and Women's Sports? No Comparison!" *USA Today*

defunct:
no longer existing

5. Underline the topic sentence.

6. What does this paragraph compare? _____

   _____

7. What pattern of comparison does the author follow? Circle the best answer.

   a. Point by point   b. Topic by topic

8. What does the author focus on? Circle the correct answer.

   a. Similarities   b. Differences

vo•cab•u•lar•y BOOST

Brainstorming Opposites

Work with a partner, and brainstorm words that have the opposite meaning to the words listed below. Try to come up with as many antonyms (words that have the opposite meaning) as possible.

Example: tiny   *huge, immense, gigantic*

shy   _____

ugly   _____

happy   _____

run   _____

spicy   _____

Explore Topics

In the Warm Up, you will try an exploring strategy to generate ideas about different topics.

The Writer's Desk   Warm Up

Think about the following questions, and write down the first ideas that come to your mind. Try to think of two to three ideas for each topic. Then decide if a good paragraph would be about similarities or differences.

EXAMPLE: What are some key features of two cultural traditions?

My mother's tradition: Diwali	My father's tradition: Hanukkah
festival of lights	*festival of lights*
share gifts with siblings	*light the Menorah*
great desserts	*gold-wrapped chocolates*

My paragraph will focus on __X__ similarities _____ differences

1. What are some stereotypes about your nationality? What is the reality about your nationality?

Stereotypes	Reality
_____	_____
_____	_____
_____	_____

This paragraph will focus on _____ similarities _____ differences.

2. What were your goals when you were a child? What are your goals today?

Goals in childhood	Goals today
_____	_____
_____	_____
_____	_____

This paragraph will focus on _____ similarities _____ differences.

3. Write down the names of two famous or prominent actors, politicians, or music stars. Choose one who is accomplished and respected, and choose another who is less respected. List some interesting characteristics of each person.

Person 1: _____	Person 2: _____
_____	_____
_____	_____
_____	_____

This paragraph will focus on _____ similarities _____ differences.

When you plan your comparison and contrast paragraph, decide whether you want to focus on comparing (looking at similarities), contrasting (looking at differences), or both. In a paragraph, it is usually best to focus on either comparing or contrasting. In a larger essay, you could more easily do both.

ESSAY LINK

In a comparison and contrast essay, the thesis statement expresses the main point of the essay.

DEVELOPING

The Topic Sentence

In a comparison and contrast paragraph, the topic sentence indicates what is being compared and contrasted and expresses a controlling idea.

Although all dogs make good house pets, large dogs are much more useful than small dogs.

Topic: Large dogs versus small dogs
Controlling idea: One is more useful than the other.

PRACTICE 2

Read each topic sentence, and then answer the questions that follow. State whether the paragraph would focus on similarities or differences.

EXAMPLE:

Although coffee and tea can both be caffeinated, tea is a much healthier drink than coffee.

a. What is being compared? *Coffee and tea*

b. What is the controlling idea? *One is healthier than the other.*

c. What will the paragraph focus on? Circle the correct answer.

Similarities   (Differences)

1. Many media pundits complain about reality television; however, reality shows are just as good as regular scripted shows.
   a. What is being compared? _____

   _____

   b. What is the controlling idea? _____

   _____

   c. What will the paragraph focus on? Circle the correct answer.

       Similarities   Differences

2. Before the baby comes, people expect a beautiful world of soft coos and sweet smells, but the reality is quite different.
   a. What is being compared? _____

   _____

   b. What is the controlling idea? _____

   _____

   c. What will the paragraph focus on? Circle the correct answer.

       Similarities   Differences

3. Teenagers are as difficult to raise as toddlers.
   a. What is being compared? _____

   _____

   b. What is the controlling idea? _____

   _____

   c. What will the paragraph focus on? Circle the correct answer.

       Similarities   Differences

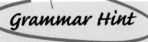 *Grammar Hint*   **Comparing with Adjectives and Adverbs**

When comparing or contrasting two items, ensure that you have correctly written the comparative forms of adjectives and adverbs. For instance, never put *more* with an adjective ending in *-er*.

    Living alone is ~~more~~ quieter than living with a roommate.

If you are comparing two actions, remember to use an adverb instead of an adjective.

                    more quickly
    My roommate cleans ~~quicker~~ than I do.

See Chapter 29 for more information about making comparisons with adjectives and adverbs.

The Writer's Desk Write Topic Sentences

For each topic, write whether you will focus on similarities or differences. Then, write a topic sentence for each one. You can look for ideas in the Writer's Desk Warm Up on pages 141–142. Your topic sentence should include what you are comparing and contrasting, as well as a controlling idea.

> **EXAMPLE:** Topic: Two cultural traditions
>
> Focus: *Similarities*
>
> Topic sentence: *Diwali and Hanukkah have some surprising similarities.*

1. Topic: Stereotypes and reality about my nation

   Focus: _____

   Topic sentence: _____

   _____

2. Topic: Goals in childhood and goals in adulthood

   Focus: _____

   Topic sentence: _____

   _____

3. Topic: Two famous people

   Focus: _____

   Topic sentence: _____

   _____

ESSAY LINK

In a comparison and contrast essay, place the thesis statement in the introduction. Each supporting idea becomes a distinct paragraph with its own topic sentence.

The Supporting Ideas

After you have developed an effective topic sentence, generate supporting ideas. In a comparison and contrast paragraph, think of examples that help clarify the similarities or differences. To generate supporting ideas, you might try using a Venn diagram. In this example, you can see how the writer draws two circles to contrast Diwali and Hanukkah. Where the circles overlap, the writer includes similarities. If you are focusing only on similarities or differences, then you can make two separate circles.

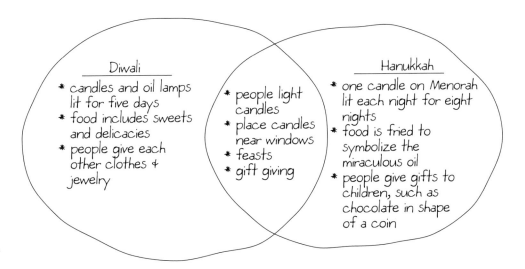

The Paragraph Plan

Before you write a comparison and contrast paragraph, it is a good idea to make a paragraph plan. Decide which pattern you will follow: point by point or topic by topic. "**A**" and "**B**" written alongside your topics can indicate which side they support. Then add supporting details. Make sure that each detail supports the topic sentence.

TOPIC SENTENCE: <u>Diwali and Hanukkah have some surprising similarities.</u>

POINT BY POINT

A/B Both celebrations are festivals of light.
  Details: -People light candles.
  -They place candles near windows.

A/B Both have traditions of feasts.
  Details: -People eat fried sweets for Diwali.
  -Everyone loves fried food for Hanukkah.

A/B Both celebrations include gift giving.
  Details: -In Hanukkah, people give gifts of money to children.
  -In Diwali, people give clothing and jewelry to each other.

TOPIC BY TOPIC

A Diwali is a festival of light.
  Details: -Candles and oil lamps are lit for five days.

A Diwali includes feasts.
  Details: -Food includes sweets and delicacies.

A During one day of the Diwali festival, people give gifts to each other.
  Details: -Clothes and jewelry are given.
  -Children get the most gifts.

B Hanukkah is also a festival of light.
  Details: -Menorah has eight candles.
  -People light one candle each night.

B People have feasts during Hanukkah.
  Details: -Food is fried to symbolize the miraculous oil.

B People give gifts to children during Hanukkah.
  Details: -Gifts usually resemble money such as chocolate in the shape of a coin.

The Writer's Desk **Write a Paragraph Plan**

Write a detailed paragraph plan in a point-by-point or side-by-side pattern. You can refer to the information you generated in previous Writer's Desk exercises. You can use the letters **A** and **B** to indicate which side you are discussing in your plan. Include details about each supporting idea.

Topic sentence: _____

_____

Support 1: _____

Details: _____

_____

Support 2: _____

Details: _____

_____

Support 3: _____

Details: _____

_____

Support 4: _____

Details: _____

_____

Support 5: _____

Details: _____

_____

Support 6: _____

Details: _____

_____

The First Draft

After you outline your ideas in a plan, you are ready to write the first draft. Remember to write complete sentences. You might include transitional words or expressions to help your ideas flow smoothly.

Transitional Words and Expressions

In comparison and contrast paragraphs, there are some transitional words and expressions that you might use to explain either similarities or differences.

To Show Similarities		To Show Differences	
additionally	in addition	conversely	nevertheless
at the same time	in the same way	however	on the contrary
equally	similarly	in contrast	then again

The Writer's Desk Write the First Draft

Write the first draft of your comparison and contrast paragraph. Before you write, carefully review your paragraph plan to see if you have enough support for your points and topics.

REVISING AND EDITING

Revise and Edit a Comparison and Contrast Paragraph

When you finish writing a comparison and contrast paragraph, carefully review your work and revise it to make the comparison or contrast as clear as possible to your readers. Check that you have organized your paragraph logically, and remove any irrelevant details.

PRACTICE 3

Read the following student paragraph and answer the questions.

The Hindu and Jewish faiths have distinct religious celebrations. However, Diwali and Hanukkah have surprising similarities. For Hindus, Diwali is known as the festival of light, and it symbolizes the victory of good over evil. For five nights, celebrators are lighting as many small oil lamps as possible to symbolize hope and the victory of good over evil. Similarly, Hanukkah is a festival of lights, and people light a Menorah containing eight candles or oil lamps, one per night for eight nights. In Hanukkah, the candles celebrate the miracle of an oil lamp found in the Temple, which burned for eight days and nights even though it only had a day's worth of oil in it. Furthermore, both Hindu and Jewish faithful place the lights near windows so that people passing by can see them. Another similarity: feasts. People celebrating Diwali and Hanukkah have special meals. The Diwali feast includes fried sweets and other desserts. In the same way, during Hanukkah, people eat food fried in oil, such as potato pancakes and donuts. Finally, both Hanukkah and Diwali involve gift-giving, with children as the major beneficiaries of the largesse. Hanukkah celebrants give gifts of money or coin-shaped chocolate. During Diwali, children receive gifts of clothing or jewelry, and siblings give gifts to each other. Thus, people of the Jewish and Hindu faiths celebrate some festivals in a similar way.

Revising

1. What is the writer comparing? _____

2. What does the writer focus on?
   a. similarities   b. differences

3. Number the three main arguments.

4. Underline six transitional words or expressions that appear at the beginnings of sentences.

Editing

5. This paragraph contains one fragment, or incomplete sentence. Identify and correct it.

6. Identify and correct one verb-tense error.

GRAMMAR LINK

See the following chapters for more information about these grammer topics:
   Fragments, Chapter 20
   Verb Tenses, Chapter 24

The Writer's Desk Revise and Edit Your Paragraph

Revise and edit the paragraph that you wrote for the previous Writer's Desk. Ensure that your paragraph has unity, adequate support, and coherence. Also correct any errors in grammar, spelling, punctuation, and mechanics.

REFLECT ON IT

Think about what you have learned in this chapter. If you do not know an answer, review that topic.

1. Define the words *comparing* and *contrasting*.

a. Comparing: _____

b. Contrasting: _____

2. Explain the following comparison and contrast patterns.

a. Point by point: _____

_____

b. Topic by topic: _____

_____

 The Writer's Room

Topics for Comparison and Contrast Paragraphs

WRITING LINK

More Comparison and Contrast Writing Topics

Chapter 21, Writer's Room topic 2 (page 339)

Chapter 28, Writer's Room topic 3 (page 434)

Chapter 32, Writer's Room topic 1 (page 490)

Writing Activity 1

Choose any of the following topics, or choose your own topic. Then write a comparison and contrast paragraph.

General Topics

Compare or contrast . . .

1. two types of music
2. people from two different regions
3. your current home and a home that you lived in before
4. expectations about marriage and the reality of marriage
5. real-life heroes and movie heroes
6. a clean person and a messy person

College and Work-Related Topics

Compare or contrast . . .

7. two different types of students
8. high school and college
9. two career options
10. working indoors and working outdoors
11. leaving a child in day care and leaving a child with a family member
12. working mainly with your hands and working mainly with your head

Writing Activity 2

Examine the photos on the following page, and think about things that you could compare and contrast. Some ideas might be two types of fashion, two

READING LINK

More Comparison and Contrast Readings

"Religious Faith Versus Spirituality" by Neil Bissoondath (page 558)

"Body over Mind" by Mitch Albom (page 570)

generations, two youth subcultures, or two types of rebellion. Then write a comparison and contrast paragraph.

1920s flappers

James Dean, 1950s rebel

COMPARISON AND CONTRAST PARAGRAPH CHECKLIST

As you write your comparison and contrast paragraph, review the checklist on the inside front cover. Also ask yourself the following questions.

☐ Does my topic sentence explain what I am comparing and/or contrasting?

☐ Does my topic sentence make a point about the comparison?

☐ Does my paragraph have a point-by-point or topic-by-topic pattern?

☐ Does my paragraph focus on either similarities or differences?

☐ Do all of my supporting examples clearly relate to the topics that I am comparing or contrasting?

How Do I Get a Better Grade?

Visit www.mywritinglab.com for audio-visual lectures and additional practice sets about comparison and contrast writing.

Get a better grade with MyWritingLab!

Cause and Effect

Do not go where the path may lead; go instead where there is no path and leave a trail.

—RALPH WALDO EMERSON
American essayist and poet (1803–1882)

Pollution is a major problem in our world. What causes dirty air, water, and soil? What are the results of a contaminated environment? Cause and effect writing helps to explain the answers to these types of questions.

Writers' Exchange

Your instructor will divide the class into two groups. You should work with a partner or a team of students. Your group will discuss one of the following topics.

Why do people have children?
What are the effects of having children on a person's life?

What Is Cause and Effect?

Cause and effect writing explains why an event happened or what the consequences of such an event were. A cause and effect paragraph can focus on causes, effects, or both.

You often analyze the causes or effects of something. At home, you may worry about what causes your siblings or your own children to behave in a certain manner, or you may wonder about the effects of certain foods on your health. In a U.S. history course, you might analyze the causes of the Civil War, or you might write about the effects of industrialization on American society. At work, you may wonder about the causes or effects of a promotion or a pay cut.

Cause and Effect at Work

In this memo from the file of a fourth-grade student, early childhood educator Luisa Suarez explains some causes and effects of the child's behavioral and learning problems.

Mark frequently expresses his dislike of school and reading. He continues to read at a second-grade level and is behind his classmates in the acquisition of knowledge expected from fourth-grade students. In interviews with the child, he has stated that he never reads at home and spends most of his time watching television. Because he is so far behind his peers in the classroom, he is embarrassed to show his lack of reading skills for fear of ridicule. It is easier for him to "act out," thus distracting others from his deficiency in reading. He displays a low level of self-confidence and appears to have given up trying.

The Cause and Effect Paragraph

When you write a cause and effect paragraph, focus on two main points.

1. **Indicate whether you are focusing on causes, effects, or both.** Because a paragraph is not very long, it is often easier to focus on either causes or effects. If you do decide to focus on both causes and effects, make sure that your topic sentence announces your purpose to the reader.

2. **Ensure that your causes and effects are valid.** Determine real causes and effects and do not simply list things that happened before or after the event. Also verify that your assumptions are logical.

Illogical: The product does not work because it is inexpensive.

(This statement is illogical; quality is not always dictated by price.)

Better: The product does not work because it is constructed with poor-quality materials.

PRACTICE I

Read the following paragraph and answer the questions.

When I played football, I learned to be an animal. Being an animal meant being fanatically aggressive and ruthlessly competitive. If I saw an arm in front of me, I trampled it. Whenever blood was spilled, I nodded approval. Broken bones (not mine of course) were secretly seen as little victories within the bigger struggle. The coaches taught me to "punish the other man," but little did I suspect that I was devastating my own body at the same time. There were broken noses, ribs, fingers, toes and teeth, torn muscles and ligaments, bruises, bad knees, and busted lips, and the gradual pulverizing of my spinal column that, by the time my jock career was long over at age 30, had resulted in seven years of near-constant pain. It was a long road to the surgeon's office.

—Don Sabo, "Pigskin, Patriarch, and Pain"

1. Underline the topic sentence.

2. What does this paragraph focus on? Circle the best answer.

   a. Causes   b. Effects

3. Who is the audience? _____

4. List the supporting details.

   _____

   _____

   _____

   _____

   _____

Explore Topics

In the Warm Up, you will try an exploring strategy to generate ideas about different topics.

Imagine that you had to write a cause and effect paragraph about employee absenteeism. You might brainstorm and think of as many causes and effects as possible.

Causes
- Child is sick
- Employee is sick
- Personal problems such as marital strife, depression
- Lack of motivation

Employee absenteeism

Effects
- Other employees do more
- May lose job
- Could get demoted
- Develop financial problems

 **Grammar Hint** **Do Not Confuse *Effect* and *Affect***

Generally, *affect* is used as a verb, and *effect* is used as a noun. *Affect* (verb) means "to influence or change" and *effect* (noun) means "the result."

verb
How will your new job <u>affect</u> your family?

noun
What <u>effect</u> will moving to a new city have on your spouse's career?

Effect can also be used as a verb that means "to cause or to bring about." It is generally used in the following phrases: "to effect a change" or "to effect a plan."

The union members demonstrated to <u>effect</u> changes in their working conditions.

The Writer's Desk Warm Up

Write some possible causes and effects for the following topics. Then decide if your paragraph will focus on causes or effects.

EXAMPLE: smoke-free work zones

Causes	Effects
workers complain about smoke	*employees smoke in entrances*
new legislation	*cigarette litter outside building*
lobby groups asking for smoke-free zones	*smokers influence non-smokers*
lack of ventilation in offices	*smokers take long breaks*

Focus on: _____ *Effects*

1. cheating

Causes	Effects
_____	_____
_____	_____
_____	_____
_____	_____

Focus on: _____

2. popularity of fast food

Causes	Effects
_____	_____
_____	_____
_____	_____
_____	_____

Focus on: _____

3. teenage rebellion

Causes	Effects
_____	_____
_____	_____
_____	_____
_____	_____

Focus on: _____

DEVELOPING

The Topic Sentence

The topic sentence in a cause and effect paragraph must clearly demonstrate whether the focus is on causes, effects, or both. Also, make sure that you have clearly indicated your controlling idea. For example, read the topic sentences. Notice that the controlling ideas are underlined.

ESSAY LINK

In a cause and effect essay, the thesis statement expresses whether the essay will focus on causes, effects, or both.

topic   controlling idea (causes)

The Civil War was fought for many reasons.

topic   controlling idea (effects)

The Civil War changed the values of American society in a profound way.

topic   controlling idea (causes and effects)

The Civil War, which was fought for many reasons, changed the values of American society in a profound way.

PRACTICE 2

Carefully read the following topic sentences. Decide whether each sentence focuses on causes, effects, or both. Look for key words that give you clues. Circle the best answer.

1. People become homeless due to difficult life circumstances.
   a. Causes   b. Effects   c. Both

2. Homeless people must deal with difficult situations in their day-to-day lives.
   a. Causes   b. Effects   c. Both

3. Because of many problems at the Chernobyl nuclear site, the environment in Ukraine has changed forever.
   a. Causes   b. Effects   c. Both

4. Scientists have proposed many theories that explain the disappearance of the dinosaurs.
   a. Causes   b. Effects   c. Both

---

vo•cab•u•lar•y BOOST

Using your thesaurus, come up with three synonyms for *cause* and three synonyms for *effect*.

The Writer's Desk Write Topic Sentences

Write a topic sentence for each of the following topics. You can look for ideas in the Writer's Desk Warm Up on pages 154–155. Determine whether you will focus on the causes, effects, or both in your paragraph.

EXAMPLE: Topic: Smoke-free work zones

Topic sentence: *Smoke-free work zones, implemented for obvious reasons, have had surprising consequences for employees.*

1. Topic: Cheating

   Topic sentence: _____

   _____

2. Topic: Popularity of fast food

   Topic sentence: _____

   _____

3. Topic: Teenage rebellion

   Topic sentence: _____

   _____

The Supporting Ideas

After you have developed an effective topic sentence, generate supporting ideas. When planning a cause and effect paragraph, think of examples that clearly show the causes or effects. Then arrange your examples in emphatic order. **Emphatic order** means that you can place your examples from the most to the least important or from the least to the most important.

Hint **Do Not Oversimplify**

Avoid attributing a simple or general cause to a complex issue. When you use expressions such as *it appears that* or *a possible cause is*, you show that you are aware of the complex factors involved in the situation.

Oversimplification:	The high murder rate in cities is caused by easily obtained firearms.
	(This is an oversimplification of a complicated problem.)
Better:	A possible cause of the high murder rate in cities is the abundance of easily obtained firearms.

The Writer's Desk Generate Supporting Ideas

Choose one of the topic sentences from the Writer's Desk on the previous page. Then list either causes or effects.

EXAMPLE: Topic sentence: *Smoke-free work zones, implemented for obvious reasons, have had surprising consequences for employees.*

Supports: *polluted entrances of buildings*

smokers need long breaks

smokers influence nonsmokers

Topic sentence: _____

_____

Supports: _____

_____

_____

_____

ESSAY LINK

In a cause and effect essay, place the thesis statement in the introduction. Then use body paragraphs, each with its own topic sentence, to support the thesis statement.

The Paragraph Plan

In many courses, instructors ask students to write about the causes or effects of a particular subject. Plan your paragraph before you write your final version. Also think about the order of ideas. Arrange the supporting details in a logical order. As you make your plan, ensure that you focus on causes, effects, or both.

TOPIC SENTENCE: Smoke-free work zones, implemented for obvious reasons, have had surprising consequences for employees.

Support 1:   Smokers stand at entrances to have their cigarettes.
  Details: —drop their cigarette butts on the ground
           —heavy smoke at the entrances
Support 2:   Smokers take more breaks.
  Details: —need frequent cigarette breaks
           —not fair to others who must do extra work
Support 3:   Smoking culture influences nonsmokers.
  Details: —nonsmokers take breaks with their smoking friends
           —some nonsmokers become smokers

The Writer's Desk **Write a Paragraph Plan**

Refer to the information you generated in previous Writer's Desk exercises and create a paragraph plan. If you think of new details that will explain your point more effectively, include them here.

Topic sentence: _____

_____

Support 1: _____

  Details: _____

_____

_____

Support 2: _____

  Details: _____

_____

_____

Support 3: _____

  Details: _____

_____

_____

The First Draft

After you outline your ideas in a plan, you are ready to write the first draft. Remember to write complete sentences. You might include transitional words or expressions to help your ideas flow smoothly.

Transitional Words and Expressions

The following transitional expressions are useful for showing causes and effects.

To Show Causes	To Show Effects
for this reason	accordingly
the first cause	as a result
the most important cause	consequently

The Writer's Desk Write the First Draft

Write the first draft of your cause and effect paragraph. Before you write, carefully review your paragraph plan and make any necessary changes.

REVISING AND EDITING

Revise and Edit a Cause and Effect Paragraph

When you finish writing a cause and effect paragraph, review your work and revise it to make the examples as clear as possible to your readers. Make sure that your sentences relate to the topic sentence and flow together smoothly.

PRACTICE 3

Read the next student paragraph and answer the questions.

> Smoke-free work zones, implemented for obvious reasons, have had
>
> surprising consequences for employees. First, smokers light up outside
>
> the main entrances of buildings, and nonsmokers must pass through a
>
> cloud of heavy smoke to get inside. Additionally, the ground outside
>
> entrances is littered with cigarette butts, which smokers do not consider

as pollution. Moreover, smokers get more breaks because they frequently leave their workstations to have cigarettes. Some people smoke cigars, and others smoke pipes. The nonsmokers must work more harder to cover for their smoking colleagues, and this makes the nonsmokers resentful. An other surprising consequence is that the smoking culture influences nonsmokers. Former smokers, or those who have never smoked, sometimes get into the habit of smoking in order to socialize with their colleagues during the many breaks. Although no-smoking rules are in the public interest, the consequences of such rules should be examined more thoroughly.

Revising

1. Does the paragraph focus on causes, effects, or both? _____

2. List the causes or effects given. _____

_____

_____

_____

3. There is one sentence in the paragraph that does not relate to the topic sentence. Cross out that sentence.

Editing

4. There is one error with the comparative form. An adverb is incorrectly formed. Correct the error directly on the text.

5. This paragraph contains two misspelled words. Identify and correct them.

GRAMMAR LINK

See the following chapters for more information about these grammar topics:

   Adjectives and Adverbs, Chapter 29
   Spelling, Chapter 32

The Writer's Desk **Revise and Edit Your Paragraph**

Revise and edit the paragraph that you wrote for the previous Writer's Desk. Ensure that your paragraph has unity, adequate support, and coherence. Also correct any errors in grammar, spelling, punctuation, and mechanics.

REFLECT ON IT

Think about what you have learned in this chapter. If you do not know an answer, review that topic.

1. What is the difference between the words *affect* and *effect*?

   Affect: _____

   Effect: _____

2. Brainstorm to think of three possible causes for each option.

   a. Starting to smoke _____

   _____

   b. A car crash _____

   _____

3. Brainstorm to think of three possible effects for each option.

   a. Pollution: _____

   _____

   b. War: _____

   _____

 *The Writer's Room*   **Topics for Cause and Effect Paragraphs**

Writing Activity 1

Choose any of the following topics, or choose your own topic. Then write a cause and effect paragraph.

General Topics

Causes and/or effects of . . .

1. having a close friendship
2. having a caffeine addiction
3. getting a higher education
4. having a poor body image
5. spoiling a child
6. seeing a therapist

College and Work-Related Topics

Causes and/or effects of . . .

7. having low (or high) marks in college
8. not keeping up with college workload
9. skipping classes
10. working with a family member
11. working at home
12. getting a promotion

WRITING LINK

More Cause and Effect Writing Topics
Chapter 19, Writer's Room topic 2 (page 316)
Chapter 26, Writer's Room topic 3 (page 397)
Chapter 35, Writer's Room topic 2 (page 526)

READING LINK

More Cause and Effect Readings

"Growing Up in Cyberspace" by Brent Staples (page 566)

"Dying to Be Bigger" by H.D. (page 573)

Writing Activity 2

Think about a day when you felt frustrated. What causes you to feel like screaming? What are the effects when you scream at someone or when someone screams at you? Write a paragraph about the causes or effects of screaming.

 CAUSE AND EFFECT PARAGRAPH CHECKLIST

As you write your cause and effect paragraph, review the checklist on the inside front cover. Also ask yourself the following questions.

- Does my topic sentence indicate clearly that my paragraph focuses on causes, effects, or both?

- Do I have adequate supporting examples of causes and/or effects?

- Do I make logical and valid points?

- Do I use the terms *effect* and/or *affect* correctly?

How Do I Get a Better Grade?

 Visit www.mywritinglab.com for audio-visual lectures and additional practice sets about cause and effect writing. *Get a better grade with MyWritingLab!*

Argument

> *Do not fear to be eccentric in opinion, for every opinion now accepted was once eccentric.*
>
> — BERTRAND RUSSELL
> *British author and philosopher (1872–1970)*

CONTENTS

Lawyers have to make effective arguments to persuade a judge and jury. In argument writing, you try to convince readers to agree with your point of view.

Writers' Exchange

For this activity, you and a partner will take turns debating an issue. To start, choose which one of you will begin speaking. The first speaker chooses one side of any issue listed below, and then argues about that issue, without stopping, for a set amount of time. Your instructor will signal when to switch sides. After the signal, the second speaker talks nonstop about the other side of the debate. If you run out of ideas, you can switch topics when it is your turn to speak.

Possible topics:

Dogs are better than cats.	Cats are better than dogs.
It's better to be married.	It's better to be single.
Life is easier for men.	Life is easier for women.

What Is Argument?

When you use **argument,** you take a position on an issue and try to defend your position. You try to convince somebody that your point of view is the best one.

Argument is both a writing pattern and a purpose for writing. In fact, it is one of the most common aims or purposes in most college and work-related writing. For example, in Chapter 10, there is a paragraph about teen fashion, and the author uses comparison and contrast as the predominant pattern. At the same time, the author uses argument to convince the reader that fashions have not become more shocking over the years. Therefore, in most of your college and work-related writing, your purpose is to persuade the reader that your ideas are compelling and valid.

You use argument every day. You might write a persuasive letter to a newspaper to express your views about public policy. At college, in a sociology class, you might take a position on capital punishment or on gun control. At work, you might have to convince your manager to give you a raise.

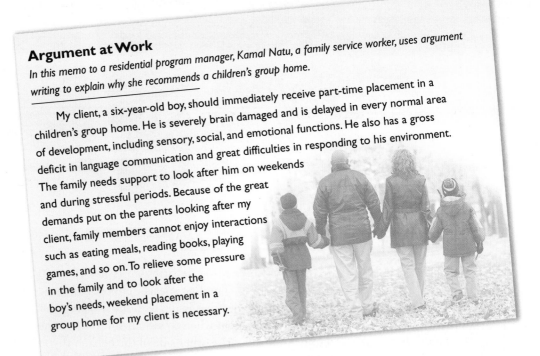

Argument at Work

In this memo to a residential program manager, Kamal Natu, a family service worker, uses argument writing to explain why she recommends a children's group home.

My client, a six-year-old boy, should immediately receive part-time placement in a children's group home. He is severely brain damaged and is delayed in every normal area of development, including sensory, social, and emotional functions. He also has a gross deficit in language communication and great difficulties in responding to his environment. The family needs support to look after him on weekends and during stressful periods. Because of the great demands put on the parents looking after my client, family members cannot enjoy interactions such as eating meals, reading books, playing games, and so on. To relieve some pressure in the family and to look after the boy's needs, weekend placement in a group home for my client is necessary.

The Argument Paragraph

ESSAY LINK

When you write argument essays, also keep these four points in mind.

When you write an argument paragraph, remember the following four points.

- **Choose a subject that you know something about.** It would be very difficult to write a good text about space research funds, capital punishment, or conditions in federal prisons, for example, if you have never had experience with, or read about, these issues. On the other hand, if you, or someone close to you, cannot find good day care, then you could likely write a very effective paragraph about the necessity of having better day-care services.

- **Consider your readers.** What do your readers already know about the topic? Will they likely agree or disagree with you? Do they have specific concerns? Consider what kind of evidence would be most effective with your audience.

- **Know your purpose.** In argument writing, your main purpose is to persuade the reader to agree with you. Your specific purpose is more focused. You may want the reader to take action, you may want to support a viewpoint, you may want to counter somebody else's argument, or you may want to offer a solution to a problem. Ask yourself what your specific purpose is.

- **Take a strong position and provide supporting evidence.** The first thing to do in the body of your paragraph is to prove that there is, indeed, a problem. Then back up your point of view with a combination of facts, statistics, examples, and informed opinions.

 **Be Passionate!**

When you are planning your argument paragraph, try to find a topic that you feel passionate about. If you care about your topic, and if you express your enthusiasm, your audience will be more likely to care about it, too.

PRACTICE I

Read the next paragraph and answer the questions.

Ordinary families would benefit greatly from a plan that provided health insurance to those now uninsured. It is true that at any given moment most middle-income families have insurance, but people lose their jobs, companies go bankrupt, and benefits get suddenly slashed. Over any given two-year period, roughly a third of Americans spend some time without health insurance; over longer periods, the risk of losing health insurance is very significant for most families. When a family without health insurance suffers illness, the results are often catastrophic—either serious conditions go untreated or the family faces financial ruin. Our inadequate insurance system is one important reason why America, the richest country in the world, has lower life expectancy and higher child mortality than most other advanced nations. If American families knew what was good for them, then most of them—all but a small, affluent minority—would cheerfully give up any tax cuts in return for a guarantee that health care would be there when needed. And even the affluent might prefer to live in a society where no sick child was left behind.

—Paul Krugman, *New York Times* editorial

1. Underline the topic sentence.

2. Who is the author's audience? _____

3. What is the author's specific purpose? _____

_____

_____

4. What health-care issues might concern the audience?

_____

_____

_____

_____

5. Underline some examples that the author gives to show that there is a problem.

6. Look at the author's supporting evidence, and circle a statistic.

Explore Topics

In the Warm Up, you will try an exploring strategy to generate ideas about different topics.

The Writer's Desk Warm Up

Think about the following questions, and write down the first ideas that come to mind. Try to think of two or three ideas for each topic.

EXAMPLE: Should officials place more speed bumps on city streets?

Yes, I think so. Then speeding cars would have to slow down. Kids often play on the streets. Speeding cars are dangerous for kids who often play on the streets. Of course, speed bumps may create traffic jams. But in the long term, I think speed bumps are necessary.

1. Sometimes minors steal, vandalize, go joyriding, and do other illegal acts. Should parents be required to pay for damages when their children break the law?

_____

_____

_____

2. In some countries, all youths must do two years of military service. What do you think about compulsory military service?

_____

_____

_____

3. What are some of the major controversial issues in your neighborhood, at your workplace, at your college, or in the news these days?

_____

_____

_____

DEVELOPING

The Topic Sentence

In the topic sentence of an argument paragraph, state your position on the issue. In the following topic sentence, notice that the controlling idea has been underlined.

controlling idea   topic

<u>Our government should severely punish</u> **corporate executives who commit fraud.**

Your topic sentence should be a debatable statement. It should not be a fact or a statement of opinion.

Fact: In some public schools, students wear uniforms.

(This is a fact. It cannot be debated.)

Opinion: I think that it is a good idea for public school students to wear uniforms.

(This is a statement of opinion. Nobody can deny that you like school uniforms. Therefore, do not use phrases such as *In my opinion, I think,* or *I believe* in your topic sentence.)

Argument: Public school students should wear uniforms.

(This is a debatable statement.)

PRACTICE 2

Evaluate the following statements. Write *F* for a fact, *O* for an opinion, or *A* for a debatable argument.

1. I think that competitive sports are unhealthy.   _____

2. The legal driving age is too low in Florida.   _____

3. Greedy athletes have hurt professional sports.   _____

4. In most states, the legal drinking age is twenty-one.   _____

5. In my opinion, some college students drink too much. _____

6. Some students engage in binge drinking on our college campus. _____

7. The proposed "No Binge Drinking" campaign should be scrapped because underage drinking is not a serious problem in our college. _____

8. I believe that most students are responsible and do not abuse alcohol. _____

 Be Direct

You may feel reluctant to state your point of view directly. You may feel that it is impolite to do so. However, in academic writing, it is perfectly acceptable, and even desirable, to state an argument in a direct manner.

In argument writing, you can make your topic debatable by using *should, must,* or *ought to* in the topic sentence or thesis statement.

Although daily prayer is important for many people in the United States, it **should** not take place in the classroom.

The Writer's Desk **Write Topic Sentences**

Write a topic sentence for the following topics. You can look for ideas in the previous Writer's Desk Warm Up. Make sure that each topic sentence clearly expresses your position on the issue.

EXAMPLE:

Topic: More speed bumps on city streets

Topic sentence: *With the increased traffic flow in the community, speed bumps should be put in place to decrease the number of speeders and increase public safety.*

1. Topic: Parents paying for children's crime sprees

   Topic sentence: _____

   _____

2. Topic: Compulsory military service

   Topic sentence: _____

   _____

3. Topic: A controversial issue in your neighborhood, at work, at college, or in the news

   Topic sentence: _____

   _____

The Supporting Ideas

When you write an argument paragraph, it is important to support your point of view with examples, facts, statistics, and informed opinions. It is also effective to think about some answers you can give to counter the opposition's point of view, and you can consider the long-term consequences if something does not occur. Therefore, try to use several types of supporting evidence.

ESSAY LINK

In an argument essay, body paragraphs should contain supporting details such as examples, facts, informed opinions, logical consequences, or answers to the opposition.

- **Examples** are pieces of information that illustrate your main argument. For instance, if you want to argue that there are not enough day-care centers in your area, you can explain that one center has over one hundred children on its waiting list.

   Another type of example is the **anecdote.** To support your main point, you can write about a true event or tell a personal story. For example, if you think that rebellious teenagers hurt their families, you might tell a personal story about your brother's involvement with a gang.

- **Facts** are statements that can be verified in some way. For example, the following statement is a fact: "According to the World Health Organization, secondhand smoke can cause cancer in nonsmokers." **Statistics** are another type of fact. When you use statistics, ensure that the source is reliable, and remember to mention the source. For example, if you want to argue that underage drinking is a problem, you could mention the following statistic from the *Journal of the American Medical Association:* "Underage drinkers consume about 20 percent of all the alcohol imbibed in this country."

- Sometimes experts in a field express an **informed opinion** about an issue. An expert's opinion can give added weight to your argument. For example, if you want to argue that the courts treat youths who commit crimes too harshly or leniently, then you might quote a judge who deals with juvenile criminals. If you want to argue that secondhand smoke is dangerous, then you might quote a lung specialist or a health organization.

- Solutions to problems can carry **logical consequences.** When you plan an argument, think about long-term consequences if something does or does not happen. For example, in response to the terrorist attacks of September 11, 2001, many governments enacted antiterrorism legislation. However, in some cases, the new laws could be used to suppress legitimate dissent or free speech. Also, those new laws could be misused or misinterpreted by future governments.

- In argument writing, try to **answer the opposition.** For example, if you want to argue that drinking laws are ineffective, you might think about the arguments that your opposition might make. Then you might write, "Drinking age laws do a fine job of keeping young people out of clubs and bars; however, these laws do nothing to keep young people from getting access to alcohol from other places." Try to refute some of the strongest arguments of the opposition.

 Avoid Circular Reasoning

When you write an argument paragraph, ensure that your main point is supported with facts, examples, informed opinions, and so on. Do not use circular reasoning. Circular reasoning means that you restate your main point in various ways.

Circular	The abundance of spam is not harmless; in fact, a lot of junk e-mail is offensive. People receive many copies of junk mail and the content offends them. Most people complain when they receive too much junk e-mail, and they feel especially unhappy when the junk e-mail has offensive images.
Not Circular	The abundance of spam is not harmless; in fact, a lot of junk e-mail is offensive. According to Odin Wortman of Internet Working Solutions, about 30 percent of unwanted e-mail is pornographic. Children and older people open such mail hoping for a message from a friend, only to see an offensive picture. Another 30 percent of junk mail advertises fraudulent schemes to get rich quickly and hawks products of questionable value or safety.

PRACTICE 3

You have learned about different methods to support a topic. Read each of the following topic sentences and think of a supporting reason for each item. Use the type of support suggested in parentheses.

1. Boys should be encouraged to express their emotions.

   (Logical Consequence) _____

   _____

   _____

2. Unleashed dogs should not be allowed on public streets.

    (Example) _____

    _____

    _____

3. The attendance policy at this college is (or is not) effective.

    (Fact) _____

    _____

    _____

4. Teen magazines should not show ads with extremely thin models.

    (Logical Consequence) _____

    _____

    _____

5. When a couple goes on a date, the person who earns the most money
    should always pay the bill.

    (Answer the opposition.) _____

    _____

    _____

READING LINK

For more information about avoiding plagiarism and evaluating and documenting sources, refer to Chapter 15, "Enhancing Your Writing with Research."

 Hint   **Using Research**

You can enhance your argument essay with **research** by including information from an informed source. You can look for information in textbooks, newspapers, magazines, and on the Internet.

When you use the Internet for research, make sure that your sources are from legitimate organizations or from reputable magazines, newspapers, or government sites. For example, for information about the spread of AIDS, you might find statistics on the World Health Organization's Web site. You would not go to someone's personal rant or conspiracy theory site.

Consider Both Sides of the Issue

Once you have decided what to write about, try to think about both sides of the issue. Then you can predict arguments that your opponents might make, and you can plan your answer to the opposition.

EXAMPLE: Speed bumps

For	**Against**
—slows down speeders	—slows down emergency vehicles
—increases safety in residential neighborhoods	—increases noise from braking cars
—children will be able to play freely without being hit by a speeding car	—increases wear and tear on a car
—may reduce traffic accidents	—may increase traffic jams
—may discourage heavy traffic in residential neighborhoods	—may cause some drivers back pain

The Writer's Desk Consider Both Sides of the Issue

Write arguments for and against each of the following topics.

1. Parents paying for children's crimes

   For   **Against**

   _____   _____

   _____   _____

   _____   _____

   _____   _____

2. Compulsory military service

   For   **Against**

   _____   _____

   _____   _____

   _____   _____

   _____   _____

3. A controversial issue: _____

   For   **Against**

   _____   _____

   _____   _____

   _____   _____

   _____   _____

Avoid Common Errors

When you write an argument paragraph or essay, avoid the following pitfalls.

Do not make generalizations. If you begin a statement with *Everyone knows* or *It is common knowledge*, then the reader may mistrust what you say. You cannot possibly know what everyone else knows. It is better to refer to specific sources.

Generalization:	Everyone knows that sending troops to Iraq was necessary.
Better:	Prominent politicians such as Donald Rumsfeld stated that sending troops to Iraq was necessary.

Use emotional arguments sparingly. Certainly, the strongest arguments can be emotional ones. Sometimes the most effective way to influence others is to appeal to their sense of justice, humanity, pride, or guilt. However, do not rely on emotional arguments. If you use emotionally charged words (for example, if you call someone *ignorant*) or if you try to appeal to base instincts (for example, if you appeal to people's fear of other ethnic groups), then you will seriously undermine your argument.

Emotional:	Bleeding-heart liberals did not want the United States to send troops to Iraq.
Better:	Many sectors of society, including several student activists, actors, educators, and business groups, did not want the United States to send troops to Iraq.

Do not make exaggerated claims. Make sure that your arguments are plausible.

Exaggerated:	If military forces had not captured Iraq's leader, Saddam Hussein, eventually the United States would have been destroyed.
Better:	If military forces had not captured Saddam Hussein, the tyrant would have continued to terrorize his people.

---

vo•cab•u•lar•y BOOST

Looking at Associated Meanings

Some words have neutral, positive, or negative associations. With a partner, try to find the most neutral word in each list. Categorize the other words as positive or negative.

1. macho, jerk, hunk, lout, hottie, man, stud, sweetheart, bully
2. large boned, shapely, plump, fat, big, monstrous, heavy, muscular, curvy
3. nation, homeland, refuge, kingdom, fatherland, country, motherland, axis of evil
4. childish, young, immature, innocent, naïve, gullible, inexperienced, youthful, pure
5. freedom fighter, terrorist, anarchist, believer, radical, fanatic, revolutionary, rebel, soldier, activist

---

The Paragraph Plan

Before you write your argument paragraph, make a plan. Think of some supporting arguments, and think about details that can help illustrate each argument. Ensure that every example is valid and that it relates to the topic sentence. Also, arrange your ideas in a logical order.

TOPIC SENTENCE:	With the increased traffic flow in Swan Creek, speed bumps should be put in place to decrease the number of speeders and to increase public safety.
Support 1:	By placing speed bumps evenly throughout the community, pedestrians will not have to worry about being hit by cars.
Details:	—Often children play sports on streets. —Sometimes people cross the street without looking both ways.
Support 2:	Speed bumps can help unify a community.
Details:	—A community can petition the city to put speed bumps on certain streets. —Neighbors form friendships based on a common cause.
Support 3:	Speed bumps may reduce traffic accidents.
Details:	—Traffic accidents are often caused by excess speed. —Some drivers have no regard for the speed limits.

The Writer's Desk **Write a Paragraph Plan**

Choose one of the topic sentences that you wrote for the Writer's Desk on page 168, and write a detailed paragraph plan. You can refer to the information you generated in previous Writer's Desk exercises, and if you think of examples that will explain your point more effectively, include them here.

Subject: _____

Topic sentence: _____

_____

Support 1: _____

Details: _____

_____

_____

Support 2: _____

Details: _____

_____

_____

Support 3: _____

Details: _____

_____

_____

The First Draft

After you outline your ideas in a plan, you are ready to write the first draft. Remember to write complete sentences. You might include transitional words or expressions to help your ideas flow smoothly.

Transitional Words and Expressions

The following transitional words and expressions can introduce an answer to the opposition or the support for an argument.

To Answer the Opposition	To Support Your Argument
admittedly	certainly
however	consequently
nevertheless	furthermore
of course	in fact
on one hand/on the other hand	obviously
undoubtedly	of course

The Writer's Desk **Write the First Draft**

Write the first draft of your argument paragraph. Before you write, carefully review your paragraph plan and make any necessary changes.

REVISING AND EDITING

Revise and Edit an Argument Paragraph

When you finish writing an argument paragraph, carefully review your work and revise it to make the supporting examples as clear as possible to your readers. Check that the order of ideas is logical, and remove any irrelevant details.

PRACTICE 4

College student Craig Susanowitz wrote the following paragraph. Read the paragraph and answer the questions.

> With the increased traffic flow in Swan Creek, speed bumps should be put in place to decrease the number of speeders and to increase public safety. Of course, some people argue that speed bumps increase the wear and tear on a car, cause drivers back pain, and increase traffic jams. But such arguments are idiotic when it comes to public safety. By constructing speed bumps in residential neighborhoods, pedestrians will not have to worry about being hit by speeding cars. Often, in such residential areas, children play sports on the street. As children, my friends and I often played street hockey on roller blades. We wondered why did cars screech to a stop near us. It was a bit scary. In addition, children as well as adults sometimes cross the street without paying attention to the traffic. If a car is going over the speed limit, it may not be able to stop in time if a pedestrian steps into traffic. Next, speed bumps can help unify a community. Neighbors can petition city officials to put speed bumps on certain streets. Being involved in such a worthwhile cause can bring strangers together in a community spirit. Furthermore, speed bumps will prevent car accidents. Traffic accidents are often caused by excess speed because drivers do not have enough time to react to surprises on the road. Many dudes are in a hurry and have no regard for the posted 25 m.p.h. speed limit. So, in closing, speed bumps should be implemented in Swan Creek to ensure the safety of our community's residents.

Revising

1. Underline the topic sentence.

2. The writer uses an emotionally charged word. Find and replace the word with a more appropriate word.

Emotionally charged word: _____

Replacement: _____

3. List three arguments that support the topic sentence.

_____

_____

_____

4. The writer also acknowledges the opposition. List the arguments he acknowledges.

_____

Editing

5. Find a slang word and substitute it with a standard English word.

Slang: _____   Standard English: _____

6. This paragraph contains a dangling modifier. The modifier has no subject. Underline the error and write the correct sentence below.

_____

_____

7. This paragraph contains an embedded question error. Underline the error and write the correct phrase below.

_____

> ### GRAMMAR LINK
>
> See the following chapters for more information about these grammar topics:
>   Slang versus standard
>   English, Chapter 31
>   Dangling modifiers, Chapter 30
>   Embedded questions, Chapter 18

Grammar Hint   **Using Embedded Questions**

When you embed a question inside a larger sentence, you do not need to use the question word order. Ensure that your embedded questions are correctly written.

our nation doesn't have
People wonder why ~~doesn't our nation have~~ universal health care.

The Writer's Desk Revise and Edit Your Paragraph

Revise and edit the paragraph that you wrote for the previous Writer's Desk. Ensure that your paragraph has unity, adequate support, and coherence. Also correct any errors in grammar, spelling, punctuation, and mechanics.

REFLECT ON IT

Think about what you have learned in this chapter. If you do not know an answer, review that topic.

1. What is the main purpose of an argument paragraph or essay?

   _____

2. What is the difference between a statement of opinion and a statement of argument?

   _____

   _____

3. What five types of supporting evidence can you use in argument writing?

   _____   _____

   _____   _____

   _____

4. In argument writing, you should avoid circular reasoning. What is circular reasoning?

   _____

   _____

5. Why is it important to avoid using emotionally charged words?

   _____

   _____

WRITING LINK

More Argument Writing Topics

Chapter 19, Writer's Room topic 4 (page 316)

Chapter 21, Writer's Room topic 3 (page 339)

Chapter 24, Writer's Room topic 3 (page 376)

Chapter 26, Writer's Room topic 4 (page 397)

Chapter 28, Writer's Room topic 4 (page 434)

Chapter 30, Writer's Room topics 3–4 (page 461)

Chapter 32, Writer's Room topics 2–3 (page 490)

 *The Writer's Room*

Topics for Argument Paragraphs

Writing Activity 1

Choose any of the following topics, or choose your own topic. Then write an argument paragraph. Remember to narrow your topic and to follow the writing process.

General Topics

1. fame
2. the voting age
3. disciplining children
4. chat room relationships
5. alternative medical therapies
6. home schooling

College and Work-Related Topics

7. drug testing
8. value of a college education
9. compulsory physical education in college
10. longer vacations for workers
11. office relationships
12. labor unions

Writing Activity 2

Examine the photo, and think about arguments that you might make about marriage. For example, you might argue about the high cost of weddings, the best type of wedding, why people should or should not marry, or the benefits of premarital counseling. Then write an argument paragraph.

READING LINK

More Argument Readings

"Nothing But Net" by Mark McFadden (page 564)

"It's Class, Stupid!" by Richard Rodriguez (page 577)

✔ ARGUMENT PARAGRAPH CHECKLIST

As you write your argument paragraph, review the checklist on the inside front cover. Also ask yourself the following questions.

Does my topic sentence clearly state my position on the issue?

Do I make strong supporting arguments?

Do I include facts, examples, statistics, logical consequences, or answers to the opposition?

Do my supporting arguments provide evidence that directly supports the topic sentence?

How Do I Get a Better Grade?

Visit www.mywritinglab.com for audio-visual lectures and additional practice sets about argument writing. **Get a better grade with MyWritingLab!**

The Essay

Each body paragraph begins with a topic sentence.

The introductory paragraph introduces the essay's topic and contains its thesis statement.

The title gives a hint about the essay's topic.

The thesis statement contains the essay's topic and its controlling idea.

What Is an Essay?

An *essay* is a series of paragraphs that support one main or central idea. Essays differ in length, style, and subject, but the structure of an essay generally consists of an *introductory paragraph,* several *body paragraphs,* and a *concluding paragraph.*

Before you begin reading the following chapters, become familiar with the parts of the common five-paragraph essay.

Alternative Culture

In an era when alternative has become mainstream, what's an angst-ridden teenager to do? Dyeing hair punk colors has become passé. Goths with white face powder, dark lipstick, and lots of eyeliner no longer attract even a second glance. Everyone listens to "alternative" music. It has become increasingly hard for a teenager to rebel against the mainstream.

In other eras, youths had something to rebel about. The 1960s had the hippie era, as young adults rebelled by protesting against injustice, the Vietnam War, and the restrictions of society. LSD, marijuana, and free love reigned. Flash forward to the 1970s, when the punk movement came into existence with bands such as the Sex Pistols, and unemployed youths railed against consumerism. Kurt Cobain in the early 1990s became the rallying cry for a new generation of teenagers disillusioned with the confines of society. But what is happening now? Nobody is in the streets. Nobody is rising up.

Furthermore, bizarre fashion statements have become acceptable. Previously, rebellious teenagers had to resort to shopping in thrift stores or making their own clothes to attain their desired fashion statement. Luckily (or unluckily) for them, society now makes it easy to dress like an individual. Companies make jeans that already have holes in them so they do not have to wait around to have that punk look. If they want to look different, they can try Urban Outfitters, the trendy chain store for people who are fed up with trendy chain stores, where they can look "unique" just like everyone else who shops there.

With this watering down of alternative culture, it has become harder and harder to shock anyone or gain any notorious press. Marilyn Manson, the press's former whipping boy and scapegoat for music as a cause of violence in society (witness the aftermath of the Columbine shootings), has faded from the public's view. Then Eminem became a strange symbol for the increasingly difficult quest to be different from everyone else and to shock society into paying attention. He got some press for his song about killing his wife, but today, nobody is paying attention.

Today's teens, with little to rebel against, find themselves wearing clothing that is mainstream and espousing ideas that shock no one. Perhaps to be truly alternative, adolescents must think for themselves. Authentic is best, no matter what that might be. They can dress as punk or as preppy as they like. They should not let society's version of "alternative" control their actions. The truly cool can think for themselves.

The concluding paragraph brings the essay to a satisfactory close.

Each body paragraph contains details that support the thesis statement.

—*Veena Thomas, student*

> *Without words, without writing, and without books there would be no history, and there could be no concept of humanity.*
>
> —HERMANN HESSE
> *German author (1877–1962)*

Completed in 1973, the Sydney Opera House in Australia has tons of concrete, steel, and glass supporting its structure. In the same way, an essay is a sturdy structure that is supported by a strong thesis statement and solid body paragraphs held together by plenty of facts and examples.

EXPLORING

Explore Topics

There are limitless topics for writing essays. Your knowledge and personal experiences will help you find topics and develop ideas when you write your essay.

When you are planning your essay, consider your topic, audience, and purpose. Your **topic** is who or what you are writing about. Your **audience** is your intended reader, and your **purpose** is your reason for writing. Do you hope to entertain, inform, or persuade the reader?

Narrowing the Topic

Your instructor may assign you a topic for your essay, or you may need to think of your own. In either case, you need to narrow your topic (make it more specific) to ensure that it suits your purpose for writing and fits the size of the assignment. To narrow your topic, you can use some exploring methods such as questioning or brainstorming.

> **WRITING LINK**
>
> For more information about exploring strategies, see Chapter 1.

When you narrow your topic, keep in mind that an essay contains several paragraphs; therefore, an essay topic can be broader than a paragraph topic. In the following examples, you will notice that the essay topic is narrow but is slightly larger than the paragraph topic.

Broad Topic	Paragraph Topic	Essay Topic
Job interview	Dressing for the interview	Preparing for the interview
Rituals	College orientation week	Initiation rituals

 **Choosing an Essay Topic**

Paragraphs and essays can also be about the same topic. However, an essay has more details and concrete examples to support its thesis.

Do not make the mistake of choosing an essay topic that is too broad. Essays that try to cover a large topic risk being superficial and overly general. Make sure that your topic is specific enough that you can cover it in an essay.

DAVID NARROWS HIS TOPIC

Student writer David Raby-Pepin used both brainstorming and questioning to narrow his broad topic, "music." His audience was his English instructor, and the purpose of his assignment was to persuade.

– Should street performers be required to have a license?

– downloading music

– difference in earning power between classical and pop musicians

– Why do some rock bands have staying power?

– how to be a successful musician

– What is hip-hop culture?

– the popularity of shows like *American Idol*

– difference between poetry and song lyrics

The Writer's Desk Narrow the Topics

Practice narrowing five broad topics.

EXAMPLE:

Money: – *reasons it doesn't make you happy*

– *teach children about value of money*

– *best ways to be financially successful*

1. Crime: _____

_____

_____

2. Volunteer work: _____

_____

_____

3. Fashion: _____

_____

_____

4. Advertising: _____

_____

_____

5. Education: _____

_____

_____

DEVELOPING

The Thesis Statement

Once you have narrowed the topic of your essay, develop your thesis statement. The **thesis statement**—like the topic sentence in a paragraph—introduces the topic of the essay and arouses the interest of the reader.

Characteristics of a Good Thesis Statement

A thesis statement has three important characteristics.

- It expresses the main topic of the essay.
- It contains a controlling idea.
- It is a complete sentence that usually appears in the essay's introductory paragraph.

Here is an example of an effective thesis statement.

topic   controlling idea
Marriage has lost its importance for many young people in our society.

Writing an Effective Thesis Statement

When you develop your thesis statement, ask yourself the following questions.

1. **Is my thesis statement a complete statement that has a controlling idea?**
   Your thesis statement should always reveal a complete thought and make a point about the topic. It should not announce the topic or express a widely known fact.

Incomplete:	Gambling problems.
	(This statement is not complete.)
Announcement:	I will write about lotteries.
	(This statement announces the topic but says nothing relevant about the topic. Do not use expressions such as *I will write about . . .* or *My topic is . . .*)
Thesis statement:	A lottery win will not necessarily lead to happiness.

2. **Does my thesis statement make a valid and supportable point?** Your thesis statement should express a valid point that you can support with evidence. It should not be a vaguely worded statement, and it should not be a highly questionable generalization.

Vague:	Workplace relationships are harmful.
	(For whom are they harmful?)
Invalid point:	Women earn less money than men.
	(Is this really true for all women in all professions? This generalization might be hard to prove.)
Thesis statement:	Before coworkers become romantically involved, they should carefully consider possible problems.

3. **Can I support my thesis statement in an essay?** Your thesis statement should express an idea that you can support in an essay. It should not be too broad or too narrow.

Too broad:	There are many museums in the world.
	(It would be difficult to write an essay about this topic.)
Too narrow:	The Spy Museum is in Washington.
	(What more is there to say?)
Thesis statement:	Washington's Spy Museum contains fascinating artifacts related to the secret world of espionage.

 **Give Specific Details**

Give enough details to make your thesis statement focused and clear. Your instructor may want you to guide the reader through your main points. To do this, mention both your main point and your supporting points in your thesis statement. In other words, your thesis statement provides a map for the readers to follow.

| Weak: | My first job taught me many things. |
| Better: | My first job taught me about responsibility, organization, and the importance of teamwork. |

PRACTICE I

Identify the problem in each thesis statement. Then revise each statement to make it more interesting and complete.

Announces   Invalid   Broad
Incomplete   Vague   Narrow

EXAMPLE:

I will write about human misery on television news.

Problem: *Announces*

Revised statement: *Television news programs should not treat personal tragedies as big news.*

1. I think that college friendships are important.

   Problem: _____

   Revised statement: _____

   _____

2. Scholarships go to athletes, so academic excellence is not appreciated in colleges.

   Problem: _____

   Revised statement: _____

   _____

3. Scientific discoveries have changed the world.

   Problem: _____

   Revised statement: _____

   _____

4. The streets are becoming more dangerous.

   Problem: _____

   Revised statement: _____

   _____

5. How to use a digital camera.

   Problem: _____

   Revised statement: _____

   _____

6. This essay will talk about security and privacy on the Internet.

   Problem: _____

   Revised statement: _____

   _____

The Writer's Desk **Write Thesis Statements**

For each item, choose a narrowed topic from the Writer's Desk on pages 180–181. Then write an interesting thesis statement. Remember that each thesis statement should contain a controlling idea.

EXAMPLE: Topic: Money

Narrowed topic: *Winning a lottery*

Thesis statement: *Rather than improving your life, a lottery win can lead to feelings of guilt, paranoia, and boredom.*

1. Topic: Crime

   Narrowed topic: _____

   Thesis statement: _____

   _____

2. Topic: Volunteer work

   Narrowed topic: _____

   Thesis statement: _____

   _____

3. Topic: Fashion

   Narrowed topic: _____

   Thesis statement: _____

   _____

4. Topic: Advertising

   Narrowed topic: _____

   Thesis statement: _____

   _____

5. Topic: Education

   Narrowed topic: _____

   Thesis statement: _____

   _____

The Supporting Ideas

The thesis statement expresses the main idea of the entire essay. In the following illustration, you can see how the ideas flow in an essay. Topic sentences relate to the thesis statement, and details support the topic sentences; therefore, every single idea in the essay is unified and supports the thesis.

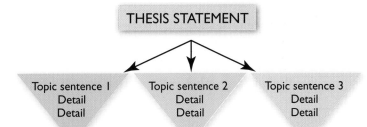

PRACTICE 2

Read the following essay. After you have finished reading, do the following:

1. Create an effective thesis statement. It should sum up the point of the entire essay.

2. Write a topic sentence at the beginning of each body paragraph. The topic sentence should sum up the main point of the paragraph in an interesting way.

Introduction:
    Danger has always been synonymous with travel. In past centuries, pirates on the high seas attacked passing ships. Land travelers were not much safer; bandits could attack their covered carriages. Even trains were not safe; in 1877 the masked outlaw Sam Bass held up a train in Nebraska and robbed the passengers. Today, with modern communication and with high-speed trains and planes, travel is quick and relatively risk-free. Nonetheless, there are still certain hazards inherent in traveling. **Thesis statement:** _____

_____

    Body paragraph 1 topic sentence: _____

_____

For example, before you arrive in a new town, find an address and phone number for affordable lodging, and book a room for your first night. If you are a budget traveler, you can always find cheaper accommodations the next day. If you are going to visit a large city, plan to arrive during the daylight hours. It is dangerous to arrive at night and then try to find your way around. Also, make sure that you have a map of your destination. You can download maps on the Internet.

    Body paragraph 2 topic sentence: _____

_____

Do not flash your money in public places. You might wear a money belt under your clothing. One innovative solution is to sew long, extended pockets on the insides of your clothes; you could keep your checks and passport there. In a small, easily accessible purse or wallet, keep small amounts of local currency for your daily spending.

Body paragraph 3 topic sentence: _____

_____

For example, you could bring along a first aid kit that includes bandages and pain relievers. Wear hats in very hot, sunny places. If you are visiting a tropical country, make sure you have the proper vaccinations. Be careful about where you eat and what you eat, and buy bottled drinking water. Your health is important. Obviously, if you get sick, you are not going to enjoy your trip.

Conclusion:

Although robberies can happen, it is unlikely that someone will physically hurt you. If you take risks with your health, if you are careless with your money and passports, or if you underestimate thieves, you may have an unpleasant experience. Of course, if you are careful, you should have a perfectly safe and exciting trip.

Generating Supporting Ideas

An effective essay has **unity** when the body paragraphs support the thesis statement. When you develop supporting ideas, make sure that they all focus on the central point that you are making in the thesis statement. To generate ideas for body paragraphs, you could use exploring strategies such as brainstorming, clustering, or freewriting.

DAVID'S SUPPORTING IDEAS

David created a list to support his thesis statement. Then he reread his supporting points and removed ideas that he did not want to develop in his essay.

THESIS STATEMENT: Rap and hip-hop artists use their music to share their positive cultural values with others.

— use lyrics to reveal their religious opinions
— Christian lyrics
— ~~hip hop inspired breakdancing~~
— praise Allah
— want to promote peace
— some address issues of violence
— ~~some hip hop artists have been jailed~~
— advise fans about healthy lifestyles
— warn about drugs
— talk about AIDS

The Writer's Desk **List Supporting Ideas**

Choose two of your thesis statements from the previous Writer's Desk on page 184, and create two lists of possible supporting ideas.

Thesis 1: _____ Thesis 2: _____

_____ _____

Support: _____ Support: _____

_____ _____

_____ _____

_____ _____

_____ _____

_____ _____

_____ _____

_____ _____

_____ _____

_____ _____

_____ _____

Organizing Your Ideas

After you have examined your list of supporting ideas, choose three or four that are most compelling and most clearly support your statement. Highlight your favorite ideas, and then group together related ideas. Finally, make your essay as clear and coherent as possible by organizing your ideas in a logical manner using time, space, or emphatic order.

WRITING LINK

For more information about time, space, and emphatic order, see Chapter 2, "Developing."

DAVID'S EXAMPLE

David underlined his three best supporting points, and he grouped related ideas using emphatic order.

3
- use lyrics to reveal their religious opinions
- Christian lyrics
- hip hop inspired breakdancing
- praise Allah

1
- want to promote peace
- some address issues of violence
- some hip hop artists have been jailed

2
- advise fans about healthy lifestyles
- warn about drugs
- talk about AIDS

The Writer's Desk **Organize Your Ideas**

Look at the list you produced in the previous Writer's Desk, and then follow these steps.

1. Highlight at least three ideas from your list that you think are most compelling and most clearly illustrate the point you are making in your thesis statement.

2. Group together any related ideas with the three supporting ideas.

3. Organize your ideas using time, space, or emphatic order.

The Essay Plan

An **essay plan** or an **outline** can help you organize your thesis statement and supporting ideas before writing your first draft. To create an essay plan, follow these steps.

- Look at your list of ideas and identify the best supporting ideas.
- Write topic sentences that express the main supporting ideas.
- Add details under each topic sentence.

In the planning stage, you do not have to develop your introduction and conclusion. It is sufficient to simply write your thesis statement and an idea for your conclusion. Later, when you develop your essay, you can develop the introduction and conclusion.

DAVID'S ESSAY PLAN

David wrote topic sentences and supporting examples and organized his ideas into a plan. Notice that he begins with his thesis statement, and he indents his supporting ideas.

THESIS STATEMENT:	Rap and hip-hop artists use their music to share their positive cultural values with others.
Body paragraph 1:	Many musicians shout out a powerful message of nonviolence. — They promote peace. — Some artists address the issue of violence.
Body paragraph 2:	Some advise fans about responsible and healthy lifestyles. — They discuss the importance of good parenting. — They talk about drug addiction or AIDS.

Body paragraph 3:   These urban musicians use their poetry to reveal their religious beliefs.
— Some show their Christian faith through the lyrics.
— Others praise Allah.

Concluding sentence: Finally, music is a way for rap musicians to share their personal culture with the world.

Writing a Formal Essay Plan

Most of the time, a basic essay plan is sufficient. However, in some of your courses, your instructor may ask you to make a formal plan. A formal plan uses Roman numerals and letters to identify main and supporting ideas.

Thesis statement: _____

   I. _____

      A. _____

      B. _____

  II. _____

      A. _____

      B. _____

 III. _____

      A. _____

      B. _____

Concluding idea: _____

PRACTICE 3

Create an essay plan based on Veena Thomas's essay "Alternative Culture" on page 178.

_____

_____

_____

_____

_____

_____

_____

_____

_____

_____

_____

_____

_____

_____

PRACTICE 4

Complete the following essay plan. Add details under each supporting point. Make sure that the details relate to the topic sentence.

Thesis statement: Rather than improving your life, a lottery win can lead to feelings of guilt, paranoia, and boredom.

I.   Feelings of guilt are common in newly rich people.

Details: A. _____

_____

B. _____

_____

C. _____

_____

II.   Lottery winners often become paranoid.

Details: A. _____

_____

B. _____

_____

C. _____

_____

III. After lottery winners quit their jobs, they commonly complain of boredom and loneliness.

Details: A. _____

_____

B. _____

_____

C. _____

_____

Concluding idea: _____

_____

_____

The Writer's Desk **Write an Essay Plan**

Write an essay plan using one of your thesis statements and supporting details you came up with in the previous Writer's Desk.

Thesis statement: _____

_____

I. _____

Details: A. _____

B. _____

C. _____

II. _____

Details: A. _____

B. _____

C. _____

III. _____

Details: A. _____

B. _____

C. _____

Concluding idea: _____

_____

The Introduction

After you have made an essay plan, you develop the sections of your essay by creating an effective introduction, linking paragraphs, and writing a conclusion.

The **introductory paragraph** introduces the subject of your essay and contains the thesis statement. A strong introduction will capture the reader's attention and make him or her want to read on. Introductions may have a lead-in, and they can be developed in several different ways.

The Lead-In

You can begin the introduction with an attention-grabbing opening sentence, or lead-in. There are three common types of lead-ins.

- Quotation
- Surprising or provocative statement
- Question

Introduction Styles

You can develop the introduction in several different ways. Experiment with any of these introduction styles.

- **Give general or historical background information.** The general or historical information gradually leads to your thesis. For example, in an essay about winning a lottery, you could begin by giving a brief history of lotteries.
- **Tell an interesting anecdote.** Open your essay with a story that leads to your thesis statement. For example, you might begin your lottery essay by telling the story of a real-life lottery winner.
- **Present a vivid description.** Give a detailed description, and then state your thesis. For example, you might describe the moment when a lottery winner realizes that he or she has won.
- **Present an opposing position.** Open your essay with an idea that contradicts a common belief, and build to your thesis. For instance, if most people want to win the lottery, you could begin your essay by saying that you definitely do not want to be a millionaire.
- **Give a definition.** Define a term, and then state your thesis. For example, in an essay about the lottery, you could begin by defining *happiness*.

> ### Hint ⟩ Placement of the Thesis Statement
>
> Although a paragraph often begins with a topic sentence, an introduction does not begin with a thesis statement. Rather, most introductory paragraphs are shaped like a funnel. The most general statement introduces the topic. The following sentences become more focused and lead to a clear, specific thesis statement. Therefore, the thesis statement is generally the last sentence in the introduction.

PRACTICE 5

In introductions A through E, the thesis statement is underlined. Read each introduction and then answer the questions that follow. Look at David's example for some guidance.

DAVID'S INTRODUCTION

Can hip-hop, with its obscene lyrics and violent culture, have any redeeming qualities? Hip-hop and rap music originated from poor, minority-inhabited neighborhoods located in New York City. Since the residents did not have enough money to buy musical instruments, they began creating beats with their mouths. This raw form of music rapidly became popular within these communities because it gave people a way to express themselves and to develop their creative abilities. Rap and hip-hop artists use their music to share their positive cultural values with others.

1. What type of lead-in does David use? ___*Question*___

2. What introduction style does he use?
   a. Description
   b. Definition
   (c.) Background information
   d. Opposing position

3. What is his essay about? ___*The positive message of hip-hop and rap music*___

A. "I never saw the blow to my head come from Huck. Bam! And I was on all fours, struggling for my equilibrium." These are the words of Kody Scott, a former member of a Los Angeles street gang. Kody is describing part of the initiation ritual he endured in order to join a local branch (or "set") of the Crips. First, he stole an automobile to demonstrate his "street smarts" and willingness to break the law. Then he allowed himself to be beaten, showing both that he was tough and that he was ready to do whatever the gang required of him. He completed the process by participating in a "military action"—killing a member of a rival gang. Initiations like this are by no means rare in today's street gangs. Kody, by the way, was just eleven years old.

—Linda L. Lindsey and Stephen Beach, "Joining the Crips," *Essentials of Sociology*

1. What type of lead-in does the author use? _____

2. What introduction style does the author use?
   a. Anecdote
   b. Definition
   c. Background information
   d. Opposing position

3. What is this essay about? _____

B. What is there about alternative medicine that sets it apart from ordinary medicine? The term refers to a remarkable heterogeneous group of theories and practices that are as disparate as homeopathy, therapeutic touch, imagery, and herbal medicine. What unites them? Eisenberg et al. defined alternative medicine (now often called complementary medicine) as "medical interventions not taught widely at U.S. medical schools or generally available at U.S. hospitals." That is not a very satisfactory definition, especially since many alternative remedies have recently found their way into the medical mainstream.

—Adapted from Marcia Angell and Jerome P. Kassirer, "Alternative Medicine: The Risks of Untested and Unregulated Remedies," *The New England Journal of Medicine*

4. What type of lead-in does the author use? _____

5. What introduction style does the author use?
   a. Anecdote
   b. Definition
   c. Description
   d. Opposing position

6. What is this essay about? _____

C. High school is a waste of time. In fact, it is a baby-sitting service for teens who are too old to be baby-sat. In England, fifteen-year-olds graduate and can choose technical or university streams of education. They are free to choose what to study, or they can stop schooling and get jobs. In short, they are treated like mature adults. In our country, we prolong the experience of forced schooling much longer than is necessary. We should abolish high schools and introduce a system of technical or pre-university schooling.

—Adelie Zang, Student

7. What type of lead-in does the author use? _____

8. What introduction style does the author use?
   a. Anecdote   b. Definition
   c. Background information   d. Opposing position

9. What is this essay about? _____

D. When I was 8 years old, I read a story about a boy who built a robot out of junkyard scraps. The robot in the story could move, talk, and think, just like a person. For some reason, I found the idea of building a robot very appealing, so I decided to build one of my own. I remember optimistically collecting body parts: pipes for arms and legs, motors for muscles, light bulbs for eyes, and a big tin can for the head, fully expecting to assemble the pieces into a working mechanical man. After nearly electrocuting myself a few times, I began to get my parts to move, light up, and make noises. I felt I was making progress. If I only had the right tools and the right parts, I was sure that I could build a machine that could think.

—Danny Hillis, "Can They Feel Your Pain?"

10. What introduction style does the author use?
    a. Anecdote   b. Definition
    c. Background information   d. Opposing position

11. What is this essay about? _____

E. The story of how Christianity ultimately conquered the Roman Empire is one of the most remarkable in history. Christianity faced the hostility of the established religious institutions of its native Judea and had to compete not only against the official cults of Rome and the sophisticated philosophies of the educated classes, but also against "mystery" religions like the cults of Mithra, Isis, and Osiris. The Christians also suffered formal persecution, yet Christianity finally became the official religion of the empire.

—Albert M. Craig et al., *The Heritage of World Civilizations*

12. What introduction style does the author use?
    a. Description
    b. Definition
    c. Historical information
    d. Opposing position

13. What is this essay about? _____

The Writer's Desk **Write Three Introductions**

In the previous Writer's Desk, you made an essay plan. Now, write three different styles of introductions for your essay. Use the same thesis statement in all three introductions. Later, you can choose the best introduction for your essay.

The Conclusion

A **conclusion** is a final paragraph that rephrases the thesis statement and summarizes the main points in the essay. To make your conclusion more interesting and original, you could close with a prediction, a suggestion, a quotation, or a call to action.

DAVID'S CONCLUSION

David concluded his essay by restating his main points.

> Finally, music is a way for hip-hop and rap musicians to share their personal culture with the world. This cultural facet can be reflected through different values, religious beliefs, and ways of life.

He could then close his essay with one of the following:

Prediction: If you are concerned about hip-hop portraying negative images, don't abandon the music yet. There are many artists who promote and will continue to promote positive values through upbeat lyrics.

Suggestion: Hip-hop fans should encourage musicians to continue to give a positive message through their music.

Call to action: If you are concerned by the negative message of hip-hop music, make your opinions heard by joining the debate on hip-hop blogs and buying CDs from musicians who only write positive lyrics.

Quotation: According to hip-hop artist Doug E. Fresh, "Hip Hop is supposed to uplift and create, to educate people on a larger level, and to make a change."

PRACTICE 6

Read the following conclusions and answer the questions.

A. As soon as smoking is banned in all public places, we will see the benefits. Our hospitals will treat fewer smoking-related illnesses, and this will save money. Non-smokers will be saved from noxious fumes, and smokers, who will be forced to smoke outdoors, might feel a greater desire to give up the habit. In the future, we will have a world where a non-smoker can go through life without having to breathe in someone else's cigarette smoke.

—Jordan Lamott, "Butt Out!"

1. What method does the author use to end the conclusion?
   a. Prediction
   b. Suggestion
   c. Quotation
   d. Call to action

B. Ultimately, spam is annoying, offensive, time consuming, and expensive. There is nothing good to say about it. Spam marketers will argue that we get junk in our mail, and that cannot be denied, but we do not get crates of junk mail every week. If we did, paper junk mail would be banned in a hurry. The only real solution is for governments around the world to work together in order to make spam production illegal. Governments should actively hunt down and prosecute spammers.

—Adela Fonseca, "Ban Spam"

2. What method does the author use to end the conclusion?
   a. Prediction
   b. Suggestion
   c. Quotation
   d. Call to action

C. Every once in a while the marketing wizards pay lip service to today's expanding career options for women and give us a Scientist Barbie complete with a tiny chemistry set as an accessory. But heaven forbid should little Johnnie plead for his parents to buy him that Scientist Barbie. After all, it is acceptable for girls to foray, occasionally, into the world of boy-style play, but for boys the opposite "sissified" behavior is taboo. Why is this? One commentator, D. R. Shaffer, says, "The major task for young girls is to learn how not to be babies, whereas young boys must learn how not to be girls."

—Dorothy Nixon, "Put GI Barbie in the Bargain Bin"

3. What method does the author use to end the conclusion?
   a. Prediction
   b. Suggestion
   c. Quotation
   d. Call to action

 **Avoiding Conclusion Problems**

In your conclusion, do not contradict your main point, and do not introduce new or irrelevant information. David initially included the next sentences in his conclusion.

> The rap and hip-hop movement is not restrained only to the musical scene. It influences many other facets of art and urban culture as well. It can be found in dance and fashion, for instance. Thus, it is very versatile.

He revised his conclusion when he realized that some of his ideas were new and irrelevant information. His essay does not discuss dance or fashion.

The Writer's Desk Write a Conclusion

In previous Writer's Desks, you wrote an introduction and an essay plan. Now write a conclusion for your essay.

The First Draft

After creating an introduction and conclusion, and after arranging the supporting ideas in a logical order, you are ready to write your first draft. The first draft includes your introduction, several body paragraphs, and your concluding paragraph.

The Writer's Desk Write the First Draft

In previous Writer's Desks, you wrote an introduction, a conclusion, and an essay plan. Now write the first draft of your essay.

REVISING AND EDITING

Revising and Editing the Essay

Revising your essay is an extremely important step in the writing process. When you revise your essay, you modify it to make it stronger and more convincing. You do this by reading the essay critically, looking for faulty logic, poor organization, or poor sentence style. Then you reorganize and rewrite it, making any necessary changes.

    Editing is the last stage in writing. When you edit, you proofread your writing and make sure that it is free of errors.

WRITING LINK

To practice revising for unity and support, see Chapter 3, "Revising and Editing."

Revising for Unity

To revise for **unity,** verify that all of your body paragraphs support the thesis statement. Also look carefully at each body paragraph: ensure that the sentences support the topic sentence.

 **Avoiding Unity Problems**

Here are two common errors to check for as you revise your body paragraphs.

- **Rambling paragraphs.** The paragraphs in the essay ramble on. Each paragraph has several topics, and there is no clearly identifiable topic sentence.
- **Artifical breaks.** A long paragraph is split into smaller paragraphs arbitrarily, and each smaller paragraph lacks a central focus.

To correct either of these errors, revise each body paragraph until it has *one* main idea that supports the thesis statement.

Revising for Adequate Support

When you revise for adequate **support,** ensure that there are enough details and examples to make your essay strong and convincing. Include examples, statistics, quotations, or anecdotes.

Revising for Coherence

When you revise for **coherence,** ensure that paragraphs flow smoothly and logically. To guide the reader from one idea to the next, or from one paragraph to the next, try using **paragraph links.**

You can develop connections between paragraphs using three methods.

1. **Repeat words or phrases from the thesis statement in each body paragraph.** In the next example, *violent* and *violence* are repeated words.

Thesis statement:	Although some will argue that <u>violent</u> movies are simply a reflection of a <u>violent</u> society, these movies actually cause a lot of the <u>violence</u> around us.
Body paragraph 1:	Action movie heroes train children to solve problems with <u>violence</u>.
Body paragraph 2:	<u>Violent movies</u> are "how to" films for many sick individuals.

2. **Refer to the main idea in the previous paragraph, and link it to your current topic sentence.** In body paragraph 2, the writer reminds the reader of the first point (the newly rich feel useless) and then introduces the next point.

Thesis statement:	A cash windfall may cause more problems than it solves.
Body paragraph 1:	The newly rich often lose their desire to become productive citizens, and they end up <u>feeling useless</u>.
Body paragraph 2:	Apart from <u>feeling useless</u>, many heirs and lottery winners also tend to feel guilty about their wealth.

3. **Use a transitional word or phrase to lead the reader to your next idea.**

   Body paragraph 2: <u>Furthermore,</u> the newly rich often feel guilty about their wealth.

WRITING LINK

Furthermore is a transition. For a list of transitions, see page 47 in Chapter 3.

Revising for Style

Another important step in the revision process is to ensure that you have varied your sentences and that you have used concise wording. When you revise for sentence style, ask yourself the following questions.

- Do I use a variety of sentence patterns? (To practice using sentence variety, see Chapter 19.)
- Do I use exact language? (To learn about slang, wordiness, and overused expressions, see Chapter 31.)
- Are my sentences parallel in structure? (To practice revising for parallel structure, see Chapter 21.)

Editing

When you edit, you proofread your essay and correct any errors in punctuation, spelling, grammar, and mechanics. There is an editing guide on the inside back cover of this book that provides you with a list of things to check for when you proofread your text.

ESSAY LINK

To practice your editing skills, see Chapter 36, "Editing Paragraphs and Essays."

DAVID'S ESSAY

David Raby-Pepin revised and edited this paragraph from his essay about hip-hop culture.

Furthermore, some
~~Some~~ rappers advise fans about responsible and healthy lifestyles.
they are
Several hip-hop artists divulge the fact that ~~their~~ are parents and discuss the importance of good parenting. Others announce their
and encourage
choice of a monogamous lifestyle. ~~They~~ encourage their fans to have respectful relationships. Some rappers mention past drug addictions
avoid
and advise listeners to ~~be avoiding~~ drugs. Others rap about the dangers of sexually-transmitted diseases. The rapper Ludacris, for
example, warns
~~example. He~~ warns his fans about AIDS and HIV and advises them to be careful and to have protected sexual relationships. Such
extremely
messages are ~~extremely~~ important since many young people do not take precautions with their health.

> ### *The Writer's Desk* Revising and Editing Your Essay
>
> In the previous Writer's Desk, you wrote the first draft of an essay. Now revise and edit your essay. You can refer to the checklist at the end of this chapter.

ESSAY LINK

For more information about punctuating titles, see pages 513–515 in Chapter 34.

The Essay Title

It is a good idea to think of a title after you have completed your essay because then you will have a more complete impression of your essay's main point. The most effective titles are brief, depict the topic and purpose of the essay, and attract the reader's attention.

When you write your title, place it at the top center of your page. Capitalize the first word of your title, and capitalize the main words except for prepositions (*in, at, for, to,* etc.) and articles (*a, an, the*). Leave about an inch of space between the title and the introductory paragraph.

Descriptive Titles

Descriptive titles are the most common titles in academic essays. They depict the topic of the essay clearly and concisely. Sometimes, the author takes key words from the thesis statement and uses them in the title. Here are some descriptive titles.

> The Importance of Multiculturalism in a Democratic Society
>
> Why Mothers and Fathers Should Take Parenting Seriously

Titles Related to the Writing Pattern

You can also relate your title directly to the writing pattern of your essay. Here are examples of titles for different writing patterns.

Illustration:	The Problems with Elections
Narration:	My Visit to Las Vegas
Description:	Graduation Day
Process:	How to Dress for an Interview
Definition:	What It Means to Be Brave
Classification:	Three Types of Hackers
Comparison and contrast:	Fast Food Versus Gourmet Food
Cause and effect:	Why People Enter Beauty Pageants
Argument:	Barbie Should Have a New Look

 **Avoiding Title Pitfalls**

When you write your title, watch out for problems.

- Do not view your title as a substitute for a thesis statement.
- Do not put quotation marks around the title of your essay.
- Do not write a really long title because it can be confusing.

PRACTICE 7

1. List some possible titles for the essay about travel in Practice 2 (pages 185–186).

   _____

   _____

2. List some alternative titles for David's essay about rap and hip-hop music, which appears below.

   _____

   _____

The Final Draft

When you have finished making the revisions on the first draft of your essay, write the final copy. This copy should include all the changes that you have made during the revision phase of your work. You should proofread the final copy of your work to check for grammar, spelling, mechanics, and punctuation errors.

DAVID'S ESSAY

David Raby-Pepin revised and edited his essay about hip-hop culture. This is his final draft.

Positive Messages in Hip-Hop Music

Can hip-hop, with its obscene lyrics and violent culture, have any redeeming qualities? Hip-hop and rap music mainly originated from poor, minority-inhabited neighborhoods located in New York City. Since the residents did not have enough money to buy musical instruments, they began creating beats with their mouths. This raw form of music rapidly became popular within these communities because it gave people a way to express themselves and to develop their creative abilities. The rap and hip-hop artists use their music to share their positive cultural values with others.

Many of these musicians shout out a powerful message of non-violence. They promote peace by denouncing the fighting that takes place within their own communities. Many leading hip-hop and rap artists are breaking away from the "gangsta rap" lyrics and writing music that shows a productive way to resolve social issues.

Furthermore, some rappers advise fans about responsible and healthy lifestyles. Several hip-hop artists divulge the fact that they are parents and discuss the importance of good parenting. Others announce their choice of a monogamous lifestyle and encourage their fans to have respectful relationships. Some rappers mention past drug addictions and advise listeners to avoid drugs. Others rap about the dangers of sexually-transmitted diseases. The rapper Ludacris, for example, warns his fans about AIDS and HIV and advises them to be careful and to have protected sexual relationships. Such messages are extremely important since many young people do not take precautions with their health.

Moreover, these urban musicians also use their lyrics to reveal their religious beliefs. Some show their Christian faith by including God in their texts. "Tommy is on the other side talking with God, understanding why he had it so hard," is from the song "Tommy" by Mathematics. Members of the band Killarmy praise Allah in their lyrics. Hip-hop and rap musicians generally do not criticize other religions through their songs. They only use this form of communication to support their own religious opinions. Hip-hop and rap music can be a way for individuals to show their faith or to pass it on to members of their audience.

Finally, music is a way for rap musicians to share their personal culture with the world. This cultural facet can be reflected through different values, religious beliefs, and ways of life. According to hip-hop artist Doug E. Fresh, "Hip Hop is supposed to uplift and create, to educate people on a larger level, and to make a change."

The Writer's Desk **Writing Your Final Draft**

At this point, you have developed, revised, and edited your essay. Now write the final draft. Before you hand it to your instructor, proofread it one last time to ensure that you have found as many errors as possible.

REFLECT ON IT

Think about what you have learned in this unit. If you do not know an answer, review that topic.

1. What is a thesis statement? _____

_____

2. What are the five different introduction styles?

_____   _____

_____   _____

_____

3. What are the four different ways to end a conclusion?

_____   _____

_____   _____

4. What are the three different ways you can link body paragraphs?

_____

_____

_____

 The Writer's Room   **Essay Topics**

Writing Activity 1

Choose any of the following topics, or choose your own topic. Then write an essay. Remember to follow the writing process.

General Topics

1. values
2. having a roommate
3. differences between generations
4. advertising
5. peer pressure

College and Work-Related Topics

6. juggling college and family life
7. having a job and going to college
8. workplace problems
9. a stressful work environment
10. an important issue in the workplace

REVISING AND EDITING CHECKLIST FOR ESSAYS

Revising

☐ Does my essay have a compelling introduction and conclusion?

☐ Does my introduction have a clear thesis statement?

☐ Does each body paragraph contain a topic sentence?

☐ Does each body paragraph's topic sentence relate to the thesis statement?

☐ Does each body paragraph contain specific details that support the topic sentence?

☐ Do all of the sentences in each body paragraph relate to its topic sentence?

☐ Do I use transitions to smoothly and logically connect ideas?

☐ Do I use a variety of sentence styles?

Editing

☐ Do I have any errors in grammar, spelling, punctuation, and capitalization?

How Do I Get a Better Grade?

Visit www.mywritinglab.com for audio-visual lectures and additional practice sets about writing the essay.
Get a better grade with MyWritingLab!

Essay Patterns

CHAPTER 14

"The act of writing is the act of discovering what you believe."

—DAVID HARE
American Playright (1947–)

CONTENTS

Fashion designers choose fabric patterns that are appropriate for the articles of clothing that they wish to make. In the same way, writers choose essay patterns that best suit their purposes for writing.

In Chapters 4 through 12, you read about and practiced using nine different paragraph patterns. In this chapter, you will learn how to apply those patterns when writing essays. Before you begin working through this chapter, take a moment to review nine writing patterns.

Pattern	Use
Illustration	To illustrate or prove a point using specific examples
Narration	To narrate or tell a story about a sequence of events that happened
Description	To describe using vivid details and images that appeal to the reader's senses
Process	To inform the reader about how to do something, how something works, or how something happened
Definition	To define or explain what a term or concept means by providing relevant examples
Classification	To classify or sort a topic to help readers understand different qualities about that topic
Comparison and contrast	To present information about similarities (compare) or differences (contrast)

| Cause and effect | To explain why an event happened (the cause) or what the consequences of the event were (the effects) |
| Argument | To argue or to take a position on an issue and offer reasons for your position |

Most college essay assignments have one dominating essay pattern. However, you can use several essay patterns to fulfill your purpose. For example, imagine that you want to write a cause and effect essay about youth crime, and the purpose of the essay is to inform. The supporting paragraphs might include a definition of youth crime and a narrative about an adolescent with a criminal record. You might incorporate different writing patterns, but the dominant pattern would still be cause and effect.

Each time you write an essay, remember to follow the writing process that you learned in Chapter 13, "Writing the Essay."

The Illustration Essay

PARAGRAPH LINK

For more information about developing ideas with examples, refer to Chapter 4, "Illustration."

When writing an illustration essay, you use specific examples to illustrate or clarify your main point. Illustration writing is a pattern that you frequently use in college essays and exams because you must support your main idea with examples.

The Thesis Statement

The thesis statement in an illustration essay controls the direction of the body paragraphs. It includes the topic and a controlling idea about the topic.

topic   controlling idea
A second language <u>provides students with several important advantages.</u>

The Supporting Ideas

In an illustration essay, the body paragraphs contain examples that support the thesis statement. You can develop each body paragraph in two different ways. To give your essay variety, you could use both a series of examples and extended examples.

- **Use a series of examples** that support the paragraph's topic sentence. For example, in an essay about bad driving, one body paragraph could be about drivers who do not pay attention to the road. The paragraph could list the things that those drivers do, such as choosing songs on an iPod, using a cell phone, eating, and putting on makeup.
- **Use an extended example** to support the paragraph's topic sentence. The example could be an anecdote or a description of an event. In an essay about bad driving, for example, one paragraph could contain an anecdote about a driver who always wanted to be faster than other drivers.

An Illustration Essay Plan

Read the next essay plan and answer the questions.

Introduction
Thesis statement: New technologies have had a profound impact on self-employed workers.
I. Hand-held organizers help such workers maintain a portable office.

      A. They store e-mails, schedules, phone lists, and more.
      B. Models are lightweight and fit in a pocket.
      C. Messenger services provide means to communicate in real time.
  II. Portable computers provide workers with the ability to do complicated things anywhere.
      A. They can format and design documents using graphs, tables, and art.
      B. They can write, revise, and edit simultaneously.
      C. There is no need to carry large paper files; computers can store hundreds of files.
      D. The self-employed can access the Internet while traveling.
 III. Computer printers have useful features for the self-employed worker.
      A. There are integrated scanners and photocopiers.
      B. Fax machines allow easy sending and receiving of messages.
      C. Laser printers can quickly print out large volumes of documents.
Conclusion: As technologies evolve, more people will work at home.

PRACTICE 1

1. Circle the topic and underline the controlling idea in the thesis statement.

2. How does the writer develop each body paragraph? Circle the best answer.
   a. With an extended example   b. With a series of examples

3. Write another topic sentence that could support the writer's thesis statement.

_____

_____

An Illustration Essay

Read the next essay by journalist Stephen Lautens and answer the questions.

Down Time

1   As I write this, my phone is ringing. I am also doing my Internet banking and refilling the fax machine with paper. How did we all get so busy? We eat our breakfast and check our voice mail on the drive to work. The ATM line is the perfect place to call an estranged relative or answer our pager. What we have done is successfully eliminated the concept of spare time. It seems like we are not happy unless we have filled every waking moment of our lives with something to do.

2   My father knew how to relax. I remember him sitting on the big green couch under a reading lamp for hours at a time, carefully going through the newspaper. It was as if time stood still. Sometimes he would just listen to music. It is amazing because all he was doing was listening to music—not trying to balance his checkbook and make a stock trade at the same time.

3   Some of my best times as a kid were days when I had nothing planned. Nothing was sweeter than the first day of the vast summer holiday, without a

valiantly: bravely

single thing to fill it. My mother tried **valiantly** to send us off to camp, but I refused to go. I took goofing around very seriously. Much to my mother's dismay, I never had any interest in hockey, soccer, or any other organized sport that made me get up early or lose any teeth.

4   Technology has given us some terrific benefits, but now we feel that we are wasting valuable time unless we are doing six things at once. I am not knocking vaccines, airbags, or NSYNC CDs, but there is something wrong when everyone has to have a website. (I am guilty as charged.) We feel we have to be an expert on the high-tech stocks—otherwise how can we expect to be a dot-com millionaire by the age of twelve? Electronic appointment books are being marketed for children so they can schedule their play dates. No doubt they can also keep track of all the other six-year-olds' e-mail addresses and cell phone numbers. There is a TV commercial on right now where a little boy puts his playmates on a conference call, which is probably good practice for the day when he has to eat his lunch at his desk with a phone in his ear.

5   Now when I get a few days off, it is so packed with errands and obligations that I am worn out by Monday morning. Maybe it is just part of growing up. If it is, I do not recommend it to anyone. Do not get me wrong. I like to be busy, but we have forgotten the need to slow down. We feel the need to be connected all the time. So go ahead. Turn off the phone and have a nap. I guarantee the world will still be there when you wake up, and it will look better, too.

PRACTICE 2

1. Underline the thesis statement of the essay.

2. Underline the topic sentence in each body paragraph.

3. In which paragraph(s) does the author give an extended example?

    _____

4. In which paragraph(s) does the author list ideas to illustrate his point?

    _____

5. What suggestion does the author make in the conclusion of the essay?

    _____

    _____

PARAGRAPH LINK

To practice illustration writing, you could develop an essay about one of the topics found in Chapter 4, "Illustration."

 The Writer's Room   **Topics for Illustration Essays**

Writing Activity 1

Write an illustration essay about one of the following topics.

General Topics

1. ridiculous fads or fashions
2. characteristics of a good friend
3. stereotypes on television
4. useless products or inventions
5. activities that relieve stress
6. commercialized holidays

College and Work-Related Topics

7. characteristics of a good boss
8. qualities of an ideal workplace
9. skills that you need for your job
10. temptations that college students face
11. important things to know about doing your job
12. your employment history

Writing Activity 2

Read the following quotations. Find one that you agree or disagree with, or find one that inspires you in some way. Then write an illustration essay based on the quotation.

> Sports serve society by providing vivid examples of excellence.
> —George F. Will, American editor and columnist

> After climbing a great hill, one only finds that there are many more hills to climb.
> —Nelson Mandela, former South African president

> Everything has its beauty, but not everyone sees it.
> —Confucius, ancient Chinese philosopher and educator

> Everyone I meet is in some way my superior.
> —Ralph Waldo Emerson, American author

> Creativity comes from looking for the unexpected and stepping outside your experience. Computers simply cannot do that.
> —Masaru Ibuka, Japanese businessman

✔ ILLUSTRATION ESSAY CHECKLIST

As you write your illustration essay, review the essay checklist on the inside front cover. Also ask yourself the following questions.

☐ Does my thesis statement include a topic that I can support with examples?

☐ Does my thesis statement make a point about the topic?

☐ Do my body paragraphs contain sufficient examples that clearly support the thesis statement?

☐ Do I smoothly and logically connect the examples?

PARAGRAPH LINK

For more information about narrative writing, refer to Chapter 5, "Narration."

The Narrative Essay

When you write a narrative essay, you tell a story about what happened, and you generally explain events in the order in which they occurred.

There are two main types of narrative writing. In **first-person narration**, you describe a personal experience using *I* or *we*. In **third-person narration**, you describe what happened to somebody else, and you use *he*, *she*, or *they*.

The Thesis Statement

The thesis statement controls the direction of the body paragraphs. To create a meaningful thesis statement for a narrative essay, you could ask yourself what you learned, how you changed, or how the event is important.

controlling idea   topic

<u>Something wonderful happened</u> **that summer I turned fifteen.**

The Supporting Ideas

Here are some tips to remember as you develop a narrative essay.

- Make sure that your essay has a point. Do not simply recount what happened. Try to indicate why the events are important.
- Organize the events in time order (the order in which they occurred). You could also reverse the order of events by beginning your essay with the outcome of the events, and then explaining what happened that led to the outcome.
- Make your narrative essay more interesting by using some descriptive language. For example, you could use images that appeal to the senses.

To be as complete as possible, a good narrative essay should provide answers to most of the following questions.

- *Who* is the essay about?
- *What* happened?
- *When* did it happen?
- *Where* did it happen?
- *Why* did it happen?
- *How* did it happen?

GRAMMAR LINK

For information about punctuating quotations, see Chapter 34.

 Using Quotations

One effective way to enhance your narrative essay is to use dialogue. Include direct and/or indirect quotations.

A **direct quotation** contains the exact words of an author, and the quotation is set off with quotation marks. When you include the exact words of more than one person, you must start a new paragraph each time the speaker changes.

> Sara looked at me sadly: "Why did you betray me?"

> "I didn't mean to do it," I answered.

> She looked down at her hands and said, "I don't think I can ever forgive you."

An **indirect quotation** keeps the author's meaning but is not set off by quotation marks.

> Sara asked why I had betrayed her.

A Narrative Essay Plan

Read the next essay plan and answer the questions that follow.

Introduction

Thesis statement: Stephen Glass, a promising young writer in Washington, D.C., shocked the world of journalism with his fabricated stories.

I. After his first small falsehood, his lying escalated.
    A. He invented a quotation in 1995.
    B. He invented sources to back up his stories.
    C. He knew about fact checkers, so he created false memos, meeting notes, etc.
    D. Soon entire stories were filled with lies.

II. Glass's career came to a crashing end.
    A. *Forbes* magazine wanted to follow up a Glass story about hackers.
    B. Glass was unable to produce documents about sources.
    C. Glass invented more lies to cover up his initial lies.
    D. Realizing Glass was unethical, the editor of the *New Republic* fired him in 1998.

III. The Glass scandal erupted, shocking publishers and readers.
    A. The story became front-page news.
    B. His editor's competency was questioned.
    C. Fact checkers were exposed as not being thorough enough.
    D. Readers wondered if journalists could be trusted.

Conclusion: The world of journalism is still recovering from the Glass scandal.

PRACTICE 3

1. Who is this essay plan about? _____

2. What happened? _____

3. When and where did this happen? _____

4. What type of narration is this? Circle the best answer.
    a. First person   b. Third person

A Narrative Essay

In the next essay, Jeff Kemp recounts what happened during his early years as a professional football player. Read the essay and answer the questions.

A Lesson in Humility

1   We live in an age when, too often, rules are scorned, values are turned upside down, principles are replaced by **expediency,** and character is sacrificed for popularity. Individual athletes are sometimes the worst offenders, but not as often as one might think. In fact, sports teach important moral lessons that athletes can apply on and off the playing field.

expediency: convenience; self-interest

2   Many people dream of being a professional athlete. For me, the dream seemed to be within reach because my father, Jack Kemp, an outstanding

designated: selected

quarterback, played for the American Football League's Buffalo Bills (prior to the AFL's 1970 merger with the National Football League). The trouble was, I was not very good! I was a third-string football player through most of junior high and high school and for two years at Dartmouth College. I was not anyone's idea of a "hot prospect." After graduation, I was passed over by NFL scouts. When I was finally asked to join the Los Angeles Rams in 1981 as a free agent, I was **designated** as fifth-string quarterback.

3   It was a 50-to-1 shot that I would survive training camp. Rookies were the only players required to show up for the first week of camp. There were dozens competing for the few spots open on the team. After two days, a young boy approached me as I was walking off the field. He asked if he could carry my helmet to the locker room. It was a long way, but I said, "Sure, I think you can handle that." The next morning, he showed up before practice and offered to carry my helmet and shoulder pads, and he was there again after practice offering the same service. So it went for the rest of the week.

4   On the last day, as we were departing the field, my young assistant said, "Jeff, can I ask you a question?" (We were on a first-name basis by then.)

5   I thought, "This is my first fan! He is going to ask me for an autograph."

6   He then inquired, "When do the good football players come to camp?" Right then and there, I learned a lesson in humility from a seven-year-old boy.

7   In my first three NFL seasons, I was forced to learn the same lesson over and over again. During that time, I threw just 31 passes. Nevertheless, by 1984, I had managed to outlast the five NFL quarterbacks who had been ahead of me. With the Rams' record standing at 1–2, I took over for injured quarterback Vince Ferragamo and earned my first start against the Cincinnati Bengals, eventually leading the Rams to nine more victories and a playoff berth.

8   The next season, I returned to the bench as a backup quarterback. Humility, I was compelled to remind myself, was a good thing. It helped me appreciate what I had and avoid dwelling on what I did not have. It prevented complaining, which drains the spirit and unity of any group. It also led me to persevere and be ready whenever opportunity presented itself.

PRACTICE 4

1. What type of narration is this text? Circle the best answer.
    a. First person   b. Third person

2. Underline the thesis statement of the essay.

3. What introduction style does Kemp use? Circle the best answer.
    a. Definition   b. Anecdote
    c. General information   d. Historical information

4. List the main events that Kemp recounts in his essay.

    _____

    _____

    _____

    _____

_____

_____

_____

5. What organizational method does Kemp use? Circle the best answer.
   a. Time order   b. Space order   c. Emphatic order

6. Write down one example of an indirect quotation from the essay.

_____

7. Write down one example of a direct quotation from the essay.

_____

8. Narrative writers do more than simply list a series of events. Kemp explains why the events were meaningful. What did Kemp learn?

_____

_____

_____

The Writer's Room   Topics for Narrative Essays

PARAGRAPH LINK

To practice narrative writing, you could develop an essay about one of the topics found in Chapter 5, "Narration."

Writing Activity 1

Write a narrative essay about one of the following topics.

General Topics

1. a family legend
2. an illuminating moment
3. a surprising coincidence
4. a poor financial decision
5. an important event in the world
6. when you learned to do something new

College and Work-Related Topics

7. life lessons that college teaches you
8. what your previous job taught you
9. your best or worst job
10. your first job
11. when you worked with a team
12. a scandal at work or college

Writing Activity 2

Read the following quotations. Find one that you agree or disagree with, or find one that inspires you in some way. Then write a narrative essay based on the quotation.

Drama is life with the dull bits cut out.

—Alfred Hitchcock, British filmmaker

When your mouth stumbles, it's worse than feet.

—Oji proverb

Those who cannot remember the past are condemned to repeat it.

—George Santayana, Spanish poet and philosopher

> If you tell the truth, then you don't have to remember everything.
> —Mark Twain, American author

> We can draw lessons from the past, but we cannot live in it.
> —Lyndon B. Johnson, American politician

✔ NARRATIVE ESSAY CHECKLIST

As you write your narrative essay, review the essay checklist on the inside front cover. Also ask yourself the following questions.

- ☐ Does my thesis statement clearly express the topic of the narration, and does it make a point about that topic?

- ☐ Does my essay answer most of the following questions: *who, what, when, where, why, how?*

- ☐ Do I use transitional expressions that help clarify the order of events?

- ☐ Do I include details to make my narration more interesting?

PARAGRAPH LINK

For more information about descriptive writing, refer to Chapter 6, "Description."

The Descriptive Essay

When writing a descriptive essay, use words to create a vivid impression of a subject. Use details that appeal to the five senses: sight, smell, hearing, taste, and touch. You want your readers to be able to imagine all that you are describing.

The Thesis Statement

In a descriptive essay, the thesis statement includes what you are describing and makes a point about the topic.

topic   controlling idea

Walking down the streets of New York, I was filled with a sense of wonder.

The Supporting Ideas

When you develop your descriptive essay, make sure it gives a **dominant impression.** The dominant impression is the overall feeling that you wish to convey. For example, the essay could convey an impression of tension, joy, nervousness, or anger.

You can place the details of a descriptive essay in space order, time order, or emphatic order. The order that you use depends on the topic of your essay. For example, if you describe a place, you can use space order, and if you describe a difficult moment, you can use time order.

 **Using Figurative Devices**

When writing a descriptive essay, you can use figurative devices such as simile, metaphor, or personification. These devices use comparisons and images to add vivid details to your writing.

- A **simile** is a comparison using *like* or *as*.

    Just imagine me with no flaws
    like a parking lot with no cars . . . —Mya, "Movin' On"
    My son's constant whining felt like a jackhammer on my skull.

- A **metaphor** is a comparison that does not use *like* or *as*.

    I'm a genie in a bottle . . . —Christina Aguilera, "Genie in a Bottle"
    The mind is a battlefield.

- **Personification** is the act of attributing human qualities to an inanimate object or animal.

    The wind kicked the leaves.   —Kurt Vonnegut, Jr., "Next Door"
    The sauce hissed on the stove.

PRACTICE 5

Practice using figurative language. Use one of the following to describe each item: simile, metaphor, or personification. If you are comparing two things, try to use an unusual comparison.

EXAMPLE:

Surprising: *Her sudden appearance was as surprising as a 4 a.m. phone call. (simile)*

1. Truck: _____

2. Road: _____

3. Crowd: _____

4. Annoying: _____

5. Relaxed: _____

A Descriptive Essay Plan

Read the next essay plan and answer the questions that follow.

Introduction
Thesis statement: Walking down the streets of Manhattan, tourists are filled with a sense of wonder.

I.   Times Square buzzes with bright lights, bustling crowds, and eclectic sounds.
    A.   The lights on the billboards glow.
    B.   There are theaters on every corner.
    C.   The streets are filled with the chatter of many different languages.
    D.   The salty pretzels are a delight.

II. Central Park is an oasis in the center of Manhattan.
   A. The joggers pass by on the running paths.
   B. The hansom drivers with their beautiful horses wait for
       passengers.
   C. The smell of the hot dogs and sausages is pervasive.
   D. The saxophone player, the bird lady, and the mime ply their trades.
III. Battery Park, on the southern tip of the island, is impressive.
   A. Visitors hear the roar of the waves crashing.
   B. The chilly wind whips people's faces.
   C. The Statue of Liberty stands tall in the distance.
   D. The shouts of the vendors fill the air.
Conclusion: "Outside America, New York is America, and its skyscraper a
symbol of the spirit of America" (Thomas Adams, 1931).

PRACTICE 6

1. This essay plan contains imagery that appeals to the senses. Find one
    example of imagery for each sense.

    a. Sight: _____

    b. Sound: _____

    c. Smell: _____

    d. Taste: _____

    e. Touch: _____

2. Which type of imagery is most prevalent? _____

3. What is the dominant impression of this essay? Circle the best answer.
    a. Desire   b. Suspicion   c. Joy and awe   d. Sadness

A Descriptive Essay

Read the following essay by Catherine Pigott, a freelance writer. Pay close attention
to the descriptive details.

Chicken Hips

1   The women of the household clucked disapprovingly when they saw me.
It was the first time I had worn African clothes since my arrival in tiny, dusty
Gambia, and evidently they were not impressed. They adjusted my head-tie
and pulled my *lappa*, the ankle-length fabric I had wrapped around myself,
even tighter. "You're too thin," one of them pronounced. "It's no good." They
nicknamed me "Chicken-hips."

2   I marveled at this accolade, for I had never been called thin in my life.
It was something I longed for. I would have been flattered if those ample-
bosomed women hadn't looked so distressed. It was obvious I fell far short of
their ideal of beauty.

3   I had dressed up for a very special occasion—the baptism of a son. The
women heaped rice into tin basins the size of laundry tubs, shaping it into
mounds with their hands. Five of us sat around one basin, thrusting our
fingers into the scalding food. These women ate with such relish, such joy.

They pressed the rice into balls in their fists, squeezing until the bright-red palm oil ran down their forearms and dripped off their elbows.

4   I tried desperately, but I could not eat enough to please them. It was hard for me to explain that I come from a culture in which it is almost unseemly for a woman to eat too heartily. It's considered unattractive. It was even harder to explain that to me thin is beautiful, and in my country we deny ourselves food in our pursuit of perfect slenderness.

5   That night, everyone danced to welcome the baby. Women swiveled their broad hips and used their hands to emphasize the roundness of their bodies. One needed to be round and wide to make the dance beautiful. There was no place for thinness here. It made people sad. It reminded them of things they wanted to forget, such as poverty, drought, and starvation. They never knew when the rice was going to run out.

6   I began to believe that Africa's image of the perfect female body was far more realistic than the long-legged leanness I had been conditioned to admire. There, it is beautiful—not shameful—to carry weight on the hips and thighs, to have a round stomach and heavy, swinging breasts. Women do not battle the bulge; they celebrate it. A body is not something to be tamed and molded.

7   The friends who had christened me Chicken-hips made it their mission to fatten me up. It wasn't long before a diet of rice and rich, oily stew twice a day began to change me. Every month, the women would take a stick and measure my backside, noting with pleasure its gradual expansion. "Oh Catherine, your buttocks are getting nice now!" they would say.

8   What was extraordinary was that I, too, believed I was becoming more beautiful. There was no sense of panic, no shame, and no guilt-ridden resolves to go on the miracle grape-and-water diet. One day, I tied my *lappa* tight across my hips and went to the market to buy beer for a wedding. I carried the crate of bottles home on my head, swinging my hips slowly as I walked. I felt transformed.

PRACTICE 7

1. In this essay, what is the author describing?_____

    _____

2. Underline at least five descriptive verbs.

3. What is the dominant impression? Circle the best answer.
    a. homesickness   b. tension   c. admiration

4. The writer appeals to more than one sense. Give an example for each type of imagery.

    a. Sight: _____

    _____

    b. Sound: _____

    _____

    c. Touch: _____

    _____

5. How does the writer change physically and emotionally during her time in Africa?

    _____

    _____

PARAGRAPH LINK

To practice descriptive writing, you could develop an essay about one of the topics in Chapter 6, "Description."

The Writer's Room

Topics for Descriptive Essays

Writing Activity 1

Write a descriptive essay about one of the following topics.

General Topics

1. a celebration
2. a future car or house
3. a painting or photograph
4. a shopping area
5. a physical and psychological self-portrait
6. a train or bus station, or a hospital waiting room

College and Work-Related Topics

7. your first impressions of college
8. a gymnasium
9. a past or current workplace
10. your college or workplace cafeteria or food court
11. a memorable person with whom you have worked
12. a pleasant or unpleasant task

Writing Activity 2

Read the following quotations. Find one that you agree or disagree with, or find one that inspires you in some way. Then write a descriptive essay based on the quotation.

> The real voyage of discovery consists not in seeking new landscapes but in having new eyes.
>
> —Marcel Proust, French author

> There is no need to go to India or anywhere else to find peace. You will find that deep place of silence right in your room, your garden, or even your bathtub.
>
> —Elisabeth Kubler-Ross, Swiss author

> Speak when you are angry—and you will make the best speech you'll ever regret.
>
> —Laurence J. Peter, American educator and author

> All sanity depends on this: that it should be a delight to feel heat strike the skin, a delight to stand upright, knowing the bones are moving easily under the flesh.
>
> —Doris Lessing, British author

> Iron rusts from disuse, and stagnant water loses its purity and in cold weather becomes frozen; even so does inaction sap the vigor of the mind.
>
> —Leonardo Da Vinci, Italian artist and inventor

✔ **DESCRIPTIVE ESSAY CHECKLIST**

As you write your descriptive essay, review the essay checklist on the inside front cover. Also ask yourself the following questions.

- Does my thesis statement clearly show what I will describe in the rest of the essay?

- Does my thesis statement make a point about the topic?

- Does my essay have a dominant impression?

- Does each body paragraph contain supporting details that appeal to the reader's senses?

- Do I use figurative language (simile, metaphor, or personification)?

The Process Essay

A **process** is a series of steps done in chronological order. When you write a process essay, you explain how to do something, how something happens, or how something works. There are two main types of process essays.

1. **Complete a process.** Explain how to complete a particular task. For example, you might explain how to create a sculpture or how to give first aid to a choking victim. Each step you describe helps the reader complete the process.

2. **Understand a process.** Explain how something works or how something happens. In other words, the goal is to help the reader understand a process rather than do a process. For example, you might explain how a law is passed or explain how a previous war began.

> **PARAGRAPH LINK**
>
> For more information about process writing, refer to Chapter 7, "Process."

The Thesis Statement

The thesis statement in a process essay includes the process you are describing and a controlling idea. In the introduction of a process essay, you should also mention any tools or supplies that the reader would need to complete the process.

topic   controlling idea
Choosing a college <u>requires some careful thinking and planning.</u>

topic   controlling idea
Pregnancy <u>consists of several stages.</u>

 **List Specific Steps**

You can write a thesis statement that contains a map, or guide, to the details that you will present in your essay. To guide your readers, you could mention the main steps in your thesis statement.

topic   controlling idea
It is possible to quit smoking <u>if you focus on your goal, find alternative</u> <u>relaxing activities, and enlist the support of friends and family.</u>

The Supporting Ideas

The body paragraphs in a process essay should explain the steps in the process. Each body paragraph should include details and examples to explain each step.

 **Using Commands**

When writing an essay to help readers complete a process, you can use commands when you explain each step in the process. It is not necessary to write *you should*.

command
First, **introduce** yourself to your roommate.

command
Ask your roommate about his or her pet peeves.

A Process Essay Plan

Read the next essay plan and answer the questions that follow.

Introduction
Thesis statement: By introducing yourself, joining groups, and organizing events, you will have a better chance of making friends in a new neighborhood.

I. Introduce yourself to your neighbors.
    A. Find a good moment.
    B. Explain that you are new to the neighborhood.
    C. Ask a few questions about the area.
II. Have an outdoor party and invite your neighbors.
    A. Find a pretext (holiday, birthday).
    B. Keep the party casual (the point is to have a relaxing time).
    C. Do not worry if some neighbors turn you down.
    D. Aim to find at least one good friend in your area.
III. Get involved in your community.
    A. Volunteer to work at the library.
    B. Become politically active in local elections.
Conclusion: With a bit of effort, you can make friends in any neighborhood.

PRACTICE 8

1. What kind of process essay is this? Circle the best answer.
    a. Complete a process   b. Understand a process

2. Add another supporting idea to body paragraph 3.

    _____

    _____

3. What organizational method does the writer use? Circle the best answer.
    a. Time   b. Space   c. Emphatic

A Process Essay

In the following essay, Jake Sibley, a musician who maintains an online music site, explains how to become a successful musician. Read the essay and answer the questions.

Steps to Music Success

1   Before you can achieve anything, you must first imagine it. If you are serious about becoming a successful musician, it will serve you well to look not only at the next step, but also to look down the road to where you ultimately want to be. There is no question that regularly revisiting the fundamentals is critical to success in any long-term **endeavor.** With that in mind, there are some basic things to consider while pursuing your musical dreams.

endeavor: attempt

2   First, setting specific goals and giving them regular attention is **vital** to achieving success at any level in the music business. Goals give direction to your action. Furthermore, achieving goals is a tasty reward that will build your esteem and motivate you to reach even higher. So pick your endpoint, and then write down the steps to get there. If you are just beginning in music, then resolve to take lessons. If you are taking lessons, then resolve to get in a performing band. If you are already performing, then resolve to join a paid project. There is no obstacle that can prevent you from reaching your dream. You just have to plan it and then do it.

vital: extremely important

3   It is also important to spend time, not money, on your dream. Most likely you have seen rookie musicians with stacks of absurdly expensive gear. Certainly I am guilty of walking into a music store and **ogling** the top-end instruments, convinced that if I could afford that equipment, my sound would improve by leaps and bounds: "If I had that guitar, I would practice *every day.*" If you are not practicing every day already, a new guitar won't change that. The only investment that will improve your success as a musician is *time*— time spent practicing, time spent learning, and time spent pursuing your goals. The lure of expensive gear is a tempting but false road to better musicianship.

ogling: staring at with desire

4   Furthermore, if you really want to improve, play with others. Music is a form of conversation between human beings. It may well be the oldest language, used for millennia by musically inclined people to jointly convey their own rage, sorrow, hope, and joy to other human beings. Learning music without this community is as futile as learning to play football by yourself. Although hours spent alone with your instrument are certainly necessary for success, engaging in musical conversations and performances is an equally vital element to your progress. A very common weakness among amateur musicians is their inability to make music with other artists—a flaw that can be easily remedied with experience. Even if you are a beginner, get out and play with others and stage a few performances if you can. Without even realizing it, you will begin to assimilate fundamental lessons about listening, interacting, and performing in a live setting that are critical to your future success.

5   Finally, practice, practice, practice! There is simply no other way to ensure your own progress as a musician. Have you been spending hours on the Internet, combing for information on how to market your music, or cheaply record a CD, or win a music competition? That's great, but have you been

spending as least as much time alone with your instrument? If not, you should reconsider your priorities. If you are not practicing several times a week at least, the music you market, or record cheaply, or submit to a competition is not going to get very far. As a musician seeking success at any level, practicing your instrument should be your number-one priority.

6   If you're serious about music, keep focused on your goal. Take the time to learn your craft, and share your gift with others. Do not let anyone else hold you back from what you know you can achieve.

PRACTICE 9

1. Underline the thesis statement of the essay.

2. What type of process essay is this? Circle the best answer.
   a. Complete a process
   b. Understand a process

3. In process essays, the support is generally a series of steps. List the steps to music success.

   _____

   _____

   _____

   _____

   _____

4. What organizational method does the author use?
   a. Time order   b. Emphatic order   c. Space order

5. Circle the transitional expressions that Sibley uses to introduce each new paragraph.

6. In which paragraph does Sibley use an anecdote to support his point?

   _____

7. Who is the audience for this essay? _____

8. How could this essay have relevance for people who never play music?

   _____

   _____

PARAGRAPH LINK

To practice process writing, you could develop an essay about one of the topics in Chapter 7, "Process."

 The Writer's Room

Topics for Process Essays

Writing Activity 1

Write a process essay about one of the following topics.

General Topics	**College and Work-Related Topics**
1. how to be a good person	7. how to manage your time
2. how to become an adult	8. how education changed somebody's life
3. how to learn a new language	9. how to plan a project
4. how someone became famous	10. how to do your job
5. how something works	11. how to be a better student
6. how to deal with a problematic teenager	12. how to find satisfaction in your work life

Writing Activity 2

Read the following quotations. Find one that you agree or disagree with or one that inspires you in some way. Then write a process essay based on the quotation.

> Treat the earth well. It was not given to you by your parents; it was loaned to you by your children.
>
> —Native American proverb

> If you judge people, you have no time to love them.
>
> —Mother Teresa, Catholic nun

> Know how to listen, and you will profit even from those who talk badly.
>
> —Plutarch, ancient Greek philosopher

> Every child is an artist. The problem is how to remain an artist once he [or she] grows up.
>
> —Pablo Picasso, Spanish artist

> If you can spend a perfectly useless afternoon in a perfectly useless manner, you have learned how to live.
>
> —Lin Yutang, Chinese author

✓ PROCESS ESSAY CHECKLIST

As you write your process essay, review the essay checklist on the inside front cover. Also ask yourself the following questions.

☐ Does my thesis statement make a point about the process?

☐ Does my essay explain how to do something, how something works, or how something happened?

☐ Do I include all of the steps in the process?

☐ Do I clearly explain the steps in the process or in the event?

☐ Do I mention the tools or equipment that my readers need to complete or understand the process?

PARAGRAPH LINK

For more information about definition writing, refer to Chapter 8, "Definition."

The Definition Essay

A definition tells you what something means. When you write a **definition essay,** you give your personal definition of a term or concept. Although you can define most terms in a few sentences, you may need to offer extended definitions for words that are particularly complex. For example, you could write an essay or even an entire book about the term *love.* The way that you interpret love is unique, and you would bring your own opinions, experiences, and impressions to your definition essay.

The Thesis Statement

In your thesis statement, indicate what you are defining, and include a definition of the term. Look at the three ways you might define a term in your thesis statement.

1. **Definition by synonym.** You could give a synonym for the term.

   term   +   synonym

   Some consumers insist that Frankenfood, or genetically modified food, be labeled.

2. **Definition by category.** Decide what larger group the term belongs to, and then determine the unique characteristics that set the term apart from others in that category.

   term   +   category   +   detail

   A groupie is a fanatical devotee of a musician or band.

3. **Definition by negation.** Explain what the term is not, and then explain what it is.

   term   +   what it is not   +   what it is

   Stalkers are not misguided romantics; they are dangerous predators.

The Supporting Ideas

In a definition essay, you can support your main point using a variety of writing patterns. For example, in a definition essay about democracy, one supporting paragraph could give historical background about democracy, another could include a description of a functioning democracy, and a third paragraph could compare different styles of democracy. The different writing patterns would all support the overriding pattern, which is definition.

 **Enhancing a Definition**

One way to enhance a definition essay is to begin with a provocative statement about the term. Then in the body of your essay, develop your definition more thoroughly. This technique arouses the interest of the readers and makes them want to continue reading. For example, the next statement questions a common belief.

According to Dr. W. Roland, attention deficit disorder is an invented disease.

A Definition Essay Plan

Read the next essay plan and answer the questions that follow.

Introduction

Thesis statement: Depression is not just the blues; it is a serious health problem.

I. A depressed person cannot just "snap out of it."
    A. Depression is not a sign of self-indulgence.
    B. Some people battle the illness for years and need specific treatment.
    C. Offer the example of Katie Rowen, who has been hospitalized several times.
    D. Include quotations from people suffering from depression: William Styron says, "Nightfall seemed more somber"; Mike Wallace calls it "endless darkness."

II. Symptoms are not always obvious and can be overlooked.
    A. People feel excess fatigue and lack of energy.
    B. They may have unexplained bouts of sadness.
    C. Another symptom is extreme irritability for no obvious reason.
    D. Academic and work performance may suffer.

III. Depression has impacts on a person's physical and emotional life.
    A. A person may neglect nutrition, leading to excess weight gain or weight loss.
    B. He or she may neglect appearance and hygiene.
    C. He or she may alienate family and coworkers.
    D. A depressed person may suffer job loss, leading to financial consequences.

Conclusion: Depression is a serious illness that affects many people in our society.

PRACTICE 10

1. What type of definition does the writer use in the thesis statement? Circle the best answer.
    a. Definition by synonym   b. Definition by category
    c. Definition by negation

2. The writer uses many types of supporting details. Underline a quotation, and circle an anecdote.

3. What organizational strategy does the writer use? Circle the best answer.
    a. Time order   b. Emphatic order   c. Space order

A Definition Essay

In the next essay, student writer Diego Pelaez defines a sports fanatic. Read the essay and answer the questions.

Sports Fanatics

1   The opposing team's greatest player received the ball with time running low. His team down a point, he went to work on his defender. Faking a rush to the basket, he stepped back and rose for the deciding jump shot of the game. He released the ball with a good arc, and sure enough, it found its target, winning the game and the championship. I watched silently and shared the sorrow of my team—the losing team—for I am a sports fanatic. When a beloved team loses, the true sports fanatic feels like he or she has been through a personal tragedy. For sports fanatics, the game is not just a game; it is one of life's most significant events.

2   Sports fanatics never hesitate to show devotion to the team, for devotion is what separates a true sports fanatic from the average, casual sports fan. The casual fan may express **complacency** when the team loses. A sports fanatic feels each defeat with stretches of sorrow and answers each victory with **jubilation.** When my team lost that championship game, I was **despondent** for over a week. I kept going over the game in my head, imagining what might have happened had the game ended a few seconds earlier.

3   Statistics are a vital part to the full understanding of any sport, and sports fanatics know this fact. Fanatics learn everything that they can about the game. They can usually rattle off at least a few statistics that can make regular people question the fanatics' use of their spare time. Yet despite the opinions of others, true sports fans wear their ability to memorize statistics as a badge of honor and as proof of their undying dedication. For example, when I meet a fellow fanatic, I excitedly recite numbers, names, and dates, often competing to show that I have amassed more information about my favorite sport than others.

4   True sports fanatics are not crazy; they simply have an **avid** fantasy life. Millions of kids imitate Joe Montana or Michael Jordan, dreaming of becoming a major leaguer. Even if the sports fanatic is a poor player, he or she has usually played the game in order to fully understand the sport. In essence, the thrill of the sports fanatic is to **live vicariously** through the people talented enough to achieve the fanatic's childhood dreams. I spend many pleasurable moments imagining that I can hear the roar of the crowd when I make that winning jump shot.

5   The sports fanatic is a hard creature to understand. Others may wonder why die-hard fans care so much about sports. The point is, fanatics have a purpose in life: they truly care about something, and they express their devotion wholeheartedly. Some of the greatest athletes are sports fanatics too. Growing up, Michael Jordan was passionate about baseball and basketball. Wayne Gretzky spent his childhood absorbing everything that he could about hockey. So instead of regarding sports fanatics as crazy, people should commend them for their commitment and love of the game.

complacency: contentment

jubilation: extreme joy

despondent: miserable

avid: full, enthusiastic

live vicariously: to imagine participating in someone else's experience

PRACTICE 11

1. Underline the thesis statement of the essay.

2. What introduction style does the writer use? Circle the best answer.
    a. Anecdote   b. Historical information   c. Shocking statement

3. In paragraph 2, the writer compares a fanatic with a casual fan. What is the main difference between the two?

    _____

    _____

4. Using your own words, list the main supporting ideas in this essay.

   a. _____

   b. _____

   c. _____

5. Look in the body of the essay, and underline an example of definition by negation.

6. What method does the writer use to end this essay? Circle the best answer.

   a. Quotation   b. Suggestion   c. Prediction

 The Writer's Room   **Topics for Definition Essays**

Writing Activity 1

Write a definition essay about one of the following topics.

PARAGRAPH LINK

To practice definition writing, you could develop an essay about one of the topics found in Chapter 8, "Definition."

General Topics

1. propaganda
2. a pacifist
3. street smarts
4. a control freak
5. our disposable culture
6. a generation gap

College and Work-Related Topics

7. a McJob
8. a perfectionist
9. a whistle-blower
10. an ineffective boss
11. a conspiracy theory
12. downsizing

Writing Activity 2

Read the following quotations. Find one that you agree or disagree with, or find one that inspires you in some way, and use it as the basis for a definition essay.

> A cult is a religion with no political power.
> —Tom Wolfe, American author

> Tact is the ability to describe others as they see themselves.
> —Abraham Lincoln, former American president

> One of the keys to happiness is a bad memory.
> —Rita Mae Brown, American activist

> A leader who does not hesitate before he sends his nation into battle is not fit to be a leader.
> —Golda Meir, former Israeli prime minister

> Opportunity is missed by most people because it is dressed in overalls and looks like work.
> —Thomas A. Edison, American inventor

✔ **DEFINITION ESSAY CHECKLIST**

As you write your definition essay, review the essay checklist on the inside front cover. Also ask yourself the following questions.

Does my thesis statement explain what term I am defining?

Does each topic sentence clearly show some aspect of the definition?

Do my supporting paragraphs include examples that help illustrate the definition?

Do I use concise language in my definition?

PARAGRAPH LINK

For more information about classification writing, refer to Chapter 9, "Classification."

The Classification Essay

Classifying means "to sort a subject into more understandable categories." When you are planning a classification essay, find a topic that you can divide into categories. Each of the categories must be part of a larger group, yet they must also be distinct. For example, if your essay is about types of lawyers, you might sort them into criminal lawyers, divorce lawyers, and corporate lawyers.

The Thesis Statement

The thesis statement in a classification essay mentions the categories of the subject and contains a controlling idea. In this type of essay, the controlling idea is your classification principle, which is the overall method that you use to sort the items. For example, if your essay topic is "crime," you might sort crime according to types of criminals, categories of violent crimes, or categories of bank-machine crimes.

controlling idea (classification principle)   topic   categories

There are three very effective types of **bank-machine crimes**: no-tech, low-tech, and high-tech.

 **List Specific Categories**

You can guide your reader by listing the specific categories you will cover in your thesis statement.

topic   controlling idea

Children learn gender roles through the family, the school, and the media.

The Supporting Ideas

In a classification essay, each body paragraph covers one category. To organize your categories and supporting details, you can use a classification chart or a more traditional classification essay plan.

A Classification Chart

A classification chart helps you plan your ideas by providing a visual representation of how you wish to classify a subject. In this sample chart, the thesis statement appears at the top, and all of the categories branch from it.

Historically, three types of marital unions have been practiced around the world.

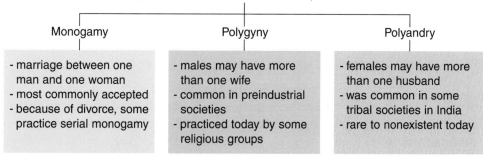

Monogamy	Polygyny	Polyandry
- marriage between one man and one woman - most commonly accepted - because of divorce, some practice serial monogamy	- males may have more than one wife - common in preindustrial societies - practiced today by some religious groups	- females may have more than one husband - was common in some tribal societies in India - rare to nonexistent today

A Classification Essay Plan

A classification essay plan also helps you organize your essay's categories and details. Read the following essay plan and answer the questions.

Introduction

Thesis statement: There are three main types of bad jokes: overused children's jokes, practical jokes, and insulting jokes.

I. Overused children's jokes bore the listener.
    A. Knock-knock jokes are dull.
    B. The "what is it" jokes are overused.
    C. Nobody likes "why did the chicken cross the road" jokes.
    D. Silly riddles are boring.
II. Practical jokes humiliate the victims.
    A. Whoopee cushions can embarrass people.
    B. The plastic wrap on the toilet seat leads to a humiliating mess.
    C. The "paint can over the door" trick can hurt others.
    D. The "kick me" note on a person's back is not funny.
III. Insulting jokes can seriously hurt or offend others.
    A. Jokes about ethnic groups or religious groups can be awful.
    B. Cruel jokes about a person's appearance (big nose jokes, blond jokes) can be hurtful.
    C. Jokes about a profession (lawyer jokes) can insult professionals.

Conclusion: Let's hope that people come up with better jokes.

PRACTICE 12

1. What is the classification principle? That is, what main principle unifies the three categories?

    _____

2. Why is each type of joke considered bad? Underline the reason in each topic sentence.

3. The author organizes the main ideas in emphatic order. How are they arranged? Circle the best answer.

    a. From most to least offensive   b. From least to most offensive

4. How does the writer support the main ideas? Circle the best answer.

    a. Examples   b. Anecdotes   c. Statistics

A Classification Essay

Read the next essay by Saundra Cicarelli, which is from her textbook *Psychology*.

Phobias

1   Anxiety can take very specific forms. There's a difference between anxiety that is realistic and has a known source and the kind of anxiety found in disorders. If final exams are coming up and a student hasn't studied enough, that student's anxiety is understandable and realistic. But if a student who has studied, has done well on all the exams, and is very prepared still worries excessively, that student is showing an unrealistic amount of anxiety. One of the more specific anxiety disorders is a phobia, an irrational, persistent fear of something. Irrational anxieties, or phobias, come in three categories.

2   Social phobias involve a fear of interacting with others or being in a social situation. People with a social phobia are afraid of being evaluated in some negative way by others, so they tend to avoid situations that could lead to something embarrassing or humiliating. They are very self-conscious as a result. Common types of social phobia are stage fright, fear of public speaking, and fear of urinating in a public restroom. Not surprisingly, people with social phobias often have a history of being shy as children.

3   A specific phobia is an irrational fear of some object or specific situation, such as a fear of darkness or a fear of being enclosed in a small space (claustrophobia). Other specific phobias include a fear of injections, a fear of dental work, a fear of blood, and a fear of heights. Many people experience a fear of specific animals such as a fear of dogs, snakes, or spiders. Mysophobia is a fear of germs, and pyrophobia is a fear of fire.

4   A third type of phobia is agoraphobia, a Greek name that literally means "fear of the marketplace." Although that makes it sound like a social phobia, agoraphobia is a little more complicated. It is actually the fear of being in a place or situation (social or not) from which escape is difficult or impossible if something should go wrong. So agoraphobics are often afraid of not only crowds but also crossing bridges, traveling in a car or plane, eating in restaurants, and sometimes even of leaving the house. To be in any of these situations or to even think about being in such situations can lead to extreme feelings of anxiety and even panic attacks.

5   People with specific phobias can usually avoid the object or situation without too much difficulty, and people with social phobias may simply avoid jobs and situations that involve meeting people face-to-face. But people with agoraphobia cannot avoid their phobia's source because it is simply being outside in the real world. A severe case of agoraphobia can make a person's home a prison, leaving the person trapped inside unable to go to work, shop, or engage in any kind of activity that requires going out of the home.

PRACTICE 13

1. What is the essay's classification principle? _____

_____

2. What are the three main categories? _____

_____

3. Underline the topic sentences in body paragraphs 2, 3, and 4.

4. Do the categories overlap? Explain your answer. _____

_____

_____

5. To better understand how the author organizes this essay, make a classification chart. Write the categories on the lines and examples in the boxes. Use your own words to explain each category.

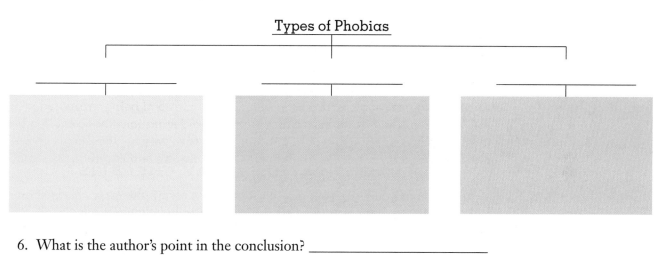

Types of Phobias

6. What is the author's point in the conclusion? _____

_____

_____

 The Writer's Room   **Topics for Classification Essays**

Writing Activity 1

Write a classification essay about one of the following topics.

General Topics

1. addictions
2. marriage ceremonies
3. extreme sports
4. things that cause allergic reactions
5. youth subcultures
6. punishment

College and Work-Related Topics

7. annoying customers or clients
8. art
9. competition
10. success
11. conversational topics at work
12. fashions in the workplace

PARAGRAPH LINK

To practice classification writing, you could develop an essay about one of the topics found in Chapter 9, "Classification."

Writing Activity 2

Read the following quotations. Find one that you agree or disagree with, or find one that inspires you in some way. Then write a classification essay based on the quotation.

Work saves us from three great evils: boredom, vice, and need.

—Voltaire, French author and philosopher

There are three kinds of lies: lies, damned lies, and statistics.

—Benjamin Disraeli, British politician

Nothing is particularly hard if you divide it into small jobs.

—Henry Ford, American inventor

There appears to be three types of politicians: leaders, lobbyists, and professionals.

—R. Ravimohan, Indian journalist

Never bear more than one trouble at a time. Some people bear three kinds—all they have had, all they have now, and all they expect to have.

—Edward Everett Hale, American author and clergyman

✔ CLASSIFICATION ESSAY CHECKLIST

As you write your classification essay, review the essay checklist on the inside front cover. Also ask yourself the following questions.

- Do I clearly identify which categories I will discuss in my thesis statement?

- Do I use a common classification principle to unite the various items?

- Do I include categories that do not overlap?

- Do I clearly explain one of the categories in each body paragraph?

- Do I use sufficient details to explain each category?

- Do I arrange the categories in a logical manner?

PARAGRAPH LINK

For more information about this pattern, refer to Chapter 10, "Comparison and Contrast."

The Comparison and Contrast Essay

You **compare** when you want to find similarities and **contrast** when you want to find differences. When writing a comparison and contrast essay, you explain how people, places, things, or ideas are the same or different to prove a specific point.

Before you write, you must make a decision about whether you will focus on similarities, differences, or both. As you explore your topic, make a list of both similarities and differences. Later, you can use some of the ideas in your essay plan.

The Thesis Statement

The thesis statement in a comparison and contrast essay indicates if you are making comparisons, contrasts, or both. When you write a thesis statement, indicate what you are comparing or contrasting and the controlling idea.

Although neat people have a very nice environment, messy people are more relaxed.

Topics being contrasted: Neat people and messy people

Controlling idea: Messy people are more relaxed.

Alice's daughter wants to be her own person, but she is basically very similar to her mother.

Topics being compared: Mother and daughter

Controlling idea: Very similar personalities

The Supporting Ideas

In a comparison and contrast essay, you can develop your body paragraphs in two different ways.

1. In a **point-by-point** development, you present *one* point about Topic A and then *one* point about Topic B. You keep following this pattern until you have a few points for each topic.

    Paragraph 1: Topic A, Topic B
    Paragraph 2: Topic A, Topic B
    Paragraph 3: Topic A, Topic B

2. In a **topic-by-topic** development, you discuss one topic in detail, and then you discuss the other topic in detail.

    Paragraphs 1 and 2: All of Topic A
    Paragraphs 3 and 4: All of Topic B

A Comparison and Contrast Essay Plan

Read the next essay plan and answer the questions that follow.

Introduction

Thesis statement: Soccer is a more exciting, active, and popular sport than baseball.

I. Soccer is fast-paced and thrilling to watch, whereas baseball is boring.
    A. In soccer, fans watch the ball as it gets kicked constantly around the field.
    B. In soccer, there are very few quiet moments; the game has constant action.
    C. In baseball, spectators get bored while watching the pitcher think, consider, and eventually pitch.
    D. Baseball games have very few seconds of excitement because home runs are so rare.

II. Those who play soccer get more exercise than those who play baseball.
    A. During soccer games, players constantly run to cover the opposing player.
    B. After games, soccer players are drenched with sweat.
    C. Baseball players generally stand on bases or in the outfield simply waiting for action.
    D. When baseball players are at bat, they spend most of their time waiting for their turn.

III. The World Cup is more popular than the World Series.
  A. Soccer is the number one sport in South America, Africa, Asia, and Europe.
  B. According to Japan's Market Monthly, the number of World Cup viewers is about 40 billion.
  C. Baseball is mainly popular in North America and Japan.
  D. During baseball's 2004 World Series, only 25 million people watched the Boston Red Sox beat the St. Louis Cardinals.
Conclusion: Learn about soccer because it is a fantastic sport.

PRACTICE 14

1. The writer compares and contrasts two things in this essay plan. What are they?

   _____

2. Look at the thesis statement. What is the controlling idea?

   _____

3. What will this essay focus on? Circle the best answer.
   a. Similarities   b. Differences

4. What pattern of comparison does the writer use in this essay? Circle the best answer.
   a. Point by point   b. Topic by topic

A Comparison and Contrast Essay

In the next essay, college student Emily Hotte compares two eras. Read the essay and answer the questions.

The Unchanging Generation

1   In the 1920s, life was more difficult for most people than it is today. There were no electric washers, dryers, or dishwashers. Racism was more rampant, and so was sexism. Women were expected to work in the home, and few universities accepted female students. Entertainment was different, too. People listened to radios and watched silent films. They did not have televisions, iPods, computers, or cellular phones. Yet in spite of these differences, young people in the 1920s were very much like young people today.

2   Today, young people want to be popular, and they go to great lengths to fit in with their friends, yet this was also true in the 1920s. F. Scott Fitzgerald wrote stories and novels that describe the 1920s, and he portrayed a world where young people were divided among those who were popular and those who were not. In his short story "Bernice Bobs Her Hair," the main character is a shy, socially awkward girl who feels a "vague pain that she was not at present engaged in being popular" (26). In a desperate effort to make friends, Bernice changes her style and modifies her personality in order to be accepted by her peers. Today's youths also worry about popularity. Those who are not part of the "in" crowd are often ridiculed and rejected, and those at the top of the social hierarchy are imitated, envied, and admired. In several highly publicized cases of school violence, the perpetrators complained of being unpopular outcasts who were bullied by more popular students.

3   Teens of the 1920s, like teens today, tried to distinguish themselves from previous generations. In the 1920s, young "flapper" women stopped wearing corsets, they wore skirts that showed their legs, and, in an act of extreme rebellion, they cut their long hair short. In Fitzgerald's story, Bernice calls bobbed hair on women "immoral" but then notes that "you've either got to amuse people or feed 'em or shock 'em" (21). Today, teenagers also differentiate themselves from their elders in an attempt to forge their own identities and create a sense of independence. To the chagrin of their parents, teens color their hair distinctive shades and tattoo or pierce body parts. Some commentators lament the deplorable state of youth fashion, complaining that their daughters expose too much skin and their sons wear poorly fitting clothing.

4   In contemporary subcultures, music is an element that can bond youths together but enrage parents, and the same was true in the 1920s. Fitzgerald called the 1920s the "Jazz Age" and said that youths were a jazz-nourished generation. Jazz, which was created by African Americans, was noted for its forceful rhythms and improvisations. Many parents associated the music with immoral behavior; however, that did not stop armies of kids from crowding jazz clubs. Today, virtually all youth subcultures identify with a particular music style. Punk, alternative, rap, and hip-hop are just some musical styles associated with various youth groups. Often, the music, with its violent or sexual lyrics, enrages older generations. In fact, in the early 2000s, a Senate subcommittee looked at the impact of violent lyrics on urban youths.

5   Although many things have changed since the 1920s, the characteristics of adolescents have remained fundamentally the same. Rebellious youths in the 1920s attacked social conventions by adopting new and shocking styles and by dancing to music that was considered **licentious.** Today, youths do much the same things. Perhaps the association of youth and rebellion is simply part of the human condition. In fact, about two thousand years ago, Seneca, a Roman philosopher and statesman, said, "It is a youthful failing to be unable to control one's impulses."

licentious: immoral or shameful

PRACTICE 15

1. Underline the thesis statement of the essay.

2. In the thesis statement, what two things does the writer compare?

_____

3. What does this essay focus on? Circle the best answer.
    a. Similarities   b. Differences

4. What pattern of comparison does the writer follow in paragraph 2? Circle the best answer.
    a. Point by point   b. Topic by topic

5. Using your own words, list the writer's main supporting points.

_____

_____

_____

6. In the conclusion, how does the quotation support the writer's main point?

_____

_____

 The Writer's Room **Topics for Comparison and Contrast Essays**

PARAGRAPH LINK

To practice comparison and contrast writing, you could develop an essay about one of the topics found in Chapter 10, "Comparison and Contrast."

Writing Activity 1

Write a comparison and contrast essay about one of the following topics.

General Topics

Compare and/or contrast . . .

1. a good host and a bad host
2. expectations about parenthood versus the reality of parenthood
3. two different interpretations of an event
4. living together and getting married
5. manners today and manners fifty years ago
6. a book and a film about the same topic

College and Work-Related Topics

Compare and/or contrast . . .

7. male and female college athletes
8. working with others and working alone
9. a good manager and a bad manager
10. a stay-at-home parent and an employed parent
11. student life and professional life
12. expectations about a job and the reality of that job

Writing Activity 2

Read the following quotations. Find one that you agree or disagree with, or find one that sparks your imagination. Then write a comparison and contrast essay based on the quotation.

> My grandfather once told me that there are two kinds of people: those who work and those who take the credit. He told me to try to be in the first group; there was less competition there.
>> —Indira Gandhi, Indian politician

> People are more violently opposed to fur than leather because it is safer to harass rich women than motorcycle gangs.
>> —Unknown

> Happy families are all alike. Every unhappy family is unhappy in its own way.
>> —Leo Tolstoy, Russian author

> Commandments for wives:
> 1. Don't bother your husband with petty troubles and complaints when he comes home from work.

2. Let him relax before dinner, and discuss family problems after the "inner man" has been satisfied.

Commandments for husbands:

1. Remember your wife wants to be treated as your sweetheart.
2. Compliment her new dress, hair-do, and cooking.
  —Edward Podolsky, American author of 1947 self-help manual

The first half of our lives is ruined by our parents, and the second half is ruined by our children.
  —Clarence Darrow, American defense lawyer

COMPARISON AND CONTRAST ESSAY CHECKLIST

As you write your comparison and contrast essay, review the essay checklist on the inside front cover. Also ask yourself the following questions.

 Does my thesis statement explain what I am comparing or contrasting?

 Does my thesis statement make a point about my topic?

 Does my essay focus on either similarities or differences?

 Does my essay include point-by-point and/or topic-by-topic patterns?

 Do all of my supporting examples clearly relate to the topics that are being compared or contrasted?

 Do I use transitions that will help readers follow my ideas?

The Cause and Effect Essay

When writing a cause and effect essay, you explain why an event happened or what the consequences of such an event were.

PARAGRAPH LINK

For more information about this pattern, refer to Chapter 11, "Cause and Effect."

The Thesis Statement

The thesis statement in a cause and effect essay contains the topic and the controlling idea. The controlling idea indicates whether the essay will focus on causes, effects, or both.

topic   controlling idea (causes)

Chronic insomnia is caused by many factors.

topic   controlling idea (effects)

Chronic insomnia can have a serious impact on a person's health.

topic   controlling idea (causes and effects)

Chronic insomnia, which is caused by many factors, can have a serious impact on a person's health.

 **Thinking About Effects**

If you are writing about the effects of something, you might think about both the short-term and long-term effects. By doing so, you will generate more ideas for the body of your essay. You will also be able to structure your essay more effectively by moving from short-term to long-term effects.

For example, look at the short- and long-term effects of a smoke-free work zone.

Short term: Inside air is cleaner.
              The smokers get more coffee breaks.

Long term: Fewer smoke-related illnesses occur in nonsmokers.
              Some smokers might quit smoking.

The Supporting Ideas

The body paragraphs in a cause and effect essay focus on causes, effects, or both. Make sure that each body paragraph contains specific examples that clarify the cause and/or effect relationship.

A Cause and Effect Essay Plan

Read the next essay plan and answer the questions that follow.

Introduction

Thesis statement: People become vegetarians for three important reasons.

I. They cannot justify killing something with a nervous system.
    A. They do not want to hurt living creatures.
    B. Animals with a nervous system suffer horribly when they are killed for food.
    C. Methods used in slaughterhouses are inhumane.
II. A vegetarian diet is healthier than a meat-based diet.
    A. In modern agricultural practices, steroids are given to farm animals.
    B. Meat products have higher cholesterol levels than plant and grain products.
    C. Vegetables and beans ensure an adequate supply of nutrients and proteins.
III. A vegetarian diet is inexpensive.
    A. Vegetables are cheaper than meat.
    B. It is cheaper to produce one pound of vegetables than one pound of beef.
    C. People can grow their own vegetables.

Conclusion: A vegetarian diet is a healthy alternative.

PRACTICE 16

1. In the thesis statement, circle the topic and underline the controlling idea.

2. Does this essay focus on causes or effects? _____

3. Who is the audience for this essay? _____

A Cause and Effect Essay

Read the next essay by student writer Jim Baek and then answer the questions that follow.

Why Small Businesses Fail

1   Last spring, Pablo Ortiz rented a tiny pizzeria in his neighborhood to turn it into a taco restaurant. Full of enthusiasm, he bought supplies, paid for advertisements, and posted a large menu in the window of his new venture, called Taco Heaven. Ten months later, Taco Heaven closed, and Ortiz declared bankruptcy. He was not alone. The Small Business Administration Office reports that close to half of all new businesses fail within the first five years. Causes of small business failures are numerous.

2   First, inexperienced business owners often neglect to do market research to find out if community members are interested in the product. In Ortiz's case, he thought that area residents would appreciate the chance to buy hearty chicken or pork tacos. However, there were three other Mexican fast-food restaurants in the area, so Ortiz's competitors took most of the business.

3   Second, inadequate pricing can hurt new businesses. Maggie Stevens, owner of a successful restaurant in Los Angeles, sells stuffed Belgian waffles to an eager clientele. Before pricing her waffles, she calculated the exact cost of each plate, right down to the strawberry that adorned the waffle and the touch of cream next to it. She also considered other costs beyond that of the ingredients, including the cost of labor and food spoilage. Her final price for each dish was 60 percent higher than her base cost. Ortiz, on the other hand, had absolutely no idea what he really spent to make each taco. He ended up underpricing his product and losing money.

4   Additionally, many small business owners have insufficient funds to run their ventures successfully. According to accountant Louis Polk, most small businesses operate for four years before they break even, let alone actually make money. Therefore, owners need a cash reserve to get through the first slow years. Ortiz, expecting to make a decent profit right away, did not realize that he would have to use up his savings to keep his business afloat.

5   Finally, inexperienced merchants may underestimate the sheer volume of work involved in running a business. Ortiz admits he was very naive about the workload. Taco Heaven had to be open 15 hours a day, 7 days a week. Ortiz also had to shop for ingredients and do the accounting. After months of grueling work and little to no pay, he burned out.

6   People who plan to open small businesses should become informed, especially about potential pitfalls. Inexperience, lack of proper planning, and insufficient funds can combine to create a business failure.

PRACTICE 17

1. Underline the thesis statement of the essay.

2. Does this essay focus on causes, effects, or both? _____

3. Underline a statistic and an anecdote.

4. Using your own words, list the four supporting points.

_____

_____

_____

_____

 The Writer's Room **Topics for Cause and Effect Essays**

PARAGRAPH LINK

To practice cause and effect writing, you could develop an essay about one of the topics found in Chapter 11, "Cause and Effect."

Writing Activity 1

Write a cause and effect essay about one of the following topics.

General Topics

Causes and/or effects of . . .

1. a new law or policy
2. rejecting or adopting a religion
3. patriotism
4. getting a divorce
5. bad parenting
6. leaving your home or homeland

College and Work-Related Topics

Causes and/or effects of . . .

7. being a parent and college student
8. taking time off before college
9. having an office romance
10. losing a job
11. gossiping in the office
12. changing jobs or career paths

Writing Activity 2

Read the following quotations. Find one that you agree or disagree with or one that inspires you in some way, and use it as the basis for a cause and effect essay.

When a man tells you that he got rich through hard work, ask him, "Whose?"
—Don Marquis, American humorist

Another possible source of guidance for teenagers is television, but television's message has always been that the need for truth, wisdom, and world peace pales by comparison with the need for toothpaste that offers whiter teeth and fresher breath.
—Dave Barry, American author and humorist

Sometimes when we are generous in barely detectible ways, it can change someone else's life forever.
—Margaret Cho, American comedian

All human actions have one or more of these seven causes: chance, nature, compulsion, habit, reason, passion, and desire.
—Aristotle, ancient Greek philosopher

One of the symptoms of an approaching nervous breakdown is the belief that one's work is terribly important.
—Bertrand Russell, British author and philosopher

✔ **CAUSE AND EFFECT ESSAY CHECKLIST**

As you write your cause and effect essay, review the essay checklist on the inside front cover. Also ask yourself the following questions.

☐ Does my essay clearly focus on causes, effects, or both?

☐ Do I have adequate supporting examples of causes and/or effects?

☐ Do I avoid using faulty logic (a mere asumption that one event causes another or is the result of another)?

☐ Do I use the terms *effect* and/or *affect* correctly?

The Argument Essay

When you write an **argument essay,** you take a position on an issue, and you try to defend your position. In other words, you try to persuade your readers to accept your point of view.

PARAGRAPH LINK

For more information about argument writing, refer to Chapter 12, "Argument."

The Thesis Statement

The thesis statement in an argument essay mentions the subject and a debatable point of view about the subject. Do not include phrases such as *in my opinion, I think,* or *I am going to talk about* in your thesis statement.

topic   controlling idea
Building a wall on the Mexican border **is an ineffective way to deal with illegal immigration.**

 **List Specific Arguments**

Your thesis statement can further guide your readers by listing the specific arguments you will make in your essay.

controlling idea   topic   (arguments)   1
Colleges should implement **work terms** to help students acquire job skills,
                          2   3
make professional contacts, and earn money for expenses.

The Supporting Ideas

In the body of your essay, give convincing arguments. Try to use several types of supporting evidence.

PARAGRAPH LINK

For more detailed information about types of evidence, see pages 168–169 in Chapter 12, "Argument."

- **Include anecdotes.** Specific experiences or pieces of information can support your point of view.
- **Add facts.** Facts are statements that can be verified in some way. **Statistics** are a type of fact. When you use a fact, ensure that your source is reliable.

- **Use informed opinions.** Opinions from experts in the field can give weight to your argument.
- **Think about logical consequences.** Consider long-term consequences if something does or does not happen.
- **Answer the opposition.** Think about your opponents' arguments, and provide responses to their arguments.

RESEARCH LINK

For more information about doing research, see Chapter 15, "Enhancing Your Writing with Research."

 **Quoting a Respected Source**

One way to enhance your essay is to include a quotation from a respected source. Find a quotation from somebody in a field that is directly related to your topic. When you include the quotation as supporting evidence, remember to mention the source.

According to Dr. Tom Houston, co-director of the American Medical Association's SmokeLess States campaign, secondhand smoke "can lead to serious health consequences, ranging from ear infections and pneumonia to asthma."

An Argument Essay Plan

Read the next essay plan and answer the questions that follow.

Introduction
Thesis statement: America should institute longer vacation time for employees.

I. Paid vacations in America are much shorter than they are in other countries.
    A. My friend Jay complains because he has only one week of paid vacation.
    B. According to Perri Capell (*Wall Street Journal*), many American employees get only a one-week vacation during their first year of work.
    C. Most European countries give employees five weeks of vacation time during their first year of work.
    D. My sister lives in London and gets five weeks off each year.

II. Longer vacations allow employees to have a family life.
    A. Employees with children need time for the children.
    B. With current rules, many children must spend the summer in day camps.
    C. One week is not enough time to have adequate family holidays.

III. Employees with too little time off may burn out.
    A. According to psychologist Brenda Armour, "employees face stress-related illnesses because they don't get enough time off."
    B. Add anecdote about Ted M., who had a nervous breakdown.
    C. The physical health of employees deteriorates when they lack vacation time.

Conclusion: To improve the health and the morale of employees, the government needs to legislate more vacation time.

PRACTICE 18

1. Circle the topic and underline the controlling idea in the thesis statement.

2. The author uses many types of supporting material. Do the following:
   a. Underline three anecdotes.   b. Circle two informed opinions.

3. Write a few sentences that could appear in the introduction before the thesis statement. (For ideas about how to write an introduction, look in Chapter 13, "Writing the Essay.")

_____

_____

_____

_____

An Argument Essay

The next essay was written by college student Christine Bigras.

The Importance of Music

1   Most parents want their children to receive a well-rounded education. Students study traditional subjects like math, science, English, history, geography, and physical education, but many educators and parents have come to believe that school children should also be taught fine arts subjects. Thus, often school boards offer art, dance, and music, if not as core courses, then at least as extracurricular activities. Although the study and practice of all these arts develop sensitivity and creativity in students, learning music is the most beneficial to all-around student success.

2   First, music makes a child smarter. Everybody has already heard about scientists or doctors who are also musicians. A child who studies music may not become a genius; nevertheless, several research findings have shown that music lessons can enhance IQ and develop intelligence. One of the most recent and conclusive studies, "Music Lessons Enhance IQ," was conducted by E. Glenn Schellenberg from the University of Toronto and was published by *American Psychological Society Magazine* in 2004. This work concluded that there was a link between children who studied music and their academic success because music and schoolwork may develop similar problem-solving skills in children.

3   Furthermore, music education improves a child's physical and psychological health. Playing music is excellent exercise for the heart, especially for those who play a wind instrument. A child will also learn to stand straight and adopt good posture. Playing music also decreases stress and anxiety. Through music, the apprentices will learn concentration and listening skills. Furthermore, high school students who participate in band or orchestra are less interested in the use of all illegal substances (alcohol, tobacco, and drugs) according to the Texas Commission on Drug and Alcohol Abuse Report. The National Data Resource Center states that about 12 percent of students are labeled "disruptive" whereas only 8 percent of students in music programs have that label.

4   Finally, music education helps a child's social development. Playing music may facilitate students to connect to each other better, particularly through participation in orchestra or a choir. No matter if a child is ugly, poor, big, or shy, he or she is as important as any other musician in the group. Music is the great equalizer. Therefore, musicians will learn how to respect each other, how to cooperate, and how to build constructive relationships with others. When Yoko Kiyuka entered my former high school, she was very shy and lonely. The music program changed her life. The connections she made helped her integrate into the school and feel valued. "Music has the power to unite us. It proves that by working together, we can create something truly beautiful," said Pinchas Zukerman, Music Director of the National Arts Centre of Canada. Therefore, music may help a child to become a better citizen, another outstanding reason to encourage children to learn music.

5   Many school boards are removing music education from the curriculum. They argue that music is not a necessary or useful course. However, the benefits conveyed by music education are tremendous. By developing a child's brain, body, and feelings, music gives him or her a better chance to be confident in life. Parents of elementary or secondary school children can play an active role in the success of their children by encouraging them to learn music. Music can make the difference in a child's life.

PRACTICE 19

1. Underline the thesis statement of the essay.

2. What introductory styles open this essay? Circle the best answer.
   a. Definition   b. Historical information
   c. General information   d. Opposing viewpoint

3. Underline the topic sentence in each body paragraph.

4. In which paragraph does the author address the opposition? _____

5. Find an example in the essay for each of the following types of evidence.

   a. Statistic: _____

   _____

   b. Anecdote: _____

   _____

   c. Quotation from informed source: _____

   _____

6. With what does the writer conclude her essay? Circle the best answer.
   a. Prediction   b. Quotation   c. Suggestion

The Writer's Room   **Topics for Argument Essays**

PARAGRAPH LINK

To practice argument writing, you could develop an essay about one of the topics found in Chapter 12, "Argument."

Writing Activity 1

Write an argument essay about one of the following topics. Remember to narrow your topic and follow the writing process.

General Topics

1. state-sponsored gambling
2. beauty contests
3. gun control
4. talk shows
5. driving laws
6. the health-care system

College and Work-Related Topics

7. outsourcing of jobs
8. great reasons to choose your college
9. the cost of a university education
10. student activism
11. the retirement age
12. dress codes at work

Writing Activity 2

Read the following quotations. Find one that you agree or disagree with or one that inspires you in some way, and use it as the basis for an argument essay.

> Advertising is legalized lying.
> —H. G. Wells, British author

> An eye for an eye leads to a world of the blind.
> —Mahatma Gandhi, Indian activist

> Peace is not merely a distant goal that we seek, but the means by which we arrive at that goal.
> —Dr. Martin Luther King, Jr., American civil rights leader

> The thing that impresses me the most about America is the way that parents obey their children.
> —King Edward VIII, British monarch

> Choice has always been a privilege of those who could afford to pay for it.
> —Ellen Frankfort, American journalist

✓ **ARGUMENT ESSAY CHECKLIST**

As you write your argument essay, review the essay checklist on the inside front cover. Also ask yourself the following questions.

☐ Does my thesis statement clearly state my position on the issue?

☐ Do I include facts, examples, statistics, logical consequences, or answers to my opponents in my body paragraphs?

☐ Do my supporting arguments provide evidence that directly supports each topic sentence?

☐ Do I use transitions that will help readers follow my ideas?

How Do I Get a Better Grade?

Enhancing Your Writing with Research

> *Research is formalized curiosity. It is poking and prying with a purpose.*
>
> —ZORA NEALE HURSTON
> *American playwright and author (1891–1960)*

CONTENTS

When you want to seek more information about something, you might talk to other people, look for resources in libraries, bookstores, and museums, make phone calls, search the Internet, and so on. You can use the same tools when looking for details to include in your writing.

What Is Research?

When you **research,** you look for information that will help you better understand a subject. For example, when you plan to see a movie and read movie reviews in the newspaper, you are engaging in research to make an informed decision. At college, you are often asked to quote outside sources in your essays. And, if you have ever looked for a job, you might have read the newspaper's classified ads, talked to employment counselors, or spoken to potential employers.

This chapter gives you some strategies for researching information and effectively adding it to your writing.

Research for Academic Writing

There is a formal type of writing called the research paper. However, many types of academic essays, especially those with the purpose of persuading, can benefit from research. Additional facts, quotations, and statistics can back up your arguments.

Student writer David Raby-Pepin prepared an argument for an essay about rap music. You may have read his essay in Chapter 13. His purpose was to persuade the reader that rap musicians share positive cultural values. The following paragraph is from his essay.

David's Paragraph Without Research

Many of these musicians shout out a powerful message of nonviolence. They promote peace by denouncing the fighting that takes place within their own community. Many leading hip-hop and rap artists are breaking away from the "gangsta rap" lyrics and writing music that shows a productive way to resolve social issues.

David's paragraph, although interesting, is not entirely convincing. He refers to artists who are writing about social issues, but he doesn't mention the names of those artists. David decided to do some research and support his points with specific details. He found many Internet sites about his topic that are run by hip-hop fans, but he worried that his readers might be skeptical if he used those sources. He kept searching and found two quotations from reputable sources.

David's Paragraph with Research

Many of these musicians shout out a powerful message of nonviolence. They promote peace by denouncing the fighting that takes place within their own community. The hip-hop artists 4Peace write lyrics promoting an end to gun violence; their mission "is to sell peace as aggressively as other rappers peddle sex and violence" (Kahn). To open up the debate on violent behavior, the National Hip-Hop Summit Youth Council has developed projects to encourage discussion of aggression in the music community. Many leading hip-hop and rap artists support the Council's work and are breaking away from the "gangsta rap" lyrics. They write music that shows a productive way to resolve social issues. Chuck D. of Public Enemy states, "Too often, rap artists focus on the 'gangsta fairy tale' without mentioning the repercussions" (Marks).

◄ David added two quotations from respected publications. He included the authors' last names in parentheses. Because the publications were on Web sites, he did not include page numbers in the parentheses.

Later, at the end of his essay, David also included a "Works Cited" page with the following information. (You will learn more about the Works Cited page later in this chapter.)

Works Cited

Kahn, Joseph P. "The Message." Boston Globe 10 Oct. 2006. 23 May
   2007 <http://www.boston.com/yourlife/articles/2006/10/10/
   the_message>.
Marks, Alexandra. "Hip Hop Tries to Break Images of Violence."
   Christian Science Monitor 14 Nov. 2002. 23 May 2007 <http://
   www.csmonitor.com/2002/1114/p01s04-ussc.html>.

 **Avoid Plagiarism!**

Plagiarism is the act of using someone else's words or ideas without giving that person credit. Plagiarism is a very serious offense and can result in expulsion from college or termination from work.

The following actions are examples of plagiarism.

- Buying another work and presenting it as your own
- Using another student's work and presenting it as your own
- Failing to use quotation marks or properly set off an author's exact words
- Using ideas from another source without citing that source
- Making slight modifications to an author's sentences but presenting the work as your own

off the mark.com   by Mark Parisi

YOUR TERM PAPER ON "THE GROWING PROBLEM OF PLAGIARISM IN SOCIETY" IS EYE-OPENING...ESPECIALLY SINCE IT'S THE THIRD TIME I'VE SEEN IT...

To avoid plagiarism, always cite the source when you borrow words, phrases, or ideas from an author. Include the author's name, the title of the work, and the page number (if it is available).

Gathering Information

To find information that will bolster your essay, consult sources in the library or on the Internet.

Using the Library

When you first enter a library, ask the reference librarian to help you locate information using various research tools, such as online catalogues, CD-ROMs, and microforms.

- **Search the library's online catalogue.** You can search by keyword, author, title, or subject. When you find a listing that interests you, remember to jot down the title, author, and call number. You will need that information when you search the library shelves.
- **Use online periodical services in libraries.** Your library may have access to *EBSCOhost®* or *INFOtrac*. By typing keywords into EBSCO*host®*, you can search through national or international newspapers, magazines, and reference books. When you find an article that you need, print it or cut and paste it in a Word file and then e-mail the document to yourself. Remember to print or copy the publication data because you will need that information when you cite your source.

Using the Internet

The Internet is a valuable research tool. You will be able to find information about almost any topic online. Here are some tips to help you with your online research.

- **Use efficient search engines** such as *Google*, *Yahoo!*, or *Ixquick*. Those sites can rapidly retrieve thousands of documents from the Internet. However, most people do not need as many documents as those engines can generate.

- **Choose your keywords with care.** Narrow your search by putting in very specific key words. For example, to bolster an essay about binge drinking, you might try to find information about deaths due to alcohol poisoning. By placing quotation marks around your key words, you further limit your search. For example, when you input the words *alcohol poisoning deaths* into Google without quotation marks, you will have over a million hits. When the same words are enclosed with quotation marks, the number of hits is reduced to about five hundred, and the displayed web pages are more relevant.

- **Use bookmarks.** When you find information that might be useful, create a folder where you can store the information so that you can easily find it later. (The bookmark icon appears on the toolbar of your search engine.)

- **Use academic search engines.** Sites such as *Google Scholar* (scholar.google.com) or *Virtual Learning Resources Center* (virtuallrc.com) help you look through academic publications.

Hint   **Useful Internet Sites**

The following Web sites could be useful when you research on the Internet.

Statistics

Statistics from over one hundred government agencies	www.fedstats.gov
Bureau of Labor Statistics	www.stats.bls.gov
U.S. Census Bureau	www.census.gov

News Organizations

Addresses of hundreds of online magazines	newsdirectory.com
Access to newspapers from all over the world	www.newspapers.com
New York Times site for college students	www.nytimes.com/college

Other Sites

Job sites	www.monster.com
	www.jobs.org
Internet Public Library	www.ipl.org/reading
Online encyclopedias	www.encyclopedia.com
	www.britannica.com

Academic Research Sites

Google Scholar	scholar.google.com

Evaluating Sources

Be careful when you use Internet sources. Some sites contain misleading information, and some sites are maintained by people who have very strong and specific biases. Remember that the content of Internet sites is not always verified for accuracy. When you view Web sites, try to determine who benefits from the publication. What is the site's purpose?

 **Evaluating a Source**

When you find a source, ask yourself the following questions:

- Will the information support the point that I want to make?
- Is the information current? Check the date of publication of the material you are considering.
- Is the source reliable and highly regarded? For instance, is the source from a respected newspaper, journal, or Web site?
- Is the author an expert on the subject?
- Does the author present a balanced view, or does he or she clearly favor one viewpoint over another? Ask yourself if the author has a financial or personal interest in the issue.
- On various sites, do different authors supply the same information? Information is more likely to be reliable if multiple sources cite the same facts.

PRACTICE I

Imagine that you are writing an essay about the dangers of online gambling. Your audience is other college students. To enhance your argument, you want to add some facts, statistics, anecdotes, and quotations to your essay. Answer the questions by referring to the list of Web sites below.

1. Which sites would likely contain useful information? For each site that you choose, explain why it could be useful.

   _____

   _____

   _____

2. Which sites are probably not useful for your essay? For each site you choose, explain why.

   _____

   _____

   _____

   _____

A. **Bill to Ban Gambling Online Gets 4th Chance—washingtonpost.com**
Online poker players will have to fold their hands if a Virginia congressman gets his way. www.washingtonpost.com

B. **Petition to: Ban Online Gambling In The UK.**
I wish that the Goverment would ban online gambling Web sites like JackpotJoy as these online sites a . . . petitions.pm.gov.uk/remotegambling/-

C. **Gambling.com—Casino Sites**
One of the major benefits of online gambling is that it gives the gambler a lot more choice in deciding on where they are going to place their bets. . . . www.gambling.com/best/casino-sites.htm

D. **The Chronicle: Daily News Blog: Gambling Addiction Blamed as . . .**
A former student at Lehigh University pleaded guilty this morning to a felony charge of robbing a bank in order to finance an online gambling addiction, . . . chronicle.com/news/article/

E. **MedlinePlus Medical Encyclopedia: Pathological gambling**
. . . Like alcohol or drug addiction, pathological gambling is a chronic disorder that tends to get worse without treatment. . . . www.nlm.nih.gov/medlineplus/ency/article/001520.htm

F. **Derek's Rantings and Musings: Poker Archives**
I'm not sure if it's a testament to self-control (and, obviously, the fact that I am not a gambling addict *grin*), or if it's simply an indication of how . . . blog.megacity.org/archives/cat_poker.php

Web Addresses

When you evaluate Internet sites, you can often determine what type of organization runs the Web site by looking at the last three letters of the Uniform Resource Locator (URL) address.

URL Ending	Meaning	Example
.com	Company	www.nytimes.com
.edu	Educational institution	univ.phoenix.edu
.gov	Government	www.irs.gov
.net	Network	www.jobs.net
.org	Organization	www.magazines.org

Keeping Track of Sources

When you find interesting sources, make sure that you record the following information. Later, when you incorporate quotations or paraphrases into your work, you can quickly find the source of the information. (You will learn how to cite sources later in this chapter.)

Book, Magazine, Newspaper	**Web Site**
Author's full name	Author's full name
Title of article	Title of article
Title of book, magazine, or newspaper	Title of Web site
Publishing information (name of publisher, city, and date of publication)	Date of publication or last printing
Pages used	Date you accessed the site
	Complete Web site address

 **Hint**   **Finding Complete Source Information**

Source information is easy to find in most print publications. It is usually on the second or third page of the book, magazine, or newspaper. On many Internet sites, however, finding the same information can take more investigative work. When you research on the Internet, look for the home page to find the site's title. The Modern Language Association (MLA) recommends that you find and cite as much source information as is available on the Web site (author's name, title of article, date of publication, etc.).

RESEARCH LINK

To find out more about the MLA and its guidelines, visit the MLA Web site at www.mla.org.

Add a Paraphrase, Summary, or Quotation

To add research to a piece of writing, you can paraphrase it, summarize it, or quote it.

- When you **paraphrase,** you use your own words to present someone's ideas. A paraphase is about the same length as the original selection.
- When you **summarize,** you briefly state the main ideas of another work. A summary is much shorter than the original selection.
- When you **quote,** you either directly state a person's exact words (with quotation marks) or report them (without quotation marks).

All of these are valid ways to incorporate research in your writing, as long as you give credit to the author or speaker.

Paraphrasing and Summarizing

Both paraphrases and summaries present the ideas that you have found from another source. Before you can restate someone's ideas, you must ensure that you have a very clear understanding of those ideas. Thus, the first thing you must do when you paraphrase or summarize is to read the text carefully.

How to Paraphrase

When you paraphrase, you keep the length and order of the original selection, but you restate the ideas using your own words. To paraphrase, do the following steps.

- Read the original text carefully and underline any key ideas. Ensure that you understand the text.
- Use your own words to restate the key ideas of the original text. To help prevent copying, do not look again at the original source.
- Use approximately the same number of words as the original passage.
- Do not change the meaning of the original text. Do not include your own opinions.
- Document the source. State the author and title of the original text.
- Reread your paraphrase. Verify that you have respected the order and emphasis of the original source.

How to Summarize

A summary is much shorter than a paraphrase, and it presents a global view. To summarize, do the following steps.

- Read the original text carefully. Ensure that you understand the main point.
- Ask yourself *who, what, when, where, why,* and *how* questions. These questions will help you to synthesize the ideas of the original text.
- Restate the essential ideas in your own words.
- Maintain the original meaning of the text. Do not include your own opinions.
- Document the source. State the author and title of the original text.
- Reread your summary. Verify that you have explained the central message.

 **Consider Your Audience**

When you decide whether to paraphrase or summarize, think about your audience.

- Paraphrase if your audience needs detailed information about the subject.
- Summarize if the audience needs to know only general information.

PRACTICE 2

The next selection, written by Adam Liptak, appeared in the August 24, 2003 edition of the New York Times on page A16. Read the selection, the paraphrase, and the summary, and then answer the questions that follow.

Original Selection

Gerald Sanders, 48, will spend the rest of his life in an Alabama prison because he stole a $16 bicycle. He had a five-year history of burglaries, none of them involving violence, and that record was enough under the state's habitual offender law to require a judge to send him away forever. Since California enacted a law requiring tough sentences for many third offenses in 1994, the trend in many states has been toward long, fixed sentences, even for nonviolent crimes.

Paraphrase

Adam Liptak, in the New York Times, reports that an Alabama citizen who committed a minor crime has been sentenced to life imprisonment. Because of a bicycle theft and a series of previous robberies, Gerald Sanders will die in jail. Following California's lead, Alabama and numerous other states have enacted strict three-strike laws that punish habitual offenders, including those who are not violent (A16).

Summary

Numerous states have followed California's lead and enacted three-strike laws, giving long prison sentences to habitual offenders. This law applies even to those who do not use violence, according to Adam Liptak in the New York Times (A16).

1. In the paraphrase and summary, does the writer express an opinion? _____

2. In the paraphrase and summary, the writer gives three pieces of information about the source. What are they?

_____

_____

_____

3. What is the main difference between a paraphrase and a summary?

_____

_____

 **Paraphrasing and Summarizing**

When you paraphrase or summarize, avoid looking at the original document. After you finish writing, compare your version with the original and ensure that you have not used too many words from the original document.

PRACTICE 3

Read the following selections and answer the questions. The original selection, written by Martin Seligman, appeared in the <u>APA Monitor</u> on page 97.

Original Selection

Unfortunately it turns out that hit men, genocidal maniacs, gang leaders, and violent kids often have high self-esteem, not low self-esteem. A recipe for their violence is a mean streak combined with an unwarranted sense of self-worth. When such a boy comes across a girl or parents or schoolmates who communicate to him that he is not all that worthy, he lashes out.

Summary 1

In the <u>APA Monitor</u>, Martin Seligman says that hit men and genocidal maniacs often have high self-esteem. Their mean streak combines with an unwarranted sense of self-worth and creates a recipe for violence (97).

1. How does this summary plagiarize the original piece of writing?

_____

_____

_____

_____

Summary 2

Violent youths, like hired assassins and other murderers, often have self-esteem that is too high. Such youths lash out when others question their worthiness.

2. How does this summary plagiarize the original piece of writing?

_____

_____

_____

_____

 **Mention Your Source**

When you paraphrase or summarize, remember to mention the name of the author and the title of the publication. If the page number is available, place it in parentheses.

PRACTICE 4

Paraphrase and summarize the original selection. Remember that a paraphrase respects the length and order of the original document, whereas a summary is a very condensed version of the original. The next selection, written by Carol R. Ember and Melvin Ember, appeared on page 239 of their book Cultural Anthropology.

Original Selection

Religious beliefs and practices are found in all known contemporary societies, and archaeologists think they have found signs of religious belief associated with Homo sapiens who lived at least 60,000 years ago. People then deliberately buried their dead, and many graves contain the remains of food, tools, and other objects that were probably thought to be needed in an afterlife.

Paraphrase: _____

_____

_____

_____

_____

_____

_____

_____

Summary: _____

_____

_____

_____

_____

Quoting Sources

An effective way to support your arguments is to include quotations. Use quotations to reveal the opinions of an expert or to include ideas that are particularly memorable and important. When quoting sources, remember to limit how many you use in a single paper and to vary your quotations by using both direct and indirect quotations.

> **GRAMMAR LINK**
>
> To find out more about using quotations, see Chapter 34.

Direct and Indirect Quotations

A **direct quotation** contains the exact words of an author, and the quotation is set off with quotation marks.

A survey released by the Police Foundation states, "There are enough guns in private hands to provide every adult in America with one."

An **indirect quotation** keeps the author's meaning but is not set off by quotation marks.

A survey released by the Police Foundation states that there are so many privately owned guns in the United States that every adult could be given one.

How to Introduce or Integrate a Quotation

Quotations should be integrated into sentences. To learn how to introduce or integrate quotations in your writing, read the following original selection and then view three common methods. The selection, written by John E. Farley, appeared on page 97 of his book, <u>Sociology</u>.

Original Selection

Human history abounds with legends of lost or deserted children who were raised by wild animals. Legend has it, for example, that Rome was founded by Romulus and Remus, who had been raised in the wild by a wolf.

1. **Phrase introduction**

   You can introduce the quotation with a phrase followed by a comma. Capitalize the first word in the quotation. Place the page number in parentheses.

   In <u>Sociology</u>, John E. Farley writes, "Human history abounds with legends of lost or deserted children who were raised by wild animals" (97).

   Alternatively, you can place the phrase after the quotation. End the quotation with a comma instead of a period.

   "Human history abounds with legends of lost or deserted children who were raised by wild animals," writes John E. Farley in <u>Sociology</u> (97).

2. **Sentence introduction**

   Introduce the quotation with a sentence followed by a colon. Capitalize the first word in the quotation.

   In his book <u>Sociology</u>, John E. Farley suggests that such stories are not new: "Human history abounds with legends of lost or deserted children who were raised by wild animals" (97).

3. **Integrated quotation**

   Integrate the quotation as a part of your sentence. Place quotation marks around the source's exact words. Do not capitalize the first word in the quotation.

   In <u>Sociology</u>, John E. Farley mentions a legend about the twin founders of Rome "who had been raised in the wild by a wolf" (97).

 **Words That Introduce Quotations**

One common way to introduce a quotation is to write, "The author says . . ." However, there are a variety of other verbs that you can use.

admits	concludes	mentions	speculates
claims	explains	observes	suggests
comments	maintains	reports	warns

PRACTICE 5

Practice integrating quotations. Read the following selection and then write direct and indirect quotations. The selection, written by Daniel R. Brower, appeared on page 371 of his book, <u>The World in the Twentieth Century</u>.

> The collapse of German communism began with the regime's desperate decision to grant complete freedom of travel to East Germans. On the night of November 9, the gates through the Berlin Wall were opened to all. The city became the center of an enormous celebration by East and West Berliners. Some of them climbed the wall itself to celebrate.

1. Write a direct quotation.

_____

_____

_____

_____

2. Write an indirect quotation.

_____

_____

_____

_____

Cite Sources Using MLA Style

Each time you use another writer's words or ideas, you must **cite the source,** giving complete information about the original document from which you borrowed the material. When quoting, paraphrasing, or summarizing, you can offset the source information using parentheses. These **in-text citations**, also known as **parenthetical citations**, allow you to acknowledge where you obtained the information. You must also cite your sources in an alphabetized list at the end of your essay. The Modern Language Association (MLA) refers to the list as Works Cited.

 **Choose a Documentation Style**

The three most common styles for documenting sources are the Modern Language Association (MLA) format, <u>Chicago Manual of Style</u> (CMS) format, and the American Psychological Association (APA) format. Before writing a paper, check with your instructor to see which documentation style you should use and to learn where you can find more information about it.

Citing the Source in the Body of Your Essay

When you introduce a quotation or idea, try to mention the source directly in your paragraph or essay. The next examples show how you can cite some common sources using MLA style.

1. **Mention the author and page number in parentheses.**

   Put the author's last name and the page number in parentheses. Place the final period after the parentheses, not inside the quotation marks.

Successful people fight to succeed: "They have determined that nothing will stop them from going forward" (Carson 224).

2. **Mention the page number in parentheses.**

If you mention the author's name in the introductory phrase, put only the page number in the parentheses. Place the final period after the parentheses.

> According to Ben Carson, "Successful people don't have fewer problems" (224).

3. **Mention the Internet site.**

If you are using a Web-based source, no page number is necessary. If you do not know the author's name, then put the title of the Web page in parentheses.

> Furthermore, according to the Bureau of Statistics for the U.S. Department of Labor, elephant trainers have a hazardous job, and "the relative risk is 68 times greater than for the typical worker" ("Dangerous").

GRAMMAR LINK

To find out more about writing titles, see pages 513–515 in Chapter 34.

 **Hint**   **Writing Titles for Borrowed Material**

Place the title of a short work (article, short story, or individual page on a Web site) in quotation marks, and underline the title of a longer work (book, magazine, newspaper, or the name of an entire Web site). If you are using a computer, you can choose to italicize or underline the titles of longer works.

Underlined: "Addicted to Exercise" appears in <u>Newsweek</u>.

Italicized: "Addicted to Exercise" appears in *Newsweek*.

Preparing a Works Cited Page

Sometimes called a References list or Bibliography, the Works Cited page gives details about each source you have used and appears at the end of your paper. To prepare a Works Cited page, use this format.

- Write Works Cited at the top of the page and center it.
- List each source alphabetically, using the last names of the authors.
- Indent the second line and all subsequent lines of each reference.

Here are some examples of how to cite different types of publications. Notice that the author's name and title are separated by periods, not commas. Also, publishers' names are shortened: for example, Random House is cited as Random.

Book

> Last name, First name. <u>Title of Book</u>. City of publication: Publisher, Year.

- **One author**

  Tan, Amy. <u>The Joy Luck Club</u>. New York: Random, 1990.

- **Two or more authors**

  Ember, Carol R., and Melvin Ember. <u>Cultural Anthropology</u>. Upper Saddle River: Prentice, 2002.

- **Essay in an anthology**

  Budnitz, Judy. "Nadia." <u>The Best American Nonrequired Reading</u>. Ed. Dave Eggers. Boston: Houghton, 2006.

- **Encyclopedia**

  "Haiti." <u>Columbia Encyclopedia</u>. 6th ed. 2005.

Periodical

Last name, First name. "Title of Article." <u>Title of Magazine or Newspaper</u>
Date: pages.

- **Magazine**

  Stix, Gary. "Spice Healer." <u>Scientific American</u> Feb. 2007: 66-69.

- **Newspaper**

  Knight, Heather. "The Final Farewell." <u>San Francisco Chronicle</u> 15 Apr.
  2007: A1.

Print Journal

Last name, First name. "Title of Article." <u>Title of Journal</u> Volume
Number.Issue (Year): pages.

Seligman, Martin. "The American Way of Blame." <u>APA Monitor</u> 29.7 (1998): 97.

Electronic Source

If the information was published on the Internet, include as much of the following
information as you can find. Keep in mind that some sites do not contain complete
information. Please note that you must add a period after the title of the Web site
unless the site is an online periodical. No period is required after the titles of
online magazines or newspapers.

Author. "Title of Article." <u>Title of Site or Online Publication</u>. Date of publication
or most recent update. Date you accessed the site <network address>.

- **Online Periodical**

  Slator, Dashka. "It's All Fun and Games." <u>Salon.com</u> 26 Mar. 2007. 15 May
  2007 <http://www.salon.com/mwt/feature/2007/03/26/fun/index.html>.

- **A Document from an Internet Site**

  Nankani, Gobind. "Creating Shared Wealth in Africa." <u>The World Bank</u>.
  6 Dec. 2004. 11 June 2007 <http://go.worldbank.org/OR0UE8SGT0>.

Other Sources

- **Personal Interview**

  Include the person's name, the words "Personal interview," and the date, as
  shown below.

  Anaya, Lourdes. Personal interview. 12 Sept. 2008.

- **Film, Video, or DVD**

  Include the name of the film, the director, the studio, and the year of release.

  <u>Friday Night Lights</u>. Dir. Peter Berg. DVD. Universal Studios. 2004.

- **Television Program**

  Include the segment title, the program name, the network, and the broadcast date.

  "Turning the Tables." <u>Primetime</u>. ABC News. 26 Dec. 2006.

- **Sound Recording**

Include the name of the performer or band, the title of the song, the title of the CD-ROM, the name of the recording company, and the year of release.

Charles, Ray. "Fever." Genius Loves Company. Hear Music, 2004.

 **Placement and Order of Works Cited**

The works cited should be at the end of the research paper. List sources in alphabetical order using the author's last names. If there is no author, list the title (but ignore *A*, *An*, or *The*, which may appear at the beginning of the title).

Knight, Heather. "The Final Farewell." San Francisco Chronicle 15 Apr. 2007: A1.

Slator, Dashka. "It's All Fun and Games." Salon.com 26 Mar. 2007. 15 May 2007 <http://www.salon.com/mwt/feature/2007/03/26/fun/index.html>.

"Test Vote Leaves Immigration Bill in Doubt." CNN.com. 2007. 7 June 2007. <http://www.cnn.com/2007/POLITICS/06/07/congress.immigration.ap/index.html>.

PRACTICE 6

The four sources below were used in a research paper about humor and creativity. Arrange the sources for a Works Cited list using MLA style.

- Some quotations are from a book called Creative Intelligence by Alan J. Rowe. The book was published by Pearson Education in Upper Saddle River, New Jersey, in 2004.
- A summary is of a newspaper article by Steve Winn called "Offensive Language." It appeared in the April 15, 2007, edition of The San Francisco Chronicle on page A1.
- Some quotations are from a magazine article that Louise Dobson wrote called "What's Your Humor Style?" The article appeared in the August 2006 issue of Psychology Today on pages 74 to 77.
- A paraphrase is from an article called "Humor in the Workplace" by Maggie Finefrock. The article was on the Web site The Learning Project, which was last updated on March 9, 2004. The student viewed the article on May 2, 2008. The Web site address is http://thelearningproject.com/humor.htm.

Works Cited

_____

_____

_____

_____

_____

_____

_____

_____

_____

_____

Sample Research Essay Using MLA Style

Read a complete student essay. Notice how the student integrates paraphrases, summaries, and quotations.

Alapi 1

Zachary Alapi

Mrs. Wheatcroft

ARH LFA 01

April 24, 2006

Goya's Greatest Work

Francisco José de Goya y Lucientes (1746–1828) is one of the most renowned and famous Spanish artists whose work has had a tremendous and lasting impact on the world of art. One of Goya's most famous paintings is titled The Shootings of May 3, 1808. It is an extremely powerful and evocative work that captures the brutality of the French occupation of Spain during the reign of Napoleon. There is little doubt that Goya's message regarding his feelings on religious hypocrisy and the elevation of the common Spaniard are clearly visible in The Shootings of May 3, 1808.

The Shootings of May 3, 1808 was painted in the context of the French occupation of Spain under Napoleon. For the Spanish, this was a war of independence against the oppression and tyrannical rule of Napoleon, as well as an attempt to rid the country of the political corruption that was so rampant (Gassier and Wilson 205). Spanish guerrilla fighters launched attacks on French troops, which led to French firing squads killing captured Spanish guerrilla fighters (Alexander 194). The Spaniards killed at the hands of the firing squads became heroes and martyrs for the Spanish cause. In the work, Goya elevates the common Spaniard to a seemingly Christ-like status against the faceless oppressive French soldiers.

The unique and revolutionary techniques in painting used by Goya throughout his career can be seen in The Shootings of May 3, 1808. Goya used a fairly limited color palette and his scheme of light, shadow, line, and color was generally subordinate to the cartoon-like subject matter (Myers 20). His aim seems to be to shock the viewer with a harsh and brutally realistic portrayal of the scene. Compositionally, "Goya seems to have related his form in a positive way to the edge of the canvas or wall area," which essentially means that the majority of the action in his work takes place in a lit central oval surrounded by darkness, leaving the corners of the canvas empty (Myers 24). This focus is important in the context of the The Shootings of May 3, 1808 because the top half and the bottom right corner of the canvas are completely dark. "Both the night and symmetrical composition of the subjects emphasize the drama" ("Goya"). The light, which shines specifically on the central peasant figure, captures the attention of the viewer and places the emphasis on what is happening to the peasant. This painting technique makes his defiance toward the firing squad even more poignant and emphatic.

◄ Double-space your name, instructor's name, course title, and date.

◄ Title in middle. (Notice that the title is not underlined, boldfaced, or italicized.)

◄ Double-space the body of the essay.

◄ Acknowledge sources of borrowed ideas.

◄ Notice that a paraphrase of someone's idea is acknowledged.

◄ Place author's name and page number in parentheses.

◄ For an Internet source, place the title of the Web page in parentheses.

Alapi 2

Goya identified closely with the Spanish people, and through his depiction of them in The Shootings of May 3, 1808, he shows how he shares their sentiments (Lassaigne 96). While the common peasant is the martyr, the monk cowers at his feet, unable to stand up to the firing squad. Religion, which is supposed to provide stability and courage for the people, is depicted as weak and not carrying out its duties, forcing the peasant to stand up to the executioners. Furthermore, the monastery in the background is shrouded in an inauspicious darkness, which is juxtaposed by the light shining on the central peasant figure, thereby suggesting that the courage of the common man is to be celebrated, not the church, which is weak and hypocritical.

The Shootings of May 3, 1808 is a powerful and important painting that explores the elevation of the common Spanish peasant to a seemingly divine status and criticizes the hypocrisy of the church. The realistic representation of the subject matter accentuates the emotions and messages depicted. Through his brutally honest depiction of the shootings, Goya conveys a sense of suffering, courage, and human sacrifice by his glorification of the common man, who is the eternal victim of war and its inhumanity.

Alapi 3

Works Cited

Alexander, Don. "French Replacement Methods during the Peninsular War, 1808–1814." Military Affairs 44.4 (1980): 192-197.

Gassier, Pierre, and Juliet Wilson. The Life and Complete Work of Francisco Goya. New York: Reynal, 1971.

"Goya." Spanish Arts. 2003. 22 Jan. 2007 <http://www.spanisharts.com/prado/ goya.htm>.

Lassaigne, Jacques. Spanish Painting from Velazquez to Picasso. Cleveland: World, 1952.

Myers, Bernard. Goya. London: Spring, 1964.

Center the title of the Works Cited page. ➤

Double-space sources. ➤

Place sources in alphabetical order. ➤

Indent the second line of each source by ½ inch. ➤

REFLECT ON IT

Think about what you have learned in this chapter. If you do not know an answer, review that topic.

1. What are the differences between a paraphrase and a summary?

   Paraphrase   **Summary**

   _____   _____

   _____   _____

   _____   _____

   _____   _____

2. What are the differences between direct and indirect quotations?

   Direct   **Indirect**

   _____   _____

   _____   _____

   _____   _____

3. What is a Works Cited page?

   _____

   _____

   _____

   _____

 The Writer's Room **Research**

Writing Activity 1

Choose a paragraph or an essay that you have written, and research your topic to get more detailed information. Then insert at least one paraphrase, one summary, and one quotation into your work. Remember to acknowledge your sources.

Writing Activity 2

Write an essay about one of the following topics. Your essay should include research (find at least three sources). Include a Works Cited page at the end of your assignment.

1. Write about a contemporary issue that is in the news. In your essay, give your opinion about the issue.

2. Write about your career choice. You could mention job opportunities in your field, and you could include statistical information.

3. Write about the importance of a college education. Does a college education help or hurt a person's career prospects? Find some facts, examples, or statistics to support your view.

How Do I Get a Better Grade?

Visit www.mywritinglab.com for audio-visual lectures and additional practice sets about enhancing your writing with research.

mywritinglab

Get a better grade with MyWritingLab!

PART

The Editing Handbook

Why Is Grammar So Important?

When you speak, you have tools such as tone of voice and body language to help you express your ideas. When you write, however, you have only words and punctuation to get your message across. Naturally, if your writing contains errors in style, grammar, and punctuation, you may distract readers from your message, and they may focus, instead, on your inability to communicate clearly. You increase your chances of succeeding in your academic and professional life when you write in clear standard English.

The chapters in this Editing Handbook can help you understand important grammar concepts and ensure that your writing is grammatically correct.

16 Simple Sentences

CHAPTER

Section Theme **CULTURE**

CONTENTS

In this chapter, you will read about topics related to advertising *and* consumerism.

The Writer's Desk Warm Up

What is your cultural background? How would you identify yourself culturally? Write a paragraph about your cultural identity.

Identify Subjects

A **sentence** contains one or more subjects and verbs, and it expresses a complete thought. Although some sentences can have more than one idea, a **simple sentence** expresses one complete thought. The **subject** tells you who or what the sentence is about. The **verb** expresses an action or state. If a sentence is missing a subject or a verb, it is incomplete.

Singular and Plural Subjects

Subjects may be singular or plural. To determine the subject of a sentence, ask yourself who or what the sentence is about.

A **singular subject** is one person, place, or thing.

> **Oprah Winfrey** is known around the world.

> **Chicago** is her hometown.

A **plural subject** is more than one person, place, or thing.

> Contemporary **musicians** try to reach a mass audience.

> Many **countries** import American products.

Pronouns

A **subject pronoun** (*he, she, it, you, I, we, they*) can act as the subject of a sentence, and it replaces the noun.

> Reese Witherspoon stars in many films. **She** is known around the world.

> Directors make many action films. **They** hope the films will interest young males.

Gerunds (-*ing* words)

Sometimes a gerund (-*ing* form of the verb) is the subject of a sentence.

> **Relaxing** is important.

> **Business planning** is an ongoing process.

Compound Subjects

Many sentences have more than one subject. *Compound* means "multiple." Therefore, a **compound subject** contains two or more subjects.

> **Men** and **women** evaluate products differently.

> The **accountants, designers,** and **advertisers** will meet to discuss the product launch.

> ## Hint > Recognizing Simple and Complete Subjects
>
> In a sentence, the **simple subject** is the noun or pronoun. The complete name of a person, place, or organization is a simple subject.
>
> | he | dancer | Homer Simpson | Sony Music Corporation |
>
> The **complete subject** is the noun, plus the words that describe the noun. In the next examples, the descriptive words are in italics.
>
> | *new electric* piano | *the old, worn-out* shoes | *Anna's green* convertible |
>
> In the following sentences, the simple and complete subjects are identified.
>
> simple subject
> The glossy new **magazine** contained interesting articles.
> complete subject

PRACTICE I

Underline the complete subject and circle the simple subject(s).

EXAMPLE:

Academic institutions teach popular culture.

1. Popular music, films, books, and fashions are the sources of our common culture.

2. University professors and administrators did not see the value of popular culture in the past.

3. Classical music, art, and literature were standard subjects.

4. Well-known academics made a distinction between "high" and "low" culture.

5. Opinions changed in the 1980s.

6. Some colleges began offering courses on popular culture.

7. Reality television is considered worthy of study today.

8. An old, highly respected college has a course about television game shows.

9. Alison Anthony and James O'Reilly teach popular culture.

10. They and their students enjoy discussing current trends.

Special Subject Problems
Unstated Subjects (Commands)

In a sentence that expresses a command, the subject is unstated, but it is still understood. The unstated subject is *you*.

> Remember to use your coupon.

> Pay the cashier.

here/there

Here and *there* are not subjects. In a sentence that begins with *Here* or *There*, the subject follows the verb.

> There are five <u>ways</u> to market a product.
> (The subject is *ways*.)

> Here is an interesting <u>brochure</u> about cosmetics.
> (The subject is *brochure*.)

PRACTICE 2

Circle the simple subject(s). If the subject is unstated, then write the subject (*you*) before the verb.

EXAMPLE:

you

To see the announcement, watch carefully.

1. There are many advertisements on the streets of our cities.

2. Look at any bus shelter, billboard, store window, or newspaper.

3. Certainly, some ads appear in surprising places. 4. There are framed announcements on the doors of hotel bathrooms, for example.

5. Furthermore, there are commercials hidden in the middle of the action in movies and television shows. 6. For instance, soft-drink and car companies advertised during the popular reality show *American Idol.*

7. There were soft drinks on the table in front of the show's judges.

8. The show's singers sang a tribute to an American automobile company. 9. View advertising with a critical eye.

Identify Prepositional Phrases

A **preposition** is a word that links nouns, pronouns, or phrases to other words in a sentence. It expresses a relationship based on movement or position. Here are some common prepositions.

Common Prepositions

about	before	during	near	through
above	behind	except	of	to
across	below	for	off	toward
after	beside	from	on	under
against	between	in	onto	until
along	beyond	inside	out	up
among	by	into	outside	with
around	despite	like	over	within
at	down			

A **phrase** is a group of words that is missing a subject, a verb, or both and is not a complete sentence. A **prepositional phrase** is made up of a preposition and its object (a noun or a pronoun). In the following phrases, an object follows the preposition.

Preposition	**+**	**Object**
in		the morning
among		the shadows
over		the rainbow
with		some friends

 **Be Careful**

Because the object of a preposition is a noun, it may look like a subject. However, the object in a prepositional phrase is *never* the subject of the sentence. For example, in the next sentence, the subject is *child*, not *closet*.

subject
In the closet, the **child** found the hidden gift.

Sometimes a prepositional phrase appears before or after the subject. To help you identify the subject, you can put parentheses around prepositional phrases or mark them in some other way. In each of the following sentences, the subject is in boldface type and the prepositional phrase is in parentheses.

(In spite of the costs,) **Ruth Handler** took the assignment.

(On a trip to Germany,) **she** saw an interesting product.

Her **company,** (after 1959,) expanded greatly.

Sometimes a sentence can contain more than one prepositional phrase.

prepositional phrase   prepositional phrase
(In the late 1950s,) (during a period of prosperity,) a new and original **doll** appeared in American stores.

 According to . . .

When a sentence contains *according to,* the noun that immediately follows the words *according to* is *not* the subject of the sentence. In the following sentence, *Jack Solomon* is not the subject.

subject
(According to Jack Solomon,) **Americans** are tired of fantasy advertisements.

PRACTICE 3

Place parentheses around the prepositional phrase(s) in each sentence. Then circle the simple subject.

EXAMPLE:

(In 1995,) a successful online company began.

1. In Pierre Omidyar's living room, an idea took shape.
2. With friend and co-founder Jeff Skoll, Omidyar decided to create an online flea market.
3. For several years, the company expanded.
4. Then, in 1998, a Harvard business graduate was asked to join the company.
5. Meg Whitman, with a team of top managers, helped turn eBay into a billion-dollar business.

6. Buyers and sellers, with a click of a mouse, can enter a virtual marketplace.

7. For a small fee, sellers can list items on the site.

8. Buyers, with only a picture and description to evaluate, then bid on the item.

9. At the end of the auction, an eBay employee contacts the buyer and seller.

10. In spite of some initial problems, the online auction has been tremendously successful.

PRACTICE 4

Look at the underlined word in each sentence. If it is the subject, write *C* (for "correct") beside the sentence. If the underlined word is not the subject, then circle the correct subject(s).

EXAMPLES:

In past <u>eras</u>, bustling markets sold consumer goods. _____

Enclosed shopping <u>malls</u> are a fairly recent development. _*C*_

1. In Edina, <u>Minnesota</u>, the first indoor mall was built. _____

2. The world's largest <u>mall</u> has 800 stores. _____

3. For some <u>consumers</u>, the local dress shop is a dangerous place. _____

4. On her twenty-second <u>birthday</u>, Amber Wyatt divulged a secret. _____

5. During the previous four years, <u>she</u> had piled up $60,000 in credit card debts. _____

6. She acknowledges, with a shrug, her shopping <u>addiction</u>. _____

7. Today, with a poor credit <u>rating</u>, Amber is unable to get a lease. _____

8. Her <u>brother</u>, boyfriend, and aunt have lent her money. _____

9. Her <u>parents</u>, with some reluctance, allowed their daughter to move back home. _____

10. Many <u>American</u> men and women, according to a recent survey, have a shopping addiction. _____

Identify Verbs

Every sentence must contain a verb. The **verb** either expresses what the subject does or links the subject to other descriptive words.

Action Verbs

An **action verb** describes an action that a subject performs.

In 2006, China <u>launched</u> an electric car called the Zap Xebra.

Engineers <u>designed</u> the car's energy-efficient engine.

Linking Verbs

A **linking verb** connects a subject with words that describe it, and it does not show an action. The most common linking verb is *be*.

The marketing campaign <u>is</u> expensive.

Some advertisements <u>are</u> very clever.

Other linking verbs refer to the senses and indicate how something appears, smells, tastes, and so on.

The advertising photo <u>looks</u> grainy.

The glossy paper <u>feels</u> smooth.

Common Linking Verbs

appear	feel	smell
be (am, is, are, was, were, etc.)	look	sound
become	seem	taste

Compound Verbs

When a subject performs more than one action, the verbs are called **compound verbs.**

Good advertising <u>informs</u>, <u>persuades</u>, and <u>convinces</u> consumers.

Members of the public either <u>loved</u> or <u>hated</u> the logo.

 **Hint**   **Infinitives Are Not the Main Verb**

Infinitives are verbs preceded by *to* such as *to fly, to speak,* and *to go.* An infinitive is never the main verb in a sentence.

       V   infinitive   V   infinitive
Kraft <u>wants</u> **to compete** in Asia. The company <u>hopes</u> **to sell** millions of products.

PRACTICE 5

Underline one or more verbs in these sentences.

EXAMPLE:

Some companies <u>use</u> buzz appeals.

1. Buzz marketers entice consumers to talk about a brand.

2. Some companies hire students to chat about a particular brand of clothing in online forums.

3. To promote *America's Next Top Model*, the network gave free party kits to five hundred young girls.

4. The teenage girls were the target audience for the campaign.

5. The network asked the girls to invite four friends to their homes to watch the series.

6. Occasionally, buzz advertising backfires.

7. A car company placed people in chatrooms to discuss a new SUV model.

8. However, people in the chatroom became angry about the SUVs and criticized them.

9. Guerrilla marketers ambush consumers with promotional content in unexpected places.

10. Turner Broadcasting placed electronic boards with a light-up cartoon character around Boston, Massachusetts, as part of a guerrilla marketing campaign.

11. The campaign to advertise *Aqua Teen Hunger Force* caused a panic.

12. The campaign created havoc but promoted a new cartoon series at the same time.

Helping Verbs

A verb can have several different forms, depending on the tense that is used. **Verb tense** indicates whether the action occurred in the past, present, or future. In some tenses, there is a **main verb** that expresses what the subject does or links the subject to descriptive words, but there is also a helping verb.

The **helping verb** combines with the main verb to indicate tense, negative structure, or question structure. The most common helping verbs are forms of *be*, *have*, and *do*. **Modal auxiliaries** are another type of helping verb; they indicate ability (*can*), obligation (*must*), possibility (*may, might, could*), advice (*should*), and so on. For example, here are different forms of the verb *open*. The helping verbs are underlined.

<u>is</u> opening	<u>had</u> opened	<u>will</u> open	<u>should have</u> opened
<u>was</u> opened	<u>had been</u> opening	<u>can</u> open	<u>might be</u> open
<u>has been</u> opening	<u>would</u> open	<u>could be</u> opening	<u>could have been</u> opened

The **complete verb** consists of the helping verb and the main verb. In the following examples, the helping verbs are indicated with *HV* and the main verbs with *V*.

               HV HV   V
American culture <u>has been</u> <u>spreading</u> across the globe for years.

        HV HV V
You <u>must have</u> <u>seen</u> the news articles.

In **question forms,** the first helping verb usually appears before the subject.

    HV   subject HV   V
<u>Should</u> the coffee chain <u>have</u> <u>expanded</u> so quickly?

    HV   subject   V
<u>Will</u> the coffee and cakes <u>sell</u> in Moscow?

Interrupting words may appear between verbs, but they are *not* part of the verb. Some interrupting words are *easily, actually, not, always, usually, sometimes, frequently, often, never,* and *ever.*

                             HV   V

Consumers <u>have</u> often <u>complained</u> about product quality.

                        HV   HV   V

The car maker <u>should</u> not <u>have</u> <u>destroyed</u> its electric cars.

GRAMMAR LINK

For information on the position of mid-sentence adverbs, such as *often, sometimes,* and *never,* see page 441 in Chapter 29.

PRACTICE 6

Underline the helping verbs once and the main verbs twice.

EXAMPLE:

    The modern consumerism movement <u>has</u> <u>been</u> strong since the 1960s.

1. In 1961, President John F. Kennedy outlined the Consumer Bill of Rights.

2. Products should not be dangerous or defective.

3. A single company should never have a monopoly.

4. Businesses must provide consumers with honest information.

5. Some companies have been sued for defective products.

6. Merck, a pharmaceutical company, was forced to remove the drug Vioxx from the market.

7. To protect consumers, the Federal Trade Commission has implemented rules to prevent misleading advertising.

8. Some companies have been fined for deceptive marketing methods.

9. In a Volvo ad, a monster truck ran over a row of cars and crushed all but the Volvo station wagon.

10. In fact, the Volvo's structure had been reinforced.

11. Volvo was fined $150,000 for deceptive marketing.

12. How should companies respond to consumer complaints?

PRACTICE 7

Circle the simple subjects and underline the complete verbs. Remember to underline all parts of the verb.

EXAMPLE:

    Japanese (products) <u>have captured</u> the imaginations of children around the world.

1. In 1974, a Japanese greeting card company created a white cat with vacant, staring eyes. The cat was given the name "Hello Kitty." Soon, purses, toasters, cameras, and T-shirts had the image of the little animal. For some reason, the strange cat with a bow on one ear and a missing

mouth has become a fashion icon for teenagers worldwide. Thirty years after its debut, Hello Kitty's popularity remains constant.

2. A self-taught illustrator from Japan has created another cute and creepy character. At first glance, you might not notice the details on Mori Chack's bear. The fuzzy pink toy seems to be sweet and cuddly. However, after a closer look, you will see the long, pointed claws and the drop of blood on the bear's mouth. Like Hello Kitty, Gloomy Bear has become trendy. The bear's likeness appears on clothing, key chains, and coffee mugs.

3. Some journalists, including Julia Dault and Kjeld Duits, have written about the trends. They credit Japanese animators with an ability to add a sinister twist to images of saccharine sweetness. Of course, the characters do not simply appeal to children. Gloomy Bear sells briskly to those in their twenties and thirties.

The Writer's Desk Revise and Edit Your Warm Up

Read the sentences that you wrote for the Warm Up at the beginning of this chapter. Circle the subject(s) and underline the verb(s) in each sentence. Remember to underline both the helping verbs and the main verbs. Write *V* over each main verb.

REFLECT ON IT

Think about what you have learned in this chapter. If you do not know an answer, review that concept.

1. What is a sentence? _____

_____

2. What does the subject of a sentence do? _____

_____

3. Write an example of a simple subject and a complete subject.

   a. Simple: _____

   b. Complete: _____

4. What is a verb? _____

_____

5. Write examples of action verbs and linking verbs.

   a. Action: _____

   b. Linking: _____

Circle the best answers.

6. Can the object of a preposition be the subject of a sentence?   No   Yes

7. Can a sentence have more than one subject?   No   Yes

8. Can a sentence have more than one verb?   No   Yes

FINAL REVIEW

Circle the simple subjects and underline the complete verbs. Underline *all* parts of the verb. Remember that infinitives such as *to go* or *to run* are not part of the main verb.

EXAMPLE:

In the late 1950s, during a period of prosperity, an original new (doll) appeared on American store shelves.

1. Kristin Riddick, in her book *Barbie: The Image of Us All*, describes the history of a popular toy. 2. The hard plastic doll with an exaggerated figure was a very unusual item. 3. Before Barbie, most dolls in the United States looked like babies or small children. 4. The new toy from the Mattel Toy Company was a grown-up woman.

5. On a Monday morning, in her living room, Mattel founder Ruth Handler observed her daughter, Barbara, playing with paper dolls. 6. Barbara and her friends loved to dress their paper dolls in various pieces of paper clothing. 7. In a moment of

inspiration, Handler had a great idea. 8. A three-dimensional adult-looking doll could be a best-seller. 9. Later, during a trip to Germany, Handler saw a shapely doll. 10. The sexy Lilli doll, with a tiny waist and a large chest, was based on a German comic-strip character. 11. The experience reinforced Handler's determination to create a new doll.

12. After returning home, Handler decided to work on the Barbie doll. 13. She wanted it to look like an innocent American teenager. 14. Ruth and Elliot Handler, with the help of a team of inventors, created the Barbie doll.

15. In the middle of winter, at a toy fair in New York City, the first Barbies were sold. 16. Then, in 1962, in response to requests from the public, a male companion was created for Barbie. 17. Barbie accessories and clothing in a variety of shapes and colors became an indispensable part of the Barbie empire.

18. Many other companies, in an effort to get part of the lucrative toy market, have tried to replace Barbie. 19. However, until now, no doll has outsold Mattel's toy. 20. In fact, according to a Barbie Internet site, somewhere in the world a Barbie is being sold right now.

How Do I Get a Better Grade?

Visit www.mywritinglab.com for audio-visual lectures and additional practice sets about simple sentences.
Get a better grade with MyWritingLab!

CHAPTER 17

Compound Sentences

Section Theme **CULTURE**

CONTENTS

- Compare Simple and Compound Sentences
- Combine Sentences Using Coordinating Conjunctions
- Combine Sentences Using Semicolons
- Combine Sentences Using Transitional Expressions

In this chapter, you will read about topics related to **fads** *and* **fashions**.

The Writer's Desk Warm Up

Do you have body art such as tattoos and piercings? In a paragraph, explain why you do or do not have body art.

Compare Simple and Compound Sentences

When you use sentences of varying lengths and types, your writing flows more smoothly and appears more interesting. You can vary sentences and create relationships between ideas by combining sentences.

Review the differences between simple and compound sentences.

A **simple sentence** is an independent clause. It expresses one complete idea, and it stands alone. Simple sentences can have more than one subject and more than one verb.

One subject and verb:	Tattooing <u>is</u> not a new fashion.
Two subjects:	<u>Tattooing</u> and <u>body piercing</u> <u>are</u> not new fashions.
Two verbs:	<u>Della McMahon</u> <u>speaks</u> and <u>writes</u> about current trends.

A **compound sentence** contains two or more simple sentences. The two complete ideas can be joined in several ways.

Trey is a drummer. + He also sings.

Add a coordinator:	Trey is a drummer, **and** he also sings.
Add a semicolon:	Trey is a drummer; he also sings.
Add a semicolon and conjunctive adverb:	Trey is a drummer; **moreover,** he sings.

Combine Sentences Using Coordinating Conjunctions

A **coordinating conjunction** joins two complete ideas and indicates the connection between them. The most common coordinating conjunctions are *for, and, nor, but, or, yet,* and *so.*

Complete idea,   **coordinating conjunction**   complete idea.

Review the following chart showing coordinating conjunctions and their functions.

Coordinating Conjunction	Function	Example
for	to indicate a reason	Henna tattoos are good options, **for** they are not permanent.
and	to join two ideas	Jay wants a tattoo, **and** he wants to change his hairstyle.
nor	to indicate a negative idea	Cosmetic surgery is not always successful, **nor** is it particularly safe.
but	to contrast two ideas	Tattoos hurt, **but** people get them anyway.
or	to offer an alternative	Jay will dye his hair, **or** he will shave it off.
yet	to introduce a surprising choice	He is good-looking, **yet** he wants to get cosmetic surgery.
so	to indicate a cause and effect relationship	He saved up his money, **so** he will get a large tattoo.

 **Recognizing Compound Sentences**

To be sure that a sentence is compound, place your finger over the coordinating conjunction, and then ask yourself whether the two clauses are complete sentences.

> **Simple:**   The fashion model was tall **but** also very thin.
>
> **Compound:**   The fashion model was tall, **but** she was also very thin.

PRACTICE I

Indicate whether the following sentences are simple (*S*) or compound (*C*). Underline the coordinating conjunction in each compound sentence.

EXAMPLE:

There are many ways to alter your appearance.   *S*

1. Many humans permanently alter their bodies, and they do it for a variety of reasons.   _____

2. Body altering is not unique to North America, for people in every culture and in every historical period have found ways to permanently alter their bodies.   _____

3. In past centuries, some babies in South America had boards tied to their heads, and their soft skulls developed a long, high shape.   _____

4. In Africa, Ubangi women used to extend their lower lips with large, plate-sized pieces of wood.   _____

5. In the 1700s, wealthy European men and women ate tiny amounts of arsenic to have very pale complexions.   _____

6. Then, in the next century, European and American women wore extremely tight corsets, and they suffered from respiratory and digestive problems.   _____

7. Today, some people want to improve their physical appearance, so they sculpt their bodies with cosmetic surgery.   _____

8. Others have images tattooed on their skin for decorative, religious, or political reasons.   _____

9. Body altering can be painful, but people do it anyway.   _____

PRACTICE 2

Read the following passages. Insert an appropriate coordinating conjunction in each blank. Choose from the list below, and try to use a variety of coordinating conjunctions.

for   and   nor   but   or   yet   so

EXAMPLE:

Fashions usually take awhile to be accepted, __*but*__ fads appear and vanish quickly.

1.   In the twentieth century, there were some bizarre fashion fads, _____ many people adopted them. For example, in the 1920s, the styles of World War I flyers became popular, _____ young women wore goggles, scarves, and leather aviator helmets and jackets.

2.   Men also followed fashion fads, _____ they were generally more conservative than women. In the 1940s, zoot suits were associated with rebellious behavior, _____ they were extremely popular. The name *zoot* came from urban jazz culture, _____ it meant "something extravagant or outrageous." The suit could be in dark, conservative colors, _____ it could be in pastel shades such as light blue. During World War II, the War Production Board restricted the amount of fabric in men's clothing, _____ the zoot suit lost popularity.

3. In the 1950s, boys grew the front part of their hair to at least eight inches in length, _____ then they greased their hair back into a "ducktail." The style took a lot of effort to maintain, _____ many boys carried combs and hair pomade with them. In the late 1970s, punk fashion spread throughout Europe and America. Parents reacted with shock, ____ they hated the spiked, colored hair and the torn clothing. At first, only "punks" dyed their hair blue or green, _____ even some of today's more conservative types now add bright color to their hair.

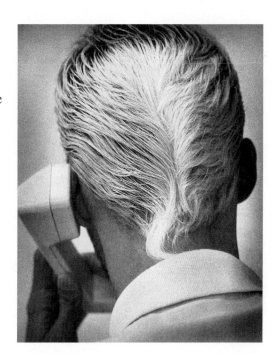

Ducktail haircut

4. Designers may try to create unique new styles, _____ they may look to past styles for inspiration. Not all old fashions make a comeback, _____ are all of them practical for today's lifestyles.

 > **Place a Comma Before the Coordinating Conjunction**

Add a comma before a coordinating conjunction if you are certain that it joins two complete sentences. If the conjunction joins two nouns, verbs, or adjectives, then you do not need to add a comma before it.

Comma: The word *fashion* refers to all popular styles, **and** it does not refer only to clothing.

No comma: The word *fashion* refers to all popular styles **and** not only to clothing.

PRACTICE 3

Create compound sentences by adding a coordinating conjunction and another complete sentence to each simple sentence. Remember to add a comma before the conjunction.

EXAMPLE:

Many people deny it ___ *, but they worry about their personal style.* ___

1. My hair is too long _____

_____

2. You can wear those pants _____

_____

3. Today, hairstyles are varied _____

_____

4. Those shoes are expensive _____

_____

5. You may be surprised _____

_____

Combine Sentences Using Semicolons

Another way to form a compound sentence is to join two complete ideas with a semicolon. The semicolon replaces a coordinating conjunction.

Complete idea   ;   complete idea.

Advertisers promote new fashions every year; they effectively manipulate consumers.

PRACTICE 4

Insert the missing semicolon in each sentence.

EXAMPLE:

Tattoos are applied with needles ; ink is inserted under the skin.

1. Primitive tribes used sharp, thin instruments to introduce color into the skin methods of tattooing have not changed much over the years.

2. In 1990, in the Alps, Austrian hikers found a 5,000-year-old man they photographed the frozen, tattooed body.

3. The body had long straight lines tattooed on the ankles other lines appeared on the stomach region.

4. An Austrian professor, Konrad Spindler, has a theory about the tattoos he published his ideas in a journal.

5. Perhaps the ancient man received tattoos to cure an illness he may have had intestinal problems.

6. In the past, some tattoos celebrated war victories others honored religious figures.

7. The warriors of the Marquesas Islands wanted to intimidate their enemies they tattooed a staring eye on the insides of their arms.

8. A tribesman would raise his arm to attack an opponent his enemy would then see the staring eye and feel frightened.

9. In the early twentieth century, in Western cultures, tattoos were often associated with the lower classes sailors, soldiers, and criminals would get tattoos.

10. Tattoos have had a strong resurgence in our culture people from gang members to Hollywood actors have gotten tattoos.

 **Use a Semicolon to Join Related Ideas**

Do not use a semicolon to join two unrelated sentences.

Incorrect:	Some societies have no distinct word for art; I like to dress in bright colors.
	(The second idea has no clear relationship with the first idea.)
Correct:	Some societies have no distinct word for art; art is an intrinsic part of their cultural fabric.
	(The second idea gives further information about the first idea.)

PRACTICE 5

Write compound sentences by adding a semicolon and another complete sentence to each simple sentence. Remember that the two sentences must have related ideas.

EXAMPLE:

Last year my sister had her tongue pierced; _she regretted her decision._

1. Youths rebel in many ways _____

   _____

2. I dislike a recent fashion _____

   _____

3. At age thirteen, I dressed like other teens _____

   _____

4. Many fashions are recycled _____

   _____

Combine Sentences Using Transitional Expressions

A third way to combine sentences is to join them with a semicolon and a transitional expression. A **transitional expression** can join two complete ideas together and show how they are related. Most transitional expressions are **conjunctive adverbs** such as *however* or *furthermore*.

Transitional Expressions

Addition	Alternative	Contrast	Time	Example or Emphasis	Result or Consequence
additionally	in fact	however	eventually	for example	consequently
also	instead	nevertheless	finally	for instance	hence
besides	on the contrary	nonetheless	later	namely	therefore
furthermore	on the other hand	still	meanwhile	of course	thus
in addition	otherwise		subsequently	undoubtedly	
moreover					

If the second part of a sentence begins with a transitional expression, put a semicolon before it and a comma after it.

Complete idea;   **transitional expression,**   complete idea.

Miriam is not wealthy**; nevertheless,** she always wears the latest fashions.
                    ; however,
                    ; nonetheless,
                    ; still,

PRACTICE 6

Punctuate the following sentences by adding any necessary semicolons and commas.

EXAMPLE:

A bizarre fashion style can become accepted; however, future generations may find the style ridiculous.

1. Often, a popular personality adopts a fashion later others copy the style.

2. King Louis XIV originally disliked wigs however he started to go prematurely bald and changed his mind about the fashion.

3. The king started to wear high, curly wigs subsequently others copied his style.

4. The heavy, elaborate wigs were expensive hence only middle- and upper-class Europeans wore them.

5. The wigs required constant care in fact they needed to be cleaned, powdered, and curled.

6. Later, the king's mustache started to go gray therefore he shaved it off.

7. Others noticed the king's bare face consequently all the fashionable men removed their mustaches too.

8. Not all new fashions are frivolous in fact some fashions signal a change in a group's status.

9. In the 1920s, women gained the right to vote meanwhile pants became associated with women's new freedom.

10. Other fashions have also made political statements for example in the 1970s, the Afro hairstyle signaled black power.

PRACTICE 7

Combine sentences using one of the following transitional expressions. Choose an expression from the following list, and try to use a different expression in each sentence.

in fact	for example	~~however~~	of course	for instance
therefore	eventually	nevertheless	thus	in contrast

EXAMPLE:

                                     ; however, young

Today's parents often complain about their children. ~~Young~~ people are not more violent and rebellious than those of past generations.

1. Youth rebellion is not new. In each era, teenagers have rebelled.

2. Teenagers distinguish themselves in a variety of ways. They listen to new music, create new dance styles, wear odd fashions, and break established social habits.

3. The most visible way to stand out is to wear outrageous fashions. Teenagers try to create original clothing and hairstyles.

4. In the past fifty years, rebellious teens have done almost everything to their hair, including growing it long, buzzing it short, dyeing it, spiking it, shaving it off, and coloring it blue. It is difficult for today's teenagers to create an original hairstyle.

5. Sometimes a certain group popularizes a style. Hip-hop artists wore baggy clothing in the late 1980s.

6. Many parents hated the baggy, oversized pants. Boys wore them.

7. Before the 1990s, most women just pierced their ears. It is now common to see a pierced eyebrow, tongue, or cheek.

8. "Retro" hair and clothing styles will always be popular. People often look to the past for their inspiration.

 **Subordinators versus Conjunctive Adverbs**

A **subordinator** is a term such as *when, because, until,* or *although.* Do not confuse subordinators with conjunctive adverbs. When a subordinator is added to a sentence, the clause becomes incomplete. However, when a conjunctive adverb is added to a sentence, the clause is still complete.

Complete:	She wore fur.
Incomplete (with subordinator):	When she wore fur.
Complete (with conjunctive adverb):	Therefore, she wore fur.

When you combine two ideas using a conjunctive adverb, use a semicolon.

No punctuation:	She was criticized <u>when she wore fur.</u>
Semicolon:	It was very cold; <u>therefore, she wore fur.</u>

PRACTICE 8

Create compound sentences by using the next transitional expressions. Try to use a different expression in each sentence.

in fact   however   therefore   furthermore   consequently   for example

EXAMPLE:

I have my own style *; therefore, I refuse to spend money following the latest fad.*

1. Many people like to wear fashionable clothing _____

_____

2. Designer clothing is expensive _____

_____

3. American fashions borrow ideas from different cultures _____

_____

4. Some new fashions are attractive _____

_____

5. Americans spend billions of dollars on clothing _____

_____

The Writer's Desk Revise and Edit Your Warm Up

Review the sentences that you wrote for the Warm Up at the beginning
of the chapter. Verify that you have punctuated any compound
sentences correctly. If you have no compound sentences, then create
two for your paragraph.

REFLECT ON IT

Think about what you have learned in this unit. If you do not know an answer, review
that concept.

1. a. What is a simple sentence? _____

_____

   b. Write a simple sentence. _____

2. a. What is a compound sentence? _____

_____

   b. Write a compound sentence. _____

3. What are the seven coordinating conjunctions? _____

_____

4. Circle the best answer: When two sentences are joined by a coordinating
   conjunction such as *but*, should you put a comma before the conjunction?   Yes   No

5. When you join two simple sentences with a transitional expression, how should you
   punctuate the sentence?

_____

_____

FINAL REVIEW

Read the following essay. Create at least ten compound sentences by adding semicolons, transitional expressions (*however*, *therefore*, and so on), or coordinating conjunctions (*for*, *and*, *not*, *but*, *or*, *yet*, *so*). You may choose to leave some simple sentences.

EXAMPLE:

; for example, top

The fashion industry does not hire average-sized models. ~~Top~~ models are very tall and thin.

1.   The fashion industry promotes a specific body type. Advertisers also prefer a specific look. They use tall, skinny models to sell fashion. The average person does not have the body dimensions of a top model. This type of appearance is unfeasible for most people. A public backlash has developed against the skinny top model image. People on both sides of the controversy have an opinion. They may love the fashion industry. They may hate it.

2.   Critics blame the fashion industry for depicting unrealistic body types. First, top models are far too thin. Their Body Mass Index (BMI) is less than 18.5. A healthy woman should have a BMI between 18.5 and 25. The industry pressures models to remain uncommonly lean. Young girls compare themselves to models. They develop negative body images. Emaciated women are found in fashion magazines, on billboards, and on television. According to psychologists, such images contribute to eating disorders in adolescents. The images may also lead to yo-yo dieting.

3.   Some in the fashion industry have chosen to present more realistic body types. In 2006, one Madrid fashion organizer banned overly skinny models from fashion runways. About 30 percent of the models could not participate in the show. A well-known cosmetics company has launched a regular-women campaign. Dove uses ordinary women to promote a line of body creams. According to a Dove spokesperson, the company wants to encourage debate about body image.

4.   However, many in the fashion industry are reacting negatively to the critics' demands. For example, Lucio Guerrero is a reporter for the *Chicago Sun-Times*. He is offended by the Dove regular-women campaign. He does not want to see women with big thighs. Also, the Dove campaign is hypocritical. Dove sells anti-cellulite creams and anti-aging creams. At the same time, the company tells women to accept their own bodies. Furthermore, according to some critics, clothes look better on thin people. The fashion industry is trying to sell clothes. It must make consumers buy into the fantasy of thin, glamorous models. The models wear beautiful clothes.

5.   Clearly, there will be no immediate end to the body image controversy. Such a debate is important. It may never be resolved. Perhaps consumers will influence the direction of the fashion industry in the future.

How Do I Get a Better Grade?

Visit www.mywritinglab.com for audio-visual lectures and additional practice sets about compound sentences. **Get a better grade with MyWritingLab!**

18 CHAPTER

Complex Sentences

Section Theme **CULTURE**

In this chapter, you will read about topics related to **activity fads.**

The Writer's Desk **Warm Up**

What types of sports or activities do you like? Choose one type of activity that you enjoy, and write a paragraph explaining why you like it.

What Is a Complex Sentence?

Before you learn about complex sentences, it is important to understand some key terms. A **clause** is a group of words containing a subject and a verb. There are two types of clauses.

An **independent clause** has a subject and a verb and can stand alone because it expresses one complete idea.

Laban Nkete won the race.

A **dependent clause** has a subject and verb, but it cannot stand alone. It "depends" on another clause to be complete.

Although he had injured his heel

A **complex sentence** combines both a dependent and an independent clause.

dependent clause   independent clause
Although he had injured his heel, Laban Nkete won the race.

 More About Complex Sentences

Complex sentences can have more than two clauses.

               1

    Although women have played organized football for over a century, their salaries

   2   3

   are not very high because their games are rarely televised.

You can also combine compound and complex sentences. The next example is a **compound-complex sentence.**

        complex

   Although Kyra is tiny, she plays basketball, and she is a decent player.

                         compound

Use Subordinating Conjunctions

An effective way to create complex sentences is to join clauses with a subordinating conjunction. When you add a **subordinating conjunction** to a clause, you make the clause dependent. *Subordinate* means "secondary," so subordinating conjunctions are words that introduce secondary ideas. Here are some common subordinating conjunctions followed by examples of how to use these types of conjunctions.

Common Subordinating Conjunctions

after	as though	if	though	where
although	because	provided that	unless	whereas
as	before	since	until	wherever
as if	even if	so that	when	whether
as long as	even though	that	whenever	while

Main idea	**subordinating conjunction**	secondary idea.

Crowds cheered **whenever** the team won.

Subordinating conjunction	secondary idea,	main idea.

Whenever the team won, crowds cheered.

PRACTICE 1

The following sentences are complex. In each, circle the subordinating conjunction, and then underline the dependent clause.

EXAMPLE:

(Even if) we cannot know for sure, early humans probably played games and sports.

1. When humans shifted from being food gatherers to hunters, sports probably developed in complexity.

2. It would be important to practice cooperative hunting before humans attacked mammoths or other large creatures.

3. Early humans also practiced war games so that they could win battles with other tribes.

4. Spectator sports evolved when societies had more leisure time.

5. In many places, spectators watched while young boys passed through their initiation rituals.

6. Whenever early humans played sports or games, they tested their physical, intellectual, and social skills.

Meanings of Subordinating Conjunctions

Subordinating conjunctions create a relationship between the clauses in a sentence.

Subordinating Conjunction	Indicates	Example
as, because, since, so that	A reason, a cause, or an effect	Eric learned karate **because** he wanted to be physically fit.
after, before, once, since, until, when, whenever	A time	**After** he received his black belt, he returned to the United States.
as long as, even if, if, provided that, so that, unless	A condition or result	He will not fight with a stranger **unless** he feels threatened.
although, even though, though, whereas	A contrast	**Although** karate is difficult to learn, millions of people study it every year.
where, wherever	A location	**Wherever** you travel, you will find karate enthusiasts.

PRACTICE 2

In each of the following sentences, underline the dependent clause. Then, indicate the type of relationship between the two parts of the sentence. Choose one of the following relationships.

      condition or result   reason or cause   time
      contrast   location

EXAMPLES:

<u>When someone decided to attach wheels to a plank of wood</u>, a new sport began.   *time*

The name *skateboard* came about <u>because the device was literally a board with roller-skating wheels attached to it.</u>   *reason or cause*

1. Although kids occasionally rode skateboards and scooters, bicycles were more popular for the next forty years. _____

2. In the prosperous 1950s, the quality of skateboards improved when modifications were made to the device that holds the wheels. _____

3. Teenagers bought skateboards so that they could practice an inexpensive and thrilling hobby. _____

4. Although the sport was quite dangerous, skaters tried doing a variety of tricks. _____

5. Many surfers took up skateboarding because the sports required similar skills. _____

6. Wherever surfing was popular, skateboarding was popular too. _____

7. When the first skateboard movie (*Skater Dance*) was released, over 50 million skateboards had been sold. _____

8. In 1965, the popularity of skateboarding plummeted because too many people had serious skateboarding accidents. _____

9. Many cities threatened to ban skateboarding unless manufacturers could develop a safer product. _____

10. According to Michael Brooke, author of *The Concrete Wave*, many accidents happened because the wheels on early skateboards did not grip the road well. _____

11. After companies created unbreakable boards with urethane wheels, the skateboarding fad peaked again. _____

12. Today, skateboarding is once again an important part of popular culture even though it is not exactly a new activity. _____

CHAPTER 18

> ⟨ *Hint* ⟩ **Punctuating Complex Sentences**
>
> If you use a subordinator at the beginning of a sentence, put a comma after the dependent clause. Generally, if you use a subordinator in the middle of the sentence, you do not need to use a comma.
>
> **Comma:**   **Even though** he is afraid of heights, Malcolm tried skydiving.
>
> **No comma:**   Malcolm tried skydiving **even though** he is afraid of heights.

PRACTICE 3

Correct eight errors in the following selection by adding the missing commas. If the sentence has a subordinating conjunction, then underline the conjunction.

EXAMPLE:

<u>Although</u> most sports are quite safe, some sports are extremely hazardous.

1. Each year, many people are killed or maimed when they practice a sport. Although skydiving and bungee jumping are hazardous extreme sports like base jumping, free diving, and rodeo events are even more dangerous.

2. Even though they may get arrested many people try base jumping. Wherever there are tall structures there may also be base jumpers. The jumpers wear parachutes and dive off buildings and bridges so that they can feel an adrenaline rush. Because the parachute may get tangled on the structure base jumping is an extremely dangerous sport.

3. Another extreme sport is free diving. Free divers hold their breath until they are as deep as possible underwater. So that they can break existing records some free divers have dived almost 400 feet. Sometimes when their brains lack oxygen they have to be resuscitated.

4. Although most rodeo sports can be safe bull riding is dangerous. Many bull riders are injured or even killed because the bull throws them off and tramples them.

5. Surprisingly, most sports-related injuries occur when people participate in an innocent-sounding sport. According to the American Academy of Orthopedic Surgeons, almost half a million people are injured each year when they ride bicycles. So, what is the best policy? When playing a sport take precautions to protect yourself.

PRACTICE 4

Add a missing subordinating conjunction to each sentence. Use each subordinating conjunction once.

although	even though	~~when~~	whereas
because	unless	whenever	

EXAMPLE:

____*When*____ you refer to a "football" in Europe, Africa, or Asia, most people assume you are talking about a round black-and-white ball.

1. British people will assume you are speaking about soccer _____ you specifically say "American football."

2. Soccer is the world's most popular sport _____ it is inexpensive to play. _____ someone decides to join a soccer team, he or she does not require expensive padding or equipment.

3. _____ a lot of Americans love to play soccer, there are not many professional teams in the United States. Sports such as basketball, baseball, and football have professional teams and are shown on network television _____ soccer is not widely viewed.

4. _____ soccer has yet to become as popular as other sports in the United States, it is this country's fastest-growing sport, according to the American Soccer Federation. Perhaps soccer sensation David Beckham will help raise soccer's profile in our country.

Hint **Put a Subject After the Subordinator**

When you form complex sentences, always remember to put a subject after the subordinator.

                       it
Wrestling is like theater because involves choreographed maneuvers.

                       they
Boxers do not know who will win the round when enter the ring.

CHAPTER 18

PRACTICE 5

Add four missing subjects to the next paragraph.

EXAMPLE:

                                                  it

    Bullfighting is popular in Mexico and Spain although is controversial.

        Each bullfight is an elaborate ceremony with three parts. In the first part, when the matador enters the arena, is dressed in a fine suit embroidered with gold. Holding a red cape, the matador tries to entice the bull. The spectators cheer when see the bull charging at the cape. In the second part, the banderilleros, or matador's assistants, push short spears into the bull until is tired and angry. In the third part, the matador enters the ring again holding a smaller cape and a sword. After has performed well, the matador kills the bull.

PRACTICE 6

Combine the next sentence pairs with subordinating conjunctions. Write each sentence twice: once with the dependent clause at the beginning of the sentence, and once with the dependent clause at the end. Properly punctuate the sentences.
    Use one of the following conjunctions. Use a different conjunction each time.

~~because~~   while   when   even though   although

EXAMPLE:

    I try to exercise. It is important.

    I try to exercise because it is important.

    Because it is important, I try to exercise.

1. I am not very athletic. I will join a team.

    _____

    _____

2. The line is long. I will wait for my turn.

    _____

    _____

3. The game is over. The winners will receive a trophy.

    _____

    _____

4. I was leaving the field. I heard people cheering.

    _____

    _____

Use Relative Pronouns

A **relative pronoun** describes a noun or pronoun. You can form complex sentences by using relative pronouns to introduce dependent clauses. Review the most common relative pronouns.

who   whom   whomever   whose   which   that

That

Use *that* to add information about a thing. Do not use commas to set off clauses that begin with *that*.

> In 1947, Jackie Robinson joined a baseball team **that** <u>was located in Brooklyn</u>.

Which

Use *which* to add nonessential information about a thing. Generally, use commas to set off clauses that begin with *which*.

> Football, **which** <u>was segregated in 1945</u>, included African-American players the following year.

Who

Use *who* (*whom, whomever, whose*) to add information about a person. When a clause begins with *who*, you may or may not need a comma. Put commas around the clause if it adds nonessential information. If the clause is essential to the meaning of the sentence, do not add commas. To decide if a clause is essential or not, ask yourself if the sentence still makes sense without the *who* clause. If it does, the clause is not essential.

> Most women **who** <u>play sports</u> do not earn as much money as their male counterparts.
> (The clause is essential. The sentence would not make sense without the *who* clause.)

> Tennis player Maria Sharapova, **who** <u>has won many tournaments</u>, earns millions of dollars in endorsement deals.
> (The clause is not essential.)

Using *That* or *Which*

Both *which* and *that* refer to things, but *which* refers to nonessential ideas. Also, *which* can imply that you are referring to the complete subject and not just a part of it. Compare the next two sentences.

> Local baseball teams that have very little funding can still succeed.
> (This sentence suggests that some teams have good funding, but others don't.)

> Local baseball teams, **which** have very little funding, can still succeed.
> (This sentence suggests that all of the teams have poor funding.)

GRAMMAR LINK

For more information about punctuating relative clauses, refer to Chapter 33, "Commas."

PRACTICE 7

Using a relative pronoun, combine each pair of sentences to form a complex sentence.

CHAPTER 18

EXAMPLE:

The Olympic Games celebrate excellence in sports. They occur once every four years.

The Olympic Games, which occur once every four years, celebrate

excellence in sports.

1. Steroids can enhance your ability in sports. They are dangerous to your body and mind.

   _____

   _____

2. Some people use steroids. They may experience severe side effects or even death.

   _____

   _____

3. Steroids were first banned at the 1973 Olympic Games. The drugs continue to be used by some athletes.

   _____

   _____

4. Dr. Wade Exum is a respected professional. He ran the U.S. Olympic Committee's doping control program.

   _____

   _____

5. According to Dr. Exum, many U.S. athletes were caught using steroids. Those athletes were not punished.

   _____

   _____

6. In 2000, Dr. Exum quit his Olympic Committee job in disgust. He expressed his concerns in a report.

   _____

   _____

PRACTICE 8

Add a dependent clause to each sentence. Begin each clause with a relative pronoun (*who*, *which*, or *that*). Add any necessary commas.

EXAMPLE:

Teams *that have good leadership* often win tournaments.

1. The player _____ might be hired to promote running shoes.

2. An athlete _____ should be suspended for at least one game.

3. Bungee jumping is an activity _____

4. I would like to try an extreme sport _____

5. Skydiving _____ is a sport I would like to try.

6. Athletes _____ should be warned about the dangers of steroids.

Use Embedded Questions

It is possible to combine a question with a statement or to combine two questions. An **embedded question** is a question that is set within a larger sentence.

Question:	How old are the Olympic Games?
Embedded question:	The sprinter wonders <u>how old the Olympic Games are</u>.

In questions, there is generally a helping verb before the subject. However, when a question is embedded in a larger sentence, you need to remove the helping verb or place it after the subject. As you read the following examples, pay attention to the word order in the embedded questions.

Combine two questions.

Separate:	Do you know the answer? Why **do** they like bullfighting?
	(The second question includes the helping verb *do*.)
Combined:	Do you know <u>why they like bullfighting</u>?
	(The helping verb *do* is removed from the embedded question.)

Combine a question and a statement.

Separate:	I wonder about it. When **should** we go to the arena?
	(In the question, the helping verb *should* appears before the subject.)
Combined:	I wonder <u>when we should go to the arena</u>.
	(In the embedded question, *should* is placed after the subject.)

>  **Use the Correct Word Order**
>
> When you edit your writing, ensure that you have formed your embedded questions properly. Remove question form structures from the embedded questions.
>
>   *he thought*
> He wonders why ~~do~~ people like bullfighting. I asked him what ~~did he think~~ about the sport.

PRACTICE 9

Correct six embedded question errors.

EXAMPLE:

   people can
The writer explains how ~~can people~~ love dangerous sports.

One activity that generates controversy is bullfighting. Some people wonder why should bulls die for entertainment. They question how can bullfighting be so popular. Many call it a brutal activity because the bull is weakened and then slaughtered. For others, bullfighting is a strong and respected tradition.

Spanish matador Mario Carrión wonders why do some people call bullfighting a sport. In sports, the goal is to win points in a confrontation with an opponent. In Carrión's view, a bullfight is not a sport because a human cannot compete against a thousand-pound beast. He defines bullfighting as "a dramatic dance with death."

Bullfight enthusiasts ask themselves why does bullfighting have a bad reputation. They wonder why is it rejected by so many nations. Do you know what can they do to improve the reputation of bullfighting?

The Writer's Desk   Revise and Edit Your Warm Up

Review the sentences that you wrote for the Warm Up at the beginning of the chapter. Ensure that your complex sentences are correctly punctuated. If you have no complex sentences, then create two for your paragraph.

When you have finished, look at another paragraph that you have written. Try combining sentences into complex sentences.

REFLECT ON IT

Think about what you have learned in this chapter. If you do not know an answer, then review that concept.

1. Write six subordinating conjunctions. _____

_____

2. Write a complex sentence. _____

_____

3. List six relative pronouns. _____

4. Correct the error in the following sentence.

Clayton wonders why should he wear a helmet when he goes skateboarding.

FINAL REVIEW

The following paragraphs contain only simple sentences. To give the paragraphs more variety, form at least ten complex sentences by combining pairs of sentences. You will have to add some words and delete others.

EXAMPLE:

When   *, they*

~~Some~~ people pierce their tongues. ~~They~~ risk getting an infection.

1. Many activity fads come and go. Many of these fads are ridiculous.

Why do fads become so popular? Nobody knows the answer. There

were some unusual fads in the 1950s. College students did phone-booth

stuffing. Students entered a phone booth one by one. They tried to

stuff as many people as possible into the closed space. Later, hula hoops

hit the market. In the 1960s, millions of people bought and used the

circular plastic tubes. The hula hoop fad did not last long. It briefly

provided people with an innovative way to exercise. People put the

hoops around their waists. They would gyrate to keep the hoops

spinning.

2.   In the spring of 1974, a streaking fad began. It occurred on college campuses in Florida and California. Young people stripped naked. They may have felt embarrassed. They ran through public places such as football stadiums and malls. They wanted to shock people. The actor David Niven was presenting at the 1974 Academy Awards. A nude streaker dashed behind him. The streaker made a peace sign. Millions of viewers were watching the show. They saw the streaker.

3.   Flash mobbing, a recent trend, is organized on Web sites. Flash mobs first appeared in New York City in the summer of 2003. For no obvious reason, a large group of people gathered on a stone wall in Central Park. They chirped like birds. In Berlin, Germany, about forty people shouted "Yes." They were in a subway car. They shouted into their cell phones at exactly the same moment. In Montreal, Canada, a large group of people began quacking. They were throwing rubber ducks into a fountain. Do you know the answer to the following question? Why do certain Web sites promote flash mobbing? They do it for a simple reason. They hope to add vibrancy to dull modern life.

How Do I Get a Better Grade?

Visit www.mywritinglab.com for audio-visual lectures and additional practice sets about complex sentences. *Get a better grade with MyWritingLab!*

Sentence Variety

Section Theme **CULTURE**

In this chapter, you will read about topics related to cultural icons.

The Writer's Desk   Warm Up

Would you like to be famous? What are some problems that could be associated with fame? Write a paragraph about fame.

What Is Sentence Variety?

In Chapters 17 and 18, you learned how to write different types of sentences. This chapter focuses on sentence variety. **Sentence variety** means that your sentences have assorted patterns and lengths. In this chapter, you will learn to vary your sentences by consciously considering the length of sentences, by altering the opening words, and by joining sentences using different methods.

Combine Sentences

A passage filled with simple, short sentences can sound choppy. When you vary the lengths of your sentences, the same passage becomes easier to read and flows more smoothly. For example, read the following two passages about cultural icon Rosa Parks. In the first paragraph, most of the sentences are short, and the style is repetitive and boring. In the second paragraph, there is a mixture of simple, compound, and complex sentences.

GRAMMAR LINK

If you forget what compound and complex sentences are, refer to Chapters 17 and 18.

Simple Sentences

We know the story. A woman left work. She boarded a bus for home. She was tired. Her feet ached. This was Montgomery, Alabama. It was in December 1955. The bus became crowded. The driver yelled at the black woman to give her seat to a white passenger. She remained seated. Her decision was important. It led to the changes in the South. It ushered in a new era.

Simple, Compound, and Complex Sentences

We know the story. One December evening, a woman left work and boarded a bus for home. She was tired; her feet ached. But this was Montgomery, Alabama, in December 1955, and as the bus became crowded, the woman, a black woman, was ordered to give up her seat to a white passenger. When she remained seated, that simple decision eventually led to the disintegration of institutionalized segregation in the South, ushering in a new era of the civil rights movement.

—Rita Dove, "The Torchbearer"

Hint **Be Careful with Long Sentences**

If a sentence is too long, it may be difficult for the reader to understand. If you have any doubts, break up a longer sentence into shorter ones.

Long and complicated:	Elvis Presley is a cultural icon who achieved the American dream by using his musical skills and his raw sexual energy to transform himself from a truck driver into a rock-and-roll legend, yet he did not handle his fame very well, and by the end of his life, he was unhappy and addicted to painkillers.
Better:	Elvis Presley is a cultural icon who achieved the American dream. Using his musical skills and his raw sexual energy, he transformed himself from a truck driver into a rock-and-roll legend. However, he did not handle his fame very well. By the end of his life, he was unhappy and addicted to painkillers.

PRACTICE I

Modify the following paragraph so that it has both long and short sentences. Make sure you write some compound and complex sentences.

A cultural icon can be an object, a person, or a place. Cultural icons

symbolize a belief or a way of life. Each country has its own icons. They

become part of that country's history. For example, Mickey Mouse is a familiar image. The cartoon character symbolizes American optimism. Ellis Island and the Statue of Liberty are cultural icons. People can be icons, too. In Mexico, revolutionary leader Emiliano Zapata is a cultural icon. In America, Elvis Presley is an icon. These icons reflect a shared cultural experience.

Include a Question, a Quotation, or an Exclamation

The most common type of sentence is a statement. A simple but effective way to achieve sentence variety is to do the following:

- Ask and answer a **question.** You could also insert a **rhetorical question,** which does not require an answer but is used for effect.

    Did Elvis really do anything shocking?

- Include the occasional **exclamation** to express surprise. However, do not overuse exclamations because they make your writing look less academic.

    Elvis's swinging hips were considered obscene!

- Add a **direct quotation,** which includes the exact words that somebody said.

    Elvis said, "I didn't copy my style from anybody."

In the next passage, a question, an exclamation, and a quotation add variety.

> Norma Jeanne Baker was born to a mentally unstable mother and an absent father. The shy little girl spent her childhood being shuffled between an orphanage and foster parents. From such inauspicious beginnings, a cultural icon was born. Norma, who later changed her name to Marilyn Monroe, bleached her hair, had plastic surgery on her nose, and became one of Hollywood's most recognizable figures. **Why is she remembered?** Perhaps her fame is   ◄ Question
> partly due to her untimely death at the age of thirty-six. She is also remembered for her sensuality and her childlike vulnerability. **Even at the height of fame, she exuded unhappiness and once complained, "Everybody is always tugging at you. They'd like a**   ◄ Quotation
> **chunk out of you."** Some argue that she was not talented, and others suggest that people will forget her. **But the truth is, even half a century after her death, her image is one of the most recognized in**   ◄ Exclamation
> **America!**

 **Punctuating Quotations**

If you introduce your quotation with a phrase, put a comma after the phrase and before the opening quotation marks. Put the final period inside the closing quotation marks.

Marilyn Monroe once complained, "Everybody is always tugging at you."

If the end of the quotation is not the end of the sentence, place a comma inside the final quotation mark.

"They were terribly strict," she once said.

GRAMMAR LINK

For more information about punctuating quotations, refer to Chapter 34.

PRACTICE 2

Read the following passage. Change one sentence to a question, one to an exclamation, and one to a quotation.

EXAMPLE:

> *Why do most*   ?
> ~~Most~~ people want to be famous⁄

The last one hundred years was a century of celebrities. Many ordinary people achieve almost saintly status. In previous centuries, heroes were those who fought bravely in wars or who rescued others. Today, actors, musicians, politicians, and athletes are routinely deified. Even criminals such as Al Capone and Charles Manson become household names. In the words of Daniel J. Boorstin, celebrity worship and hero worship should not be confused. However, we confuse them every day.

Vary the Opening Words

An effective way to make your sentences more vivid is to vary the opening words. Instead of beginning each sentence with the subject, you could try the following strategies.

Begin with an Adverb

An **adverb** is a word that modifies a verb, and it often (but not always) ends in *-ly. Slowly, usually,* and *suddenly* are adverbs. Other adverbs include words such as *sometimes, never, however,* and *often.*

> Generally, a cultural icon arouses strong feelings in members of that culture.

> Often, an extremely gifted and famous person becomes an icon.

Begin with a Prepositional Phrase

A **prepositional phrase** is a group of words made up of a preposition and its object. *Under the chair*, *in the beginning*, and *after the fall* are prepositional phrases.

<u>In New York's harbor</u>, the Statue of Liberty welcomes visitors.

<u>At dawn</u>, we photographed the statue.

 **Comma Tip**

Generally, when a sentence begins with an adverb or a prepositional phrase, place a comma after the opening word or phrase.

Cautiously, the reporter asked another question to the volatile star.

Without any warning, she stood up and left the room.

PRACTICE 3

Rewrite the following sentences by placing an adverb or prepositional phrase at the beginning. First, strike out any word or phrase that could be moved. Then, rewrite that word or phrase at the beginning of the sentence. Finally, correctly punctuate your new sentence.

EXAMPLE:

<u>*Actually, the*</u>   ~~The~~ United States' most recognizable symbol was ~~actually~~ made in France.

1. _____ A group of French intellectuals, in 1865, met in a restaurant and discussed the United States.

2. _____ The French artists and thinkers carefully criticized their oppressive emperor, Napoleon III.

3. _____ They then expressed in quiet voices admiration for America's new democratic government.

4. _____ A sculptor gradually developed the idea of creating a gift for the United States.

5. _____ Frederic-Auguste Bartholdi searched for a site to place his sculpture during a visit to the United States.

6. _____ He crafted "Lady Liberty" with the help of many workers.

7. _____ The 305-foot statue was completed in 1884.

8. _____ Bartholdi unfortunately died in 1883 without seeing the completed work.

PRACTICE 4

Add an opening word or phrase to each sentence. Use the type of opening that is indicated in parentheses. Remember to punctuate the sentence properly.

EXAMPLE:

Adverb

Surprisingly, playwright Naomi Iizuka loves the 50-foot Hollywood sign.

1. (Adverb) _____ the sign is more than just white letters that spell "Hollywood."

2. (Prepositional phrase) _____ the sign is like a beacon to aspiring actors.

3. (Prepositional phrase) _____ thousands of people arrive with dreams of stardom.

4. (Adverb) _____ some people make it, but many do not.

5. (Adverb) _____ the sign is an important American symbol.

Combine Sentences with a Present Participle

You can combine two sentences with a present participle. A **present participle** is a verb that ends in *-ing*, such as *believing*, *having*, and *using*. Combine sentences using an *-ing* modifier only when the two actions happen at the same time.

Separate sentences:	He looked across the harbor. He saw the Statue of Liberty.
Combined sentences:	<u>Looking</u> across the harbor, he saw the Statue of Liberty.

PRACTICE 5

Combine the next sentences by converting one of the verbs into an *-ing* modifier.

EXAMPLE:

Odessa and Cassius Clay looked at their tiny son. They had no idea of their boy's future fame.

Looking at their tiny son, Odessa and Cassius Clay had no idea of their boy's future fame.

Having no idea of their boy's future fame, Odessa and Cassius Clay looked at their tiny son.

1. Cassius Clay competed in the 1960 Olympics. He won a gold medal.

   _____

   _____

   _____

2. He used a unique boxing method. Clay won many fights.

   _____

   _____

   _____

3. He changed his name to Mohammad Ali. He professed his loyalty to Islam.

   _____

   _____

   _____

4. He spoke in rhymes. Ali became the original rapper.

   _____

   _____

   _____

5. Ali voiced his own opinions. He promoted black power and antiwar beliefs.

   _____

   _____

   _____

6. He proclaimed his opposition to the Vietnam War. He was arrested as a draft dodger.

   _____

   _____

Mohammad Ali

   _____

7. He refused to back down. He lost his boxing license from 1967 to 1970.

   _____

   _____

   _____

8. Ali knocked out George Foreman in 1974. He regained his boxing title.

   _____

   _____

   _____

GRAMMAR LINK

For a complete list of irregular past participles, see Appendix 2.

Combine Sentences with a Past Participle

Another way to combine sentences is to use a past participle. A **past participle** is a verb that has an *-ed* ending (although there are many irregular past participles, such as *gone, seen, broken,* and *known.*)

You can begin a sentence with a past participle. To do this, you must combine two sentences, and one of the sentences must contain a past participle.

Separate sentences:	Jesse Owens was raised in Alabama. He became a famous athlete.
Combined sentences:	<u>Raised in Alabama,</u> Jesse Owens became a famous athlete.

PRACTICE 6

Combine each pair of sentences into one sentence beginning with a past participle.

EXAMPLE:

Jesse Owens was born in 1913. He was the son of sharecroppers and the grandson of slaves.

Born in 1913, Jesse Owens was the son of sharecroppers and

the grandson of slaves.

1. Jesse Owens was excluded from team sports in college. The African-American athlete excelled at individual sports such as track and field.

_____

_____

_____

2. He was invited to the 1936 Olympic Games. He competed in twelve events.

_____

_____

_____

3. The 1936 Olympic Games were held in Berlin. They were a showcase for the Nazi party.

_____

_____

_____

4. Owens went on to win four gold medals. He was encouraged by his fans.

_____

_____

_____

5. Hitler was surprised at Owens's success. He refused to shake the medal winner's hand.

_____

_____

_____

6. The athlete was treated like a hero upon his return. He basked in glory for a short while.

_____

_____

_____

7. Owens was forbidden to ride in the front of a bus. He expressed sadness about the segregation laws in his state.

_____

_____

_____

8. A Berlin street was renamed Jesse Owens Strasse in 1984. The street leads to the Olympic stadium.

_____

_____

_____

Combine Sentences with an Appositive

An **appositive** is a word or phrase that gives further information about a noun or pronoun. You can combine two sentences by using an appositive. In the example, the italicized phrase could become an appositive because it describes the noun *Bob Marley.*

Two sentences: Bob Marley was *a founding member of The Wailers.* He went on to have a solo career.

You can place the appositive directly before the word that it refers to or directly after that word. Notice that the appositives are set off with commas.

appositive
Combined: A founding member of The Wailers, **Bob Marley** went on to have a successful solo career.

appositive
Combined: **Bob Marley,** a founding member of The Wailers, went on to have a successful solo career.

> ## Hint Finding an Appositive
>
> To find an appositive, look for a word or phrase that describes or renames a noun. The noun could be anywhere in the sentence.
>
> Bob Marley popularized a new fashion trend. He wore dreadlocks.
>
> In the preceding sentences, "dreadlocks" describes the new fashion trend. You could combine the sentences as follows:
>
> appositive
> Bob Marley popularized **a new fashion trend,** <u>dreadlocks.</u>

PRACTICE 7

Combine the following pairs of sentences. In each pair, make one of the sentences an appositive. Try to vary the position of the appositive. In some sentences, you could put the appositive at the beginning of the sentence, and in others, you could put the appositive after the word that it describes. The first one has been done for you.

EXAMPLE:

Bob Marley was a Jamaican. He greatly popularized reggae music.

Bob Marley, a Jamaican, greatly popularized reggae music.

1. Bob Marley brought international attention to reggae music. He was a great musician.

   _____

   _____

2. Marley was biracial. He was born in 1945 in Jamaica.

   _____

   _____

3. Marley's father was a sailor. His father died when Marley was young.

   _____

   _____

4. At the age of 14, Marley started jam sessions with Joe Higgs. Higgs was a Rastafarian and reggae musician.

   _____

   _____

5. Reggae music started in Jamaica in the 1960s. It was a blend of Caribbean and African music.

   _____

   _____

6. Marley's first group performed ska and rocksteady music. The group was called The Wailers.

   _____

   _____

7. Jamaicans loved the reggae sound of The Wailers. The group was one of the most famous bands in the country.

   _____

   _____

8. In 1974, The Wailers gained international acclaim when Eric Clapton recorded one of Marley's songs. The song was called "I Shot the Sheriff."

   _____

   _____

9. Marley wrote about political protest, poverty, love, and religion in his music. Marley was a devout Rastafarian.

   _____

   _____

10. Bob Marley contributed greatly to twentieth-century music. He is a music icon.

    _____

    _____

The Writer's Desk   Revise and Edit Your Paragraph

In the Warm Up at the beginning of this chapter, you wrote a short paragraph about the problems associated with fame. Revise your paragraph for sentence variety, and check it for errors.

REFLECT ON IT

Think about what you have learned in this unit. If you do not know an answer, review that topic.

1. Why is sentence variety important? _____

_____

2. Write a sentence that begins with an adverb. _____

_____

3. Write a sentence that begins with a present participle. _____

_____

4. Write a sentence that begins with a past participle. _____

_____

5. Write a sentence that begins with an appositive. _____

_____

FINAL REVIEW

The next essay lacks sentence variety. Use the strategies that you have learned in this chapter to create at least ten varied sentences.

EXAMPLE:

, believing

People are obsessed with fame. ~~Perhaps they believe~~ that fame will make them immortal.

1. Andy Warhol was an artist. He made a fortune with silkscreens of famous icons such as Marilyn Monroe and Mick Jagger. He predicted that everyone would be famous for fifteen minutes. Today television is filled with ordinary people. They hope to achieve celebrity status. We wonder why this is happening. Our society elevates celebrities above the common human. Certainly, celebrities often have great talent. The talent includes exceptional musical ability, great athletic prowess, or a compelling ability to act. However, many celebrities lack moral character. They are models of bad behavior. Celebrities often make poor role models.

2. Some celebrities in the twentieth century were emotionally fragile. There are people such as Marilyn Monroe, Jimi Hendrix, and Kurt Cobain. They turned to drugs to cope with their pain. For example, Cobain and Hendrix abused heroin. Monroe abused prescription drugs. Some argue that these celebrities are simply troubled people. They cannot be blamed for their addictions. Others suggest that such celebrities provide children with negative role models. The celebrities make drugs appear glamorous and exciting.

3. Other celebrities have promoted violence. This includes Tupac Shakur and many other rap artists. Shakur certainly had a difficult childhood. He was raised in Baltimore, Maryland. He was accepted to the prestigious Baltimore School for the Arts. He developed his music and writing skills. He also became involved in gangs. He was arrested on several occasions. His rap music often mentioned the thug life. It told stories of gunfights and gang rivalries. He was gunned down during a trip to Las Vegas, Nevada. The rapper died violently.

4. Impressionable youngsters want to emulate their heroes. They do not think about the dangers of drugs or gang life. Some people do not care what celebrities do. Artists are entitled to make mistakes. Others argue that celebrities have a certain responsibility. No matter what your opinion is, people leading public lives will always be under scrutiny.

READING LINK

Culture

"The Old-Time Pueblo World" by Leslie Marmon Silko (page 546)

"Bound Feet" by Jung Chang (page 548)

"I'm a Banana and Proud of It" by Wayson Choy (page 551)

"Fads" by David A. Locher (page 554)

The Writer's Room Topics for Writing

Choose one of the following topics and write a paragraph or an essay. When you write, remember to follow the writing process.

1. Define *hero*. What makes a person a hero?

2. Why do so many people crave fame? How does celebrity status affect people? Write about the causes or effects of fame.

3. Think of a sport or activity that you have tried. Explain how to play or participate in the activity.

4. Some people argue that humans should not wear animal fur. Others support the fur industry. What is your opinion?

The Writers' Circle

Work with a team of about three students. Using the six words below, create a paragraph. Include simple, compound, and complex sentences in your paragraph.

hero	disappointment	clothing
talent	leader	icon

When you finish, exchange paragraphs with another team. Verify whether the other team has used a variety of sentences. Then, edit the other team's paragraph, looking for any errors in punctuation or sentence form.

How Do I Get a Better Grade?

Visit www.mywritinglab.com for audio-visual lectures and additional practice sets about sentence variety.

Get a better grade with MyWritingLab!

Fragments and Run-Ons

Section Theme **PSYCHOLOGY**

CONTENTS

- Fragments
- Run-Ons

In this chapter, you will read about topics related to psychological profiles.

The Writer's Desk Warm Up

Do you remember your dreams? Do you think that dreams have a purpose? Write a short paragraph about dreams.

Fragments

A **sentence** must have a subject and verb, and it must express a complete thought. A **fragment** is an incomplete sentence. Either it lacks a subject or verb, or it fails to express a complete thought. You may see fragments in newspaper headlines and advertisements (*Wrinkle-free skin in one month*). However, in college writing, it is unacceptable to write fragments.

Sentence: Sigmund Freud was a famous psychologist.

Fragment: Considered to be the founder of psychoanalysis.

Phrase Fragments

A phrase fragment is missing a subject or a verb. In the following examples, the fragments are underlined.

CHAPTER 20

No verb:	<u>First, Gestalt theory.</u> It focuses on an individual's perception.
No subject:	Wolfgang Kohler was born in 1887. <u>Founded the Gestalt theory of psychology.</u>

How to Correct Phrase Fragments

To correct a phrase fragment, either add the missing subject or verb, or join the fragment to another sentence. Here are two ways you can correct the phrase fragments in the previous examples.

Join sentences:	First, Gestalt theory focuses on an individual's perceptions.
Add word:	Wolfgang Kohler was born in 1887. **He** founded the Gestalt theory of psychology.

   **Incomplete Verbs**

A sentence must have a subject and a complete verb. If a sentence has an incomplete verb, it is a phrase fragment. The following example contains a subject and part of a verb. However, it is missing a helping verb; therefore, the sentence is incomplete.

Fragment: Many books about psychology written by Carl Jung.

To make this sentence complete, you must add the helping verb.

Sentence: Many books about psychology <u>were</u> written by Carl Jung.

PRACTICE I

Underline and correct six phrase fragments.

EXAMPLE:

<u>A childhood trauma.</u> ~~It~~ can be the source of an irrational fear.

1. First, superstitions. People sometimes have irrational beliefs. Many compulsive gamblers, for example, think that they can control the spin of slot machine reels by carrying good luck charms. Some carry a four-leaf clover. Or a rabbit's foot. The illusion of control.

2. Many athletes have rituals or lucky items of clothing. A lucky number on their jersey. Rams running back Marshall Faulk always wears black to the stadium. Another football player, Chris Hale. He believes that dressing in a particular sequence is lucky. Also, Michael Jordan played each game. With blue North Carolina College shorts under his Bulls uniform.

Fragments with *-ing* and *to*

A fragment may begin with a **present participle,** which is the form of the verb that ends in *-ing* (*running, talking*). It may also begin with an **infinitive,** which is *to* plus the base form of the verb (*to run, to talk*). These fragments generally appear before or after another sentence that contains the subject. In the examples, the fragments are underlined.

-ing fragment:	<u>Thinking about positive outcomes.</u> It helps people cope with stress.
to fragment:	Oprah Winfrey has developed a resilient attitude. <u>To overcome her childhood traumas.</u>

How to Correct *-ing* and *to* Fragments

To correct an *-ing* or *to* fragment, either add the missing words, or join the fragment to another sentence. Here are two ways to correct the previous examples.

Join sentences:	Thinking about positive outcomes helps people cope with stress.
Add words:	Oprah Winfrey has developed a resilient attitude **because she had** to overcome her childhood traumas.

> *Hint* **When the *-ing* Word Is the Subject**
>
> Sometimes a gerund (*-ing* form of the verb) is the subject of a sentence. In the next example, *listening* is the subject of the sentence.
>
> **Correct:** <u>Listening</u> is an important skill.
>
> A sentence fragment occurs when the *-ing* word is part of an incomplete verb string or when the subject was mentioned in a previous sentence.
>
> **Fragment:** Oprah Winfrey has achieved success. <u>Listening to people's problems.</u>

PRACTICE 2

Underline and correct six *-ing* and *to* fragments.

EXAMPLE:

<u>Living through a childhood trauma.</u> ~~It~~ can be the source of an irrational fear.

Relating characteristics and physical health. Doctors Myer Friedman and Ray Rosenman divided people into personality types. Acting extremely competitive. Type A personalities are workaholics. They feel a strong pressure. To be busy. Type B personalities tend to be easygoing. Feeling relaxed and at peace. They can spend hours lying in the sun. Other researchers identified a Type C personality. Type C people are usually very

pleasant but cannot easily express anger. To avoid conflict. They internalize strong emotions. According to Friedman and Rosenman. The personality type at greatest risk of developing heart disease is Type A. However, researchers at Duke University have found that only extremely hostile Type A profiles are at increased risk of coronary disease.

Explanatory Fragments

An **explanatory fragment** provides an explanation about a previous sentence and is missing a subject, a complete verb, or both. Such fragments are sometimes expressed as an afterthought. These types of fragments begin with one of the following words.

also	especially	for example	including	particularly
as well as	except	for instance	like	such as

In each example, the explanatory fragment is underlined.

Fragment: Carl Jung studied with many prominent psychologists. <u>For instance, Sigmund Freud.</u>

Fragment: Psychologists analyze behavior. <u>Particularly through methods of observation.</u>

How to Correct Explanatory Fragments

To correct explanatory fragments, add the missing words, or join the explanation or example to another sentence. Here are two ways to correct the fragments in the previous examples.

Add words: Carl Jung studied with many prominent psychologists. For instance, **he worked with** Sigmund Freud.

Join sentences: Psychologists analyze behavior particularly through methods of observation.

PRACTICE 3

Underline and correct six explanatory fragments. You may need to add or remove words.

EXAMPLE:

loyal, especially

Some fans are very loyal. <u>Especially Red Sox fans.</u>

Stephen Dubner wrote *Confessions of a Hero Worshipper*. He describes the personality of sports fans, and his book has interesting anecdotes. For example, the 1994 World Cup. The saliva in male soccer fans was tested before and after an important match. The chosen fans were from

Brazil. As well as Italy. The testosterone level in the fans of the winning team rose quickly. Particularly during the final minutes of the game. The losing fans' testosterone level decreased. Researcher Paul Bernhardt was surprised. Especially by the percentages. The fans of the winning team, with a 20 percent increase, had the same level of testosterone as the athletes. The findings may explain aggressive episodes. Such as soccer hooliganism. Immediately after a testosterone surge, some males may act more aggressively. Especially when provoked.

Dependent-Clause Fragments

A **dependent clause** has a subject and verb, but it cannot stand alone. It *depends* on another clause to be a complete sentence. Dependent clauses may begin with subordinating conjunctions (subordinators) or relative pronouns. The following are some of the most common words that begin dependent clauses.

Common Subordinating Conjunctions				Relative Pronouns
after	before	though	whenever	that
although	even though	unless	where	which
as	if	until	whereas	who(m)
because	since	what	whether	whose

The next two examples contain dependent-clause fragments. In each example, the fragment is underlined.

Fragment:	<u>Although I cross my fingers for luck.</u> I know that it is a silly superstition.
Fragment:	I will not walk under a ladder. <u>That is leaning against a wall.</u>

How to Correct Dependent-Clause Fragments

To correct dependent-clause fragments, either join the fragment to a complete sentence or add the necessary words to make it a complete idea. You could also delete the subordinating conjunction. Here are two ways to correct the fragments in the previous examples.

Delete the subordinator:	I cross my fingers for luck. I know that it is a silly superstition.
Join sentences:	Although I cross my fingers for luck, I know that it is a silly superstition. I will not walk under a ladder that is leaning against a wall.

PRACTICE 4

Underline and correct five dependent-clause fragments.

EXAMPLE:

Whenever they blame themselves. ~~Negative~~ *, negative* thinkers make their problems larger.

1.   Andrew Shatte is a University of Pennsylvania researcher. Who worked on the Resiliency Project. For the project, graduate psychology students taught seventy children. That they can become more resilient. Children learned the difference between productive and self-defeating thinking. After they looked at their own fears. The children had to test their expectations and see if they were realistic.

2.   One child in the program who came from a tough inner-city neighborhood had convinced himself that he would probably end up in a gang. Even though he hated violence. The program taught this boy. That there are other possible outcomes. He learned that he did not have to focus on worst-case scenarios.

PRACTICE 5

The next paragraphs contain phrase, explanatory, *-ing*, *to*, and dependent-clause fragments. Correct fifteen fragment errors.

EXAMPLE:

Many people had ~~nightmares. When~~ *nightmares when* they were children.

1.   In ancient times. People thought that dreams had heavenly origins. The ancient Egyptians thought that dreams had a prophetic function.

The Babylonians and Assyrians also. Some Egyptian pharaohs recorded their strange dreams. For example, Thutmose IV. He dreamed that the Sphinx spoke to him. Using a familiar language. The Sphinx, which was buried in sand, asked Thutmose to remove the sand. If he obeyed. He would then become king. Thutmose cleared the sand off the Sphinx. Soon after, became king.

2. Some psychologists believe that dreams are meaningless. Although others disagree. Dreams have a significant purpose. According to Sigmund Freud. Freud believed that dreams could lead to understanding the unconscious mind. He proposed that dreams appeared in symbols or in disguised forms. That dreams had hidden meanings. Freud theorized that dream symbols showed the dreamer's desires. Either sexual or aggressive in nature.

3. Two modern theories about dreams. In the first theory, some psychologists propose that dreaming is necessary. Because a dream's purpose is to rid the mind of useless data. We forget our dreams because we no longer need the information in them. The second theory. Dreams have no function at all. Some psychologists believe that the brain is responding to high levels of stimuli. Therefore, people have inexplicable dreams. Such as dreams about someone that they have never met. Certainly, there are many psychological theories. To help explain the meanings of dreams.

Run-Ons

A **run-on sentence** occurs when two or more complete sentences are incorrectly joined. In other words, the sentence runs on without stopping. There are two types of run-on sentences.

- A **fused sentence** has no punctuation to mark the break between ideas.

    Incorrect: Psychologists describe human behavior they use observational methods.

- A **comma splice** uses a comma incorrectly to connect two complete ideas.

    Incorrect: Wilhelm Wundt was born in 1832, he is often called the founder of modern psychology.

PRACTICE 6

Read the following sentences. Write *C* beside correct sentences and *RO* beside run-ons.

EXAMPLE:

Sigmund Freud and Carl Jung were two famous psychologists they profoundly influenced the field of psychology.   *RO*

1. Psychologists study human behavior, researchers have developed many theories on human nature.   _____

2. Instinct theory is one model developed by psychologists it proposes that behavior is based on biology.   _____

3. Learning theory suggests that humans learn through experience. _____

4. Trait theories focus on human characteristics, psychologists describe personality types. _____

5. Freud developed a theory about personality in which he divided the mind into three parts. _____

6. Freud named the parts the *id, ego,* and *superego* his theory became enormously influential. _____

7. Psychoanalysis started to lose its popularity by the 1940s, at that time other personality theories were developing. _____

8. One psychologist, William Sheldon, tried to connect personality to body shapes. _____

9. Sheldon's types were mesomorphic or lean, endomorphic or fat, and ectomorphic or tall and thin. _____

10. Human personalities vary greatly it is difficult to categorize them. _____

How to Correct Run-Ons

You can correct run-on sentences in a variety of ways. Read the following run-on sentence, and then review the four ways to correct it.

> **Run-On:**   Thomas Bouchard Jr. studies twins, he is interested in genetic influences on behavior.

1. Make two separate sentences by adding end punctuation, such as a period.

    Thomas Bouchard Jr. studies twins. **He** is interested in genetic influences on behavior.

2. Add a semicolon.

    Thomas Bouchard Jr. studies twins**;** he is interested in genetic influences on behavior.

3. Add a coordinator (*for, and, nor, but, or, yet, so*).

    Thomas Bouchard Jr. is interested in genetic influences on behavior, **so** he studies twins.

4. Add a subordinator (*after, although, as, because, before, since, when, while*).

    Thomas Bouchard Jr. studies twins **because** he is interested in genetic influences on behavior.

PRACTICE 7

A. Correct each run-on by making two complete sentences.

EXAMPLE:

> . They
> The twins are identical, they have brown hair and eyes.

1. Until the 1960s, twins put up for adoption were generally separated they were often adopted by two different families.

2. Psychologists are interested in studying twins raised in different families, they want to determine whether genetics or the environment plays a dominant role in behavior.

3. An amazing case involves Tamara Rabi and Adriana Scott they met each other in 2003.

B. Correct each run-on by joining the two sentences with a semicolon.

EXAMPLE:

The girls are remarkably similar; they both love to dance.

4. Tamara and Adriana were born in Mexico they were separated and raised by different families.

5. The girls were adopted by American families they lived just twenty-five miles apart.

6. Tamara Rabi was raised by a Jewish family in a city Adriana Scott was raised by a Catholic family in a suburb.

C. Correct the next run-ons by joining the two sentences with a coordinator such as *for, and, nor, but, or, yet,* or *so.*

EXAMPLE:

                        , but

A boy named Justin dated Adriana there was no mutual attraction.

7. Justin still wanted to find a girlfriend, his friend set him up with another girl.

8. Justin met Tamara he was astounded at her similarity to his previous girlfriend, Adriana.

9. Justin convinced the girls to meet each other, they met in a McDonald's parking lot.

D. Correct the next run-ons by joining the two sentences with a subordinator such as *although*, *because*, *where*, or *when*.

EXAMPLE:

because
The girls were happy to meet they each wanted a sister.

10. The twins did not go to the same type of school their families were not in the same income bracket.

11. They received different qualities of education, they were both B students.

12. The girls flew to Mexico they met their birth mother.

PRACTICE 8

Write *F* beside fragments, *RO* beside run-on sentences, and *C* beside correct sentences.

EXAMPLE:

The origins of certain fears.   _F_

1. Maggie Juato, a public relations executive, becomes breathless and dizzy whenever she sees one.   _____

2. The red nose, the curly green hair, and the large floppy shoes.   _____

3. The fear of clowns is known as coulrophobia.   _____

4. The clown's painted face is frightening.   _____

5. With a large mocking grin painted over the clown's real mouth.   _____

6. Professional clowns are aware of the problem they do not approach the fearful.   _____

7. Perhaps the phobia is caused by clown horror movies.   _____

8. Stephen King's movie *It*, for example.   _____

9. In the film, actor Tim Curry plays the evil clown, Pennywise, he smacks his lips every time he is about to murder a child.   _____

10. While such movies are terrifying.   _____

11. Real clowns are actors and comedians who need the work, they entertain children in hospitals and the elderly in nursing homes.   _____

12. Certain psychologists can help patients overcome their clown phobias.   _____

PRACTICE 9

Correct fifteen fragment and run-on errors.

EXAMPLE:

About 3 percent of births in the United States are twins ~~the~~ *, but* the percentage is increasing.

1.　　Thomas Bouchard Jr. and some colleagues at the University of Minnesota began studying twins in 1979. Bouchard had read about twins. Who had been raised apart. He contacted them to study their similarities and differences.

2.　　By 1990, Bouchard's team had studied seventy-seven sets of identical twins. The majority of the separated twins had astounding similarities. For example, two men named Jim. They had been separated at birth. They met in 1979 they found that they were similar in many ways. They smoked the same brand of cigarettes, they were both volunteer firefighters. The men also had the same hobbies. For example, working with wood. Amazingly, the Jims had both built white benches, they placed the benches near a tree.

Jim Lewis and Jim Springer

3.　　In the study, one set of twins was unusual. Japanese-born twins were adopted by different families in California. They shared some similarities, researchers were puzzled by their differences. One twin had 20/20 vision, but the other wore glasses. One was afraid to travel by airplane, the other had no such fear. One twin was quite timid, the other was easygoing and friendly.

4.　　Researchers suspect that the environment may play a role. In twin differences. For example, one twin could be malnourished, the other could have a healthy diet. The differences in diet could affect the development of the twins' brains. And bodies. Birthing problems may also result in differences. Between twins. One twin may receive less oxygen during delivery.

5.   The separated-twin studies suggest certain possibilities, for example, twins raised separately may be more similar than twins raised together. Twins raised together may emphasize their differences. Twins raised apart would have no need. To search for their individuality. Much more research is needed to know how genes influence behavior.

CHAPTER 20

The Writer's Desk Revise and Edit Your Warm Up

In the Warm Up at the beginning of the chapter, you wrote several sentences about dreams. Edit your paragraph. Make sure that sentences are complete and that there are no fragments or run-ons.

REFLECT ON IT

Think about what you have learned in this unit. If you do not know an answer, review that concept.

1. What is a sentence fragment? _____

    _____

2. What are the types of fragments?

    _____   _____

    _____   _____

3. What is a run-on? _____

    _____

4. Define a comma splice. _____

    _____

5. Define a fused sentence. _____

    _____

6. Explain the four ways to correct a run-on sentence.

    a. _____

    b. _____

    c. _____

    d. _____

FINAL REVIEW

Correct fifteen fragment and run-on errors.

EXAMPLE:

> *First, dreams express our deepest fears.*
> ~~First, dreams and fears.~~

1. "To sleep, perchance to dream," wrote Shakespeare in his play *Hamlet*. Many great writers have written about dreams. Such as Lewis Carroll. His famous work *Alice in Wonderland* is dreamlike, in the story, Alice has an adventure with a white rabbit. Another bizarre character is the Queen of Hearts. Who wants to cut off Alice's head.

2. Dreams sometimes leave the dreamer feeling uncomfortable. In Franz Kafka's novella *Metamorphosis*, the main character, Gregor Samsa, wakes up feeling uneasy. Because he has had bad dreams during the night. When he wakes up, Samsa finds himself transformed into a grotesque insect, he realizes that it is not a dream.

3. The meaning of dreams. Sigmund Freud and his student Carl Jung proposed a theory, they wrote that dreams have a specific purpose. Jung believed that dreamers could learn from their dreams. In his book *Memories, Dreams, and Reflections*. Jung wrote that dreams forced him to think about important things. Such as life and death.

4. Dreams have been the source of inspiration to many people. According to the Koran. God revealed many truths to Mohammad through dreams. Mohammad then recorded these revelations. In the Bible. God appeared in dreams to many people. Including Joseph. Others have also drawn inspiration from dreams. For instance, the Japanese filmmaker Akira Kurosawa. He recorded his dreams he stated that man is a genius when he is dreaming.

5.   Dreams have inspired artists, writers, and religious figures. If you have recurring dreams, you might write them down, dreams can be the source of fascinating stories.

How Do I Get a Better Grade?

Visit www.mywritinglab.com for audio-visual lectures and additional practice sets about fragments and run-ons. **Get a better grade with MyWritingLab!**

Faulty Parallel Structure

Section Theme **PSYCHOLOGY**

In this chapter, you will read about topics related to psychological experiments.

The Writer's Desk Warm Up

Write a short paragraph comparing your personality to that of a family member or friend. Describe how your personalities are similar and different.

What Is Parallel Structure?

Parallel structure occurs when pairs or groups of items in a sentence are balanced. In the following sentences, the underlined phrases contain repetitions of grammatical structure but not of ideas. Each sentence has parallel structure.

Internet sites, magazines, and newspapers published the results of the experiment.

(The nouns are parallel.)

Psychologists <u>observe</u> and <u>predict</u> human behavior.
(The present tenses are parallel.)

The experiment was <u>fascinating</u>, <u>groundbreaking</u>, and <u>revolutionary</u>.
(The adjectives are parallel.)

To get to the psychology department, go <u>across the street</u>, <u>into the building</u>, and <u>up the stairs</u>.
(The prepositional phrases are parallel.)

There are some test subjects <u>who develop a rash</u> and some <u>who have no reactions</u>.
(The "who" clauses are parallel.)

PRACTICE I

All of the following sentences have parallel structures. Underline the parallel items.

EXAMPLE:

Students in my psychology class <u>listened to the instructor</u>, <u>took notes</u>, and <u>asked questions</u>.

1. Professor Stanley Milgram taught at Yale, conducted a famous experiment, and wrote a book about his research.

2. Milgram's experiment was controversial, provocative, and surprising.

3. His experiment tried to understand how humans reacted to authority, how they obeyed authority, and how they felt about authority.

4. For his experiment, Milgram used one actor in a lab coat, one actor with glasses, and one unsuspecting subject in street clothes.

5. The psychologist told the subject to sit at the desk, to watch the "patient" behind the glass, and to listen to the experiment "leader."

6. The leader told the subject when to start electric shocks, when to increase the level of shocks, and when to stop the experiment.

7. Milgram's experiment raised important questions, ended in astonishing results, and gave valuable insight into human behavior.

8. Psychologists continue to perform experiments, give lectures, and debate issues.

Identify Faulty Parallel Structure

It is important to use parallel structure when using a series of words or phrases, paired clauses, comparisons, and two-part constructions.

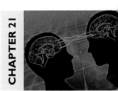

Series of Words or Phrases

Use parallel structure when words or phrases are joined in a series.

Not parallel: Students, administrators, and people who teach sometimes volunteer for psychology experiments.

Parallel: Students, administrators, and teachers sometimes volunteer for psychology experiments.
(The nouns are parallel.)

Not parallel: I plan to study for tests, to attend all classes, and listening to the instructor.

Parallel: I plan to study for tests, to attend all classes, and to listen to the instructor.
(The verbs are parallel.)

Paired Clauses

Use parallel structure when independent clauses are joined by *and, but,* or *or.*

Not parallel: The experimenter placed two probes on her head, and her wrist is where he attached a monitor.

Parallel: The experimenter placed two probes on her head, and he attached a monitor to her wrist.
(The prepositional phrases are parallel.)

Not parallel: She felt dizzy, and she also had a feeling of fear.

Parallel: She felt dizzy, and she also felt afraid.
(The adjectives are parallel.)

 **Hint** **Use Consistent Voice**

When a sentence has two independent clauses and is joined by a coordinating conjunction, use a consistent voice. In other words, if one part of the sentence is active, the other should also be active.

Not parallel: The researcher conducted the experiment, and then a report was written by him.

Parallel: The researcher conducted the experiment, and then he wrote a report.
(Both parts use the active voice.)

GRAMMAR LINK

To learn more about active and passive voice, see pages 361–365 in Chapter 23.

PRACTICE 2

Correct the faulty parallel structure in each sentence.

EXAMPLE:

original.
Some psychology experiments are bold, pioneering, and ~~show their originality.~~

1. Ivan Pavlov was a Russian physiologist, a research scientist, and he won a Nobel prize.

2. Pavlov became interested in dog salivation, and digestion also interested him.

3. To get to his lab, Pavlov walked through the door, up the stairs, and the department is where he entered.

4. Pavlov used many sound-making devices to stimulate his dogs, such as metronomes, whistles, and he also used tuning forks.

5. Pavlov noticed that the dogs heard the noise, saw the food dish, and were salivating.

6. Some of the dogs were excited, nervous, and expressed enthusiasm.

7. Western scientists found Pavlov's experiments to be astounding, innovative, and thought they were important.

8. Ivan Pavlov worked quickly and was very efficient.

Comparisons

Use parallel structure in comparisons containing *than* or *as*.

Not parallel:	Creating new experiments is more difficult than to re-create an earlier experiment.
Parallel:	<u>Creating a new experiment</u> is more difficult than <u>re-creating an earlier experiment</u>. (The *-ing* forms are parallel.)
Not parallel:	His home was as messy as the way he kept his laboratory.
Parallel:	His <u>home</u> was as messy as his <u>laboratory</u>. (The nouns are parallel.)

Two-Part Constructions

Use parallel structure for the following paired items.

either . . . or	not . . . but	both . . . and
neither . . . nor	not only . . . but also	rather . . . than

Not parallel:	My psychology class was both informative and a challenge.
Parallel:	My psychology class was both <u>informative</u> and <u>challenging</u>. (The adjectives are parallel.)
Not parallel:	I would rather finish my experiment than leaving early.
Parallel:	I would rather <u>finish</u> my experiment than <u>leave</u> early. (The verbs are parallel.)

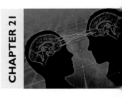

PRACTICE 3

Correct ten errors in parallel construction.

EXAMPLE:

                                interesting.

Philip Zimbardo is creative and ~~an interesting person.~~

1.   Philip Zimbardo created an experiment that was both unique and startled others. The Stanford Prison Experiment examined how ordinary people would react when placed in positions of power. He chose twenty-four students who were healthy, stable, and they abided by the law. Each subject would be either a guard or a prisoner for a two-week period.

2.   On the first day of the experiment, each guard was told to wear a uniform, carry a baton, and sunglasses were put on. Ordinary people who had committed no crime, who had broken no laws, and been honest were placed in a cold room. The prisoners were not only arrested but the guards also deloused them.

3.   Immediately, the experimenters observed shocking behavior. Some of the guards started to act controlling, sadistic, and they abused the prisoners. On the second day, the prisoners rioted and the guards attacked. Some prisoners decided that they would rather leave than continuing with the experiment.

4.   During the next few days, officials, priests, and teachers observed the experiment. Nobody questioned the morality of the proceedings. Then, on the sixth day, another psychologist arrived. She was appalled and she felt horror when she realized what was happening.

5. Zimbardo realized that his student actors were taking the experiment too seriously. Both the prisoners and the people playing the guards had to stop the experiment. Zimbardo worried that the student actors would be seriously hurt, distressed, and suffer from depression.

PRACTICE 4

Correct nine errors in parallel construction.

EXAMPLE:

Information about bystander apathy is surprising and ~~of interest.~~ *interesting.*

1. Bystander apathy is the unwillingness of an individual to help another in an emergency. In the 1960s, psychologists started to collect data, investigate behaviors, and proposing theories about bystander apathy. One celebrated instance of bystander apathy is the Kitty Genovese case.

2. On March 13, 1964, Kitty Genovese was on her way to her apartment in Queens, New York. She was walking quietly and her steps were quick. Suddenly, she saw a strange man. He attacked her, and she screamed for help. Kitty Genovese died slowly, violently, and in tragic circumstances.

3. The police investigation was complete, thorough, and done with precision. The results of the investigation were both astounding and nobody expected them. Apparently, thirty-eight people heard the victim screaming, and the attack was watched by some of them, but no one called the police.

4. Many psychologists have studied the phenomenon of bystander apathy, and the results have been published by them. There are many reasons a bystander may not help someone in trouble. Bystanders may not want to risk their own lives, they may not have the skills to help in an emergency, or legal problems could be incurred. In addition, many people do not want to look stupid or be seen as being foolish if there is no real emergency. Psychologists believe that these are only some possible reasons for bystander apathy.

PRACTICE 5

Write sentences using parallel structure with the following grammatical items.

1. Parallel nouns: _____

_____

2. Parallel verbs: _____

_____

3. Parallel adjectives: _____

_____

4. Parallel *who* clauses: _____

_____

The Writer's Desk Revise and Edit Your Warm Up

In the Warm Up at the beginning of the chapter, you wrote a short paragraph comparing your personality to that of a family member or friend. Check for any sentences that contain faulty parallel structure and correct your mistakes.

REFLECT ON IT

Think about what you have learned in this chapter. If you do not know an answer, review that concept.

1. What is parallel structure? _____

_____

2. Why is parallel structure important? _____

_____

Fill in the blanks of the following sentences. Make sure the grammatical structures are parallel.

3. The college I attend is both _____ and

_____.

4. In my spare time, I _____ , _____ ,

and _____ .

FINAL REVIEW

Correct twelve errors in parallel construction.

EXAMPLE:

                              counselors
Psychiatrists, psychologists, and ~~other people who are counselors~~ help patients deal with their mental health problems.

1.   In 1972, psychologist David Rosenhan was young, intelligent, and had

enthusiasm. He asked eight of his friends to participate in a psychology

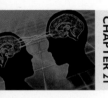

experiment. There were some psychologists, a pediatrician, a psychiatrist, a man who was a painter, a homemaker, and a graduate student. Rosenhan told the participants that for five days they had to stop showering, they had to look unclean, and to wear old clothes. At the end of the fifth day, the participants traveled to different parts of the country and entered various psychiatric hospital emergency rooms. The psychiatric hospitals were either private and expensive or public and they cost very little. The participants told the admitting psychiatrists that they heard voices. They told the truth about everything else in their lives.

2.   Psychiatrists looked for and were finding serious psychological illnesses in the patients. They diagnosed all eight patients with paranoid schizophrenia. The doctors institutionalized the patients from eight to fifty-eight days. Rosenhan's experiment showed that psychiatric evaluation had to be both stringent and have no bias.

3.   Lauren Slater is a researcher, psychologist, and she writes. In 2003, she decided to reenact Rosenhan's experiment to see if assessment methods in psychiatry had changed. She became the guinea pig in her own experiment. Like Rosenhan's friends, she looked scruffy, she visited different psychiatric institutions, and told the psychiatrists about voices in her head. Psychiatrists asked her neither about her religious beliefs, nor was she asked anything about her cultural background. The examining psychiatrists asked her some general questions, took her temperature, and she was diagnosed by them with depression.

4.   Slater knew she did not really suffer from depression because she had asked her real doctor, her family, and her people who were her friends to assess her mental state. Unlike the psychiatrists in Rosenham's experiment, Slater's psychiatrists did not admit her to their hospitals, but they all prescribed antipsychotic and antidepressant drugs for her. She wrote about her experiences in her book *Opening Skinner's Box*. Her book is fascinating, illuminating, and it is of interest.

The Writer's Room — **Topics for Writing**

Choose one of the following topics and write a paragraph or an essay. When you write, remember to follow the writing process.

1. Explain why people are superstitious, and list some common superstitions.
2. Describe a set of twins. Compare the twins, looking at their similarities and differences.
3. What are some different ways that people deal with their fears? Classify responses to fear into three categories.

 ### The Writers' Circle

When you apply for a job, the employer often asks you what your strengths and weaknesses are. Work with a team of students to do the following activity.

STEP 1 Think of a successful person. You could choose a person from any of the next categories.

A business tycoon	A politician	A movie star
A musician	An athlete	A writer or artist

STEP 2 Brainstorm one list of that person's strengths and another list of that person's weaknesses.

STEP 3 Write a short paragraph about that successful person, discussing the person's strengths and weaknesses.

STEP 4 Exchange paragraphs with another team. Proofread the other team's paragraph, checking especially for fragments, run-ons, and parallel structure.

READING LINK

Psychology

"I'm a Banana and Proud of It" by Wayson Choy (page 551)

"Dancing with Fear" by Bebe Moore Campbell (page 556)

"Religious Faith Versus Spirituality" by Neil Bissoondath (page 558)

"Dying to Be Bigger" by H.D. (page 573)

"Dealing with People" by Greg McGrew (page 588)

"Interview with Jimmy Baca" by Elizabeth Farnsworth (page 598)

How Do I Get a Better Grade?

Visit www.mywritinglab.com for audio-visual lectures and additional practice sets about faulty parallel structure.
Get a better grade with MyWritingLab!

Present and Past Tenses

Section Theme **ESPIONAGE**

In this chapter, you will read about topics related to the history of espionage.

The Writer's Desk Warm Up

Write a short paragraph describing the last spy or suspense movie that you have seen. Describe what happened in the movie.

What Is Verb Tense?

A verb shows an action or a state of being. A **verb tense** indicates when an action occurred. Review the various tenses of the verb *work*.

Present time: She <u>works</u> alone.

Past time: The agent <u>worked</u> in Monaco last summer.

Future: She <u>will work</u> in the Middle East next year.

Use Standard Verb Forms

Nonstandard English is used in everyday conversation, and it may differ according to the region in which you live. **Standard American English** is the common language generally used and expected in schools, businesses, and government institutions in the United States. Most of your instructors will want you to write using Standard American English.

Nonstandard:	He <u>don't</u> have <u>no</u> time.	She <u>be</u> busy.
Standard:	He <u>does not</u> have <u>any</u> time.	She <u>is</u> busy.

The Simple Present Tense

In English there are two forms of the present tense. The **simple present tense** indicates that an action is a general fact or habitual activity.

Fact: The Spy Museum <u>contains</u> many interesting spy artifacts.

**Habitual
activity:** The undercover agent <u>meets</u> her superiors once a month.

CHAPTER 22

(past)	JANUARY ▼	FEBRUARY ▼	MARCH ▼	APRIL ▼	(future)
	They meet.	They meet.	They meet.	They meet.	

 **The Present Progressive**

The **present progressive tense** indicates that an action is in progress at this moment. In this chapter, you will focus on the simple present and past forms.

present progressive tense
Right now, the agent <u>is taking</u> pictures with her spy camera.

Forms of the Simple Present Tense

Simple present tense verbs (except *be*) have two forms.

- **Base form:** When the subject is *I, you, we,* or *they,* or the equivalent (*women, the Rocky Mountains*), do not add an ending to the verb.

    Nations <u>rely</u> on spies to gather secret information.

    Many agents <u>speak</u> several languages.

- **Third-person singular form:** When the subject is *he, she, it,* or the equivalent (*Mark, Carol, Miami*), add an *-s* or *-es* ending to the verb.

    That woman <u>works</u> as a spy. She <u>has</u> several code names.

Look at the singular and plural forms of the verb *work.*

GRAMMAR LINK

For more information about progressive forms, see pages 367–369 in Chapter 24.

Present Tense of Work	Singular	Plural
First person:	I work.	We work.
Second person:	You work.	You work.
Third person:	He works.	They work.
	She works.	
	It works.	

Irregular Present Tense Verbs (*be* and *have*)

In the present tense, *be* and *have* do not follow the regular pattern for verb endings. Be particularly careful when writing these verbs.

Present Tense of *Be*

I am	He is	You are
	She is	We are
	It is	They are

Present Tense of *Have*

I have	He has	You have
	She has	We have
	It has	They have

GRAMMAR LINK

For more information about subject-verb agreement, see Chapter 25.

> *Hint*   **Make Your Subjects and Verbs Agree**
>
> In the present tense, the subject and verb must **agree** in number. If the subject is third-person singular (*he, she, it*), the corresponding verb must have the singular form, too.
>   Although plural nouns usually end in -*s*, plural verbs do not. Instead, singular verbs have the -*s* or -*es* ending. Notice the errors in subject-verb agreement in the next sentences.
>
>
>
> Edward Rowen ~~work~~ for the Central Intelligence Agency. Why ~~do~~ the agency
>   *does*
> investigate candidates? It ~~do~~ not want to hire people with criminal records.

PRACTICE 1

Circle the correct present tense form of the verbs in parentheses.

EXAMPLE:

Spying (seem, (seems)) like an exciting job.

1. Men and women (betray, betrays) their country for many reasons.

2. According to Christopher Andrew, co-author of *The Sword and the Shield*, the acronym *mice* (sum, sums) up the reasons why a person may become a traitor.

3. *Mice* (stand, stands) for "money, ideology, compromise, and ego."

4. According to Andrew, the most popular reason (is, are) money.

5. Some agents (receive, receives) millions in cash, jewelry, and so on.

6. Another reason (is, are) ideology.

7. Maybe the agent (dislike, dislikes) his or her own political system.

8. Sometimes people (believe, believes) that another country's way of life is better.

9. Some men and women (become, becomes) spies because they are ashamed of something that they have done.

10. For example, if a government bureaucrat (steal, steals) money and another person (find, finds) out, the bureaucrat can be blackmailed to become a spy.

11. Finally, many people (think, thinks) that spying (is, are) an exciting profession.

12. Andrew (say, says) that "an interesting minority want to be secret celebrities" in their own little world of espionage.

The Simple Past Tense

The **simple past tense** indicates that an action occurred at a specific past time. In the past tense, there are regular and irregular verbs. **Regular verbs** end in *-d* or *-ed* (*talked, ended, watched*). **Irregular verbs** do not follow a regular pattern and do not end in any specific letter (*knew, saw, met*).

Yesterday morning, the spy satellite **passed** over my home.

YESTERDAY MORNING   TODAY

The satellite **passed.**

> **Hint**   **The Past Progressive**
>
> The **past progressive tense** indicates that an action was in progress at a particular past moment. In this chapter, you will focus on the simple past.
>
> past progressive tense
> While the detectives <u>were watching</u> the house, the suspect escaped.

Regular Past Tense Verbs

Regular past tense verbs have a standard *-d* or *-ed* ending. Use the same form for both singular and plural past tense verbs.

Singular subject: One well-known agent **learned** to speak twelve languages.

Plural subject: During World War II, secret agents **used** codes to communicate.

Spell Regular Past Tense Verbs Correctly

Most regular past tense verbs are formed by adding -*ed* to the base form of the verb.

walk<u>ed</u>   question<u>ed</u>

However, there are some exceptions.

- When the regular verb ends in -*e*, just add -*d*.

realize<u>d</u>   appreciate<u>d</u>

- When the regular verb ends in consonant + -*y*, change the *y* to *i* and add -*ed*.

reply, repl<u>ied</u>   try, tr<u>ied</u>

- When the regular verb ends in the vowel + -*y*, just add -*ed*.

play<u>ed</u>   employ<u>ed</u>

- When the regular verb ends in a consonant-vowel-consonant combination, double the last consonant and add -*ed*.

tap, tap<u>ped</u>   plan, plan<u>ned</u>

GRAMMAR LINK

See Chapter 32, "Spelling and Commonly Confused Words," for information about the spelling of verbs.

PRACTICE 2

Write the simple past form of each verb in parentheses. Make sure you spell the past tense verb correctly.

EXAMPLE:

The U.S. government (form) ___*formed*___ the Federal Bureau of Investigation in 1908 to detect enemy spies in the country.

1.   In 1924, the FBI (hire) _____ J. Edgar Hoover to be the

director of the Bureau. During the Hoover years, the FBI (improve)

_____ training. The agency (plan) _____ to use modern

technological investigative methods. During the 1930s, Americans (treat)

_____ Hoover as a hero because the FBI (carry) _____ out

raids against gangsters such as Al Capone.

2.   However, Hoover also had a dark side. His agents (snoop)

_____ on politicians and celebrities. For example, agents (spy)

_____ on the Kennedy brothers and on Dr. Martin Luther King Jr.

According to King's widow and others, the FBI director (act)

_____ unethically.

3.   In 1994, biographer Anthony Summer wrote a book about Hoover.

According to Summer, Hoover (study) _____ the private lives

of the eight presidents whom he served under. Some presidents
(worry) _____ that Hoover would disclose secrets about them.
Hoover (retain) _____ his top position at the FBI for forty-eight
years, until his death in 1972.

Irregular Past Tense Verbs

Irregular verbs change internally. Because their spellings change from the present
to the past tense, these verbs can be challenging to remember.

> The prisoner <u>wrote</u> with invisible ink. (**wrote** = past tense of *write*)

> The guards <u>sent</u> the letter. (**sent** = past tense of *send*)

> The prisoners <u>began</u> a revolt. (**began** = past tense of *begin*)

> *Hint*   **Do Not Confuse *Past* and *Passed***
>
> Some people confuse *past* and *passed*. *Past* is a noun that means "in a previous time" or
> "before now."
>
> > She has many secrets in her <u>past</u>.
>
> *Passed* is the past tense of the verb *pass*, which has many meanings. In the first example
> below, it means "to go by." In the second example, it means "to take something and give
> it to someone." In the last example, it means "to successfully complete."
>
> > Many days <u>passed</u>, and the nights got shorter.
> >
> > Please <u>pass</u> the salt. I <u>passed</u> you the butter a moment ago.
> >
> > He <u>passed</u> the entrance test. Did you <u>pass</u> your test?

PRACTICE 3

Write the correct past form of each verb in parentheses. Some verbs are regular
and some are irregular. If you do not know the past form of an irregular verb,
consult Appendix 2.

EXAMPLE:

> During the American Revolution, armies (write) _____*wrote*_____ letters
> with invisible ink.

1.   In 1775, an American soldier named Benjamin Thompson (combine)

_____ ferrous sulphate and water. When mixed together, the

substances (turn) _____ into invisible ink. Later, the reader of the

letter (hold) _____ it over a candle flame, and the ink (become)

_____ brown. The lines with the invisible ink (appear)

_____ between the lines of the regular letter.

2.   More recently, during World War II, a mysterious person (send)

_____ a postcard to Jacob Rosenblum, a resident of Bucharest,

GRAMMAR LINK

See Appendix 2 for a complete list
of irregular verbs.

Romania. The postcard, dated August 20, 1943, (come) _____ from a death camp and (have) _____ one line. In German, the letter (say) _____, "My darling, I remember you with love" and was signed "Lola." Underneath the black writing, a message (appear) _____ in invisible ink. In that message, the author (speak) _____ of "starvation, degradation, killing by gas," and "an agonizing hell." The letter writer also (request) _____ signal pistols and invisible ink. The letter (end) _____ with the mysterious words "K is fulfilling his mission. We will do what we have to do."

3.   During past wars, people (find) _____ many ways to make invisible ink, and they (pass) _____ secret messages to others. For example, soldiers (make) _____ ink out of acidic liquids such as lemon juice and vinegar. When a soldier (write) _____ with such substances, the ink would later turn brown when heated. In the past, some prisoners of war even (use) _____ their own sweat and saliva to make invisible ink.

be (*was or were*)

Past tense verbs generally have one form that you can use with all subjects. However, the verb *be* has two past forms: *was* and *were*.

Past Tense of Be		
	Singular	**Plural**
First person:	I was	We were
Second person:	You were	You were
Third person:	He was She was It was	They were

PRACTICE 4

Write *was* or *were* in each space provided.

EXAMPLE:

Robert Barron _____*was*_____ not an ordinary artist.

1.   During the 1970s, Robert Barron worked for the Pentagon. He _____ not happy with his parking spot because he always had to

walk a long way to get to his office. One day, when he _____
alone, he created a perfect fake parking permit. Some other employees
_____ aware of what Barron had done, and they told superior
officers about it. Barron had to pay a fine. As it happened, some CIA agents
_____ impressed with Barron's artistic talents.

2.   Soon, Barron joined the graphic arts department at the CIA. He
became an expert at creating disguises for secret agents, and he
_____ happy with his new job. Barron and other artists
_____ very creative, and they made false noses, foreheads, and
chins so that agents could look completely different. Some artists
_____ experts at creating false mustaches, beards, wigs, and teeth.
The disguises _____ important because disguised defectors needed
to pass army checkpoints and borders.

Problems with *be, have,* and *do*

Some writers find it particularly difficult to remember how to use the irregular
verbs *be*, *have*, and *do* in the past tense. Here are some helpful guidelines.

Avoiding Common Errors with *be*

- Use *were* in the past tense when the subject is plural. Do not use *was*.

  > *were*
  > The spies ~~was~~ arrested in 1995.

- Use the standard form of the verb (*is* or *was*), not *be*.

  > *was*
  > The camera ~~be~~ small enough to fit in a pen.

Avoiding Common Errors with *have*

- Use the past form of the verb (*had*), not the present form (*have* or *has*), when
  speaking about a past event.

  > *had*
  > The prisoner ~~has~~ to write messages with invisible ink during the war.

Avoiding Common Errors with *do*

- Use *done* only when it is preceded by a helping verb (*was done, is done,* and so on).

  > *did*
  > Barron ~~done~~ an interview with the press yesterday.

PRACTICE 5

Correct ten verb errors. If the verb is incorrectly formed, or if the verb is in the
wrong tense, write the correct form above it.

EXAMPLE:

> *have*
> Some people ~~has~~ very little respect for pigeons.

1.   Most city dwellers believes that pigeons are nuisances. For example, at my apartment building, the owner done many things last year to keep pigeons off the balconies. However, people undervalue pigeons. During past wars, the homing pigeon has an important role in international espionage.

2.   During the Napoleonic wars, homing pigeons gived officials a crucial way to communicate. The small birds carried and delivered secret messages because they was able to fly over enemy territories. Those pigeons be able to transmit messages faster than soldiers on horses, and they haved legendary endurance.

3.   According to Richard Platt's book *Spy*, Roman emperor Julius Caesar also used birds to send messages. Pigeons be valued for their speed, size, and reliability. Additionally, over half a million pigeons taked messages to soldiers during World War I, and some soldiers actually hided pigeons in their pockets and cared for them on battlefields. We should appreciate pigeons because they played an important role in previous wars.

Negative and Question Forms

In the present and past tenses, you must add a helping verb (*do*, *does*, or *did*) to question and negative forms. In the present tense, use the helping verb *do*, or use *does* when the subject is third-person singular. Use *did* in the past tense.

Questions: **Do** you know about the Spy Museum in Washington?
Does the museum open on weekends?
Did you visit the spy museum last summer?

Negatives: We **do** not live in Washington.
The museum **does** not open on holidays.
We **did** not visit the spy museum last summer.

When the main verb is *be* (*is*, *am*, *are*), no additional helping verb is necessary.

Questions: **Is** the spy story suspenseful?
Were foreign spies in New York during the 2005 World Summit?

Negatives: The story **is not** suspenseful.
Foreign spies **were not** in New York during the event.

A Note about Contractions

In informal writing, it is acceptable to contract negative verb forms. However, you should avoid using contractions in your academic writing.

does not
The CIA ~~doesn't~~ have enough multilingual interpreters.

> **Hint**   **Use the Correct Question and Negative Forms**
>
> In question and negative forms, always use the base form of the main verb, even when the subject is third-person singular.
>
> *have*
> Why does the Spy Museum ~~has~~ so many spy gadgets?
>
> *discuss*
> In 1914, Mata Hari did not ~~discussed~~ her identity.

PRACTICE 6

Write questions for each answer. Remember to add a helping verb (*do*, *does*, or *did*) when necessary.

EXAMPLES:

   Where is the International Spy Museum?

The International Spy Museum is in Washington.

   What does it contain?

It contains hundreds of spy gadgets.

1. _____

   The Spy Museum opened in 2002.

2. _____

   The spy gadgets are from nations around the world.

3. _____

   Yes, the museum is open on Sundays.

4. _____

   Yes, the camera has a powerful lens.

5. _____

   Yes, many tourists visit the museum each year.

PRACTICE 7

Combine the words in parentheses to form negatives. Remember to add a helping verb (*do*, *does*, or *did*) when necessary.

EXAMPLE:

   Washington's Spy Museum has hundreds of spy gadgets, but it (have, not)
   ____*does not have*____ paintings.

1.   Washington's International Spy Museum contains many interesting

   gadgets. For example, on display is a tube of lipstick called "The Kiss

   of Death." The tube (have, not) _____ an obvious

function. It (add, not) _____ color to a person's lips. Instead, the lipstick tube conceals a tiny pistol. In 1965, a female Russian spy carried the pistol in her purse, and the people she met (know, not) _____ about her hidden weapon.

2.   The museum also displays interesting spy cameras. The best spy camera, the Minox, (be, not) _____ very large. It has a high-resolution lens, and it (need, not) _____ to be frequently reloaded. These days, with microtechnology, cameras and recording devices (be, not) _____ as large as they used to be. In the 1960s, recording devices (be, not) _____ very sensitive. Nowadays, microphones (have, not) _____ to be in a particular room to pick up a conversation.

3.   Clearly, the Spy Museum is an extremely interesting place. Tourists (have, not) _____ to spend the entire day at the museum because it (be, not) _____ a very large place.

> ### Hint   Use the Base Form After *To*
>
> Remember to use the base form of verbs that follow *to* (infinitive form).
>
> > *study*
> > Greenstein wanted to ~~studied~~ the postcard.

PRACTICE 8

The next selection contains verb tense, spelling, and *past* versus *passed* errors. Correct fifteen errors.

EXAMPLE:

> *describe*
> Many books ~~describes~~ the Navajo code talkers of World War II.

1.   Navajo be an incredibly complex language with complicated syntax and tonal qualities. It has no alphabet or written forms, and only Native Americans in the Southwest speaks it. During World War II, Navajo natives maked an important contribution to the Allied war effort.

2.   During the war, Japanese and German troops tapped Allied communication lines and listen to the messages. Japanese code breakers was particularly capable. They managed to figured every code that the

Allies came up with. In 1942, the Marines get hundreds of Navajo volunteers to relayed coded messages about military plans. The Navajos past messages using their language, and they be very efficient code talkers. They call fighter planes "hummingbirds" and submarines "iron fish."

3. The Japanese tought that they could figure out the messages. They work hard, but they did not managed to break the Navajo code. After the war ended, the Navajos did not received recognition for their important work as code talkers until 1969.

Avoid Double Negatives

A double negative occurs when a negative word such as *no, nothing, nobody,* or *nowhere* is combined with a negative adverb such as *not, never, rarely,* or *seldom.* The result is a sentence that has a double negative. Such sentences can be confusing because the negative words cancel each other.

> The agent <u>does not</u> have <u>no</u> children.
> (According to this sentence, the agent has children.)

> He <u>didn't</u> know <u>nothing</u> about it.
> (According to this sentence, he knows something about it.)

How to Correct Double Negatives

There are several ways to correct double negatives.

- Completely remove one of the negative forms.

Incorrect:	The agent doesn't have no children.
Correct:	The agent **doesn't** have children.
	The agent has **no** children.

Incorrect:	He didn't know nothing about the crime.
Correct:	He knew **nothing** about the crime.
	He **didn't** know about the crime.

- Change *no* to *any (anybody, anything, anywhere).*

Incorrect:	The agent doesn't have no children.
Correct:	The agent doesn't have **any** children.

Incorrect:	He didn't know nothing about the crime.
Correct:	He didn't know **anything** about the crime.

PRACTICE 9

Correct the six errors with double negatives. You can correct each error in more than one way.

EXAMPLES:

any
Mata Hari didn't have ~~no~~ close friends.

had
Mata Hari ~~didn't have~~ no close friends.

1.   In 1875, Mata Hari's Dutch parents named her Margareta Zelle. At the age of eighteen, she married a much older naval officer. Her husband was an alcoholic, and Zelle didn't see no reason to stay with him. Zelle left, and she didn't take none of her furniture or clothing.

2.   Zelle didn't have no marketable skills. She decided to become an exotic dancer. She changed her name to Mata Hari and performed authentic Hindu temple dances. She never said nothing to her parents about her new career choice.

3.   Due to her beauty, she attracted many influential men such as the German crown prince and high-ranking German officers. Their wives didn't say nothing nice about Mata Hari. Her career as a dancer lasted for about ten years.

4.   According to her biographer Erika Ostrovsky, Mata Hari became a spy for the Germans in 1914, and her code name was H 21. One day, French officials intercepted a German secret service telegram. They identified

Mata Hari's code name and accused her of espionage. Mata Hari said that she didn't do nothing wrong. However, the French courts found her guilty of espionage. In 1918, a firing squad executed her.

The Writer's Desk Revise and Edit Your Warm Up

Review the sentences that you wrote for the Warm Up at the beginning of this chapter. Make sure that your regular and irregular verbs are spelled correctly.

REFLECT ON IT

Think about what you have learned in this chapter. If you do not know an answer, review that concept.

1. What are the present and past forms of the verb *be*?

	Present	**Past**
I	_____	_____
he, she, it	_____	_____
you, we, they	_____	_____

2. Write an example of a regular past tense verb. _____

3. Write an example of an irregular past tense verb. _____

4. What is the simple past form of the following verbs?

    a. think: _____   c. have: _____

    b. mention: _____   d. go: _____

5. Correct one verb tense error in each of the following sentences.

    a. In 1954, a Russian agent surrender to the United States.

    b. Khokhlov defected because he did not wanted to kill another Russian agent.

    c. Khokhlov past many days and nights wondering whether he should give himself up.

    d. The agent owned a cigarette case that be a secret weapon.

    e. The cigarette case fired bullets that was poisonous.

CHAPTER 22

FINAL REVIEW

Correct fifteen errors in present and past tense verbs.

EXAMPLE:

> *think*
> When people talk about espionage, they generally ~~thinks~~ about secret agents who work for governments.

1.   Industrial espionage occurs when companies spy on each other. It be a major problem. A nation's economic survival depend on its ability to be innovative in the industrial sector. For example, in 1994, a large company develop a new highly efficient and low-cost engine. It wanted to be the first company to put that engine on the market. That company had to protected its information so that competitors could not put the product out first.

2.   Last year, Max B. worked as a spy, and he easily finded top-secret information. A large corporation hire Max as a temporary worker. He begun his job last August. When he be inside the company, he done an unethical thing. He used his computer to access the company's database. He discover an important new project just by looking at the electronic file folder titled "Priorities." The company directors never knowed what Max was doing. When Max left the job, he brung home important documents.

3.   Computers is everywhere, and they are not secure machines. Hackers works on finding new ways to break codes every day. Today, businesses is more vulnerable than ever. Our government needs to take industrial espionage seriously.

How Do I Get a Better Grade?

Visit www.mywritinglab.com for audio-visual lectures and additional practice sets about present and past tenses.
Get a better grade with MyWritingLab!

Past Participles

Section Theme **ESPIONAGE**

CONTENTS

In this chapter, you will read about fictional and real spies.

The Writer's Desk Warm Up

Reflect on how children were disciplined in the past and how they are disciplined today. Write a paragraph explaining how the disciplining of children has changed over the years.

Past Participles

A **past participle** is a verb form, not a verb tense. You cannot use a past participle as the only verb in a sentence; instead, you must use it with a helping verb such as *have, has, had, is, was,* or *were.*

GRAMMAR LINK

For a list of irregular past participles, see Appendix 2.

	helping verbs	past participle
Ian Fleming	was	<u>raised</u> in England.
His novels	have	<u>become</u> very popular.

Regular Verbs

The past tense and the past participle of regular verbs are the same.

Base Form	Past Tense	Past Participle
walk	walked	walked
try	tried	tried
use	used	used

Irregular Verbs

The past tense and the past participle of irregular verbs may be different. For a complete list of irregular past participles, see Appendix 2.

Base Form	Past Tense	Past Participle
begin	began	begun
go	went	gone
speak	spoke	spoken

PRACTICE 1

Each group of verbs contains one error. Underline the error, and write the correct word in the space provided.

EXAMPLE:

Base Form	Past Tense	Past Participle	
lose	<u>losed</u>	lost	*lost*

	Base Form	Past Tense	Past Participle	
1.	cost	cost	costed	_____
2.	come	came	came	_____
3.	build	builded	built	_____
4.	sink	sank	sank	_____
5.	bring	brang	brought	_____
6.	write	wrote	wrote	_____
7.	choose	choosed	chosen	_____
8.	fall	felt	fallen	_____
9.	feel	felt	fell	_____
10.	blow	blew	blowed	_____
11.	tear	tore	tore	_____
12.	take	taked	taken	_____
13.	bite	bited	bitten	_____
14.	sit	sat	sitten	_____
15.	grow	grew	growed	_____

PRACTICE 2

In the following selection, all irregular past participles are underlined. Correct ten past participle errors.

EXAMPLE:

                                  put

Many parents have <u>putted</u> video cameras in their home.

1.   Spying on children is not new; in fact, parents have <u>did</u> it for centuries. Parents have <u>read</u> their children's diaries, and some have <u>gone</u> through their children's belongings. However, in recent years, the methods used to spy have <u>became</u> more sophisticated.

2.   According to John Stossel of ABC News, some parents have <u>bought</u> video cameras and miniature tape recorders to spy on their children. For example, in 2002, the Roy family bought a small video camera. It was <u>hided</u> behind a plant in the living room, and their son, Samuel, was not <u>told</u> that the camera was there. One evening, while his parents were out, Samuel was <u>catched</u> on the video camera smoking and drinking with friends. When the boy was <u>shown</u> the tape, he admitted that he had <u>taked</u> the alcohol. The parents insist that they have <u>tought</u> their child a valuable lesson.

3.   Another spy tool can track the speed of a driver. A Miami father, Ed Jarvis, has <u>putted</u> the device in his car so that he can monitor his son's driving. Recently, Ed punished his son, David, when he realized that the boy had <u>broke</u> the law. The device proved that David had <u>drove</u> over the speed limit. David's reaction was harsh: "The only thing my father has <u>done</u> is make me angry. He has no faith in me."

4.   The issue about spying on children is controversial. Some people believe that parents should snoop. Parents have the right to know if their teenagers have <u>maked</u> serious mistakes. Others claim that spying can break the bonds of trust between a parent and a child. If you were a parent, would you spy on your children?

The Present Perfect Tense: *have/has* + Past Participle

A past participle combines with *have* or *has* to form the **present perfect tense.** You can use this tense in two different circumstances.

- Use the present perfect to show that an action began in the past and continues to the present time. You will often use *since* and *for* with this tense.

PAST   NOW

I **have been** a James Bond fan for five years.

- Use the present perfect to show that one or more completed actions occurred at unspecified past times.

PAST (unspecified past times)   NOW
?   ?   ?   ?

I **have watched** at least four James Bond movies.

Hint   **Use Time Markers**

Time markers are words that indicate when an action occurred.

Simple Past Tense
To refer to a completed incident that occurred at a specific past time, use the following time markers.

yesterday	ago	when I was . . .	last (week, month, year . . .)
in the past	in 2005	during the 1970s	in the early days of . . .

Ian Fleming **wrote** his first novel in 1953.

Present Perfect Tense

- To refer to an action that began in the past and is still continuing, use the following time markers.

since	for (a period of time up to now)	ever
up to now	so far	not . . . yet

Spy films **have been** popular since the 1930s.

- To refer to an action that occurred at unspecified past times, use the following time markers.

once	lately	several times	three times
many	twice	recently	

I **have seen** *The World is Not Enough* once and *Die Another Day* twice.

Look at the difference between the past and the present perfect tenses.

Simple past: In 1962, Sean Connery <u>appeared</u> in the first James Bond film, *Dr. No.*
(This event occurred at a known past time.)

Present perfect: Many different actors <u>have played</u> James Bond.
(We do not really know when the actors played James Bond.)

James Bond movies <u>have been</u> popular for more than forty years.
(The action began in the past and continues to the present.)

PRACTICE 3

Write the simple past or present perfect form of each verb in parentheses.

EXAMPLE:

For the last six years, my cousin Mike (be) _____*has been*_____ a James Bond fanatic.

1.   Spy fans around the world (watch) _____ James Bond movies since the mid-1960s. Although most people (hear) _____ of James Bond, few people know about the man behind the movies.

2.   Ian Fleming was born in 1906, and his father (be) _____ a successful stockbroker. As a result, Ian (spend) _____ his youth living a high-class lifestyle. In the 1940s, the British Secret Service (draft) _____ Ian Fleming because he could easily mix with upper-class officials.

3.   In 1953, Fleming (use) _____ his experiences to create his first James Bond book. Since then, James Bond (be) _____ extremely popular. Over the last forty years, viewers around the world (see) _____ the sophisticated spy in action.

4.   Since the first film, the James Bond character (age, never) _____. For more than forty years, beautiful women (try) _____ to seduce him and villains _____ to kill him. Over and over, Bond (escape) _____ danger by using his intelligence, his fast cars, and his secret weapons. Since its debut, the James Bond character (capture) _____ the audience's imagination.

The Past Perfect Tense: *had* + Past Participle

The **past perfect tense** indicates that one or more past actions happened before another past action. It is formed with *had* and the past participle.

PAST PERFECT · · · · · PAST · · · · · NOW

The robbers **had left** when the police arrived.

Notice the differences between the simple past, the present perfect, and the past perfect tenses.

Simple past: Last night I <u>watched</u> a documentary on double agents.
(The action occurred at a known past time.)

Present perfect: I <u>have read</u> many articles about spying.
(The actions occurred at unspecified past times.)

Past perfect: The government <u>had suspected</u> the agent for a long time before he was arrested as a spy.
(All of the actions happened in the past, but one action happened before another.)

PRACTICE 4

Circle the correct verb forms. You may choose the simple past, the present perfect, or the past perfect tense.

EXAMPLE:

Before his death, Alexander Litvinenko (criticized/ has criticized) the Russian government many times.

1. Alexander Litvinenko, a former KGB agent, (was / has been) born in 1962 and (died / had died) in 2006. He (worked / has worked) for the Russian spy agency between 1986 and 2000. By the time Russia became a democracy, Litvinenko (was / had become) disillusioned with the secret service agency. One of his jobs with the security forces (was / had been) to protect a Russian billionaire, Boris Berezovsky, a man who (accumulated / had accumulated) a lot of enemies. In 2000, Berezovsky criticized President Putin. Authorities tried to arrest the billionaire, but it was too late because he (fled / had fled) to London.

2. In 1998, Litvinenko (blamed / has blamed) the Russian government for plotting to assassinate the Russian businessman. A few years later, a bomb (explode / exploded) in an apartment building in Moscow, killing

many Chechen separatists. After the explosion, Litvinenko also (claimed / has claimed) that Russian President Putin (has ordered / had ordered) the bomb. Russian security forces (wanted / have wanted) to arrest Litvinenko. Fearing for his life, he (asked / had asked) for political asylum in England.

3.   In November, 2006, Litvinenko (became / has become) very ill because of a rare radioactive poison. He (stated / has stated) that he (had / had had) lunch with Russian spies the day before his illness occurred. He (said / has said) those spies (put / had put) poison in his meal the previous day. Since his death, Litvinenko's wife (accused / has accused) the Russian government of murdering her husband. Since that time, the British authorities (have held / had held) several press conferences about the case.

The Passive Voice: *be* + Past Participle

In sentences with the **passive voice**, the subject receives the action and does not perform the action. Look carefully at the next two sentences.

Active: The diplomat **gave** secret documents to an undercover agent.
(This is active because the subject, *diplomat,* performed the action.)

Passive: Secrets documents **were given** to an undercover agent.
(This is passive because the subject, *documents,* was affected by the action and did not perform the action.)

To form the passive voice, use the appropriate tense of the verb *be* plus the past participle.

Verb Tenses	Active Voice (The subject performs the action.)	Passive Voice: *be* + Past Participle (The subject receives the action.)
Simple present	She writes spy stories.	Spy stories are written (by her).
Present progressive	is writing	are being written
Simple past	wrote	were written
Present perfect	has written	have been written
Future	will write	will be written
Modals	can write	can be written
	could write	could be written
	should write	should be written
	would have written	would have been written

PRACTICE 5

Decide whether each underlined verb is active or passive. Write *A* (for "active") or *P* (for "passive") above each verb.

EXAMPLE:

Many ordinary citizens <u>have been recruited</u> [P] as spies even though the work <u>is</u> [A] dangerous.

1. During times of war, armies <u>have used</u> both scouts and spies. Army scouts <u>can wear</u> their full uniform. They <u>are sent</u> ahead of advancing forces. Spies, on the other hand, <u>wear</u> disguises and <u>try</u> to blend in with the regular population.

2. Spying <u>is</u> much more dangerous than scouting because captured scouts <u>are treated</u> as prisoners of war. A captured spy, on the other hand, <u>may be executed</u> immediately. In spite of the obvious dangers, many people <u>are attracted</u> to the field of espionage because they <u>love</u> excitement and danger.

> **The by . . . Phrase**
>
> In many passive sentences, it is not necessary to write the *by* . . . phrase because the noun performing the action is understood.
>
> > CIA agents are selected according to their abilities.
> > (Adding "by CIA recruiters" after "selected" is not necessary.)

PRACTICE 6

A. Complete the following sentences by changing each italicized verb to the passive form. Do not alter the verb tense. Note: You do not have to include the *by* . . . phrase.

EXAMPLE:

The supervisor *spies* on the workers.

The workers ___*are spied on (by the supervisor).*___

1. Sometimes employers *place* spy cameras in their factories.

    Sometimes spy cameras _____

    _____

2. Last year, Mr. Roy *installed* three surveillance cameras.

    Last year, three surveillance cameras _____

    _____

3. The video cameras *filmed* some sleeping workers.

   Some sleeping workers _____

   _____

4. As a result, the boss *has fired* three technicians.

   As a result, three technicians _____

   _____

B. The following sentences are in the passive voice. Change them to the active voice, but do not alter the verb tense.

EXAMPLE:

The workers *are spied* on by the bosses.

The bosses   *spy on the workers.* _____

5. For months, Kurt's privacy *has been violated* by the cameras.

   For months, the cameras _____

   _____

6. Last week, a complaint *was made* to the American Civil Liberties Union by Kurt.

   Last week, Kurt _____

   _____

7. The case *will be investigated* by the union.

   The union _____

   _____

8. Complaints about privacy *are often ignored* by companies.

   Companies _____

   _____

Hint **Avoid Overusing the Passive Voice**

Generally, use the active voice instead of the passive voice. The active voice is more direct and less wordy than the passive voice. For example, read the next two versions of the same message.

Passive voice:	The problem has been rectified by us, and a new order is being prepared for you. You will be contacted by our sales department.
Active voice:	We have corrected the problem and are preparing a new order for you. Our sales department will contact you.

In rare cases when you do not know who did the action, the passive voice may be more appropriate.

James Bond's miniature camera was made in Italy.

(You do not know who made the camera.)

PRACTICE 7

Underline examples of the passive voice in the following letter. Then rewrite the letter using the active voice.

Dear Parents,

Security cameras have been installed in our school for several reasons. First, intruders have been seen by students. Also, if fighting is done by students, the scenes will be recorded and the culprits will be caught. In addition, any vandalism to school property can be viewed by our staff. For further information, we can be contacted at any time during school hours.

Sincerely,
Tony Romano, Principal, Rosedale High School

_____

_____

_____

_____

_____

_____

_____

_____

 **Be Careful!**

In the passive voice, sometimes the verb *be* is suggested but not written. The following sentence contains the passive voice.

that were
Many activities done in the 1920s are still common today.

PRACTICE 8

Underline and correct twelve errors in past participles.

EXAMPLE:

written
Military historians have <u>wrote</u> about American military strategies in Vietnam.

1. One of the most complex wars in American history was the Vietnam

    War. Many military strategies were develop to win the war against

    communist forces in Vietnam.

2.   By 1967, American military experts had discover the existence of the

Ho Chi Minh Trail, and they wanted to spy on the North Vietnamese

communists. The Americans knew that the trail, well hid by vegetation,

was use to supply the Viet Cong in the south. It was consider an

important supply line to the Viet Cong. The Americans needed to gather

information, so aircraft were send to drop remote sensors on the trail. The

sensors were activate by sound or heat. Information was collect by signals

and processed by a computer near the Thai border. Then fighter planes

were launch to drop napalm and other bombs on the trail.

3.   The operation was not successful. The trail had too many secondary

routes that were not expose by the sensors. Also, the sensors were

sometimes trigger by animals. Therefore, the supply lines were not disrupt.

The Writer's Desk   **Revise and Edit Your Warm Up**

Review the sentences that you wrote in the Warm Up at the beginning
of the chapter. Identify all verbs, and verify that each verb is used and
formed correctly. Correct any incorrect or nonstandard verbs.

REFLECT ON IT

Think about what you have learned in this chapter. If you do not know an answer, review
that concept.

1. What are the simple past and past participle forms of the following verbs?

    EXAMPLE: grow: *grew*_____   *grown*_____

    a. fly: _____ _____   b. ring: _____ _____

    c. break: _____ _____   d. read: _____ _____

2. Give two circumstances in which you would use the present perfect tense.

    _____

    _____

    _____

    _____

3. When do you use the past perfect tense? _____

_____

4. How do you form the passive voice? _____

_____

5. Identify and correct the errors in the following sentences.

   a. Robert Ludlum's first book was publish in 1971.

   b. By 2000, he had wrote twenty-one spy novels.

   c. Millions of people have buyed his novel *The Bourne Identity*.

   d. Have you ever saw a movie that was based on a book by Ludlum?

FINAL REVIEW

Fill in each blank with the appropriate verb tense. The sentence may require active or passive voice.

EXAMPLE:

Cell phone cameras (be) _____*have been*_____ on the market since 2003.

1.   Since their debut, cell phone cameras (criticize) _____ by those who are worried about privacy issues. For example, in 2003, cell phone cameras (ban) _____ in many health clubs. In January 2004, clients in a European spa (film) _____ by a voyeur in the women's locker room. Additionally, since 2003, schoolteachers and others who work with the public (complain) _____ to authorities about the possible misuse of cell phone cameras in public places. In fact, in 2004, one government employee's rage (record) _____ by an astute member of the public.

2.   On the other hand, since their first appearance, cell phone cameras (help) _____ some people. In August 2003, a fifteen-year-old boy (approach) _____ by a stranger in a white car. The boy (ask) _____ by the strange man to get into the car. The boy refused and walked away after he (take) _____ a photograph of the man's car with his cell phone camera. The boy (congratulate) _____ by the police after the motorist (catch) _____ by a detective.

3.   Clearly, the cell phone camera (cause) _____ a lot of controversy since its appearance in the marketplace. Last year, many complaints (register) _____ with authorities about cell phone camera misuse. However, since 2003, cell phone cameras (help) _____ people in emergency situations. Since its debut, the cell phone camera (change) _____ the way we communicate.

How Do I Get a Better Grade?

Visit www.mywritinglab.com for audio-visual lectures and additional practice sets about past participles.

mywritinglab

Get a better grade with MyWritingLab!

Other Verb Forms

Section Theme **ESPIONAGE**

CONTENTS

- Problems with Progressive Forms (*-ing* verbs)
- Nonstandard Forms: *gonna, gotta, wanna*
- Problems with Conditional Forms
- Nonstandard Forms: *would of, could of, should of*

In this chapter, you will read about topics related to spy mysteries.

The Writer's Desk Warm Up

In your opinion, is it ethical to use cameras to spy on nannies, babysitters, or other caregivers? Write a paragraph about the issue.

Problems with Progressive Forms (*-ing* Verbs)

Most verbs have progressive tenses. The **progressive tense** indicates that an action is, was, or will be in progress. For example, the present progressive indicates that an action is happening right now or for a temporary period of time.

Simple present: Detective Jonkala **spies** on cheating spouses everyday.

Present progressive: Today, he **is following** Ms. Wang.

Every day, he spies on cheating spouses.

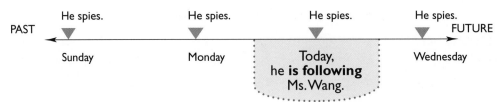

To form the progressive, use the appropriate tense of the verb *be* with the *-ing* verb.

Present progressive: Right now, Detective Jonkala is watching the suspect.

Past progressive: He was taking notes when the suspect left the hotel.

Future progressive: Tomorrow, at 6 a.m., Natasha will be following the suspect.

Present perfect progressive: Detective Jonkala has been working for the police since 1994.

Past perfect progressive: Detective Jonkala had been waiting in his car when his partner arrived.

Common Errors with the Progressive Form

- Do not use the progressive form when an action happens regularly.

  complains
  Every day he ~~is complaining~~ about his job.

- In the progressive form, use the correct form of the verb *be*.

  is
  Right now the nanny ~~be~~ playing with the children.

- In the progressive form, always include the complete helping verb.

  are   *have*
  Right now, the agents examining the photos. They been working for hours.

 **Nonprogressive Verbs**

Some verbs do not take the progressive form because they indicate an ongoing state or a perception rather than a temporary action. Here are some examples of nonprogressive verbs.

Perception Verbs	Preference Verbs	State Verbs	Possession
admire	care*	believe	have*
hear	desire	know	own
feel*	doubt	mean	possess
look*	hate	realize	
smell*	like	recognize	
see	love	suppose	
seem	prefer	think*	
taste*	want	understand	

*The verbs marked with an asterisk have more than one meaning and can also be used in the progressive tense. Compare the next pairs of sentences.

Nonprogressive	**Progressive**
He **has** a video camera. (Expresses ownership)	He **is having** a bad day.
I **think** it is unethical. (Expresses an opinion)	I **am thinking** about you.

PRACTICE I

Each sentence has errors with progressive forms. Correct each error.

EXAMPLE:

> *have been*
> I been working as a nanny for years.

1. Generally, I am loving my job, but this morning something terrible happened.

2. I was watching TV while the baby be sleeping, and I couldn't believe what was on one of the family's videos.

3. When I pressed the "Play" button, I was shocked because I was recognizing myself on the video.

4. The video had been taken months ago while I be reading to the family's children.

5. There is a hidden video camera in the house, and for months the parents been spying on me.

6. I cannot believe that the parents would use a nanny camera to see what I been doing.

7. I am a good nanny, and every day I am conducting myself professionally.

8. I do not think that families should spy on nannies unless the children been acting upset or the nanny been displaying strange behavior.

Nonstandard Forms: *gonna, gotta, wanna*

Some people commonly say *I'm gonna, I gotta,* or *I wanna*. These are nonstandard forms, and you should not use them in written communication.

- Write *going to* instead of *gonna*.
  > *going to*
  > The nanny is ~~gonna~~ sue her employer.

- Write *have to* instead of *gotta*.
  > *have to*
  > The Smiths ~~gotta~~ go to court to fight the lawsuit.

- Write *want to* instead of *wanna*.
  > *want to*
  > They ~~wanna~~ win their case.

PRACTICE 2

Underline and correct eight incorrect verb tenses or nonstandard verbs.

EXAMPLE:

want to

I really ~~wanna~~ solve the CIA sculpture code.

1.   Spies have always relied on codes and ciphers to hide and send secret messages. Cryptology refers to systems that use letters of the alphabet to represent other letters. A ciphered message is unintelligible to someone who is not familiar with the code. There are many codes and ciphers that remain unsolved. Code hobbyists are understanding that those who wanna solve codes gotta be very patient and clever.

2.   One of the most intriguing unsolved codes is the "Beale Ciphers." In 1822, Thomas Beale gave a Virginian innkeeper a box with three coded texts. These texts were directions to an enormous treasure. The innkeeper was gonna try to solve the puzzle, but he died shortly after receiving the box. A friend of the innkeeper was also desiring to decipher the code for many years but was unsuccessful. To this day, no one has been able to crack the code. There is great debate about whether the Beale Ciphers are a hoax.

3.   The CIA is owning a more contemporary puzzle. In 1990, artist Jim Sanborn created a granite-and-copper sculpture for the courtyard of the CIA headquarters. The sculpture contains a 2,000-character message in code. Only the CIA director and the artist know what the message says. Many people wanna solve the code, but they gotta realize how difficult it is to solve. There are Web sites, articles, and blogs about the encrypted message. So far, only three passages of the message have been decoded. The fourth passage still remains a mystery.

Problems with Conditional Forms

In **conditional sentences,** there is a condition and a result. There are three types of conditional sentences, and each type has two parts, or clauses. The main clause depends on the condition set in the *if* clause.

First Form: Possible Present or Future

The condition is true or very possible.

If + present tense,   . . . future tense . . .

    condition (*if* clause)   result

If you **buy** the book, you **will learn** about satellites.

Second Form: Unlikely Present

The condition is not likely and will probably not happen.

If + past tense,   . . . *would* (expresses a condition) . . .
If + past tense,   . . . *could* (expresses a possibility) . . .

condition (*if* clause)   result

If I **saw** a UFO, I **would take** a picture of it.

Note: In formal writing, when the condition contains the verb *be*, always use *were* in the *if* clause.

If Jenna **were** a scientist, she would study UFOs.

Third Form: Impossible Past

The condition cannot happen because the event is over.

If + past perfect tense,   . . . *would have* (+ past participle) . . .

       condition (*if* clause)   result

If aliens **had visited** the earth in 1947, someone **would have photographed** them.

> ### *Hint* Be Careful with the Past Conditional
>
> In the third type of conditional sentence, the impossible past, the writer expresses regret about a past event or expresses the wish that a past event had worked out differently. In the *if* part of the sentence, remember to use the past perfect tense.
>
> *If* + past perfect tense,   . . . *would have* (past participle) . . .
>
>   had listened
> If CIA agents ~~would have listened~~ to the tape, they **would have discovered** the agent's identity.

PRACTICE 3

Write the correct conditional form of each verb in parentheses.

EXAMPLE:

If I buy a book about the Cambridge Four, perhaps I (be) ___*will be*___ able to understand why they spied for the Soviets.

1.   One of the most interesting spy rings of the twentieth century

       was known as The Cambridge Four. In the 1930s, if England (be)

_____ stable economically, perhaps communism (appeal, not)

_____ to British youth. However, at that

time, Russia recruited many young men who were communist sympathizers.

2.   The infamous Cambridge Four were recruited as undergraduates from Cambridge University's Trinity College in the 1930s. The Russians wanted recruits who would eventually be in positions of influence. For example, Anthony Blunt came from an upper-class family. If he (come)

_____ from a working class background, the

Russians (recruit, never) _____ him. In

college, the four spies behaved normally. If the Cambridge Four (behave)

_____ erratically, perhaps someone (denounce)

_____ them as spies sooner.

3.   During World War II, the four men revealed many American and British secrets to the Russians. By 1951, they fell under suspicion. British code breakers deciphered a message showing that someone had leaked nuclear secrets to the Russians. If this information about the leak (reach,

not) _____ one of the traitors, the British authorities

(catch) _____ the Cambridge Four. Instead, two of the

spies successfully fled to Russia, and the other two were never prosecuted.

Nonstandard Forms: *would of, could of, should of*

Some people commonly say *would of, could of,* or *should of.* They may also say *woulda, coulda,* or *shoulda.* These are nonstandard forms, and you should avoid using them in written communication. When you use the past forms of *should, would,* and *could,* always include *have* + the past participle.

                                      would have

If I had been alive in 1963, I ~~woulda~~ tried to meet President Kennedy.

                                               should have

Unfortunately, he was assassinated. The president ~~should of~~ traveled in a

bulletproof car.

PRACTICE 4

Correct the ten errors in conditional forms or in the past forms of *could* and *should*.

EXAMPLE:

have
The assassination should not ~~of~~ happened.

1. One of the biggest mysteries of the twentieth century surrounds the death
    of President John Fitzgerald Kennedy (JFK). On November 22, 1963, at
    12:30 p.m., JFK was shot. Some people suggest that Lee Harvey Oswald
    acted alone and killed the president. Others say that Oswald could not of
    done the crime by himself. In 1964, Justice Earl Warren headed a
    commission that investigated the case.

2. The strongest evidence is home movie footage of the actual assassination
    taken by a man named Abraham Zapruder. The Warren Commission
    printed out still images of the Zapruder film in the wrong order. If the
    investigators would have printed the photos of the assassination in the
    correct order, they would of known that the bullets came from the front
    of the car and not behind it. If Zapruder would not have taken his home
    movie, we would not of known about the directions of the bullets.

3. The Warren Commission declared that Lee Harvey Oswald was the sole
    assassin. However, many witnesses at the scene said that some of the shots
    could not of come from the library building where Oswald was hiding.
    Perhaps the investigators shoulda considered eyewitness accounts. On the
    other hand, maybe the eyewitnesses were unreliable.

4. Oswald's motive was unclear. Investigators pointed out that Oswald had
    spent many years living in Russia. If he would have lived in Russia, then he
    could have been a spy. They argued that Oswald was deeply involved in
    espionage, and he had secretly passed secrets to the communists. However,
    others insisted that if Oswald had been a spy, the government woulda
    arrested him sooner.

5. Today, the mystery surrounding JFK's assassination is still unsolved. No accepted truth has emerged, and some say we will never know what happened on that day. If you would have been alive in 1964, would you have believed the Warren Commission report?

The Writer's Desk **Revise and Edit Your Warm Up**

In the Warm Up at the beginning of the chapter, you wrote a short paragraph about spying on nannies and other caregivers. Check your paragraph and ensure that you have formed your verbs correctly. Correct any errors.

REFLECT ON IT

Think about what you have learned in this chapter. If you do not know an answer, review that concept.

1. When do you use the progressive form of verbs? _____

_____

2. Circle five nonprogressive verbs in the list below. Nonprogressive verbs cannot take the *-ing* form to indicate continuing action.

go	understand	walk	appreciate
believe	carry	know	watch
talk	speak	hear	listen

3. Write your own examples of the three types of conditional sentences.

First form: _____

_____

Second form: _____

_____

Third form: _____

_____

4. Correct the following sentences by writing the standard form of each nonstandard verb.

a. If you wanna succeed, you gotta work hard.

b. J. Rowen been investigating UFOs since 1978.

c. If Kennedy would have taken another route, maybe he woulda lived.

d. Maybe one day somebody is gonna tell the truth about the Kennedy case.

FINAL REVIEW

Correct fifteen errors with verbs.

EXAMPLE:

       want to
Many adults ~~wanna~~ go back to school to develop new careers.

Dear Mrs. Adams:

I am an adult student, but I be going back to college because I gotta change my life. I could of gone back last year, but I decided to continue working at a local company. I had a job helping a private detective named Kenneth Rolland. In my job, I had to wait outside motels and take pictures of people who been cheating on their spouses. I also had to write reports, but the job was depressing. Then, one day while I sitting at my desk, I realized that even though I was in my thirties, it was not too late to change my life.

I know that I should of gone to college when I was in my twenties. However, if I would have tried that, I would of wasted a lot of time because I did not know what to do with my life. Now that I am older, I am more settled, and I am thinking that I have a better idea about what I am good at. In fact, I am understanding a lot of things these days. I know that if I wanna reach my goals, I gotta take the steps myself. Nobody else is gonna show me how to succeed.

Thank you for reading this letter. I wanna go to your college. I am motivated now, and I think that I am gonna be a great student.

Yours truly,

D. Mathers

The Writer's Room   Topics for Writing

Choose one of the following topics and write a paragraph or an essay. When you write, remember to follow the writing process.

1. How would your life have been different if you had lived one hundred years ago? List some ways.

2. What are some types of spies? Think of at least three different categories of spies.

3. Today, many police departments have installed traffic cameras on busy streets. Drivers receive tickets for traffic violations in the mail. Police departments argue that the cameras deter crimes, but others say that such cameras invade our privacy. Should there be cameras on public streets?

4. Define an ideal spy. What qualities should a great spy have?

The Writers' Circle

READING LINK

Espionage

"How Spies Are Caught"
(page 562)

"Nothing But Net" by Mark
McFadden (page 564)

Divide students into groups of four or five. Each team will have the opportunity to compose several short stories. Ask each student to use one sheet of paper.

STEP 1   Look at the following present-tense verbs. Write the past form of each verb at the top of your sheet of paper.

be	catch	buy	drink	think
drive	break	shake	grow	take

STEP 2   Choose one verb from the list. Write a sentence using the past form of that verb. The sentence can be serious or silly. On the list, cross off the verb that you have chosen.

STEP 3   After you have written your sentence, pass your piece of paper to the student on your left. That student must choose another past-tense verb from the list and add another sentence to the story. The second sentence must make sense and must link to the first sentence in some way. Students continue passing the sheets until everyone in the group has a sheet with ten sentences.

STEP 4   Team members read their paragraphs and then the team chooses the most interesting paragraph to hand in. Revise and edit the paragraph together to make it more complete and grammatically correct.

How Do I Get a Better Grade?

Visit www.mywritinglab.com for audio-visual lectures and additional practice sets about other verb forms.

Get a better grade with MyWritingLab!

Subject-Verb Agreement

Section Theme **COLLEGE LIFE**

In this chapter, you will read about topics related to college issues.

The Writer's Desk Warm Up

In a short paragraph, express your opinion about the extracurricular activities on your campus.

Basic Subject-Verb Agreement Rules

Subject-verb agreement simply means that a subject and verb agree in number. A singular subject needs a singular verb, and a plural subject needs a plural verb.

                          S   V

Singular subject: <u>Mr. Connor</u> **teaches** in a community college.

                          S   V

Plural subject: The <u>students</u> **appreciate** his approach.

GRAMMAR LINK

For more information about the present tense, see Chapter 22.

Simple Present Tense Agreement

Writers use **simple present tense** to indicate that an action is habitual or factual. Review the following rules for simple present tense agreement.

- When the subject is *he, she, it,* or the equivalent (*Adam, Maria, Florida*), add an *-s* or *-es* ending to the verb. This is also called the **third-person singular form.**

  Singular: Michael **works** in the college bookstore. (one person)

  This neighborhood **needs** a medical clinic. (one place)

  The trophy **belongs** to the best athlete in the college. (one thing)

- When the subject is *I, you, we, they,* or the equivalent (*the Zorns, the mountains, Amber and Tom*) do not add an ending to the verb.

  Plural: College students **have** many options. (more than one person)

  Some cities **have** colleges and four-year universities. (more than one place)

  The benefits **include** a higher standard of living. (more than one thing)

For example, review the present tense forms of the verb *talk.*

Present Tense of *Talk*

	Singular	**Plural**
First person:	I talk	We talk
Second person:	You talk	You talk
Third person:	He talks	They talk
	She talks	
	It talks	

 **Question and Negative Forms**

To create present tense question and negative forms, add *do* or *does,* and use the base form of the main verb.

- Add *do* when the subject is *I, you, we, they,* or the equivalent.

  Anne and Jay **live** together.

  Do they **live** together?

  They **do** not **live** together.

- Add *does* when the subject is *he, she, it,* or the equivalent.

  The library **needs** repairs.

  Does it **need** repairs?

  It **does** not **need** repairs.

PRACTICE I

Write the correct present tense form of each verb in parentheses.

EXAMPLE:

Mila Zahn's family (live) _____*lives*_____ near Hamburg, Germany.

1. Mila Zahn is a German exchange student, and she (study) _____ in an American college.

2. Zahn (see) _____ many glaring cultural differences between Americans and Germans.

3. Many American students (juggle) _____ work and school.

4. For example, Mila's friend Amber (do) _____ not have much money.

5. Amber (work) _____ part time so that she can pay for her studies.

6. However, in Germany, the state (sponsor) _____ all levels of education, so students (do) _____ not feel financial pressure.

7. (Do) _____ the average American student pay too much for higher levels of education?

8. (Do) _____ you work and go to college?

Troublesome Present Tense Verbs: *be, have, do*

Some present tense verbs are formed in special ways. Review the verbs *be, have,* and *do.*

	Be	**Have**	**Do**
Singular forms			
First person:	I am	I have	I do
Second person:	You are	You have	You do
Third person:	He is	He has	He does
	She is	She has	She does
	It is	It has	It does
Plural forms			
First person:	We are	We have	We do
Second person:	You are	You have	You do
Third person:	They are	They have	They do

> **Hint** **Do Not Use _Ain't_**
>
> Although some people say _ain't_ in informal conversation, it is a nonstandard form and should not be used in written communication. Instead, write _is not, are not,_ or _am not._
>
>   _are not_   _is not_
> They ~~ain't~~ sure about the evidence. It ~~ain't~~ accurate.

PRACTICE 2

In the next selection, each verb is underlined. Correct twelve errors in subject-verb agreement or the incorrect use of _ain't_.

EXAMPLE:

                                     study
Many exchange students <u>studies</u> in the United States.

1.   Emi Kawamura <u>is</u> a Japanese exchange student. According to Emi, some American students <u>has</u> many misguided ideas about the Japanese. Emi <u>remind</u> people that she <u>do</u> not <u>fit</u> any stereotype. For example, her math skills <u>is</u> poor and she rarely <u>uses</u> computers.

2.   The educational system in Japan <u>differ</u> from that in the United States. Japanese students <u>has</u> a longer school year than American students. Japanese college entrance exams <u>is</u> very difficult, and students <u>experience</u> high levels of stress. Emi's brother, Jin, <u>attends</u> a private "cramming" school called a juku. He <u>have</u> to study six days a week because he <u>hopes</u> to get into a good university.

3.   Because of complaints from parents and students, Japanese officials <u>wants</u> to reform the educational system. One plan <u>is</u> to place less emphasis on entrance exams. The current system <u>ain't</u> healthy for students.

4.   Although the average Japanese student <u>have</u> a stressful experience in high school, the situation <u>changes</u> in college. American college courses <u>is</u> more difficult than those in Japan, in Emi's opinion.

Simple Past Tense Agreement

In the past tense, all verbs except *be* have one past form.

Regular:	I worked.	He worked.	You worked.	We worked.	They worked.
Irregular:	I ate.	He ate.	You ate.	We ate.	They ate.

Exception: *Be*

In the past tense, the only verb requiring subject-verb agreement is the verb *be*, which has two past forms: *was* and *were*.

Was	**Were**
I was	We were
He was	You were
She was	They were
It was	

Present Perfect Tense Agreement

When writing in the present perfect tense, which is formed with *have* or *has* and the past participle, use *has* when the subject is third-person singular.

My college **has** raised tuition fees. Other colleges **have** not raised their fees.

Agreement in Other Tenses

When writing in most other verb tenses, and in modal forms (*can, could, would, may, might*, and so on), use the same form of the verb with every subject.

Future:	I will **work**; she will **work**; they will **work**; you will **work**; we will **work**.
Past perfect:	I had **met**; she had **met**; they had **met**; you had **met**; we had **met**.
Modals:	I can **talk**; she should **talk**; they could **talk**; you might **talk**; we would **talk**.

GRAMMAR LINK

For more information about using the present perfect tense, see Chapter 23.

PRACTICE 3

In the next selection, each verb is underlined. Correct ten subject-verb agreement errors.

EXAMPLE:

     exists

A problem exist in many colleges and universities.

1.   Hazing occur on many American campuses. When a new student want

to gain admittance to a club or organization, the student undergoes an

initiation ritual.

2.   For example, in 2004, at the University of Central Florida, some fraternity members <u>was wrapped</u> in plastic and tied to a tree. One student <u>was</u> also <u>covered</u> in shaving cream, chocolate syrup, and vegetable oil. Many students <u>was</u> upset when they heard about the incident. Since that time, other fraternity members <u>has denied</u> their involvement in hazing.

3.   Sometimes hazing rituals <u>is</u> dangerous. Hank Newar <u>is</u> a professor and journalist, and he <u>have written</u> a book called *Broken Pledges: The Deadly Rite of Hazing*. Newar <u>states</u>, "Collegiate hazing <u>has resulted</u> in at least fifty-nine fraternity deaths" since the 1970s.

4.   Although hazing <u>has been banned</u> in most states, many clubs <u>continues</u> to perform illegal rituals. When hazing rituals <u>is reported</u>, the offending club <u>can loses</u> its affiliation with the university.

More Than One Subject

There are special agreement rules when there is more than one subject in a sentence.

and

When subjects are joined by *and*, use the plural form of the verb.

> <u>Colleges</u>, <u>universities</u>, and <u>trade schools</u> **prepare** students for the job market.

or, nor

When two subjects are joined by *or* or *nor*, the verb agrees with the subject that is closer to it.

> plural
> Neither Amanda Jackson nor her <u>students</u> **use** the computer lab.

> singular
> Either the students or <u>Amanda</u> **uses** the department's portable laptop computer.

PRACTICE 4

Circle the correct verb in each sentence. Make sure the verb agrees with the subject.

EXAMPLE:

Colleges and universities (have, has) various interesting programs.

1. Both Theo and Amber (study, studies) nursing.

2. Amber and her mother (live, lives) in Los Angeles.

3. Two buses or a train (transport, transports) Amber to her college campus.

4. Theo and his mother (reside, resides) in a small town outside San Francisco.

5. Neither of the two local colleges nor the university (offer, offers) nursing programs.

6. Each day, Theo and his girlfriend (travel, travels) to Samuel Merrit College in Oakland.

7. Neither Theo nor his parents (has, have) a lot of money.

8. Each year, either two fast-food restaurants or the local hardware store (sponsor, sponsors) low-income students.

9. Work and careful planning (pay, pays) off for college students.

Special Subject Forms

Some subjects are not easy to identify as singular or plural. Two common types are indefinite pronouns and collective nouns.

Indefinite Pronouns

Indefinite pronouns refer to a general person, place, or thing. Carefully review the following list of indefinite pronouns.

Indefinite Pronouns

Singular	another	each	nobody	other
	anybody	everybody	no one	somebody
	anyone	everyone	nothing	someone
	anything	everything	one	something
Plural	both, few, many, others, several			

Singular Indefinite Pronouns

In the following sentences, the verbs require the third-person singular form because the subjects are singular.

> <u>Everyone</u> **knows** that career colleges offer practical, career-oriented courses.

> <u>Nothing</u> **stops** people from applying to a career college.

You can put one or more singular nouns (joined by *and*) after *each* and *every*. The verb is still singular.

> <u>Each</u> man and woman **knows** the stories about secret societies.

Plural Indefinite Pronouns

Both, few, many, others, and *several* are all plural subjects. The verb is always plural.

Many **apply** to high-tech programs.

Others **prefer** to study in the field of health care.

PRACTICE 5

Underline the subjects and circle the correct verbs.

EXAMPLE:

Many people (chooses /(choose) career colleges to further their studies.

1. Lucas Vigoletti (study/ studies) Programming and Systems Analysis at Beaumont College. The program (is / are) very demanding, and everyone in his class (work/ works) very hard. Everybody (know / knows) that a good grade will help him or her find an interesting career. No one (expect / expects) the program to be easy.

2. Lucas (is / are) married to Virginia, and he (have / has) a part-time job as a telemarketer. Therefore, he (have / has) to schedule his study time well. All courses (require / requires) reading a lot of material, participating in workshops, and engaging in student discussions. Lucas and his classmates (have / has) to learn programming codes, (find / finds) computer viruses, and (review / reviews) notes from the previous day. Many (stay / stays) up past midnight studying.

3. Lucas and his friend Joshua also (practice / practices) interviewing techniques. They (prepare / prepares) lists of questions and (take / takes) turns "interviewing" each other. Some students (do / does) group interviews, while others (observe / observes) taped authentic interviews. Everybody (feel / feels) confident that such preparation will be helpful in a formal interview situation. Nobody (expect / expects) to pass the courses without working hard.

Collective Nouns

Collective nouns refer to a group of people or things. These are common collective nouns.

army	class	crowd	group	population
association	club	family	jury	public
audience	committee	gang	mob	society
band	company	government	organization	team

Generally, each group acts as a unit, so you must use the singular form of the verb.

The <u>jury</u> **is** ready to read the verdict.

If the members of the group act individually, use the plural form of the verb. It is a good idea to use a phrase such as *members of*.

Acceptable: The <u>jury</u> **are** not able to come to an agreement.

Better: The <u>members of the jury</u> **are** not able to come to an agreement.

   Police Is Plural

The word *police* is always thought of as a plural noun because the word *officers* is implied but not stated.

The police **have** arrested a suspect.

The police **are** patrolling the neighborhood.

PRACTICE 6

In each sentence, underline the subject and circle the correct verb.

EXAMPLE:

The <u>government</u> (offer / (offers)) financial aid for some students.

1.   A career college (is / are) a sensible choice for many students wanting practical work skills. Such institutions (offer / offers) a variety of career-related programs. For example, my college (have / has) programs in high-tech, health care, business, and hospitality.

2.   My friend Santosh (studies / study) in the hospitality program. Santosh (was / were) a cook in the army, but now he (want / wants) a career in

adventure tourism. The army (provide / provides) financial help to Santosh for his studies. In fact, the military (encourage / encourages) its employees to continue education and training. Santosh's family also (give / gives) him encouragement.

3.   People (need / needs) social, math, communication, and organizational skills when entering the hospitality business. Everyone (enter / enters) this field knowing that he or she must be able to get along with people during stressful situations. The industry (is / are) growing, but it (is / are) very important to have the right education. Career colleges (give / gives) students an advantage in this highly competitive market.

Verb Before the Subject

Usually the verb comes after the subject, but in some sentences, the verb comes before the subject. In such cases, you must still ensure that the subject and verb agree.

there or here

When a sentence begins with *there* or *here*, the subject always follows the verb. *There* and *here* are not subjects.

>   V   S   V   S
> Here **is** the college course <u>list</u>.   There **are** many night <u>courses</u>.

Questions

In questions, word order is usually reversed, and the main or helping verb is placed before the subject. In the following example, the main verb is *be*.

>   V   S   V   S
> Where **is** the <u>cafeteria</u>?   **Is** the <u>food</u> good?

However, in questions in which the main verb isn't *be*, the subject usually agrees with the helping verb.

>   HV   S   V   HV   S   V
> When **does** the <u>library</u> **close**?   **Do** <u>students</u> **work** there?

PRACTICE 7

Correct any subject-verb agreement errors. If the sentence is correct, write *C* in the blank.

EXAMPLE:

~~Has~~ you ever won a competition?   *Have*

1. There is many athletic scholarships in colleges.   _____

2. Has many students benefited from the scholarships? _____

3. Does athletes get preferential treatment? _____

4. Is there a reason to stop giving scholarships to athletes? _____

5. There is many pressures on student athletes. _____

6. Why do Wayne Brydon want to be play basketball professionally? _____

7. Do female athletes have the same opportunities? _____

8. According to Selma Rowen, there have not been enough attention given to academically successful students. _____

9. On the other hand, there is many people who support athletes. _____

10. In addition to doing their course work, do college athletes have to train for several hours each day? _____

Interrupting Words and Phrases

Words that come between the subject and the verb may confuse you. In these cases, look for the subject and make sure that the verb agrees with the subject.

>   S   interrupting phrase   V
> Some <u>rules</u> regarding admission to this college **are** controversial.

>   S   prepositional phrase   V
> A <u>student</u> in two of my classes **writes** for the college newspaper.

Hint   **Identify Interrupting Phrases**

When you revise your paragraphs, add parentheses around words that separate the subject and the verb. Then you can check to see whether your subjects and verbs agree.

>   S   prepositional phrase   V
> A <u>student</u> (in two of my classes) **writes** for the college newspaper.

When interrupting phrases contain *of the* or similar words, the subject appears before the phrase.

>   S   prepositional phrase   V
> <u>One</u> (of my biggest problems) **is** my lack of organization.

PRACTICE 8

Underline the subject in each sentence. Add parentheses around any words that come between each subject and verb. Then circle the correct form of the verb.

EXAMPLE:

<u>One</u> (of the most controversial issues on campus) (**is**)/**are** affirmative action.

1. Some colleges in this country **have/has** more relaxed admission standards

   for students from ethnic minorities. Such colleges, with good reason,

   want/wants to have a vibrant and diverse student population. However, arguing that they have been discriminated against, students from across the nation **have/has** sued their colleges. Judges in courtrooms **have/has** had to consider whether affirmative action is unfair.

2. People in favor of affirmative action **have/has** compelling arguments. Historically, some ethnic groups in the United States **has/have** not had access to a higher education. Many factors such as poverty **contribute/contributes** to the problem. University of California professor Norman Matloff, in an article for *Asian Week*, **suggest/suggests** that society suffers when there is a large, poorly educated underclass. Additionally, affirmative action **help/helps** create a diverse student body.

3. Opponents of affirmative action **feel/feels** that admissions should be based purely on test scores. Barbara Grutter, a white student and an applicant to the University of Michigan, **argue/argues** that affirmative action is reverse discrimination. One of her best arguments **is/are** compelling: Grutter, as a forty-year-old single mother, **add/adds** to the university's diversity. On June 23, 2003, a decision about Grutter's affirmative action case **was/were** made. Although justices in the Supreme Court **were/was** divided, they ruled that race can be used as one of the factors in college admissions.

4. For some people, regulations to safeguard affirmative action **help/helps** equalize opportunities in our society. For others, such regulations **is/are** unfair to certain groups. What is your opinion?

Interrupting Words: *who, which, that*

If a sentence contains a clause beginning with *who*, *which*, or *that*, then the verb agrees with the subject preceding *who*, *which*, or *that*.

There is a <u>woman</u> in my neighborhood *who* **counsels** students.

Here are some old <u>newspapers</u> *that* **discuss** steroid abuse.

One <u>article</u>, *which* **contains** stories about hazing, is very interesting.

PRACTICE 9

Correct ten subject-verb agreement errors.

EXAMPLE:

                                               opens

The English department has a help center that ~~open~~ weekdays.

1. Students who needs help with their English can go to the help center. My friend who never speak English at home often goes to the help center. He does exercises that helps him. He says that the woman who work there is friendly.

2. There is some computers in the help center. If a student who have an assignment due need to use a computer, one is available. There is also several tutors available who help the students.

3. Sometimes the administrators who control the budget threatens to close the help center. When that happens, students who uses the center protest. Then the center remains open.

The Writer's Desk Revise and Edit Your Warm Up

In the Warm Up at the beginning of this chapter, you wrote a short paragraph about extracurricular activities on campus. Check for any subject-verb agreement errors.

REFLECT ON IT

Think about what you have learned in this unit. If you do not know an answer, review that concept.

1. When should you add -s or -es to verbs? _____

_____

2. Some indefinite pronouns are singular, and the verbs that follow them require the -s or -es ending. List six singular indefinite pronouns.

_____ _____ _____

_____ _____ _____

3. Look at the following nouns. Circle all the collective nouns.

family	people	army	committee
judge	crowd	brothers	audience

4. When do you use *was* and *were*?

Use *was* _____

Use *were* _____

5. Circle and correct any subject-verb agreement errors in the following sentences.

a. There is many colleges in Florida.

b. Yale is a university that have several secret societies.

c. Either the Edwards sisters or Simon have been initiated.

d. One of our cousins go to Yale.

e. There is no hazing rituals on our campus.

FINAL REVIEW

Correct twenty errors in subject–verb agreement.

EXAMPLE:

looks
This college campus ~~look~~ peaceful.

1.   Two years ago, Elmira Reed left home for the first time and went to her

state college. Today, Reed, a biology major, has a private dorm room on

campus. She admits that she love the feeling of independence. However,

last March, Reed's purse and book bag was stolen from her car, and in May,

there was robberies in several dorm rooms.

2.   College campuses is not always the peaceful and safe places that they appears to be. In fact, according to the *New York Times Magazine*, there is over eight assaults or other violent crimes per year on the average college or university campus. However, if each student take a few simple precautions, he or she can reduce the risk of being a crime victim.

3.   First, everyone who live in campus dorms need to act responsibly. Neither Reed nor her roommate take proper precautions. Sometimes, when Reed's roommate go out for the evening, she posts information about her whereabouts on her room door. However, such information provide thieves with an invitation to break in. Students should not leave notes posted on their doors, and they should always lock their room doors even if they plan to be absent for only a short while.

4.   Furthermore, students should familiarize themselves with campus security locations. There is usually call boxes in certain buildings, and students should know where to find those emergency phones. Also, if someone want to study in a secluded location at night, he or she should inform campus security. Some campuses has "walk home" services for students who uses the library late at night. New students need to find out what the campus has to offer.

5.   Ultimately, anyone who live on campus need to think about security. If nobody take precautions, then more robberies will occur. Remember that colleges are public places, buildings are open late, and there is not always a lot of security guards on campus. Therefore, it is important to be sensible.

How Do I Get a Better Grade?

Visit www.mywritinglab.com for audio-visual lectures and additional practice sets about subject-verb agreement. **Get a better grade with MyWritingLab!**

Tense Consistency

Section Theme **COLLEGE LIFE**

In this chapter, you will read about people who have made difficult choices.

The Writer's Desk **Warm Up**

How do images in the media influence the way that people judge their own bodies? Write a short paragraph about the media and body image.

Consistent Verb Tense

When you write, the verb tense you use gives the reader an idea about the time when the event occurred. A **tense shift** occurs when you shift from one tense to another for no logical reason.

Tense shift:	College reporter Erica Santiago interviewed a protester and <u>asks</u> about his political philosophy.
Correct:	College reporter Erica Santiago interviewed a protester and <u>asked</u> about his political philosophy.

Sometimes the time frame in a text really does change. In those circumstances, you would change the verb tense. The following example accurately shows two different time periods. Notice that certain key words (*during my childhood, today*) indicate what tense the writer should use.

past   present

During my childhood, I <u>ate</u> a lot of fast food. Today, I <u>try</u> to eat a healthy diet.

PRACTICE I

Identify and correct each tense shift. If the sentence is correct, write *C* in the space.

EXAMPLE:

Many adults go back to college and ~~received~~ training in
new careers.   *receive*

1. Career change is a frightening experience for many people because they lost the security and familiarity of a job, and they have to go back to school to become requalified. _____

2. Last year, Lee Kim was at a crossroads in his life because he is about to change careers. _____

3. For the previous ten years, Lee had been working as a computer service technician for a small company, but a year ago, the company downsized, and he lost his job. _____

4. Suddenly, at the age of thirty-five, Lee is faced with having to change careers, and he was scared. _____

5. Lee met with a career counselor; she advises Lee to check out the different programs in various career colleges. _____

6. Lee researched the courses at different institutions, and he finds that the medical laboratories program was a good option for him. _____

7. Now, Lee is enrolled as a student at Holly Fields Career College, but he admits that going back to college after many years is intimidating. _____

8. Nowadays, Lee had to budget his money and has to relearn how to be a student. _____

 **Would and Could**

When you tell a story about a past event, use *would* instead of *will*, and use *could* instead of *can*.

could

In 1996, college wrestler Robert Burzak knew that he <u>can</u> bulk up if he used

would

steriods, but he promised his coach that he <u>will</u> not.

PRACTICE 2

Underline and correct ten tense shifts.

EXAMPLE:

broke
Robert began weight training after he <u>breaks</u> his leg.

1.   In 2003, Robert Burzak joined a health club and tries weightlifting. He knew that he can have a sculpted body if he worked out. After a few months of weight training, he starts to get impatient. He wanted to get larger muscles very quickly, so, after a training partner told him about steroids, he decides to try them.

2.   Robert started by taking steroids in pill form. Within weeks he noticed a difference. Soon, he graduated to steroid injections. Others noticed his large muscles, and Robert feels proud of his "six-pack" stomach and his large biceps. He realized that his new look conformed to the images of male beauty seen in the media.

3.   Unfortunately, after Robert began to use steroids, side effects kick in. Robert developed acne on his back. Most worrisome, he felt wild mood swings, and he will alternate between violent outbursts and periods of depression. He cannot stop taking the pills because each time he tried to stop, his weight will plummet.

4.   Finally, in 2005, Robert gave up steroids. He knew that the risks to his health outweighed the benefits of having a sculpted body. Furthermore, his girlfriend said that she will leave him if he could not stay off the drugs. Today, Robert is drug free.

The Writer's Desk Revise and Edit Your Warm Up

In the Warm Up at the beginning of the chapter, you wrote a short paragraph about the media and body image. Check the paragraph for any tense shifts.

REFLECT ON IT

Think about what you have learned in this unit. If you do not know an answer, review that concept.

1. What is tense inconsistency? _____

_____

2. If you are writing a paragraph about a past event, what word should you use instead of these two?

a. will: _____   b. can: _____

3. Read the following paragraphs and find five tense inconsistencies. Correct the errors.

> *wants*
> **EXAMPLE:**   Kaitlin diets because she ~~wanted~~ to look thinner.

In 2001, college student Amy Heller became severely malnourished. In an attempt to lose weight, Heller ingested diet pills, and she severely restricts her intake of food. When others suggested that she had a problem, Heller will deny it. By July 2004, she weighs only 88 pounds. Heller finally sought treatment, and soon she can eat regular meals.

In 2001, Wendy Hoyt made a study about body image and college students. She asked over two hundred students to rate their level of satisfaction with their own bodies. Her results showed that women are more dissatisfied with their weight than men were. She attributed the diverse statistics to the influence of the media.

FINAL REVIEW

Correct fifteen tense shifts in the next student essay.

EXAMPLE:

> *got*
> In the 1970s, many college students ~~get~~ involved in politics, and they joined protest marches.

1.   In 2002, Eric Longley wrote an article about draft laws in the *Gale Encyclopedia of Popular Culture*. According to Longley, young people of college age are often forced to participate in wars. For example, during the Civil War, the U.S. government passed a draft law to ensure that there will be enough soldiers to fight.

2.   In the twentieth century, Congress repeatedly passed draft laws. In fact, during both World Wars I and II, young men cannot volunteer for the army. According to Longley, the government "chose to rely solely on the draft for its military needs." After World War II, the ban was lifted, so men can volunteer for the armed services. However, the draft laws were still in effect until 1973.

3.   Draft dodging was common during previous wars. For example, during the Civil War, wealthy young Americans can escape the draft by paying for a "substitute" soldier. During World War II, the government will not draft married men. In 1940, after the draft law passes, five times more men got married than in the previous year. After World War II, young men who were in college can avoid the draft. During the Vietnam War, many men will register in college to avoid going to war. However, when the Vietnam War escalated, the government introduces a lottery system, and college students can be drafted. Finally, a popular way to avoid the draft during previous wars was to flee to another country. In a 2004 interview, V. A. Smith said that he fled to Canada in 1970 when his lottery number is picked because he does not want to fight in Vietnam.

4.   In 2001, many young men and women entered the National Guard to get a free college education. Then, many of them had to fight overseas. For example, during the Iraq War, wounded soldier Jessica Lynch said that she just wants to get an education when she enlists.

5.   Do the poorest members of society face a larger risk of fighting overseas? Some argue that a military draft penalizes working-class men and women. Others believed that a military draft is the only fair way to ensure that armies have enough soldiers. As long as conflicts between nations exist, the military will need to find recruits.

The Writer's Room **Topics for Writing**

Choose one of the following topics and write a paragraph or an essay. When you write, remember to follow the writing process.

1. Describe your college campus. You might describe an interesting building or area of the campus.

2. What are some things that new students should know about your college? Explain how to survive the first few semesters in college.

3. Sometimes fraternities, sororities, clubs, and teams make new students undergo initiation rituals. Why do groups do this? How might such rituals affect new students? Explain your view.

4. What is your opinion of the military draft? Should governments force young people to join the armed forces? Should college students and married students be exempt from the draft?

 The Writers' Circle

Work with a team of students and create a short survey. Form at least five interesting questions about college life.

Then one team member should remain seated, and the other team members should split up and sit with other groups in the class to ask the questions. After each member has gathered information, the original group should get together and write a summary of the results.

READING LINK

College Life

"Body over Mind" by Mitch Albom (page 570)

"Dying to Be Bigger" by H.D. (page 573)

"It's Class, Stupid!" by Richard Rodriguez (page 577)

"The Case for Affirmative Action" by Dave Malcolm (page 579)

CHAPTER 26

How Do I Get a Better Grade?

Visit www.mywritinglab.com for audio-visual lectures and additional practice sets about tense consistency.

Get a better grade with MyWritingLab!

CHAPTER 27

Nouns, Determiners, and Prepositions

Section Theme **INVENTIONS AND DISCOVERIES**

CONTENTS

In this chapter, you will read about topics related to inventions *and* discoveries.

The Writer's Desk Warm Up

Write a short paragraph describing the most interesting invention from the last century. Explain why the invention is important.

Singular and Plural Nouns

Nouns are words that refer to people, places, or things. Nouns are divided into common nouns and proper nouns.

- **Common nouns** refer to general people, places, or things and begin with a lowercase letter. For example, *books, computer,* and *city* are common nouns.
- **Proper nouns** refer to particular people, places, or things and begin with a capital letter. For example, *Benjamin Franklin, Microsoft,* and *Kitty Hawk* are proper nouns.

Nouns are either singular or plural. A **singular noun** refers to one of something, while a **plural noun** refers to more than one of something. Regular plural nouns end in *-s* or *-es*.

	Singular	**Plural**
People:	inventor	inventors
	writer	writers
Places:	town	towns
	village	villages
Things:	computer	computers
	aspirin	aspirins

 **Adding -es**

When a noun ends in s, x, ch, sh, or z, add -es to form the plural.

business/business**es**   tax/tax**es**   church/church**es**

Irregular Plural Nouns

Nouns that do not use *-s* or *-es* in their plural forms are called **irregular nouns.** Here are some common irregular nouns.

Singular		**Plural**	
person	woman	people	women
child	tooth	children	teeth
man	foot	men	feet

Some nouns use other rules to form the plural. It is a good idea to memorize both the rules and the exceptions.

- For nouns ending in *f* or *fe*, change the *f* to *v* and add *-es*.

Singular	**Plural**	**Singular**	**Plural**
knife	kni**ves**	thief	thie**ves**
wife	wi**ves**	leaf	lea**ves**

Some exceptions: belief, beliefs; roof, roofs; safe, safes.

- For nouns ending in a consonant + *y*, change the *y* to *i* and add *-es*.

Singular	**Plural**	**Singular**	**Plural**
lady	lad**ies**	baby	bab**ies**
berry	berr**ies**	cherry	cherr**ies**

If a vowel comes before the final *y*, then the word retains the regular plural form.

Singular	**Plural**	**Singular**	**Plural**
day	day**s**	key	key**s**

- Some nouns remain the same in both singular and plural forms.

Singular	**Plural**	**Singular**	**Plural**
fish	fish	deer	deer
moose	moose	sheep	sheep

CHAPTER 27

- Some nouns are thought of as being only plural and therefore have no singular form.

  Plural Form Only

clothes	goods	pants	scissors
eyeglasses	proceeds	savings	series

- Some nouns are **compound nouns,** which means that they are made up of two or more words. To form the plural of compound nouns, add -*s* or -*es* to the last word of the compound noun.

Singular	**Plural**	**Singular**	**Plural**
bus stop	bus stop**s**	artificial heart	artificial heart**s**
air conditioner	air conditioner**s**	jet airplane	jet airplane**s**

  In hyphenated compound nouns, if the first word is a noun, add -*s* to the noun.

Singular	**Plural**	**Singular**	**Plural**
senator-elect	senator**s**-elect	runner-up	runner**s**-up
sister-in-law	sister**s**-in-law	husband-to-be	husband**s**-to-be

- Some nouns that are borrowed from Latin keep the plural form of the original language.

Singular	**Plural**	**Singular**	**Plural**
millennium	millennia	paparazzo	paparazzi
datum	data	phenomenon	phenomena

 *Hint*   **Persons versus People**

There are two plural forms of *person. People* is the most common plural form.

Some <u>people</u> have great ideas. Many <u>people</u> patent their ideas.

Persons is used in a legal or official context.

The patent was stolen by <u>persons</u> unknown.

PRACTICE 1

Correct ten errors in plural noun forms.

1. Most inventions are made by ordinary persons who are able to think

   outside the box. Many inventions are unplanned. Back in 1905, an eleven-

   year-old boy named Frank Epperson mixed powdered fruit and water with

   a stick and accidentally left the drink on his back porch. Overnight, the

   temperature plummeted. In the morning, he pulled his frozen drink out of

   his glass and showed it to the other childrens at school. When he was in his

twentys, he remembered his invention and patented it. He called his
product a "popsicle."

2. In 1869, a wire factory worker named Alan Parkhouse was at a company
gathering with several familys. His two sister-in-laws complained about the
lack of places to hang their coats. Parkhouse bent a piece of wire into two
ovales and created a hook between them, thus inventing the first cloths
hanger.

3. In 1853, George Crum, a chef, was cutting potatos when he heard some
customers complain about the thickness of his French fries. Then he cut
thinner fries, but the two womans still complained. Finally, Crum looked
through his selection of knifes and chose the sharpest one. He cut fries that
were so thin they could not be eaten with a fork. The potato chip was
born!

PRACTICE 2

Fill in the blanks with either the singular or plural form of the noun. If the noun
does not change, put an *X* in the space.

EXAMPLES:

Singular	Plural
man	*men*
X	goggles

1. person _____
2. loaf _____
3. _____ mice
4. brother-in-law _____
5. lady _____
6. _____ pants
7. _____ jeans
8. sheep _____
9. calf _____
10. _____ binoculars
11. child _____

12. _____   shelves

13. _____   sunglasses

14. alarm clock   _____

15. bathing suit   _____

Key Words for Singular and Plural Nouns

Some key words will help you determine whether a noun is singular or plural.

- Use a singular noun after words such as *a, an, one, each, every,* and *another.*

   As **a** <u>young mother</u>, Dorothy Gerber prepared homemade baby food for her daughter.

   Gerber tried to sell her product to **every** <u>grocery store</u> in her town.

- Use a plural noun after words such as *two, all, both, many, few, several,* and *some.*

   Very **few** <u>companies</u> produced food targeted to children.

   Today, **many** <u>babies</u> eat Gerber's baby food.

 **Hint**   **Using Plural Nouns After of the**

Use a plural noun after the expressions *one (all, two, each, few, lots, many, most, several) of the....*

   <u>One of the most</u> useful **items** ever invented is the zipper.

PRACTICE 3

Circle the correct noun in each set of parentheses.

EXAMPLE:

   In the future, some of the most useful (invention /(inventions)) will be in the energy sector.

1.   Very few (government / governments) would deny that carbon reduction

      is important. Every (year / years), engineers try to come up with an

      automobile (prototype / prototypes) that is fuel efficient and economical.

      Today, many (person / people) discuss electric cars, but did you know that

      such automobiles are not a new (invention / inventions)?

2.   In 1897, electric (taxi / taxis) roamed New York's streets. By 1900, 28

      percent of all (car / cars) in the United States were powered by electricity.

However, during the 1920s, the mass production of combustion

(engine / engines) wiped out electric vehicles for the next forty years.

3.   Then, on October 16, 1973, something happened. All of the

(member / members) of the Organization of Petroleum Exporting

Countries (OPEC) cut production of oil and announced that they would no

longer ship oil to western nations. One of the (result / results) of the crisis

was that people discussed electric cars again. Today, engineers in almost

every (nation / nations) want to develop an efficient electric

(vehicle / vehicles).

Count Nouns and Noncount Nouns

In English, nouns are grouped into two types: count nouns and noncount nouns. **Count nouns** refer to people or things that you can count, such as *engine*, *paper*, or *girl*. Count nouns usually can have both a singular and plural form.

She read a <u>book</u> about inventions. She read five <u>books</u> about inventions.

Noncount nouns refer to people or things that you cannot count because you cannot divide them, such as *electricity* and *music*. Noncount nouns usually have only the singular form.

The <u>furniture</u> in the inventor's house looked expensive.

Inventors usually have a lot of specialized <u>equipment</u>.

To express a noncount noun as a count noun, refer to it in terms of types, varieties, or amounts.

The patent office has **a variety of** <u>furniture</u>.

My friend works for an entertainment company where he listens to **many styles of** <u>music</u>.

The clerk at the patent office likes to drink coffee with **four cubes of** <u>sugar</u>.

Here are some common noncount nouns.

Common Noncount Nouns

Categories of Objects		Food	Nature	Substances	
clothing	machinery	bread	air	chalk	hair
equipment	mail	honey	earth	charcoal	fur
furniture	money	meat	electricity	coal	
homework	music	milk	energy	ink	
jewelry	postage	fish	radiation	paint	
luggage	software	rice	water	paper	

Abstract Nouns

advice	evidence	information	progress
attention	effort	knowledge	proof
behavior	health	luck	research
education	help	peace	violence

PRACTICE 4

Change the italicized words to the plural form, if necessary. If you cannot use the plural form, write *X* in the space. If the word ends in *y*, you may have to change the *y* to *i* for the plural form.

EXAMPLE:

In written communication, there have been many useful *discovery* _ies_ .

1. Since the beginning of *history*_____, people have used various

    *method*_____ to compose in written form. Early *human*_____ used

    *substance*_____ such as *charcoal*_____, *chalk*_____, and *paint*_____ to

    write on *wall*_____ and *paper*_____ . Eventually, a lot of *information*_____

    was recorded using ink and a quill.

2. In 1884, Lewis Waterman patented one of the most useful *invention*_____.

    Although Waterman's fountain *pen*_____ worked reasonably well, they

    were unreliable, and ink could leak onto *clothing*_____ and

    *furniture*_____ .

3. Since the 1930s, a lot of *progress*_____ has been made in written

    communication. In 1938, Ladislo Biro was one of the best-known

    *journalist*_____ in Hungary. He spent a lot of *time*_____ thinking about

    different *type*_____ of writing *tool*_____ . Using quick-drying ink that was

    common in printing *press*_____, and using a small ball bearing, he created

    the first ballpoint pen.

4. These days, *company*_____ do a lot of *research*_____ because they

    want to develop a new, better writing tool. In fact, there are many different

    *kind*_____ of *pen*_____ on the market.

CHAPTER 27

Determiners

Determiners are words that help to determine or figure out whether a noun is specific or general.

> Arthur Scott used **his** imagination and created **a** new invention, **the** paper towel.

You can use many words from different parts of speech as determiners.

Articles:	a, an, the
Demonstratives:	this, that, these, those, such
Indefinite pronouns:	any, all, both, each, every, either, few, little, many, several
Numbers:	one, two, three
Possessive nouns:	Jack's, the teacher's, a man's
Possessive adjectives:	my, your, his, her, its, our, their, whose

Commonly Confused Determiners

Some determiners can be confusing because you can use them only in specific circumstances. Review this list of some commonly confused determiners.

a, an, the

A and *an* are general determiners, and *the* is a specific determiner.

> general   specific
> I need to find a new car. The cars in that showroom are expensive.

- Use *a* and *an* before singular count nouns but not before plural or noncount nouns. Use *a* before nouns that begin with a consonant (*a man*), and use *an* before nouns that begin with a vowel (*an invention*).

  > An ordinary woman created a very useful product.

- Use *the* before nouns that refer to a specific person, place, or thing. Do not use *the* before languages (*he studies Greek*), sports (*we played football*), and most city and country names (*Biro was born in Hungary*).

  > In 1885, Karl Benz invented the first automobile while living in the city of Mannheim, Germany.

many, few, much, little

- Use *many* and *few* with count nouns.

  > Many **people** have tried to develop new products, but few **inventions** are really successful.

- Use *much* and *little* with noncount nouns.

  > Manu Joshi spent too much **money** on very little **research.**

this, that, these, those

- Use *this* and *these* to refer to things that are physically close to the speaker or at the present time. Use *this* before singular nouns and *these* before plural nouns.

This **computer** in my purse measures three by five inches. These **days,** computers are very small.

- Use *that* and *those* to refer to things that are physically distant from the speaker or in the past or future. Use *that* before singular nouns and *those* before plural nouns.

  In the 1950s, computers were invented. In those **years,** computers were very large. In that **building,** there is a very old computer.

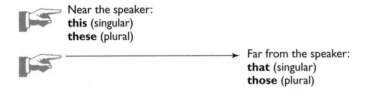

Near the speaker:
this (singular)
these (plural)

Far from the speaker:
that (singular)
those (plural)

PRACTICE 5

Write *a*, *an*, or *the* in the space before each noun. If no determiner is necessary, write *X* in the space.

EXAMPLE:

A modern convenience like ___*a*___ car can make traveling much easier.

CHAPTER 27

1.   Most of us admire _____ beautiful, shiny new automobiles, but we do

not give _____ same admiration to _____ windshield wipers. Indeed, we

take _____ windshield wiper for granted, yet it is _____ extremely

necessary tool when we are driving. In fact, before _____ invention of

_____ windshield wiper, drivers had to stop to clean the front window of

their vehicles.

2.   In 1902, when she was on _____ trip to New York City, Mary

Anderson observed that streetcar drivers had to look through open

windows when they were driving in bad weather. In 1903, she invented

_____ gadget that could clean car windows. Her wipers consisted of rubber

blades on _____ outside of the windshield and _____ handle on _____

inside of the car. Drivers could turn _____ wipers by turning the handle.

3.   Anderson received _____ patent for her invention, and by 1916, all

American-made cars had _____ windshield wipers as _____ regular

feature.

PRACTICE 6

Underline the appropriate determiner in parentheses. If the noun does not require a determiner, underline X.

EXAMPLE:

Most inventions begin with (X / <u>a</u> / the) great idea.

1. (This / These) days, (much / many) people want to get rich quickly

    by developing (a / the / X) great new product. They also hope to make

    (X / the) life easier for others. (Every / Some / X) inventions are extremely

    useful, while others are totally absurd.

2. (Few / little) inventions are as bizarre as (a / X / the) "Twelve Gauge

    Golf Club." It requires very (few / little) equipment. It contains (the / a)

    barrel, (the / a) muzzle, and (the / a) trap door to load explosives. (A / The / X)

    firing pin is in (an / the / X) exact spot where (a / the / X) club is

    supposed to hit (the / X) ball. (The / An) inventor received (X / a) patent in

    1979. There were many odd patents (this / that) year. The device does not

    cost (much / many) money to produce. However, it has produced very

    (few / little) interest among consumers.

3. Although (much / many) absurd inventions never earn a penny, a

    (few / little) of them become successful. In 2005, (a / the) cell phone

    company in China created a breathalyzer phone. People can program

    (a / the) phone to block certain numbers such as that of the boss. If the

    phone user is inebriated, he or she cannot dial (that / those) numbers.

    Although people in North America do not have (much / many) information

    about the phone, it is extremely popular in (the / X) Korea. Over 200,000

    people bought the phones because they wanted to avoid making

    (a / the / X) embarrassing phone calls.

4. (This / That) year, thousands of people will patent their ideas. With a

    (few / little) time and (some / many) research, perhaps you can come up

    with a great invention.

PRACTICE 7

Correct fifteen errors in singular nouns, plural nouns, and determiners.

EXAMPLE:

One of the most interesting ~~idea~~ *ideas* is a self-cleaning house.

In her autobiography, Agatha Christie wrote that most invention arise from laziness. Peoples invent to save themselves trouble. Christie's comments apply perfectly to Frances Gabe of Newberg, Oregon. Gabe, after a lot of researches, has invented and patented the world's first self-cleaning house. A house will appeal to anyone who hates to clean. On the ceiling of each rooms in Gabe's house, there is a cleaning and drying machines. At the touch of a buttons, each units first sprays soapy water over the room, then rinses and blow-dries the entire area. The rooms' floors are sloped slightly so that excess waters runs to a drain. The furnitures is made of waterproof material, and there are no carpets. There are not much decorations in the house. In the kitchen, all dish are cleaned, dried, and stored inside dishwasher cupboards. Every sink, tub, and toilets is self-cleaning. Gabe created the architectural plans and the designs for the specialized equipments. This days, Gabe actually lives in her patented prototype home.

Prepositions

Prepositions are words that show concepts such as time, place, direction, and manner. They show connections or relationships between ideas.

Scientists made many important discoveries **during** World War II.

American scientists raced **to** build the first atomic bomb.

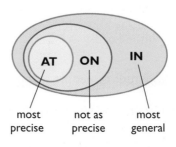

Prepositions	Prepositions of Time	Prepositions of Place
at	at a specific time of day (at 8:30 p.m.) at night at breakfast, lunch, dinner	at an address (at 15 Maple Street) at a specific building (at the hospital)
on	on a day of the week (on Monday) on a specific date (on June 16) on a specific holiday (on Martin Luther King Day) on time (meaning "punctual") on my birthday	on a specific street (on 17th Avenue) on technological devices (on TV, on the radio, on the phone, on the computer) on a planet (on Earth) on top
in	in a year (in 2005) in a month (in July) in the morning, afternoon, evening in the spring, fall, summer, winter	in a city (in Boston) in a country (in Spain) in a continent (in Africa)
from ... to	from one time to another (from 6 a.m. to 8 p.m.)	from one place to another (from Las Vegas to Miami)
for	for a period of time (for six hours)	for a distance (for ten miles)

Commonly Confused Prepositions

to vs. at

Use *to* after verbs that indicate movement from one place to another.

> Each morning, Albert <u>walks</u> **to** the library, he <u>goes</u> **to** the coffee shop, and he <u>returns</u> **to** his office.

Exception: Do not put *to* directly before *home*.

> Albert returned ~~to~~ home after he won his prize. He didn't go to his friend's home.

Use *at* after verbs that indicate being or remaining in one place (and not moving from one place to another).

> In the afternoon, he <u>stays</u> **at** work. He <u>sits</u> **at** his desk and <u>looks</u> **at** his inventions.

for vs. during

Use *during* to explain when something happens. Use *for* to explain how long it takes to happen.

> **During** <u>the month of August</u>, the patent office closes **for** <u>two weeks</u>.

> The inventors of the bomb experimented **for** <u>many years</u> **during** <u>World War II</u>.

PRACTICE 8

Write the correct preposition in each blank. Choose *in, on, at, to, for, during,* or *from.*

EXAMPLE:

_At_ 5:15 a.m. we heard the news.

1. One of the most influential inventions _____ history was the creation of the atomic bomb.

2. _____ Germany, scientists were trying very hard to develop the atomic bomb _____ the beginning of World War II.

3. _____ August 2, 1939, Albert Einstein wrote a letter to President Franklin Delano Roosevelt about Germany's progress making the bomb.

4. _____ that day, Einstein went _____ his office _____ 1 p.m., and he sat _____ his desk _____ several hours while he composed the letter.

5. Roosevelt was _____ his office speaking _____ the telephone when he heard about Einstein's letter.

6. Roosevelt's advisors were _____ breakfast when the president called them, and they hastily rushed _____ the White House.

7. The president and his advisers stayed _____ Washington and discussed the information _____ two days. _____ the crisis, the President remained calm.

8. _____ 1941, the U.S. government decided to develop the atomic bomb.

9. The U.S. government spent around $2 billion on the Manhattan Project, which lasted _____ 1939 _____ 1945.

PRACTICE 9

Correct five errors with prepositions.

EXAMPLE:

for

The zipper has been popular <s>during</s> many years.

Whitcomb Judson patented a new type of fabric fastener on 1893.

Several others contributed to the design of the fastener. Today, the zipper is the source of many "fly" jokes. For example, last semester, I went at my science class to make a presentation, and I did not realize that my zipper was down. During twenty minutes, I spoke, and some students giggled. During a month, others teased me. I must have heard "you're flying low" a hundred times. Now, when I go at college, I ensure that my zipper is firmly fastened.

Common Prepositional Expressions

Many common expressions contain prepositions. These types of expressions usually express a particular meaning.

EXAMPLE:

verb   preposition

This morning I <u>listened</u> **to** the radio.

Here is a list of common prepositional expressions.

accuse (somebody) of	escape from	prevent (someone) from
acquainted with	excited about	protect (someone) from
add to	feel like	proud of
afraid of	familiar with	provide (someone) with
angry with	fond of	qualify for
angry about	forget about	realistic about
agree with	forgive (someone) for	refer to
apologize for	friendly with	related to
apply for	good for	rely on
approve of	grateful for	rescue from
argue with	happy about	responsible for
ask for	hear about	sad about
associate with	hope for	satisfied with
aware of	hopeful about	scared of
believe in	innocent of	search for
belong to	insist on	similar to
capable of	insulted by	specialize in
care about	interested in	stop (something) from
care for	introduce to	succeed in
commit to	jealous of	take advantage of
comply with	keep from	take care of
concern about	located in	thank (someone) for
confronted with	long for	think about
consist of	look forward to	think of
count on	opposed to	tired of
deal with	participate in	upset with
decide to	patient with	upset about
decide on	pay attention to	willing to
depend on	pay for	wish for
be disappointed with	pray for	worry about
be disappointed about	prepared to	
dream of	prepared for	

PRACTICE 10

Write the correct preposition in each blank. Use the preceding list of prepositional expressions to help you.

EXAMPLE:

Many American citizens participated __*in*__ the war effort.

1. During World War II, many people believed _____ science. Robert Oppenheimer was interested _____ physics. He heard _____ the rise of fascism in Germany. He decided _____ become a scientist with the U.S. government.

2. Oppenheimer was excited _____ working on atomic bombs for the Manhattan Project. Officials searched _____ a secluded location to develop the bomb and chose a desert area near Los Alamos, New Mexico. Oppenheimer dealt _____ a large team of scientists.

3. When he saw an atomic bomb test, Oppenheimer became afraid _____ its power. Later, when a bomb called Little Boy was dropped on Hiroshima, he felt partially responsible _____ changing the world with his discovery.

4. After the war, Oppenheimer argued _____ some other physicists and politicians about atomic weapons. He worried _____ the impact of the atomic bomb, and he came to believe that the nuclear arms race was not good _____ society. During the 1950s, Oppenheimer was accused _____ having communist sympathies. He was disappointed _____ the government for taking away his security clearance.

5. At the end of his career, Oppenheimer took advantage _____ his experience with the Manhattan Project and wrote about ethics and morality. In 1967, the world heard _____ Oppenheimer's death from throat cancer.

> ### *The Writer's Desk* **Revise and Edit Your Warm Up**
>
> In the Warm Up at the beginning of the chapter, you wrote a few sentences about the most interesting inventions of the last century. Edit your sentences to check for any errors with nouns, determiners, and prepositions.

REFLECT ON IT

Think about what you have learned in this chapter. If you do not know an answer, review that concept.

1. What is the definition of a noun? _____

_____

2. Give examples of five noncount nouns.

_____ _____ _____ _____ _____

3. Make the following nouns plural.

   a. tooth: _____

   b. backseat driver: _____

   c. bride-to-be: _____

   d. kiss: _____

   e. homework: _____

   f. loaf: _____

4. Correct the errors in the following sentences.

                                   many
   EXAMPLE: Leonardo da Vinci had ~~much~~ ideas.

   a. He invented much things.

   b. He developed a idea for a parachute.

   c. Da Vinci is one of the most famous artist in the world.

   d. Little of his other works are as famous as the *Mona Lisa*.

FINAL REVIEW

Correct fifteen errors in singular nouns, plural nouns, determiners, and prepositions.

EXAMPLE:

                          a
George de Mestral had ~~the~~ splendid idea.

One summer day on 1948, George de Mestral decided to go for a hike. As he

was walking through some tall weed, burrs stuck to his pants and to his dog's furs.

This had happened much times before. However, on that day, de Mestral decided to examine some of the burrs with the microscope, and he discovered some interesting informations. He noticed that each burrs was made up of little hooks that helped it cling to material. He was very interested of this discovery. He thought on a way to use the hook system of the burrs to develop a products for the home. After much attempts, George patented his invention in 1951 and called it Velcro. This days, Velcro is used on different type of products such as shoes, clothings, and toys. Now, many manufacturers depend of Velcro.

How Do I Get a Better Grade?

Visit www.mywritinglab.com for audio-visual lectures and additional practice sets about nouns, determiners, and prepositions.
Get a better grade with MyWritingLab!

CHAPTER 27

Section Theme **INVENTIONS AND DISCOVERIES**

In this chapter, you will read about topics related to ancient civilizations.

The Writer's Desk Warm Up

Write a short paragraph describing a historical figure whom you admire. You could write about a famous politician, actor, writer, artist, scientist, or explorer. Explain what that person did that was admirable.

Pronoun Case

Pronouns are words that replace nouns (people, places, or things), other pronouns, and phrases. Use pronouns to avoid repeating nouns.

Machu Picchu is an ancient city located high in the Andes. ~~Machu Picchu~~ *It* was discovered in 1911.

Pronouns are formed according to the role they play in a sentence. A pronoun can be the subject or object of the sentence, or it can show possession. The next chart shows the three main pronoun cases: subjective, objective, and possessive.

Pronouns

			Possessives	
Singular	**Subjective**	**Objective**	**Possessive Adjective**	**Possessive Pronoun**
1st person	I	me	my	mine
2nd person	you	you	your	yours
3rd person	he, she, it, who, whoever	him, her, it, whom, whomever	his, her, its, whose	his, hers
Plural				
1st person	we	us	our	ours
2nd person	you	you	your	yours
3rd person	they	them	their	theirs

Subjective Case

A **subject** performs an action in a sentence. When a pronoun is the subject of the sentence, use the subjective form of the pronoun.

> **She** liked to read mystery novels set in ancient times.

> **We** watched a horror movie about mummies.

Objective Case

An **object** receives an action in a sentence. When a pronoun is the object in the sentence, use the objective form of the pronoun.

> The audience gave **him** an ovation for the lecture on ancient China.

> My sister saw **us** at the lecture.

Possessive Case

A possessive pronoun shows ownership.

- **Possessive adjectives** are always placed before the noun that they modify. In the next sentences, *her* and *their* are possessive adjectives.

> She finished **her** book about the pyramids, but they did not finish **their** books.

- **Possessive pronouns** replace the possessive adjective and noun. In the next sentence, *her* is a possessive adjective and *theirs* is a possessive pronoun.

    She finished **her** <u>book</u> about the pyramids, but they did not finish **theirs**.

Problems with Possessive Pronouns

When using the possessive pronouns *hers* and *theirs*, be careful that you do not add an apostrophe before the *s*.

hers   *theirs*

The archeology book is ~~her's~~. The papyrus map is ~~their's~~.

Some possessive adjectives sound like certain contractions. When using the possessive adjectives *their*, *your*, and *its*, be careful that you do not confuse them with *they're*, *you're*, and *it's*.

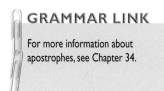

GRAMMAR LINK

For more information about apostrophes, see Chapter 34.

Their is the possessive adjective.	<u>Their</u> flight to Mexico City was late.
They're is the contraction of *they are*.	<u>They're</u> not going to be on time for the bus tour.
Your is the possessive adjective.	<u>Your</u> tour guide has a map of the Tulum Mayan ruins.
You're is the contraction of *you are*.	<u>You're</u> going to enjoy visiting this ancient site.
Its is the possessive adjective.	The Temple of the Frescoes has a beautiful mural on <u>its</u> wall.
It's is the contraction of *it is*.	<u>It's</u> an important piece of Mayan history.

CHAPTER 28

 **Choosing *His* or *Her***

To choose the correct possessive adjective, think about the possessor (not the object that is possessed).

- If something belongs to a female, use *her* + noun.

    Cecilia packed <u>her</u> luggage.

- If something belongs to a male, use *his* + noun.

    Tony booked <u>his</u> flight.

PRACTICE I

Underline the correct possessive adjective or possessive pronoun in each set of parentheses.

EXAMPLE:

Historians often cite Greece and (<u>its</u> / it's) ancient monuments as important to the study of western civilization.

1.   Societies in the ancient world revered (their / there) monuments. The Greeks especially loved (their / theirs). Greek society encouraged (its / it's) philosophers to create lists of wonderful architecture of that time because Greek leaders wanted to encourage (they're / there / their) citizens to be proud of the Greek heritage. Different philosophers put a variety of items on (their / theirs) lists. Unfortunately, many of the lists have not survived up to (our / ours) time.

2.   The oldest surviving list of ancient wonders was written by Antipater of Sidon around 140 BCE. Antipater, of course, was a Greek male, and (her / its / his) list mainly consisted of Greek structures. He listed such things as the pyramids at Giza, the Hanging Gardens of Babylon, the statue of Zeus at Olympia, and the Lighthouse of Alexandria, among others. Most of those structures are no longer standing. For example, the Lighthouse was destroyed by an earthquake and (it's / its) aftershocks.

3.   My professor, Aspasia Jones, gave a slide show of (her / hers) trip to the pyramids. Many people, of course, have taken photographs of the pyramids, but (her / hers) were particularly interesting. She had permission to go into a chamber closed to the public, and we were able to see (it's / its) contents. Her assistant, Milo, used (his / its) new camera to take the photos.

4.   Would you like to go to Aspasia's next slide show? Could we use (your / your're / yours) car? (My / Mine) is getting repaired. Call me on (my / mine) cell phone.

Pronouns in Comparisons with *than* or *as*

Avoid making errors in pronoun case when the pronoun follows *than* or *as*. If the pronoun is a subject, use the subjective case, and if the pronoun is an object, use the objective case.

   If you use the incorrect case, your sentence may have a meaning that you do not intend it to have. For example, people often follow *than* or *as* with an objective pronoun when they mean to follow it with a subjective pronoun. Look at the differences in the meanings of the next sentences.

objective case

I like ancient history as much as **him.**

(I like ancient history <u>as much as I like him.</u>)

subjective case

I like ancient history as much as **he.**

(I like ancient history <u>as much as he likes ancient history.</u>)

 **Complete the Thought**

If you are unsure which pronoun case to use, test by completing the thought. Look at the following examples.

He likes to visit museums more than **I** (like to visit museums).

He likes to visit museums more than (he likes to visit) **me.**

Pronouns in Prepositional Phrases

In a prepositional phrase, the words that follow the preposition are the objects of the preposition. Therefore, always use the objective case of the pronoun after a preposition.

<u>To</u> **her,** learning about history is not important.

<u>Between</u> **you** and **me,** our history class is very interesting.

Pronouns with *and* or *or*

Use the correct case when nouns and pronouns are joined by *and* or *or.* If the pronouns are the subject, use the subjective case. If the pronouns are the object, use the objective case.

	He and I
Subjective:	~~Him and me~~ had to do a presentation on the Incas.

	him and me
Objective:	The instructor asked ~~he and I~~ to present first.

 **Finding the Correct Case**

An easy way to determine whether your case is correct is to say the sentence with just one pronoun.

The librarian asked her and (I, me) to speak quietly.

Choices: The librarian asked I . . . *or* The librarian asked me. . . .

Correct: The librarian asked her and <u>me</u> to speak quietly.

PRACTICE 2

Correct any errors with pronoun case. Write *C* in the space if the sentence is correct.

EXAMPLE:

Last summer, my friend and ~~me~~ *I* visited Mexico.

1. My friend, Maria, is older than me. _____

2. Maria gave me a book on the Maya civilization because she is as interested in the subject as me. _____

3. Maria and me took a bus to Chichén Itzá, an ancient site that was built around the middle of the sixth century. _____

4. At the site, we asked a young man to take a picture of we girls. _____

5. Maria's camera was newer than mine, so we used her's. _____

6. The young man, whose name was Karl, climbed with Maria and me to the top of the pyramid. _____

7. Him and his friend Pedro told us that they were afraid of heights. _____

8. Between you and I, I was also getting a bit dizzy, so we decided to climb down. _____

9. Our tour guide told Pedro and me that the Maya abandoned Chichén Itzá in the tenth century. _____

10. Karl said goodbye to us because him and Pedro had to catch the bus for Belize. _____

Relative Pronouns (*who, whom, which, that, whose*)

Relative pronouns can join two short sentences. Here is a list of relative pronouns.

who	whom	which	that	whose
whoever	whomever			

- *Who* (or *whoever*) and *whom* (or *whomever*) always refer to people. *Who* is the subject of the clause, and *whom* is the object of the clause.

  Subject: The <u>archeologist</u> **who** specializes in Mayan culture is speaking today.

  Object: The <u>archeologist</u> **whom** you met is my mother.

- *Which* always refers to things.

  The ancient city of <u>Machu Picchu</u>, **which** I have never seen, is located in the Andes.

GRAMMAR LINK

Clauses with *which* are set off with commas. For more information, see Chapter 33, "Commas."

- *That* refers to things.

   Hiram Bingham wrote a <u>book</u> **that** is about Machu Picchu.

- *Whose* always shows that something belongs to or is connected with someone or something. It usually replaces possessive pronouns such as *his*, *her*, or *their*. Do not confuse *whose* with *who's*, which means "who is."

   The <u>archaeologist</u> traced the route. <u>His</u> maps were on the table.

   The <u>archaeologist</u>, **whose** maps were on the table, traced the route.

 Choosing *Who* or *Whom*

If you are unsure whether to use *who* or *whom*, test yourself in the following way. Replace *who* or *whom* with another pronoun. If the replacement is a subjective pronoun such as *he* or *she*, use *who*. If the replacement is an objective pronoun such as *her* or *him*, use **whom.**

   I know a man **who** works in a museum.
   (He works in a museum.)

   The man to **whom** you gave your portfolio is the director of the museum.
   (You gave your portfolio <u>to him</u>.)

CHAPTER 28

PRACTICE 3

Write the correct relative pronoun in each blank.

EXAMPLE:

   The Khmer civilization, *which* built the temples of Angor, lost its power by the fifteenth century.

1. The Hindu temples of Angkor, _____ are among the most magnificent examples of architecture, were built between the ninth and twelfth centuries. The ancient Khmer kings, _____ kingdom was between present-day Cambodia and the Bay of Bengal, commissioned around a hundred temples at the site. King Suryavaram II, _____ was a devout Hindu, started to build the temples to honor the Hindu god Vishnu. The temple _____ portrays Hindu cosmology is at Angkor Wat.

2.   During the powerful reign of the Angkor kings, many people _____ were Vishnu devotees made pilgrimages to the temples. The Angkor kings, to _____ religion was important, preserved these temples for many centuries. The temples were abandoned around 1432 due to political instability.

3.   The temples, _____ were very beautiful, were almost forgotten for the next few centuries. Although Buddhist monks for _____ the temples represented an important religious site did visit, it was the French explorer Henri Mouhot _____ popularized the spot for Europeans. Mouhot visited the area _____ the jungle had hidden. On his journey, Mouhot encountered tigers, spiders, and leeches, _____ made his journey difficult.

4.   Today, many tourists _____ are interested in ancient monuments visit the site. However, looters, _____ steal priceless objects to sell to collectors and tourists, are destroying the temples _____ are a world heritage site.

Reflexive Pronouns (-*self*/-*selves*)

Use **reflexive pronouns** when you want to emphasize that the subject does an action to himself or herself.

I asked **myself** many questions.

History often repeats **itself.**

Do not use reflexive pronouns for activities that people do to themselves, such as washing or shaving. However, you can use reflexive pronouns to draw attention to a surprising or an unusual action.

The little boy fed **himself.**
(The boy probably could not feed himself at a previous time.)

The next chart shows subjective pronouns and the reflexive pronouns that relate to them.

Pronouns That End with *-self* or *-selves*		
Singular	**Antecedent**	**Reflexive Pronoun**
1st person	I	myself
2nd person	you	yourself
3rd person	he, she, it	himself, herself, itself
Plural		
1st person	we	ourselves
2nd person	you	yourselves
3rd person	they	themselves

 **Common Errors with Reflexive Pronouns**

Hisself and *theirselves* do not exist in English. These are incorrect ways to say *himself* or *themselves*.

themselves
The tourists went by ~~theirselves~~ to the museum.

himself.
Croesus visited the oracle by ~~hisself.~~

PRACTICE 4

Fill in the blanks with the correct reflexive pronouns.

EXAMPLE:

He wanted to explore the forest by *himself*.

1.   Our guide was upset because she had twisted her ankle while walking by _____ through the jungle. She had forgotten how easily she could hurt _____ by tripping on a tree root.

2.   Our guide looked at us and said, "Go to the temple by _____. You are all capable of finding it."

3.   Because our guide could not go with us, we had to climb the steps of the temple by _____. One member of the group, Matt, decided we were too slow for him, so he decided to climb up by _____.

4.   I thought to _____ that he would probably get lost. Sure enough, he did get lost. When we found him, he told us that he had lost his footing and cut _____ on some of the crumbling pieces of rock. We offered him some first aid supplies so he could patch _____ up.

5.   After we found Matt, we got _____ back on track. We reached the top of the temple and felt very pleased with _____.

Pronoun–Antecedent Agreement

A pronoun must agree with its **antecedent,** which is the word to which the pronoun refers. Antecedents are nouns, pronouns, and phrases that the pronouns have replaced, and they always come before the pronoun. Pronouns must agree in person and number with their antecedents.

The archeologist was frustrated because **she** could not raise enough money for **her** expedition.
(*The archeologist* is the antecedent of *she* and *her*.)

My instructor went on a vacation to Peru. **He** took **his** family with **him.**
(*My instructor* is the antecedent of *he, his,* and *him*.)

China has many ancient salt mines. **They** date back to the fourth century B.C.
(*Salt mines* is the antecedent of *they*.)

CHAPTER 28

GRAMMAR LINK

For a list of collective nouns, see page 385 in Chapter 25.

 Using Collective Nouns

Collective nouns refer to a group of people or things. The group acts as a unit; therefore, it is singular.

The association had **its** meeting on Monday.

The government tried to implement **its** policies.

PRACTICE 5

Fill in the blank spaces with the appropriate pronouns or possessive adjectives.

EXAMPLE:

Many people are fascinated with the lost city of Troy, and ___*they*___ are curious about the city's history.

1.   The archeologist Heinrich Schliemann believed that finding the lost city of Troy would bring _____ fame and fortune. He was convinced

that _____ idea about the location of Troy was correct. Archeologists at that time thought that the city of Troy was a myth and that they would waste _____ time hunting for _____.

2.   Schliemann was a millionaire who spent _____ time and money pursuing _____ archeological interests. In 1868, Schliemann met Frank Calvert, a businessman who owned land around Hisarlik, Turkey. Both men were convinced that _____ could find the lost city of Troy. Calvert provided the funding, and Schliemann began to excavate on Calvert's land.

3.   Schliemann began digging in 1870. The Turkish government had not yet given Schliemann _____ approval for the excavation. As the work progressed, he made _____ first discovery when he uncovered many stone blocks. In 1873, Schliemann and _____ wife Sophia also discovered gold at the site. Schliemann dismissed the workers because he did not want _____ to know about the gold.

4.   The couple then uncovered a larger hoard of gold, silver, and jewelry. They smuggled _____ treasures out of Turkey. Sophia, Schliemann's wife, wore some of the jewelry around _____ neck. The Turkish authorities were furious because treasures had been removed without _____ permission. Eventually Schliemann got control over the treasures, and he presented _____ to the city of Berlin. The treasures somehow disappeared from Berlin after World War II, and _____ were recently rediscovered in Moscow.

Indefinite Pronouns

Use **indefinite pronouns** when you refer to people or things whose identity is not known or is unimportant. The next chart shows some common singular and plural indefinite pronouns.

Indefinite Pronouns

Singular	another	each	nobody	other
	anybody	everybody	no one	somebody
	anyone	everyone	nothing	someone
	anything	everything	one	something
Plural	both, few, many, others, several			
Either singular or plural	all, any, some, none, more, most, half (and other fractions)			

Singular

When you use a singular indefinite antecedent, also use a singular pronoun to refer to it.

Everybody feels amazed when **he or she** sees China's terracotta army for the first time.

Nobody should forget to visit China's terracotta army in **his or her** lifetime.

Plural

When you use a plural indefinite antecedent, also use a plural pronoun to refer to it.

The two objects are ancient, and both have **their** own intrinsic value.

The world has many illegal excavation sites; there are several operating in China, but **they** cannot be controlled.

Either Singular or Plural

Some indefinite pronouns can be either singular or plural, depending on the noun to which they refer.

Many archeologists came to the site. All were experts in **their** field.
(*All* refers to archeologists; therefore, the pronoun is plural.)

We excavated all of the site and **its** artifacts.
(*All* refers to the site; therefore, the pronoun is singular.)

> *Hint* **Using of the Expressions**
>
> In sentences containing the expression *one of the . . .* or *each of the . . .* , the subject is the indefinite pronoun *one* or *each*. Therefore, any pronoun referring to that phrase must be singular.
>
> One of the statues is missing **its** weapon.
>
> Each of the men has **his** own map.

PRACTICE 6

Identify and correct nine errors in pronoun-antecedent agreement. You may change either the antecedent or the pronoun. If you change any antecedents, make sure that your subjects and verbs agree.

EXAMPLE:

                      their

Some of the soldiers had ~~his~~ own swords.

1.   In 1974, in Xi'an, China, some local men were digging a well when they made an astounding discovery. One of the men uncovered a clay soldier with their bare hands. Then others, using their shovels, discovered more clay soldiers at the site. Someone rode their bicycle to the local communist party headquarters. The worker described what he and the others had found.

2.   The local communist party sent some archeologists to the site. When they arrived, everyone expressed shock at the sight before their eyes. They realized that the find was significant. The central government sent a message to the local peasants. Each had to leave their land and move to another location. Nobody was allowed to remain in their home.

3.   Over the next years, specialists excavated the site. They uncovered more than 8,000 terracotta soldiers. The soldiers are life-size, and many have his own unique physical features, representing every ethnic group in China. Different male artists sculpted groups of the soldiers. Each engraved their name on the statues.

4.   The clay soldiers have been guarding an ancient emperor for over 2,000 years. Everybody in the all-male army, including generals, officers, cavalry, and archers, had their own life-sized weapon. Today the site is a major tourist attraction in China. Anybody who goes to China on their holiday should try to visit the terracotta army.

Avoid Sexist Language

Terms like *anybody, somebody, nobody,* and *each* are singular antecedents, so the pronouns that follow those words must be singular. At one time, it was acceptable to use *he* as a general term meaning "all people"; however, today it is more acceptable to use *he or she*.

Sexist:	Everyone had to leave his home.
Solution:	Everyone had to leave his or her home.
Better solution:	The citizens had to leave their homes.

Exception: If you know for certain that the subject is male or female, then use only *he* or only *she*.

PRACTICE 7

Circle the correct pronouns in the following paragraphs.

EXAMPLE:

Some people say that history is not important because (its, it's) information is not relevant to people's everyday lives.

1.   History courses offer information about the past, but many people

wonder whether they should spend (his or her, their) time studying the

past. In fact, somebody might feel it is more important to think about

(his or her, their) future. In other words, some people may not consider

history and (it's, its) lessons to be as important as other subjects that are

more practical.

2.   In the past, historians and (their, theirs) supporters memorized names

and dates. Everybody believed that (his or her, their) knowledge of history

indicated a high level of education. Between you and (I, me), I do not think

that this reason for studying history is valid. I think that history should

be studied for (its, it's) own merits. For example, history tells us about

societies and (their, theirs) past behaviors. History also informs us about

a critical moment in the past and (its, it's) influence on today's

lifestyles. Furthermore, history helps us understand more about

(yourselves, ourselves).

3.   I like studying history; however, my brother has always liked it far more than (I, me). He became really interested when we were children. (He, Him) and (I, me) used to read stories about World War I. After school, while the other neighborhood kids were playing outside, my brother preferred to spend hours watching war films (who, that) had great battle scenes.

4.   Now my brother is a historian. He is a man (who, whom) believes that everybody should take (his or her, their) history lessons seriously. In fact, my brother met (his, her) future wife in history class. He was sitting by (hisself, himself, herself) when she sat near him. The rest, of course, is history.

Vague Pronouns

Avoid using pronouns that could refer to more than one antecedent.

Vague: Frank asked his friend where <u>his</u> map of ancient Greece was.
(Whose map is it: Frank's or his friend's?)

Clearer: **Frank** wondered where **his** map of ancient Greece was, so he asked his friend about it.

Avoid using confusing pronouns such as *it* and *they* that have no clear antecedent.

Vague: <u>They</u> say that people should get vaccines before traveling to certain countries.
(Who are *they?*)

Clearer: **Health authorities** say that people should get vaccines before traveling to certain countries.

Vague: <u>It</u> stated in the magazine that the tower of Copán in Honduras has more hieroglyphic inscriptions than any other Maya ruin.
(Who or what is *it?*)

Clearer: **The magazine article** stated that the tower of Copán in Honduras has more hieroglyphic inscriptions than any other Maya ruin.

This, *that*, and *which* should refer to a specific antecedent.

Vague: The teacher told us that we should study hard for our history exams because they were going to be difficult. <u>This</u> caused all of us to panic.
(What is *this?*)

Clearer: The teacher told us that we should study hard for our history exams because they were going to be difficult. **This information** caused all of us to panic.

> **Avoid Repeating the Subject**
>
> When you clearly mention a subject, do not repeat the subject in pronoun form.
>
> Egypt's pyramids, ~~they~~ are more than 4,000 years old.
>
> The book ~~it~~ is really interesting.

PRACTICE 8

Each sentence has either a vague pronoun or a repeated subject. Correct the errors. You may need to rewrite some sentences.

EXAMPLE:

> *The radio reporter announced*
> ~~They said on the radio~~ that archeologists have discovered a new burial ground along the Yangzte River.

CHAPTER 28

1. Professor Schmitt told Mark that a book about the Great Wall of China is on his desk.

2. It states that the Great Wall of China is more than 2,000 years old.

3. They built the wall to protect the Chinese empire from northern invasions.

4. This also helped unify China.

5. The history book it contains information on the emperor Oin Shi Huang.

6. They say that the emperor ordered construction of the Great Wall.

7. They persecuted anyone who disagreed with the emperor.

8. The book it has many other interesting facts about the Great Wall of China.

9. For example, the wall it is over 1,500 miles in length.

10. They say the only man-made object that can be seen from space is the Great Wall.

Pronoun Shifts

If your writing contains unnecessary shifts in person or number, you may confuse your readers. Carefully edit your writing to ensure that your pronouns are consistent in number and person.

Making Pronouns Consistent in Number

Pronouns and antecedents must agree in **number**. If the antecedent is singular, then the pronoun must be singular. If the antecedent is plural, then the pronoun must be plural.

> singular   *his or her*
> The **director** of the museum encouraged ~~their~~ employees to be on time.

> plural   *they*
> When **tourists** visit an excavation site, ~~he~~ should be careful not to touch the artifacts.

Making Pronouns Consistent in Person

Person is the writer's perspective. In some writing assignments, you may use first person (*I, we*). For other assignments, especially most college and workplace writing, you may use second person (*you*) or third person (*he, she, it, they*).

When you shift your point of view for no reason, your writing may become unclear, and you may confuse your readers. If you begin writing from one point of view, do not shift unnecessarily to another point of view.

> *we*
> If ~~one~~ considered the expenses involved in visiting another country, **we** would probably never travel.

>   *we*
> **We** visited the pyramids at Teotihuacán, but ~~you~~ could not climb one of them because archeologists were working on it.

 **Hint**   **Avoiding Pronoun Shifts in Paragraphs**

Sometimes it is easier to use pronouns consistently in individual sentences than it is in larger paragraphs or essays. When you write paragraphs and essays, always check that your pronouns agree with your antecedents in person and in number. In the next example, the pronouns are consistent in the first two sentences; however, they shift in person in the third sentence.

> **We** went to Mexico City last year. **We** traveled around on the subway to visit
>
> various archeological sites. Sometimes the subway was so crowded that ~~you~~ *we*
>
> could barely move.

PRACTICE 9

Correct eight pronoun shift errors.

EXAMPLE:

> *we*
> We visited the pyramids at Giza, Egypt. The lines were so long that ~~you~~ had to wait for hours.

1. An Egyptian pharaoh built the Great Pyramid as a tomb. All the powerful pharaohs believed that material goods must be buried in their tombs to help you on their journey in the afterlife.

2. Napoleon invaded Egypt in 1798. Napoleon and his soldiers were amazed when they saw the pyramids. After the army invaded Egypt, they returned to France with many artifacts. Napoleon thought that you had the right to take anything from a country that you had invaded.

3. One of Napoleon's soldiers discovered the Rosetta Stone but did not realize the importance of their discovery. In 1801, British soldiers invaded Egypt and found the Rosetta Stone. They took the stone and brought them back to England.

4. When tourists go to the British Museum in London, one may see many antiquities from Egypt. Every year, people go to see the Rosetta Stone because you know it is impressive.

The Writer's Desk **Revise and Edit Your Warm Up**

In the Warm Up at the beginning of the chapter, you described a historical figure whom you admire. Check your paragraph for any problems with pronouns.

REFLECT ON IT

Think about what you have learned in this chapter. If you do not know an answer, review that concept.

1. What is a pronoun? _____

_____

2. Write a sentence that includes an objective pronoun. _____

_____

3. When do you use possessive pronouns (*my, mine, his, hers,* etc.)? _____

_____

4. Circle the best answer: In a sentence, *whom* replaces

   a. the subject.   b. the object

5. What is an antecedent? _____

_____

6. Circle the best answer: Pronouns must agree with their antecedents:

   a. only in number.   b. only in person.

   c. both in number and in person.   d. neither in number nor in person.

FINAL REVIEW

Correct fifteen errors with pronouns in the next paragraphs.

EXAMPLE:

> *A prominent archeologist*
> ~~It~~ says that the dispute between many countries is about cultural property rights.

1.   People learn important things about history by visiting museums filled

with historical artifacts. For example, Britain and France they have

obtained antiquities from countries around the world. The British

government believes in it's right to keep the treasures who are exhibited in

museums. However, countries such as Greece and Egypt want their

treasures back because they view antiquities as a part of its cultural

heritage. Returning antiquities to its native countries is a complicated issue.

2.   The removal of artifacts such as mummies has created an ethical problem

for the Egyptian government and their archeologists. An interesting science article it says that a lot of information can be acquired from the scientific study of burial sites. Although some people believe it is always unethical to dig up the dead, every archeologist who studies Egyptian mummies increases their knowledge of ancient Egypt. For example, centuries ago, the pharaohs believed that they could get to heaven faster if you were buried with food and treasures for the voyage. Each pharoah decided for hisself what he would take on his journey to the afterlife. When a pharaoh died, priests mummified the body and buried them in the pyramids. Therefore, archeologists whom have excavated burial sites not only find mummies, but they find valuable artworks and other artifacts.

3.   They say that the dispute between countries such as Egypt and Britain will not be resolved. They say that international policy should regulate ownership of national treasures. Everybody has their own opinion about the issue.

 The Writer's Room   **Topics for Writing**

Choose one of the following topics and write a paragraph or an essay. Remember to follow the writing process.

1. In the past one hundred years, what events have changed the world? List some events.
2. Tell a story about an ideal vacation. Where would you go, and what would you do? Use descriptive language in your writing.
3. Think about a recent invention. Contrast people's lives before and after that invention.
4. How important is history as a school subject? Should history be a compulsory subject?

The Writers' Circle

Take turns interviewing a partner. Discover at least five interesting things about each other. Then write a paragraph about your partner.

When you have finished, exchange paragraphs with your partner. Proofread your partner's paragraph. Look carefully at nouns, pronouns, and determiners. Discuss any errors that you find.

How Do I Get a Better Grade?

Visit www.mywritinglab.com for audio-visual lectures and additional practice sets about pronouns.
Get a better grade with MyWritingLab!

READING LINK
Great Discoveries
"Nothing but Net" by Mark McFadden (page 564)
"Growing Up in Cyberspace" by Brent Staples (page 566)

CHAPTER 28

Adjectives and Adverbs

Section Theme **HEALTH CARE**

*In this chapter, you will read about topics
related to* health care.

The Writer's Desk Warm Up

Write a short paragraph describing how people can best protect their
health. List several examples in your paragraph.

Adjectives

Adjectives describe nouns (people, places, or things) and pronouns (words that
replace nouns). They add information explaining how many, what kind, or which
one. They also help you appeal to the senses by describing how things look, smell,
feel, taste, and sound.

The **intelligent** woman, Justina Ford, became the first **African American** female in Colorado to be a licensed physician.

Justina Ford delivered more than **seven thousand** babies.

Dr. Ford had to overcome **difficult** obstacles in her career.

Placement of Adjectives

You can place adjectives either before a noun or after a linking verb such as *be, look, appear, smell,* or *become.*

Before the noun: The **young unemployed** man received a scholarship for **medical** school.

After the linking verb: He was **shocked**, but he was **happy**.

PRACTICE I

Underline the adjectives in the next sentences.

EXAMPLE:

About 47 million Americans had no medical insurance in 2005.

1. Self-employed entrepreneurs and small-business owners struggle to get adequate health care.

2. Also, certain groups of elderly Americans cannot afford sufficient, reliable medical treatment.

3. For example, Timothy Evans is disappointed and angry because he cannot afford to see a heart specialist.

4. Furthermore, prescription drug costs are higher in the United States than they are in other countries such as England, Switzerland, Canada, and Sweden.

5. Where the average American citizen pays one dollar for a prescription drug, a British citizen pays only sixty-four cents and a Canadian citizen pays only fifty-seven cents.

CHAPTER 29

6. The average annual profit of the top ten drug companies is over three billion dollars.

7. Drug companies argue that they do groundbreaking research on new drugs.

8. Politicians are trying to come up with decent and fair legislation about health-care issues.

Problems with Adjectives

You can recognize many adjectives by their endings. Be particularly careful when you use the following adjective forms.

Adjectives Ending in -*ful* or -*less*

Some adjectives end in -*ful* or -*less*. Remember that -*ful* ends in one *l* and -*less* ends in double *s*.

> Alexander Fleming, a **skillful** scientist, conducted many **useful** experiments.

> His work appeared in **countless** publications.

Adjectives Ending in -*ed* and -*ing*

Some adjectives look like verbs because they end in -*ing* or -*ed*.

- When the adjective ends in -*ed*, it describes the person's or animal's expression or feeling.

  > The **overworked** and **tired** scientist presented her findings to the public.

- When the adjective ends in -*ing*, it describes the quality of the person or thing.

  > Her **compelling** and **promising** discovery pleased the public.

 **Keep Adjectives in the Singular Form**

Always make an adjective singular, even if the noun following the adjective is plural. In the next example, "year" acts as an adjective.

>   *year*   *other*
> Paul was a nine-~~years~~-old boy when he broke his arm while playing with ~~others~~ children.

PRACTICE 2

Correct eight adjective errors. The adjectives may have the wrong form, or they may be misspelled.

EXAMPLE:

      surprising
Many ~~surprised~~ medical findings happen by accident.

1. One of the world's amazed scientifics discoveries happened by pure chance. Born in 1881, Alexander Fleming was a tireles medical doctor. He worked in his small London clinic where he treated famous people for venereal disease. He also conducted many biologicals experiments.

2. One day in 1928, he put some *Staphylococcus* bacteria in a culture dish. Two weeks later, Fleming, who was a carefull researcher, discovered that a clear ring encircled the yellow-green mold on the dish. A mold spore had flown into the dish from a laboratory on the floor below. At that point, Fleming made an insightfull observation. He had an astounded revelation. He realized that the mold somehow stopped the growth of bacteria in the culture dish.

3. Fleming named the new product penicillin. During World War II, the drug saved millions of lives, and it continues to be used today to treat differents infections.

Adverbs

Adverbs add information to adjectives, verbs, or other adverbs. They give more specific information about how, when, where, and to what extent an action or event occurred.

         verb   adverb

Doctors in ancient Rome performed surgeries **seriously.**

               adverb   adverb

These surgeons could remove cataracts **quite** quickly.

          adverb   adjective

The ancient Romans were **highly** innovative.

Forms of Adverbs

> ⟨*Hint*⟩   **Some Adverbs and Adjectives Have the Same Form**
>
> Some adverbs look exactly like adjectives. The only way to distinguish them from adjectives is to see what they are modifying or describing. The following words can be either adjectives or adverbs.
>
> | early | fast | high | often | right |
> |-------|------|------|-------|-------|
> | far | hard | late | past | soon |
>
>   adjective   adverb
> Dr. Greenbay has a **hard** job. She works **hard.**

Adverbs often end in -*ly*. In fact, you can change many adjectives into adverbs by adding -*ly* endings.

- If you add -*ly* to a word that ends in *l*, then your new word will have a double *l*.

                  scornful + ly
  Many ancient Romans viewed surgeons **scornfully.**

- If you add -*ly* to a word that ends in *e*, keep the *e*. Exceptions to this rule are *truly* and *duly*.

         extreme + ly
  Doctors were **extremely** careful when they operated on patients.

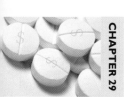

CHAPTER 29

PRACTICE 3

Circle the correct adjectives or adverbs in each sentence.

EXAMPLE:

Many groups (loud, ⟨loudly⟩) debate the subject of euthanasia.

1.   The average life span for human beings has increased (great, greatly) due to advances in medical technology. Yet (certain, certainly) debilitating diseases decrease the quality of life. Therefore, society has to deal (frequent, frequently) with the issue of a patient's right to choose to die. A debate has (rapid, rapidly) developed among medical professionals on the ethics of prolonging the life of people with debilitating diseases. Many people have (strong, strongly) opinions on the subject of euthanasia.

2.   The term *euthanasia* refers to a third party (intentional, intentionally) causing the death of a patient at the patient's request. For example, a doctor removing a life support machine is committing euthanasia. *Assisted suicide* refers to a third party (clear, clearly) helping a patient commit the act of dying. For example, a family member who (knowing, knowingly) supplies a patient with drugs is assisting suicide if the patient takes the (powerful, powerfully) drugs to die. To date, Oregon is the only state that allows people to participate in assisted suicide (legal, legally).

Placement of Frequency Adverbs

Frequency adverbs are words that indicate how often someone performs an action or when an event occurs. Common frequency adverbs are *always, ever, never, often, sometimes,* and *usually.* They can appear at the beginning of sentences, or they can appear in the following locations.

- Place frequency adverbs before regular present tense and past tense verbs.

    Medical doctors **always** <u>recite</u> the Hippocratic oath.

- Place frequency adverbs after all forms of the verb *be (am, is, are, was, were).*

    My patients <u>are</u> **usually** punctual for appointments.

- Place frequency adverbs after helping verbs.

    I <u>have</u> **never** broken any bone in my body.

CHAPTER 29

PRACTICE 4

Correct six errors in the placement of frequency adverbs.

EXAMPLE:

           must sometimes take
Medical students ~~must take sometimes~~ a course on the history of medicine.

1.   Hippocrates was born around 460 B.C. in Greece. Medical professionals claim generally that Hippocrates is the founder of modern medicine. In ancient Greece, physicians thought that a patient's illness usually was due to evil spirits. Hippocrates rejected often such explanations. He believed that there was a connection between good health and a good diet. He often was criticized for his beliefs.

2.   Hippocrates traveled sometimes through Greece teaching medicine. On the island of Cos, Hippocrates founded a school of medicine and also developed his famous oath. To show their respect for Hippocrates, doctors take always the Hippocratic oath before they begin to practice medicine.

Problems with Adverbs

Use the Correct Form

Many times, people use an adjective instead of an adverb after a verb. Ensure that you always modify your verbs using an adverb.

really quickly
Ancient Greek medicine advanced ~~real quick~~ after the time of Homer.

slowly
However, patients recovered very ~~slow~~.

PRACTICE 5

Correct nine errors in adjective and adverb forms.

EXAMPLE:

really
Euthanasia is a ~~realy~~ difficult issue.

CHAPTER 29

1.   People who oppose the "right-to-die" movement argue that many patients who wish for euthanasia may be extremelly depressed. Patients may also have incomplete information about other options such as long-term care and real effective pain control. Opponents of legal euthanasia also suggest that many desperately people could be coerced into committing euthanasia quick.

2.   People who want to legalize euthanasia feel profound that the quality of a person's life is the most important consideration in this debate. They say that if a patient has become severe disabled due to illness, his or her quality of life is drastically reduced. They believe that a patient should have the right to die with dignity if he or she chooses. Proponents of euthanasia have real firm beliefs. They think that laws can prevent abuse or coercion of the patient.

3.	Legislators act slow when it comes to making policy decisions about euthanasia. People on both sides of the issue express their opinions forcefuly. There is no consensus.

Using *Good* and *Well,* *Bad* and *Badly*

Good is an adjective, and *well* is an adverb.

    Adjective: Louis Pasteur had a **good** reputation.

    Adverb: He explained his theories **well.**

    Exception: Use *well* to describe a person's health: I do not feel **well.**

Bad is an adjective, and *badly* is an adverb.

    Adjective: My father has a **bad** cold.

    Adverb: His throat hurts **badly.**

PRACTICE 6

Circle the correct adjectives or adverbs.

EXAMPLE:

Generally, patients who communicate (good, (well)) with their doctors receive ((good), well) advice.

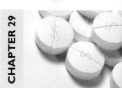

1.	Mary Mallon was feeling (good, well) on the day that she was arrested.

2.	Her (bad, badly) cooked food made many people ill.

3.	The public had some (good, well) luck when authorities found Mary Mallon.

4.	Mallon was accused of having (bad, badly) habits in the kitchen and of spreading typhoid fever through food.

5.	She reacted (bad, badly) to these accusations.

6.	She did not believe that the authorities had (good, well) intentions when they took her to the police station.

CHAPTER 29

7. Although she cooked (good, well), the public health authorities wanted her to stop cooking for others.

8. Mary behaved (bad, badly) and continued to cook for people, so the police forced her to move to an isolated island near the Bronx.

9. She became known as Typhoid Mary and lived in (good, well) conditions in a house on North Brother Island for more than twenty years.

Comparative and Superlative Forms

Use the comparative form to show how two persons, things, or items are different.

Adjectives:	Dr. Jonas Salk was a <u>better</u> researcher than his colleague.
	Dr. Sabin is <u>more famous</u> for his research on the polio virus than Dr. Enders.
Adverbs:	Dr. Salk published his results <u>more quickly</u> than Dr. Drake.
	Dr. Salk debated the issue <u>more passionately</u> than his colleague.

Use the **superlative form** to compare three or more items.

Adjectives:	Dr. Salk was the <u>youngest</u> scientist to receive funding for polio research at the University of Michigan.
	Polio was one of the <u>most destructive</u> diseases of the twentieth century.
Adverbs:	Dr. Parekh talked the <u>most rapidly</u> of all the doctors at the conference.
	She spoke the <u>most effectively</u> of all of the participants.

How to Write Comparative and Superlative Forms

You can write comparative and superlative forms by remembering a few simple guidelines.

Using -er and -est endings

Add -*er* and -*est* endings to one-syllable adjectives and adverbs.

Adjective or Adverb	Comparative	Superlative
tall	tall**er** than	the tall**est**
hard	hard**er** than	the hard**est**
fast	fast**er** than	the fast**est**

Double the last letter when the adjective ends in one vowel + one consonant.

hot	hot**ter** than	the hot**test**

Using *more* and *the most*

Add *more* and *the most* to adjectives and adverbs of two or more syllables.

Adjective or Adverb	Comparative	Superlative
dangerous	**more** dangerous than	**the most** dangerous
effectively	**more** effectively than	**the most** effectively
nervous	**more** nervous than	**the most** nervous

When a two-syllable adjective ends in *y*, change the *y* to *i* and add *-er* or *-est*.

Adjective	Comparative	Superlative
happy	happ**ier** than	the happ**iest**

Using Irregular Comparative and Superlative Forms

Some adjectives and adverbs have unique comparative and superlative forms. Study this list to remember how to form some of the most common ones.

Adjective or Adverb	Comparative	Superlative
good, well	better than	the best
bad, badly	worse than	the worst
some, much, many	more than	the most
little (a small amount)	less than	the least
far	farther, further	the farthest, the furthest

> **GRAMMAR LINK**
>
> *Farther* indicates a physical distance. *Further* means "additional." For more commonly confused words, see Chapter 32.

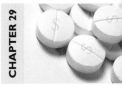

CHAPTER 29

PRACTICE 7

Underline the appropriate comparative or superlative form of the words in parentheses.

EXAMPLE:

Some drug ads are (<u>more</u> / most) effective than others.

1. In the past, there was (less, least) drug research than there is today.

    Anybody could claim to have the (better, best) medicine on the market. For

    example, in the early twentieth century, one of the (more, most) successful

    products was Miss Lydia E. Pinkham's Vegetable Compound. The vial,

    which contained 20 percent alcohol content, promised to cure "female

    complaints." It had (more, most) alcohol than beer, and it was the (more,

    most) popular cure of its era.

2. In 1927, the Food and Drug Administration was formed. The FDA's (more, most) important goal was to regulate drug advertising. Companies could no longer say that their products were (better, best) than the competitors, and they could not claim to have the (less, least) side effects of all medications.

3. Today, drug companies spend billions on advertising. Critics claim that companies spend (more, most) on convincing consumers to buy their products than they do on testing their products. Those who are against drug advertising say that it makes medications (more, most) expensive than they were before. Companies spend billions convincing consumers that their products are the (more, most) effective on the market. Consumers then pressure their doctors to give a certain well-known drug, even if there are (better, best) alternative products. On the other hand, advertisements must list side effects, so in some respects, consumers are (better, best) informed than they were in the past.

CHAPTER 29

PRACTICE 8

Complete the sentences by writing either the comparative or superlative form of the word in parentheses.

EXAMPLE:

Some people have (thin) _____*thinner*_____ bones than others.

1. By about age thirty-five, all adults lose some bone mass. Then, as people age, bone deteriorates (rapidly) _____ than before. With osteoporosis, bones become (brittle) _____ than previously. Some people become (short) _____ than they were in their youth because osteoporosis can cause the vertebra in the back to collapse.

2.   Osteoporosis is much (common) _____ in women

than in men because women have (little) _____ bone

mass than men do. In women, the rate of bone loss is (quick)

_____ after menopause than it is in pre-menopausal

women.

3.   Some in the medical community say that calcium pills are the

(effective) _____ way to slow the onset of the disease.

Yet women from Asian and African nations who consume very little

calcium have much (low) _____ osteoporosis rates

than American women. Osteoporosis is one of the (little)

_____ understood chronic diseases in the world.

Problems with Comparative and Superlative Forms

Using *more* and *-er*

In the comparative form, never use *more* and *-er* to modify the same word. In the superlative form, never use *most* and *-est* to modify the same word.

> ~~~~~~~~~~~~~~~~~~~~~~~~~~~~~~~~~~~~*better*
> Some people thought that Salk's vaccine was ~~more better~~ than Sabin's
> ~~~~~~~~~~~~~~~~~~~~~~~~~~~~~~~~~~~~~~~*best*
> vaccine. The polio vaccine was one of the ~~most best~~ discoveries of our
> times.

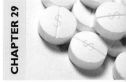

CHAPTER 29

Using *fewer* and *less*

In the comparative form, never use *less* to compare two count nouns. Use *less* to compare two noncount nouns. (Noncount nouns are nouns that cannot be divided, such as *information* and *music*.) Use *fewer* to compare two count nouns.

> ~~~~~~~~~~*fewer*
> Today, ~~less~~ people get vaccinated than in previous decades because
> ~~~~~~*Less*
> some question the safety of certain vaccinations. ~~Fewer~~ information
> about vaccines was available in the 1950s than is available today.

GRAMMAR LINK

For a list of noncount nouns, refer to pages 403–404 in Chapter 27.

> **Using *the* in the Comparative Form**
>
> Although you would usually use *the* in superlative forms, you can use it in some two-part comparatives. In these expressions, the second part is the result of the first part.
>
> action   result
> <u>The more</u> you exercise, <u>the better</u> your health will be.

PRACTICE 9

Correct fifteen adjective and adverb errors.

EXAMPLE:

                      continually
Americans debate ~~continual~~ on the ethics of organ transplants.

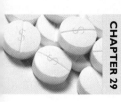

1.   One of the most greatest miracles of modern medicine is organ transplants. Organ transplants save most lives than ever before. With donor organs, many recipients can lead more better lives than previously imagined. However, a public debate about organ transplants is growing rapid.

2.   The source of donor organs is a controversial issue. Given the scarcity of organs, some individuals who need transplants quick have obtained organs through unscrupulous methods. For instance, some have bought organs from the most poorest segments of the population in developing countries. Destitute people sometimes sell their organs to rich buyers because they need money real badly.

3.   Who should receive an organ transplant? Given the scarcity of supply, should a person who smokes heavy or drinks too much receive a lung or liver transplant? Obviously, the more a person smokes, the worst his or her health will be. Should such people be refused access to organ transplants?

4.   In addition, money is an issue in this debate. Hospital administrators are concerned about the high cost of transplants. Less people have

adequate medical insurance than ever before. Should those with health insurance be treated more better than those without? According to most experts, the richest a patient is, the best his or her chances are to receive a transplant.

5.   Waiting for an organ transplant is one of the worse experiences anyone can go through. Hopefully, in future years, the number of people who sign donor cards will be more higher than it is now.

The Writer's Desk **Revise and Edit Your Warm Up**

In the Warm Up at the beginning of this chapter, you wrote a short paragraph about the ways people can protect their health. Check the paragraph for any adjective and adverb errors.

REFLECT ON IT

Think about what you have learned in this unit. If you do not know an answer, review that concept.

1. What is an adjective? _____

   _____

2. What is an adverb? _____

   _____

3. Write the correct adjective or adverb in each blank.

   a. My doctor treats her patients (good, well) _____. She is one of the (better, best) _____ eye surgeons in Berlin.

   b. My brother has (less, fewer) _____ work experience than I do, but he also has (less, fewer) _____ responsibilities.

4. The following sentences contain adjective or adverb errors. Correct each mistake.

   a. We had a real nice time at the medical conference.

   b. Everyone was dressed casual.

   c. My sister changes often her mind about her career.

   d. The advancing medical textbook is my sister's.

FINAL REVIEW

Underline and correct twenty errors in adjectives and adverbs.

1.   Health care is one of the most fastest growing fields in the world. In our nation, the aging population is making the demand for nurses more and more intenser. According to *Health Affairs*, an online magazine, there is an acute nursing shortage. Less people enter the nursing profession than in the past. In fact, the number of people in their early twenties entering the nursing profession is at its lower point in forty years. The shortage is worldwide. Canada, England, and many other nations have a more greater shortage than the United States has. As a possible career, more people should consider the nursing profession.

2.   First, nurses have a greater responsibility and more diversely role than most people realize. In states such as California, nurses can write prescriptions and nurse midwives can deliver babies. Forensic nurses treat traumatizing victims of violent crime. Furthermore, hospitals are not the only places where nurses can work. Nursing jobs are available in walk-in clinics, schools, vacation resorts, and medical equipment firms. Even film studios hire sometimes on-set nurses.

3.   Also, nursing can be an extreme rewarding career. Joan Bowes, a nurse in Oregon, says that she feels as if she is doing something usefull each day. Occasionally, her actions help to save lives. Last month, a young patient who had been injured really bad was admitted to the hospital where Joan works. A few days later, Joan noticed that the patient was unable to move his head as easy as before. She quick alerted a specialist who then diagnosed a meningitis infection. Joan's observation helped to save the patient's life. Joan's husband Keith is a home-care nurse. He is compassionate, and he interacts good with his patients. As one of a growing number of men in the

profession, Keith feels that entering nursing was the better decision he has
ever made.

4.   Nurses are more better compensated than in the past. In the 1970s,
salaries for nurses were much worst than they are today. In fact, nurses
were paid the less among health care professionals. Nowadays, because
nurses are in such high demand, many hospitals give signing bonuses,
decent schedules, and real good salaries.

5.   Potential nurses should enjoy helping people. For those who want to
have a rewarding career with decent benefits, nursing is an excellent career
choice. The more society appreciates nurses, the best health care will be.

How Do I Get a Better Grade?

Visit www.mywritinglab.com for audio-visual lectures
and additional practice sets about adjectives and adverbs.
Get a better grade with MyWritingLab!

CHAPTER 30

Mistakes with Modifiers

Section Theme **HEALTH CARE**

In this chapter, you will read about topics related to alternative medicine.

The Writer's Desk Warm Up

Would you ever consult an acupuncturist, a homeopath, or any other alternative healing practitioner? Why or why not? Write a paragraph about your attitude toward alternative medicine.

Misplaced Modifiers

A **modifier** is a word, phrase, or clause that describes or modifies nouns or verbs in a sentence. For example, *holding the patient's hand* is a modifier. To use a modifier correctly, place it next to the word(s) that you want to modify.

modifier   words that are modified

<u>Holding the patient's hand</u>, **the doctor** explained the procedure.

A **misplaced modifier** is a word, phrase, or clause that is not placed next to the word it modifies. When a modifier is too far from the word that it is describing, then the meaning of the sentence can become confusing or unintentionally funny.

> I saw a pamphlet about acupuncture sitting in the doctor's office.
> (How could a pamphlet sit in a doctor's office?)

Commonly Misplaced Modifiers

As you read the sample sentences for each type of modifier, notice how the meaning of the sentence changes depending on where the modifier is placed. In the examples, the modifiers are underlined.

Prepositional Phrase Modifiers

A prepositional phrase is made of a preposition and its object.

Confusing: Cora read an article on acupuncture written by reporter James Reston <u>in a café.</u>
(Who was in the café: James or Cora?)

Clear: <u>In a café</u>, Cora read an article on acupuncture written by reporter James Reston.

Present Participle Modifiers

A present participle modifier is a phrase that begins with an *-ing* verb.

Confusing: James Reston learned about acupuncture <u>touring China.</u>
(Can acupuncture tour China?)

Clear: While <u>touring China,</u> James Reston learned about acupuncture.

Past Participle Modifiers

A past participle modifier is a phrase that begins with a past participle (*walked, gone, known*, and so on).

Confusing: <u>Called meridians,</u> acupuncturists claim there are two thousand pathways on the body.
(What are called meridians: the acupuncturists or the pathways?)

Clear: Acupuncturists claim there are two thousand pathways <u>called meridians</u> on the body.

Limiting Modifiers

Limiting modifiers are words such as *almost, nearly, only, merely, just,* and *even.* In the examples, notice how the placement of *almost* changes the meaning.

> **Almost** all of the doctors went to the lecture that disproved acupuncture.
> (Some of the doctors did not attend, but most did.)

> All of the doctors **almost** went to the lecture that disproved acupuncture.
> (The doctors did not go.)

All of the doctors went to the lecture that **almost** disproved acupuncture.
(The lecture did not disprove acupuncture.)

 Other Types of Modifiers

There are many other types of modifiers. For example, some modifiers begin with relative clauses and some are appositives.

Relative Clause

Confusing:	The treatments involved acupuncture needles <u>that were expensive</u>.
	(What was expensive: the treatment or the needles?)
Clear:	The treatments <u>that were expensive</u> involved acupuncture needles.

Appositive

Confusing:	<u>A very sick man</u>, Monica helped her uncle find a doctor.
	(How could Monica be a very sick man?)
Clear:	Monica helped her uncle, <u>a very sick man</u>, find a doctor.

PRACTICE I

Circle the letter of the correct sentence in each pair. Underline the misplaced modifier in each incorrect sentence.

EXAMPLE:

   a. Simon Weiss learned about acupuncture <u>with enthusiasm</u>.

   (b.) With enthusiasm, Simon Weiss learned about acupuncture.

1. a. Simon read about acupuncture, which is based on an ancient philosophy.
    b. Based on an ancient philosophy, Simon read about acupuncture.

2. a. By licensed practitioners, many U.S. states allow acupuncture to be performed.
    b. Acupuncture can be performed by licensed practitioners in many U.S. states.

3. a. Only seventeen states allow acupuncturists to practice without medical supervision.
    b. Seventeen states only allow acupuncturists to practice without medical supervision.

4. a. In a hurry, Simon asked for information about acupuncture.
    b. Simon asked for information about acupuncture in a hurry.

5. a. Needing treatment, Mr. Lo examined the patient.
    b. Mr. Lo examined the patient needing treatment.

6. a. Faced with chronic headaches, Mr. Lo was prepared to treat Simon.
    b. Faced with chronic headaches, Simon was prepared to try Mr. Lo's treatment.

7. a. Carefully guiding the needles, Mr. Lo gently pierced Simon's skin.

   b. Carefully guiding the needles, Simon's skin was gently pierced by Mr. Lo.

8. a. Mr. Lo treated Simon wearing a mask.

   b. Wearing a mask, Mr. Lo treated Simon.

 Correcting Misplaced Modifiers

To correct misplaced modifiers, do the following:

- Identify the modifier.
  Manuel saw the accident <u>walking past the hotel.</u>
- Identify the word or words that are being modified.
  Who walked past the hotel? **Manuel**
- Move the modifier next to the word(s) being modified.
  <u>Walking past the hotel,</u> **Manuel** saw the accident.

PRACTICE 2

Underline the misplaced modifiers in the following sentences. Then, rewrite the sentences. You may have to add or remove words to give the sentence a logical meaning.

EXAMPLE:

<u>Acting recklessly,</u> the motorcycle was driven too quickly by the young man.

Acting recklessly, the young man drove the motorcycle too quickly.

1. In a wheelchair, the nurse sat near the patient.

2. The patient took the medication with red hair.

3. Ross was a teenager with a cast on his leg weighing 120 pounds.

4. Dr. Zimboro talked to Ross carrying a medical chart.

5. Not wearing a helmet, the accident could have killed the young man.

6. By all motorcyclists, many medical professionals believe that helmets should be worn.

   _____

   _____

7. Citing freedom of expression, a fight against helmet laws is being proposed by cycling enthusiasts.

   _____

   _____

8. Scared of having another accident, the motorcycle will not be driven again by Ross.

   _____

   _____

Dangling Modifiers

A **dangling modifier** opens a sentence but does not modify any words in the sentence. It "dangles" or hangs loosely because it is not connected to any other part of the sentence.

To avoid having a dangling modifier, make sure that the modifier and the first noun that follows it have a logical connection.

Confusing: While talking on a cell phone, the ambulance drove off the road.

(Can an ambulance talk on a cell phone?)

Clear: While talking on a cell phone, the ambulance **technician** drove off the road.

Confusing: To get into medical school, high grades are necessary.

(Can high grades get into a school?)

Clear: To get into medical school, **students** need high grades.

PRACTICE 3

Read each pair of sentences. Circle the letter of each correct sentence.

EXAMPLE:

   a. Having taken a pill, the results were surprising.

   (b.) Having taken a pill, I was surprised by the results.

1. a. With the patient's budget in mind, the least expensive drugs were prescribed.
   b. With the patient's budget in mind, the doctor prescribed the least expensive drugs.

2. a. Believing in their effects, placebos are often given to patients.
   b. Believing in their effects, Doctor Zimboro sometimes gives placebos to patients.

3. a. After taking a sugar pill, patients often feel relieved.

   b. After taking a sugar pill, there is often a feeling of relief.

4. a. Surprised, the word *placebo* means "to please."

   b. Surprised, I read that the word *placebo* means "to please."

5. a. Thinking about the mind-body relationship, scientist Esther Sternberg conducted an experiment.

   b. Thinking about the mind-body relationship, an experiment was conducted.

6. a. Frustrated, Sternberg's temptation was to give up.

   b. Frustrated, Sternberg was tempted to give up.

7. a. Using laboratory rats, Sternberg discovered a link between the mind and body.

   b. Using laboratory rats, a link was discovered between the mind and body.

8. a. Given an antidepressant, the arthritis disappeared.

   b. Given an antidepressant, some rats no longer had arthritis.

9. a. Excited about her discovery, Sternberg wrote an article for a medical journal.

   b. Excited about her discovery, an article was written for a medical journal.

 Correcting Dangling Modifiers

To correct dangling modifiers, do the following:

- Identify the modifier.

    While dieting, self-control is necessary.

- Decide who or what the writer aims to modify.

    Whose self-control is necessary? **People's**

- Add the missing subject (and in some cases, also add or remove words) so that the sentence makes sense.

    While dieting, **people** need to have self-control.

PRACTICE 4

In each sentence, underline the dangling modifier. Then rewrite each sentence, adding or removing words to provide a logical meaning.

EXAMPLE:

Worried about their weight, a lot of diet books are bought.

Worried about their weight, Americans buy a lot of diet books.

1. When dieting, obsessing about food is common.

_____

_____

2. To buy that diet book, $13.95 is required.

_____

_____

3. The chicken was roasting while reading my diet book.

_____

_____

4. Not eating any bread, rice, or pasta, weight fell off easily.

_____

_____

5. Feeling skeptical, the benefits of a meat-based diet are questioned.

_____

_____

6. Indulging in fatty foods, heart problems can occur.

_____

_____

7. Working with celebrities, diet books are promoted on television.

_____

_____

8. When uncertain about which diet to follow, the advice of a nutritionist can be helpful.

_____

_____

CHAPTER 30

PRACTICE 5

Some sentences in this practice have dangling or misplaced modifiers. Write *M* next to misplaced modifiers, *D* next to dangling modifiers, and *C* next to correct sentences. If the modifier is misplaced, move it. If the modifier is dangling, add words to make the sentence complete.

EXAMPLE:

                          people try different therapies.
Hoping to live a long life, ~~different therapies are tried.~~   *D*

1. Called Ayurveda therapy, ancient Indians developed a school

   of medicine.   _____

2. Originally written on palm leaves, researchers found

   2,000-year-old texts.   _____

3. Possibly causing diseases, Ayurvedic medicine teaches about

   an imbalance in mental and physical energies. _____

4. Ayurvedic medicine is widely followed by people in India. _____

5. Doing meditation and yoga, essential parts of this alternative

   therapy are learned. _____

6. Dr. Shah spoke about traditional Indian medicine in a state

   of excitement. _____

7. Called homeopathy, India has produced a therapy that uses

   plants, animals, and minerals to cure a patient's illness. _____

8. Later, a German doctor organized the rules of homeopathic

   treatment wearing glasses. _____

9. In the 1800s, homeopathy became popular in the United States. _____

10. Feeling skeptical, the merits of homeopathy are questioned. _____

11. In fact, many conventionally trained doctors do not believe

    in alternative medical therapies. _____

12. Having tried many different therapies, the effectiveness

    of the treatments were discussed. _____

CHAPTER 30

The Writer's Desk Revise and Edit Your Warm Up

In the Warm Up at the beginning of the chapter, you wrote a short
paragraph about your attitude toward alternative health care. Edit the
paragraph. Identify any modifiers and ensure that they are not dangling
or misplaced. Then correct any modifier errors.

REFLECT ON IT

Think about what you have learned in this unit. If you do not know an answer, review that concept.

1. What is a modifier? _____

_____

2. What is a misplaced modifier? _____

_____

3. What is a dangling modifier? _____

_____

4. What type of modifier error is in each sentence? Write *M* for "misplaced" and *D* for "dangling." Then correct the sentence.

a. Overeating, a weight problem was developed.

_____

b. The doctor examined the X-ray in the lab coat.

_____

CHAPTER 30

FINAL REVIEW

Underline ten dangling or misplaced modifier errors in the next selection. Then, correct each error. You may need to add or remove words to ensure that the sentence makes sense.

EXAMPLE:

young girl got a surprising result.
Working on her school project, a ~~surprising result occurred.~~

1.   There are many fraudulent claims in alternative medicine. In fact, feeling desperate, fortunes are spent on suspect therapies. It is difficult for members of the public to determine which therapies are valid and which are pure quackery. At an important medical conference, some doctors discussed healing touch eating lunch together. In recent years, critics have attacked healing touch therapy.

2.   Based on several ancient healing practices, Dolores Krieger developed therapeutic touch therapy. According to touch therapists, a skilled practitioner can pass his or her hands over a patient's body and remove

obstacles in the energy field. Using the method all over the United States, therapeutic touch is actively promoted.

3.   Named Emily Rosa, an experiment at school was conducted by a nine-year-old girl. In 1998, Emily tested twenty-one therapeutic touch practitioners wearing a school uniform. A therapist would place both hands, palms facing up, on the table. A screen prevented the therapist from seeing Emily. Emily then placed her own hand over one of the therapist's hands. Emily asked the therapist which hand was nearest to her own. Unable to see Emily, the guesses were correct only 44 percent of the time.

4.   Emily's results were published in the *Journal of the American Medical Association*. Emily's parents proudly read the article drinking coffee. Dr. George D. Lundberg believes that therapeutic touch practitioners should disclose the results of Emily's experiment to patients. However, those in the therapeutic touch community criticize the experiment feeling angry. They believe that Emily was too healthy for the experiment to work. They also feel that there were too few practitioners in the experiment. Rejecting the results, therapeutic touch continues to be popular.

CHAPTER 30

 The Writer's Room Topics for Writing

Choose one of the following topics and write a paragraph or an essay. Remember to follow the writing process.

1. Have you ever been to an acupuncturist, a massage therapist, a naturopath, a homeopath, or any other alternative healing practitioner? Describe the treatment that you received.

2. Do you have a scar, or have you ever had an accident? Explain what happened.

3. Right now, millions of Americans are uninsured for medical care. Should the government provide health care for all citizens, just as Canada and many European nations do? Why or why not?

4. Should terminally ill patients have the right to die? What are the possible problems if euthanasia is legalized? Write about euthanasia.

 The Writers' Circle

Work with a group of students on the following activity.

READING LINK

Health Care

"Bound Feet" by Jung Chang (page 548)

"Dancing with Fear" by Bebe Moore Campbell (page 556)

"Dying to Be Bigger" by H.D. (page 573)

"Control Your Temper" by Elizabeth Passarella (page 583)

STEP 1   Write down adjectives, adverbs, and phrases that describe the following people.

> **EXAMPLE:**   A good boss: <u>*honest, listens well, supportive*</u>
>
> a. A good doctor: _____
>
> _____
>
> b. A bad doctor: _____
>
> _____

STEP 2   Rank the qualities from most important to least important.

STEP 3   As a team, write a paragraph about doctors. Compare the good with the bad.

STEP 4   When you finish writing, edit your paragraph and ensure that you have written all the adjectives and adverbs correctly.

CHAPTER 30

How Do I Get a Better Grade?

Visit www.mywritinglab.com for audio-visual lectures and additional practice sets about mistakes with modifiers. ***Get a better grade with MyWritingLab!***

Exact Language

Section Theme **THE LEGAL WORLD**

In this chapter, you will read about topics related to crimes and criminals.

The Writer's Desk Warm Up

Write a paragraph that summarizes the events of a well-known crime. Describe what happened.

Use Specific and Detailed Vocabulary

Great writing evokes an emotional response from the reader. Great writers not only use correct grammatical structures, but they also infuse their writing with precise and vivid details that make their work come alive.

When you proofread your work, revise words that are too vague. **Vague words** lack precision and detail. For example, the words *nice* and *bad* are vague. Readers cannot get a clear picture from them.

Compare the following sets of sentences.

Vague: The movie was bad.

Precise: The crime drama contained violent, gory scenes.

Vague: Our instructor told us about the death of Julius Caesar.

Precise: Our history instructor, Dr. London, recounted how Julius Caesar was murdered in 44 B.C.

Creating Vivid Language

When you choose the precise word, you convey your meaning exactly. Moreover, you can make your writing clearer and more impressive by using specific and detailed vocabulary. To create vivid language, try the following strategies.

- **Modify your nouns.** If your noun is vague, make it more specific by adding one or more adjectives. You could also rename the noun with a more specific term.

    Vague: the man

    Vivid: the shopkeeper   the thin, nervous soldier

- **Modify your verbs.** Use more vivid and precise verbs. You could also use adverbs.

    Vague: walk

    Vivid: saunter   stroll   march briskly

- **Include more details.** Add detailed information to make the sentence more complete.

    Vague: Several signs foretold of Caesar's murder.

    Precise: Several ominous signs, such as Caesar's horses getting loose and a soothsayer's warning, foretold of Caesar's impending death.

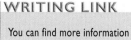

WRITING LINK

You can find more information about appealing to the five senses in Chapter 6, "Description."

CHAPTER 31

 Use Imagery

You can make your writing come alive by using **imagery,** which is description using the five senses: sight, sound, smell, touch, and taste. In the examples, the underlined words add details to the sentence and contribute to a more exact description.

The <u>one-eyed</u>, <u>scar-faced</u> pirate <u>jabbed</u> his sword at the <u>frightened</u> crew.

PRACTICE I

Replace the familiar words in parentheses with more vivid words or phrases, and add more specific details. Use your dictionary or thesaurus if you need help.

EXAMPLE:

Graffiti artists (write) *scrawl words and pictures* on walls.

1. Many cities spend a lot of money (cleaning) _____

   _____ graffiti.

2. (Youths) _____ spray paint on many (places)

   _____

3. They worry about getting caught by (someone) _____

   _____

4. Some cities permit graffiti artists to paint on (certain locations) _____

   _____

5. Sometimes graffiti artists use (bad words) _____

   _____

6. Governments could combat the problem (with many solutions) _____

   _____

7. Some people think graffiti artists should be (treated harshly) _____

   _____

PRACTICE 2

Underline all the words in the paragraph that add vivid details to the description.

EXAMPLE:

The <u>tappity-tap-tap</u> and the <u>thin bell</u> and <u>muffled whir</u> of Effie Perine's typewriting came through the <u>closed</u> door.

Somewhere in a neighboring office a power-driven machine vibrated dully. On Spade's desk a limp cigarette smoldered in a brass tray filled with the remains of limp cigarettes. Ragged gray flakes of cigarette-ash dotted the yellow top of the desk and the green blotter and the papers that were there. A buff-curtained window, eight or ten inches open, let in from the court a current of air faintly scented with ammonia. The ashes on the desk twitched and crawled in the current.

—Dashiell Hammett, *The Maltese Falcon*

 **Adding Appositives**

An appositive is a word or phrase that gives further information about a noun or pronoun. You can write sentences that are more exact and detailed by adding appositives.

appositive   appositive
Sherlock Holmes, <u>the famous detective</u>, was helped by his friend, <u>Dr. Watson</u>.

Avoid Wordiness and Redundancy

Sometimes students fill their writing assignments with extra words to meet length requirements. However, good ideas can get easily lost in work that is too wordy. Also, if the explanations are unnecessarily long, then writing becomes boring.

To improve your writing style, use only as many words or phrases as you need to fully explain your ideas.

> The police department was a distance of two blocks from the municipal library.
>
> (A block is a measure of a distance, so it is unnecessary to repeat that information.)

Correcting Wordiness

You can cut the number of words needed to express an idea by substituting a wordy phrase with a single word. You could also remove the wordy phrase completely.

> *Because*
> ~~By virtue of the fact that~~ we did a survey, we found that most young college students do not study criminology.

Some Common Wordy Expressions and Substitutions

Wordy	Better	Wordy	Better
at that point in time	then, at that time	gave the appearance of	looked like
big, small in size	big, small	great, few in number	great, few
in close proximity	close *or* in proximity	in order to	to
a difficult dilemma	a dilemma	in spite of the fact	in spite of
due to the fact	because	in the final analysis	finally, lastly
equally as good as	as good as	period of time	period
exactly the same	the same	past history	past *or* history
exceptions to the rule	exceptions	return again	return
final completion	end	still remain	remain
for the purpose of	for	a true fact	a fact

CHAPTER 31

PRACTICE 3

In the next sentences, cross out all unnecessary words or phrases, or modify any repeated words.

EXAMPLE:

> *many*
> In 1970, ~~a great number of~~ people were interested in Charles Manson's trial.

1. In 1969, Los Angeles citizens were terrified due to the fact that a killer was in their midst.

2. At that point in time, nobody knew why innocent people were being murdered.

3. Eventually, the crimes were traced to a gang living in close proximity to Los Angeles.

4. Although Manson's gang was small in size, it was very dangerous.

5. The group of killers gave the appearance of being young and carefree hippies.

6. At the final completion of Manson's trial, he was sentenced to death.

7. In 1972, judges on the California Supreme Court faced a difficult dilemma, and they voted to abolish the death penalty.

8. There were no exceptions to the rule, so Manson's sentence was changed to life in prison.

9. In spite of the fact that his crimes were horrific, Manson has become famous.

10. Manson and some of his gang members still remain in a California prison.

Avoid Clichés

Clichés are overused expressions. Because they are overused, they lose their power and become boring. You should avoid using clichés in your writing.

> She was <u>as busy as a bee</u>.
> Local businesses had to <u>cough up</u> money.

Some Common Clichés

a drop in the bucket	easier said than done
as light as a feather	keep your eyes peeled
as luck would have it	last but not least
axe to grind	top dog
between a rock and a hard place	tried and true
break the ice	under the weather
calm, cool, and collected	work like a dog

Correcting Clichés

When you modify a cliché, you can change it into a direct term. You might also try playing with language to come up with a more interesting description.

Cliché:	She was as busy as a bee.
Direct language:	She was extremely busy.
Interesting description:	She was as busy as an emergency room nurse.

PRACTICE 4

Cross out ten clichéd expressions, and then replace them with fresh or direct language.

EXAMPLE:

deal with

Police forces have to ~~bear the burden of~~ organized criminal groups.

1.   The American Mafia, also known as the Cosa Nostra, flourished during the years of Prohibition. Criminals hustled and bustled to meet a demand for alcohol and other illegal services such as prostitution. As Prohibition progressed, Mafia members kept their noses to the grindstone to provide services in cities such as Chicago and Detroit. Law-enforcement agents kept their eyes peeled and tried to stop the Mafia's criminal activities, but that was easier said than done.

2.   According to Frank Schmalleger in his book *Criminal Justice Today*, the Cosa Nostra has twenty-four families in the United States. Their illegal revenue is estimated to be $60 billion a year, which provides them with the finer things in life. Each Cosa Nostra family is based on a pyramid-shaped model of authority. The top dog is the Godfather. Under the Godfather, there are lieutenants and, last but not least, soldiers. Soldiers are Mafia members who do the criminal activities.

3.   Currently, authorities have arrested many crime bosses, but that is just a drop in the bucket. Other gangs such as the Russian mafia are gaining influence and power in the blink of an eye. The police are now working like dogs to investigate criminal organizations that are made up of many different ethnic groups.

CHAPTER 31

Standard English Versus Slang

Most of your instructors will want you to write using **standard American English.** The word *standard* does not imply "better." Standard American English is the common language generally used and expected in schools, businesses, and government institutions in the United States.

Slang is nonstandard language. It is used in informal situations to communicate common cultural knowledge. In any academic or professional context, do not use slang.

Slang:	My friends and I <u>hang</u> together. Last weekend, we watched a movie that was <u>kinda weird but also pretty sweet</u>. It was called *The Untouchables*, and it was about the Mafia during Prohibition.
Standard American English:	My friends and I <u>spend a lot of time</u> together. Last weekend, we watched a movie that was <u>unusual but fascinating</u>. It was called *The Untouchables*, and it was about the Mafia during Prohibition.

 Do Not Use Slang in Academic Writing

Slang is very informal and should be avoided in academic writing. Keep in mind that slang changes depending on generational, regional, cultural, and historical influences. For example, rather than saying "I have to *leave*," people in one group might say *scram* or *split* while those in another group might say *bail* or *bounce*. Avoid using slang expressions in your writing because they can change very quickly—so quickly, in fact, that you might remark that this textbook's examples of slang are "lame."

PRACTICE 5

Substitute the underlined slang expressions with the best possible choice in standard American English.

EXAMPLE:

Every day, <u>the cops</u> deal with gangs.   *police officers*

1. Gang members can be <u>guys or chicks</u>.   _____

2. Some young people think that gangs are <u>cool</u>.   _____

3. It takes a lot of <u>guts</u> to refuse to join a gang.   _____

4. Someone may join a gang because he or she

   does not want to look <u>like a wimp</u>.   _____

5. Others join gangs because they want to

   earn <u>megabucks</u>.   _____

CHAPTER 31

6. Sometimes people <u>hang</u> with gangs because they feel more protected.   _____

7. It is <u>dicey</u> to be in a gang.   _____

8. Police try to <u>keep their cool</u> when they deal with gangs.   _____

9. Gang members are often on the lookout for <u>narcs</u>.   _____

10. Many gang members end up in <u>the joint</u>.   _____

The Writer's Desk Revise and Edit Your Warm Up

In the Warm Up at the beginning of this chapter, you wrote a few sentences about a well-known crime. Revise and edit your sentences. Identify and correct vagueness, wordiness, overused expressions, and slang.

REFLECT ON IT

Think about what you have learned in this unit. If you do not know an answer, review that concept.

1. What is vivid language? _____

_____

2. Why should you add details to your writing? _____

_____

3. Edit the following sentences for wordiness and redundancy. Cross out any unnecessary phrases or modify them to make them more concise.

a. The suspect lived in close proximity to the bank that he had robbed.

b. Hakim wrote the final completion of his paper on *The Great Train Robbery*.

4. Edit the following sentences for clichés and overused expressions. Replace the clichés with your own words.

a. Peter will be in for a rude awakening if he does not study for his law-enforcement exams.

b. Peter is feeling under the weather today.

5. Edit the following sentences for slang. Replace the slang words with standard American English.

a. Replacing the contents of a stolen wallet is such a drag.

b. I read a cool biography about Al Capone.

FINAL REVIEW

Edit the following paragraphs for slang, clichés, and vague language.

Part A

In the next paragraph, five vague words are underlined. Replace these words with specific details to make the paragraph more interesting. Also correct three wordy expressions.

EXAMPLE:

     flamboyant criminal
The ~~man~~ convinced wealthy victims to part with their money.

1.   Christopher Rocancourt is a con artist. Small in size, Rocancourt was the son of an alcoholic house painter and a teenage prostitute. He lived in an orphanage, and then he was adopted at age twelve. Perhaps, as a result of the fact that he grew up in poverty, Rocancourt decided to reinvent himself. He has pretended to be a venture capitalist, the son of a movie director, and a boxing champion. For over fifteen years, he has managed to steal money from rich <u>people</u> in Hollywood and elsewhere. He says that he simply wanted to have a <u>better</u> life. Rocancourt claims his life has been <u>interesting</u>. He spent the past few years <u>running</u> from authorities. At this point in time, <u>he</u> is in prison.

Part B

Replace twelve slang or clichéd expressions.

EXAMPLE:

                   a skilled manipulator
Christopher Rocancourt is <u>a strange dude.</u>

2.   While in Hollywood, Rocancourt stayed in the Beverly Wilshire Hotel. He managed to pull the wool over many people's eyes. Some actors knew him

as Christopher De Laurentiis, the nephew of filmmaker Dino De Laurentiis. To others, he was Christopher de la Renta, nephew of fashion designer Oscar de la Renta. He claimed to be friends with Robert De Niro, Jean-Claude Van Damme, and the Sultan of Brunei. Posing as an investor, he persuaded his wealthy friends to give him tons of dough. Promising to triple or quadruple their money, he easily messed with people's heads. Rocancourt earned millions with his cons. When his wealthy friends learned the truth about him, they were blown away. Today, a lot of his former friends have an axe to grind with Christopher Rocancourt.

3.   Nowadays, the con artist is surprisingly unrepentant. While rapping with a journalist from CBS News, Rocancourt said that he is not a thief. He claims that he simply borrows from friends, and then he doesn't repay them. Certainly, he is a slick piece of work who preys on people who are as dumb as doorknobs. Most of his victims wanted to turn a quick buck, and he was happy to let them believe that they could benefit from his financial expertise. Nowadays, those victims are understandably bummed. It will be a cold day in hell before any of the wealthy friends recoup their money. Rocancourt's sweet gig, which included driving Hummers, dating wealthy women, and befriending millionaires, seems to be over.

CHAPTER 31

How Do I Get a Better Grade?

Visit www.mywritinglab.com for audio-visual lectures and additional practice sets about exact language.
Get a better grade with MyWritingLab!

Spelling and Commonly Confused Words

Section Theme **THE LEGAL WORLD**

In this chapter, you will read about topics related to controversial crimes.

The Writer's Desk Warm Up

Do you think that celebrities who commit crimes are treated differently than regular people? Write a paragraph expressing your opinion about celebrity criminals.

Spelling Rules

It is important to spell correctly. Spelling mistakes can detract from good ideas in your work. You can become a better speller if you always proofread your written work and if you check a dictionary for the meaning and spelling of words about which you are unsure. To help you improve your spelling, here are some spelling rules.

READING LINK
For more information about using a dictionary, see pages 544–545 in Part V, "Reading Strategies" (Chapter 37).

 **Using a Dictionary**

If you are unsure about the spelling or meaning of a word, consult a dictionary. Try to use a recent edition. Also, get to know the features of your dictionary.

Writing *ie* or *ei*

Remember the following rule so that you know when to use *ie* or *ei*. Write *i* before *e* except after *c* or when *ei* is pronounced *ay*, as in *neighbor* and *weigh*.

i before e:	achieve	believe	friend	
ei after c:	ceiling	conceive	perceive	
ei pronounced *ay*:	beige	vein	weigh	

Exceptions:	efficient	either	foreigner	height
	leisure	neither	science	seize
	society	species	their	weird

PRACTICE I

Circle the correct spelling of each word.

EXAMPLE:

   recieve/(receive)

1. decieve/deceive
2. foreigner/foriegner
3. grief/greif
4. hieght/height
5. vien/vein
6. science/sceince

7. efficient/efficeint
8. theif/thief
9. deciet/deceit
10. chief/cheif
11. wieght/weight
12. sufficeint/sufficient

CHAPTER 32

Adding Prefixes and Suffixes

A **prefix** is added to the beginning of a word, and it changes the word's meaning. For example, *con-*, *dis-*, *pre-*, *un-*, and *il-* are prefixes. A **suffix** is added to the ending of a word, and it changes the word's tense or meaning. For example, *-ly*, *-ment*, *-ed*, and *-ing* are suffixes.

When you add a prefix to a word, keep the last letter of the prefix and the first letter of the main word.

   u**n** + **n**atural = u**nn**atural   di**s** + **s**atisfaction = di**ss**atisfaction

When you add the suffix *-ly* to words that end in *l*, keep the *l* of the root word. The new word will have two *l*'s.

   persona**l** + **l**y = persona**ll**y   actua**l** + **l**y = actua**ll**y

 **Words Ending in -ful**

Although the word *full* ends in two *l*'s, when *-ful* is added to another word as a suffix, it ends in one *l*.

careful   successful   hopeful

Notice the unusual spelling when *full* and *fill* are combined: fulfill.

PRACTICE 2

Read the following words and decide if they are correctly spelled. If the word is correct, write *C* in the space provided. If the word is incorrect, write the correct word in the space.

EXAMPLES:

factualy   *factually*＿＿＿＿   untrue   *C*＿＿＿＿＿

1. naturally ＿＿＿＿＿＿   7. beautifull ＿＿＿＿＿＿

2. ilogical ＿＿＿＿＿＿   8. iresponsible ＿＿＿＿＿

3. continually ＿＿＿＿＿   9. unusual ＿＿＿＿＿＿

4. imoral ＿＿＿＿＿＿   10. carefuly ＿＿＿＿＿＿

5. unecessary ＿＿＿＿＿   11. fataly ＿＿＿＿＿＿

6. mispell ＿＿＿＿＿＿   12. fulfilled ＿＿＿＿＿＿

Adding -s or -es

Add *-s* to nouns and to present tense verbs that are third-person singular. However, add *-es* to words in the following situations.

- When words end in *s*, *sh*, *ss*, *ch*, or *x*, add *-es*.

    Noun: church–church**es**   **Verb:** fix–fix**es**

- When words end with the consonant *y*, change the *y* to *i* and add *-es*.

    Noun: berry–berr**ies**   **Verb:** marry–marr**ies**

- When words end in *o*, add *-es* in most cases.

    Noun: hero–hero**es**   **Verb:** do–do**es**

    Exceptions: piano–piano**s**; radio–radio**s**; logo–logo**s**; patio–patio**s**.

- When words end in *f* or *fe*, change the *f* to *v* and add *-es*.

    leaf–lea**ves**   knife–kni**ves**

    Exceptions: belief–belief**s**; roof–roof**s**.

PRACTICE 3

Add *-s* or *-es* to each word. Write the new word in the space provided.

EXAMPLE:

reach   *reaches*＿＿＿＿＿＿＿＿

1. hero _____   7. potato _____

2. crutch _____   8. candy _____

3. fix _____   9. miss _____

4. echo _____   10. fly _____

5. carry _____   11. teach _____

6. dish _____   12. scarf _____

Adding Suffixes to Words Ending in -e

When you add a suffix to a word ending in *e*, make sure that you follow the next rules.

- If the suffix begins with a vowel, drop the *e* on the main word. Some common suffixes beginning with vowels are *-ed, -er, -est, -ing, -able, -ent,* and *-ist*.

    hope–hop**ing**   encourage–encourag**ing**

    Exceptions: For some words that end in *ge*, keep the *e* and add the suffix.

    courage–courag**eous**   change–change**able**

- If the suffix begins with a consonant, keep the *e*. Some common suffixes beginning with consonants are *-ly, -ment, -less,* and *-ful*.

    sure–sure**ly**   like–like**ness**

    Exceptions: Some words lose their final *e* when a suffix is added.

    acknowledge–acknowledgment   true–truly
    argue–argument

PRACTICE 4

Rewrite each word with the suggested ending.

EXAMPLE:

use + ed   *used*_____

1. achieve + ment _____   7. large + er _____

2. strange + est _____   8. endorse + ment _____

3. argue + ment _____   9. argue + ing _____

4. love + ing _____   10. nine + ty _____

5. active + ly _____   11. write + ing _____

6. true + ly _____   12. change + able _____

Adding Suffixes to Words Ending in -y

When you add a suffix to a word ending in *y*, make sure that you follow the next rules.

- If the word has a consonant before the final *y*, change the *y* to an *i* before adding the suffix.

    beauty–beaut**i**ful   supply–suppl**i**ed

- If the word has a vowel before the final *y*, if it is a proper name, or if the suffix is *-ing*, do not change the *y* to an *i*.

    day–days   try–trying   the Vronsky family–the Vronskys

    Exceptions: Some words do not follow the previous rule.

    day–da**i**ly   lay–la**i**d   say–sa**i**d   pay–pa**i**d

PRACTICE 5

Rewrite each word with the suggested ending.

EXAMPLE:

try + ed   *tried*_____

1. happy + est   _____
2. play + er   _____
3. pretty + er   _____
4. Connolly + s   _____
5. lonely + ness   _____

6. envy + able   _____
7. angry + ly   _____
8. day + ly   _____
9. say + ing   _____
10. dirty + est   _____

Doubling the Final Consonant

Sometimes when you add a suffix to a word, you must double the final consonant. Remember the next tips.

One-Syllable Words

- Double the final consonant of one-syllable words ending in a consonant-vowel-consonant pattern.

    bat–ba**tt**er   plan–pla**nn**ed   prod–pro**dd**ed

- Do not double the final consonant if the word ends in a vowel and two consonants or if it ends with two vowels and a consonant.

    cool–coolest   park–parking   clean–cleaner

Words of Two or More Syllables

- Double the final consonant of words ending in a stressed consonant-vowel-consonant pattern.

    pre<u>fer</u>–prefe**rr**ed   oc<u>cur</u>–occu**rr**ed

- If the word ends in a syllable that is not stressed, then do not double the last letter of the word.

    <u>hap</u>pen–happened   <u>vis</u>it–visiting

CHAPTER 32

PRACTICE 6

Rewrite each word with the suggested ending.

EXAMPLES:

	Add -ed		**Add -ing**
stop	_stopped_	try	_trying_

1. slip	_____	6. smile	_____
2. load	_____	7. stay	_____
3. mention	_____	8. enter	_____
4. plan	_____	9. begin	_____
5. open	_____	10. refer	_____

PRACTICE 7

Correct twelve spelling mistakes in the next selection.

EXAMPLE:

                                        angrily
The parents reacted ~~angryly~~ when they were convicted.

1.   In the United States, every state except New Hampshire has a parental

responsibility statute. Such laws make parents legaly responsible for their

children's criminal acts. The first parents who were ever tryed and

convicted under such laws were from St. Claire Shores, Michigan. In 1995,

a sixteen-year-old boy commited a series of crimes after he was released

from juvenile detention. The state questionned why the parents could not

control their son. The prosecutor was successfull in convicting the parents,

and the case brought national attention to the issue. Since then, many

parents have been convicted. For example, in one case, a couple's son set

the nieghbor's house on fire. The parents had to pay $60,000 to the

victim.

2.   Those who are against such laws argue that holding parents responsible

definitly does nothing to stop juvenile delinquents from committing

crimes. At a certain age, peer groups become more influential than parents.

It is unecessary and unfair to force parents to pay for damages. Such laws are ilogical and simply attempt to fix a problem after the fact instead of helping the parents deal with the child before any serious crimes occur.

3.   Some people, argueing for the laws, say parents must be encouraged to take a more active role in their children's lifes. If parents know that they may be charged for their child's actions, they will likly intervene and try to get their child some help before serious crimes can occur. Some supporters also argue that taxpayers should not have to pay for vandalism and other damage caused by juveniles.

Spelling Two-Part Words

Some one-word indefinite pronouns sound as if they should be two separate words, but they are not. Here are some examples of one-word indefinite pronouns.

Words with *any*:   anything, anyone, anybody, anywhere
Words with *some*:   something, someone, somebody, somewhere
Words with *every*: everything, everyone, everybody, everywhere

---

 Hint   **Spelling *another* and *a lot***

Another is always one word: Bonnie committed <u>another</u> crime.
A lot is always two words: She robbed <u>a lot</u> of banks.

PRACTICE 8

Correct ten spelling errors in the next paragraph.

EXAMPLE:

Another
~~An other~~ scandal occurred last year.

Alot of professional athletes have committed criminal acts. Some times the crimes are not serious. For example, Florida State football player Peter Warrick was charged with theft in a designer clothing scheme. Pete Rose is an other athlete who let greed draw him into imoral activities when he bet against his own team. However, some athletes have assaulted, raped, or killed. Ice skater Tonya Harding and her husband hired some body to hit her skating rival in the knee. Boxer Mike Tyson was accused and eventualy convicted of rape, and several professional football players have been charged with murder. Because television and newspapers present professional athletes as icons, many fans refuse to accept that their heroes have done any thing wrong. Basketball fan Trevor Nixon says, "Any body can make accusations. Unfair attacks on successfull athletes can cause their families much greif." Perhaps the public should accept that athletes are not always heroic.

120 Commonly Misspelled Words

The next list contains some of the most commonly misspelled words in English.

CHAPTER 32

absence	ceiling	exercise	medicine
absorption	cemetery	extraordinarily	millennium
accommodate	clientele	familiar	minuscule
acquaintance	committee	February	mischievous
address	comparison	finally	mortgage
aggressive	competent	foreign	necessary
already	conscience	government	ninety
aluminum	conscientious	grammar	noticeable
analyze	convenient	harassment	occasion
appointment	curriculum	height	occurrence
approximate	definite	immediately	opposite
argument	definitely	independent	outrageous
athlete	desperate	jewelry	parallel
bargain	developed	judgment	performance
beginning	dilemma	laboratory	perseverance
behavior	disappoint	ledge	personality
believable	embarrass	leisure	physically
business	encouragement	license	possess
calendar	environment	loneliness	precious
campaign	especially	maintenance	prejudice
careful	exaggerate	mathematics	privilege

probably	schedule	thorough	Wednesday
professor	scientific	tomato	weird
psychology	separate	tomatoes	woman
questionnaire	sincerely	tomorrow	women
receive	spaghetti	truly	wreckage
recommend	strength	Tuesday	writer
reference	success	until	writing
responsible	surprise	usually	written
rhythm	technique	vacuum	zealous

 **Spelling Strategies**

Here are some useful strategies to improve your spelling.

- Keep a record of words that you commonly misspell in your spelling log, which could be in a journal or binder. Have a friend read from your list of misspelled words to give you a spelling quiz. See Appendix 7 for more information about spelling logs.
- Use memory cards or flash cards to help you memorize the spelling of difficult words.
- Write down the spelling of difficult words at least ten times to help you remember how to spell them.

PRACTICE 9

Circle the correctly spelled word in each pair.

EXAMPLE:

foreigner/foriegner

1. ceiling/cieling
2. ancient/anceint
3. noticable/noticeable
4. echos/echoes
5. writting/writing
6. accommodate/accomodate
7. definitely/definitly
8. sincerly/sincerely
9. running/runing
10. appealled/appealed
11. comittee/committee
12. embarrassed/embarassed

13. recommend/recommand
14. absence/absense
15. wierd/weird
16. niece/neice
17. personallity/personality
18. exaggerate/exagerate
19. butterflys/butterflies
20. responsible/responsable
21. efficeint/efficient
22. fryed/fried
23. independent/independant
24. appointment/apointment

PRACTICE 10

Correct fifteen spelling mistakes in the next selection.

EXAMPLE:

outrageous
Detectives may never solve some ~~outragous~~ crimes.

1.   In 1888, in England, a series of sickening and vicious murders horrifyed London society. A serial killer, known only as Jack the Ripper, attacked women in London's East End with a razor blade. He caught the imagineation of the public.

2.   Newspaper articles and editorials on the Ripper's crimes appearred every day, but some of the stories were filled with exagerations. London citizens were extremly afraid of the serial killer, and they wanted to know who was responsable for the crimes. Politicians recommanded that the Ripper be executed for his crimes. As time passed, London police felt embarassed because they could not find the killer.

3.   Although there was much speculation at that time, the identity of the Ripper was never discovered. A myth has developped about him, and today some people are hopefull that the puzzle can be solved. An American crime writer, Patricia Cornwell, has proposed that the well-known British impressionist painter Walter Sickert was the Ripper. In the early 1900s, Sickert made graphic paintings of murdered women, and he had studioes near the crime scenes. In an interview with *ABC News*, Cornwell said, "Some of his paintings, if you juxtapose them with some of the morgue photos, are extraordinarilly chilling." Cornwell has used her own money to verify DNA evidence from a letter supposedly writen by the Ripper. However, her evidence is inconclusive, so the controversy remains.

4.   Not everybody beleives Cornwell's theory, and people have offered other explanations about who Jack the Ripper actualy was. Perhaps the case will remain an unsolved mystery.

 **Using a Spelling Check**

The spelling and grammar tool on a computer will highlight most misspelled words and provide suggested corrections. Be aware that a spelling checker's abilities are limited; it cannot verify that you have used commonly confused words accurately. For example, it cannot determine whether you should use *your* or *you're*.

Because a spelling checker is not 100 percent reliable, remember to proofread for spelling errors before you submit your final work.

Look-Alike and Sound-Alike Words

Sometimes two English words can sound very much alike but have different spellings and different meanings. For example, two commonly confused words are *defiantly*, which means "to resist or challenge something," and *definitely*, which means "finally" or "decisively." Dictionaries will give you the exact meaning of unfamiliar words. Read the next list to get familiar with many commonly confused words.

Word	Meaning	Example
accept	to receive; to admit	The police sergeant <u>accepted</u> an award for outstanding work.
except	excluding; other than	None of his colleagues, <u>except</u> his wife, knew about the award.
affect	to influence	Writer's block <u>affects</u> a person's ability to write.
effect	the result of something	Writer's block can have bad <u>effects</u> on a person's ability to write.
been	past participle of the verb *to be*	Patrick Fitzgerald has <u>been</u> a prosecutor for many years.
being	present progressive form (the *-ing* form) of the verb *to be*	He was <u>being</u> very nice when he signed autographs.
by	preposition meaning *next to*, *on*, or *before*	The defendant sat <u>by</u> her lawyer. <u>By</u> 10 a.m., the jury was getting restless. Everyone hoped the case would be over <u>by</u> the weekend.
buy	to purchase	The lawyer will <u>buy</u> a new car with the client's money.
complement	to add to; to complete	The car will be a nice <u>complement</u> to her other possessions.
compliment	to say something nice about someone	Chicago's mayor <u>complimented</u> the detectives.
conscience	a personal sense of right or wrong	The robber had no <u>conscience</u>.
conscious	to be aware; to be awake	The robber was <u>conscious</u> of his terrible crime.

(continued)

Word	Meaning	Example
disinterested	to be impartial	The trial judge was disinterested, favoring neither side.
uninterested	to lack interest in something	The robber looked uninterested when told of his sentence.
elicit	to get or draw out	The police tried to elicit a confession from the gang member.
illicit	illegal; unlawful	The police found evidence of the gang's illicit activities.
everyday	ordinary; common	Crime is an everyday occurrence.
every day	during a single day; each day	The police watch the gang members every day.
imply	to suggest	The reporter implied that the police need more time to investigate.
infer	to conclude	The police inferred from the clues the gang's whereabouts.
imminent	soon to happen	The police stated that an arrest was imminent.
eminent	distinguished; superior	Patrick Fitzgerald is an eminent prosecutor.
its	possessive case of the pronoun *it*	The judge's desk is large and its legs are ornate.
it's	contraction for *it is*	It's generally known that he is very good at solving crimes.
knew	past tense of *know*	Fitzgerald knew that the newspaper executive was guilty.
new	recent; unused	He had new evidence to present to the court.
know	to have knowledge of	Many people know about Fitzgerald's work.
no	a negative	The police made no arrests.
lose	to misplace or forfeit something	The police did not want to lose track of the stolen money.
loose	too big or baggy; not fixed	Detectives sometimes wear loose clothing as part of their disguises.
loss	a decrease in an amount; a serious blow	The company experienced a serious loss when the money was stolen.
peace	calm sensation; a lack of violence	The two rival gangs finally made peace. They felt a sense of peace when hostilities stopped.
piece	a part of something else; one item in a group of items	The thieves ate a piece of cake to celebrate the successful heist.
personal	private	The criminal has a lot of personal problems.
personnel	employees; staff	The police must hire new personnel.
principal	main person; director of a school	The principal detective talked to the principal of our school.
principle	a rule or standard	The police try to follow the principle of law.

Word	Meaning	Example
quiet	silent	The thieves remained quiet when arrested.
quite	very	The public is becoming quite angry at the increase in crime.
quit	stop	The detective sometimes wants to quit the force.
taught	past tense of *teach*	Drake taught a class on criminology.
thought	past tense of *think*	He thought his students were intelligent.
than	word used in comparisons	Fitzgerald is more determined than other prosecutors.
then	at a particular time; after a specific time	Cornwell investigated the case, and then she wrote about it.
that	word used to introduce a clause	She wrote that Walter Sickert was the Ripper.
their	possessive form of *they*	The police officers went to their favorite restaurant.
there	a place	They went there by police van.
they're	contraction of *they are*	They're both interesting people.
through	in one side and out the other; finished	The police cruiser passed through a tunnel. Then they were through for the day.
threw	past tense of *throw*	Somebody threw a rock at the officer's car.
thorough	complete	They did a thorough investigation of the crime scene.
to	indicates direction or movement; part of an infinitive	I want to go to the film.
too	also; very	The robber was too young to be given a prison sentence. Her friend was, too.
two	the number after one	There were two witnesses to the holdup.
where	question word indicating location	The police knew where the diamonds were hidden.
were	past tense of *be*	The diamonds were in a safe place.
we're	contraction of *we are*	We're going to meet the detectives.
write	to draw symbols that represent words	Patricia Cornwell will write about the crime.
right	correct; the opposite of the direction left	The police knew that they had arrested the right criminal. They found the diamonds in her right pocket.
who's	contraction of *who is*	The police sergeant, who's very well known, spoke to reporters.
whose	pronoun showing ownership	Criminals, whose crimes hurt society, must be punished.

CHAPTER 32

PRACTICE 11

Circle the correct word in each sentence.

1. Many people (buy, by) mystery novels.

2. Successful writers of detective fiction receive many (complements, compliments) for their ingenious plots.

3. Edgar Allan Poe and Herman Melville are (excepted, accepted) as being the first American mystery writers.

4. Arthur Conan Doyle and Agatha Christie are two (eminent, imminent) British mystery writers.

5. The (principal, principle) characters in their works are Sherlock Holmes and Hercule Poirot, both of whom are detectives.

6. To solve the mystery, both Holmes and Poirot try to (elicit, illicit) clues by talking to various characters.

7. The public has also (thought, taught) highly of other mystery writers such as Earl Stanley Gardner and Dashiell Hammett.

8. Many students were (quite, quiet) when Margaret Hamilton started to give her lecture about detective fiction.

PRACTICE 12

Correct twenty-five errors in the following passages. Look for the commonly confused words that are indicated in parentheses.

EXAMPLE:

> *too*
> He is ~~to~~ busy these days.

1. (*to, too, two*)

   Hollywood has been the center of many famous crimes. In 1995, the

   O. J. Simpson criminal trial kept Americans glued too their televisions.

   Simpson was accused of killing to people. Nicole Simpson was killed,

   and her friend Ronald Goldman was killed, to. Some analysts believe

   that there was to much media coverage during the trial. The police tried

   to find clues too solve the murder. On October 3, 1995, Simpson was

   declared not guilty, although he was later convicted in a civil trial.

2. (*then, than, that*)

   Another celebrity accused of murder was record producer Phil

   Spector, a man who produced The Beatles, the Ramones, and others.

In recent years, Spector has become more eccentric and reclusive then he was in the past. In 2007, prosecutors stated than Spector murdered a guest in his home. Apparently, Lana Clarkson, a night-club hostess and actress, was visiting Spector on the night of February 3. Spector claimed than she played with his gun, and than she committed suicide. However, immediately after her death, Spector told the police than he had just killed someone. His lawyers stated than his admission of guilt was not valid because Spector had been suffering from prescription drug withdrawal, and the producer was less lucid then he should have been. The case was more highly publicized then most murder cases. On September 26, 2007, the trial ended in a hung jury.

3. (*threw, through, thorough*)

Wynona Ryder, another famous Hollywood actor, was accused of shoplifting in 2002. Store detectives claimed that Ryder passed threw the store taking items and then left threw the front doors when she was finished shopping. Store detectives intercepted Ryder as she was leaving and did a through search of her bags. They then charged her with theft of merchandise worth $4,800. In court, the judge threw out some evidence, but he accepted testimony from the store detectives. When the trial was threw, the jury found Ryder guilty, but she did not have to spend time in prison.

4. (*it's, its*)

The preceding three celebrities have received a lot of attention from the media and it's readership. Many people think that its wrong for celebrities to profit from crimes they have been accused of doing. Other people think that its fair if celebrities profit in the long term.

5. (*who's, whose*)

People of all ages idolize celebrities who have committed crimes. However, the public should remember that celebrities who commit crimes are criminals. A person whose famous should not behave criminally. Celebrities who's profession puts them in the public spotlight should be aware of the influence they have, especially on young people.

6. (*their, there, they're*)

However, supporters of celebrities who have committed crimes say that although celebrities lead public lives, there human. They should not be punished for the rest of there lives for making a mistake. Their is much debate about this issue.

The Writer's Desk Revise and Edit Your Warm Up

In the Warm Up at the beginning of this chapter, you wrote about celebrity criminals. Edit your paragraph for errors with spelling or commonly confused words.

REFLECT ON IT

Think about what you have learned in this unit. If you do not know an answer, review that concept.

1. a. In a word containing *ie*, when does *i* come before *e*?

   _____

   b. When does *e* come before *i*?

   _____

2. Circle the correctly spelled words. Correct each misspelled word.

   realy   finally   unatural   illogical   plentifull

3. Write down three pairs of words that you commonly confuse.

   _____   _____

   _____   _____

   _____   _____

4. Correct eight mistakes in the next passage.

   Crimes are quiet a common occurrence in my nieghborhood. The police are planing to increase there surveillance in this area. The public, to, can help. Its important to report any unnusual events. Eventualy, such actions will help lower the crime rate.

FINAL REVIEW

Underline and correct twenty spelling errors and mistakes with commonly confused words in the essay.

EXAMPLE:

applied
Sometimes, laws are unfairly <u>applyed</u>.

1. Three strikes laws have stired up controversy in the United States. Such laws state that if a person is convicted of two felonys, the felon will recieve a life sentence if convicted of a third crime. The laws aim to make career criminals take responsability for their actions.

2. The first three strikes law was passed in California in 1994, and it grew out of the public's sense of frustration. The public percieved that there was a steady increase in crime, so the state decided to implement an action plan. Lawmakers excepted the public's viewpoint and designed a law they taught would be tough on criminals. However, the law continus to be debated.

3. Proponents of this controversial law argue that criminals need a strong deterrent to stop doing ilegal activities. In fact, they claim that the crime rate has definitly droped since the three strikes law was passed. Moreover, supporters say that other states have passed the same law because it has being so successfull in California.

4. Critics of this law claim that buy harshly punishing criminals who have committed minor crimes, this law ensures that everybody looses. Three strikes laws go against the principal of the punishment fitting the crime. Furthermore, opponents argue that the laws should be applyed only to violent felons. They also say that the cost of enforcing this type of law is great and that the money should not be wasted on jailing those who comit minor offenses such as stealing food or shoplifting.

5. Critics forcefuly condemn three strikes laws, argueing that such laws are inhumane, expensive, and unfair. Supporters do not want the laws to be modified. Both sides have valid points of view; therefore, three strikes laws will continue to generate controversy.

The Writer's Room Topics for Writing

Choose one of the following topics and write a paragraph or an essay. Remember to follow the writing process.

1. Compare and contrast graffiti with another type of art.

2. Do you believe that three strikes laws are fair and effective?

3. Should juveniles who commit serious crimes be treated as harshly as adults?

4. What are some steps that parents can take to prevent their children from breaking laws or becoming criminals?

The Writers' Circle

Work with a partner or a small group of students and compose a paragraph about the qualities of a good comic book hero. In your paragraph, tell a story about an heroic action that the superhero does. Use slang words and clichés in your paragraph. Make sure that your paragraph is double-spaced, and make sure that the writing is clear.

When you have finished your paragraph, exchange sheets with another team of students. Edit the other team's paragraph and imagine that the audience is a college instructor. Change all clichés and slang expressions into standard American English.

READING LINK

The Legal World

"Why I Worked with La Migra" by Veronica Ortega (page 591)

"When the Legal Thing Isn't the Right Thing" by Deborah Mead (page 594)

"A Faith in Others Versus Security" by Barbara Card Atkinson (page 596)

"Interview with Jimmy Baca" by Elizabeth Farnsworth (page 598)

CHAPTER 32

How Do I Get a Better Grade?

mywritinglab

Visit www.mywritinglab.com for audio-visual lectures and additional practice sets about spelling and commonly confused words.

Get a better grade with MyWritingLab!

Section Theme **THE WORKPLACE**

In this chapter, you will read about business etiquette and wise business decisions.

The Writer's Desk Warm Up

Have you ever thought about having your own business? What type of business would you like to have? Write a paragraph about owning a business.

What Is a Comma?

A **comma** (,) is a punctuation mark that helps keep distinct ideas separate. There are many ways to use a comma. In this chapter, you will learn some helpful rules about comma usage.

Notice how comma placement changes the meaning of the following sentences.

The dog bites, the cat laughs, and then she has a nap.

The dog bites the cat, laughs, and then she has a nap.

Commas in a Series

Use a comma to separate items in a series of three or more items. Remember to put a comma before the final *and* or *or.*

unit 1	,	unit 2	,	and or	unit 3

Miami, Los Angeles, and New York have many employment opportunities.

The job search requires courage, perseverance, and energy.

You can network, contact employers directly, or use a placement service.

> ## Hint **Punctuating a Series**
>
> In a series of three or more items, do not place a comma after the last item in the series (unless the series is part of an interrupting phrase).
>
> **Incorrect:**   Her poise, simplicity, and kindness, impressed us.
>
> **Correct:**   Her poise, simplicity, and kindness impressed us.
>
> Do not use commas to separate items if each item is joined by *and* or *or.*
>
> It is not possible to study <u>and</u> listen to music <u>and</u> have a conversation at the same time.

PRACTICE I

Underline series of items in the next selection. Then add eighteen missing commas where necessary.

EXAMPLE:

Some <u>individuals, small-business owners, and home-based workers</u> design and print their own business cards.

1.   Many small companies do not have the money to advertise, so their only means of promoting their product is to hand out cards to friends neighbors and strangers who might be interested in the business. The type of card that people carry depends on the type of business that they have. Photographers pastry chefs artists and musicians often have colors and images on their cards. Doctors lawyers and accountants tend to use a simple black-and-white design printed on good-quality paper.

2.   Your business card should transmit more than just your name position telephone number and address. According to consultant Frank Yeoman,

people are attracted to cards that have clear simple and direct messages. At the same time, a business card should stand out in some way, so it is a good idea to think about the color texture and design of the card. The card should be eye-catching.

3.   Yeoman says that you should never put your photo on your business cards unless you are a model or an actor. As trends change, you may be embarrassed to have hundreds of business cards depicting you with an unfashionable hairstyle outdated glasses and an unattractive shirt. You get only one chance to make an impression on new customers, so it is important to put some time effort and planning into your business card design.

Commas After Introductory Words and Phrases

Use a comma after an **introductory word.** The introductory word could be an interjection such as *yes, no,* or *well,* it could be an adverb such as *usually* or *generally,* or it could be a transitional word such as *however* or *therefore.*

> <u>Introductory word(s)</u>   **,**   sentence.
>
> <u>Yes</u>, I will help you complete the order.
>
> <u>Frankly</u>, you should reconsider your customer service promise.
>
> <u>However</u>, the job includes a lot of overtime.

Use a comma to set off **introductory phrases** of two or more words. The phrase could be a transitional expression such as *of course* or *on the contrary,* or it could be a prepositional phrase such as *on a warm summer evening.* The introductory phrase could also be a modifier such as *running out of fuel* or *born in France.*

> <u>On the other hand</u>, his career was not going well.
>
> <u>In the middle of the meeting</u>, I received a phone call.
>
> <u>Speaking to the crowd</u>, the manager explained the stock's performance.

PRACTICE 2

Underline each introductory word or phrase. Then add ten missing commas.

EXAMPLE:

<u>In today's job market</u>, people must remain flexible.

1. For the first time in history workers can expect to outlive the organizations that they work for. For example many high-tech companies came and went during the stock market boom of the late 1990s. Additionally many businesses go bankrupt each year.

2. Furthermore those working in successful companies may see their jobs become obsolete. In fact the majority of the nation's bank tellers were laid off in the 1990s. As a result many people in the banking industry have had to retrain or change jobs.

3. According to Myriam Goldman the average person should plan for three different careers. Of course some people love their jobs and have no desire to look elsewhere. However even those in secure jobs may get bored and long for a career change down the road. Working in a volatile job market workers should remain open and flexible.

Commas Around Interrupting Words and Phrases

Interrupting words or phrases appear in the middle of sentences. Such interrupters are often asides that interrupt the sentence's flow but do not affect its overall meaning. Some interrupters are *by the way*, *as a matter of fact*, and *for example*. Prepositional phrases can also interrupt sentences.

My sister, for example, has never invested in stocks.
The market, by the way, has been down recently.
Mrs. Jayson, frankly, never acknowledges her employees.
My manager, in the middle of a busy day, decided to go to a movie!

CHAPTER 33

Hint   Using Commas with Appositives

An appositive gives further information about a noun or pronoun. The appositive can appear at the beginning, in the middle, or at the end of the sentence. Set off appositives with commas.

beginning
A large city in Florida, Miami has a variety of public learning centers.

middle
Dr. Anex, a senior surgeon, recommends the transplant.

end
The office is next to Graham's, a local eatery.

PRACTICE 3

The next sentences contain introductory words and phrases, interrupters, and series of items. Add the missing commas. If the sentence is correct, write *C* in the space provided.

EXAMPLE:

E-mail, voice mail ^,^ and cell phones are changing the way that
people do business. _____

1. Jamaal Khabbaz a marketing manager, complains about high-tech

    gadgets in the workplace such as pagers, cell phones and personal

    organizers. _____

2. Many workers in his opinion break rules of basic etiquette. _____

3. He gets annoyed, for example when a lunch meeting is

    interrupted by a ringing cell phone. _____

4. Unfortunately, many people do not consider it rude to answer

    a call in the middle of a meal. _____

5. According to Kabbaz the workplace needs new business

    etiquette rules. _____

6. Electronic mail, a convenient way to send and receive

    messages is not private. _____

7. Without a doubt, it is offensive to read other people's mail. _____

8. Some people, however have no qualms about standing next to

    a computer and reading over the shoulder of an e-mail recipient. _____

9. E-mail junkies, those addicted to electronic messages cause the

    most problems. _____

10. In the middle of a busy day the e-mail addict sends cartoons,

    videos and messages to co-workers. _____

11. Most shocking of all, some employees download offensive films

    and send them to others. _____

12. One company, a producer of electronic surveillance equipment

    fired six employees for sending pornographic e-mails to each other. _____

Commas in Compound Sentences

A **compound sentence** contains two or more complete sentences joined by a coordinating conjunction (*for, and, nor, but, or, yet, so*).

> Sentence   , and   sentence.

I want a job **,** **so** I will look in the classified ads.
Some interesting companies are nearby **,** **and** maybe they are hiring.
I will work in an office **,** **but** I do not want to work from nine to five.

PRACTICE 4

Add six commas that are missing from this letter.

EXAMPLE:

I am punctual **,** and I am hardworking.

> Dear Ms. Graham:
>
> I saw an ad in the *Miami Herald* stating that you need a junior accountant. I am interested in the job so I have enclosed a résumé highlighting my skills in this field. I have an aptitude for computers and I am able to solve problems in creative ways.
>
> I have taken several courses in accounting at Marshall College but I have not completed the program. I am comfortable with spreadsheets and I have worked with income tax preparation programs.
>
> I am available for an interview at any time so please do not hesitate to contact me. Thank you for your consideration and I look forward to hearing from you.
>
> Yours sincerely,
>
> *Marcus Fisher*
>
> Marcus Fisher

CHAPTER 33

Commas in Complex Sentences

A **complex sentence** contains one or more dependent clauses (or incomplete ideas). When you add a **subordinating conjunction**—a word such as *because, although,* or *unless*—to a clause, you make the clause dependent.

dependent clause   independent clause
<u>**When** the stock market opened</u>, he sold his shares.

Use a Comma After a Dependent Clause

If a sentence begins with a dependent clause, place a comma after the clause. Remember that a dependent clause has a subject and a verb, but it cannot stand alone. When the subordinating conjunction comes in the middle of the sentence, it is not necessary to use a comma.

	Dependent clause **,** main clause.
Comma:	<u>After the meeting ends</u>, we will go to lunch.

	Main clause dependent clause.
No comma:	We will go to lunch <u>after the meeting ends</u>.

Use Commas to Set Off Nonrestrictive Clauses

Clauses beginning with *who, that,* and *which* can be restrictive or nonrestrictive. A **restrictive clause** contains essential information about the subject. Do not place commas around restrictive clauses.

No commas:	The only local company <u>that does computer graphics</u> has no job openings.
	(The underlined clause is essential to understand the meaning of the sentence.)

A **nonrestrictive clause** gives nonessential information. In such sentences, the clause gives additional information about the noun but does not restrict or define the noun. Place commas around nonrestrictive clauses.

Commas:	Her book, <u>which is in bookstores</u>, is about successful entrepreneurs.
	(The underlined clause contains extra information, but if you removed that clause, the sentence would still have a clear meaning.)

 **Which, That, Who**

which
Use commas to set off clauses that begin with *which.*

    ImClone, **which** was founded in 1983, creates pharmaceutical products.

that
Do not use commas to set off clauses begining with *that.*

    The company **that** <u>Sam Waksal founded</u> creates pharmaceutical products.

(continued)

> **who**
> When a clause begins with *who*, you may or may not need a comma. If the clause contains nonessential information, put commas around it. If the clause is essential to the meaning of the sentence, it does not require commas.
>
> **Essential:** Many people **who** buy stocks think that they will earn a profit.
>
> **Not essential:** Domestic guru Martha Stewart, **who** became a multimillionaire, was convicted of obstructing justice in 2004.

PRACTICE 5

Edit the following practice by adding fifteen missing commas.

EXAMPLE:

Many charitable foundations have donated money, time, and expertise to alleviate inequality.

1. The Bill and Melinda Gates Foundation which began in 2000 is the largest charity in the world. The couple created a foundation to help reduce economic inequality in the world. Their foundation has three branches: the Global Health Program the Global Development Program, and the United States Program. Recently, Warren Buffet who is a rich financier gave the Gates Foundation 10 million shares of his company Berkshire Hathaway. Buffet, who has a reputation of being frugal made a vow to give most of his fortune to charity. Although Buffet is an astute businessman he thought that Bill and Melinda Gates could donate his money better than he could. With his donation, the foundation, which is based in Seattle is worth about $33 billion.

2. A foundation, which is not strictly a business must function like a business to amass enough money to continue its charitable work. Even though a foundation cannot pay its directors it must pay its employees, researchers, and suppliers. Therefore, income that a charitable foundation generates must offset such expenses. The BMG Foundation, for example invests in

other companies. It has invested in oil firms drug companies and other multinational corporations. However critics argue that such companies often contribute to the unequal distribution of resources that the foundation is trying to eradicate. The Foundation, which remains highly effective stands behind its investment choices.

Commas in Business Letters

When you write or type a formal letter, ensure that you use commas correctly in the following parts of the letter.

Addresses

In the address at the top of the letter, insert a comma between the following elements.

- The street name and apartment number
- The city and state or country

Do not put a comma before the zip code.

> Dr. Brent Patterson
>
> 312 Appleby Road, Suite 112
>
> Cleveland, OH 45678

If you include an address inside a complete sentence, use commas to separate the street address from the city and the city from the state or country. If you just write the street address, do not put a comma after it.

Commas: The building at 11 Wall Street, New York, contains the Stock Exchange.

No comma: The building at 11 Wall Street contains the New York Stock Exchange.

Dates

In the date at the top of the letter, add a comma between the full date and the year. If you just write the month and the year, then no comma is necessary.

> May 21, 2006   January 2006

If you include a date inside a complete sentence, separate the elements of the date with commas.

> We visited Washington on Monday, July 26, 2008.

 **Writing Numbers**

In letters, it is not necessary to write ordinal numbers such as *first* (1st), *second* (2nd), *third* (3rd), or *fourth* (4th). Instead, just write the number: 1, 2, 3, 4, and so on.

> February 24, 2001   October 11, 1966

CHAPTER 33

Salutations

Salutations are formal letter greetings. The form "To Whom It May Concern" is no longer used regularly by North American businesses. The best way to address someone is to use his or her name followed by a comma or a colon. The colon is preferred in business letters.

Dear Ms. Lewin: Dear Sir or Madam: Dear Mom,

Complimentary Closings

Place a comma after the complimentary closing. Notice that the first word of the closing is capitalized.

Respectfully,   Yours sincerely,   Many thanks,

Sample Letter of Application

You send a sample letter of application to an employer when you apply for a job. Review the parts of the following letter.

Sender's address ➤
(name, phone, and possibly
an e-mail address)

Seamus O'Brien
10 Santa Fe Boulevard
Seattle, WA 90001
(661) 234-5678

Date ➤

September 12, 2005

Recipient's address ➤

Avant Garde Computers
Adelaide and Sinclair Corporation
6116 Greenway Avenue
Seattle, WA 98711

Subject line ➤

Subject: Position of junior programmer

Salutation ➤

Dear Ms. Roebok:

I saw an ad in Saturday's *Seattle Times* stating that you need a junior programmer. I have enclosed a résumé highlighting my skills in this field. I have an aptitude for computers, and, when I was fourteen years old, I created my first game program.

I have just finished a diploma program in computer programming at Marshall College. I took courses in several computer languages. I have also completed a six-week training program, and I have enclosed a letter of reference from the owner of that company.

If you require further information, please contact me. I am available for an interview at any time and could start work immediately. Thank you for your consideration.

Closing (After the closing, ➤
put your handwritten
signature followed by your
typed name.)

Sincerely,

S. O'Brien

Seamus O'Brien

Enclosures: résumé
             letter of reference

PRACTICE 6

The next letter contains ten errors. Add seven missing commas and remove three unnecessary commas.

Red River Publications
1440 Cliff Street
Austin Texas 76780

April 2 2005

Graham Britt
214 Regents Road,
Austin Texas 77787

Dear Mr. Britt:

On Monday March 12 2004 we received your manuscript. We are pleased to inform you that your article will be published in the May, issue of *Phoenix Magazine*.

Could you please meet with me at our branch office? I will be at 44 Hillside Road, during the last week of the month. You can stop by the office at anytime during that week. We are looking forward to meeting with you.

Yours truly

Lydia Halburton

Lydia Halburton

The Writer's Desk Revise and Edit Your Warm Up

Read the paragraph that you wrote for the Warm Up at the beginning of this chapter. Verify that you have used commas correctly. Then add two more sentences to the paragraph. In one sentence, include a restrictive clause. In another sentence, include a nonrestrictive clause.

REFLECT ON IT

Think about what you have learned in this unit. If you do not know an answer, review that concept.

1. Explain the rules of comma usage in the following situations.

   a. Series of items: _____

   _____

   b. Introductory words or phrases: _____

   _____

   c. Interrupting phrases: _____

   _____

   d. Compound sentences: _____

   _____

2. What is a nonrestrictive clause? _____

   _____

3. Should you place commas around nonrestrictive clauses? _____ Yes _____ No

4. Write a sentence that contains a nonrestrictive clause.

   _____

   _____

5. Write three common closings for a business letter.

   _____

   _____

FINAL REVIEW

Edit the next essay by adding seventeen missing commas and removing three unnecessary commas.

EXAMPLE:

Entertainers, including comedians, actors ˄ and musicians, should consult with a financial advisor.

1.   Horace Madison co-founder of Madison Smallwood Financial Group,

   manages the careers of top urban rappers, hip-hop artists and blues musicians. Madison grew up in Harlem and he had a middle-class childhood. He heard about many high-profile artists and musicians M. C. Hammer, for example, who ended up going broke. When he began to work on Wall Street, he decided to focus on entertainers, who were at risk of mismanaging their funds.

2.   Madison handles every aspect of his clients' lives. He helps them pay their bills, collect their revenue and plan their investment portfolios. According to Madison, some of his new artists desperately want to buy expensive jewelry or cars. In many cases they have just signed a million-dollar record deal. The artists, explains Madison do not always realize that they owe the record label for some of the money spent on music videos, marketing and travel. In fact, some artists can sell a million records and still end up owing money to the company. Furthermore new artists face pressure from family and friends. When their friends see the artist in a music video they call up the artist asking for a handout or a job.

3.   Madison helps artists set up a budget and he carefully monitors what his clients spend. If a client wants to waste an outrageous amount on a frivolous luxury item Madison forces the client to sign a "stupid letter." He wants his clients to understand, that they are making a stupid financial move so the letter states that such spending is against the advice of Madison's firm. In an interview with Mitchell Raphael a journalist with the *National Post* newspaper, Madison told an anecdote. He said that a client wanted to rent a Ferrari for $1,000 a day. Madison without a pause, asked the client to sign the stupid letter. The client, a rapper rethought his plans and decided to rent a different car for $300 a day.

4.   Ultimately, excessive spending is not smart. Hip-hop artists must think about their long-term future, because they have a career span of only three or four years. Madison and Smallwood Financial Group have helped a variety of artists manage the minefield of fame. In fact, Eve, a hip-hop artist has thanked Madison for helping her spend her money wisely.

How Do I Get a Better Grade?

Visit www.mywritinglab.com for audio-visual lectures and additional practice sets about commas.
Get a better grade with MyWritingLab!

CHAPTER 33

The Apostrophe, Quotation Marks, and Titles

Section Theme **THE WORKPLACE**

CONTENTS

In this chapter, you will read about topics related to success stories and controversies.

The Writer's Desk Warm Up

Would you like to own your own business? If so, what type would you like to own? Describe your dream business.

The Apostrophe (')

An **apostrophe** is a punctuation mark showing a contraction or ownership.

      ownership   contraction
Daymond **John's** business is very successful, and **it's** still growing.

Using Apostrophes in Contractions

To form a **contraction,** join two words into one and add an apostrophe to replace the omitted letter(s).

Apostrophe replaces *o*	is + n**o**t = isn't
Apostrophe replaces *a*	I + **am** = I'm

Common Contractions

The following are examples of the most common contractions.

- **Join a verb with *not*.** The apostrophe replaces the letter *o* in *not*.

is + not = isn't	has + not = hasn't
are + not = aren't	have + not = haven't
could + not = couldn't	should + not = shouldn't
do + not = don't	would + not = wouldn't
does + not = doesn't	

  Exceptions: will + not = won't, can + not = can't

- **Join a subject and a verb.** Sometimes you must remove several letters to form the contraction.

I + will = I'll	she + will = she'll
I + would = I'd	Tina + is = Tina's
he + is = he's	they + are = they're
he + will = he'll	we + will = we'll
Joe + is = Joe's	who + is = who's
she + has = she's	who + would = who'd

  Exception: Do not contract a subject with the past tense of *be*. For example, do not contract *he + was* or *they + were*.

 Hint   **Contractions with Two Meanings**

Sometimes one contraction can have two different meanings.

    I'd = I had or I would   **he's** = he is or he has

When you read, you should be able to figure out the meaning of the contraction by looking at the words in context.

    She's hiring new personnel.   **She's** seen several interesting candidates.
    (She is)   (She has)

CHAPTER 34

PRACTICE I

Add nine missing apostrophes to the next selection.

EXAMPLE:

          isn't
Starting a business ~~isnt~~ a simple process.

1.   Back in 1992, Daymond John wasnt happy with his job, so he decided

to create his own business. He recruited his three best friends, and they

designed and sold hats. Since then, theyve created hockey jerseys, baseball caps, shoes, shirts, and pants. They called their company Fubu, meaning "For us, by us."

2.   They havent always been successful. In the first years, they made some mistakes. For example, John mortgaged his house to finance the business. Today, he says that he shouldnt have done that. He didnt know that he could have asked for a line of credit from a bank.

3.   Sometimes the Fubu owners couldnt pay their bills. They werent familiar with common business practices. For example, when they sent orders to stores, theyd get paid four months later. They didnt realize that most businesses operate that way. During the first year of business, Daymond John almost lost his house, but today he is very successful.

PRACTICE 2

Look at each underlined contraction, and then write out the complete word.

EXAMPLE:

They <u>weren't</u> ready to start a business.   *were not*

1. Carol <u>Simon's</u> very happy with her bridal gown company.   _____
2. <u>She's</u> been an entrepreneur for seven years.   _____
3. <u>She's</u> an extremely friendly, ambitious woman.   _____
4. I wish <u>I'd</u> had the same idea as Carol.   _____
5. <u>I'd</u> like to have my own company, too.   _____

Using Apostrophes to Show Ownership

You can also use apostrophes to show ownership. Review the next rules.

Possessive Form of Singular Nouns

Add -'s to a singular noun to indicate ownership, even if the noun ends in *s*.

> **Daymond's** best friends joined his company.
>
> **Somebody's** house became a factory.
>
> **Ross's** dad has his own business.

Possessive Form of Plural Nouns

When a plural noun ends in *s*, just add an apostrophe to indicate ownership. Add -'s to irregular plural nouns.

CHAPTER 34

Many **companies'** Web sites are down.

The four **friends'** business is very successful.

The **children's** clothing company is expanding.

Possessive Form of Compound Nouns

When two people have joint ownership, add -*'s* to the second name. When two people have separate ownership, add -*'s* to both names.

Joint ownership: Daymond and **Carl's** company is successful.

Separate ownership: **Daymond's** and **Carl's** offices are in different buildings.

PRACTICE 3

Write the singular and plural possessive forms.

EXAMPLE:

	Singular Possessive	**Plural Possessive**
Mr. Cohen	*Mr. Cohen's*	*the Cohens'*

1. client   _____ _____

2. boss   _____ _____

3. secretary   _____ _____

4. Mr. Ness   _____ _____

5. woman   _____ _____

6. salesperson _____ _____

PRACTICE 4

Write the possessive forms of the following phrases.

EXAMPLE:

the sister of the doctor   ___*the doctor's sister*___

1. the locker of the employee   _____

2. the supplies of the employees   _____

3. the profits of the company   _____

4. the directors of the companies   _____

5. the house of Jan and Ted   _____

6. the car of Omar and the car of Roy _____

Using Apostrophes in Expressions of Time

When an expression of time (*day, week, month, year*) appears to possess something, use the possessive form of that word.

CHAPTER 34

Singular: The customer won a **year's** supply of paper.

Plural: Mike Roy gave two **weeks'** notice before he left the company.

When writing the numerals of a decade or century, do not put an apostrophe before the final -*s*.

In the **1800s,** many immigrants arrived at Ellis Island.

Many Internet companies failed in the **1990s.**

 **Hint**   **Common Apostrophe Errors**

Do not use apostrophes before the final *s* of a verb.

       wants
Simon ~~want's~~ to open a franchise.

Do not confuse contractions with possessive pronouns that have a similar sound. For example, the contraction *you're* sounds like the pronoun *your*. Remember that possessive pronouns never have apostrophes.

           Its
The company is growing. ~~It's~~ slogan is catchy.
               theirs.
That is my idea. It is not ~~their's.~~

PRACTICE 5

Correct fifteen errors with apostrophes and possessive pronouns.

EXAMPLE:

    aren't   *don't*
If you ~~arent~~ willing to work hard, ~~do'nt~~ start your own business.

1.   If your thinking of starting a business, you should plan carefully.

Spend a few year's learning about the business before you invest your life

savings. In an interview with *Smart Money* magazine, Daymond John said

that he would'nt have started his Fubu clothing business so soon if hed

known how complicated it was. He think's that he should have interned at

other fashion companies to learn the business. According to John, "When I

started Fubu in 1992, I just thought about the designs. But if you do'nt

understand distribution, shipping, financing, and product timing, you can

have the greatest designs in the world and still end up losing."

CHAPTER 34

2.   John say's that he made a lot of mistakes in the 1990's. He and his partner's werent aware of common business practices. They didnt know that they could get salespeople whod work on commission. He advises, "Know how everything works, from the mailroom to the advertising department. If you cant operate every part of your company, then youre dependent on other people. You never know if they are doing their jobs to the fullest or just wasting your money. And if they decide to leave, youll have to teach their replacements, or maybe do the jobs yourself."

Quotation Marks (" ")

Use **quotation marks** to set off the exact words of a speaker or writer. If the quotation is a complete sentence, there are some standard ways that it should be punctuated.

- Capitalize the first word of the quotation.
- Place quotation marks around the complete quotation.
- Place the end punctuation inside the closing quotation marks.

| . . . declared | , | "Complete sentence." |

Here is an example of a sentence with a quotation.

> Poet William Butler Yeats declared, "Education is not the filling of a pail but the lighting of a fire."

Generally, when using quotations, attach the name of the speaker or writer to the quotation in some way. Review the following rules.

Introductory Phrase

Place a comma after a phrase introducing a quotation.

| . . . says | , | "_____." |

> Malcolm Forbes jokes, "It is unfortunate we can't buy many business executives for what they are worth and sell them for what they think they are worth."

Interrupting Phrase

When a quotation is interrupted, do the following:

- Place a comma after the first part of the quotation.
- Place a comma after the interrupting phrase.

| "_____," | . . . says, | "_____." |

> "I don't know the key to success," Bill Cosby said, "but the key to failure is to try to please everybody."

Ending Phrase

When you place a phrase at the end of a quotation, end the quotation with a comma instead of a period.

"_____," says _____.

"You're fired," said Donald Trump.

If your quotation ends with other punctuation, put it before the final quotation mark.

"_____?" says _____.

"You can't fire me!" she shouted.

"Why can't I fire you?" he asked.

Introductory Sentence

You can introduce a quotation with a complete sentence. Simply place a colon (:) after the introductory sentence.

He explains his views: "_____."

Albert Highfield explains why businesses fail: "They try to grow too quickly."

Inside a Quotation

If one quotation is inside another quotation, use single quotation marks (' ') around the inside quotation.

"Main quotation, 'Inside quotation.' "

According to Shannon Dowell, "Good parents always say, 'Clean up your own mess.' "

 **Hint** ▸ **When the Quotation Is an Incomplete Sentence**

If the quotation is not a complete sentence and you simply integrate it into your sentence, do not capitalize the first word of the quotation.

Sir Francis Bacon once said that an artist's job is to **"deepen the mystery."**

PRACTICE 6

In each sentence, the quotation is in bold. Add quotation marks and commas or colons. Also capitalize the first word of the quotation if necessary.

EXAMPLE:

                                  : "A

Comedian Bob Hope made fun of financial institutions **a̶ bank is a place**

that will lend you money if you can prove that you don't need it."

1. According to novelist Lisa Alther **any mother could perform the jobs of several air traffic controllers with ease.**

2. U.S. educator Laurence J. Peter believes that everyone is useful **a miser, for example, makes a wonderful ancestor.**

3. Fred Delaney proclaimed **a celebrity is a person who works hard all his life to become well known, and then wears dark glasses to avoid being recognized.**

4. **In the future, a wall could become a computer screen** according to journalist Kate McNamara.

5. Comedian Mel Brooks believes that humor provides people with a **defense against the universe.**

6. Muhammad Ali describes his profession as a boxer **grass grows, birds fly, waves pound the sand, and I beat people up.**

7. **Success only breeds a new goal** observed actress Bette Davis.

8. **Hard work never killed anybody** declared comedian Edgar Bergen **but why take a chance?**

9. My mother once said **remember the words of humorist Erma Bombeck do not confuse fame with success.**

10. Executive Robert Townsend proclaimed **a leader needs to have a compass in his head and a bar of steel in his heart.**

11. Author Stephen Beach says that Americans are **socialized into a strong work ethic.**

12. Actress Mae West expressed her views **to err is human, but it feels divine.**

CHAPTER 34

Punctuation of Titles

When using a title within a sentence, place quotation marks around the title of a short work and underline or italicize the title of a longer work. Here are some guidelines for both.

Short Works	Long Works
Short story: "The Lottery"	**Novel:** The Grapes of Wrath
Web article: "Music Artists Lose Out"	**Web site:** CNET News.com
Chapter: Chapter 1, "Exploring"	**Book:** The Writer's World
Newspaper article: "Missing in Action"	**Newspaper:** New York Times
Magazine article: "Young Entrepreneurs"	**Magazine:** Forbes
Essay: "Downsizing"	**Textbook:** Writing Guidelines
TV episode: "The Election"	**TV series:** Prison Break
Song: "Don't Panic"	**CD:** Parachutes
Poem: "Howl"	**Anthology:** Collected Poems of Beat Writers
	Movie: The Matrix

Capitalizing Titles

When you write a title, capitalize the first letter of the first and last words and all the major words.

> The Catcher in the Rye   War and Peace   "Stairway to Heaven"

Do not capitalize *.com* in a Web address. Also do not capitalize the following words except as the first or last word in a title.

Articles:	a, an, the
Coordinators:	for, and, nor, but, or, yet, so
Prepositions:	by, in, of, off, out, to, up . . .

 **Hint**   **Your Own Essay Titles**

When writing the title of your own essay, do not put quotation marks around the title. However, you should capitalize key terms.

A Cultural Icon Is Born

PRACTICE 7

A. Add twenty missing capital letters to the titles in the next paragraph.

EXAMPLE:

                  B   W

The magazine *business week* featured successful female entrepreneurs.

1.   In recent years, some ambitious, multitalented women have become

incredibly successful in different fields. Madonna, for example, has released about ten CDs, including one called *american life*. Her popular songs include "hollywood" and "like a prayer." She has written children's books, such as *the english roses*. She has also appeared in many movies, including *desperately seeking susan* and *swept away*. Critics have not always been kind to the Michigan native. In his article "no madonna is an island," *new york times* film critic A. O. Scott called Madonna a poor actress.

B. Underline or add quotation marks to the eight titles in the next paragraph.

EXAMPLE:

In 2005, the magazine <u>Ebony</u> featured an interesting article about Queen Latifah.

Queen Latifah

2.   Queen Latifah is a versatile performer. She is a rapper, model, and actress. In 1988, Queen Latifah got her big break with the song Princess of the Posse, which became a hit single on her album All Hail the Queen. She received a Grammy for another hit, U.N.I.T.Y. from the CD Black Reign. In the 1990s, Queen Latifah continued experimenting with her musical style, and she also ventured into acting. From 1993 to 1998, she had a role in a sitcom, Living Single. She also had a part in Spike Lee's hit film Jungle Fever. She became a household name when she received an Oscar for her role as Mama Morton in the film Chicago. Becoming an instant celebrity, she was on the cover of many magazines, including Essence. She continues to achieve great success in her music and acting careers.

CHAPTER 34

PRACTICE 8

Correct twelve errors with quotation marks, titles, apostrophes, or capital letters.

EXAMPLE:

Paul Salopek, in an article titled "Children ~~s~~eeking ~~r~~oyalties," denounced the treatment of a South African composer.

1.   Every time a song is placed on a CD or album, the writer receives a royalty. Lee Ann Arbringer, in an article called "How royalties work," says,

"currently, the statutory rate is eight cents for each song." To combat illegal file sharing on the Internet, some legal music site's have opened up, but not all artists are happy about it. "I earn almost nothing from the legal file-sharing sites because the users just rent songs", says Jimmy Dee, a guitarist. Roz Hillman, an accountant, agrees, noting that the artist gets "Next to nothing."

2.   Some artists have lost the rights to their own compositions. One of the greatest songs in the last century was written by a nearly unknown South African singer, Solomon Linda. Paul Salopek, of the <u>Chicago tribune</u>, wrote about him. In 1939, Linda wrote a song called "Mbube" and sold the rights to Gallo Records for a mere ten shillings, which is less than $2. Since then, Linda song has been rerecorded almost two hundred times, most famously in the 1961 version "The Lion sleeps tonight." The song is on the soundtrack of fifteen movies, including Disney's The Lion King. Solomon Linda died a pauper. "We are sad because he died without praise." said his daughter, Elizabeth.

The Writer's Desk **Revise and Edit Your Paragraph**

Read the paragraph that you have written about your dream business. Check that you have used any apostrophes correctly. Also verify that you have punctuated any song titles properly.

CHAPTER 34

REFLECT ON IT

Think about what you have learned in this unit. If you do not know an answer, review that concept.

1. In contractions, which letter does the apostrophe replace in the word *not*? _____

2. Write the possessive forms of the following phrases.

   EXAMPLE: the wife of my brother: *my brother's wife* _____

   a. the music of Jennifer Lopez: _____

   b. the books of the professor: _____

   c. the house of Rob and Ann: _____

   d. the cases of the lawyers: _____

3. When a sentence ends with a quotation, the period should be

   a. inside the final quotation marks.

   b. outside the final quotation marks.

4. The titles of short works such as essays, articles, and poems should be

   a. underlined or italicized.

   b. set off with quotation marks.

5. The titles of longer works, such as magazines, newspapers, and movies, should be

   a. underlined or italicized.

   b. set off with quotation marks.

FINAL REVIEW

Edit the following paragraphs for fifteen errors with apostrophes, quotations, or underlining. Also, ensure that titles and quotations have the necessary capital letters.

EXAMPLE:

Musician Steve Miller complains' "My royalties have dropped 80 percent since 1999."
                                       ^

1. In recent year's, some recording artists and music companies have

   complained about the proliferation of music-sharing sites on the Internet.

   According to a reporter for *Fox News* "An estimated 60 million people

   participate in file-sharing networks". Opinions about file sharing differ

   greatly.

2. File sharing among college students is common. Roz Mingue, a student

   at Austin Community College, frequently downloads free music. Roz' friend, Melissa Peng, says: "What is the big deal? They can't stop us." Some students think the record companies are simply too greedy. "Music companies say, "Don't do that,' but they still make a lot of money, so they should stop complaining," argues Peng.

3.   Recording companies have decided to fight back. Cary Sherman, president of the Recording Industry Association of America (RIAA), compares file swappers to shoplifters. In a press conference, Sherman said, "there comes a time when you have to stand up and take appropriate action". In the 1990s, Napster was successfully sued and shut down. The recording industrys latest tactic is to take individual music file sharers to court.

4.   The online magazine Wired News reports that hundreds of downloaders have been sued. Journalist Katie Dean writes "The defendants include a working mom, a college football player, and a 71-year-old grandpa." Joel Selvin and Neva Chonin are reporters for the <u>San Francisco chronicle</u>. Their article, "Artists Blast Record companies," contains quotations from artists who are unhappy with the lawsuits.

5.   A prominent rocker points out that artists earn more from touring than from CD sales. "Bruce Springsteen probably earned more in ten nights at Meadowlands last month than in his entire recording career." said rocker Huey Lewis. Certainly music file sharing will not stop anytime soon. David Draiman of the rock band The Disturbed think's that artists should stop fighting because they can't win.

How Do I Get a Better Grade?

Visit www.mywritinglab.com for audio-visual lectures and additional practice sets about the apostrophe, quotation marks, and titles.
Get a better grade with MyWritingLab!

35

Capitalization and Other Punctuation Marks

Section Theme **THE WORKPLACE**

In this chapter, you will read about topics related to innovators.

The Writer's Desk **Warm Up**

Do you buy products online? Why or why not? Express your opinion about online shopping.

Capitalization

There are many instances in which you must use capital letters. Always capitalize the following words:

- **the pronoun *I* and the first word of every sentence**

    My co-workers and I share an office.

- **days of the week, months, and holidays**

    Tuesday   May 22   Labor Day

    Do not capitalize the seasons: summer, fall, winter, spring.

- **titles of specific institutions, departments, companies, and schools**

    Apple Computer   Department of Finance   Daleview High School

    Do not capitalize general references.

    the company   the department   the school

- **the names of specific places such as buildings, streets, parks, cities, states, and bodies of water**

    Market Street   Times Square   Los Angeles, California
    Sunset Boulevard   Mississippi   Lake Erie

    Exception: Do not capitalize general references.

    the street   the state   the lake

- **the names of specific languages, nationalities, tribes, races, and religions**

    Spanish   Mohawk   Buddhist   an Italian restaurant

- **titles of specific individuals**

    General Dewitt   President Abraham Lincoln   Dr. Blain
    Professor Cruz   Prime Minister Tony Blair   Mrs. Ellen Ross

    Do not capitalize titles if you are referring to the profession in general, or if the title follows the name.

    my doctor   the professors   Edward M. Kennedy, a senator

- **specific course and program titles**

    Economics 201   Topics in Electrical Engineering   Nursing 402

    Do not capitalize if you refer to a course but do not mention the course title.

    an economics course   an engineering program   a nursing class

- **major words in titles of literary or artistic works**

    Washington Post   *The Golden Compass*   *Lord of the Flies*

- **historical events, eras, and movements**

    World War II   Cubism   the Middle Ages

 **Capitalizing Computer Terms**

Always capitalize software titles, as well as the following computer terms.

    Internet   World Wide Web   Microsoft Office

PRACTICE I

Add fifteen missing capital letters.

EXAMPLE:

> *Oregon's*
> One of ~~oregon's~~ best-known artists is Matt Groening.

1. Born on february 15, 1954, Matt Groening grew up with an interest in comic book art. In 1977, he moved to Los angeles with the intention of becoming a writer. He held many different types of jobs, including chauffeur and ghostwriter for an elderly movie producer. He started writing his own comic strip called *Life in hell*. The strip appeared in the *Los Angeles reader* in 1980 and went into syndication in 1983.

2. In 1987, Groening created a short animated series that served as extra material for the *Tracy Ullman show*. Picked up by Fox in 1990, *The Simpsons* has become the longest-running cartoon show in television history. The fate of the show was at first in doubt because many people, including former First lady Barbara Bush, criticized the show's portrayal of a dysfunctional family.

3. The show's characters are named after people in Groening's family. Groening's father is named Homer, his mother is Marge, and his two sisters are Lisa and Maggie. The show's central character is a scheming ten-year-old, and the name Bart was created by rearranging the letters in the word *brat*. In the television series, the Simpson family lives in Springfield next to Ned Flanders, a devout christian. Both families live on a street called evergreen terrace.

4. The show satirizes american society. It contains stereotypical characters such as Wiggum, the corrupt, donut-eating police chief. In addition, at Ainsworth elementary school, principal Skinner takes orders from his mother and punishes students erratically.

CHAPTER 35

5.   Although the show is a cartoon, both adults and children enjoy it. To appeal to adults, some of the show's stories are based on famous literary works such as Edgar Allan Poe's "The raven." The show has been translated into spanish and other languages, and it has been watched by millions of people around the world.

Other Punctuation Marks

Colon (:)

Use a colon for the following purposes.

- To introduce a quotation with a complete sentence

    The writer Oscar Wilde stated his opinion: "All art is quite useless."

- To introduce a series or a list after a complete sentence

    The United States has produced some great writers: Emily Dickinson, F. Scott Fitzgerald, Ernest Hemingway, John Steinbeck, and William Faulkner.

- After the expression *the following*

    Please do the following: read, review, and respond.

- To introduce an explanation or example

    In 1929, investors witnessed a tragedy: the Stock Market Crash.

- To separate the hour and minutes in expressions of time

    The meeting will begin at 11:45.

Hyphen (-)

Use a hyphen in the following situations.

- When you write the complete words for numbers between twenty-one and ninety-nine.

    twenty-six   ninety-nine   seventy-two

- When you use a compound adjective before a noun. The compound adjective must express a single thought.

    No hyphen: The new employee must work under high pressure.

    Hyphen: The new employee has a <u>high-pressure</u> **job.**

    (You cannot say a "high job" or a "pressure job." *High* and *pressure* must go together.)

    No hyphen: Our boss is thirty years old.

    Hyphen: We have a <u>thirty-year-old</u> **boss.**

    (The words *thirty, year,* and *old* express a single thought. You cannot remove one of those words.)

    If the adjectives before a noun function independently, do *not* add hyphens.

    No hyphen: They renovated an old red barn.

    (The two adjectives function separately.)

> **Hint** **Nonhyphenated Compound Adjectives**
>
> Some compound adjectives never take a hyphen, even when they appear before a noun.
>
> World Wide Web   high school senior   real estate agent

PRACTICE 2

Add ten missing colons and hyphens.

EXAMPLE:

top-notch

The World Wide Web is a ~~top notch~~ communications system.

1.   Some revolutionary inventions in human communication are the

following paper, the printing press, the personal computer, and the World

Wide Web. Tim Berners-Lee, a respected fifty-three year old man, created

the World Wide Web while working as a researcher for the European

Laboratory for Particle Physics. His invention has had long term effects in

the field of communications.

2.   Born in 1955 in London, England, Berners-Lee showed an early

interest in mathematics. He had many childhood hobbies designing

cardboard computers, doing mental mathematical calculations, and

experimenting with electronics. Because his parents were interested in

computers, Berners-Lee became a computer savvy child.

CHAPTER 35

3.   In 1986, while he was working in Geneva, he had two great ideas

designing a software system that linked information on his computer to

information on his colleagues' computers, and sharing his program with

scientists around the world. The system allowed scientists to communicate

with each other by accessing information on each other's computers.

Berners-Lee envisioned a web like system of communications links. He

named the new system the World Wide Web.

4.   Since 1991, the Internet has become an extremely user friendly

research tool. Berners-Lee did not profit monetarily from his creation. In

fact, he fights hard to keep it free so that everyone can benefit from it.

Ellipsis Marks (. . .)

You may want to quote key ideas from an author, but you do not always want to quote an entire paragraph. Use ellipsis marks to show that you have omitted information from a quotation.

When you type an ellipsis mark, leave a space before and after each period. If the omitted section includes complete sentences, then add a period before the ellipses. In the next examples, notice how the quotation changes when ellipses are used.

Original Selection

I submit that an individual who breaks a law that conscience tells him is unjust, and who willingly accepts the penalty of imprisonment in order to arouse the conscience of the community over its injustice, is in reality expressing the highest respect for the law.

—Martin Luther King Jr.

Quotation with Omissions

I submit that an individual who breaks a law that conscience tells him is unjust . . . is in reality expressing the highest respect for the law.

—Martin Luther King Jr.

> **GRAMMAR LINK**
>
> For more information about quotations, see Chapter 34.

PRACTICE 3

Write quotations incorporating material from each of the next passages. Use ellipses to show where you omit words, and remember to keep important information.

1. Normal thoughts of my future (not pertaining to football), friends, family, reputation, moral status, etc., were entirely beyond me.

    —From H.D.'s "Dying to Be Bigger"

According to H. D., _____

_____

_____

2. To top it off, our kids are imbued with victimology, which today has become the American way of blame. It is too routine for adults and their kids to explain all their problems as victimization. When a boy in trouble sees himself as a victim, this festers into seething anger. With easy availability of guns, it can explode as murder.

    —From Martin Seligman's "The American Way of Blame"

Martin Seligman says, _____

_____

_____

_____

_____

The Writer's Desk   Revise and Edit Your Warm Up

In the Warm Up, you wrote about online shopping. Edit your paragraph to ensure that you have punctuated it correctly.

REFLECT ON IT

Think about what you have learned in this unit. If you do not know an answer, review that concept.

1. List five types of words that require capitalization. For instance, the days of the week begin with capital letters.

    _____

    _____

2. Add hyphens, where necessary, to the following sentences.

    He is a twenty five year old man who carries a small red book in his back pocket.

    He has a high pressure job, but he remains relaxed at work.

3. Correct the six errors in punctuation and capitalization.

    The famous cuban-american actor Andy Garcia was born in havana on april 12,

    1956. He has made many films *The Godfather: Part III, Ocean's eleven,* and *The*

    Untouchables.

FINAL REVIEW

Correct fifteen capitalization and punctuation (colon and hyphen) errors in the next selection. Count each hyphen, colon, or capital letter as one error.

EXAMPLE:

> *highly motivated*
> Some ~~highly motivated~~ people risk their careers to become whistle-blowers.

1.   The U.S. government passed an act in 1990 to protect whistle-blowers

from retaliation in the workplace. However, many people are frightened to

come forward for the following reasons their colleagues might think of them as traitors, they might become the target of bad publicity, or they might lose their jobs.

2.   In 2002, three women were honored by *Time* Cynthia Cooper, Coleen Rowley, and Sherron Watkins. Cooper worked for WorldCom, Rowley worked for the Federal bureau of investigation, and Watkins worked for Enron. They became the focus of public scrutiny because they revealed their employers' criminal business practices.

3.   These risk taking women upheld ethical standards. Cooper revealed WorldCom's illegal accounting practices. The company had inflated its profits, and the multibillion dollar fraud caused many shareholders to lose their investments. In may 2002, Rowley wrote a memo to FBI director Robert Mueller about the agency's failure to investigate a possible terrorist who was later linked to attacks on the United States. Watkins, in a letter to chairman Kenneth Lay, warned of accounting discrepancies at Enron. Later, when the company failed, many employees and investors lost their life savings.

4.   Another important whistle-blower is New York Attorney general Eliot Spitzer. In june 2001, forty-three year old Spitzer investigated the illegal actions of Merrill Lynch, a wall street financial firm. Merrill Lynch was accused of illegally downgrading the stock value of a company.

5.   Whistle-blowers risk their careers and their reputations to do the right thing. They should be recognized as heroes because they expose corruption and incompetence.

CHAPTER 35

The Writer's Room   Topics for Writing

Choose one of the following topics and write a paragraph or an essay. Remember to follow the writing process.

1. What is *success*? In your paragraph or essay, define success. As a supporting example, describe a successful person whom you know.

2. What reasons do people give for downloading music and films? What are the effects of their actions? Write about the causes or the effects of illegal downloading.

3. What types of jobs does society place a high value on? Describe at least three different categories or types of workers who get a lot of respect.

4. Describe your work environment.

The Writers' Circle

Work with a partner and think about a job that would interest you. Find a job advertisement from a newspaper, a magazine, or an Internet site. You could refer to one of the following sites.

www.monster.com   www.jobs.net   www.jobs.org

Compose a letter of application. In the first paragraph, explain what job you want, and tell where you heard about the job. In the second paragraph, briefly detail your qualities and experience. Then, in a third paragraph, explain your availability and how you can be contacted. Ask your partner to help you compose each part of the letter.

Remember to be as direct as possible. After you finish writing, proofread your letter and ensure that you have used correct punctuation and capitalization. Exchange letters with your partner, and proofread your partner's letter.

CHAPTER 35

How Do I Get a Better Grade?

Visit www.mywritinglab.com for audio-visual lectures and additional practice sets about capitalization and other punctuation marks.

Get a better grade with MyWritingLab!

Editing Paragraphs and Essays

EDITING PRACTICE

In this chapter, you will have opportunities to edit different pieces of writing.

After you finish writing the first draft of a paragraph or essay, it is important to edit your work. When you edit, you carefully review your writing to verify that your grammar, punctuation, sentence structure, and capitalization are correct. In this chapter, you can practice editing the types of written pieces that you see every day, including e-mail messages, paragraphs, essays, and business correspondence.

PRACTICE I   EDIT A PARAGRAPH

Correct ten underlined errors in the next student paragraph. An editing symbol appears above each error. To understand the meaning of each symbol, refer to the revising and editing symbols at the end of this book on the inside back cover.

Reading <u>teach</u> [agr] me a lot of important things. Through books, I

discover that other people have problems just as I do, and I learn about

different ways to solve problems. For <u>exemple</u> [sp], in Jane Austen's *Emma*,

the main character <u>try</u> [agr] to control her <u>friend's</u> [p] lives, but she really

makes things <u>worst</u> [ad] for them. I saw myself in the story, and now I try to

be less controlling. Through reading, I also learn about different

religions and <u>cultures, I</u> [ro] realize that people have the same concerns all

over the world. <u>Also, exploring other places.</u> [frag] Reading allows me to visit

distant countries. I cannot afford to fly to India, but when I read

Arundhati Roy's *The God of Small Things,* I learned about the life and

culture there. <u>Finaly</u> [sp], in books, I learn that ordinary people can have

extraordinary lives, and it <u>make</u> [agr] me appreciate that I am living my own

<u>interresting</u> [sp] story.

PRACTICE 2   EDIT AN ESSAY

Correct twenty underlined errors in the next student essay. An editing symbol
appears above each error.

Family Dynamics

1   One day, my brothers and <u>me</u> [pro] were discussing our childhood. We

had very distinct viewpoints about our experiences. We realized that

                      vt

our opinions were <u>influence</u> by our birth position in the family.

Certainly, birth order has an impact on a person's personality.

        p   agr

2   <u>First time</u> parents, unsure of what to do, <u>tends</u> to put a lot of pressure

                                  shift

on the firstborn child. Although the oldest child <u>benefited</u> from the

                                  ad

undivided attention of the parents, he or she also feels <u>more</u> stronger

pressure than the younger siblings. Oldest children are most likely to

                p

conform to their <u>parents</u> expectations and are often compliant high

achievers. For example, my brother made my parents proud

       m

<u>who became a lawyer.</u>

                        ad   agr

3   Middle children have <u>certains</u> qualities that <u>sets</u> them apart.

Immediately, they must fight for their place in the limelight,

                          wc

especially if they are the same sex <u>than</u> the eldest child. Middle

children, therefore, tend to learn how to manipulate others to get

          ro

what they <u>want, they</u> sometimes act out to get their parents'

attention. I am a middle child, and I rebelled. Of course, the

        wc   agr

attention <u>than</u> I received from my parents <u>were</u> not always positive,

but attention is attention, and I needed it.

                                    ad

4   By the time the youngest child is born, the parents are <u>real</u>

             wc

relaxed and have <u>less</u> financial worries. Therefore, they tend to

spoil the baby of the family, letting the youngest get away with

mischief. In my family, my youngest brother did things that I would

wc   frag

<u>of</u> been punished for. <u>Including staying out late and taking the car</u>

<u>without permission.</u>

                                                      //

5   Being a parent is time-consuming, heartbreaking, and <u>a reward</u>.

Knowing about birth order can help people become better parents.

Nancy Samalin, in her book *Love and Anger: The Parental Dilemma*,

wrote, "Children will observe one another closely and take

                                        p

advantage of any edge they can <u>achieve"</u>.

PRACTICE 3   EDIT A PARAGRAPH

There are no editing symbols in the next paragraph. Proofread it as you would your own writing, and correct twelve errors.

     Physicians overprescribe antibiotics and this practice is having a terrible effect on our health system. First, antibiotics are completely useless against viruses, yet alot of patients ask for and receive it when they have a simple cold. When drugs are overprescribed, some bacterial infections become drugs-resistant. Malaria and tuberculosis for example, are more difficult to treat than they were twenty years ago. The problem is especialy serious in hospitals. According to Dr. Ricki Lewis, antibiotic-resistant infections spread rapidly in a hospital environment. Furthermore, patients who are criticaly ill requires large doses of drugs who cause bacteria to mutate rapidly. We should remember that the body can fight many illnesses on its own. For instance, some common ear infections.

Before accepting a prescription, consumers should ask whether antibiotics are necessary. There are problems enough in this world, the population does not need to create new illnesses by overusing antibiotics.

PRACTICE 4 EDIT A PARAGRAPH

There are no editing symbols in the next paragraph. Proofread it as you would your own writing, and correct fifteen errors.

Identity theft is the ilegal use of someones personal information. It is a serious crime, in fact, last year there was over 10 million cases of identity theft in the United States. To find identities, thieves go threw recycling bins, empty garbage cans, and stealing mail to obtain somebodys personal information. Computer hackers can even steal identities by tapping into personal information that persons keep on their computers. When a criminal has stolen a name, birthplace, address, and social security number, they can take out credit cards in the victim's name. For example, my co-worker, Nick Matsushita. He came home one day and found a large bill from a credit card company. Somebody had use his personal information to apply for credit. Nick and me are good friends, and I know that the identity theft has caused him alot of pain. He says that if he would have known about the way identity thieves work, he would have been more careful with his personal papers. Certainly, victims of identity theft loose time and money trying to fix the problem. To avoid being a victim, be prudent when sharing personal information.

PRACTICE 5   EDIT A WORKPLACE MEMO

Correct eight errors in the next excerpt from a memo.

Re: Summer vacations

As many of you know, each summers everybody wants to take their
vacation at the same time. For this reason, employees are being ask
to state your vacation preferences before next friday. Please sign the
sheet posted on the bulletin board stating when you wanna take your
time off. If you gotta good reason for needing a specific time period,
please send Judy or I a memo explaining why.

Michael Rosen

Human Resources Department

PRACTICE 6   EDIT AN ESSAY

Correct twenty errors in the next essay.

1.   Many courageous explorers has attempted expeditions to the Antarctic.
     Robert Falcon Scott did not want to become an explorer. In fact, he
     once said "I may as well confess that I had no predilection for polar
     exploration". However, he went on to lead two expeditions to the
     South Pole.

2.   His first expedition, which took place from 1901 to 1904 was
     unsuccessful. Scott and his crew experienced many problems. Because of
     the harsh climate and terrain. For example many crew members develop
     scurvy due to a lack of vitamin C. They had traveled 960 miles and was

only 480 miles short of the South Pole when they had to give up. In 1905, Scott wrote a book about his journey, *The Voyage of discovery*.

3.   On June 10 1910, on a ship called the *Terra Nova*, Scott raced to the South Pole again. Unfortunately, when Scott reached his destination, he found that a norwegian expedition had arrived there first. Every member of Scotts team were disappointed.

4.   On the return journey, Scott and his crew faced terrible blizzards. "Great God! This is an awful place." Scott wrote in his journal. One man, Captain Oates, had severe frostbite on his feet. Knowing that he would never make it to the supply camp Oates decided to leave the group and walk to certain death. So that he would not have to depend of his friends. When they were only eleven miles from the supply camp, Scott and the remaining crew members set up their tents. Their frozen bodies were discover a few months later. Forty-three-year-old Scott was the last to die.

5.   Although Scott was not the first person to reach the South Pole his decision to undertake important and dangerous explorations inspired many others. In Cambridge, England, the Scott Polar research Institute was named after the explorer.

CHAPTER 36

PRACTICE 7   EDIT A LETTER OF COMPLAINT

Correct fifteen errors in this excerpt from a letter of complaint.

We, the employees of Echo Industries, would like to formaly complain about the presence of cameras in company hallways, and rest areas. We wonder why are there so many cameras in those areas. The cameras they are invading are privacy.

We know the managements point of view. Senior managers argue that the cameras increases security. They also claim that employees take less breaks when the cameras are in leisure areas.

Feeling spied on, there is now an atmosphere of mistrust in our company. We don't have no privacy. We feel insulted, mistreated, and getting no respect. What we do during our breaks should not concern our employers. As long as we obey company rules, we should have the rite to rest and socialize in private. We done nothing to warrant such treatment. Please take our comments serious. We are confident than we can resolve this issue.

PRACTICE 8 EDIT A FORMAL LETTER

Correct ten punctuation and capitalization errors in the next formal letter.

Ari Praz

278 First avenue

New York, NY 10009

July 6, 2007

New York Department of Finance

Hearing-by-Mail Unit

P.O. Box 29201

Brooklyn, New York 11202

Subject: Ticket #4089-01411

Attention: Finance Department

I am writing to explain why I am pleading "not guilty" to a parking

ticket I received on the morning of friday, june 24, 2007. Please read

the following explanation and refer to the enclosed documents.

On the evening of june 23, I parked a rented car on the south side of

18th street. I knew I could park there legally overnight until 8:30 a.m.

At approximately 8:15 friday morning, I went to move the car from that

parking space. When I arrived, I discovered that the front tire on the

passenger side was flat. Unable to move the car, and unable to change

the tire myself, I immediately returned to my apartment a few blocks

away to phone the rental companys hotline. I estimated that I made

the call at about 8:30 a.m. On the photocopies of Continentals service records, you will see they dispatched someone at 8:39 a.m. Unfortunately, while I was away from the car making that call, I received a ticket. The ticket was written at 8:40 a.m.

I'm sure you can see why I am pleading "not guilty" to this parking offense. I had every intention of moving the car by the specified time, I was not able to do so until roadside assistance arrived to replace the flat tire.

Yours Truly,

Ari Praz

Ari Praz

Enclosures: 2

PRACTICE 9   EDIT AN ESSAY

Correct twenty errors in the next essay.

1   During world war II, the United States had it's own version of Mata Hari. A debutante by the name of Amy Thorpe became one of the wars most successful secret agents.

2   At the age of nineteen, Thorpe met and married a much older British diplomat, Arthur Pack. At the beginning of the spanish civil war, the Packs was sent to Spain. During a hot summer day, five desperate Nationalist soldiers approached Amy Pack. With some hesitation, she agreed to smuggle them past enemy lines. The soldier's hid inside the trunk of her car and past through a

checkpoint. On that momentous occasion, the young woman discovered her true calling.

3   In a revolt against her sheltered upbringing, the diplomats wife desired a life of danger and excitement. In the summer of 1937, Amy Thorpe separated from her husband and becomes a spy for Britain. With the code name of Cynthia, she obtained secret information about Hitlers plan to invade Czechoslovakia.

4   One of her most dangerous mission occurred in Vichy, France. Posing as an American journalist, "Cynthia" seduced Charles Brousse, an official at the french Embassy, and convinced him to work with her. Thorpe's mission was to photograph secret Nazi codebooks. The couple met in the embassy for several nights and convinced the night watchmen that they were simply an amorous couple. On the third night, they enterred the code room, opened the window, and let a professionnal safecracker into the room. Suddenly, Thorpe had a hunch, and, to the surprise of the men, she decided to remove her clothing. Seconds later, the door opened, and the night watchmans flashlight beamed into the room. When he saw the naked woman, he apologized and retreated. Thorpe quickly dressed. The safecracking expert then opened the safe, Thorpe photographed the codebooks.

5   Although most Americans have never heard of her, Amy Thorpe's wartime actions were extreme important. Amy Thorpe has been credited with saving over 100,000 Allied lives.

CHAPTER 36

PRACTICE 10 EDIT AN ESSAY

Correct twenty errors in the next essay.

1 Sports surround us every day in the papers, on television, and on the radio. Some people criticize our sports-driven culture. Sports critics say that colleges' put young athletes on pedestals and do not emphasize the achievments of students in academic programs. In fact, athletes do not receive enough praise.

2 First, colleges with good sports teams gets a lot of publicity. For example, during the football season, three national television channels covers the games CBS, NBC, and ABC. During the basketball playoffs, March Madness CBS covers the games. The publicity that colleges receive from sports bring more students to the academic programs. Sports help these programs, they do not harm them.

3 In addition, colleges and universities make money from their student athletes. For example, the National Collegiate athletic association (NCAA), the organization devoted to the administration of intercollegiate athletics in the United States, showed $422.2 millions in revenue in its 2002–2003 budget. A large part of this money come from television. Most of the money is redistributed to colleges and universities. Educational institutions use the funds not only for their sports programs but also are giving money to academic programs. Clearly, colleges show good long-term planning when they promote star athletes.

4 Moreover, sports are a motivation for athletes to go to college. Last year, there was about 360,000 student athletes in NCAA-affiliated colleges. Over 126,000 of thoses athletes received either a partial or a full scholarship. Therefore, they were real motivated. To attend postsecondary institutions.

5　Colleges and universities are right to pay special attention to athletes and sports programs. Because of the extra effort that student athletes must give to suceed, and because of the publicity and money that educational institutions receive from sports programs and their athletes colleges and universities have a serious obligation to encourage there athletes.

Reading Strategies and Selections

PART V

In the first part of Chapter 37, you will learn strategies that can help you improve your reading skills. Later in the chapter, you will see a number of thought-provoking essays that present a wide range of viewpoints about topics related to culture, psychology, espionage, great discoveries, college life, health care, the legal world, and the workplace.

As you read each essay, think about how the writer achieves his or her purpose using one or more of these writing patterns:

- **Illustration**
- **Narration**
- **Description**
- **Process**
- **Definition**
- **Classification**
- **Comparison and Contrast**
- **Cause and Effect**
- **Argument**

From Reading to Writing

CHAPTER 37

> ❝ *Reading is to the mind what exercise is to the body.* ❞
>
> —SIR RICHARD STEELE
> *Irish author*

Aspiring songwriters and musicians study different musical styles to determine which lyrics, notes, rhythms, and so on work well together. In the same way, by reading different pieces of writing, you can observe which elements other writers use and how they use them. Then, you can try applying the same principles to your own writing.

Reading Strategies

When you read, you also develop your writing skills. You expand your vocabulary and learn how other writers develop topics. In addition, you learn to recognize and use different writing patterns. Finally, reading helps you find ideas for your own paragraphs and essays.

The next strategies can help you become a more successful reader and writer. They guide you through the reading process and provide useful tips for getting specific information from a piece of writing.

Previewing

Previewing is like window shopping; it gives you a chance to see what the writer is offering. When you preview, look quickly for visual clues so that you can determine the selection's key points. Review the following:

- Titles or subheadings (if any)
- The first and last sentences of the introduction
- The first sentence of each paragraph

- The concluding sentences of the selection
- Any photos, graphs, or charts

Finding the Main Idea

After you finish previewing, read the selection carefully. Search for the **main idea,** which is the central point that the writer is trying to make. In an essay, the main idea usually appears somewhere in the first few paragraphs in the form of a thesis statement. However, some professional writers build up to the main idea and state it only in the middle or at the end of the essay. Additionally, some professional writers do not state the main idea directly.

> **Making a Statement of the Main Idea**
>
> If a reading does not contain a clear thesis statement, you can determine the main idea by asking yourself *who, what, when, where, why,* and *how* questions. Then, using the answers to those questions, write a statement that sums up the main point of the reading.

Making Inferences

If a professional writer does not state the main idea directly, you must look for clues that will help you **infer** or figure out what the writer means to say. For example, read the next paragraph and try to infer the writer's meaning.

> The band cost about $4,500 for the night. The hall rented for $900, and we figured we got a good deal. We had to decorate it ourselves. There were flowers on every table ($25 for each bouquet), rented china and silverware ($1,850), and tablecloths, tables, and chairs ($900). The catered food worked out to be $40 per person, multiplied by 300. This is not counting the dresses, the tuxedos, the photographer, or the rented limos. Sure, it was a special night. It is too bad the guests of honor split up three months later.

PRACTICE I

Read the preceding paragraph. Then answer the following questions.

1. What is the subject of the paragraph? _____

2. What is the writer's relationship to the guests of honor? _____

   _____

3. What is the writer's main point? _____

Finding the Supporting Ideas

Different writers use different types of supporting ideas. They may give steps for a process, use examples to illustrate a point, give reasons for an argument, and so on. Try to identify the author's supporting ideas.

Highlighting and Making Annotations

After you read a long text, you may forget some of the author's ideas. To help you remember and quickly find the important points, you can highlight key ideas and make annotations. An **annotation** is a comment, question, or reaction that you write in the margin of a page.

Each time you read a passage, follow the next steps.

- Look in the introductory and concluding paragraphs. Underline sentences that sum up the main idea. Using your own words, rewrite the main idea in the margin.
- Underline or highlight supporting ideas. You might even number the arguments or ideas. This will allow you to understand the essay's development.
- Circle words that you do not understand.
- Write questions in the margin if you do not understand the author's meaning.
- Write notes beside passages that are interesting or that relate to your own experiences.
- Jot down any ideas that might make interesting writing topics.

Here is a highlighted and annotated passage from an essay titled "The New Addiction" by Josh Freed.

1   Is the cell phone the cigarette of our times? That's what I've been asking myself lately as the scourge of smokers slowly disappears from city life and a scourge of cell-phone users takes their place. Everywhere you look, people hold cell phones up to their mouths, instead of cigarettes, and nonusers react as intolerantly as nonsmokers ever did. How does the cell phone resemble the cigarette? Let me count the ways.

   ◄ Why?
   ◄ What is "scourge"?
   ◄ General background

   ◄ Main point suggests cell phones are like cigarettes.

2   It's an oral habit. For many users, the cell phone is an obvious substitute for smoking. It's a nervous habit that gives you something to do with your hands—whether you're dialing, checking your messages, or just fondling the buttons. Just like cigarettes, the phone sits in your breast pocket or on a restaurant table, ready to bring quickly to your mouth. Often, it's in a fliptop case that pops open as easily as a cigarette pack.

   ◄ Good example. I play with my phone.

   ◄ "Fondling"?

Understanding Difficult Words

When you read, you will sometimes come across unfamiliar words. You can try to guess the word's meaning, or you can circle it and look it up later.

Using Context Clues

Context clues are hints in the text that help define a word. To find a word's meaning, try the following strategies.

- **Look at the word.** Is it a noun, a verb, or an adjective? Sometimes it is easier to understand a word if you know how that word functions in the sentence.
- **Look at surrounding words.** Look at the sentence in which the word appears and try to find a relation between the difficult word and the words that surround it. Maybe there is a **synonym** (a word that means the same

thing) or an **antonym** (a word that means the opposite). Maybe other words in the sentence help define the word.

- **Look at surrounding sentences.** Sometimes you can guess the meaning of a difficult word by looking at the sentences, paragraphs, and punctuation surrounding the word. When you use your logic, the meaning becomes clear.

PRACTICE 2

1. Can you easily define the word *disseminates?*   No   Yes

2. Can you easily define the word *parity?*   No   Yes

3. If you do not understand the meanings of those two words, then read them in the context of the next paragraph. You will notice that it is much easier to guess their meanings.

> Christina Hoff Sommers, author of *The War Against Boys*, argues that boys are being neglected in order to help girls succeed in school. For years, she argues, feminist groups have spread myths about the disadvantaged girls, yet boys are actually the disadvantaged sex. The Department of Education **disseminates** hundreds of documents about gender equity, Sommers says. While the documents suggest ways to help girls succeed, none of them explain how educators can help boys achieve academic **parity** with girls.

Now write your own definition of the words as they are used in the paragraph.

a. disseminates: _____

b. parity: _____

 **Cognates**

Cognates, or word twins, are English words that may look and sound like words in another language. For example, the English word *responsible* is similar to the Spanish word *responsable*, although the words are spelled differently.

If English is not your first language, and you read an English word that looks similar to a word in your language, check how it is being used in context. It may, or may not, mean the same thing in English as it means in your language. For example, in English, *assist* means "to help." In Spanish, *assistar* means "to attend." If you are not sure of a word's meaning, consult a dictionary.

Using a Dictionary

If you do not understand the meaning of an unfamiliar word after using context clues, look up the word in a dictionary. A dictionary is useful if you use it correctly. Review the following tips for dictionary usage.

- **Look at the dictionary's frontmatter.** The preface contains explanations about the various symbols and abbreviations.

- **Read all of the definitions listed for the word.** Look for the meaning that best fits the context of your sentence.
- **Look up root words, if necessary.** If the difficult word has a prefix such as *un-* or *anti-*, you may have to look up the root word.

Here is an example of how dictionaries set up their definitions.

Word Division
Your dictionary may use black dots to indicate places for dividing words.

Stress symbol (′) and Pronunciation
Some dictionaries provide the phonetic pronunciation of words. The stress symbol (′) lets you know which syllable has the highest or loudest sound.

Parts of Speech
The *n* means that *deception* is a noun. If you don't understand the parts of speech symbol, look in the front or the back of your dictionary for a list of symbols and their meanings.

de•cep′tion / [di-sep′shən] / *n* 1, the act of misleading. 2, a misrepresentation; artiface; fraud.

From *The New American Webster Handy College Dictionary* (New York: Signet, 2000) 606.

From Reading to Writing

After you finish reading a selection, try these strategies to make sure that you have understood it.

- **Summarize the reading.** When you summarize, you use your own words to write a condensed version of the reading. You leave out all information except the main points.
- **Outline the reading.** An outline is a visual plan of the reading. First, write down the main idea of the essay, and then note the most important idea from each paragraph. Under each idea, include a detail or an example.

Make a Written Response

Your instructor may ask you to write about your reaction to a reading. These are some questions you might ask yourself before you make a written response.

- What is the writer's main point?
- What is the writer's purpose? Is the writer trying to entertain me, persuade me, or inform me?
- Who is the audience? Is the writer directing his or her message at someone like me?
- Do I agree or disagree with the writer's main point?
- What aspects of the topic can I relate to?

After you answer the questions, you will have more ideas to use in your written response.

Reading Selections

Themes: Culture and Psychology

READING I

The Old-Time Pueblo World
Leslie Marmon Silko

> Born in 1948 on a Laguna Pueblo reservation near Albuquerque, New Mexico, Leslie Marmon Silko has a mixed heritage—white, Native American, and Mexican. An award-winning author, Silko has written novels, short stories, poems, articles, and film scripts. In the following example of an illustration essay, the author discusses some characteristics of Pueblo communities. As you read, also look for elements of narration and description writing.

1   In the view of the old-time people, we are all sisters and brothers because the Mother Creator made all of us—all colors and all sizes. In everyday Pueblo life, not much attention was paid to one's physical appearance or clothing. Ceremonial clothing was quite elaborate but was used only for the sacred dances. The traditional Pueblo societies were communal and strictly **egalitarian,** which means that no matter how well or how poorly one might have dressed, there was no social ladder to fall from. All food and other resources were strictly shared so that no one person or group had more than another. I mention social status because it seems to me that most of the definitions of beauty in contemporary Western culture are really codes for determining social status. People no longer hide their face-lifts, and they discuss their liposuctions because the point of the procedures isn't just cosmetic, it is social. It says to the world, "I have enough spare cash that I can afford surgery for cosmetic purposes."

2   In the old-time Pueblo world, beauty was manifested in behavior and in one's relationships with other living beings. Beauty was as much a feeling of harmony as it was a visual, aural, or sensual effect. The whole person had to be beautiful, not just the face or the body; faces and bodies could not be separated from hearts and souls. Health was foremost in achieving this sense of well-being and harmony; in the old-time Pueblo world, a person who did not look healthy inspired feelings of worry and anxiety. A healthy person, of course, is in harmony with the world around her; she is at peace with herself too. Thus, an unhappy or spiteful person would not be considered beautiful.

3   In the old days, strong, sturdy women were most admired. One of my most vivid preschool memories is of the crew of Laguna women in their forties and fifties who came to cover our house with **adobe** plaster. They handled the ladders with great ease, and while two women ground the adobe mud on stones and added straw, another woman loaded the **hod** with mud and passed it up to the two women on ladders who were smoothing the plaster on the wall with their hands. Since women owned the houses, they did the plastering. At Laguna, men did the basket making and the weaving of fine textiles; men helped a great deal with the childcare too. Because the Creator is female, there is no stigma on being female; gender is not used to control behavior. No job was a man's job or a woman's job; the most able person did the work.

egalitarian:
supporting equal rights for all

adobe:
sun-dried mud

hod:
a trough fixed on a long handle for carrying mortar or bricks

4   When I was growing up, there was a young man from a nearby village who wore nail polish and women's blouses and permed his hair. People paid little attention to his appearance; he was always part of a group of other young men from his village. No one ever made fun of him. Pueblo communities were and still are very interdependent, but they also have to be tolerant of individual eccentricities because survival of the group means everyone has to cooperate. Differences were celebrated as signs of the Mother Creator's grace. People born with exceptional physical or sexual differences were highly respected and honored because their physical differences gave them special positions as mediators between this world and the spirit world. The great Navajo medicine man of the 1920s, the Crawler, had a hunchback and could not walk upright, but he was able to heal even the most difficult cases.

5   New life was so precious that pregnancy was always appropriate, and pregnancy before marriage was celebrated as a good sign. Since the children belonged to the mother and her clan, and women owned and bequeathed the houses and farmland, the exact determination of paternity wasn't critical. Although fertility was prized, infertility was no problem because mothers with unplanned pregnancies gave their babies to childless couples within the clan in open adoption arrangements. Children called their mothers' sisters "mother" as well, and a child became attached to a number of parent figures.

6   In the sacred kiva ceremonies, men mask and dress as women to pay homage and to be possessed by the female energies of the spirit beings. Because differences in physical appearance were so highly valued, surgery to change one's face and body to resemble a model's face and body would be unimaginable. To be different, to be unique, was blessed and was best of all.

VOCABULARY AND COMPREHENSION

1. In paragraph 6, what does *pay homage* mean? Circle the best answer.
    a. give money to   b. show respect for   c. sacrifice

2. What role did women play in the old-time Pueblo society?

    _____

    _____

    _____

3. List four ways in which attitudes in the old-time Pueblo world were different from those in contemporary society. Give examples from the essay to support your answer.

    _____

    _____

    _____

    _____

    _____

CRITICAL THINKING

4. In your opinion, what is Silko's motivation for writing this essay?

    _____

    _____

5. What is Silko's attitude toward her subject?

_____

_____

_____

6. What is her purpose? Why is she describing this old-time Pueblo world?

_____

_____

_____

_____

_____

WRITING TOPICS

Write about one of the following topics. Remember to explore, develop, and revise and edit your work.

1. Compare the values and attitudes of contemporary society with the attitudes and values of the old people in Laguna Pueblo culture. How are they similar or different? Use examples to illustrate your point.
2. What do you think about the description of the old Pueblo world? Is Silko's depiction of that world too idealistic? Do you think a utopian society can exist? Why or why not?
3. Reflect on Maugham's quotation. Is the past important? Why or why not? Use examples to support your point.

> **I can't think of the past. The only thing that matters is the everlasting present.**
> —W. SOMERSET MAUGHAM, ENGLISH AUTHOR

READING 2

Bound Feet

Jung Chang

Jung Chang was born in Yibin, China, and teaches Oriental and African studies at London University. In the next excerpt from her novel, _Wild Swans, Three Daughters of China_, Chang writes about her grandmother. As you read this descriptive essay, also look for elements of the narration and process writing patterns.

1   My grandmother was a beauty. She had an oval face with rosy cheeks and lustrous skin. Her long, shiny black hair was woven into a thick plait reaching down to her waist. She could be demure when the occasion demanded, which was most of the time, but underneath her composed exterior she was bursting with suppressed energy. She was petite, about five feet three inches, with a slender figure and sloping shoulders, which were considered the ideal.

2   But her greatest assets were her bound feet, called in Chinese "three-inch golden lilies" (_san-tsun-gin-lian_). This meant she walked "like a tender young **willow shoot** in a spring breeze," as Chinese connoisseurs of women traditionally put it. The sight of a woman **teetering** on bound feet was supposed to have an erotic effect on men, partly because her vulnerability induced a feeling of protectiveness in the onlooker.

willow shoot:
the new growth of a willow tree

teetering:
walking unsteadily

3   My grandmother's feet had been bound when she was two years old. Her mother, who herself had bound feet, first wound a piece of white cloth about twenty feet long round her feet, bending all the toes except the big toe inward and under the sole. Then she placed a large stone on top to crush the arch. My grandmother screamed in agony and begged her to stop. Her mother had to stick a cloth into her mouth to gag her. My grandmother passed out repeatedly from the pain.

4   The process lasted several years. Even after the bones had been broken, the feet had to be bound day and night in thick cloth because the moment they were released they would try to recover. For years my grandmother lived in relentless, **excruciating** pain. When she pleaded with her mother to untie the bindings, her mother would weep and tell her that unbound feet would ruin her entire life and that she was doing it for her future happiness.

excruciating: extremely painful

5   In those days, when a woman was married, the first thing the bridegroom's family did was to examine her feet. Large feet, meaning normal feet, were considered to bring shame on the husband's household. The mother-in-law would lift the hem of the bride's long skirt, and if the feet were more than about four inches long, she would throw down the skirt in a demonstrative gesture of **contempt** and stalk off, leaving the bride to the critical gaze of the wedding guests, who would stare at her feet and insultingly mutter their **disdain.** Sometimes a mother would take pity on her daughter and remove the binding cloth, but when the child grew up and had to endure the contempt of her husband's family and the disapproval of society, she would blame her mother for having been too weak.

contempt: disapproval

disdain: disapproval

6   The practice of binding feet was originally introduced about a thousand years ago, allegedly by a concubine of the emperor. Not only was the sight of women hobbling on tiny feet considered erotic, men would also get excited playing with bound feet, which were always hidden in embroidered silk shoes. Women could not remove the binding cloths even when they were adults, as their feet would start growing again. The binding could only be loosened temporarily at night in bed, when they would put on soft-soled shoes. Men rarely saw naked bound feet, which were usually covered in rotting flesh and stank when the bindings were removed. As a child, I can remember my grandmother being in constant pain. When we came home from shopping, the first thing she would do was soak her feet in a bowl of hot water, sighing with relief as she did so. Then she would set about cutting off pieces of dead skin. The pain came not only from the broken bones, but also from her toenails, which grew into the balls of her feet.

7   In fact, my grandmother's feet were bound just at the moment when foot-binding was disappearing for good. By the time her sister was born in 1917, the practice had virtually been abandoned, so she escaped the torment. However, when my grandmother was growing up, the prevailing attitude in a small town like Yixian was still that bound feet were essential for a good marriage.

VOCABULARY AND COMPREHENSION

1.   Find a word in paragraph 1 that means "modest, quiet, and reserved."

   _____

2.   In the past, why were Chinese women's feet bound?

   _____

   _____

   _____

3. Did the author's grandmother choose to have bound feet? Support your answer with evidence from the reading.

_____

_____

_____

4. The author describes the process of binding feet. List the steps in the process.

_____

_____

_____

_____

CRITICAL THINKING

5. Why would women who had been through the pain of foot-binding subject their daughters to the same torture? Think of some reasons.

_____

_____

_____

6. What are some of the most effective images in Chang's narrative?

_____

_____

7. What is the narrator's point of view about her grandmother's bound feet? Look for clues in the text.

_____

_____

_____

WRITING TOPICS

Write about one of the following topics. Remember to explore, develop, and revise and edit your work.

1. This reading describes a painful process that Chinese women went through in the past. Although foot binding seems shocking and distasteful, there are parallels in contemporary society. Explain how people alter their bodies today. Try to use descriptive imagery.

2. Describe an incident from the childhood of your parent or grandparent. Try to use descriptive imagery.

3. Reflect on Thoreau's quotation. Compare and contrast some old fashions that people laugh at and new fashions that they follow.

> 66 *Every generation laughs at the old fashions, but follows religiously the new.* 99
> —HENRY DAVID THOREAU, AMERICAN AUTHOR

READING 3

I'm a Banana and Proud of It

Wayson Choy

> Wayson Choy grew up in Vancouver's Chinatown district and has written about his experiences. He is the author of several books, including *The Jade Peony* and *All That Matters.* In this definition essay, also look for the narration, illustration, and cause and effect writing patterns.

1   My father and mother arrived separately to the British Columbia coast in the early part of the century. Because both my parents came from China, I look Chinese. But I cannot read or write Chinese and barely speak it. I love my North American citizenship. I don't mind being called a "banana," yellow on the outside and white on the inside. I'm proud I'm a banana. After all, in Canada and the United States, native Indians are "apples" (red outside, white inside); blacks are "Oreo cookies" (black and white); and Chinese are "bananas." These metaphors assume, both rightly and wrongly, that the North American culture has been primarily anglo-white. Cultural history has made me a banana.

2   My parents came as unwanted "aliens." It's better to be an alien here than to be dead of starvation in China. But after the Chinese Exclusion laws were passed in North America (late 1800s, early 1900s), no Chinese immigrants were granted citizenship in either Canada or the United States. Like those Old China village men from *Toi San* who, in the 1850s, laid down cliff-edge train tracks through the Rockies and the Sierras, or like those first women who came as mail-order wives or concubines and who as bond-slaves were turned into cheaper laborers or even prostitutes—like many of those men and women—my father and mother survived ugly, unjust times. In 1918, two hours after he got off the boat from Hong Kong, my father was called "chink" and told to go back to China. "Chink" is a hateful racist term, stereotyping the shape of Asian eyes: "a chink in the armor," an undesirable slit. For the Elders, the past was humiliating.

3   Eventually, the Second World War changed hostile attitudes toward the Chinese. During the war, Chinese men volunteered and lost their lives as members of the American and Canadian military. When hostilities ended, many more were proudly in uniform waiting to go overseas. Record Chinatown dollars were raised to buy War Bonds. After 1945, challenged by such money and ultimate sacrifices, the Exclusion laws in both Canada and the United States were revoked. Chinatown residents claimed their citizenship and sent for their families. By 1949, after the Communists took over China, those of us who arrived here as young children, or were born here, stayed. No longer aliens, we became legal citizens of North America. Many of us also became bananas.

4   Historically, banana is not a racist term. Although it clumsily stereotypes many of the children and grandchildren of the Old Chinatowns, the term actually follows the old Chinese tendency to assign endearing nick-names to replace formal names. The semicomic nicknames keep one humble. Thus, "banana" describes the generations who assimilated well into North American life. In fact, our families encouraged members of my generation in the 1950s and 1960s to get ahead, to get an English education, and to get a job with good pay and prestige. "Don't work like me," Chinatown parents said. "Work in an office!" The *iao wahkiu*, the Chinatown old-timers, also warned, "Never forget—you still be Chinese!"

5   None of us ever forgot. The mirror never lied. Many of us Chinatown teenagers felt we didn't quite belong in either world. We looked Chinese but thought and behaved North American. Impatient Chinatown parents wanted the best of both worlds for us, but they bluntly labeled their children and grandchildren *juk-sing* or even *mo no*. Not that we were totally "shallow bamboo butt-ends" or entirely "no brain," but we had less and less understanding of Old China traditions and less and less interest in their village histories. Father used to say we lacked Taoist ritual and Taoist manners. We were, he said, *mo ii*.

6   He was right. Chinatown's younger brains, like everyone else's of whatever race, were being colonized by "white bread" U.S. family television programs. We began to feel Chinese home life was inferior. We co-operated with English-language magazines that showed us how to act and what to buy. Seductive Hollywood movies made some of us secretly weep that we did not have movie star faces. American music made Chinese music sound like noise. By the seventies and eighties, many of us had consciously or unconsciously distanced ourselves from our Chinatown histories. We became bananas.

7   Finally, for me, in my forties, with the death first of my mother, then my father, I realized I did not belong anywhere unless I could understand the past. I needed to find the foundation of my Chineseness. I needed roots. I spent my college holidays researching the past. I read Chinatown oral histories, located documents, and searched out early articles. Those early citizens came back to life for me. Their long toil and blood sacrifices, and the proud record of their patient, legal challenges, gave us all our present rights as citizens. Canadian and American Chinatowns set aside their family tongue differences and encouraged each other to fight injustice. There were no borders. "After all," they affirmed, *"Daaih ga tohng yahn. . . . We are all Chinese!"*

8   In my book, *The Jade Peony*, I tried to recreate this past, to explore the beginnings of the conflicts trapped within myself, the struggle between being Chinese and being North American. I discovered a truth: These "between world" struggles are universal. In every human being, there is "the Other"—something that makes each of us feel how different we are from everyone else, even family members. Yet, ironically, we are all the same, wanting the same security and happiness. I know this now.

9   I think the early Chinese pioneers actually started "going bananas" from the moment they first settled upon the West Coast. They had no choice. They adapted. They initiated assimilation. If they had not, they and their families would have starved to death. I might even suggest that all surviving Chinatown citizens eventually became bananas. Only some, of course, were riper than others.

10   That's why I'm proudly a banana: I accept the paradox of being both Chinese and not Chinese. Now at last, whenever I look in the mirror or hear ghost voices shouting, "You still Chinese," I smile. I know another truth: In immigrant North America, we are all Chinese.

VOCABULARY AND COMPREHENSION

1.   According to the author, what is a "banana"?

_____

2.   Underline the thesis statement.

3.   Why did Choy's parents emigrate from China?

_____

4. How did the position of Chinese immigrants change after their participation in World War II?

_____

_____

_____

CRITICAL THINKING

5. What experiences did early Chinese immigrants have in North America?

_____

_____

_____

6. The author describes himself as a "banana." What connotations does such a term hold?

_____

_____

7. How did integration into North America affect the different generations of the Chinese community?

_____

_____

_____

_____

8. What three life lessons does the author learn about himself and others?

_____

_____

_____

WRITING TOPICS

Write about one of the following topics. Remember to explore, develop, and revise and edit your work.

1. What is your ethnicity? Do you identify with a particular ethnic group? Give examples of traditions or customs that link you to that group. If you do not identify with a particular group, explain why.
2. Should new immigrants adapt their lifestyles to the general lifestyle in the new country, or should they attempt to retain some of their cultural differences? Argue for one side of this issue.
3. Reflect on Navratilova's quotation. Choose a label that is placed on a group of people and define it. Describe some of that label's positive or negative connotations.

> *I came to live in a country I love; some people label me a defector. I have loved men and women in my life; I've been labeled 'the bisexual defector.' Want to know another secret? I'm even ambidextrous. I don't like labels. Just call me Martina.*
>
> —MARTINA NAVRATILOVA, PROFESSIONAL TENNIS PLAYER

READING 4

Fads
David A. Locher

David A. Locher is an author and college professor at Missouri Southern State College. The next excerpt about fads is from his book *Collective Behavior.* As you read this classification essay, also look for elements of definition and illustration writing.

1   Fads can take a wide variety of forms. However, almost all fads have a common pattern. They always appear quickly. They seem to come from nowhere and suddenly occupy the attention of virtually everyone. Then, as quickly as they came, they fade from popularity. Most fads can be placed into one of three general categories: activity fads, product fads, and fashion or apparel fads.

2   Activity fads center on some leisure activity like breakdancing or rollerblading. People suddenly feel excited about taking part in an activity that has never seemed appealing before. Prior to the 1950s, nobody felt the urge to stuff themselves into a phone booth with a large number of other people, and few have done it since then. However, it was all the rage for several years in the 1950s. Disco dancing came and (thankfully) went. Manufacturers often capitalize on these fads by producing a range of accessories to go with the activity. Often, music and movies that relate to the activity are rushed into production in an attempt to cash in on the fad before it ends. The song "The Streak," by Ray Stevens, and the film *Wheels* (a skateboarding film) are both good examples of attempts to make money from fad participants.

3   Useful product fads center on the acquisition of products that serve some purpose, however unimportant. In late 1998, "onion-bloom machines" suddenly became popular. Millions of Americans bought this kitchen tool designed to cut a large onion into a ready-to-fry "bloom" similar to the popular fried "onion blooms" served in restaurants. They were advertised on television almost every night. Stores quickly sold out their supply of the devices. The product itself is relatively useful, or at least serves some function. In this case, it makes a kind of variation of onion rings. However, the product is neither particularly necessary nor terribly important. The vast majority of onion-bloom machines are probably gathering dust in kitchen cabinets and closets all over the United States. Like many products at the center of these fads, onion-bloom machines remain on the market, but prices and demand dropped dramatically once the initial excitement wore off and people no longer felt the need for such a product in their lives.

4   Frivolous product fads may be the most interesting of all. People may stand in line for hours, fight with each other, and spend hundreds or thousands of dollars just so they can own something that is useless. The Pet Rock is the ideal example of this type of fad. In late 1975, an entrepreneur marketed a plain rock in a cardboard box called "The Pet Rock" and sold over one million at five dollars each. The Pet Rock was not decorated, nor did it do anything. It was, in fact, an ordinary rock. Today it may seem difficult to understand why one million Americans would pay five dollars for a stone, particularly in 1975 when five dollars could buy a meal or two tickets to the movies. Such is the nature of useless product fads. They are always difficult to explain or understand after they end.

5   Fashion fads may or may not involve the purchase of a particular item. For example, millions of American women purchased and wore "leg warmers" in the 1980s. These wooly socks without feet were worn over pants or stockings and were used for their look, rather than practical function. Other fashion-related fads may not involve buying anything. In late 1999, at the University of Missouri in Columbia, Missouri, hundreds of young women on campus began wearing their hair loosely gathered into a small ponytail that stuck straight up from the top of their head. The only accessory required was a rubber band. No products were purchased. The rapid adoption of the unflattering look and its relatively rapid disappearance would categorize the hairstyle as a fad.

6   Fads usually seem strange or even ridiculous in hindsight. Looking back, it is hard to believe that hundreds, thousands, or even millions of Americans took part in bizarre fads such as pole sitting, phone booth stuffing, and breakdancing. What drives otherwise normal people to pay money for a rock, to jump from a bridge or crane attached to a bungee cord, or to stand in freezing weather for hours in order to run, push, shove, and fight over a thirty-dollar talking toy? According to Turner and Killian, in their book *Collective Behavior*, there is nothing wrong with the participants in fads. Most of them are ordinary people. It is the situation that is abnormal. Once confusion and uncertainty set in, people can potentially be led into unusual behavior.

VOCABULARY AND COMPREHENSION

1.   Find a slang expression in paragraph 2 that means "popular."

   _____

2.   How does Locher define a fad?

   _____

   _____

3.   Underline the thesis statement in this essay.

4.   Locher divides one of the categories mentioned in the thesis statement into two subcategories. What are they?

   _____

   _____

5.   Give examples of the characteristics of each fad Locher mentions.

   _____

   _____

   _____

   _____

   _____

   _____

CRITICAL THINKING

6.   Locher clearly dislikes some of the fads. Which fads does he directly criticize?

   _____

   _____

7.   Who benefits the most when a product becomes a fad?

_____

_____

8.   Why do fads disappear?

_____

_____

WRITING TOPICS

Write about one of the following topics. Remember to explore, develop, and revise and edit your work.

1.   What fads have you followed? Have you bought something silly, joined in an activity that was suddenly popular, or worn your hair in a trendy style? Describe one or more fads that you have followed.

2.   Write a classification paragraph or an essay about other types of fads. Make sure the fads are linked by a common classification principle. For example, you might write about types of body improvement fads or types of hair fads, or you might break down fashion fads or activity fads into categories.

3.   Reflect on Shaw's quotation. Why do you think some people are motivated to create or follow fads?

66 A fashion is nothing but an induced epidemic. 99
—GEORGE BERNARD SHAW,
IRISH AUTHOR

READING 5

Dancing with Fear
Bebe Moore Campbell

Bebe Moore Campbell, who passed away in 2006, was a newspaper writer, a commentator for National Public Radio, and a contributing editor for *Essence* magazine. She was also an award-winning novelist whose works include *Your Blues Ain't Like Mine* and *Brothers and Sisters*. In the next selection, the author expresses her thoughts about fear. As you read this definition essay, also look for elements of narration, description, and cause and effect writing.

protracted:
lasting; drawn out

1   The last day of my first marriage exploded into a final siege of screaming and hollering, doors slamming, and two cars speeding down the driveway, each in search of a demilitarized zone. The silence that followed was the kind that comes when night duty is wide-eyed and **protracted.** I woke up the next morning feeling tired, crazy, and evil. I drank two cups of black coffee and headed off to work because that is what tough sisters do. Little did I know that my weary mind was about to betray me.

2   That evening at the Metro station, I boarded the subway for home. Hemmed in by wilted commuters, I began to feel dizzy and uncomfortably light-headed. My heart started racing, perspiration dripped down my face causing my glasses to slide, and I had a hard time breathing. I felt as though I were stuck, trapped by the bogeyman of my worst childhood nightmares. I wanted to flee, but my body was frozen. There was no doubt in my mind that I was going crazy and dying at the same horrible time.

3   Somehow I managed to get off at the next stop, sit down on a bench, and slowly breathe in and out until that rhythm gradually calmed me. Several

trains passed me by. When I finally did board one, I was a changed woman: My three-minute ordeal had marked me for life. I was scared as I rode to my destination, gripping a pole so tightly that there were marks on my moist palm. It's going to happen again, my mind told me. And it did.

4   I didn't know it then, but at twenty-seven I'd just had my first panic attack.

5   Panic is to fear what a wildfire is to a match. A panic attack is fear of fear, an irrational, out-of-control emotional response to an original panic that even experts can't pinpoint the source of. Childhood experiences, stress, genetics, caffeine, and insomnia can all play a role in panic disorder. More than the occasional bout of nerves that most people experience, true panic attacks are marked by a predictable pattern of **debilitating fear** and dread in response to specific stimuli, such as crowds, enclosed spaces, and driving on a freeway.

debilitating fear:
fear that is so great one cannot function

6   Ever since my first episode, I have been vulnerable, and not just in subways. I've had panic attacks while at concerts, on street corners, in hotel rooms, and in traffic. Whenever I think I have conquered the feeling, it simply chooses another space. For years, being on airplanes was a trigger. Now elevators are my challenge. In those split seconds when the doors close and the elevator is still, I battle the sensation of being swallowed up and trapped. For a long time, I have tried to shake this affliction and be normal like everybody else. I never dreamed that so many other Americans would become as haunted by the fear of fear as I am.

7   September 11 changed the collective American psyche as much as my first panic attack altered mine. I've spoken with people who admit that they are plagued by nightmares and worry. One New York manager I know had to let go of an employee who, many weeks after the World Trade Center collapsed, was still refusing to return to her Empire State Building office. Another businesswoman told me that the Manhattan apartment building she thought she had sold fell out of **escrow** immediately after the attack. Her prospective buyers admitted that they were too frightened to live in the city.

escrow:
a conditional contract

8   I know the feeling; I avoided subways for months after my first panic attack. And guess what? My fear only increased. In fact, the one guarantee about fear is this: Run from it, and it will find you.

9   You might say that I am a veteran of my own private war against terrorism. Since that long-ago day on the subway, I've learned how to dance with fear, which, in a nation now gripped by it, is a valuable skill. As I watch friends and family grapple with war's new tensions, I am struck by how far I've come. I have by no means conquered the panic that invaded my life all those years ago, but with time and effort I have learned to cope.

Vocabulary and Comprehension

1.   What is an affliction? Look for context clues in paragraph 6.

   _____

2.   What is the author defining in her essay?

   _____

3.   What are the main symptoms of the author's panic attacks?

   _____

   _____

4. In paragraph 5, the author uses an analogy. She compares two unusual things. What is the analogy, and why does she use such an analogy?

_____

_____

_____

5. Moore Campbell uses descriptive words and phrases that appeal to the senses. Underline at least three examples of descriptive imagery.

CRITICAL THINKING

6. What may have caused the author's first panic attack?

_____

_____

7. Why does the author compare her first panic attack with the fear caused by the terrorist attacks of September 11, 2001?

_____

_____

_____

8. In the last paragraph, the author says that she has learned how to "dance with fear." What does she mean?

_____

_____

WRITING TOPICS

Write about one of the following topics. Remember to explore, develop, and revise and edit your work.

1. Compare your childhood fears with your adult fears. How are they similar or different? Remember to define your fears.
2. The author says that September 11, 2001, has changed the collective American psyche. Do you agree or disagree? Explain your answer and give examples.
3. Reflect on Young's quotation. Then define *courage*. Give examples to support your definition.

66 *Courage is one step ahead of fear.* 99
—Coleman Young, politician

READING 6

Religious Faith Versus Spirituality
Neil Bissoondath

Neil Bissoondath, a journalist and writer, was born in Trinidad and immigrated to Canada. His works include *A Casual Brutality* and *Digging Up the Mountains*. In the next selection, the author contrasts religion and spirituality. As you read this comparison and contrast essay, also look for elements of argument and descriptive writing.

1   *Wait till someone you love dies. You'll see. You'll know God exists. You'll want Him to.* The prediction, repeated with minimal variation through the years by believers challenged by my non-belief, was never offered as a promise but as a vague threat, and always with a sense of satisfied

superiority, as if the speakers relished the thought that one day I would get my comeuppance.

2   They were, without exception, enthusiastic practitioners of their respective faiths—Roman Catholics, Presbyterians, Hindus, Muslims, God-fearing people all. Which was, to me, precisely the problem: Why all this fear?

3   And then one day, without warning, my mother died. Hers was the first death to touch me to the quick. Her cremation was done in the traditional Hindu manner. Under the direction of a **pundit,** my brother and I performed the ceremony, preparing the body with our bare hands, a contact more intimate than we'd ever had when she was alive.

4   As I walked away from her flaming **pyre,** I felt myself soaring with a lightness I'd never known before. I was suddenly freed from days of physical and emotional **lassitude,** and felt my first inkling of the healing power of ritual, the solace that ceremony can bring.

5   Still, despite the pain and the unspeakable sense of loss, the oft-predicted discovery of faith eluded me. I remained, as I do today, a nonbeliever, but I have no doubt that I underwent a deeply spiritual experience. This was when I began to understand that religious faith and spirituality do not necessarily have anything to do with each other—not that they are incompatible but that they are often mutually exclusive.

6   Western civilization has spent two thousand years blurring the distinction between the two, and as we enter the third millennium we are hardly more at peace with ourselves than people were a thousand years ago. Appreciating the distinction could help soothe our anxieties about the days to come.

7   Spirituality is the individual's ability to wonder at, and delight in, the indecipherable, like a baby marveling at the wiggling of its own toes. It is to be at ease with speculation, asking the unanswerable question and accepting that any answer would necessarily be incomplete, even false. It is recognizing that if scientific inquiry has inevitable limits, so too do religious explanations, which base themselves on unquestioning acceptance of the unprovable: neither can ever fully satisfy.

8   A sense of the spiritual comes from staring deep into the formation of a rose or a hibiscus and being astonished at the intricate delicacy of its symmetry without needing to see behind its perfection of form the fashioning hand of a deity.

9   It comes from watching your child being born and gazing for the first time into those newly opened eyes, from holding that child against your chest and feeling his or her heartbeat melding with yours.

10   It comes from gazing up into the sparkling solitude of a clear midnight sky, secure in the knowledge that, no matter how alone you may feel at moments, the message of the stars appears to be that you most indisputably are not.

11   At such moments, you need no **dogma** to tell you that the world seen or unseen, near or distant, is a wonderful and mysterious place. Spirituality, then, requires neither science nor religion, both of which hunger after answers and reassurance—while the essence of spirituality lies in the opening up of the individual to dazzlement. Spirituality entails no worship.

12   At the very moment of my mother's cremation, her brother, trapped thousands of miles away in England by airline schedules, got out his photographs of her and spread them on his coffee table. He reread her old letters and spent some time meditating on the life that had been lived—his way, at the very moment flames consumed her body, of celebrating the life and saying farewell, his way of engaging with the spiritual.

pundit:
Hindu priest

pyre:
a pile of burning wood used to cremate a dead body

lassitude:
weariness, fatigue

dogma:
a doctrine or set of beliefs unquestionably accepted as true

VOCABULARY AND COMPREHENSION

1. Circle the best answer: In paragraph 1, *comeuppance* means
   a. rising up. b. punishment. c. reward.

2. Write a synonym for the word *solace* in paragraph 4. _____

3. How does Bissoondath define spirituality? Give examples from the essay.

   _____

   _____

4. Why does the author object to believers who try to challenge his nonbelief?

   _____

   _____

CRITICAL THINKING

5. How does the death of the author's mother change him?

   _____

   _____

6. Why does the author give a lesser value to science and religion than to spirituality?

   _____

   _____

   _____

   _____

7. To support his belief in spirituality, why does Bissoondath give the example of his uncle in paragraph 12?

   _____

   _____

   _____

8. Bissoondath "soared with lightness" during the traditional Hindu ceremony and mentions the "healing power of ritual." Do you believe that such words contradict his strong opinions about religion? Explain your answer.

   _____

   _____

   _____

WRITING TOPICS

Write about one of the following topics. Remember to explore, develop, and revise and edit your work.

1. People cannot learn everything by reading books. Compare and contrast knowledge acquired through books to knowledge acquired through life experiences.

2. Compare and contrast two holidays, ceremonies, or festivals.

3. Reflect on this proverb. What are some reasons that people have for believing in a god or a higher power?

❝ The believer is happy; the doubter is wise.❞
—HUNGARIAN PROVERB

The Writer's Room
Images of Culture and Psychology

The previous readings and Editing Handbook Chapters 16–21 deal with popular culture and psychology. The following activities continue developing those themes.

Writing Activity 1: Photo Writing

Reflect on the popularity of *American Idol* and write on a topic related to it. For example, you might write about the causes of its popularity, the effects of winning the contest or appearing on it, or the process of getting on the show.

Writing Activity 2: Film Writing

1. *Lords of Dogtown* depicts a group of skateborders. As they achieve success, their friendship is threatened. Describe the steps the main characters take to overcome adversity.

2. *Supersize Me* and *Fast Food Nation* both look at the fast food industry. Compare and contrast the views that are presented in those films.

3. Both *Momento* and *Eternal Sunshine of the Spotless Mind* deal with issues related to memory. Choose one of the films and write about the causes or effects of the person's problems.

4. Films can tell us a lot about the country where they were made. Choose a foreign film and explain what the film shows us about that nation. Give examples from the film to support your point. Some films you could view are *Paradise Now* (Palestine), *Close to Home* (Israel), *Volver* (Spain), *The Queen* (Great Britain), and *Water* (India).

Themes: **Espionage and Great Discoveries**

READING 7

How Spies Are Caught

This process essay recounts how spies are caught. As you read the text, also look for definition and cause and effect writing patterns.

1   Espionage is a high-risk criminal offense. The traitor must fear arrest for the rest of his or her life, as the statute of limitations does not apply to espionage. Former National Security Agency employee Robert Lipka was arrested in 1996—thirty years after he left NSA and twenty-two years after his last contact with Soviet intelligence. There are four principal ways by which spies are detected: Reporting by U.S. sources within the foreign intelligence service, routine counterintelligence monitoring, a tip from a friend or spouse, or the traitor's own mistakes.

2   Of the Americans who held a security clearance who have been arrested for espionage, about half were caught as a result of information provided by a defector from the foreign intelligence service or an agent or friend within the foreign service that the spy was working for. People who betray their country often have little fear of being caught because they think they are smarter than everyone else. They think they can easily get away with it. However, no matter how smart or clever a spy may be, he or she has no protection against U.S. Government sources within the other intelligence service.

3   If the spy is not reported by sources within the other intelligence service, there is a strong likelihood of detection through routine counterintelligence operations. Of the cleared Americans arrested for espionage or attempted espionage during the past twenty years, 26 percent were arrested before they could do any damage, and 47 percent were caught during their first year of betrayal. This is not surprising, as counterintelligence agents know many of the foreign intelligence officers active in the United States and know where they work, where they live, where they hang out, and how they ply their trade. Any would-be spy who doesn't know how the counterintelligence system works is likely to be caught in the counterintelligence web.

4   Espionage usually requires keeping or preparing materials at home, traveling to signal sites or secret meetings at unusual times and places, a change in one's financial status with no corresponding change in job income, and periods of high stress that affect behavior. All of these changes in the normal pattern of behavior often come to the attention of other people and must be explained. Other people become suspicious and pass their suspicions on. This sometimes comes out during the periodic security clearance reinvestigation.

5   Spying is a lonely business. To explain these changes in behavior, or because of a need to confide in someone else, spies often confide in a spouse or try to enlist the help of a friend. The friend or spouse in whom the spy confides often does not remain a friend or loyal spouse after he or she realizes what is going on.

6   Most people who betray their country are not thinking rationally, or they would not be involved in such a self-destructive activity. They are driven, in large part, by irrational emotional needs to feel important, successful, powerful, or to get even or to take risks. These emotional needs are out of control, so the same emotional needs that lead them to betray also cause them

to flaunt their sudden affluence or to brag about their involvement in some mysterious activity. Because they are so mixed up psychologically, they make mistakes that get them caught.

VOCABULARY AND COMPREHENSION QUESTIONS

1. Find a word in paragraph 6 that means *to show off*.

   _____

2. What are the four ways in which spies are usually caught?

   _____

   _____

   _____

3. Give an example of the following types of support.

   Statistic: _____

   _____

   Anecdote: _____

4. How might a friend or coworker suspect that someone is a spy?

   _____

   _____

CRITICAL THINKING

5. Give at least three reasons that people betray government secrets.

   _____

   _____

   _____

6. By making inferences, determine some consequences of espionage on the individual spy.

   _____

   _____

   _____

7. In your opinion, how does treachery affect a country?

   _____

   _____

WRITING TOPICS

Write about one of the following topics. Remember to explore, develop, and revise and edit your work.

1. Most people value their privacy. Should government agencies in the United States have the right to spy on citizens by any means?
2. Many people feel insecure in this post-9/11 society. What steps can people take to feel safe in their own homes? Explain.
3. Reflect on Orwell's quotation. Has our age become a time of tyranny or enlightenment? Use examples to support your point of view.

> **"**To say 'I accept' in an age like our own is to say that you accept concentration-camps, rubber truncheons, Hitler, Stalin, bombs, airplanes, tinned food, machine guns, putsches, purges, slogans, Bedaux belts, gas-masks, submarines, spies, provocateurs, press-censorship, secret prisons, aspirins, Hollywood films, and political murder.**"**
> —GEORGE ORWELL, WRITER

READING 8

Nothing But Net
Mark McFadden

> Mark McFadden is the Lead Strategist for Internet Naming and Numbering at British Telecom. In the next essay, McFadden defends privacy in this era of cyber technology. As you read this argument essay, also look for elements of the cause and effect writing pattern.

1   Once—it seems ages ago—I was asked to surreptitiously examine the content of another employee's computer to look for evidence of wrongdoing. I did it. Even though I found evidence that the employee had broken both work rules and the rules of common decency, I still felt as if I had violated someone's privacy. I was glad that it at least took some degree of technical skill to spy on my colleague down the hall. Today, that meager safeguard has disappeared. A whole market of programs has emerged that allows one to secretly record everything a person does with a computer. The emergence of these unethical snooping programs leaves me cold. Doesn't anyone have a conscience anymore?

2   One of the programs, SpectorSoft's eBlaster, promises that it will let the user "find out everything your spouse, children, and employees do online via e-mail." I can imagine some people defending the use of the program— perhaps providing a parent with warnings about drug use, gang participation, thoughts of suicide, or other threats to a child's well-being. It's also possible to imagine an employer using the spying software to ensure compliance with work rules and to detect other wrongdoing. Even so, it's wrong.

3   Defenders of this technology always seem to take the perspective of the person doing the spying and never the children, employees, or spouses he or she is spying upon. Defenders of this technology seldom use the word *trust* either.

4   Spying on children online, for instance, is almost laughable. If parents think their 14-year-old is doing, saying, or seeing things they don't approve of—it is time to move on. If I remember my teenage years correctly, children are going to do what they want whether their parents spy on them or not. If a parent blocks access to the computer in his or her house, the computer at a friend's will do just as well. **Stealthy** technology like eBlaster invites equally stealthy responses by those being spied upon. Today's technology-savvy youths are likely to find a way to disable the software while working online and then start it up again after they are finished—without their parents knowing it.

5   What about spying on an employee? The truly bad employee is going to be caught anyway—with or without spying technology. Really good employees are going to migrate to companies where there is an atmosphere of trust. The others will forever resent the image of an employer that looks over their shoulders at every possible moment. If I use the corporate e-mail to receive an emergency message from my day care provider, what need does my employer have to discover that my child has chicken pox?

6   I am well aware that the legal system today says that it is okay for companies to read their employees' e-mail and spy on them because they use the company computers. But consider this: just because companies can do it, does that make it right?

stealthy: sneaky

VOCABULARY AND COMPREHENSION

1. Find a word in paragraph 1 that means "secretly."

   _____

2. What introductory style does the author use? Circle the best answer.
   a. Definition   b. Anecdote   c. Historical background

3. Who is the audience for this essay?

   _____

4. What is the author's main point?

   _____
   _____

CRITICAL THINKING

5. Why does Mark McFadden object to snooping programs?

   _____
   _____
   _____

6. What two arguments does the author give to acknowledge the opposing point of view?

   _____
   _____
   _____

7. What two examples does the author give to defend his own position?

   _____
   _____
   _____
   _____

8. The author writes that defenders "seldom use the word *trust*" (paragraph 3). Why is trust so important to the author's argument?

   _____
   _____
   _____

WRITING TOPICS

Write about one of the following topics. Remember to explore, develop, and revise and edit your work.

1. Why do parents spy on their children? How does spying affect the parent-child relationship?
2. What are some arguments in favor of using spy technology to spy on children or employees? Write a counterargument to the essay "Nothing But Net."
3. Reflect on Folvary's quotation. What are your views about a law like the one proposed by bill 2068? Should children ever be asked to spy on their own families or friends? Explain your answer.

> *Federal and state governments in the USA have been adopting various spying techniques of totalitarian states, and they are increasingly using children as spies against their parents. California's assembly bill 2068 would require children to be asked personal questions such as whether their parents spank them, keep guns in the house, or watch violent television shows.*
>
> —FRED FOLVARY, JOURNALIST

READING 9

Growing Up in Cyberspace
Brent Staples

Brent Staples, a reporter for *The New York Times*, writes about culture and politics and has written an award-winning memoir called *Parallel Time*. In the next essay, Staples reflects on the effects of new technologies. The selection is mainly an example of cause and effect writing, but it contains elements of the comparison and contrast pattern as well.

1   My tenth-grade heartthrob was the daughter of a fearsome steelworker who struck terror into the hearts of fifteen-year-old boys. He made it his business to answer the telephone—and so always knew who was calling—and grumbled in the background when the conversation went on too long. Unable to make time by phone, the boy either gave up or appeared at the front door. This meant submitting to the intense scrutiny that the girl's father soon became known for.

2   He greeted me with a crushing handshake and then leaned in close in a transparent attempt to find out whether I was one of those bad boys who smoked. He retired to the den during the visit but cruised by the living room now and then to let me know he was watching. He let up after some weeks, but only after getting across what he expected of a boy who spent time with his daughter and how upset he'd be if I disappointed him.

3   This was my first sustained encounter with an adult outside my family who needed to be convinced of my worth as a person. This, of course, is a crucial part of growing up. Faced with the same challenge today, however, I would probably pass on meeting the girl's father—and **outflank** him on the Internet.

outflank:
go beyond the reach of somebody

4   Thanks to e-mail, online chat rooms, and instant messages—which permit private, real-time conversations—adolescents have at last succeeded in shielding their social lives from adult scrutiny. But this comes at a cost: teenagers nowadays are both more connected to the world at large than ever and more cut off from the social encounters that have historically prepared young people for the move into adulthood.

5   The Internet was billed as a revolutionary way to enrich our social lives and expand our civic connections. This seems to have worked well for elderly people and others who were isolated before they got access to the World Wide Web. But a growing body of research is showing that heavy use of the Net can actually isolate younger socially connected people who unwittingly allow time online to replace face-to-face interactions with their families and friends.

6   Online shopping, checking e-mail, and Web surfing—mainly solitary activities—have turned out to be more isolating than watching television, which friends and family often do in groups. Researchers have found that the time spent in direct contact with family members drops by as much as half for every hour we use the Net at home.

7   This should come as no surprise to the two-career couples who have seen their domestic lives taken over by e-mail and wireless **tethers** that keep people working around the clock. But a startling body of research from the Human-Computer Interaction Institute at Carnegie Mellon has shown that heavy Internet use can have a stunting effect outside the home as well.

tethers:
restraining ropes

8   Studies show that **gregarious**, well-connected people actually lost friends, and experienced symptoms of loneliness and depression, after joining

gregarious:
friendly

discussion groups and other on-line activities. People who communicated with disembodied strangers online found the experience empty and emotionally frustrating but were nonetheless seduced by the novelty of the new medium. As Professor Robert Kraut, a Carnegie Mellon researcher, told me recently, such people allowed low-quality relationships developed in virtual reality to replace higher-quality relationships in the real world.

9   No group has embraced this socially impoverishing trade-off more enthusiastically than adolescents, many of whom spend most of their free hours cruising the Net in sunless rooms. This hermetic existence has left many of these teenagers with nonexistent social skills—a point widely noted in stories about the computer geeks who rose to prominence in the early days of Silicon Valley.

10   Adolescents are drawn to cyberspace for different reasons than adults. As the writer Michael Lewis observed in his book *Next: The Future Just Happened*, children see the Net as a transformational device that lets them discard **quotidian** identities for more glamorous ones. Mr. Lewis illustrated the point with Marcus Arnold, who, as a fifteen-year-old, adopted a **pseudonym** a few years ago and posed as a twenty-five-year-old legal expert for an Internet information service. Marcus did not feel the least bit guilty and was not **deterred** when real-world lawyers discovered his secret and accused him of being a fraud. When asked whether he had actually read the law, Marcus responded that he found books "boring," leaving us to conclude that he had learned all he needed to know from his family's big-screen TV.

quotidian:
everyday

pseudonym:
false name

deterred:
discouraged; stopped

11   Marcus is a child of the Net, where everyone has a pseudonym, telling a story makes it true, and adolescents create older, cooler, more socially powerful selves any time they wish. The ability to slip easily into a new, false self is tailor-made for emotionally fragile adolescents who can consider a bout of acne or a few excess pounds an unbearable tragedy.

12   But teenagers who spend much of their lives hunched over computer screens miss the socializing, which is the real-world experience that would allow them to leave adolescence behind and grow into adulthood. These vital experiences, like much else, are simply not available in a virtual form.

VOCABULARY AND COMPREHENSION

1.   Without using a dictionary, define *hermetic* as it is used in paragraph 9. Use clues in the text to help you.

_____

2.   Underline a sentence in this essay that sums up the author's main point.

3.   What are the causes, or reasons, for young people's attraction to Internet technology, according to Staples?

_____

_____

4.   Staples gives many examples of the negative effects of Internet technology. List at least three negative effects.

_____

_____

_____

_____

_____

CRITICAL THINKING

5. What does the story about Marcus (paragraphs 10 and 11) tell us about the world of the Internet?

   _____

   _____

6. Compare Brent Staples's childhood with the childhoods of young people today. How are they different?

   _____

   _____

   _____

7. What positive effect of Internet technology does Staples mention?

   _____

   _____

8. In your opinion, what are some other ways people benefit from the Internet?

   _____

   _____

   _____

   _____

   _____

WRITING TOPICS

Write a paragraph or an essay about one of the following topics. Remember to explore, develop, and revise and edit your work.

Today every invention is received with a cry of triumph, which soon turns into a cry of fear.
—BERTOLD BRECHT, WRITER

1. Write about a new technology, and explain how it has affected your life.
2. Compare the effects of television and the Internet on you or on society in general. How are the effects similar or different?
3. Reflect on Brecht's quotation. Choose some inventions and write about their effects on our society.

The Writer's Room **Images of Espionage and Great Discoveries**

The previous three readings and Editing Handbook Chapters 22, 23, 24, 27, and 28 deal with issues related to espionage and great discoveries. The following activities continue developing those themes.

Writing Activity 1: Photo Writing

How has the technological world helped or hindered personal relationships?

Photo illustration by Tony Cenicola/The New York Times

Writing Activity 2: Film Writing

1. *The Aviator, October Sky*, and *The Astronaut Farmer* deal with inventors who had great dreams. Compare and contrast two of these films.

2. In *Disturbia*, a teen who is under house arrest believes he is living next door to a serial killer. He spies on his neighbor. Using descriptive imagery, narrate what happens in the story.

3. View one of the Bourne Identity films (*The Bourne Identity, The Bourne Supremacy,* or *The Bourne Ultimatum*). Describe the process the main character goes through.

4. View other films that deal with spying such as *Syriana, The Good Shepherd, Spy Game, Blood Simple,* and *Mission Impossible*. Write about different categories of spying.

Themes: **College Life and Health Care**

READING 10

Body over Mind
Mitch Albom

> Award-winning sports columnist Mitch Albom writes for the *Detroit Free Press*. He is also the author of eight books, including *Five People You Meet in Heaven* and *Tuesdays with Morrie*. In this comparison and contrast essay, Albom discusses the culture of college sports. As you read, also look for elements of narration, cause and effect, and argument writing.

1   The little chocolate doughnuts were in a box next to the coffee urn. Normally, high schools don't provide food for their assemblies, but today was special with all of these TV crews, radio people, and sports writers. A table was arranged near the front of the room, and a reporter set down a microphone alongside a dozen others. "Testing 1-2, testing 1-2," he said.

2   Suddenly, the whole room seemed to shift. The guest of honor had arrived. He didn't enter first. He was preceded by an entourage of friends, coaches, his grandmother, his aunt, his baby brother, more friends, more coaches, and his girlfriend. She wore a black dress and jewelry and had her hair pinned up, as if going to the prom, even though it was mid-afternoon and math classes were in progress upstairs.

3   Her boyfriend took his seat. He wore a stud earring and a colorful jacket. Only eighteen years old, he was the largest person in the room at 6-feet-9, 300 pounds. It was for his body—and what he could do with it—that these people had come.

4   "Good afternoon," Robert Traylor began, reading from a sheet of paper. His voice was deep as a businessman's, but his words were those of a nervous teen. "I'd like to welcome everyone. My dream is to play in the NBA one day. I've chosen the college that can best help me achieve my dream."

5   The crowd held its breath. For three years, a parade of grown men, employed by major universities, had been coming to Detroit to watch Robert Traylor play. They called him at home, they called his friends, and they called his relatives. They showed him videos and promised him stardom. They wooed him like a golden child.

6   "The school I will be attending," Traylor said, "will be the University of Michigan."

7   The room erupted in applause.

8   Down the hall, sitting alone by a computer, was another high school senior named Kevin Jones. Like Traylor, Jones is black, lives in Detroit, and is being raised with no father in the house. His mother supports the family by working as a janitor. Like Traylor, Jones will also be attending Michigan next fall—on a full scholarship.

9   But unlike Traylor, Jones, a thin kid with a disarming smile, got his scholarship for studying three hours a day, getting the highest grades, keeping his attendance over 95 percent, and never violating school conduct rules.

10   Kevin Jones is the most important currency in the city of Detroit, a kid with a brain. He did not announce his college decision at a press conference; he had to wait for Michigan to accept him. A letter finally arrived at the house his family shares with another family in northwest Detroit. He peeked through

the envelope and saw the word "Congratulations." He smiled. His grandmother hugged him and said, "I'm so proud of you! I'm so proud of you."

11   Back at the press conference, reporters were yelling questions: "Robert, when did you decide on Michigan?"

12   "Robert, do you think you'll start?"

13   "Robert, what did the Michigan coaches say?"

14   Traylor smiled at the last one. "I don't know. I haven't told them yet." Not that it mattered. At that moment, it was being announced all over the radio.

15   This is crazy. A press conference for a high school ballplayer? What message are we sending the other students at Murray-Wright High School who were peeking through the doors wondering what the fuss was about?

16   Don't misunderstand. Robert Traylor is a bright young man with a special talent, but why have a press conference about where he will dribble and shoot? Isn't there enough spotlight on these kids already? Besides, encouraging inner-city teens to shoot for the NBA is like encouraging them to win the lottery. Most will be disappointed.

17   Several years ago, a high school star named Chris Webber had one of these press conferences—and two years later, he held another to say he was leaving school for the pros. Someone asked Traylor about that Monday.

18   "I hope (I can) leave college in two years," he said excitedly. Later he tried to correct this, but everyone knew what he meant. In his dreams of swimming in NBA waters, college is the diving board.

19   It is more than a diving board to Kevin Jones. He has no plans of leaving early. "I want to study business and open my own one day," he said. He showed a résumé he had done himself. It noted his awards in the Navy ROTC and his computer literacy in IBM and Macintosh systems.

20   This is no nerd. This is a good-looking kid who hears bullets in his neighborhood and remembers what his grandmother said: "When there's trouble, just keep walking." He works hard because he was taught to work hard, and he doesn't read off a sheet when he says, "One day, after I get my business going, I'm going to come back to this school and teach math." That is more important than coming back to sign autographs.

21   The doughnuts were mostly gone now. Traylor's aunt was being interviewed; so were his friends, who mugged for the cameras. Traylor himself posed, wearing a maize and blue Michigan cap. Down the hall, the computer flipped on, and a young man began a new application for room and board money. He started with his name, "Kevin Jones."

22   No offense, but if there had to be a press conference Monday, it should have been Kevin's.

VOCABULARY AND COMPREHENSION

1. Why does Robert Traylor receive so much attention from the media?

_____

_____

2. Why does Kevin Jones want to attend college?

_____

_____

3. What steps has Kevin Jones taken to ensure that he can go to college?

_____

_____

_____

4. Using your own words, describe the main idea of this essay.

_____

_____

_____

CRITICAL THINKING

5. How are the personalities and physical characteristics of Robert Traylor and Kevin Jones similar? How are they different?

_____

_____

_____

_____

_____

6. The University of Michigan shows a different attitude toward Traylor and Jones as future students. How does the author suggest this difference in attitude?

_____

_____

7. Albom writes that "encouraging inner-city teens to shoot for the NBA is like encouraging them to win the lottery" (paragraph 16). Why does he make such a comparison?

_____

_____

_____

WRITING TOPICS

Write about one of the following topics. Remember to explore, develop, and revise and edit your work.

1. Argue against Albom's main point. Argue that high school athletes deserve the attention and praise that others give to them.
2. Many people tend to idolize great athletes. Think of an athlete who is deserving of public praise and adulation, and think of another who is not worthy. Compare and contrast the two sports heroes. (If you are not familiar with sports, then compare two other types of people, such as actors, writers, musicians, or politicians.)

66 I pay no attention whatsoever to anybody's praise or blame. I simply follow my own path.99

—WOLFGANG AMADEUS MOZART,
MUSICIAN AND COMPOSER

3. Reflect on Mozart's quotation. Write about how the quotation relates to the events in "Body over Mind."

READING 11

Dying to Be Bigger
H.D.

This cause and effect essay first appeared in *Seventeen* magazine and was written by a young steroid user. As you read, notice how the author also uses elements of narration and description writing.

1   I was only fifteen years old when I first started maiming my body with the abuse of anabolic steroids. I was always trying to fit in with the "cool" crowd in junior high and high school. Willingly smoking or buying pot when offered, socially drinking in excess, displaying a macho image—and, of course, the infamous "kiss and tell"—were essentials in completing my insecure mentality.

2   Being an immature, cocky kid from a somewhat wealthy family, I was not very well liked in general. In light of this, I got beat up a lot, especially in my first year of public high school.

3   I was one of only three sophomores to get a varsity letter in football. At five-foot-nine and 174 pounds, I was muscularly inferior to the guys at the same athletic level and quite conscious of the fact. So when I heard about this wonderful drug called steroids from a teammate, I didn't think twice about asking to buy some. I could hardly wait to take them and get bigger.

4   I bought three months' worth of Dianobol (an oral form of steroids and one of the most harmful). I paid 55 dollars. I was told to take maybe two or three per day. I totally ignored the directions and warnings and immediately started taking five per day. This is how eager I was to be bigger and possibly "cooler." Within only a week, everything about me started to change. I was transforming mentally and physically. My attention span became almost nonexistent. Along with becoming extremely aggressive, I began to abandon nearly all academic and family responsibilities. In almost no time, I became flustered and agitated with simple everyday activities. My **narcissistic** ways brought me to engage in verbal as well as physical fights with family, friends, and teachers, but mostly strangers.

narcissistic: self-involved

5   My bodily transformations were clearly visible. In less than a month, I took the entire three-month supply. I gained nearly thirty pounds. Most of my weight was from water retention, although at the time I believed it to be muscle. Instead of having pimples like the average teenager, my acne took the form of grotesque, cyst-like blood clots that would occasionally burst while I was lifting weights. My nipples became the size of grapes and hurt severely, which is common among male steroid users. My hormonal level was completely out of whack.

6   At first, I had such an overload of testosterone that I would have to masturbate daily, at minimum, in order to prevent having "wet dreams." Obviously, these factors enhanced my lust, which eventually led to acute perversion. My then almost-horrifying physique prevented me from having sexual encounters.

7   All of these factors led to my classification as a wretched menace. My parents grew sick and tired of all the trouble I began to get in. They were scared of me, it seemed. They cared so much about my welfare, education, and state of mind that they sent me to a boarding school that summer.

8   I could not obtain any more steroids there, and for a couple of months, it seemed I had subtle withdrawal symptoms and severe side effects. Most of the

time that summer I was either depressed or filled with intense anger, both of which were uncontrollable unless I was in a state of intoxication from any mind-altering drug.

9   After a year of being steroid-free, things started to look promising for me, and I eventually gained control over myself. Just when I started getting letters from big-name colleges to play football for them, I suffered a herniated disc. I was unable to participate in any form of physical activity the entire school year.

10   In the fall, I attended a university in the Northeast, where I was on the football team but did not play due to my injury. I lifted weights with the team every day. I wasn't very big at the time, even after many weeks of working out. Once again I found myself to be physically inferior and insecure about my physique. And again, I came into contact with many teammates using steroids.

11   My roommate was a six-foot-three, 250-pound linebacker who played on the varsity squad as a freshman. As the weeks passed, I learned of my roommate's heavy steroid use. I was exposed to dozens of different steroids I had never even heard of. Living in the same room with him, I watched his almost daily injections. After months of enduring his drug offerings, I gave in.

12   By the spring of my freshman year, I had become drastically far from normal in every way. My body had stopped producing hormones due to the amount of synthetic testosterone I injected into my system. At five-foot-eleven, 225 pounds, disproportionately huge, acne-infested, outrageously aggressive, and nearing complete sterility, I was in a terrible state of body and mind. Normal thoughts of my future (not pertaining to football), friends, family, reputation, moral status, and so on, were entirely beyond me. My entire essence had become one of a primitive barbarian.

13   This was when I was taking something called Sustunon (prepackaged in a syringe labeled "For equine use only") containing four types of testosterone. I was "stacking" (a term used by steroid users which means mixing different types) to get well-cut definition along with mass.

14   It was around this time when I was arrested for threatening a security guard. When the campus police came to arrest me, they saw how aggressive and large my roommate and I were, so they searched our room and found dozens of bottles and hundreds of dollars' worth of steroids and syringes. We had a trial, and the outcome was that I could only return the next year if I got drug-tested on a monthly basis. I certainly had no willpower or desire to quit my steroid abuse, so I transferred schools.

15   After a summer of even more heavy-duty abuse, I decided to attend a school that would cater to my instinctively backward ways. That fall I entered a large university in the South. Once again, I simply lifted weights without being involved in competition or football. It was there that I finally realized how out of hand I had become with my steroid problem.

16   Gradually, I started to taper down my dosages. Accompanying my reduction, I began to drink more and more. My grades plummeted again. I began going to bars and keg parties on a nightly basis.

17   My celibacy, mental state, aggressiveness, lack of athletic competition, and alcohol problem brought me to enjoy passing my pain onto others by means of physical aggression. I got into a fight almost every time I drank. In the midst of my insane state, I was arrested for assault. I was in really deep this time. Finally, I realized how different from everybody else I had become, and I decided not to taper off but to quit completely.

18   The average person seems to think that steroids just make one bigger. But they are a drug, and an addictive one at that. This drug does not put a person in a stupor or in a hallucinogenic state but rather gives him an up, all-around "bad-ass" mentality that far exceeds that of either normal life or any other narcotic I have tried. Only lately are scientists and researchers discovering how addictive steroids are—only now, after hundreds of thousands may have done such extreme damage to their lives, bodies, and minds.

19   One of the main components of steroid addiction is how unsatisfied the user is with his overall appearance. Although I was massive and had dramatic muscular definition, I was never content with my body, despite frequent compliments. I was always changing types of steroids, places of injection, workouts, diet, and so on. I always found myself saying, "This one ought to do it," or "I'll quit when I hit 230 pounds."

20   When someone is using steroids, he has psychological disorders that increase when usage stops. One disorder is anxiety from the loss of the superior feeling one gets from the drug. Losing the muscle mass, high energy level, and superhuman sensation that one is so accustomed to is terrifying.

21   Another ramification of taking artificial testosterone over time is the effect on the natural testosterone level (thus the male sex drive). As a result of my steroid use, my natural testosterone level was ultimately depleted to the point where my sex drive was drastically reduced in comparison to the average twenty-one-year-old male. My testicles shriveled up, causing physical pain as well as extreme mental anguish. Thus, I desired girls less. This, however, did lead me to treat them as people, not as objects of my desires. It was a beginning step on the way to a more sane and civil mentality.

22   The worst symptoms of my withdrawal after many months of drug abuse were emotional. My emotions fluctuated dramatically, and I rapidly became more sensitive. My hope is that this feeling of being trailed by isolation and aloneness will diminish and leave me free of its constant haunting.

VOCABULARY AND COMPREHENSION

1.   Find a word in paragraph 1 that means "harming." _____

2.   Circle the best answer: The word *ramification* in paragraph 21 means
     a. consequence.   b. understanding.   c. origin.

3.   Why did the author use steroids?

     _____

     _____

     _____

     _____

4.   How did the author change with continued steroid use? List physical and psychological changes that occurred.

     _____

     _____

     _____

     _____

     _____

     _____

5. The essay lists both short- and long-term effects of steroid use. What are some long-term effects?

_____

_____

_____

Critical Thinking

6. What is the significance of the title of this essay?

_____

_____

7. The author stopped using steroids for one year. Why did he start up again in college even though he knew the risks?

_____

_____

_____

8. In paragraph 18, the author refers to steroids as "a drug." List five similarities between steroids and other illegal narcotics.

_____

_____

_____

_____

_____

9. Basically, the author narrates what happened to him. What can you infer from the author's story? In other words, what is the deeper message?

_____

_____

_____

Writing Topics

Write about one of the following topics. Remember to explore, develop, and revise and edit your work.

1. What can cause a person to have a poor body image? List some examples.
2. Since 1973, performance-enhancing drugs have been banned at the Olympic Games. However, at each Olympics, athletes from nations around the world are disqualified because they have used banned substances. Should officials simply allow performance-enhancing drugs rather than trying to police the use of such drugs? Explain your answer.
3. Reflect on Morissette's quotation. What do both Morissette and the essay writer seem to be saying about body image? How are their opinions about body image similar or different?

> ❝I think of my body as an instrument rather than an ornament.❞
> —Alanis Morissette, singer and composer

READING 12

It's Class, Stupid!
Richard Rodriguez

Richard Rodriguez is a writer and an essayist who published the novel *Days of Obligation*. He also writes for the *Los Angeles Times* and *Harper's*. The next selection is an argument essay about affirmative action that originally appeared in the webzine Salon.com. As you read, also look for elements of the comparison and contrast writing pattern.

1   Some weeks ago, a law professor at the University of Texas got in trouble for saying that African Americans and Mexicans are at a disadvantage in higher education because they come from cultures that tolerate failure. Jesse Jackson flew to Austin to deliver a fiery speech; students demanded the professor's **ouster.**

ouster: dismissal

2   It was all typical of the way we have debated affirmative action for years. Both sides ended up arguing about race and ethnicity; both sides ignored the deeper issue of social inequality. Even now, as affirmative action is finished in California and is being challenged in many other states, nobody is really saying what is wrong with affirmative action: It is unfair to poor whites.

3   Americans find it hard to talk about what Europeans more easily call the lower class. We find it easier to sneer at the white poor—the "rednecks," the trailer-park trash. The rural white male is Hollywood's politically correct villain **du jour.**

du jour: French term meaning "of the day" or "at the present time"

4   We seem much more comfortable worrying about race; it's our most important metaphor for social distinction. We talk about the difference between black and white, not the difference between rich and poor. American writers—Richard Wright, James Baldwin, Toni Morrison—are brilliant at describing what it is like to be a racial minority. But America has few writers who describe as well what it is like to be poor. We don't have a writer of the stature of D.H. Lawrence—the son of an English coal miner—who grew up embarrassed by his soft hands. At the University of Texas, it was easier for the Sicilian-born professor Lino Graglia to notice that the students who dropped out of school were Mexican-American or black than to wonder if they might be poor.

5   At the same time, the angry students who accused the law professor of racism never bothered to acknowledge the obvious: Poor students *do* often come from neighborhoods and from families that tolerate failure or at least have learned the wisdom of slight expectations. Education is fine, if it works. I meet young people all the time who want to go to college, but Mama needs her oldest son to start working. It is better to have a dollar-and-cents job working at Safeway or McDonald's than a college diploma that might not guarantee a job.

6   Anyone who has taught poor children knows how hard it is to persuade students not to be afraid of success. There is the boy who is mocked by male classmates for speaking good English. There is the girl who comes from a family where women are not assumed to need, or want, education.

7   We also don't like to admit, though we have argued its merits for twenty years, that the chief beneficiaries of affirmative action—black, brown, female—are primarily middle class. It still doesn't occur to many progressives that affirmative action might be unfair to poor whites. That is because poor

whites do not constitute an officially recognized minority group. We don't even notice the presence or, more likely, the absence of the poor white on college campuses. Our only acknowledgment of working-class existence is to wear fashionable working-class denim.

8   A man I know, when he went to Harvard, had only a pair of running shoes to wear and had never owned a tie. He dropped out of Harvard after two years. I suppose some of his teachers imagined it was because he was Hispanic, not that he was dirt poor. The advantage I had, besides my parents, were my Irish nuns—who themselves had grown up working class. They were free of that middle-class fear (typical today in middle-class teachers) of changing students too much. The nuns understood that education is not an exercise in self-esteem. They understood how much education costs, the price the heart pays.

9   Every once in a while, I meet middle-class Americans who were once lower class. They come from inner cities and from West Texas trailer parks. They are successful now beyond their dreams, but bewildered by loss, becoming so different from their parents. If only America would hear their stories, we might, at last, acknowledge social class. And we might know how to proceed, now that affirmative action is dead and so many poor kids remain to be educated.

VOCABULARY AND COMPREHENSION

1.   Find a word in paragraph 6 that means "made fun of."

   _____

2.   What does the word *constitute* in paragraph 7 mean? Circle the best answer.
      a. govern   b. appoint   c. represent

3.   According to the author, what prevents many poor people from attending college? Give at least three reasons.

   _____

   _____

4.   Who benefits the most from affirmative action, according to the author?

   _____

   _____

5.   Look in the first two paragraphs and underline the thesis statement.

CRITICAL THINKING

6.   Explain why Rodriquez disagrees with affirmative action.

   _____

   _____

   _____

7.   The author compares the English writer D.H. Lawrence with American writers such as Toni Morrison. How is this comparison relevant for this essay?

   _____

   _____

   _____

   _____

8. In paragraph 1, Rodriquez includes an anecdote about a University of Texas law professor. Explain why you think the author agrees or disagrees with the professor.

_____

_____

_____

_____

9. The author writes that his teachers, Irish nuns with working-class backgrounds, "understood how much education costs, the price the heart pays." What does he mean? (Look in paragraphs 8 and 9 for clues.)

_____

_____

_____

_____

_____

WRITING TOPICS

Write about one of the following topics. Remember to explore, develop, and revise and edit your work.

1. In your employment or education, have you had any positive or negative experiences because of your economic, gender, ethnic, or racial background?
2. Do you agree or disagree with the author's argument? Support your point of view with specific examples.
3. Reflect on Baldwin's quotation. What is his deeper meaning? Do you agree with him? Give examples or anecdotes to support your views.

> _Anyone who has ever struggled with poverty knows how extremely expensive it is to be poor._
> —JAMES BALDWIN, AUTHOR

READING 13

The Case for Affirmative Action
An Open Letter to Five Justices
Dave Malcolm

> Dave Malcolm is a professor in San Diego. In 1995, the following letter was entered into the _Congressional Record_ by U.S. Representative Esteban Torres in response to anti–affirmative action decisions by the Supreme Court. In this letter, the author has used the illustration writing pattern along with the definition, comparison and contrast, and argument patterns.

1   On Monday, June 12, 1995, at 10:50 a.m., I left the office of my cardiologist having just been informed that my aortic valve implant was "leaking" and that replacement surgery would be required within the next three to six months. At 10:55 a.m., on the same date, I heard on my car radio about two new Supreme Court 5-4 decisions, each apparently placing serious additional limitations on programs of affirmative action. I drove homeward, feeling sick at heart—not from feelings of anxiety about my imminent open-heart surgery but from feelings of dismay at the direction in which the country seems to be moving, especially in regard to affirmative action.

2   You see, I know a lot about affirmative action. I count myself an expert on the subject. After all, I have benefited from it all my life. That is because I am white, I am male, I am Anglo, and I am Protestant. We male WASPs have had a great informal affirmative action program going for decades, maybe centuries. I am not speaking only of the way our "old boy networks" help people like me get into the right colleges or get jobs or get promotions. That is only the surface. Underneath, our real affirmative action is much more than just a few direct interventions at key moments in life. The real affirmative action is also indirect and at work twenty-four hours a day, seven days a week, year in and year out. Because it is informal and indirect, we tend to forget or deny just how all-important and pervasive it really is.

3   However, far be it from me to put the direct "old boy" surface stuff down. I was admitted without difficulty to the Ivy League college my father had attended. This was back in the days when the only quotas were quotas to keep certain people out, not to help them get in. There were no limits on reasonably bright kids like me—the admissions people spoke of the children of alumni as "legacies," but whether this was because the college was inheriting us as students or because the college hoped to inherit money from our families, I was never quite sure. I got a teaching job right out of college in the heart of the Depression—my father was a school superintendent well liked among his colleagues.

4   After World War II, when I became a university professor, I received promotion and tenure in minimum time, more quickly than many of my female colleagues. Of course, the decision makers knew me better; I was part of the monthly poker group and played golf every Friday afternoon. Yes, direct affirmative action—direct preferential treatment because of my gender and my color and good connections—have been good to me.

5   But, like other white males, I have benefited less obviously but far more significantly from indirect preferential treatment. Indirect affirmative action is at work to a greater or lesser degree on behalf of virtually all white males, whether one is aware of it or not. It is what did not happen to me. There were destructive, painful experiences that I did not have to endure. Early in life, I knew that boys were more important than girls and so did the girls. I have never had to worry about whether my skin color was light enough or dark enough.

6   For two of my long-time colleagues and closest personal friends, it has been a very different story. Raymond was the lightest skinned member of his family. He recalls that he was the only one who could get his hair cut downtown—but the family had to drop him off a block away from the barber shop. He once told me that he had probably spent more time worrying about his light skin than any other one thing in life. Would his fellow African Americans think he was black enough? When whites thought he was East Indian or South American, should he let them think so?

7   Maria had the opposite problem. As a child, she was called *la prieta* ("the little dark one"). Even though she knew the **diminutive** was a mark of affection, she still was aware that the label was no compliment. When she became a young woman, well-meaning whites told her, "You don't look Mexican," meaning that she looked more Spanish and hence almost white. The message always hurt deeply not simply because the speakers personally so clearly believed that there was something inferior about being Mexican but also because they had unhesitatingly assumed that she did, too, and hence would consider such a statement to be a compliment.

diminutive:
affectionate nickname

8   I have never had to endure "what-is-he-doing-here?" looks any time I walked along a residential street in a suburban area. I have not had to notice white women clutching their purses more tightly when they meet me walking along the street. I have never seen the "For Rent" or "For Sale" signs **figuratively** snatched out of the window as I walked up to the front door. I cannot even begin to imagine the insults, large and small, that send a five- or six-year-old running tearfully home to ask Mommy or Daddy, "Why can't I be white?"

figuratively:
symbolically; not literally

9   Out of the dozens of times I have crossed the border from Tijuana to San Diego, the one time I was pulled over to have my car inspected was when returning with my friend, Raymond, and another African American male as passengers. I was furious, but my friends restrained me, assuring me it was no big deal and that it happened to them all the time. That day I got some small sense of the rage and fury and helplessness and frustration that some people experience daily and are forced to smother.

10   I have never been so bombarded by negative messages that I began to internalize them and to suspect they might in part be true. As a professional person, I have never had to carry the burden of knowing that the slightest mispronunciation or grammatical error on my part will be seized upon by some people as validation of their negative stereotypes, not only about me but also about my people. But entire populations of my potential competitors have labored and are still laboring under disadvantages of this very sort as they compete with me. This is white male "affirmative action" at its most effective—the flip side of destructive life-long bombardment by negative messages.

11   Yes, affirmative action for some folks remains alive and well and unthreatened by court decisions. I ought to know. All my life I have been an indirect beneficiary because indirect affirmative action has been so effective at crippling or eliminating so many of those who might have been my competitors. As a white male, I have never had to compete with them on a level playing field.

12   The promise of the American dream is a society which is color-fair, not color-blind. Formal affirmative action programs play a dual role. They make the playing fields a bit more level, and they remind us that we still have far to go. It is no solution for society to trash its current formal efforts to make opportunity a little more equal as long as so many powerful informal barriers to equality of opportunity still persist. Think about it.

VOCABULARY AND COMPREHENSION

1.   What introduction style does the author use? Circle the best answer.
     a. General background   b. Definition
     c. Opposing position   d. Anecdote

2.   Using your own words, describe the main idea of this essay.

     _____

     _____

3.   How has the author benefited from indirect affirmative action? List some examples.

     _____

     _____

_____

_____

_____

4. What examples does the author give to illustrate that members of less-favored groups have to live with destructive, painful experiences?

_____

_____

_____

_____

_____

CRITICAL THINKING

5. Why was Malcolm promoted more quickly than his female colleagues?

_____

_____

6. Explain how a "For Rent" sign could be "figuratively snatched from a window" (paragraph 9).

_____

_____

7. What are Malcolm's main arguments for supporting affirmative action?

_____

_____

_____

_____

_____

8. Who is Dave Malcolm? What have you learned about him after reading this text? List characteristics that describe him, and make some educated guesses about his personality.

_____

_____

_____

_____

_____

_____

WRITING TOPICS

Write about one of the following topics. Remember to explore, develop, and revise and edit your work.

1. Compare Malcolm's view of affirmative action with the view expressed by Richard Rodriguez in the essay titled "It's Class, Stupid." With whom do you agree, and why?

2. List examples of ways in which people are stereotyped. You can discuss age, appearance, race, and so on.
3. Reflect on Montesquieu's quotation. What is your view about equality? Should laws protect some members of society to ensure equal access to work, education, and housing? Why or why not?

"All humans are born equal, but they cannot continue in this equality. Society makes them lose it, and they recover it only by the protection of the law."
—Charles de Montesquieu, PHILOSOPHER

READING 14

Control Your Temper
Elizabeth Passarella

Elizabeth Passarella is a freelance writer and has written for *At Home Magazine*, *Latina*, and *Allure*. As you read this process essay, look for illustration and cause and effect writing patterns.

1   You don't have to be hot-headed for steam to come out of your ears. Sometimes it seems there are triggers everywhere: the man in your life who always needs help finding his keys, the boss who never notices your hard work, or the telemarketers who call at the worst time. The next thing you know, you've snapped, shed a few tears, or had a full-blown meltdown. So how do you keep your emotions from boiling over? Read on.

2   Mind the clock and calendar. Maybe you lose your temper with your assistant every morning, or you yell at your man if you've had a stressful day at work. Whenever you lose it, take note of the time and day. "When people are tired or stressed, they are more likely not to respond properly," says Hector Machabanski, Ph.D., a clinical psychologist in Chicago. "Do a postmortem after you lose control. Learning what triggered your emotions gives you tools to manage them." Once you know when your fuses are at their lowest, you can schedule that meeting or date at a time when you tend to be calmer.

3   See the bigger picture. Being overly emotional usually stems from a deeper problem. Knowing the real issue can keep little things from making you crazy. "When you lose it, you are never attacking the real problem," says Carmen Inoa Vazquez, Ph.D., a New York City-based psychologist. Say you have a boss who always points out your mistakes. When you feel yourself ready to start crying or yelling, breathe deeply. Once you've calmed down (deep breaths are an instant emotion controller), think about how you can address the larger issue. You may realize you'll never be able to change your boss's behavior—only your reaction to it. Eventually, you'll learn to shrug him or her off.

4   Give yourself time-outs. Spend time alone, whether it's in the shower, in prayer, or at the gym, and think about why you lost control. Most important, create a strategy of self-control for next time. Maybe you need to hang up on telemarketers rather than argue with them. Or maybe you should get up fifteen minutes earlier so you can enjoy your coffee before you have to deal with the kids, instead of lashing out because they're throwing Cheerios while you're half-dressed for work.

5   Don't beat yourself up about losing control. Being emotional isn't always a bad thing. "We all rage, and we all feel sadness. And some cultures, like ours, are more expressive, more intense. It is acceptable to get excited and to shout," Vazquez says. "But we don't live on an island." In other words, if you hurt another person, you need to think about keeping your emotions in check. But if you just need to have a good cry or freak out a bit, you should. Just put away that glass vase first.

VOCABULARY AND COMPREHENSION

1. Find a word in paragraph 1 that means "activators" or "initiators."

    _____

2. Find an example of slang in paragraph 5.

    _____

3. What does this essay help readers do? Circle the best answer.
    a. complete a process   b. understand a process

4. This essay does not contain an explicit thesis statement. In your own words, write a thesis statement for this text.

    _____

    _____

5. In your own words, list the steps a person can take to control emotions.

    _____

    _____

    _____

CRITICAL THINKING

6. What is the author's specific purpose?

    _____

7. How does the author add weight to her arguments?

    _____

    _____

8. In your opinion, how are the suggestions useful or impractical?

    _____

    _____

    _____

WRITING TOPICS

Write about one of the following topics. Remember to explore, develop, and revise and edit your work.

1. Think about a time when you lost your temper. Describe the process that you went through during and after the event.
2. Passarella describes a process for controlling emotional outbursts. Describe a process that people should follow when they feel extremely sad, angry, or frustrated.
3. Reflect on Queen Elizabeth's quotation. How is it applicable in your life? You might give examples of things that make you feel angry.

“Anger makes dull men witty, but it keeps them poor.”

—QUEEN ELIZABETH I,
ENGLISH MONARCH

The Writer's Room **Images of College Life and Health Care**

The previous five readings and Editing Handbook Chapters 25, 26, 29, and 30 deal with issues related to college life and health care. The following activities continue developing those themes.

Writing Activity 1: Photo Writing

Reflect on this image and write about an issue related to it. For example, you might write an argument about preventive health care, describe healthful practices that have become popular in the last twenty years, or narrate the story of someone who used yoga, pilates, tai chi, or another type of exercise to enhance his or her life.

Writing Activity 2: Film Writing

1. *School Daze* was partially based on Spike Lee's experiences at Morehouse College in Atlanta. The film examines conflicts during a homecoming weekend. Compare and contrast the attitudes and actions of two of the main characters.

2. *Stomp the Yard*, *Orange County*, and *Good Will Hunting* all deal with college life. Choose one or more of the films and describe different categories of students. Give examples from the films.

3. The film *Million Dollar Baby* deals with euthanasia. Argue for or against the message of the film.

4. Michael Moore's film *Sicko* criticizes America's healthcare system. *Thank You For Smoking* mocks the tobacco industry. Compare and contrast these two films, or choose one of the films and express your view about the issue.

Themes: **The Legal World and the Workplace**

READING 15

Aunt Tee
Maya Angelou

Maya Angelou is a poet, historian, civil rights activist, and writer. In this next essay from her collection *I Wouldn't Take Nothing for My Journey Now*, Angelou writes about an important person in her life. As you read this description essay, also look for elements of narration and comparison and contrast.

1   Aunt Tee was a Los Angeles member of our extended family. She was seventy-nine when I met her, sinewy, strong, and the color of old lemons. She wore her coarse, straight hair, which was slightly streaked with gray, in a long braided rope across the top of her head. With her high cheekbones, old gold skin, and almond eyes, she looked more like an Indian chief than an old black woman. (Aunt Tee described herself and any favored member of her race as Negroes. *Black* was saved for those who had incurred her disapproval.)

2   She had retired and lived alone in a dead, neat ground-floor apartment. Wax flowers and china figurines sat on elaborately embroidered and heavily starched doilies. Sofas and chairs were tautly upholstered. The only thing at ease in Aunt Tee's apartment was Aunt Tee.

3   I used to visit her often and perch on her uncomfortable sofa just to hear her stories. She was proud that after working thirty years as a maid, she spent the next thirty years as a live-in housekeeper, carrying the keys to rich houses and keeping meticulous accounts.

4   "Living in lets the white folks know Negroes are as neat and clean as they are, sometimes more so. And it gives the Negro maid a chance to see white folks ain't no smarter than Negroes. Just luckier. Sometimes."

5   Aunt Tee told me that once she was housekeeper for a couple in Bel Air, California, and lived with them in a fourteen-room ranch house. There was a day maid who cleaned, and a gardener who daily tended the lush gardens. Aunt Tee oversaw the workers. When she began the job, she cooked and served a light breakfast, a good lunch, and a full three- or four-course dinner to her employers and their guests. Aunt Tee said she watched them grow older and leaner. After a few years, they stopped entertaining and ate dinner hardly seeing each other at the table. Finally, they sat in a dry silence as they ate evening meals of soft scrambled eggs, melba toast, and weak tea. Aunt Tee said she saw them growing old but didn't see herself aging at all.

6   She became the social maven. She started "keeping company" (her phrase) with a chauffeur down the street. Her best friend and her friend's husband worked in service only a few blocks away.

7   On Saturdays, Aunt Tee would cook a pot of pigs' feet, a pot of greens, fry chicken, make potato salad, and bake a banana pudding. Then, that evening, her friends—the chauffeur, the other housekeeper, and her husband—would come to Aunt Tee's **commodious** live-in quarters. There the four would eat and drink, play records and dance. As the evening wore on, they would settle down to a serious game of bid whist.

8   Naturally, during this revelry, jokes were told, fingers were snapped, feet were patted, and there was a great deal of laughter.

commodious:
large; spacious

9 Aunt Tee said that what occurred during every Saturday party startled her and her friends the first time it happened. They had been playing cards, and Aunt Tee, who had just won the bid, held a handful of trumps. She felt a cool breeze on her back and sat upright and turned around. Her employers had cracked her door open and beckoned to her. Aunt Tee, a little peeved, laid down her cards and went to the door. The couple backed away and asked her to come into the hall, and there they both spoke and won Aunt Tee's sympathy forever.

10 "Theresa, we don't mean to disturb you," the man whispered, "but you all seem to be having such a good time . . ."

11 The woman added, "We hear you and your friends laughing every Saturday night, and we'd just like to watch you. We don't want to bother you. We'll be quiet and just watch."

12 The man said, "If you'll just leave your door ajar, your friends don't need to know. We'll never make a sound." Aunt Tee said she saw no harm in agreeing, and she talked it over with her company. They said it was OK with them, but it was sad that the employers owned the gracious house, the swimming pool, three cars, and numberless palm trees, but had no joy. Aunt Tee told me that laughter and relaxation had left the house; she agreed it was sad.

13 That story has stayed with me for nearly thirty years, and when a tale remains fresh in my mind, it almost always contains a lesson which will benefit me.

14 I draw the picture of the wealthy couple standing in a darkened hallway, peering into a lighted room where black servants were lifting their voices in merriment and comradery, and I realize that living well is an art which can be developed. Of course, you need the basic talents to build upon: they are a love of life and the ability to take great pleasure from small offerings, an assurance that the world owes you nothing, and awareness that every gift is exactly that, a gift. Because of the routines we follow, we often forget that life is an ongoing adventure.

VOCABULARY AND COMPREHENSION

1. What is a *social maven* (paragraph 6)?

_____

2. What is the meaning of *revelry* in paragraph 8?

_____

3. Angelou uses descriptive imagery. Descriptive imagery includes active verbs, adjectives, and other words that appeal to the senses (sight, smell, touch, sound, taste). Underline at least six examples of descriptive imagery.

4. Why was it so important for Aunt Tee to be neat and tidy?

_____

_____

CRITICAL THINKING

5. Why does Angelou call her aunt's apartment *dead* (paragraph 2)?

_____

_____

6. In paragraph 4, Angelou quotes Aunt Tee. Why does the author use the slang word *ain't?*

   _____

   _____

7. What can you infer about the lives of Aunt Tee's wealthy employers? What types of people are they?

   _____

   _____

   _____

8. In paragraph 5, Aunt Tee says that she does not see herself aging. Why does she say this?

   _____

   _____

WRITING TOPICS

Write about one of the following topics. Remember to explore, develop, and revise and edit your work.

1. Write about a time when you saw an event that changed your perception of someone.
2. Angelou tells a story to make a point about living life to the fullest. Write about a moment in time when you felt that you were living life to its fullest. Use descriptive imagery in your writing.
3. Reflect on Rivers' quotation. Do you live in a clean, organized environment or a messy one? Describe a clean or messy room in your home. (You might reread Angelou's depiction of Aunt Tee's home to get some ideas.)

I hate housework. You make the beds, you do the dishes, and six months later you have to start all over again.
—JOAN RIVERS, ENTERTAINER

READING 16

Dealing with People
Greg McGrew

> Greg McGrew is the president of Hospitality Profit Builders. In the next essay, the author uses the classification writing pattern to describe different types of personalities.

1   It's no secret that most of our problems in life are "people" problems. Whether we are running a coffee cart or a full-service sit-down restaurant, how to solve our people problems seems to be a big secret that most of us struggle with, both in our personal lives as well as on the job. Who of us hasn't reflected on an encounter with another person and asked ourselves if we couldn't have handled the situation better? Yet there are a few people who seem to glide effortlessly through life working with a wide variety of people, achieving success in both their personal and professional lives. How do they do it? Somewhere along their life road, they have learned how to deal effectively with the four basic personality groups: dominants, expressives, analyticals, and amiables.

2   Dominants are naturally highly assertive people, and their behavior is characterized by the way they act. They tend to be active, confident, aggressive, talkative, extroverted, and confrontational. To many people, dominants are a threat to their mental well-being. However, if you know that it is important to look a dominant in the eye when talking to him or her, you can earn this person's respect and cooperation. Working with the other personality styles requires similar techniques.

3   Expressives are also highly assertive. They generally tell rather than ask and do a lot of thinking out loud. Most importantly, work has to be fun, and they will go out of their way to make it so. Expressives love touching, which makes amiables nervous. The expressive is relationship driven and has difficulty saying "no" because doing so may hurt the relationship. To get on the same wavelength with an expressive, be personable. Give the big picture first and then the details. Let the expressive know you are available at any time to talk.

4   Analyticals are thinkers. They take time to weigh everything out in their minds before they answer questions correctly the first time. To make a decision, analyticals need lots of information. They are good at making decisions; they just need a long time to get there. So, when dealing with analyticals, give them three to five seconds to answer you and ask them; do not tell them. If you do that, you will see analyticals as being logical, industrious, orderly, and systematic. Otherwise, you might think they are indecisive, unclear, and confused.

5   Amiables are very task and relationship oriented. They are naturally good listeners, and trust is key to their relationships. They are also perfectionists who like a lot of information before making decisions. To get the information, they will seek consensus from their peers. To work well with amiables, give all the information plus the result. Give them time and space to consult with others on the team. Treat them with respect and talk in a softer tone of voice.

6   Those who know how to deal with people use their knowledge of these personality styles to enhance their communication abilities, resolve conflicts more successfully, improve their working and personal relations, and recognize what motivates others. Look at the people around you and determine who are the dominants, expressives, analyticals, and amiables. Now go look that dominant customer in the eye and start communicating!

VOCABULARY AND COMPREHENSION

1.   In paragraph 3, what is the meaning of the phrase "to get on the same wavelength."

_____

2.   Underline the thesis statement in the essay.

3.   What introduction style does the author use? Circle the best answer.
     a. General background   b. Anecdote   c. Definition

4.   Describe the four personality types.

_____

_____

_____

_____

_____

_____

_____

5. Explain the author's suggestions for dealing with each personality type.

    _____

    _____

    _____

    _____

6. According to McGrew, why is it important to know personality types?

    _____

    _____

CRITICAL THINKING

7. The author states that it is important to look a dominant in the eye. Why might it be important?

    _____

    _____

8. Can you think of certain fields that each personality type might excel in?

    _____

    _____

    _____

    _____

9. Who is the audience for this essay? Circle clues in the essay that tell you about the audience.

    _____

    _____

WRITING TOPICS

Write about one of the following topics. Remember to explore, develop, and revise and edit your work.

There are two types of people in this world: The good and the bad. The good sleep better, but the bad seem to enjoy their waking hours more.

—WOODY ALLEN, COMEDIAN, ACTOR, AND FILMMAKER

1. Classify businesses into at least three categories. List characteristics of each category.
2. Do people express different aspects of their personality depending on the role they are in? In other words, could somebody be dominant in one role but amiable in another? Explain your answer.
3. Reflect on Allen's quotation. Then write about types of personalities, but do not use the same categories as Greg McGrew or Woody Allen.

READING 17

Why I Worked with La Migra

Veronica Ortega, as told to Franziska Castillo

Veronica Ortega, who crossed the border illegally as a child, worked as member of the Army National Guard stopping immigrants from entering the United States illegally. She tells why she's still conflicted over her job. In this narrative essay, also look for comparison and contrast, cause and effect, and argument writing patterns.

1   Back in the 1980s, crossing the border was easy. My mom moved smoothly between our home in Meoqui, Mexico, and the United States a couple of times a year, where she earned a living picking crops and babysitting American kids in New Mexico. We'd stay with my grandma while my mom worked tirelessly to earn a living for us, her three children. While it was hard, we understood that survival meant Mami's feet had to be grounded in both places. Even though none of my relatives had papers, the border was never a deterrent to enter the States. For instance, for a family wedding in New Mexico, we would just pack our good clothes in little plastic baggies and wade across the Rio Grande just in time to join the party. It was a constant ***va-y-viene***.

2   I was only ten the day I crossed illegally, but I don't remember being scared. My mom had a cousin who was a retired coyote. He helped my aunt, grandmother, baby brother, and little sister cross over. On the Juárez side of the Rio Grande, he told us to roll up our sleeves and take off our shoes. He had each of us climb onto his shoulders, and he took us one by one across the river. The water was pretty high, up to his neck. But he made us all feel safe.

3   Just a few minutes after being shuttled across the river, we were at a bus stop in El Paso, Texas, headed to meet my mom. It was so simple that the three of us kids imagined we were playing a big game of hide-and-seek. At that age, I just wanted to be with my mom. The boundaries or laws we were breaking never crossed my mind.

4   Ironically, nineteen years later, I ended up back on the border. This time, though, I was on patrol, helping to stop ***indocumentados*** from coming in. Of course, this was never something I'd planned on doing. After my mom brought us over, she struggled really hard to get us green cards. I learned fluent English, and right out of high school, I joined the Army National Guard. The women in my family have always been very strong, so the military was a natural path for me. For the eleven years I've been serving, the work has been rewarding: At one point, I helped dismantle drug dealers' cars to uncover hidden narcotics. After Hurricane Katrina, I was deployed to New Orleans to help the storm victims.

5   But last June, I was told that my next mission would be working for a few months to support the border patrol in New Mexico as part of Operation Jump Start, a mobilization of about 6,000 National Guardsmen that President George W. Bush was sending to ***la frontera*** to make it tougher for illegals to slip in. We were going to be stationed in the boiling-hot desert, helping the border patrol with everything from providing food and vehicles to spotting hiding immigrants.

6   My emotions were really mixed. On one hand, I kept thinking, "What if someone had stopped *me* from coming over?" But at the same time, I had signed a contract and felt obligated to fulfill my orders.

va-y-viene:
Spanish words meaning *come and go*

indocumentados:
Spanish word meaning *people without legal immigrant documents*

la frontera:
Spanish words meaning *the US/Mexican border*

7   During the first few weeks, I worked in an office, adding up the number of migrants the border patrol apprehended. I'd force myself not to think about the immigrants as people, but rather as numbers. After work, I'd go home to read books and play with my daughter to keep my mind busy with something else.

8   Then, one night, I was forced to confront the reality of my work. I was sent out to a lookout point as part of an EIT, or Entry Identification Team. EITs, using binoculars, infrared goggles, and cameras, search the desert for migrants. If we saw anything, we were supposed to radio the border patrol and guide them verbally so they could catch the immigrants.

9   A lot of people imagine the National Guard as a group walking up and down the border with M-16s, but actually being part of an EIT is as close as we get to the migrants. During my shift in the tower, everything was quiet. It was a pitch-black night, so I couldn't see anything. Even on the infrared monitor, there were no silhouettes to indicate human activity.

patrullas:
Spanish word meaning *patrols*

10   But later that night, when I was back on the ground, my partner spotted two groups. I had to radio the **patrullas** and explain to them that the UDAs—undocumented aliens—were hiding behind a big mesquite bush.

11   Turning them in was one of the hardest things I've faced in my life. I knew the migrants were scared and had saved a lot of money to make this trip a reality. Yet there I was, helping to turn them back. And still, I found myself on the radio telling an agent, "Go right. Go left. Now stop—what do you see?" Finally he said, "I see a big bush with a UDA under it," and then we lost communication. I later learned that we helped catch fourteen people that night.

12   At first, I was glad I hadn't seen their faces—I think that would have stuck with me for a long time. But the more I thought about it, the more I began to see a positive side to my role. If we hadn't stopped them right there, they would have had to walk through the desert for three days before reaching a town. People often die out here, and if I prevented their deaths, then I'm proud to have served.

las dos culturas:
Spanish word meaning *the two cultures*

13   Being out here has been an eye-opener for me. I've seen the harsh conditions the migrants face. And I've seen a lot of prejudice among Americans. A lot of times, I end up being the go-between for **las dos culturas**. Most of the soldiers and agents I've worked with have been really nice and respectful, while others are ignorant. Even some of the Latino soldiers from other states would laugh at the illegals and say, "Oh, they are so stupid. Why can't they just get a job in Mexico?" I had to work hard to stay calm and explain the facts.

14   They were usually surprised to hear I crossed the border illegally. I felt proud that my brother, sister, and I are good examples of what former illegals can accomplish; I've earned a college degree in automotive technology, and I'm working on another one in hotel, restaurant, and tourism management. My sister works for the public schools in Las Cruces, New Mexico, and my brother is a nurse.

15   I've had a lot of time to think about the immigration issue. Anti-immigrant groups say illegals take American jobs. But many Americans don't necessarily want to work more than eight hours a day; an illegal will only take eight hours a day *off*. The anti-immigrant groups also say we should seal the border. That's probably impossible; the zone where our unit worked was 54 miles long. The border patrol would need thousands, not hundreds, of agents to spot everyone. And besides, the coyotes will always find other ways to get in.

16   I think the best solution is to improve Mexico's economy. Lots of people, including my aunts and uncles in Chihuahua, don't really want to come north.

They don't have a big house, but they know everyone in their village. They share farm machinery. If they need to borrow someone's horse, they can. In the U.S., they would feel lonely and cut off. So if the economy in Mexico got stronger, they'd prefer to stay there. I'm hoping that the new president can make that happen.

17   There's a good chance I'll continue to be in the middle of the immigration issue. I recently signed up for six more years in the Guard, and by the time this article comes out, I'll probably be back out working with the border patrol. Now, the patrol's new Operation Lightning Strike will formally remove all illegal migrants caught for the first time in certain zones, including New Mexico and west Texas. If they are caught entering the country illegally again, they could face jail time. Before, a migrant had to be caught several times and sent back across the border before possibly facing a serious penalty.

18   But, *¿sabes qué?* I believe my work here is important—even helping bust immigrants. If you're smuggling human lives, I'm going to bring you down. And if you're trying to cross the border here in the desert, well, I'm going to save you.

¿sabes qué?:
Spanish question meaning *Do you know what?*

VOCABULARY AND COMPREHENSION

1.   The author uses some Spanish words in this essay. What is her purpose for doing so?

_____

_____

_____

2.   Give an example of how illegal immigrants used to cross the border into the United States when the author was young.

_____

_____

3.   How has the illegal border crossing changed from when the author was a child?

_____

_____

_____

_____

4.   Describe the author's job in the National Guard.

_____

_____

_____

_____

CRITICAL THINKING

5.   Why does the author have mixed feelings about her present job with the National Guard?

_____

_____

6. Has the author fulfilled the "American Dream"? Give examples to support your answer.

_____

_____

_____

_____

_____

7. What are some motivations for people to cross the border illegally into the United States from Mexico?

_____

_____

8. What problems might an illegal immigrant face in the United States?

_____

_____

WRITING TOPICS

Write about one of the following topics. Remember to explore, develop, and revise and edit your work.

1. Write about a time when you felt conflicted and had to make a decision. Describe what happened.
2. What are your family roots? Tell a story from your family's history.
3. Reflect on Roosevelt's quotation. Should illegal immigrants be granted amnesty so that they can live and work without fear of deportation? Explain why or why not.

> 66 *Remember, remember always, that all of us, and you and I especially, are descended from immigrants and revolutionists.* 99
> —FRANKLIN D. ROOSEVELT, AMERICAN PRESIDENT

READING 18

When the Legal Thing Isn't the Right Thing
Deborah Mead

Deborah Mead is a poet and essayist. In the next article, which appeared in the *Christian Science Monitor*, Mead reflects on a moral dilemma. As you read this illustration essay, also look for elements of narration and comparison and contrast.

1   After spending several hours at the mall, I was stuck. Traffic had slowed to a crawl on my side of the Interstate. I was in the right lane, a mile from my exit, and anxious to get home. Apparently other drivers were anxious too, because they were flying past me in the breakdown lane.

2   On most highways, driving on the shoulder is a clear no-no, but on my particular stretch of road, it's a little murkier. The shoulder functions as a travel lane on weekdays from 6 to 10 a.m. and 3 to 7 p.m. But this was 5 p.m. on a Saturday, and by some Cinderella-style governmental magic, the special 55-mile-per-hour lane had officially reverted to its lowly breakdown status.

3   As I watched the smug drivers sail by, my frustration level rising, I tried to reason my way into breaking the law, too. I told myself it's not as if the shoulder is never used as a driving lane. By establishing these windows of travel for the shoulder, the state of Massachusetts recognizes that periods of high traffic call for breaking the normal rules of the road. This was certainly one of those times.

4   I told myself the principle of putting the greater good ahead of my own didn't apply here. It is true that if everyone at a concert stood up to get a better view, all would be worse off, with the same mediocre view but sore feet. But, in this case, if everyone regarded the shoulder as a travel lane, we would all travel **incrementally** faster. If anything, my transgression would benefit society.

incrementally: increasingly

5   I told myself that I was getting off at the next exit, so in fact the shoulder would just be like a one-mile off-ramp. I would not be merging back into traffic later, and I would not be cutting anyone off. No one would be harmed.

6   I told myself all this—but, still, I couldn't turn onto the shoulder.

7   Unmoved by common sense, I sat in traffic for ten minutes to go that one mile, while other cars continued to whiz by me on the right. There was a time I would have felt morally superior to those selfish people breaking the law. I would have told myself that they had no regard for other people and congratulated myself on being a model citizen.

8   I don't feel that way anymore. Instead, I recognize that I am cowed by authority, particularly when that authority is anonymous, mere words on a sign. Somewhere in my civic upbringing, I confused obedience with goodness.

9   It's too late to reeducate myself now. As much as I reason with myself, and as much as I believe I would be justified in crossing over that solid line, I will bow to rules that make no sense. It is the legal thing to do—it may even be the moral thing to do—but I know it can't be right.

VOCABULARY AND COMPREHENSION

1.   In paragraph 4, find a word that means "a broken rule."

_____

2.   Where and when does this story take place?

_____

3.   What moral debate does Mead have with herself?

_____

_____

_____

4.   Write a sentence that sums up the essay's main idea. Use your answers to questions 2 and 3 to form your sentence.

_____

_____

_____

5.   Does Mead believe that breaking the law and driving on the shoulder is a good idea? Why or why not?

_____

_____

CRITICAL THINKING

6. How is Mead different from those who drove by her on the shoulder of the road?

_____

_____

_____

7. What does Mead mean when she says that she is "cowed by authority" (paragraph 8)?

_____

_____

8. Will Mead change her way of thinking in the future when she is confronted with similar dilemmas?

_____

_____

9. Mead says that she learned to confuse "obedience" with "goodness." Do you think that these two words mean the same thing? Why or why not?

_____

_____

WRITING TOPICS

Write about one of the following topics. Remember to explore, develop, and revise and edit your work.

1. Mead says, "I learned to confuse obedience with goodness" (paragraph 9). Reflect on the author's words. Explain when obedience may not be a sign of goodness. Use specific examples to support your opinion.
2. Do you believe that people should follow all rules and laws, or do you believe that some rules and laws are made to be broken? Explain your opinion using specific examples of rules and laws.
3. Reflect on Einstein's quotation. Do you agree with Einstein? Explain why we need or do not need laws.

> _Every kind of peaceful cooperation among men is primarily based on mutual trust and only secondarily on institutions such as courts of justice and police._
>
> —ALBERT EINSTEIN, PHYSICIST

READING 19

A Faith in Others Versus Security

Barbara Card Atkinson

Barbara Card Atkinson is a contributor to many magazines, including _The Christian Science Monitor_, _USA Today_, and _Salon_. In this narrative essay, she ponders a tough decision. As you read, also look for description, cause and effect, and argument writing patterns.

1   My running buddy and I were just finishing our cool-down stroll when the man caught my eye. He was dressed like part of a construction crew—faded denim jeans, thick, stained jacket—only it was a Sunday evening, so he had no reason to be at the building site next to the trail where we run.

2   Although the highway overpass that bridged the bike trail badly needed repair, the construction workers had halted their labor; the workers had done

neither construction nor demolition for weeks. That, and the fact that the man was on the site at dusk, poking among piles of planks, told me something wasn't right.

3   We looped back around, and I saw him again. This time he was carrying five or six of the weather-beaten boards over his shoulder. I searched his face for clues, for some way of deciding who he was. He was clean-shaven; he looked tired and determined. He caught me looking, and our eyes met. He didn't look defiant or worried or threatening. He simply held my gaze as if to say that, yes, he saw me watching him. He walked past me into the reedy, wooded overgrowth and disappeared from view.

4   This man clearly stole from the job site; I saw where he had stepped through a hole ripped in the fence. Also, the area was a busy cross-through for late-night commuters, and there had been recent reports of muggings and assaults. My friend asked if I would call the police when I got home. I wasn't sure.

5   Although I saw him walk into that no man's land near my home, I didn't know where—or to whom—he was going. The economy was bad enough; perhaps he was down on his luck and simply was trying to survive short-term homelessness. What if he had a wife or a family? If I sent authorities his way, what would I be setting into motion? Of course, the stealing was wrong, but I could be affecting irrevocably more than just the life of some scavenger. I could be tearing apart a family.

6   On the other hand, I had discovered that there was someone hidden in our midst. What would I do if it turned out that he was responsible for the growing crime in the area? If I didn't get authorities involved, what might I not be preventing? And he did, in fact, steal someone else's building material. At what point was a stranger's business my business?

7   I thought about it late into the night and the next day. I didn't call anyone; I didn't report what I saw. I believe it was his straightforward look and my conscious choice to assume the best intentions of strangers, even in the face of questionable behavior, that kept me from saying anything.

8   I'd like to believe it was optimism and not apathy that kept me quiet, but I'm not wholly comfortable with my decision. I find myself firmly unsure, equally caught between an optimistic faith in others and my concern for a community's safety. I find myself regularly checking my local newspaper's police log, and I make sure not to walk near the bushes.

VOCABULARY AND COMPREHENSION

1.   Find a word in paragraph 5 that means "permanently."

   _____

2.   A possible thesis statement for this essay would be
      a. When I saw a man stealing, I should have called the police.
      b. Never go out alone after dark because it is dangerous.
      c. Sometimes it is difficult to know what the right thing to do is.
      d. When I saw a man stealing, I faced a moral dilemma.

3.   In your own words, describe what happened to the author of this event. Answer the questions who, what, when, and where.

   _____

   _____

   _____

CRITICAL THINKING

4. In paragraph 3, the author writes that she searched the man's face "for clues." What were her reasons for doing so?

   _____

5. Give both sides of the argument that went on in the author's mind regarding the fate of the man.

   _____

   _____

   _____

   _____

   _____

6. What influenced the author not to report the man to the police?

   _____

   _____

7. What does the author seem to be suggesting in her conclusion?

   _____

WRITING TOPICS

Write about one of the following topics. Remember to explore, develop, and revise and edit your work.

1. Have you ever had to make a decision that you were not wholly comfortable with? Describe the situation and the process you went through to make your decision.
2. In your opinion, should the author have reported the man to the police? Why or why not?
3. Reflect on Russell's quotation. What are your future personal or professional goals? Do you have short and long term goals? Write about what you hope to accomplish in the future.

> *Not failure, but low aim, is crime.*
> —JAMES RUSSELL, U.S. POET
> (1819–1891)

READING 20

Interview with Jimmy Baca
Elizabeth Farnsworth

Elizabeth Farnsworth, a senior correspondent for the *The NewsHour with Jim Lehrer*, interviewed author and poet Jimmy Santiago Baca. Baca, of Chicano and Apache ancestry, was born in New Mexico. He taught himself to read and write while serving a six-year prison sentence. He has since written a memoir of his childhood called *A Place To Stand*, as well as many award-winning volumes of poetry. In the interview, Baca discusses some pivotal moments in his life.

1   ELIZABETH FARNSWORTH: You tell the story of your childhood. You were deserted by your parents, and your grandparents took care of you for a while. Then you ended up in a orphanage and finally in prison. Tell the specific story of how words and language entered your life and helped save you.

2   JIMMY SANTIAGO BACA: . . . In dark times, it seemed that words were really special to me. We didn't really have a lot of books around the house when I

was growing up except the bible. Then, of course, I never had any books until I was in county jail when I took that one book.

3   ELIZABETH FARNSWORTH: Tell us what happened.

4   JIMMY SANTIAGO BACA: Well, I stole the book from the clerk, the desk clerk, and I took it up to my cell. Late at night, I was tearing pages out of it so I could cook up some coffee. The other prisoners were yelling for their coffee. They were wondering why I wasn't coming because I was on time most of the time. As the fire beneath the coffee can was flaring, I caught a couple of words that I recognized phonetically. As I read more and more, I quit tearing the pages out of the book, and I began to read. It was about a man who was walking his dog around a lake. That triggered phenomenal memories in me of my grandfather and the love I had for him and how we went around the pond with our sheep and dog. Incidentally, the man's name that I was reading later on that night, which I fell asleep enunciating, was words—words—**Wordsworth.**

5   ELIZABETH FARNSWORTH: Eventually you had poetry published in *Mother Jones Magazine* even while you were in prison. How did you go from being almost illiterate to that?

6   JIMMY SANTIAGO BACA: It was really funny because I didn't know how to address a letter, and I didn't know people paid for poetry. I was charging people cigarettes and coffees to write letters to their mothers and write letters to their girlfriends and poems and so forth for Mother's Day. A friend of mine came by with a *Mother Jones Magazine* and said, hey, they're buying poems here. I asked how to address a letter. I took my shoebox and grabbed a bunch of poems that I had written on **baby paper.** I sent them to a place called San Francisco—never expecting to hear back from them. When $300 came in, I bought the whole cellblock ice cream that day. Everyone ate ice cream.

7   ELIZABETH FARNSWORTH: Tell us how you love language and why. You've called it almost a physical thing for you.

8   JIMMY SANTIAGO BACA: Oh, I love language. Language, to me, is what sunrise is to the birds. Language, to me, is what water is to a man that just crossed the desert. I remember, as a boy, when grown-ups looked like huge redwood trees in a storm. And the grown-ups in my life were always caught up in dramas. The one thing that they all had in common was they couldn't express that storm inside of themselves. And I was so caught up in that drama that I vowed, one day, I would grasp hold of the power that could evoke their emotions. For me, at least, I wanted to know how to say what was happening to them, and I wanted to name things.

Wordsworth:
William Wordsworth (1770–1850), renowned English Romantic poet

baby paper:
scrap paper

VOCABULARY AND COMPREHENSION

1. In paragraph 4, what is the meaning of *enunciating?* Try to guess without using a dictionary.

    _____

2. What was Baca's life like as a child?

    _____

    _____

3. How did Baca become interested in reading?

    _____

    _____

    _____

4.   Baca describes language metaphorically. A metaphor is a comparison without the word *like* or *as*. Underline two metaphors in paragraph 8.

CRITICAL THINKING

5.   Baca compares adults to "huge redwood trees in a storm" (paragraph 8). What does he mean?

_____

_____

6.   How does control over language give Baca a sense of empowerment?

_____

_____

_____

_____

7.   What lessons can be learned from Baca's life experiences?

_____

_____

WRITING TOPICS

Write about one of the following topics. Remember to explore, develop, and revise and edit your work.

1.   What experiences have you had that helped make you the person that you are today?
2.   Conduct a short interview with someone whom you think is very interesting. You might choose someone who is much older than you are. Ask questions to discover what major lessons the person has learned in life. Then write about that person.
3.   Reflect on Madwed's quotation. Describe ways in which you have invested in yourself.

66 If you want to be truly successful, invest in yourself. 99
—SIDNEY MADWED,
POET AND MOTIVATIONAL SPEAKER

The Writer's Room   **Images of the Legal World and the Workplace**

The previous readings and Editing Handbook Chapters 31–35 deal with issues related to the legal world and the workplace. The following activities continue developing those themes.

Writing Activity 1: Photo Writing

Reflect on the image on the next page and write about an idea related to it. For example, you might define the word *workaholic* and give examples of workaholics you know, narrate the story of how this man came to be sitting at his desk with his robe on, or argue for your idea of the ideal home–work balance.

Writing Activity 2: Film Writing

1. *The Waitress* and *Beauty Shop* portray women in low-paying jobs. In *The Devil Wears Prada*, the most successful woman in the film is controlling and manipulative. Using those films as examples, explain how working women are portrayed in movies. You can also discuss other films that contain working women.

2. *The Corporation* is a documentary about the inner workings of corporations. Using examples from the film, explain the causes of corruption and greed in corporations, or describe the effects of multinational corporations on nations.

3. *Fracture* is about a legal trial. Define a term related to the film.

4. Many films deal with the mafia or with well-known criminals. Examples are *The Godfather*, *The Departed*, *Goodfellas*, *Bonny and Clyde*, and *The Untouchables*. Why do people enjoy watching movies about gangsters?

Appendix 1
Grammar Glossary

The Basic Parts of a Sentence

Parts of Speech	Definition	Some Examples
Adjective	Adds information about the noun	tall, beautiful, blue, cold
Adverb	Adds information about the verb, adjective, or other adverb; expresses time, place, and frequency	friendly, quickly, sweetly, sometimes, usually, never
Conjunctive adverb	Shows a relationship between two ideas	also, consequently, finally, however, furthermore, moreover, therefore, thus
Coordinating conjunction	Connects two ideas of equal importance	for, and, nor, but, or, yet, so
Determiner	Identifies or determines if a noun is specific or general	a, an, the, this, that, these, those, any, all, each, every, many, some
Interjection	A word expressing an emotion	ouch, yikes, oh
Noun	A person, place, or thing	singular: man, dog, person plural: men, dogs, people
Preposition	Shows a relationship between words (source, direction, location, etc.)	at, to, for, from, behind, above
Pronoun	Replaces one or more nouns	he, she, it, us, ours, themselves
Subordinating conjunction	Connects two ideas when one idea is subordinate (or inferior) to the other idea	after, although, because, unless, until
Verb	Expresses an action or state of being	action: run, eat, walk, think linking: is, become, seem

PRACTICE 1

Label each word with one of the following terms.

adjective	noun	verb	adverb
conjunction	preposition	pronoun	interjection

EXAMPLE:

easy _____adjective_____

1. human _____
2. with _____
3. below _____
4. herself _____
5. wow _____

6. whispered _____
7. quickly _____
8. because _____
9. children _____
10. they _____

Types of Clauses and Sentences

Other Key Terms	Definition	Example
clause	An **independent clause** has a subject and verb and expresses a complete idea.	The movie is funny.
	A **dependent clause** has a subject and verb but cannot stand alone. It "depends" on another clause in order to be complete.	Although it is violent
complex sentence	At least one dependent clause joined with one independent clause	Although the movie is violent, it conveys an important message.
compound sentence	Two or more independent clauses that are joined together	Some movies are funny, and others are deeply moving.
compound-complex sentence	At least two independent clauses joined with at least one dependent clause	Although the movie is violent, it is very entertaining, and it conveys an important message.
phrase	A group of words that is missing a subject, a verb, or both, and is not a complete sentence	in the morning after the storm
simple sentence	One independent clause that expresses a complete idea	The movie is funny.

Appendix 2
Irregular Verbs

Base Form	Simple Past	Past Participle	Base Form	Simple Past	Past Participle
arise	arose	arisen	feel	felt	felt
be	was, were	been	fight	fought	fought
beat	beat	beat, beaten	find	found	found
become	became	become	flee	fled	fled
begin	began	begun	fly	flew	flown
bend	bent	bent	forbid	forbade	forbidden
bet	bet	bet	forget	forgot	forgotten
bind	bound	bound	forgive	forgave	forgiven
bite	bit	bitten	forsake	forsook	forsaken
bleed	bled	bled	freeze	froze	frozen
blow	blew	blown	get	got	got, gotten
break	broke	broken	give	gave	given
breed	bred	bred	go	went	gone
bring	brought	brought	grind	ground	ground
build	built	built	grow	grew	grown
burst	burst	burst	hang	hung	hung
buy	bought	bought	have	had	had
catch	caught	caught	hear	heard	heard
choose	chose	chosen	hide	hid	hidden
cling	clung	clung	hit	hit	hit
come	came	come	hold	held	held
cost	cost	cost	hurt	hurt	hurt
creep	crept	crept	keep	kept	kept
cut	cut	cut	kneel	knelt	knelt
deal	dealt	dealt	know	knew	known
dig	dug	dug	lay	laid	laid
do	did	done	lead	led	led
draw	drew	drawn	leave	left	left
drink	drank	drunk	lend	lent	lent
drive	drove	driven	let	let	let
eat	ate	eaten	lie*	lay	lain
fall	fell	fallen	light	lit	lit
feed	fed	fed	lose	lost	lost

*Lie can mean "to rest in a flat position." When lie means "tell a false statement," then it is a regular verb: lie, lied, lied.

(continued)

Irregular Verbs (continued)

Base Form	Simple Past	Past Participle	Base Form	Simple Past	Past Participle
make	made	made	speed	sped	sped
mean	meant	meant	spend	spent	spent
meet	met	met	spin	spun	spun
mistake	mistook	mistaken	split	split	split
pay	paid	paid	spread	spread	spread
prove	proved	proved, proven	spring	sprang	sprung
put	put	put	stand	stood	stood
quit	quit	quit	steal	stole	stolen
read	read	read	stick	stuck	stuck
rid	rid	rid	sting	stung	stung
ride	rode	ridden	stink	stank	stunk
ring	rang	rung	strike	struck	struck
rise	rose	risen	swear	swore	sworn
run	ran	run	sweep	swept	swept
say	said	said	swell	swelled	swollen
see	saw	seen	swim	swam	swum
sell	sold	sold	swing	swung	swung
send	sent	sent	take	took	taken
set	set	set	teach	taught	taught
shake	shook	shaken	tear	tore	torn
shine	shone	shone	tell	told	told
shoot	shot	shot	think	thought	thought
show	showed	shown	throw	threw	thrown
shrink	shrank	shrunk	thrust	thrust	thrust
shut	shut	shut	understand	understood	understood
sing	sang	sung	wake	woke	woken
sink	sank	sunk	wear	wore	worn
sit	sat	sat	weep	wept	wept
sleep	slept	slept	win	won	won
slide	slid	slid	wind	wound	wound
slit	slit	slit	withdraw	withdrew	withdrawn
speak	spoke	spoken	write	wrote	written

Appendix 3
A Quick Guide to Verb Tenses

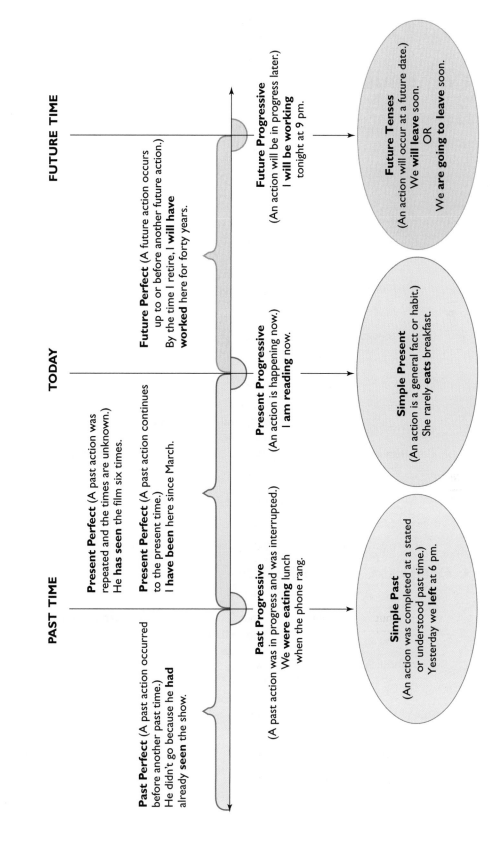

PAST TIME   TODAY   FUTURE TIME

Past Perfect (A past action occurred before another past time.) He didn't go because he **had** already **seen** the show.

Present Perfect (A past action was repeated and the times are unknown.) He **has seen** the film six times.

Present Perfect (A past action continues to the present time.) I **have been** here since March.

Future Perfect (A future action occurs up to or before another future action.) By the time I retire, I **will have worked** here for forty years.

Past Progressive (A past action was in progress and was interrupted.) We **were eating** lunch when the phone rang.

Present Progressive (An action is happening now.) I **am reading** now.

Future Progressive (An action will be in progress later.) I **will be working** tonight at 9 pm.

Simple Past (An action was completed at a stated or understood past time.) Yesterday we **left** at 6 pm.

Simple Present (An action is a general fact or habit.) She rarely **eats** breakfast.

Future Tenses (An action will occur at a future date.) We **will leave** soon. OR We **are going to leave** soon.

Making Compound Sentences

A.

Complete idea

, coordinator
, for
, and
, nor
, but
, or
, yet
, so

complete idea.

B.

Complete idea

;

complete idea.

C.

Complete idea

; transitional expression,
; however,
; in fact,
; moreover,
; therefore,
; furthermore,

complete idea.

Making Complex Sentences

D.

Complete idea

subordinator
although
because
before
even though
unless
when

incomplete idea.

E.

Subordinator
Although
Because
Before
Even though
Unless
When

incomplete idea

,

complete idea.

Appendix 5
Punctuation and Mechanics

Apostrophe (')

Use an apostrophe

- to join a subject and verb together.

    We're late.

- to join an auxiliary with *not*.

    I **can't** come.

- to indicate possession.

    Ross's computer is new.

Comma (,)

Use a comma

- to separate words in a series (more than two things). Place a comma before the final *and*.

    The doctor is kind, considerate, and gentle.

- after an introductory word or phrase.

    In the evenings, Carson volunteered at a hospital.

- around interrupting phrases that give additional information about the subject.

    Alan, an electrician, earns a good salary.

- in compound sentences before the coordinator.

    We worked for hours, and then we rested.

- around relative clauses containing *which*.

    The documents, which are very valuable, are up for auction.

- in quotations, after an introductory phrase or before an ending phrase.

    Picasso said, "Find your passion."

    "Find your passion," Picasso said.

Note: Do not join two complete sentences with a comma!

Colon (:)

Use a colon

- after a complete sentence that introduces a list, or after *the following*.

    The course has the following sections: pregnancy, labor, and lactation.

- after a complete sentence that introduces a quotation.

   Picasso's advice was clear: "Find your passion."

- before an explanation or example.

   Carlos explained what he really needed: a raise.

- to separate the hours and minutes in expressions of time.

   The mall opens at 9:30 a.m.

Semicolon (;)

Use a semicolon to join two independent but related clauses.

   Mahatma Gandhi was a pacifist; he believed in nonviolence.

Quotation Marks (" ")

Use quotation marks around direct speech. When a quotation is a complete sentence, capitalize the first word in the quotation. Place the end punctuation inside the closing quotation marks.

   In his essay, Levi said, "**W**e were interchangeable."

If the end of the quotation is not the end of your sentence, end the quotation with a comma. If your quotation ends with other punctuation, put it inside the closing quotation marks.

   "We were interchangeable," according to Levi.

   "You can't be serious!" she shouted.

   "What did you call me?" he replied.

Integrated Quotations

If you integrate a quotation in a sentence, add quotation marks around the words the speaker quoted.

   Dorothy Nixon calls herself a "**t**errible mother."

"Inside" Quotations

If one quotation is inside another quotation, add single quotation marks (' ') around the inside quotation.

   Bernice was forced to act: "She turned to Charlie Paulson and plunged. 'Do you think I ought to bob my hair?'"

Citing Page Numbers

If you are using MLA style, write the page number in parentheses and place it after the quotation. Place the final period *after* the parentheses if the quotation ends the sentence.

   In his essay, Levi says, "We were interchangeable" (4).

Capitalization

Always capitalize

- the pronoun *I* and the first word of every sentence.
- the days of the week, the months, and holidays.

    Tuesday   May 22   Labor Day

- the names of specific places, such as buildings, streets, parks, public squares, lakes, rivers, cities, states, and countries.

    Kelvin Street   Lake Erie   White Plains, New York

- the names of languages, nationalities, tribes, races, and religions.

    Spanish   Mohawk   Buddhist

- the titles of specific individuals.

    General Dewitt   Dr. Franklin   Mr. Blain

- the major words in titles of literary or artistic works.

    The Great Gatsby   *The Diviners*   *Crime and Punishment*

- the names of historical eras and movements.

    World War I   Cubism   the Middle Ages

Punctuating Titles

Place the title of short works in quotation marks. Capitalize the major words. Short works include songs, short stories, newspaper and magazine articles, essays, and poems.

> The Beatles' worst song was "Help."

Underline (or italicize, if you are writing a document for publication online) the title of a longer document. Long works include television series, films, works of art, magazines, books, plays, and newspapers.

> We watched the classic movie West Side Story.

> We watched the classic movie *West Side Story*.

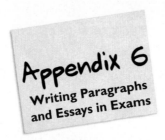

Appendix 6
Writing Paragraphs
and Essays in Exams

In many of your courses, you will have to answer exam questions with a paragraph or an essay. These types of questions often allow you to reveal your understanding of the topic. Although taking any exam can be stressful, you can reduce exam anxiety and increase your chances of doing well by following some preparation and exam-writing strategies.

Preparing for Exams

Here are some steps you can take to help prepare for exams.

- Before you take an exam, make sure that you know exactly what material you should study. Do not be afraid to ask the instructor for clarification. Also ask what materials you should bring to the exam.
- Review the assigned information, class notes, and the textbook, if any.
- Read and repeat information out loud.
- Take notes about important points.
- Study with a friend.

 **Predict Exam Questions**

An effective study strategy is to predict possible exam questions. Here are some tips:

- Look for important themes in your course outline.
- Study your notes and try to analyze what information is of particular importance.
- Look at your previous exams for the course. Determine whether any questions or subjects are repeated in more than one exam.

After you have looked through the course outline, your notes, and previous exams, write out possible exam questions based on the information that you have collected. Then practice writing the answers to your questions.

Writing Exams

Knowing your material inside and out is a large part of exam writing; however, budgeting your time and knowing how to read exam questions are important, too. When you receive the exam paper, look it over carefully and try these test-taking strategies.

Schedule Your Time

One of the most stressful things about taking an exam is running out of time. Before you write, find out exactly how much time you have. Then, plan how much time you will need to answer the questions. For example, if you have a one-hour exam and you have three questions worth the same point value, try to make sure that you spend no more than twenty minutes on any one question.

Determine Point Values

As soon as you get an exam, scan the questions and determine which questions have a larger point value. For example, you might respond to the questions with the largest point value first, or you might begin with those that you understand well. Then go to the more difficult questions. If you find yourself blocked on a certain answer, do not waste a lot of time on it. Go to another question, and then go back to the first question later.

Carefully Read the Exam Questions

It is important to read exam instructions thoroughly. Follow the next steps.

Identify Key Words and Phrases

When you read an exam question, underline or circle key words and phrases in order to understand exactly what you are supposed to do. In the next example, the underlined words highlight three different tasks.

1. Discuss how each time period differs from the other.

<u>Distinguish</u> between Paleolithic, Mesolithic, and Neolithic. <u>Place these periods in chronological order</u> and <u>describe</u> how the people lived during those times.

2. Organize the essay according to each period's date.

3. Discuss what people did for shelter, food, and leisure activities.

Examine Common Question Words

Exam questions direct you using verbs (action words). This chart gives the most common words that are used in both paragraph- and essay-style questions.

Verb	Meaning
describe discuss review	Examine a subject as thoroughly as possible. Focus on the main points.
narrate trace	Describe the development or progress of something using time order.
evaluate explain your 　point of view interpret justify take a stand	State your opinion and give reasons to support your opinion. In other words, write an argument paragraph or essay.
analyze criticize classify	Explain something carefully by breaking it down into smaller parts.
enumerate list outline	Go through important facts one by one.
compare contrast distinguish	Discuss important similarities and/or differences.
define explain what is 　meant by . . .	Give a complete and accurate definition that demonstrates your understanding of the concept.

(continued)

Verb	Meaning
explain causes	Analyze the reasons for an event.
explain effects	Analyze the consequences or results of an event.
explain a process	Explain the steps needed to perform a task.
summarize	Write down the main points from a larger work.
illustrate	Demonstrate your understanding by giving examples.

PRACTICE I

Determine the main type of response that you would use to answer each essay question.

narrate	explain a process	explain causes/effects	define
argue	classify	compare and contrast	

EXAMPLE:

Discuss the term *affirmative action*.

   define

1. Distinguish between the interest rate and the rate of return.

   _____

2. Describe what happened during the Tet Offensive.

   _____

3. List and describe five types of housing.

   _____

4. What steps are required to improve your city's transportation system?

   _____

5. List the reasons for global warming.

   _____

6. Give a short but thorough description of narcissism.

   _____

7. Discuss whether religious symbols should be banned from schools.

   _____

Follow the Writing Process

When you answer paragraph or essay exam questions, remember to follow the writing process.

Explore	▪ Jot down any ideas that you think can help you answer the question.
Develop	▪ Use the exam question to guide your topic sentence or thesis statement.
	▪ List supporting ideas. Then organize your ideas and create a paragraph or essay plan.
	▪ Write the paragraph or essay. Use transitions to link your ideas.
Revise and edit	▪ Read over your writing to make sure it makes sense and that your spelling, punctuation, and mechanics are correct.

PRACTICE 2

Choose three topics from Practice 1 and write topic sentences or thesis statements.

EXAMPLE:

Discuss the term *affirmative action*.

Topic sentence or thesis statement: *Affirmative action policies give*

certain groups in society preferential treatment to correct a history of

injustice.

1. _____

_____

_____

2. _____

_____

_____

3. _____

_____

_____

PRACTICE 3

Read the following test material and answer the questions that follow.

Essay Exam

You will have ninety minutes to complete the following test. Write your answers in the answer booklet.

A. Define the following terms (2 points each).

1. Region
2. Economic geography
3. Territoriality
4. Spatial distribution
5. Gross national product

B. Write an essay response to one of the following questions. Your essay should contain relevant supporting details. (20 points)

6. Define and contrast an open city with a closed city.
7. Discuss industrial location theories in geography, and divide the theories into groups.
8. Explain the steps needed to complete a geographical survey. List the steps in order of importance.

Schedule Your Time and Determine Point Values

1. What is the total point value of the exam? _____

2. How many questions do you have to answer? _____

3. Which part of the exam would you do first? Explain why. _____

    _____

4. Schedule your time. How much time would you spend on each part of the exam?

    Part A: _____   Part B: _____

    Explain your reasoning. _____

    _____

Carefully Read the Exam Questions

5. Identify key words in Part B. What important information is in the instructions?

    _____

6. What two things must you do in question 6?

    a. _____   b. _____

7. What type of essay is required to answer question 7?
    a. Comparison and contrast   b. Classification   c. Process

8. What type of essay is required to answer question 8?
    a. Comparison and contrast   b. Classification   c. Process

In the first few pages of your writing portfolio or on the next pages, keep spelling, grammar, and vocabulary logs. The goal of keeping spelling and grammar logs is to help you stop repeating the same errors. When you write new assignments, you can consult the lists and hopefully break some ingrained bad habits. The vocabulary log can provide you with interesting new terms that you can incorporate into your writing.

Spelling Log

Every time you misspell a word, record both the mistake and the correction in your spelling log. Then, before you hand in a writing assignment, consult your spelling log. The goal is to stop repeating the same spelling errors.

EXAMPLE: _Incorrect_   _Correct_

                       realy   _rea**ll**y_

                       exagerated   _exa**gg**erated_

Grammar Log

Each time a writing assignment is returned to you, identify one or two repeated errors and add them to your grammar log. Then, before you hand in writing assignments, consult the grammar log in order to avoid making the same errors. For each type of grammar error, you could do the following:

- Identify the assignment and write down the type of error.
- In your own words, write a rule about the error.
- Include an example from your writing assignment.

EXAMPLE: _Illustration Paragraph_   _(Feb. 12)_   _Run-On_

Do not connect two complete sentences with a comma.

                            accidents. Other

Bad drivers cause **accidents, other** drivers do not expect sudden lane changes.

Vocabulary Log

As you use this book, you will learn new vocabulary words. Keep a record of the most interesting and useful vocabulary words and expressions. Write a synonym or definition next to each new word.

EXAMPLE: _**Exasperating** means "annoying."_

Spelling Log

Grammar Log

Vocabulary Log

Credits

TEXT:

Page 10: Ember, Carol R., Ember, Melvin. *Cultural Anthropology*, 10th edition, © 2002. Reprinted with permission of Pearson Education, Inc., Upper Saddle River, NJ; **p. 11:** Reprinted by permission of Jake Sibley; **p. 23:** Lee Krystek, "Strange Science." Reprinted by permission of The Museum of Unnatural Mystery; **p. 23:** Yudkin, Jeremy, *Understanding Music*, 3rd edition, © 2002. Reprinted with permission of Pearson Education, Inc., Upper Saddle River, NJ; **pp. 23–24:** Patricia Chisholm, "The Body Builders." Reprinted with permission of Maclean's Magazine; **p. 24:** Schmalleger, Frank, *Criminal Justice Today: An Introductory Text for the 21st Century*, 7th edition © 2001. Reprinted by permission of Pearson Education, Inc., Upper Saddle River, NJ; **p. 31:** From *The Story of My Life* by Helen Keller, edited by Roger Shattuck. Copyright © 2003 by Roger Shattuck. Used by permission of W.W. Norton & Company, Inc.; **p. 31:** Fargaher, John M., Armitage, Susan, H., Buhle, Mary Jo, Czitrom, Daniel, *Out of Many, Brief Edition*, 4th edition, © 2003, Reprinted by permission of Pearson Education, Inc., Upper Saddle River, NJ; **pp. 32–33:** Reprinted by permission of Louis Tursi; **p. 61:** Reprinted by permission of Dinesh D'Souza; **p. 74:** Yudkin, Jeremy, *Understanding Music*, 3rd edition, © 2002. Reprinted with permission of Pearson Education, Inc., Upper Saddle River, NJ; **pp. 85–86:** Gene Swain, "Flight." Reprinted with permission of Gene Swain; **p. 98:** Bishop, Philip, *A Beginner's Guide to the Humanities*, 2nd edition, © 2006. Reprinted by permission of Pearson Education, Inc., Upper Saddle River, NJ; **p. 110:** Solomon, Michael R.L., Marshall, Greg W., Stuart, Elnora, *Marketing: Real People, Real Choices*, 4th edition, © 2005. Reprinted by permission of Pearson Education, Inc., Upper Saddle River, NJ; **p. 125:** Schmalleger, Frank, *Criminal Justice Today: An Introductory Text for the 21st Century*, 7th edition © 2001. Reprinted by permission of Pearson Education, Inc., Upper Saddle River, NJ; **p. 139:** Reprinted by permission of Dorothy Nixon; **p. 140:** Reprinted by permission of Ellen Zavian, Sports Attorney/Professor; **p. 165:** Copyright © 2003 by The New York Times. Reprinted with permission; **p. 174:** Reprinted with permission of Craig Susanowitz; **p. 178:** Reprinted by permission of Veena Thomas; **p. 193:** Lindsey, Linda L., Beach, Stephen, *Essentials of Sociology*, 1st edition, © 2002. Reprinted by permission of Pearson Education, Inc., Upper Saddle River, NJ; **pp. 193–194:** Wolff, Robert Paul, *About Philosophy*, 8th edition, © 2000. Reprinted by permission of Pearson Education, Inc., Upper Saddle River, NJ; **p. 194:** Craig, Albert, Graham, William A., Kagan, Donald, Ozment, Steven, Turner, Frank M., *The Heritage of World Civilizations*, 6th edition, © 2002. Reprinted by permission of Pearson Education, Inc., Upper Saddle River, NJ; **p. 196:** Reprinted by permission of Dorothy Nixon; **pp. 201–202:** Reprinted with permission of David Raby-Pepin; **pp. 207–208:** Reprinted by permission of Stephen Lautens; **pp. 211–212:** Reprinted by permission of Jeff Kemp; **pp. 216–217:** Reprinted by permission of Catherine Pigott; **pp. 221–222:** Reprinted by permission of Jake Sibley; **p. 226:** Reprinted with permission of Diego Pelaez; **p. 230:** Ciccarelli, Saundra, Meyer, Glenn E., *Psychology*, © 2006. Reprinted by permission of Pearson Education, Inc., Upper Saddle River, NJ; **pp. 243–244:** Reprinted by permission of Christine Bigras; **p. 253:** Originally published in *The New York Times*, April 25, 2003. Copyright © 2003 by the New York Times Co. Reprinted by permission; **p. 254:** Reprinted with permission of Dr. Martin E.P. Seligman; **p. 255:** Ember, Carol R., Ember, Melvin, *Cultural Anthropology*, 10th edition, © 2002. Reprinted with permission of Pearson Education, Inc., Upper Saddle River, NJ; **p. 257:** Brower, Daniel R., *The World in the Twentieth Century: From Empires to Nations*, 5th edition © 2002. Reprinted with permission of Pearson Education, Inc., Upper Saddle River, NJ; **pp. 261–262:** Reprinted with permission of Zachary Alapi; **p. 304:** Rita Dove, *Time Magazine*, Special Issue: "Time 100: Heroes and Icons of the Twentieth Century," June 14, 1999, Vol. 153, No. 23; **p. 546:** Reprinted with permission of Simon & Schuster Adult Publishing Group from *Yellow Woman and a Beauty of the Spirit* by Leslie Marmon Silko. Copyright © 1996 by Leslie Marmon Silko; **p. 548:** Copyright © 1991 Globalfair Ltd. Reprinted with permission of Aitken Alexander Associates; **p. 551:** "I'm a Banana and Proud of It," Copyright © 1997 by Wayson Choy. First published in Canada by *The Globe and Mail*. Reprinted by permission of the author; **p. 554:** Locher, David A., *Collective Behavior*, 1st edition, © 2002. Reprinted with permission of Pearson Education, Inc., Upper Saddle River, NJ; **p. 556:** Reprinted with permission of ELMA, Inc.; **p. 558:** Reprinted with permission of CBC.ca; **p. 564:** Used with permission of Mark McFadden; **p. 566:** Originally published by The New York Times, May 29, 2004; **p. 570:** Reprinted with permission of Tribune Media Services; **p. 573:** Reprinted with permission of Sterling Lord Literistics; **p. 577:** "It's Class, Stupid!" by Richard Rodriguez. Copyright © 1997 by Richard Rodriguez. (Originally appeared in *Salon*, November 10, 1997.) Reprinted by permission of George Borchardt, Inc., on behalf of the author; **p. 583:** © Latina Media Ventures, LLC; **p. 586:** From *Wouldn't Take Nothing for My Journey Now* by Maya Angelou, copyright © 1993 by Maya Angelou. Used by permission of Random House, Inc.; **p. 588:** Reprinted with permission of Greg McGrew; **p. 591:** © Latina Media Ventures, LLC; **p. 594:** Reprinted by permission of Deborah Mead; **p. 596:** Reprinted with permission of the *Christian Science Monitor*; **p. 598:** Reprinted with permission of MacNeil/Lehrer Productions.

PHOTOS:

Page 3: Lynne Gaetz; **p. 11:** © The New Yorker Collection 1999, Arnie Levin from cartoonbank.com. All Rights Reserved; **p. 18:** Violence Policy Center; **p. 19:** Lynne Gaetz; **p. 39:** Cathrine Wessel/Corbis/Bettmann; **p. 41:** Lynne Gaetz; **p. 42:** Photos.com; **p. 42 (margin):** Courtesy of www.istockphoto.com; **p. 43:** Photos.com; **p. 45:** Photos.com; **p. 46:** Photos.com; **p. 68:** Kolacz, Jerzy/Getty Images Inc.—Image Bank; **p. 70:** Courtesy Sirchie Fingerprint Laboratories, Inc., Youngsville, NC, www.sirchie.com; **p. 82:** Phil Degginger/Picturesque Stock Photo; **p. 83:** Pablo Picasso, "Mandolin and

Index

Notes

Notes

Notes

DATE DUE

11·17	
10-12-15	
	D100414
GAYLORD	PRINTED IN U.S.A.